IJS STUDIES
Research on Jesuits and the Society of Jesus

Pedro Arrupe

WITNESS OF THE TWENTIETH CENTURY, PROPHET OF THE TWENTY-FIRST

Pedro Miguel Lamet

Institute of Jesuit Sources
Boston College

Library of Congress Control Number: 2020950303

ISBN: 978-1-947617-08-7

**INSTITUTE FOR
ADVANCED JESUIT STUDIES**

BOSTON COLLEGE

IJS Studies is an imprint of the Institute of Jesuit Sources

**Pedro Arrupe:
Witness of the Twentieth Century,
Prophet of the Twenty-First**

Pedro Miguel Lamet

*Prologue by Adolfo Nicolás, S.J.
Former Superior General of the Society of Jesus*

Translated by Joseph V. Owens, S.J.

To the refugees,
fugitives,
and drug addicts
of the world,
to whom Pedro Arrupe
dedicated his final efforts
and dreams.

Contents

Prologue: The *Magis* of Father Arrupe

Adolfo Nicolás, S.J.

I respond with delight to the request of the Loyola Communications Group, which invited me to write some words to introduce the new edition of this book on the life of Father Pedro Arrupe by Pedro Miguel Lamet, S.J. The figure of Father Arrupe has played an important part in the experience of the Jesuits of my generation. He is very present to us still, so the task is a demanding one.

Pope Francis himself kept Father Arrupe very present during the Mass he celebrated with the Jesuits in Rome on the feast of Saint Ignatius in 2013. At the end of his homily, he spoke as one recalling a very familiar experience:

> I have always liked to think of the evening of a Jesuit's life, when the end is coming. Two images come to my mind: one is the classic image of Saint Francis Xavier looking longingly toward China. The other image that comes to mind as an example is the twilight of Father Arrupe who, in his last discourse at the refugee camp, told us: "Take this as my swan song: pray." Immediately after that, he boarded the plane, and when he arrived in Rome he was felled by the stroke that initiated his long and exemplary twilight. Two twilights, two images that should make us all observe carefully and remember.

After the Mass, the pope proceeded to the tomb of Pedro Arrupe, with whom he had discussed many problems in difficult times. At the tomb, he prayed and laid down a wreath of flowers; in an unexpected and surprising gesture of personal affection, he twice caressed the bas-relief with the image of Arrupe. It was clear that he wanted us all to keep alive in our hearts the never-to-be-forgotten name of Father Arrupe.

The figure of Arrupe, far from being consigned to oblivion, has been gaining greater prominence with the passage of time. In 1953, when we were scholastics finishing up our studies, we listened astounded, in the auditorium of Areneros College in Madrid, as he narrated to us his experiences in Hiroshima after the atomic bomb. Father Arrupe appeared before us as the great missionary he was: a man on fire. Being provincial superior of Japan, he was brave enough to place himself at the mercy of my hands as I practiced at barbering. He recounted with passion his long journeys, trying to collect funds and recruit Jesuits who could help with the difficult reconstruction of the vice-province of Japan.

I remember Arrupe in Rome at the beginning of the 1970s, when he would come to speak to the young Jesuits studying for their doctorates in theology. He was always concerned that we be attentive to the signs of the times, the challenges of the new emerging world, and the changes in the church, which had just experienced the Second Vatican Council (1962–65). His words were full of inspiration, prophetic vision, and penetrating intuition. That vision became more subtle and sublime with every passing year, as he demonstrated in a meeting he convoked in Hong Kong in 1972. There he made it clear to us that Japan had changed him, and his great desire was that the East would bring about a change in the Society.

Not much time would pass before the heart of Arrupe would be subjected to the distress of the cross. While meeting with major superiors in Malaysia, he centered his homily on the final months of Xavier and the great missionary's experience of failure, abandonment, and loneliness on the island of Shangchuan. Soon after that, Arrupe visited the Philippines, traveled to Bangkok, and finally flew to Rome, where he experienced his unforgiving paralysis and was placed in the infirmary. In his final letter, on love, he had spoken his definitive word. Those of us who visited him there in the infirmary witnessed his passion in silence, in prayer, in thanksgiving. It was the end of a life of complete coherence, of surrender to God and humanity, without condition or reserve.

I once heard an elderly Jesuit tell the story of a Japanese man who was baptized by Arrupe after a year of listening to his catechesis for adults. Intrigued by the man's story, the elderly Jesuit had remarked to him, "Those catechetical lessons must have been marvelous!" The man's reply, spoken quite naturally, left the Jesuit astonished:

> I didn't understand a thing. In fact, what he said seemed to me difficult and obscure. But after a year of carefully observing the father, I said to myself: If Christianity can produce a human being of such great quality, it will also be good for me. The important thing was not what he was saying but what he was living.

Arrupe lived what he believed; he radiated what he preached. As he said in one of his last talks, to the seminarians of India, he was convinced that evangelizing was not so much talking as simply being.

Arrupe's person and example continue to inspire, and his convictions and proposals, born out of the authenticity of his life, are more relevant than ever to the problems and the challenges of the twenty-first century. He was in advance of his time when he said: "We cannot respond to the problems of today with the solutions of yesterday." He never resigned himself to defensive postures. He wanted the kind of men and women who "have the future in the marrow of their bones," those who, in the language of Pope Francis, go out into the streets and travel to "the peripheries." It is no wonder, then, that twenty-three years after his death, his convictions and his proposals continue to inspire us. The world bears witness to the disenchantment with "technopolis," the injustice of globalization, and the narrowness of ideology. Arrupe spoke of "the immense spiritual vacuum that cannot be filled either by technological progress or materialist ideology." He could sense the frustrations of a consumerist society and the desperation of those citizens who, after believing true freedom was within their reach, soon found their dream fading away: "They see people completely divided, envious, and distrustful of one another, and they realize that the community, which was supposed to be their main source of security and support, was threatening to absorb them and deprive them even of their freedom and personal identity." He was describing what Pope Francis today laments as the dehumanization resulting from the "tyranny of the market."

Arrupe could discern the beginnings of a cultural crisis that would call into question the human ideal he defined as "the harmonious deployment of the whole person and of every person." He observed how, even during the 1970s, we were living in a world that was suffering the consequences of a colossal disorder: "Wealth, instead of serving to cover the basic needs of the majority of the population, is all too often misused and squandered." After assessing the vast expenditures on arms and other means of destruction, this witness of the atomic bomb argued that no solution could come about "simply by changing structures and institutions, if the people living in them did not change also." The personal change Arrupe called for became an imperative as he attempted to convert international solidarity and the global revolution into organizational forms for providing aid.

With his keen sense of reality and his far-sighted vision of the future, Arrupe brought to life and nourished many projects, of which the Jesuit Refugee Service has been the most relevant and dynamic. Pope Francis acknowledged this when he visited the Astalli Center in Rome in September 2013:

> Saint Ignatius of Loyola wanted there to be a space for receiving poor people in his residence in Rome, and Father Arrupe, when he founded the Jesuit Refugee Service in 1981, wanted the Roman offices to be located in these same places, in the heart of the city. I think it significant that, when Father Arrupe bade his spiritual farewell to Thailand, it was precisely in a refugee center. Three words sum up the program of refugee work for Jesuits and their collaborators: serve, accompany, defend.

The vision of Arrupe was also ahead of its time with regard to the unjust impoverishment of the Third World. Always in close contact with poverty, he understood "the deep mistrust and suspicion in those people, and their conviction that the industrialized countries bear the basic responsibility for their misery and for the difficulty they experience in trying to escape it." Today, we appreciate more than ever Arrupe's appreciation of the indigenous and mestizo cultures. "I have discovered the richness of this Third World: the wealth of an authentic human culture hidden beneath the poverty and the misery. I have experienced the natural energy and the extraordinary vitality of these peoples."

Arrupe also believed in young people and had a strong, optimistic faith in their desire for a better world. Staunchly opposed to convention and formalism, he was in favor of "simplicity, naturality, spontaneity, and solidarity." He appreciated the many qualities of young people: their impatient idealism, their generosity incarnated in service, their authenticity in the face of hypocrisy, their sensitivity to the human, their concern for the needy, and their universal spirit in a world that has shrunk. Arrupe was at heart a citizen of the world, as he told a Radiotelevisione Italiana (RAI) interviewer: "I feel universal. Our job really consists in working for everyone, and that is why I try to have as big a heart as possible, one that can embrace everybody." He was a citizen of the world and favored a universal passport, but he would also criticize young people at times for their "superficiality and sensationalism." He was convinced that the society of the future had to be a "frugal society"; a modest lifestyle was absolutely necessary "for the material and social survival of the human race." He was against waste-fulness and in favor of austerity. Arrupe spoke words that could appear in any of the homilies given by Pope Francis, such as these:

> To the egoistic, compulsive consumer—obsessed with the idea of possess-ing rather than being, a slave of needs he himself created, ever disgruntled and envious, whose only rule of conduct is accumulation of benefits—is opposed the person who wishes to serve, aspiring to possess nothing more, but wanting to be better and to develop his ability to serve others in solidar-ity, contenting himself with what is essential.

Arrupe the prophet seemed to foresee the present flourishing of NGOs and voluntary work, the condoning of external debt, and the rise of the anti-globalization movements. "There are some who die of starvation and oth-ers who die of excess of cholesterol. Hunger is the natural child of injustice. It is injustice the rich countries can prevent, but let us speak clearly: they do not want to." With his bold denunciations, Arrupe saw clearly how costly the Society's commitment to faith and justice would be: some one hundred Jesuits would be killed in countries of the Third World for their defense of the weak-est, out of fidelity to the Gospel of the Lord Jesus. Arrupe pioneered paths in such ground-breaking areas as inculturation, xenophobia, East–West dialogue, disarmament, ecumenism, hunger, spirituality, women, and religious life. He advocated a humanism without borders and urged Europe not to plan its own development independently of countries less favored and less developed.

History has shown that Arrupe was right. The passage of time allows us to see more clearly the exemplary character of his virtues, especially his obedience to the pope until his last breath. Hence the importance of the new edition of this book, *Pedro Arrupe: Witness of the Twentieth Century, Prophet of the Twenty-First*, by Pedro Miguel Lamet, S.J., now being published by the Institute of Jesuit Sources. This biography was truly a pioneering effort when it was first published over twenty-five years ago, when Arrupe was still alive.

In the course of time, new lives will be written of Pedro Arrupe. Pertinent historical data will be judiciously assessed, especially when scholars are able to consult all the documentation on this passionate Jesuit who was an excellent leader and a great Christian. But this biography has the merit of being the very first to trace with fidelity his human and spiritual profile and to make it available to a larger public. There is good reason, therefore, to encourage those who do not yet know this work to delve into its pages and draw close to this Jesuit who, after shaping his whole life around the Ignatian *magis*, whispered with great peace the profound sentiment so often repeated by Pope Francis: "I am only a poor human being who tries to spoil as little as possible the work of God."

—Father Adolfo Nicolás, S.J.
Superior General of the Society of Jesus
Rome, January 2014

Introduction to the New Edition:
The Twenty-Five Years of a Book

It seems only yesterday, but more than twenty-five years have passed since the first edition of this book, and during that time many important events have affected the life of the world and the church. Our perception of what we thought were the main vectors of history have been rudely changed by some of these events, such as the attack on the Twin Towers, the dominance of neoliberal thought, globalization, economic crises, the development of the internet and mobile telephones, massive migrations, the blossoming of China and other emerging economies, and a long etcetera. All these events allow this book to be seen from a new perspective, while they also reaffirm the power of the life story it tells.

In previous editions, I cited the title of Fred Zinnemann's film, *A Man for All Seasons* (1966), for it is a title that fits Arrupe perfectly. While the authenticity and coherence that characterized Arrupe are virtues that defy the passage of time, we can also see clearly today that this Basque prophet was exceptional in anticipating many of the challenges the twenty-first century has brought us.

I remember that when I undertook the task of writing this biography, I found myself facing a great challenge since few other ecclesiastical personalities of that time had come so directly under the scrutiny of public opinion. Very few others had been so passionately followed or so intensely criticized as this transparent Jesuit of aquiline profile and fiery eyes. As I considered the task, Arrupe already lay semi-conscious, entrapped by his sickness, glowing as a hot ash in a small room of the Roman headquarters of the Society of Jesus, just steps from the Vatican, where dwelled a pope who did not know how to understand him, or could not, or thought it not opportune to do so.

Expelled from Spain, like the rest of the Jesuits during the Republic, citizen of the world by vocation and formation, eyewitness of the atomic bomb, Arrupe had experienced everything: from the Nazi regime in Germany to the Second World War in Japan, passing through experiences of being accused of spying, of being imprisoned and of being misunderstood, even by some of his own brother Jesuits. But it was above all when he was the superior general of one of the Catholic Church's most influential orders that he experienced the most profound convulsions that characterized the twentieth century, and it was then that he felt most keenly the well-known tensions between the Jesuits and the Holy See. Indeed, it is safe to say that Arrupe was one of the most controversial and catalyzing figures of the church of that epoch.

While he was the center of controversy in his day, now almost everybody admires Arrupe for his apostolic spirit, his humane character, his religious leadership, and his prophetic and evangelical charism. Countless people came to know him and were honored by their friendship with him. They ranged from anonymous, humble people to presidents of nations, cardinals, theologians, intellectuals, journalists, and business people; many were those who corresponded with him or visited him on his sickbed in Rome. A Nobel Prize winner who was a non-believer confessed that he went down on his knees before Arrupe and asked for his blessing. Even Pope John Paul II went to visit him three times. He was the first superior general of the Society of Jesus to present his resignation while still alive (read by a companion since he could not speak), and upon doing so he received a more overwhelming and prolonged ovation than any other superior had ever heard in all the Jesuit assemblies that have taken place.

On other occasions (see the prologue to the 2007 edition), I have given a detailed account of the rather complex history of the writing and publishing of this book. Now it is enough to recall that, when I arrived in the land of the rising sun, an elderly Japanese man, with an enigmatic face like an ancestral samurai mask, examined me closely. He then bowed deeply and with a voice between metallic and mysterious exclaimed: *Ari-no-mama kaite kudasai*. This meant something like: "Write the things just as they are (without adding or taking away)."

That man was my first human contact after leaving the plane in Tokyo, and I must confess that those words of Kasumi Morimoto descended on me with a shock, making me aware of the great responsibility that was upon my shoulders. Then, by way of clarification, he added a frank, objective comment: "After all, you Spaniards tend to exaggerate [...]."

I got immediately to work. With the valuable assistance of my good friend Juan Masiá, S.J. and his mastery of Japanese, I interviewed dozens of Arrupe's friends and collaborators, people who had known him at the time of the atomic bomb and when he was provincial superior of Japan. I traveled to Tokyo, Kobe, Yamaguchi, Hiroshima, and Nagasaki, following his footsteps. Returning to Spain, I met with former fellow novices and companions of Arrupe in Bilbao, and especially with Father Enrique Chacón, who was brimming with memories of their university days together in Madrid. I also had the good luck of gaining access to the files of his niece Mariví Gondra, who has preserved the family correspondence and other documents. Today, many of them are no longer with us, at least not in a visible way.

Meanwhile, Arrupe, whenever he was sufficiently lucid, was busy sending me writings, as well as information about friends and other persons who might help me to collect memories, letters, and testimonies. Furthermore, Father Ignacio Iglesias did me the favor of sending a circular to all the provinces of the universal Society, asking Jesuits and others to send me whatever information concerning Arrupe they might consider opportune. I thus received dozens of letters with items of great interest, and some of them have been used to enrich this book.

At the beginning of 1989, as I was finishing my book after five years of work, a fortunate encounter with my friend, the publisher Javier de Juan, led me to Ediciones Temas de Hoy, a subsidiary of Planeta, founded and directed at the time by the intelligent, intuitive Ymelda Navajo. In the course of a meal, during which I enthusiastically explained to her the essence of the biography, she saw clearly that my book should be included in a new and successful collection that consisted of biographies of contemporary figures, especially those related to wealth and power. It contained titles that treated the lives of former Spanish prime minister Felipe González, the bankers Mario Conde, Carlo de Benedetti, the Albertos, and so on. However, at the time I was not a very well-known author, nor was Arrupe, then largely forgotten in his state of prostration, a person of such influence and importance as to render unnecessary the question of the book's viability. The conclusion of the marketing experts was that for Spaniards under the age of thirty Arrupe was an unknown figure. Despite such doubts, Temas de Hoy took the risk of publishing the book and distributing it aggressively.

Thus in October 1989 the book hit the streets, and word about it spread slowly but steadily. It was continually re-edited in different formats, including a pocket edition and translations into several languages. Its popularity was beyond all the expectations of the publishers. Curiously, while the above-cited financial and political leaders were falling into disgrace, disfavor, or decadence, people's interest in Arrupe was growing. I received and continue to receive numerous letters, including from bishops such as Cardinal Vicente Enrique y Tarancón, who praised the book and its success in evoking Arrupe's personality.

But the letters that most impressed me, and that never stopped arriving, were those of unknown persons who made statements such as these: "This book has changed my life. After reading it I decided to become a Jesuit." "I now work in a non-governmental organization." "This man was indeed a true Christian. Your book has restored my faith." My response to them was always the same: "Thank you, but I feel myself to be only a mediator between the reader and Father Arrupe." The truth is that what I have called the "Arrupe effect" was working, and it is still working. Such testimonies multiplied all the more as the result of conferences I gave on Arrupe's life and thought. Always, as I was finishing the conferences, people would come to tell me about similar experiences. Sometimes news reached me that the book was being read aloud in the dining halls of convents or monasteries.

One person who asked me to sign his copy of the book after a conference was an adolescent named Javier Burrieza. When he was only a third-year student at the college of La Salle in Valladolid, a teacher recommended the book to him. He was so impressed by the figure of Arrupe, by "his solid greatness and flexibility of spirit," that after getting a degree in modern history he decided to write his doctoral thesis about the Jesuits in Valladolid during the sixteenth and seventeenth centuries; this he did from 1997 to 2003, under the direction of Professor

Teófanes Egido. Today, he is one of the best lay specialists and researchers on the history of the Society of Jesus.

Among the many other reactions to the book, let the following message serve as an example. On the morning of July 27, 2007, while I was preparing the centenary edition of the book, I received an email from a young Colombian Jesuit named Luis Javier Sarralde. I cite it here as just one example of the many letters and testimonies I received:

> I make bold to write you not only to greet you but also to express my grati-tude (better late than never) for the great good that the Good Jesus of Naz-areth has done for me through different means, one of them being your biography of Father Arrupe.
>
> Let me explain. In September 1990, a friend from Bilbao, Francisco Abrisketa (now deceased), gave me your book, among others. Reading it little by little changed my life. I was born (sixth of seven siblings) in Pasto, a city in the south of Colombia. My family lived there, and we were all edu-cated there. The boys in the family from kindergarten on always went to the Colegio San Francisco Javier, a Jesuit school. There in 1986 I finished my secondary education at the age of eighteen. I then entered the Universidad Javeriana in Bogotá, another Jesuit school, where I studied law; I graduated as a lawyer in 1991.
>
> However, and I tell you this with a bit of shame, I had never read about the lives of either Saint Francis Xavier or Saint Ignatius of Loyola, or of any saint or priest. I always had the idea of being a good, committed Christian serving others as much as possible and indulging in politics. But your book arrived, and after reading it a couple of times, life began to take a 180-degree turn for me. It was the Ignatian year, 1991. On February 5 of that year, the good Father Arrupe went to the Lord, and I was asking myself: "Can it be that I might also follow Jesus as a priest?" In March 1992, in the midst of my work as a lawyer, I spoke with a Jesuit about my vocation for the first time. I had had Jesuit friends since college days, but we had never discussed this matter. Thus it was that I began a process of vocational discernment and entered the novitiate on January 15, 1993, leaving behind career, girlfriend, and my lawyer's office.
>
> I was ordained a priest in December 2003, and for nearly two years I was working quite happily as a parish priest in a region of my country that is beautiful but is also suffering terribly because of poverty and our violent social conflict. Now, since the law is a useful instrument, one not given to fanaticism or fundamentalism, they have decided that I should also do min-istry by using the church's law. So here I am studying in Rome since October 2005, in order to return to Colombia and teach there in our university, since I also like teaching and giving spiritual guidance.

Thus I give thanks to the Lord, to our intercessor Father Arrupe, to Ignatius of Loyola, to Francis Xavier, to everybody and to life itself, for the God of Life; and in the concrete life made history, I give thanks to the people who mediate him, among whom are you, Pedro Miguel.

Again, as we say to acknowledge a favor in my native land: "Dios te pague [May God pay you]," if you will allow me to address you as "tú." In this year of the first centenary of the birth of Pedro Arrupe.

Luis Javier, S.J.

I continued with my eventful life as writer and journalist in these complex times for church and society, but such vicissitudes and experiences go beyond the scope of this introduction. It is worth noting, though, that the present book led me to write three other books, whose aim was in part to give a fuller and better explanation of the context that provoked the drama of Arrupe. One was a biography of John Paul II, entitled *Hombre y papa* (Man and pope) (Madrid: Espasa, 1995, 2005), and the other two were *Díez-Alegría, un jesuita sin papeles* (Díez-Alegría, a Jesuit without papers) (Madrid: Temas de Hoy, 2005) and *Azul y rojo: José María de Llanos* (Blue and red: José María de Llanos) (Madrid: La Esfera de los Libros, 2013). In this way, I have attempted to complete a quadrilogy centered on key persons who catalyzed the history of the church during the twentieth century.

The years went by, and Jesuits from all over the world were petitioning for the process of Arrupe's canonization to be initiated. Many others were being raised to the altars, but the Society preferred to wait, to keep silence, to transfer Arrupe's remains discreetly from the Cementerio de Verano in Rome to the Church of the Gesù, and meanwhile to dedicate itself to other, more urgent matters. Today, with the passage of time and a new pontificate, it seems that fresh possibilities have opened up. The most recent superior general, Adolfo Nicolás, requested that testimonies on the life of Arrupe be gathered in all the provinces of the Society.

In the last decade, there has been renewed interest in the figure of Arrupe, especially in light of the fulfillment of many of his prophetic intuitions. New articles, studies, and books have appeared that provide fresh information and reflections on this exceptional man. Especially worthy of mention are *El padre Arrupe en Japón* (Father Arrupe in Japan) (Seville: Ediciones Guadalquivir, 1992), authored by Fernando García Gutiérrez, and *Aquí me tienes, Señor: Apuntes de sus Ejercicios espirituales (1965)* (Here you have me, Lord: Notes of his spiritual exercises) (Bilbao: Mensajero, 2002). The latter is an original text of Arrupe, annotated by his friend, former assistant, and devoted disciple, Iglesias, who long ago dedicated himself to delving deeply into the spirituality of Arrupe. Iglesias died in 2009 but left us a valuable posthumous work, *Misionero: Breve semblanza de Pedro Arrupe* (Brief biographical sketch of Pedro Arrupe) (Bilbao: Mensajero, 2010). Another of

Arrupe's close collaborators, the Frenchman Jean-Yves Calvez, published a study of his thought entitled *El padre Arrupe, profeta en la iglesia del concilio* (Arrupe, prophet of the church of the council) (Bilbao: Mensajero, 1998). In still another book, *Memoria siempre viva* (A memory always alive) (Bilbao: Mensajero, 2001), my companion and friend Norberto Alcover brings together a series of essays on the occasion of the tenth anniversary of Arrupe's death.

The centenary of Arrupe's birth has already brought forth two other books: an anthology of his prayers edited by José A. García under the title *Orar con el padre Arrupe* (Praying with Father Arrupe) (Bilbao: Mensajero, 2007) and a voluminous work (1,077 pages) edited by Gianni La Bella, called *Pedro Arrupe, general de la Compañía de Jesús* (Pedro Arrupe, general of the Society of Jesus) (Bilbao: Sal Terrae, 2007). This exceptional book contains a new collection of essays about specific aspects of Father Arrupe's life and governance.

The origin of La Bella's book of essays is not explained in its introduction, but the process by which it came into existence turns out to be quite instructive. Originally, there was not going to be a book at all, but simply a congress in Rome, convoked and organized by the famous Sant' Egidio Community, which always felt closely bonded to Arrupe. When soundings were made in Vatican circles regarding the appropriateness of holding such a congress, the response was that it did not seem opportune—this was during the time of John Paul II. It appears that even then the figure of Arrupe—despite his virtuous silence, his humble obedience, and his ten years of sacrificial example to the church and the world—continued to arouse the antipathy of certain curial prelates. Accordingly, instead of holding the conference it was decided to publish the abovementioned volume, which, like all collections, is uneven in the value and the relevance of its contents. Thanks to the time elapsed and the official character of the publication, the authors were favored with access to texts and documents that were forbidden territory when I wrote my own book, so soon after the events. Though the collected essays do not require any change in the substance of this biography, they contain many interesting interpretations and complementary data. The volume provides solid documentation, some of it previously unpublished, concerning the conflicts that took place during the two general congregations, and it treats especially well the resignation of Arrupe, his spirituality, and aspects of his governance on different continents. I have therefore incorporated into the present edition of my book some of those data, which I believe can enrich this work, but I have stayed within the biographical genre, leaving aside themes better suited for theoretical and monographic studies.

Furthermore, I bring a completely fresh source to this edition, one that I consider extremely valuable for an intimate understanding of Arrupe. I have selected the best fragments of the personal diary of the infirmarian, Brother Rafael Bandera, who attended to his needs day and night during the almost ten years of his prostration and silence. I am grateful for the confidence of the Jesuit provincial of Andalusia, Francisco José Pérez, for providing me access to this document. It has also seemed to me opportune, given the change of context and circumstances, to include some unedited notes from the journal I kept of the conversations I had with Arrupe during the summer of 1983. In earlier editions, I excluded them out of discretion, even though Arrupe had left it to my freedom and responsibility to publish them or not. At the time, he told me, "Decide yourself what parts of all this should be published." Finally, this edition includes a great deal of photographic material, both from my personal files and from the valuable collection of images created by Ángel Antonio Pérez Gómez on the occasion of the centenary.

Finally, I would like to respond to two criticisms that have been made of this book. The first has to do with whether Arrupe was not lacking in defects. The second is whether this volume is a work of hagiography rather than a strictly objective biography.

The problem of interpreting the life story of Arrupe as a man and as a Jesuit superior is that what for some would be a proof of his defects is for others precisely the proof of his great virtues. In a chapter on Arrupe's election included in the La Bella volume, Urbano Valero points out some of the limitations that were then being attributed to Arrupe: "Excessive idealism, a dreamy and naïve character, poor organization, excess of vision and lack of a solid plan, too little attention to concretely following up everyday business." Others might add weaknesses in his governing style, imprudence in his openness with others, exaggerated confidence in his subjects, and excessive tolerance of dissident opinions and defiant attitudes.

It is obviously possible to run some risks whenever efforts are made to read the signs of the times with a view to the future; or when individuals are respected and loved for their personal qualities, apart from the institution; or when dialogue is fostered instead of a strict chain of command. But we must ask ourselves whether this approach is not a better and more Christian alternative than the opposite. What is clear is that Pope Francis has decidedly opted for this spirit of mercy, fraternity, and dialogue in dealing with people.

Whether this book is an objective history or a biased defense is left to the reader to judge. I do not deny that it was written with passion, enthusiasm, and journalistic proximity to the events. It is not easy to dissimulate the love and admiration a writer feels for his subject. At the same time, it is quite clear that nothing has been left out here: the book recounts Arrupe's successes and failures, his bright vision of the world and his dark night of the soul, his love and his pain, his faith and his drama, the opinions of his friends and those of his enemies. No conflict is concealed, nor is any fact consciously misrepresented.

I do not know whether this book has achieved the objectivity that Kasumi Morimoto asked of me in Tokyo. Indeed, if we take seriously Immanuel Kant's universal *a priori*, such objectivity appears unobtainable even for a historian, who in the end always tints the facts with his necessarily subjective gaze. However, the reader can at least be assured that I have attempted to be objective. Moreover, in relating events experienced firsthand, I believe that a creative subjectivity can actually be more authentic than an attempt at cold objectivity that narrates only the bare facts.

It is worth recalling, nonetheless, that if every biography is only an approximation to the mystery of a human being, it is all the more so in the case of a man of such intense activity and with such a profound interior life as Father Arrupe. He used to say that "the most interesting biography is the one written without ink." This statement continues to be true for, as he also said, "the most decisive and important aspect of a life is incommunicable."

Furthermore, the life here narrated is not only that of a religious leader who had a reputation for holiness and exercised an important influence on the church; it is also the story of an exceptional witness to the turbulent century in which he lived. My experience has been that, because of his swift, intuitive, and effective response to the challenges of his time, Arrupe is of great interest to both believers and agnostics, to both Easterners and Westerners, to both intellectuals and ordinary citizens.

There remains for me only to give thanks once again to all who contributed generously and enthusiastically to the publication of this book, from those who sent me recollections and photographs to those who have accompanied me and supported me with their labor and their conviction. But I would like to express my profound gratitude most especially to Arrupe himself, who from his sickbed, when he could hardly speak, not only answered my questions and excitedly kept track of this project but also taught me something that cannot be paid for with all the gold of the world, or even with the homage of this biography, namely that it is possible to maintain one's dignity and hope in the midst of the greatest difficulty and, with an incredible interior drive, to live one's humanity to the fullest.

I want to thank the Loyola Communications Group, which has brought together the Society's publishers in Spain, for making available this new edition of Arrupe's biography, which we trust will be relevant and appealing even twenty-five years after its first appearance. I am also especially grateful to the recently deceased Father Adolfo Nicolás, S.J., general of the Society from 2008 to 2016, for being willing to write the moving prologue of this work.

Would Arrupe ever have expected that in the course of the years a companion of his, an Argentine Jesuit with whom he had shared tasks of governance, would sit on the chair of Peter? And what is more, that he would adopt some of the apostolic style that so characterized the style of "Don Pedro"? The entire world—including believers and unbelievers and especially the humble folk—has reacted enthusiastically to Francis's gestures of familiarity, simplicity, love for the poor, denunciation of injustice, and demythification of the external trappings of the papacy. The courageous steps Francis has taken to make the church's message more intelligible for people today and to restore to the Gospel its original flavor have been called a "revolution of tenderness." Readers can see for themselves, as they go through this volume, whether many of those same attitudes were not already present in germ in the thoughts, decisions, and actions of Father Arrupe.

If anyone should have doubts about this comparison of Pedro and Francis, with all their obvious differences, the pope himself made their kinship manifest when he visited the Gesù in Rome on the feast of Saint Ignatius in 2013. He did not want to leave the church before kneeling before the tomb of Father Arrupe; after making a short prayer, he twice caressed the effigy of Arrupe. It was a magnificent sign for posterity. It was as if the pope wished to acknowledge in deed, as well as in word, the spiritual and human qualities of this great Jesuit and man of God who was so terribly misunderstood in his time by highly placed clerics. It would appear that in the end history renders justice and gives the righteous their due. Truly, it seems that the "hour of Pedro Arrupe" is close at hand, if it has not arrived already.

1. The Hourless Day

Paul Tibbets checked the altimeter. The four-motor B-29, which had his mother's name, *Enola Gay*, painted on its nose, was flying at thirty thousand feet at a cruising speed of four hundred kilometers an hour. A gray, almost menacing sky stretched out over the flying fortress. Seated comfortably in the cockpit, Tibbets made sure that the "Great Artist" and the "No. 91," the companion planes charged with scientifically observing and photographing the event, were flying behind the powerful bomber without any problem. He checked to see if there, next to the panel of instruments, was his metal cigarette case, which went with him on all his flights. Yes, everything seemed to be quite in order.

"Cloud cover: less than 3/10 at all altitudes," the control tower had advised him in a coded message at 7:24 a.m. After reading the cable, he announced to his companions, not without emotion: "We are on our way to Hiroshima!"

Neither tall nor short, somewhat chubby-cheeked and quick to smile, Tibbets used gestures that gave an impression of indifference or distance. He was just another American, a mixture of would-be hero and gum-chewer. He still remembered the roguish face of Colonel Edward Lansdale of US Army intelligence when he asked him, "Have you ever heard of atomic energy?"

Tibbets had answered that he knew something about it from his physics studies and that he had heard news of experiments that the Germans were doing with heavy water in order to split the atom.

"Good," replied Professor Norman Ramsey, a twenty-nine-year old physicist at Harvard University, "because the United States has already succeeded in splitting the atom. We are building a bomb based on this discovery, a bomb that will explode with a force that is twenty thousand tons greater than a conventional explosion."

That conversation among the three men had taken place in the Second Army headquarters of the US Air Force, in Colorado, on September 1, 1944.

Just a few minutes later, Lansdale questioned Tibbets about a matter that might call into question his reputation as an able and effective pilot, almost a hero, in the Second World War. He did not hesitate to tell the truth: "Yes, I was detained on one occasion by the Miami Beach police."

"Why?"

"The police chief caught me in Surfside with a girl in the back seat of a car [...]."

After Tibbets's arrest, the intervention of a judge who was a friend of the family succeeded in hushing up the affair. The Air Force decided to ignore what was considered a sexual peccadillo. Lansdale had investigated it personally and decided to choose Tibbets, then twenty-six years old and father of a son, for the Manhattan operation.

There followed the long preparatory process, which was carefully kept top secret until *Enola Gay* took off from Tinian on the dawn of August 6, 1945. Tibbets was the only crewmember who knew the true nature of their mission. The other men had simply been told, "It will be something vital for ending the war." Tibbets still seemed to hear the voice of chaplain Downey praying before take-off:

> Hear the prayer of those who love you. We ask you to be with those who are going to battle our enemies. [...] Keep them and protect them, we ask you, so that they fly safely to their objective. May they, as we ourselves, know your force and your power; may they, with your arms, succeed in bringing this war to an end. We ask you that the war's end come soon so that we can once again experience peace on earth [...].

Once in the air, Tibbets could feel the excess weight that "Little Boy" added to his four-motor plane. That innocent name had been given to the device containing two pieces of uranium 235 that were separated by only a small space but that would be joined together by means of two conventional explosions. The new critical mass would produce the nuclear reaction. The bomb of 12.5 kilotons (one kiloton is equal to a thousand tons of TNT) had worried Tibbets from the start, but he said nothing to his crew until they came close to their objective.

It was around 4:25 a.m. Tibbets gave the controls to Robert Lewis, who in turn entrusted the plane to "George," the automatic pilot of the *Enola Gay*.

Tibbets took advantage of the free moment to look back at his companions, who were manning their respective posts. "Everything okay, colonel," called out Richard Nelson, the young radio-telegrapher, who felt very proud to hear his superior reply, "I know you're doing a good job, Dick."

Tibbets checked the padded tunnel through which the bomb was going to slide. In the rear

Colonel Paul Tibbets, pilot of the Enola Gay, *the B-29 that dropped the first atomic bomb on Hiroshima on August 6, 1945.*

cabin were George "Bob" Caron, Joe Stiborik, Robert Shumard, and Jacob Beser; the last was doing his best to stay awake. Tibbets made his way to the tail-gunner and asked him, "Bob, do you have any idea what we're going to do this morning?"

"Colonel, I wouldn't like to find myself in front of a wall when I have to fire."

Tibbets smiled, recalling that Caron had promised to keep his mouth shut and set an example for others when they had criticized him for reasons of security the previous September.

"Bob, we're on the way. You can talk now."

"Do we have on board the invention of some crackpot chemist?"

"No, not exactly."

"Then, the invention of a mad physicist?"

"Right."

Tibbets checked again the state of the launching tunnel and on his way back to the cockpit felt Caron grab his leg.

"Some problem?"

"Nothing, colonel. Just a question: Is this about split atoms?"

Tibbets continued checking the hatchway and returned to the cabin without answering. Caron had spoken that phrase without really understanding what he was saying. He had read something in a scientific magazine, but he had not the slightest idea what it meant.

By then, Hiroshima had already come into view. The base informed Tibbets that no Japanese radar had detected the plane's approach. He then quickly commanded through the intercom: "Get ready to fire and turn around immediately!"

Trailing a mile behind, the *Great Artist* was preparing to launch its measuring equipment in parachutes. Two miles farther back, the *No. 91* turned ninety degrees to put itself in the right position for taking photographs.

Major Thomas Ferebee, looking out the window of *Enola Gay*, recognized that familiar landscape from the photos he had seen. The gray and white of the undulating moors were now a smooth green; Hiroshima bay at this hour of the morning appeared intensely blue. The city buildings could be made out in the midst of a soft fog, and the main highways seemed to be drawn in ink. The slight haze that was floating over the city did not hinder visibility from the cockpit. He was able to make the two crosses in the viewfinder coincide.

"Now I've got it!"

It was eight hours, fifteen minutes, and seventeen seconds on the morning of August 6, 1945.

Some three thousand meters below, a man was looking out of a window. He did not have Asian features; he was not Japanese, but he seemed to be quite at home there in the town. His searching gaze was examining the sky. For some time, his sharp, aquiline profile had been attracting attention in that Nagatsuka neighborhood, and he was gaining a reputation. He had arrived from Yamaguchi a few years before and was known for his contagious smile and magnetic personality. He spoke Japanese with a mixture of Basque rapidity and English harshness. That day, he had been up since before five in the morning.

He had spent almost two hours making his morning prayer, seated immobile in the Japanese style, in an unfurnished Christian chapel covered with the typical bamboo mats—it was a place not to be profaned by shoes. Frequently seen riding a bicycle toward the city center, he had a spectral appearance, with a white clerical collar emerging from his black jacket and his bare forehead reflecting the sun. The people soon learned, though, that he had a wonderful smile, that he loved Japan more than his native land, and that he was always ready to help people out—at least when he was not busy with his young Japanese disciples, who wore a type of black *kimono* and were often seen reading silently or working in the garden.

That morning, the sky over Hiroshima was clear. From the window could be seen a piece of green landscape, something of the lovely hill nearby. The leaves of the trees were fluttering in the light breeze, and the first warmth of a summer day, promising as always to be humid and sticky, began to heat the fragile roof of the Japanese dwelling.

After arranging the books on his desk and making his bed more neatly, Pedro Arrupe was about to program the day's activities, anticipating the arrival of the brother who was responsible for coordinating the Jesuit novitiate. Just then, the siren sounded again.

It was 7:55 a.m. At 7:09 there had been a first siren, shortly after Radio Hiroshima had interrupted its programming to inform listeners of an air-raid alert. The sporadic siren alarms had not alarmed Father Arrupe, who, like everyone else in the city, was accustomed to such warnings of a possible air-raid. At first, the inhabitants of Hiroshima used to escape to the caves of the nearby mountains and sometimes even slept there, but they had tired of the persistent alarms and were unwilling to die of pneumonia.

And life was going on without major problems. Every day at 5:30 in the morning, Arrupe saw a B-29 fly across the sky. The flights were so constant that the Japanese with a certain irony had baptized them with the name "American mail."

For that reason, when on that August 6 a B-29 of the US Air Force disturbed the blue silence of the city with its four powerful motors, Arrupe, like many others, paid no attention and continued ordering his papers. In recent months, he had already seen formations with up to two hundred planes flying in the distance. Just then, someone called at his door. It was an older priest, coming to consult him about a minor matter.

The siren had been silent for some minutes, and a few kilometers from that tranquil setting the city was beginning to come awake, with a gingerly Japanese pace. Public transport was carrying workers to the factories, stores were opening their shutters, and uniformed children were forming lines in front of the school gates. An elderly woman was walking through the park, scattering the pigeons,

Pedro Arrupe standing before the novitiate of Nagatsuka, on the outskirts of Hiroshima. The building was transformed into an improvised hospital to provide medical services for the survivors of the bomb.

and in the rural zone to the west of Hiroshima Doctor Kaoru was looking at his watch. He would not be getting back to his clinic at least until noontime.

In the Japanese base at Shimonoseki, around a hundred miles from Hiroshima, Second Lieutenant Matsuo Yasuzawa was warming up the motors of his two-seater training plane. He was often seen flying through the skies of Hiroshima, but he had never received permission to attack the B-29s. There was no sense in risking the life of a Japanese Air Force instructor, even though he was ready to undertake a *rippa na saigo*—a "splendid death"—for the homeland, a privilege reserved for the kamikazes. Today, his mission consisted in flying to an airfield in Hatta to transport a major who was attending a communications meeting in Hiroshima. He planned to arrive about 8 a.m. and had just taken off when *Enola Gay* entered Japanese air space.

The streetcar driver, with Japanese precision, looked at his watch and sounded the departure bell. It was exactly 8:15 a.m.

Tibbets was no longer conscious of the noise of the plane's motors. He was tense, ready to turn his B-29 around immediately after concluding his secret critical mission. The "mail plane" was about to deposit its "letter."

Eight hours, fifteen minutes, seventeen seconds: the hatch doors opened. Tibbets called out: "Fire!"

At the same moment, *Enola Gay* began a ninety-degree turn toward the right. Ferebee shouted "Bombs away!" as he placed his nose against the airplane window. For a moment, the bomb appeared to be suspended in mid-air, but then it began to fall. It wobbled for a second and soon picked up speed, plunging downward toward earth.

"What was that?" exclaimed Arrupe, standing up and pointing at the window. A bright light resembling a photo flash had ripped across the blue sky. Immediately, a dull, continuous roar, more like the sound of a distant waterfall than an instantly exploding bomb, reached his ears with terrifying force. The house shook. The windowpanes shattered, and the doors twisted. The Japanese partitions of wattle and clay collapsed like so many playing cards, flattened by the explosive wave. As Arrupe and his companion instinctively covered their heads with their hands, a constant rain of wreckage fell on their motionless bodies stretched out on the floor.

When the earthquake-like event subsided, Arrupe raised his head, fearful of seeing his companion wounded, but both of them were unharmed. Worried about the thirty-five young men who lived in the house, Arrupe ran through the corridors and stairwells. As he reached the last room, he gave a sigh of relief. The explosion had caused only material damage.

But what had happened? They all went outside to the garden. Their instincts told them that they were going to find the remains of a bomb somewhere nearby, but the garden and the yard were the same as always. In contrast to that natural setting full of life was the damaged house, its tiles shattered and curiously mounted atop one another. Not a single pane of glass was intact. Behind the weirdly twisted windows, the interior of the house was filled with a cloud of dust and a jumble of fractured partitions.

"Let's climb the hill!" someone shouted. "From there, we'll be able to see what happened in the city." A desolate panorama opened up before their eyes. A huge, dark, smoking cloud hovered menacingly over a desert of ashes, the devastated remains of what had been Hiroshima.

A thousandth of a second after 8:16 a.m., a purplish-red lightning flash had extended over the city, its temperature reaching fifty million degrees Centigrade. Directly over the Shima Hospital in the center of the city, the epicenter of the first atomic bomb in history, the temperature had reached several thousand degrees Centigrade after the incredible detonation. A ball of fire like a small sun instantaneously sent out powerful radiation, and the resulting temperature difference produced an explosive wave equivalent to a typhoon. Some fifteen percent of the energy was transformed into radioactive rays, thirty-five percent into heat rays, and fifty percent into explosive force. The result was a fierce fire that extended a kilometer roundabout, scorching human skin more than three kilometers away and destroying everything within a radius of six kilometers.

Over one hundred thousand persons perished as a result of the explosion, and countless others suffered serious injury and illness. The tall columns that flanked the Shima Hospital were crushed against the pavement. The building was completely destroyed, and its inhabitants were vaporized. Of the city's ninety thousand buildings, sixty-two thousand were destroyed. Hiroshima's drainage system suffered seventy thousand ruptures. Only about twenty of the more than two hundred doctors that worked in the city had escaped the impact of the bomb and were able to help the wounded.

"Water, water, I want water!" shouted survivors who made their way to the shores of the river that ran through the city. They had to remove cadavers in order to be able to drink. The survivors appeared to be walking mummies. With their faces and bodies deformed, their clothes tattered and stuck to their skin, they walked without knowing where to go. Stupor was reflected in their gaze as they walked amid smoking ruins, burning buildings, and streetcars that had become pieces of twisted iron. Smoke, fire, ruins, screams—this was truly hell. Where a human being had been seating on the steps of the Sumitomo Bank, there could be seen only a shadow etched on the shattered granite. That image can still be contemplated in the Peace Memorial Museum of Hiroshima.

On the hill of Nagatsuka, Arrupe was speechless with fright as he viewed the inexplicable apocalypse. He had heard nobody pronounce the word "atomic." During the four years of the war, he had seen many bombs fall and many grenades explode, but this was something so new and so different that no comparison was possible. Yes, he had heard of secret weapons, especially before the defeat of the Germans, but nobody thought they were anything more than propaganda. Now there he was, standing before that most appalling spectacle of destruction of humans by other humans.

"We have to go to the city! We have to do something!" shouted Arrupe in an instinctive gesture of solidarity.

"It's impossible, Father. Fire is blocking all the roadways to the city."

"But we have to do something!"

Arrupe ran to the chapel, where one of the walls had collapsed completely. He knelt down, and in an eternal instant he asked God to enlighten him. He felt overwhelmed by the darkness surrounding him. All about him was death and destruction; he and his companions felt reduced to a terrible impotence. "And you, Lord, knowing everything, contemplating everything, are inviting us to rebuild it all."

At that moment, Arrupe suddenly recalled his past: Bilbao, his parents, his years as a medical student in Madrid, his call to Japan. He looked at his watch. It was stopped, as were thousands of watches in Hiroshima, as were hundreds of thousands of human lives, at 8:15 a.m. "That silent, paralyzed watch," he would write years later, "has been for me a symbol; it has become a phenomenon outside history. It is not a relic, but a perpetual experience of something beyond history, not measured by tick-tocks. The pendulum stopped, and Hiroshima remained burnt into our minds."

Arrupe left the chapel with a firm proposal: they would turn the novitiate into an improvised hospital, and he would make use of his medical knowledge. He told his companions of the plan, and they immediately started to work. However, the others did not yet know that Arrupe had left the chapel with something more than this practical proposal: with the watch of history stopped, his heart was in some distant place, beyond time and far above any terror that human beings could sow.

While he was rescuing his medical kit from among the ruins—he was able to find only a little iodine, a few aspirins, fruit salts, and bicarbonate—Arrupe felt helpless before the needs of two hundred thousand people suffering grievous wounds.

But he knew that God, who had brought him to this place, would guide him in the midst of that sea of anguish and destructive fire. The explosion within his heart, he realized, was even greater than the *pika-don*, that great fireball and thunder clap that had reduced Hiroshima to waste.

"Here they come, Father!" cried a novice.

They were the first walking shadows, coming in search of aid. Arrupe already had his imagination working.

High in the sky over Hiroshima, Colonel Tibbets, looking out from the cockpit of *Enola Gay* and seeing what remained of the city, exclaimed in horror, "My God, what have we done?"

2. The Adventures of "Peru"

"Don't get your sailor suit dirty! Whenever you go to the park you come back a mess!"

The voice of Doña Dolores was coming from the back of the house, a spacious second-floor apartment with more than eight rooms; its balconies looked out on Pelota Street.[1] Through the wide windows, little Pedro poked out his round face, both serious and smiling, both mischievous and responsible. He contemplated that old Bilbao neighborhood, which was then still a stately and busy place. His clear, intelligent gaze focused on a group of swarthy, broad-backed, big-nosed men, who, wearing the caps typical of the region, were singing in Basque after their first morning coffee. They later disappeared into the neighborhood of Seven Streets, a tangle of narrow lanes darkened by tall, blackish houses built along the right bank of the Nervión River, called in Basque Ibaizábal (Wide river). From the balcony of his house, Peru (the Basque diminutive for Pedro) could almost see the river with its green-black waters and its constant flow of barges. The smoke from the tall factory chimneys and the industrial ambience lent to the houses by the river, especially in the magical lights of night, an air of being part of a mythical city that pulsed amid the shadowy behemoths that forged the iron.

It was an epoch of growth for old Bilbao, which in the first decade of the century had some eighty-two thousand inhabitants. The city was beginning to spread out on the left bank of the Nervión and was host to an intense cultural life, centering especially on music and sports, in accord with the long tradition of the Basque country. The steel-making industry, through the enterprising efforts of Julio de Lazúrtegui and others, was becoming a major factor in that small, rainy city that had until then been peaceful and mistily romantic.[2]

---

1 The building and the second-floor apartment where Pedro Arrupe was born are still preserved. His baptismal certificate lists the address as 7 Pelota Street, but the number now is 5. Like so many other houses in the old center of Bilbao, the dwelling is spacious, with the old system of bedrooms opening onto the principal rooms of the house. At that time, Pelota Street, running parallel to B. Barrena and La Merced Streets, was in the city center and ended at La Ribera, not far from the San Antón market and the cathedral of Saint James. It was originally outside the walls of the first urban core. Very close by was situated the first fronton in Bilbao, which in 1790 was moved to nearby Arenal, next to the church of San Nicolás.

2 María Victoria de Gondra y Oráa, *El Bilbao de Julio Lazúrtegui: La acertada visión del futuro industrial y mercantil del País Vasco adelantada por un bilbaino del XIX* (Bilbao: Cámara Oficial de Comercio, Industria y Navegación de Bilbao, 1984). The author of this work, which gives an interesting panorama of Bilbao in that epoch, was the daughter of Pedro's cousin Fernando Gondra, who was always close to Pedro and his family. In the

"And don't be a bother to the nursemaid, since she has enough to worry about with the five of you!"

Doña Dolores Gondra de Arrupe was a tall, broad woman who wore dark clothes; she was kindly but firm, with penetrating eyes. She was possessed of a strong character, a family trait, but at the same time she was serene and knew how to smile. Born in the village of Munguía, she was one of the six children of Juan Antonio de Gondra y Urrutia and Doña Martina Robles Elorza. Don Juan Antonio, a Basque doctor who dreamed of sea adventures, had succeeded in helping two of Dolores's brothers become sailors.[3]

Lola, as they called her in the family, still recalled how her father used to show her the sword of Saint Andrew on the Gondra shield, as he told her how their ancestors had battled in Baeza; he used to show her the Torre Villela and tell of its heroic past, to which the family was also connected. She remembered the elegant Gothic church of San Pedro, where she was baptized and educated in the faith, and even the hill called "Mount Gondra" near the village, which was still property of the family.[4] What captured Lola's attention above all, though, was the stretch of green fields around Munguía, with the scattered white hamlets and the leisurely pace of the farmers; she was enchanted by that strong, serene style of living and believing of those people who were at once visionary, stubborn, and sensitive.

Suddenly, Peru came running down the stairs, accompanied by his four sisters, who from oldest to youngest were Catalina, Margarita, María, and Isabel. The younger girls, with their round hats and lace collars, seemed to be cut out of a postcard as they laughed at their rowdy brother and played jokes on him.

Basque country, above all in the cities, a new, more liberal and bourgeois society was developing alongside the traditional order. Especially affected by the changes were the maritime provinces such as Vizcaya, and cities like Bilbao and San Sebastián; less affected were places like Guipúzcoa. Throughout the Basque country, regional governments underwent modifications; by the end of the nineteenth century, the old order was maintained only in the former kingdom of Navarre and in the province of Álava; the other two provinces changed to regular governance. During the first third of the twentieth century, the city of Bilbao, Arrupe's birthplace, was known as a powerhouse of industrialization. In 1902, in order to compete better in the market, Altos Hornos de Vizcaya was created out of the fusion of three already existing firms (Iberia, Vizcaya, and Altos Hornos de Bilbao), under the sway of financial capital from the banks of Bilbao and Vizcaya. It was one of eighty-eight iron mills and other metal factories that existed in 1901 in the province of Vizcaya, many of them concentrated in the estuary of the Nervión River and a few other localities. In 1926, at the end of the period we are considering, and one month before Arrupe entered the novitiate at Loyola, the province of Vizcaya was producing fifty-eight percent of Spain's iron and 56.65 percent of its steel.

3 Testimony given by Fernando Gondra to the author of this book. Reference may be made to the attached illustration of Arrupe's genealogical tree.

4 Information provided by María Victoria Gondra.

The house where Pedro Arrupe was born on November 7, 1907: 7 Calle de la Pelota (now number 5), in the old quarter of Bilbao.

All at once there appeared in the doorway the imposing figure of Don Marcelino, the father of the five children. He smiled at them and asked, "But where are you going at this hour?"

"Out to play in the park," replied Catalina as she gave him a kiss.

Don Marcelino stroked his thick mustache and looked tenderly at his children. An architect by profession, he had, as a committed Catholic, contributed to the founding of *La gaceta del norte* (Northern gazette) along with other prestigious citizens of Bilbao, such as José María Urquijo and the Basterra brothers. Like Lola, he too was a native of Munguía, where he had been born of Pedro Arrupe Meaurio and his second wife, Inocencia Ugarte Arteche. He was coming now from a conference in the city, where he had discussed a major architectural project he was hoping to implement. He kept busy with many other important business matters, among them the limited partnership of J. B. Rochet and Company, which was involved in the purchase and sale of minerals and the operation of mines.[5] Marcelino had a distinguished bearing and an air of clarity and conviction about him; a certain pride and integrity emerged from his personality and spread to those around him.

"You're not going to take your hoop, Peru?" he asked.

Peru confessed that he had lost it, but he looked admiringly at his father, as if basking in the sensation of security and strength that emanated from that noble man for whom he felt great affection and respect.

---

5   Gondra, *El Bilbao de Julio Lazúrtegui*, 65, and photo from Archivo Gondra. Don Marcelino was the architect for a monument erected in Elorrio, along with his colleague Manuel Smith.

A Boy at Last!

Don Marcelino caressed his son's head, recalling the day he had come into the world, November 14, 1907, at nine o'clock in the morning. Lola, his wife, had shouted out joyfully: "A boy at last!"

An event-filled year had just ended. In Spain, Don Alfonso of Bourbon had been born, and Great Britain, Russia, and France had created the Triple Entente to oppose the Triple Alliance made up of Germany, Austria–Hungary, and Italy. In Transvaal, South Africa, an obscure Indian lawyer named Mahatma Gandhi, with his kind face and penetrating eyes behind round spectacles, had initiated the first movement of passive resistance. The world was experiencing a new movement in favor of human rights. Women's suffrage had been approved in Norway, and Vladimir Ilych Lenin had been exiled from Russia for the second time. In Paris, Georges Méliès was realizing that the strange apparatus of the Lumière brothers was something more than a public curiosity, and he was taking the first steps in developing motion pictures, an invention that would be important for the future of art and industry. It was also the year in which Gustav Mahler introduced his *Eighth Symphony*, in which Maxim Gorky set the basis for socialist realism with his novel *The Mother*, and in which Rudyard Kipling, with his poem, "You Will Be a Man, My Son," won the Nobel Prize for literature. In a corner of Castile, Antonio Machado, a professor who appeared to be a simple, almost crude, man, bent silently over his notebooks to sing of his *Soledades* (Solitary place):

> I go along dreamy roads
> of the twilight. Golden hills
> green pines,
> dust-laden oaks! [...]
> Where can this road lead?
> I go along singing, a traveler
> along the trail [...]
> —Night is falling now—
> once I had in my heart
> the thorn of passion;
> one day I finally drew it out,
> now I no longer feel my heart.

This important year was coming to an end when a child was born on the second floor of no. 7 Pelota Street. Nobody was aware that the infant boy would in future years travel several times around the world, speak seven languages, command thirty thousand men, make his own the lifestyles of the Orient, open up a new epoch of Christian commitment, and become an authentic explosion within the church. Nobody knew then who Pedro Arrupe Gondra would finally be.

The next day, November 15, 1907, Pedro was baptized in the cathedral of Saint James the Great, the oldest church in Bilbao, an expansive temple of Gothic origin that preserved a fourteenth-century cloister and had a Renaissance portico; it was just a short distance from the Arrupe residence. The baptism was administered by the chaplain José Cochica, and the godparents were Pedro's uncle Saturnino Gondra, a sailor in the navy, and his aunt Casta Gondra y Urcallu.[6] As he poured the water over Pedro's head, the priest did not know, nor could he dream, that he was introducing into the community of believers a human being who was going to communicate the gift of faith to thousands of persons. On Pelota Street that day there was singing and dancing until late in the evening, and wine flowed as freely as the joy and the camaraderie.

The First Farewell

What Don Marcelino could hardly have suspected in those days was that he would soon be left alone. The year was 1916. Pedrito would recall that painful experience many years later:

> I was eight years old. The sun of August was flooding the streets of Bilbao. Our house, hermetically sealed, had a very sad appearance! In a bedroom, six candles were burning around a bed. My father, my four sisters, and I were

---

6   The birth certificate states literally: "Don José Luis López Sanz, ecclesiastical administrator of the cathedral basilica of Saint James the Great of Bilbao, province of Vizcaya, diocese of Bilbao, certifies that in book no. 27 of the baptized of this parish, folio 213, no. 132, the following entry is found: 'In the city of Bilbao, dominion of Vizcaya, bishopric of Vitoria, on the fifteenth of November of the year nineteen seven, I, the below signed priest don José Gochica, chaplain, with express permission of the ecclesiastical administrator of the main parish church and basilica of Saint James the Great of this city, who also signs below, solemnly baptized a boy whom I named Pedro. He is the legitimate son of Don Marcelino de Arrupe y Ugarte, architect, and of Doña Dolores Gondra y Robles, both natives of Munguía, Vizcaya; residents and faithful of this parish. The child was born, according to his father, on the fourteenth of this present month, at nine o'clock in the morning, on Pelota Street, number seven, second floor. *Paternal grandparents*: Don Pedro Arrupe y Meaurio, native of Gautegui de Arteaga, Vizcaya, and Doña María Inocencia de Ugarte y Arteche, native of Baquio, Vizcaya. *Maternal grandparents*: Don Juan Antonio de Gondra y Urrutia, native of Baquio, and Doña Martina Robles Elorza, native of Munguía Gautegui. The godparents are Don Saturnino Gondra, native of Meñaca, Vizcaya, married, sailor in the navy, and Doña Casta Gondraondo y Urcallu, native of Munguía, Vizcaya, married; I advised both of them of the spiritual relationship and the other obligations they have acquired. And to attest to the truth of this declaration we sign it as follows: Ramón Prada, José Gochica." (In the margin is found: "Arrupe y Gondra, Pedro, received the sacred order of subdiaconate in Henday on April 29, 1936. Dr. Echevarría. On February 2, 1943, he made solemn profession in the Society of Jesus, in Hiroshimakan, Japan. Dr. Alejandro de Echevarría.") The baptismal font of red marble from Ereño, where Arrupe was christened, is still preserved in the baptismal chapel, the first in the walkway to the right.

kneeling down, praying the rosary before the still warm body of my mother. It was our last family reunion.

Someone slipped quietly into the room and whispered to me: "The priest is here and wishes to say prayers for your mother." I got up. [...] But the figure of the priest was already visible in the doorway. [...]

"Perico," he told me, "you have lost a holy mother!" Pointing out to me the image of the Virgin of Begoña that watched over the candle-lit chamber, he added, "Look, there you have your Mother, more holy still, and she never dies!" [...] Then I understood even more profoundly that the Mother of God was my mother too.[7]

That priest was the first Jesuit to enter into Pedro's life. His name was Ángel Basterra, and he was in charge of the congregation of Mary Immaculate and Saint Stanislaus Kostka in Bilbao. The boy would soon become a member.

During his mother's final illness, the children had been sent to stay with their sister Margarita, who by then was married to José Joaquín Sautu. The scene described above took place when Pedrito returned to his house after his mother's death, which had resulted from a surgical operation. The eight-year-old boy felt her absence intensely; the house seemed empty to him from that time on.

Don Marcelino made an effort to fill that empty space, but he was a quiet man, and he was finding it more difficult to be his usual cordial self. Everything had gone so well until then. "My family was very close-knit," Arrupe confessed later; "it was peaceful and patriarchal, traditionally Catholic. I felt very happy. There were no problems. We went to Mass together, and the atmosphere was one of total confidence."[8] Much time would have to pass, though, before Don Marcelino would once again sing with his magnificent tenor voice to piano accompaniment. Even so, Pedro would never forget that "he had very good, very kindly character. By temperament, he was an entertainer." Whenever he

---

7   From the collection of *Flores y frutos*, journal of the congregation of Mary Immaculate and Saint Stanislaus Kostka of Bilbao. Ángel Basterra Ortiz was born on September 4, 1870, in Bilbao, entered the Society on November 25, 1896, and died on February 7, 1947. After receiving the regular Jesuit training, he spent most of his life in the Bilbao residence (1910–43), where he was director of the congregation of the Kostkas (after Saint Stanislaus Kostka). "He looked after the spiritual formation of 4,500 young people; he made daily Mass and Communion the center of their activities and organized fifty-four closed retreats for them." Father Basterra planned and directed the apostolic activities of the congregation's members, such as the Conference of Saint Vincent de Paul; visits to prisons, hospitals, and homes for the elderly; and catechism classes for 650 children given every year by the congregation's members. He directed the congregation's journal *Flores y frutos* (see José María Margenat, "De Bilbao a Japón (1907–1938)," in *Pedro Arrupe, general de la Compañía de Jesús: Nuevas aportaciones a su biografía*, ed. Gianni La Bella [Bilbao: Ediciones Mensajero, 2007], 53–110, here 64).

8   Declarations of Father Arrupe. Jean-Claude Dietsch, *Pedro Arrupe: Itinéraire d'un jesuite* (Paris: Éditions du Centurion, 1982), 65 (*Itinéraire* hereafter).

Peru, the Basque diminutive for Pedro, at three or four years of age.

sang in the chapel of the Jesuit college of Orduña, the elderly folk of the place drew close to listen to him.[9]

Don Marcelino never missed taking part in the procession on the feast of the Sacred Heart; he would carry a large candle in his hand while Pedro would follow

---

9   *Itinéraire*, 66.

behind, proud of the small candle he was carrying. Don Marcelino often took refuge in his work, drawing up plans for many houses in Bilbao and the region. Later on, he would take part in a competition to build the tower of Begoña. He put much effort into that project; he even drew a large mock-up of the tower that he later kept in his house. He did not win the contract, however, and became seriously depressed as a result. After that, he dedicated himself mostly to business and to the education of his children; he gave up the architectural profession almost completely.[10]

During those years, Pedrito was already attending the college of the Piarist Fathers situated in the expanded part of Bilbao (between what is now Henao Street and Juan de Ajuriaguerra Street). He entered the school on October 1, 1914, at the age of seven. His school companion José Luis Isasi recalls that

> he was very happy, very open, and an excellent student. Our classes had about twenty-five or thirty students, mostly upper-middle class, though there were also some students on scholarship. We were all soccer fans, Perico as well. As you know, we would all shout together in the street: "Hurrah, hurrah, Atleti is champion." He was a very normal kid.[11]

His grades between 1916 and 1922 were excellent. Of twenty-nine subjects, he received the grade of "outstanding" in twenty-three, that of "noteworthy" in three, and that of simply "passing" in four.[12]

---

10   Testimony of Don Fernando Gondra. See also Gondra, *El Bilbao de Julio Lazúrtegui*, 110.
11   Statements made to the author by José Luis Isasi.
12   Arrupe's grades in the Piarist college were as follows: 1916–17: Spanish: outstanding; general geography: outstanding; basic arithmetic: outstanding; religion: outstanding; calligraphy: noteworthy. 1917–18: Latin 1: outstanding; geography of Spain: outstanding; arithmetic: outstanding; religion 2: outstanding; physical education 1: passing. 1918–19: Latin 2: outstanding; French 1: outstanding; history of Spain: outstanding; geometry: noteworthy; physical education 2: passing. 1919–20: precepts: outstanding; French 2: outstanding; universal history: outstanding; algebra: outstanding; drawing 1: noteworthy; psychology: outstanding; literary history: outstanding. 1920–21: psychology 1: outstanding; literary history: outstanding; physics: outstanding; physiology: outstanding; drawing 2: passing. 1921–22: ethics: outstanding; natural history: outstanding; agriculture: outstanding; chemistry: outstanding. From 1914 to 1916, Arrupe took pre-secondary courses, and from 1916 to 1922 he studied the secondary-school curriculum, known as the baccalaureate (*bachillerato*). Father Ramón Navarro was rector of the college from 1913 to 1915, and Father Luciano Moreno was rector from 1922 to 1928.
   Christian education was the basis of all the pedagogy of the Piarist schools, which tried also to impart sound instruction that would allow graduates either to continue their studies or to practice socially recognized professions. During the years of primary education, the three levels of the minor catechism were explained. Secondary education, which Arrupe began in 1916, used the major catechism of Pius X in the following order: first year, dogma; second year, morals; third year, liturgy; fourth year, history of the church; and fifth and sixth years, apologetics. After becoming general of the Society, Arrupe

"He was charming," recalls his sister María:

I loved him very much. The difference in our ages was large: I was four years older. At home, we were crazy about him, since he was the only boy. He was in no way "saintly." He liked to go to the congregation, but not much else. He always got very high grades. Sometimes I helped him with his lessons. When he got stuck in one of those difficult lessons in secondary, which could be terrible, he would say to me, "Hey, Mari, could you help me a little?" He was just a very normal kid. A good boy, and studious. When he was small, Mom used to say, "My son will be a priest," and he would repeat, "Mom says I will be a priest; well, I will be a priest!" Later, when he began his career in medicine, my mother had already died, and my father used to say, "Our little priest took another path; now he's going to be a healer of bodies."[13]

When vacation time arrived, Pedro and his family used to go regularly to Algorta, a coastal village in a secluded cove. With its granite church facing the sea, the village preserved the distinct charm of the Basque coastline, along which sailed small, brightly colored boats. Fishermen wearing berets would sew their nets while seated on stone benches; their vigorous Basque faces, gazing off into the distance, were part of the place's natural features.

Pedro and his sisters lived in the village, in one of those solid dark houses that lined the narrow streets winding down to the sea, where they would go to bathe. During the long, quiet summer evenings, Pedro used to meet with his friends to play cards or to sing old Basque songs to guitar accompaniment. Such songs, and the beloved *zortzikos*, remained fixed in his memory, and he would sing them again and again throughout his life, even when he traveled far from home, "leagues of land away, leagues of land and sea."[14]

Meanwhile, Pedrito's nose kept growing, and his forehead broadened; his head became a little oblong, and he began to display that vivacious air that would characterize him all his life. He was eleven years old and studying his first year of secondary school when, on March 29, 1918, he entered the Marian congregation directed by the already mentioned Ángel Basterra, who was famous throughout Bilbao for the great number of young people who passed through his hands.

Young Arrupe was then living at no. 7 Astarloa Street. When he came to form part of the "Kostkas," as the group's members were called, Ignacio Galdeano was president of the congregation, Carlos García Iturri was vice-president, Jesús Landa

---

always expressed his gratitude for the education he received with the Piarists. Four days after being elected in 1965, he celebrated the Eucharist in the Piarist house of Saint Pantaleon in Rome, where he also visited the former quarters of the founder, Saint Joseph Calasanz, and had breakfast with the community.

13 Statements made by Sister María Arrupe, Slave of the Sacred Heart, to the journal *Ya* (May 29, 1965).

14 Information provided by Fernando Gondra.

Don Marcelino Arrupe y Ugarte, Pedro's father, teaching his son his first letters.

y Mendo was secretary, Guillermo Videgaín Alcorta was vice-secretary, and Pedro Ruiz Mendiola was treasurer. Jesuit Luis María Abreu would later recall:

> My mother took me to the congregation to make my first Communion, and Pedro prepared me for it. He was on the council, and the director, Fr. Ángel Basterra, assigned him that job. I was studying with the Augustinians since the Jesuit school at Indauchu [Indautxu] had still not opened; Pedro studied with the Piarists. I cannot say that we became friends at that time. Our families knew one another and were friendly, but I was only seven years old, and four years of difference is very significant at that age. As was then the custom for the kids who wanted to enter the "Congre," I made my Communion on the second Sunday of Easter, in the church of the Jesuit residence of Bilbao. Pedro was very bright, very good, and very pleasant. [...] I got to know Pedro shortly after his mother died. His family was distinguished, related to the high society of Vizcaya; his father was an architect. They were rich ("millionaires," we used to say then), but they lived simply, without displaying their wealth.[15]

---

15   Thus stated in the "Commitment to the Rule," number 569, signed by "Pedro de Arrupe." Besides the names of mother and father, the document states that the congregation member promises to pay two pesetas monthly, that he is in second year of secondary at the Piarist college, and that he lives at number 7 Astarloa Street, third floor on the left. Statements of Arbeo to Margenat ("De Bilbao a Japón [1907–1938]," 65–66).

A little later, Pedro Arrupe Gondra became prefect of the prayer vigils, and he was chosen for the post of treasurer. By 1922, he was vice-president. The congregation had a small publication called *Flores y frutos* (Flowers and fruits), to which the students made literary contributions. From 1923 on, Pedro was an eager collaborator of the magazine.

In the March 1923 issue, we find a curious allusion to Japan and to the missions in an essay by Arrupe, who refers to the "tender and strained heart" of Francis Xavier: "Would that I had such a heart, [...] and could do as much good as he did!" Around the same time, two former members of the congregation, Narciso and Antonio Irala, who were Jesuit scholastics studying at Oña and would soon become missionaries in China, also wrote for *Flores y frutos*, giving witness to the missionary spirit that was abroad in those days.

University Student in Madrid

At the window of the train coming from Bilbao could be seen the face of a handsome young man; he had a wide mouth, well-defined lips, and bright eyes touched with nostalgia. The year was 1923. Pedro's hair was perfectly combed, and he wore an impeccable striped shirt and a neatly knotted tie. Looking through the window, his astonished eyes beheld the sights of multi-colored Madrid: the station guard with thick mustache and wide overalls, the newly painted cigarette stand, the haughty civil guard, the servant girl dressed in lace, and the dandy following her with his fancy coiffure and crazy remarks. Arrupe, suitcase in hand, took in all of that *Belle Époque* ambience as he walked to the house of his sister Margarita, where he would live during his first year as a university student in the capital.

Those were the years of the bay windows, the old dolls on the sofa, the pianola, and the dances at the Ritz, where nobody dared to tango because the dance had been prohibited by the archbishop of Paris. In those days, rickety Fords were the last word in elegance as they rolled through the streets of Madrid, with the driver's throat protected by a scarf. The city had still not recovered from the assassination of Prime Minister Eduardo Dato, who had been shot and killed right in the middle of the Plaza de la Independencia. Being head of government was beginning to be a dangerous occupation: Juan Prim, Antonio Cánovas, José Canalejas, and now Dato. The crises of government were taking place beneath the languid gaze of King Alfonso XIII. Meanwhile, Jacinto Benavente was about to receive the Nobel Prize for his book *Los intereses creados* (Created interests [1907]), while Santiago Ramón y Cajal was about to receive one for his scientific discoveries. The people of Madrid writhed with laughter at the humor of Pedro Muñoz Seca, or were dazzled by the lyrical beauty of Miguel Fleta's romantic novels. In Moguer, Juan Ramón Jiménez dipped his pen into nostalgia allusions to the infinite: "Heaven, a word the size of the sea / that we leave behind us in forgetfulness."

The dictatorship was on the verge of exploding. The social tensions were most evident in the class struggle and the gangsterism of Catalonia, and many problems were arising from the colonial war in Africa. These factors, along with an unviable political system that was becoming progressively more isolated, were pressing the conservative social forces to seek a political solution that would violate the 1876 Constitution. What finally sparked off the explosion was the colonial problem and the notorious Disaster of Annual (1921), where around thirteen thousand died. Rumors of a *coup d'état* were floating in the air, and not even Alfonso XIII discounted them. On the night of September 12, 1923, with the monarch's acquiescence, Spain came under the dictatorship of Miguel Primo de Rivera y Orbaneja, second marquis of Estella, lieutenant general in the army, and captain general of Catalonia. That same year, another general, Francisco Franco, married a young woman named Carmen Polo. Farther away, in legendary Tokyo, a city that for Arrupe was then only a name, a hundred thousand Japanese died in a catastrophic earthquake.

"After finishing secondary school in Bilbao," Pedro would later write,

> when I walked the streets of la Corte [in Madrid] for the first time, I experienced the fresh emotions of one who suddenly finds himself taken out the holy hothouse of an austere Christian family and thrust into the unrestrained vertigo of youthful life in the big city. However, routine also takes over one's feelings, so I soon stopped feeling that vibration. I was less moved by the history of those who had preceded me. My prime concern became my own story, with all its insignificance, but with its own heartbeat.

Arrupe spent many long hours studying, though he would with modesty write later: "I attended the medical school of San Carlos, and I studied enough to be able to get good marks, but without killing myself."[16] The fact is that Pedro, as we shall see, was a splendid student. He could be seen emerging from the old building of San Carlos in Atocha, smiling amid the swarm of students. He would walk toward the Great Way, amid the vaulted eighteenth-century edifices, while the sky darkened as in a Velázquez painting. Waiting for him at the corner would be his friend Enrique, who was studying to be a mining engineer and had a jovial, talkative manner.

"How are you, Enrique?"

"Hey, let me tell you! I'm having real problems with thermodynamics! How is it going with you?"

"My problems are with the anatomy course. The professor is extremely strict and demanding."

---

16   Pedro Arrupe, *Este Japón increíble (Memorias del P. Arrupe)* [This incredible Japan (Memoir of Father Arrupe)] (Bilbao Mensajero, 1959). Henceforth, I will refer to this work simply as *Memorias*. A later edition in Mexico has the title *Yo viví la bomba atómica* [I experienced the atomic bomb] (México: Patria, 1965). Cf. *Memorias*, 8.

Pedro with his mother, Doña Dolores Gondra y Robles, and his sisters María and Isabel.

"For you? Come on, Perico, you're an unbearable grind!"

The two friends walked up the Great Way until they reached no. 7, Pi y Margall Street. On the ninth floor was the Catholic Students' Residence, a confessional version of the "House of Troya," where a cheerful atmosphere reigned, but also one of serious study.

"At Christmastime I moved into the residence," recalls Enrique Chacón, a close friend of Arrupe in those days:

It was a wonderful place. A majority of those forty students, almost all from Bilbao and a few Catalonians, went to Mass and received Communion. We succeeded in getting rid of the old director, who was inept, and had Don Joaquín Espinosa put in his place. On the floor above lived the famous Marcelino Oreja, a deputy in the Cortes and manager of *El debate*; he would later be assassinated in Mondragón during the revolution of October 1934. Living there with us were Corral, Luis Uribe, Artaza, a very congenial group of Bilbao boys.[17]

During those years, Pedro spent his vacations in the Basque country. He received an especially welcome invitation during one of those summer periods. A Jesuit friend, the Colombian Juan María Restrepo Jaramillo, who was studying theology in Valkenburg, Holland, was going to be ordained to the priesthood. He had gotten to know Pedro during a vacation he spent in Bilbao, when Pedro was still studying with the Piarists. Juan María asked his parents that, as an ordination present, they invite his friend Perico to attend the ordination and his first Mass when they passed through Spain from Colombia, on their way to the ordination

The Colombian family did just that. In Spain, they obtained a car, and they took Pedro with them on a trip through Europe. Pedro felt like one of the family, and each night he received the blessing of the Restrepo Jaramillo couple, as was the custom in Colombia. Furthermore, the family recalls that during the trip a

---

17 Statements to the author by Enrique Chacón, S.J.

little romance developed between Pedro and one of Juan María's sisters. Years later, she would marry a famous Colombian doctor, Alberto Bernal Nicholls, and give birth to Sergio Bernal Restrepo, who would also enter the Society of Jesus in due course.[18]

First Contact with Injustice

Once back in Madrid, Enrique and Pedro decided, along with other friends, to become members of the Conference of Saint Vincent de Paul. Every day without fail, they entered earnestly into the unfamiliar world of the city slums and came into contact with the reality of injustice.

Arrupe describes his experience thus:

All that, I sincerely confess, was a totally new world for me. I met up with people suffering the terrible pain of misery and abandonment. Widows surrounded by children and asking for bread, and nobody giving them any. Sick people begging for alms to buy medicine. [...] And above all, children, many children, some half-abandoned, others abused, most of them poorly clothed, and all of them constantly hungry.

"What are you having for a snack," one day I asked a little boy.

"Nothing," he answered me crisply, while munching on a yam with satisfaction.

"Then what are you doing?" I asked, smiling.

"Having breakfast," he answered with a seriousness that chilled the smile on my lips.

"But it's four o'clock in the afternoon!"

"I know, but this is the first food I've eaten. For you it may be a snack, but for me it's breakfast." His voice resonated with something—I'm not sure whether it was forced politeness or contained anger.

"You haven't had any food all day? Doesn't your father work?"

"We hardly ever have any food. We never eat more than once a day, and my father doesn't work because I don't have one."

What a chilling analysis he made of his misery and his hunger! Like a famished dog, he wandered through the streets picking up pieces of stale,

---

18   Information provided to the author in a letter (Chicago, October 13, 1986) of Eduardo Pinzón, S.J., who claims to have heard Father Juan María Restrepo, S.J. tell this story several times. Restrepo was Arrupe's friend from the time Arrupe was studying in Bilbao with the Piarists; so close were they that Restrepo invited Arrupe to his ordination to the priesthood in Valkenburg. On that journey, Arrupe met Restrepo's sister and was attracted to her; as far as we know, this was Pedro's only romantic involvement before deciding to become a Jesuit. A further curiosity is that this woman, the only girlfriend Pedro ever had, later married and had a son who became a Jesuit: Sergio Bernal Restrepo, who was a professor of sociology in the Gregorian.

soiled bread; in that way, he helped out his mother, who was a widow with several children.

But there was another case that moved me even more deeply, because it reflected not just an isolated pain, but an extremely concentrated dose of misery. It happened in Vallecas. I was walking with my friend Enrique, and we were both gripped by the nervous emotion of experiencing something new. We were supposed to visit a family we did not know, one that would be entering into our lives for the first time. It may be true that begging out of need can be very difficult, but it can also be very hard to give when one fears that the alms will offend the recipient. […] We got closer to the place we were going, but we weren't sure of exactly where it was. To clear up our doubts, we approached a stooped old woman who was working near the entrance of a house.

"Excuse us," we said, "but do you know where Doña Luisa lives?"

We gave her all the information that we had been given ourselves.

"Just as I thought!" she answered with satisfaction, speaking her words with a whistle caused by a missing tooth. "Luisa lives in that big house across the way. Go in and take the staircase to the left. She's on the second floor, in room number 10."

"Thank you very much. I am sure with those instructions we'll find her quickly."

As we were getting ready to leave, the old woman held our attention a little longer with her inspired eloquence.

"Yes, Luisa is a very good woman. And living there with her is Luciana, the other widow."

"Yes, we want to see her also."

"Are you from the conference? Don't tell me, because I already know it. I have seen you so many times that I would recognize you from a mile away. Jesus! What handsome lads you are!" Her octogenarian flattery burst forth from her broken teeth.

"For God's sake, dear lady, don't exaggerate!"

Giving her no more time to continue analyzing our physical appearance, we took leave of her and walked to the entrance of the house where Luisa and Luciana lived.

Upon entering, we met up with a young kid who gave us further information.

With the cheekiness of a slum lad, but also with a certain respect, he spoke rapidly: "That way, gentleman, upstairs, number 10. But be careful with the stairs, since on the first landing there are some holes that you could fall through."

"Thanks, pal. Here's something for you."

I gave him a large piece of candy, which perhaps had come from La India, the famous pastry shop where we were frequent customers.

We started upstairs. The walls were dark and filthy; even touching them aroused disgust. Poverty and abandonment were everywhere evident. No note of joy was to be found anywhere. We finally reached number 10, a low door like all the rest. Some loud yelling was coming from inside, with the harsh voice of a woman standing out.

"Perico, this is like a madhouse," Enrique told me after listening for a moment.

"If that's all it is, we're okay. We'd be much worse off if we found ourselves in a lion's den full of cubs. Those shouts are really something."

We decided to knock. After knocking three times, we finally heard someone say: "What do you want?"

We looked at one another without knowing what to do. They had not invited us to enter, and we had no desire to try to explain things through the door.

"Don't answer. Let's knock again," Enrique said.

"Come on, man! Who's there?"

We decided to give a graphic explanation and so we opened the door. Everybody turned to look at us, and we were received with profound silence. Six half-naked children, hair disheveled, prudently took refuge in their mothers' skirts. The two women stood up and came toward us.

When they saw we were not from the neighborhood, they were extremely curious. Discovering that we were "from the conference," they were justifiably delighted.

We began to speak, and when they saw that we came in peace, the atmosphere of distrust created by the children's frightened silence gradually disappeared. A few handfuls of candy finally did away with all the suspicion our presence had aroused.

The room was spacious but run-down and without much furniture. There was a large bed with a shabby blanket covering the mattress, a wobbly table in the center, several chairs with missing legs and little stability, and a couple of cupboards containing assorted items.

We tried to conceal our dismay, but we were not quite able to do so. Noting our disquiet, Luisa asked us, with a sense of humor that seemed heroic in the midst of such poverty: "How do you like our palace?"

"The room is quite large," said one of us, I'm not sure which. "It's not so bad, but it depends on what the rest of the house is like."

"What house?" Luciana asked calmly.

"Why, this one, your house," we explained. "If the other rooms are the same, then it's not such a bad situation."

"They are all the same as this one," Luisa stated, "because here, where you see us, we eat and sleep. Here the kids play and we women work. On the rainy days when they can't go out, they give us headaches with their screaming. You must have heard the noise when you were outside."

Pedro dressed as a sailor and accompanied by playmates in a park of Bilbao, watched over by the nannies.

"The eight of you live here in this room?" we asked without wanting to. "And where do you sleep?"

"Where do we sleep? In the bed."

"All eight of you?"

"Yes, all eight."

We stood there in silence. So impossible did that seem to us that our expression reflected our doubts. Anxious to help us out, one of the women

During a procession through Bilbao (Pedro in center with candle), when he was a student of Piarist Fathers.

said gently: "We'll show you! Everybody get in bed, each one in place. Let these gentlemen see how you sleep."

Like a flock of birds, the six little ones went running to their nest. A moment later, they were all stretched out on the frayed blanket, which was a sickly pink color with some dark stains that gave it life.

"What do you think? Half a football team in the sack! And there they sleep the whole night without stirring or waking up. We women have a hard time sleeping there because our bodies sink down and the kids tumble on us. They are a bother, but since they're our children, we forgive them everything." Her final words were spoken with affection.

Before we could bring ourselves to say anything interesting, the other woman spoke: "The bed is the least of our worries, because the kids at least get their sleep. What is worse is the matter of food. Imagine, the poor kids have nothing more than what we can provide them, and we have no pension or widows' aid. The only income is from our work. And of course one of us always has to stay here in order to take care of the children and the house."

"What do the little ones eat?" I asked in a low voice, feeling remorse as I recalled all the sweets I had so often devoured in La India.

"Almost nothing, really. In the morning and at night, some garlic soup and whatever bread may be found. At noontime, a dish of beans or garbanzos with a piece of bread."

"And do they go outside dressed the way they are now?"

"Of course! How can we afford to buy them coats or jackets? When it gets very cold, we have them stay in bed all day, covered with the only blanket we have, but it's difficult. You know how kids are."

We continued to talk about minor matters, and we gave them our alms. We handed out more candy to the children, who cheered us, and we left the apartment taking care not to fall through the holes on the landing. I felt overwhelmed by the sight of so much misery, and Enrique even more so. After a long while, I finally asked him:

"Enrique, you know what I'm thinking?"

"What?"

"That we're going to end up doing without something."

"Without what?"

"Chantilly candy and oriental cakes."

"La India?"

"Right. How can we dare spend all our money on pastries? We'll have to revise our budget, don't you think?"

"I agree."

"Should we begin today?"

"Whatever you want."[19]

On their way home, Enrique Chacón and Pedro Arrupe hurried past the display window of La India, the pastry store, where enticing delicacies were calling out to be eaten.

This experience gave Arrupe his first clear evidence of the world's inequalities. It was his first contact with flagrant injustice, and it injected revolutionary stirrings into his Christian commitment. Around this same time, he also got to know a man of unassuming appearance who wandered around the slums of Ventanilla: it was a Jesuit named José María Rubio, who was known around Madrid for his holiness.

Enrolled in Medical School

During exam times, commotion reigned on the ninth floor of no. 7 Pi y Margall Street. A student might be seen pacing back and forth endlessly in the hallway, reciting aloud his class notes. Another might emerge from the apartment, pale as a lost soul for not having slept the whole night before. The weather in Madrid was already getting warm, and young girls could be seen flirting in El Retiro or Rosales. From a distance could be heard the calming song of a nursemaid and the soft chanting of the vendors: "Here we have water, sweets, and strong drink!" The afternoons had become long and melancholic; hot chocolate had given way to chilled fruit juice.

---

19 *Memorias*, 8ff.

Arrupe with hat and short pants, standing next to the first Jesuit he knew, Father Ángel Basterra, director of the congregation of the Kostkas of Bilbao; he ministered to Arrupe's parents on their deathbeds (March 19, 1924).

"Where are you going?"

"To study."

"Where?"

"To Arrupe's room."

"Why there?"

"Because there we don't waste time."

Indeed, Pedro's companions competed for his company, even if they were studying another career or different subjects. Just being around him was an aid to study.[20]

Enrique was having a tough time. He had much mathematical ability, but his mining courses required him to memorize the Latin names of all the fossils. His grades were going down, and one day he said to Pedro, "Perico, my father is going to kill me."

"No, Enrique, things will work out. Come to my room to study."

A few days later, Enrique spied Pedro in the hallway, and he ran up and grabbed him by the throat: "You saved me, Perico! I got a 19.5 [out of 20]!" Another of Enrique's problems was getting up in the morning. Pedro used to rouse him and then threaten to throw a basin of water on his head if he didn't get out of bed.

And the results spoke for themselves. The certificate of grades for Arrupe's three years as a medical student, now wrinkled and yellowed with age, could not be more brilliant: of the eighteen courses he took, he received a grade of "outstanding" in sixteen, and fifteen of those included a scholarship award (*matrícula de honor*).

Thus did Pedro spend his university years, amid classrooms, long hours of study, and working in the slums. He was very devout, going to Mass and receiving Communion daily, but he was a very normal guy, with a bright and jovial character. His friend Enrique had found a girlfriend and was close to finishing his engineering degree. When they could, they would escape to the theater, a concert, or the opera.

"Perico, today Fleta is singing *The Barber of Seville*. You shouldn't miss it. Are you signing up for the outing?"

---

20   Testimony of Enrique Chacón.

Arrupe would later write:

> I very much enjoyed the theater, music, opera. Especially the opera! We organized a fan club and bought our tickets at a bar where the chairs were made of metal and the silverware was attached to the tables with chains. [...] We were young!
>
> In those days, Miguel Fleta was making his debut. He had been a grocery vendor making his way through the streets of Zaragoza with a little burro. As an opera singer, he had a powerful, inspiring voice that was still untrained. He had much success in Madrid and was often interrupted by his admirers' applause. He would get down on his knees and beg the public to allow him to continue, [...] and then we would applaud him even more! [...] I liked *Aida, Lohengrin, Thais, The Barber of Seville*, and musicals like *Teresita*, which was a hit in those days.[21]

At times, there were financial difficulties on the seventh floor, and the students tried to become more independent. "It was a question of just having enough food," Arrupe later recalled:

> After reviewing the house accounts, we decided to cook for ourselves. There were twenty-five of us there at the time. Fortunately, the mother of one of the guys came to help us out. There were certainly a lot of arguments and conflicts among us, but in the end it was very agreeable period.[22]

There was no lack of the jokes typical of students. For example, Pedro and his friends once got one of the skulls used to study anatomy and tied it to a long stick. They set out to frighten the neighbors downstairs by dangling the gruesome human remnant out of the window. One day, a neighbor gave the skull such a whack with a broom that it was wrecked completely.

On another occasion, Pedro was walking through the streets of Madrid with another medical student. In front of them, a bow-legged man was hobbling along. The two students attempted to diagnose the ailment, but after arguing for a while in vain they decided to ask the man directly. Turning around and displaying a certain annoyance, the man answered, "What do I have? My problem is what I have done in my pants."[23]

Still, in the midst of that university life Pedro kept asking: What am I doing here?

> Then I began to ask myself more frequently: Why have I come into the world? To live a few years of sterile anonymity and then face the other life without having done anything worthwhile? Ignorant as I was at the time,

---

21   *Itinéraire*, 70.

22   *Itinéraire*, 68.

23   Anecdotes that Arrupe related to Luis González, S.J.

Pedro at age sixteen, when he moved to Madrid to study medicine

I was putting all the blame for those vexing questions on those six street urchins of Vallecas. If their poverty had not so overwhelmed me, I kept saying, I would be happily advancing in my university career. […] Later on, I realized that those poor urchins, living their hard, scar-filled life, had done nothing more than remove from my eyes the veil of ignorance. They made me think. They awakened in me that longing for great aspirations that I had until then been dragging behind me, lost in the flow of my unconscious. They were the ones that first alerted me that I was carelessly drifting toward a far too ordinary existence.

It was a great gift of God. Neither studies nor entertainments could ever erase the indelible emotional seal that visit to Vallecas had firmly stamped on my soul. I was at the point of crossing the bridge of my youth, but without knowing how to soar to the heights. Only because God wanted it so was I able to stop my headlong plunge and turn in a new direction.[24]

The streets of Madrid were festive, and people formed long lines to enter the theaters. The crowds joined in the noisy carnival along the Castellana promenade,

---

24 *Memorias*, 13. An article signed by "A." in *Flores y frutos* 142 (May 1, 1925) relates another episode of these apostolic experiences, in what appears to be a letter addressed to Father Basterra with the title "A Committed Veteran": "We are so busy that we hardly have time to breathe since with our classes, the Saint Vincent de Paul Conferences, catechesis, etc., the precious time we have escapes us. [...] As I told you at Christmastime, we proposed starting catechism classes in one of the outlying barrios of Madrid, in Vallecas, and from the start we have worked hard to turn our proposals into realities. The second Sunday after vacation we began to put into practice what at the beginning of the course seemed only a dream. We hold the catechesis in a college the nuns have, right at the center of the barrio. The sisters have been happy to give us space and have also helped in all sorts of other ways. The first day something exceptional happened: we announced that the first class would be on the last Sunday of January, and the sisters' chaplain said he would let everybody know. For our part, we also announced the classes among the poor people we knew, so that their children would come. What happened was that, after the eleven o'clock Mass (the time we had set for the start of class), the six of us catechists sat down waiting for the 'great crowd' to come to us. We waited till eleven-forty, quarter to twelve, twelve o'clock, [...] and not one kid showed up. Then, with all the solemnity that the grand audience required of us, we took our leave. We joked a lot about it, and it gave us a chance to tease one another; the chaplain, however, took it quite to heart and came to tell us that we should not get discouraged, that the following Sunday more children would come, etc., etc. As a result we concluded that the poor man had become quite flustered, thinking that he was almost completely to blame for what had happened.

"The next Sunday, after doing more publicity, we had eight children; since then the number has increased to about forty, and we distribute them among the seven of us catechists. As you can see, the program is much greater than we had dreamed of, since almost every Sunday some new student arrives; by the end of the term we hope to have sixty students. We are hoping to be able to borrow a projector, which would be a sure attraction for the children of the barrio, and afterward for their parents as well.

"Now we are working on a much more difficult project, namely some conferences for the adults. What is stupendous is that we had already been thinking about such a project, but now it is they (the workers) who are requesting it of us, so we just can't say no. The biggest difficulty is finding a place, but once that is resolved, as we hope it will be soon, we will begin this second part of the program, which will be much more serious than the first. The other day, we were talking with them, and they told us that they almost believed in God, but about all the rest, forget it. As you can see, it is a frightful audience; the first day we got a stone thrown at our heads when we were coming out of one of those talks."

or they showed off their abilities and their stylish outfits in the skating rink of El Retiro: "If you go to El Retiro to have a good time, / Be careful when you step out to skate, / For they've told me that many a lad / Has ended up leaving with a lifelong mate [...]." Whenever Pedro passed through the center of Madrid with books under his arm, contemplating that noisy spectacle of the twenties, his imagination would inevitably turn to the sad little houses of Vallecas, the other face, the sorrowful face of an unjust world.

3. From Doctor to Jesuit

The class beadle peered over his glasses to check his pocket watch. It was twelve noon. Then he sat up and greeted the teacher, Dr. Juan Negrín, professor of physiology. With his broad face, round spectacles, and serious intellectual mien, no one would have guessed that that socialist professor, member of the party founded by printer Pablo Iglesias, would become deeply involved in politics and be made prime minister of the Republic in 1937. But on this day he had a class to give, and he was making his way toward the classroom.

The flutter of books and notes, youthful laughter and voices, all quieted down as the professor arrived. Before proceeding to the platform and beginning his lecture, he surveyed the students. Stopping before an empty desk, he asked:

"And where is Pedro Arrupe?"

The professor's question gave rise to surprised murmuring among the students. It was not normal for a professor, especially Negrín, to take note of a student's absence. He was a figure with much influence in the Central University, along with other professors known for their agnosticism, such as Doctors Teófilo Hernando and José de Medinabeitia.

"He is in Bilbao," commented one of Arrupe's close friends, of whom there were several in that class, including Valentín Matilla, Enrique Poyuelo, and Severo Ochoa.

Shortly after Arrupe's death, Ochoa wrote to Arrupe's niece Mariví Gondra, recalling how his fellow classmate at the university had bested him to win an extraordinary prize:

> During our third year of studies, I took pharmacology and therapeutics along with other courses; among the students who got grades of "outstanding" were Arrupe and I. In the end, we were all given an exercise to decide which student would receive the *matrícula de honor*. I don't recall which other companions were competing, but I do remember that Arrupe and I were among them. He was the winner. I gave a dissertation about something I had read in a French journal of physiotherapy. I don't know what Arrupe gave his dissertation on, but the adjunct professor Dámaso Arrese explained to me the reason for my failure. Pedro Arrupe had not only studied the textbook of Dr. Teófilo Hernando, as most of us did; he had also studied the famous book on experimental pharmacology by Mayer and Gottlieb, and his mastery of the topics was evident. As we began our fourth year, and with it the clinical experience, Pedro Arrupe did not reappear in class. I learned from García Comas about his decision to enter the Society of Jesus.

In later years, Ochoa, a Nobel Prize winner in medicine and a religious agnostic, met Arrupe several times in Japan, New York, and Rome. He relates in the letter:

> I remember that on one occasion, when my wife Carmen and I were with some friends, we were speaking of Arrupe. When I mentioned what I just related, that Arrupe was by far the best student of the class, Carmen quickly commented: "Yes, and he was also the one who chose the best career."

Ochoa mentioned other meetings with his old friend and concluded: "Speaking with Arrupe was a privileged experience. What intelligence, what kindness, what a brain!"[1]

Complete Darkness

At the moment when Professor Negrín asked about his absence, Pedro was in fact in Bilbao. His tear-filled eyes were fixed on a distressing scene: his sisters gathered around the bed of Don Marcelino, who was gasping in the throes of death. Waiting at bedside, Pedro looked out the window and saw Bilbao preparing itself, as it did every year, for the Sacred Heart procession. Right in front of the Arrupe house, an altar was being set up and a carpet of flowers laid down.

Suddenly, Pedro recalled himself as a young boy with a candle in his hand, following his gigantic father through the streets of Bilbao, never missing a year. Tears again flooded his eyes, and he returned to the present reality.

"When I looked out the window," Pedro later wrote, "I saw Father Basterra coming through our gateway. I quickly went downstairs to meet him:

> "How is Don Marcelino," he asked me.
>
> "Not well! He is unconscious."
>
> "Poor Perico! How the Lord tests you! But look," he said, pointing to the statue of the Heart of Jesus that was then being placed on the altar in the street, "there you have your true father, who died for you, but who always lives at your side."
>
> From that time on, Jesus was my true father.[2]

When Don Marcelino gave his ultimate sigh, Pedro was devastated; he gazed into empty space and pondered the senselessness of death. At the age of nineteen, with all his life before him, he had been left an orphan. His sisters Margarita,

---

1   From a letter of Severo Ochoa written after Arrupe's death to Maraví Gondra, Arrupe's niece.

2   From an article quoted in *Flores y frutos* and included in *El correo español: El pueblo vasco*, May 25, 1965, 28. Father Arrupe himself confirmed the information to the author of this book. Also in *Itinéraire*, Father Arrupe states that the Sacred Heart procession was passing at that moment.

Madrid in the 1920s, where Pedro studied at the university and had his first experience of injustice.

Catalina, María, and Isabel looked at him as they sobbed and embraced him as the only hope, the only expectation and support for the family. At that moment, his vision clouded over, and he could see nothing clearly: university, books, physiology, the trips with Enrique to the slums of Madrid. He felt nothing but emptiness within himself as he walked through that house whose furniture, hallways, clocks, and mute photos recalled loved ones who were no longer there. He saw his mother, as in former times, busy with her chores in the kitchen. He saw Don Marcelino returning from work with *La gaceta* in his hand and asking, "What's up, Peru? How was school today?" Now the world had become a huge black hole, in the middle of which only a twinkle of light could be discerned.

> That psychological state of interior sadness, which none of my companions knew of or suspected in me, dulled my senses for only a moment. That sorrowful day, which I will always remember with the deepest pain, my father left us to take flight to God. Those were moments of sobbing anxiety, mitigated only by the sweet caress of faith.
>
> Only then, when pain came upon me with the heavy weight of that separation, did I forget the urgent question that had been bothering me for so long. What difference does it make, I wondered, to come into the world for one thing or another? Why should I worry about what I have to do in the world?
>
> After a few months, though, life again pursued its normal course. I became aware that slowly, very slowly, I was beginning to see life as I had

seen it before. Doubts, joys, worries—all the intimate passions of my youth began to vibrate within me again, and I heard the echoes of a kindly voice that in my days of grief I thought was gone forever.

After the first days of mourning, we all decided to travel to some quiet place where we could spend a peaceful summer, the first in which our father would not be with us.

After considerable deliberation, we decided to go to Lourdes for a month, thus putting aside the more lively possibility of visiting the northerly lands of Cantabrico.

One July day, enveloped in the mists of that sea that was so much ours, we caught the train to cross the border into Irún. Once again I was taking a step toward the unknown.[3]

Miracle Within

The train wailed as it passed through the green valleys of Lourdes. The clean, fresh air of the mountains entered through the windows, along with the white vapor from the engine. From afar, the first towers could be glimpsed. Feeling a shudder run through him, Pedro smiled and looked at his sisters, exclaiming: "Lourdes!"

He felt within himself a vague expectation, a kind of presentiment: "I arrived at Lourdes with much curiosity. I didn't know what I would find there, and it was precisely that ignorance that made me excited about the month I would spend there. There was a *kind of presentiment* that I myself didn't know how to define."

Pedro and his sisters made their way among the stretcher bearers, Boy Scouts, pilgrims, and other devotees who crowded into the train station. As he walked through the streets of the town and looked about at all the hotels and businesses, he was left confused by his first impressions: Was this a place of pilgrimage or a center of commerce? Stoves, knives, shirts, everything was bought and sold in the name of Lourdes—even miraculous water.

But when farther on he discovered the towers of Lourdes and entered into the esplanade, he felt something very special: "If Mary had not come to Lourdes, it would be just another town, lost in the anonymity and remote silence of the Pyrenees."[4]

Flowing gently in front of the church, with a soft rippling, was the Gave River, an unpretentious stream that reminded pilgrims that everything about the place was small and silent. A little farther on was the grotto, snuggled into the mountainside; separated from the religious tourism and commerce, it maintained a profound silence in which all else could be forgotten and only the quiet murmur of the water could be heard.

---

3   *Memorias*, 14.
4   *Memorias*, 15.

Arrupe (standing, second from the left) surrounded by companions at the students' residence in Madrid.

"One of the first things I obtained," Pedro later reported,

despite not having finished my medical studies, was a special certificate that allowed me to examine the sick people who were seeking to be cured through the mediation of the Virgin, and also those who were cured gradually and who gave testimony by their health that they had received a miraculous grace.

I was delighted to be able to be present in the Bureau de constatation, which verified the miracles whenever there were any. So many times I had heard some of my professors at San Carlos ranting about the "deceptions" at Lourdes.[5]

Pedro had the good fortune to witness what appeared to be three miracles in that month of July in 1927. He narrates the events himself:

The first extraordinary case was that of a nun, still young, who found herself in a state that seemed humanly hopeless. She was sick with Pott's disease and had tuberculosis in her backbone; a couple of her vertebrae were already eaten away by the pus. Half her body had long been imprisoned in a plaster cast, and she was totally immobilized by paralysis.

---

5   *Memorias*, 15ff.

But she bore her suffering with tremendous resignation! She uttered not a complaint or strong word toward those who were reluctantly making her suffer through their methods of treatment. She smiled often and offered everybody an affectionate glance and a few words, which with great difficulty slipped from her unmoving lips.

One day, she had the good fortune that they took her to the grand esplanade in front of the basilica in order to receive the blessing there.

The church doors opened, and the procession moved toward the esplanade, where people could be heard murmuring the rosary. While a hymn to the Virgin was sung in countless tongues, the cries of the sick all repeated the same phrase: "Our Lady of Lourdes, have mercy on us."

The Blessed Sacrament made its slow way forward. A bishop was blessing people with the monstrance, which stood out like a cross in the bright August sun.

During a solemn moment, as the procession continued its painfully slow pace, the two of them found themselves face to face: Jesus Christ, the same in the Eucharist and in Jerusalem, and the paralyzed nun. […] I don't know how they beheld one another, but a loving contact took place between them.

It was something instantaneous. Crying out, she sat up on the stretcher, reached out her arms toward the Eucharist and fell forward on her knees.

"I am cured!" was all she could say.

And like an immense amplifier that caught her voice, the whole crowd of people repeated: "*Le miracle!*"

A few days later, I got to see another sick woman who was miraculously cured. She had been born in Brussels. She reached the age of seventy-five in a fragile state of health. Since she had a terrible stomach cancer, the doctors performed an exploratory laparotomy in a last attempt to save her, but they finally recognized that a cure was impossible.

In order to prepare her to die well, they informed her of the gravity of her illness. […] In the doctors' opinion, she had so little time left that it would have been a crime to postpone those essential measures.

"There is no cure?" the sick woman asked in a faint voice.

"Unfortunately not. Only a miracle can save you."

She was silent for a moment. She recollected herself and with a faith and naturalness that amazed everybody, she gently suggested: "Then why don't we do what is necessary so that a miracle may happen?"

Her words were received with a silence that reflected uncertainty and fear. Could it be that she had lost her wits out of fear of her fast-approaching death?

"If I go to Lourdes, I can be cured," she continued, making herself more explicit.

Looking at one another and silently agreeing among themselves, the doctors responded unanimously: "Impossible, madam. Going to Lourdes in the condition you're in would most certainly bring on death even more quickly. Given your weakness and your sickness, you could never make a journey that required you to cross the whole of France."

Despite the formal opposition of the doctors, the old woman refused to be dissuaded. "What difference does it make, dying on the road in a week or dying here within a month? I prefer to risk losing a fortnight of my life on the chance of gaining a few years, because I am sure that the Virgin can cure me if that is what is good for me."

The next day, she set out. They transported her with great care, and she arrived at Lourdes exhausted but alive.

During the first procession after her arrival, they placed her with the other sick people so that she could receive the Lord's gaze. In the midst of a silence broken only by prayers, Christ passed before her [...], without performing a miracle.

But that woman was like the Canaanite woman or the centurion in the Gospel. She was a believer who had the kind of faith that moves mountains and gains from God whatever it seeks.

Since she was absolutely sure that she would be cured, they took her to bathe in the pool of miraculous water. After leaving the pool, she felt no immediate change at all, but when she arrived at the hospital where she was staying, she felt hungry.

She ate without feeling the least discomfort. A few hours later, she again felt an appetite that seemed inexplicable given her serious condition, and she ate again, this time more solid things, without any difficulty in digesting and assimilating everything perfectly.

Within three days, she was walking around Lourdes in perfect health. Hers was a miracle that was recognized by the experts as unquestionable. When she was x-rayed, there was not the least trace in her stomach of the cancer that she had been suffering; her organism was restored, with no sign of the earlier disease.

Her blind faith had been answered.

I want to make note of the third miracle that I saw because it involves some especially curious details.

A tremendous assembly of pilgrims had gathered together, with huge groups of innumerable sorts of people. It was an immense gathering of some twelve thousand believers, and they came together on the grand esplanade for an extraordinary manifestation of faith.

Although we had attended many processions in the days we'd spent there, the unusual number of people on this occasion attracted us irresistibly toward the basilica.

Pedro (first on left) attending a laboratory class at the Faculty of San Carlos.

On the way, we mixed with pilgrims and sick people, who were all enthusiastically seeking the most appropriate place from which to view the procession. As we crossed the street, I remember one of my sisters saying to me, "Look at how that poor fellow is riding in his wagon."

I looked to where she was pointing, and indeed I saw a young man, about twenty years old, who had the awkward appearance of someone suffering from infantile paralysis. He was being led by a uniformed nurse.

His appearance was quite notable, since he seemed completely disheartened. Walking beside him was a stricken woman, probably his mother; her face was worn, probably more from suffering than from age. Only God knows how long and with what faith she had been asking for a miracle!

As the multitude flowed onto the esplanade, the congestion became ever greater, and for a moment we were separated from the sick man. During the procession, the Eucharist passed by and blessed that fellow. Just as the priest finished the ritual of the cross, the sick man got up from the wagon and gave an emotional cry, which straight away found an echo in the crowd's "*Le miracle, le miracle!*"

Immediately, before the enthusiastic multitude could draw close, the stretcher bearers formed a human barrier around him with their straps. Their success in preventing the crowd from crushing the man with their emotional violence was a second miracle that saved his life. Everybody wanted to touch him and ask him a thousand questions.

Thanks to my doctor's certificate, I was able to examine him close-up when they were carrying out the official recognition, and so I could testify to

With the family of the Colombian Juan María Restrepo, who invited Pedro on a journey around Europe. A little romance sprung up between Pedro and Juan's sister, who in time would become the mother of the Jesuit Sergio Bernal Restrepo.

the reality of the miracle. It was an evident case: it did not allow the slightest shadow of doubt or even any room for argument.[6]

Thus far Arrupe's narrative. His experience at Lourdes was not that of some ordinary Christian eager for prodigies. Pedro had studied medicine for more than four years, receiving excellent grades. His readings and inclinations tended to concentrate less on literature and more on scientific topics: "I was inclined to read works on physics, chemistry, medicine, psychology; I was especially interested in anything having to do with the new chemistry used in therapeutics (that's how I won my big prize)."[7]

Pedro would never forget that experience. Amid the imposing silence of the grotto and the gentle murmur of the Gave River, God had spoken to him unmistakably. That summer would remain engraved forever in his imagination and in his soul.

For Arrupe, these were two worlds colliding. At the Central University of Madrid, the professors favored empiricism and boasted that science was superior to religion. Meanwhile, the God of the little ones, Jesus the friend of the poor and the outcast, the same one who spoke through the poor folks of Vallecas, was now

---

6   *Memorias*, 16ff.
7   *Memorias*, 20.

curing, by their faith, sick people who were incurable. It was as if Jesus himself was passing by.

When Pedro was riding on the train that would take him back to Bilbao, his sisters noticed that he was abstracted, gazing on the fields that were passing. He was engaged in deep meditation. A piece of his heart had tuned in to the mysterious trembling of that rare air of Lourdes:

> I felt God so close to me in his miracles that he dragged me violently behind him. And I saw him so close to those who suffer, those who weep, and those whose lives are shattered. An ardent desire burned within me to imitate him in such ready closeness to the world's human debris, to those despised by a society that doesn't even suspect that there are souls pulsating beneath such great sorrow.
>
> My old preoccupations—the ones that first arose when the urchins of Vallecas made me know, by their very misery, that the world had many sadnesses that needed consolation—found a channel that moved me toward a vocation far more sublime that any I had dreamed of up to that point.[8]

The Decision

After that vacation, Madrid appeared different to Pedro. He returned to the capital with a new sensation of being orphaned. His father's death left him feeling that he had no roots, but at the same time he had before his eyes all those human beings that had found life again at Lourdes. In the streets of Madrid, everything seemed the same: the porter was sweeping the street as always, the neighbor on the fifth floor went out to do her shopping, and the customer with the thick mustache read his newspaper at the same table in the bar while drinking his coffee. But Pedro was not the same. Slowly, within him, a decision was beginning to take shape.

Enrique noticed it right away: "What's happening, Perico?"

"I'm doing a lot of thinking, you know. I told you about Lourdes. I am wondering what to do with my life. How about you? When are you getting married? You'll soon be finished studies."

"I don't know, but soon."

With time, Arrupe became interiorly more decided. Eventually, some of his companions discovered that he was thinking of becoming a Jesuit—that was the rumor going about the medical school.

If he made that decision, some were saying, Pedro would not win the prize of five hundred pesetas, a considerable sum at the time, that was awarded to the best medical student. His becoming a novice would not go over well in the anti-clerical atmosphere of the university.

---

8   Statements of Enrique Chacón, S.J. to the author.

Don Marcelino Oreja heard the rumors with indignation and stated one day in the students' residence: "It may cost us two thousand pesetas, but believe me, they will give the five hundred to Pedro!"

Pedro traveled to Bilbao for the Christmas vacation, having finally decided to become a Jesuit. Years later, he commented:

> My decision was taking shape in a way that would be impossible to describe exactly. The process was slow, but it was the mature fruit of an evolution that kept bringing past impressions to full development. For that reason, I can't point to the last moment when I was without a vocation and the first moment when I felt I had one. The most I can say, trying to be precise, is that for a definite period I had no vocation, but that in a broad and undefined epoch afterward, I felt the absolute certainty of having one.
>
> When I returned to Madrid, the books were slipping from my hands: those classes and experiences that before so excited me now seemed so empty. […] My companions kept asking me, "What's happening to you this year? You seem lost. […]" Yes, I was a bit lost, caught up in memories and thoughts that left me every day more unsettled: that image of the monstrance blessing the people and the sight of the young man rising from his wheelchair remained in my memory and in my heart.[9]

Before returning to Bilbao, Pedro stopped at Loyola to arrange for his entrance to the novitiate. He encountered no special difficulty. By the time he arrived in the city, he had already made his application and had conversed with the examiners of the order. He would be able to enter in the coming days.

With suitcase in hand, Pedro made his way to his sisters' house. He knew that he was free. Since his parents had died, he needed no one's consent to enter the novitiate. But what to do? How should he explain it to his sisters? He was the only man of the house. He resolved on a course of action: "I won't say anything so as not to spoil their Christmas. I will tell them everything only when I have my bags packed and they think I'm returning to Madrid."

Around that same time, Enrique Chacón, in Vitoria, received the following letter signed by Arrupe:

Bilbao, December 29

Oh, *mio caro* Enrique:

I was very surprised to receive your letter, since it seems to me you have a rather dubious reputation as regards correspondence. For that reason, I

---

9   *Memorias*, 21, and *Itinéraire*, 41. Severo Ochoa, Nobel Prize winner and great friend and admirer of Arrupe, admits as much: "That year, Pedro beat me for the extraordinary award." Around that same time, Pedro made the Spiritual Exercises with Father Laburu, an experience that reinforced his decision. See "El P. Arrupe, misionero y maestro de novicios," *El siglo de las misiones* 148 (October 1950): 395.

*Reunion of Arrupe years later with former fellow
student, Severo Ochoa, Nobel Prize winner in
medicine. Pedro had beat Ochoa as best student in
the academic year 1925–26.*

answer you promptly and wish you
and your family a happy Christmas, as
well as wonderful New Year.

I see that you're rather curious to
know what has come of my resolutions,
which we discussed seriously during
our final days in Madrid. I hope to satisfy your curiosity by telling you that
my resolutions continue, that I've been
admitted to the Society of Jesus, and
that God willing I will enter their novitiate around January 10.

Around here nobody knows about
it, except Tomás and the priests who
have guided me. So, as you see, it is still a strict secret, and I entrust it to you
because of the confidence you have inspired in me. I trust that now, as on
other occasions, I will not be disappointed. You will understand perfectly
the reason for keeping this secret, since you're aware how extremely bothersome questions and comments always are: "They told me you're going to be
a Jesuit. But when? Oh, come on, where did you get that idea?" and so on.

Since you've registered your car, I hope to see you in Bilbao, though I
might also go to Vitoria, either before you come here or after. Let me know
when you hope to come this way so that we can coordinate our plans.

I see Lolita almost every day, and there's no need to say that I remember you and think of HOW HAPPY YOU'LL BE TO SEE HER IN REAL
LIFE—you were so excited even when you saw her photos. I have wonderful
information that I hope you'll like a lot. But as I told you, I don't think she
has changed a bit as regards her looks.

What is happening with the rest of the guys from Vitoria? How did
Bueso like the Exercises? And Garay's rash? And Lucio?

Since I hope to see you soon, I end wishing you and all your family a
prosperous New Year.

Your friend,
Pedro de Arrupe.[10]

---

10   From a letter provided by Enrique Chacón, S.J. to the author. Arrupe himself told the
      author regarding Chacón: "Concerning our youthful days, Chacón knows everything."

Juan Negrín, Arrupe's physiology teacher and later prime minister of the republic in 1936; he was angry when his student abandoned the study of medicine.

Pedro carried out his plan. That Christmas, he was as cheerful and friendly as ever, trying to make his sisters forget the absence of their father. But then he gave them the news—it was ten o'clock at night one unforgettable day of January 1927.

"I have decided to go to Loyola."

"Where did you get that idea, Peru! Going on a trip when we're still mourning!"

"It will be a special trip," replied Pedro; "a trip with no return."

His sisters looked at him petrified.

"But, Peru, what about your studies?"

"I can't help it. It is something bigger than me."

The young women wept with renewed grief, but then one of them, looking Pedro in the eye, told him boldly: "Go, Pedro, if you see it clearly. Without a doubt it is a grace that was obtained by dad's death."

Not one of the five slept that night.

"They were very difficult moments," wrote Arrupe later:

> They wept a lot, and taking leave was very difficult. But I cannot accuse them of trying even in the least to prevent me from following what was clearly God's will. I don't think my pain was any less great than theirs. With a sense of self-possession that God graciously gave me at that moment and that I hardly recognized as my own, I gave them all a last embrace, trying to smile so that my own anguish would not add to theirs.[11]

It was an indication of Arrupe's "normality" that nobody ever expected him to *become a priest*. In fact, the day before leaving for the novitiate he went to see a movie, as if nothing special were happening in his life.

On the Way to Loyola

Pedro's eyes drank in the moist green landscape, which became darker and more intense as he descended into the valley of Azpeitia. The bus sputtered around

---

11   Statements made to the author by Arrupe. Statements made by María and Isabel Arrupe to the journal *Ya* (May 26, 1965). Pedro's sisters insisted: "He was very likable and very good."

the curves, and at times the narrow roadway forced it to pull over to the side in order to let vehicles coming the other way pass in safety. People were getting off the bus at different stops: a woman with some hens, a couple of mule drivers, a fellow who looked like a door-to-door salesman. All the world had been reduced for Pedro to a single ambition: entering the Society of Jesus as soon as possible. He was accompanied on the journey by his brother-in-law, Sautu, who soon observed: "Look, here we are in Loyola."

Against a background of rugged mountains, the basilica of Loyola stood out against the valley's varied shades of green. Pedro immediately thought of that other Basque who had once lived in these lands: Iñigo of Loyola. He imagined that bare ancestral home to which Iñigo had retreated to recover from his battle wounds. The felled knight used to savor the heroic deeds of the saints, comparing the interior delight they gave him with the sad and bitter taste that came from contemplating the worldly feats of the knights.

Ascending a semicircular marble staircase, Pedro immediately found himself in a small inner patio, cool and dark; to the right was a sculpted monument portraying the journey of Ignatius to Loyola after he was wounded by a cannon ball in Pamplona. Suddenly, a small door opened in the large wooden gate, and a short, pale porter asked him, "What do you want?"

"My name is Pedro Arrupe, and I am entering the novitiate."

Pedro and his brother-in-law were led in to the master of novices, Father Martín de Garmendia, who greeted the young candidate: "Welcome to the novitiate, Pedro. I suppose you have brought along your documents."

"Yes, here they are."

Pedro handed the Jesuit his baptismal certificate and other papers.

"But something is missing. You haven't brought the recommendation of the bishop."

"Couldn't we send to Bilbao for them?" suggested Sautu.

"No, by no means," explained the master, who evidently was not very tolerant. "This is an indispensable requirement. Without it you cannot enter the novitiate."

"Well, Perico, then we'll have to return to Bilbao."

"No, you return," answered Pedro. "I will wait here for the recommendation."

"But where?"

"In the nearby hotel."

And there Pedro stayed for two weeks, while awaiting the arrival of the document from the bishop's office. This was a typical trait, one that would define his character throughout his life. When he was taking a step forward, no person or thing could make him retreat.[12]

---

12   Testimony of Alfonso Barandiarán, S.J., fellow novice of Arrupe and missionary in China–Taiwan.

In Madrid, meanwhile, Professor Negrín was reviewing the scholarship awards that it was his job to approve. When he came to Arrupe's, he exclaimed, despite the student's excellent grades: "No, I will not approve this!"

"But why, Dr. Negrín? Are you unhappy about his becoming a Jesuit?"

"Well, not exactly that. It's just a shame that that young man has abandoned his studies. Medicine is going to lose a great professional."

The professor made bold to write a letter to Pedro's sisters in Bilbao, telling them how foolish they were to have allowed Pedro to leave the medical profession, where he would have been a great figure. In the end, however, Negrín approved the award.

Sometime later, when the famous socialist doctor went to Loyola to visit Pedro, he confessed to him: "Pedro, I have come to give you an explanation. I tried to deprive you of the extraordinary award you'd won in order to tempt you to leave religious life and return to medicine. But I really do esteem you!"

When Pedro rewarded him with one of his most spectacular smiles, Negrín embraced him.[13] As the two men embraced there, in the shadowy valley of Azpeitia and under the watchful eyes of Ignatius of Loyola, nobody at the time could have realized that they would turn out to be the future prime minister of the Spanish Republic and the future superior general of the Society of Jesus. At that moment, they were only a professor and a former student who were in profound sympathy with one another.

---

13   *Itinéraire*, 70.

4. Rebirth in Loyola

The inopportune shock of the pre-dawn bell sounded through the long dormitory, which was divided into small chambers by curtains instead of partitions. A light sleeper, Pedro leapt from his bed, pronounced the *Hoc signum* (This is the sign of the great King [...]) and made the sign of the cross. After stammering a prayer, he washed up in the small basin in the corner. Next to his bed was a small desk with a half-dozen rule books, and these, along with a chair, a clothes rack, a broom, and a crucifix were all his furnishings.

Pedro tried to do everything perfectly, including the simple maneuver of wrapping himself in his novice's habit. He had learned well the practices used in Villagarcía, the famous Castilian novitiate that had become a school for the customs of young Jesuits, and he had also been carefully instructed by his "angel," Manuel López Uralde, a second-year novice who for many years in later life would be his close companion.

Everything in the novitiate took place with precise timing: prayer, examination of conscience, very short "free periods," and manual labor in a garden that smelled of wet grass. Sometimes, though, Pedro was able to relax and enjoy the brilliant red sunsets over the green hills strewn with villages. Often, he contemplated the small, winding river that flowed among the trees and watered farmlands sown with beans and corn.

Everything was like clockwork: the time for sweeping, the kitchen chores, reading, conversation, recreation. After a few days of being a "postulant," Pedro could put aside his regular clothes and don a religious habit, thus adopting a way of life that clashed with secular ways but had rich interior substance.

Pedro learned to lower his gaze and to hear the voice of God deep within himself. Entering into the thrilling process of the *Exercises* of Saint Ignatius, he trained himself in "discerning spirits," in distinguishing consolation from desolation, and in living as if he were "personally present" amid the scenes and the personalities of the Gospels. In this way, he became familiar with the person of Jesus: his way of walking, his tone of voice, and, above all, his way of life. Jesus was a poor, approachable king who was calling him to work side by side with him, seeking to win the world over to a new way of being human.

The Master of Novices: A Slender Basque

From the very beginning, Arrupe got along well with his novice master, a key figure in the novitiate since absolutely everything, from the daily schedule and activities to the spiritual life of each novice, depended on him.

A fellow novice of Pedro, Xavier de Liédena, described Father Martín de Garmendia with these words:

We soon reached a door with an iron gate, inside which was a tablet which read: "R.P. Maestro [Rev. Fr. Master]." When my *angel* knocked on the door, a somewhat nasal voice could be heard from inside: "Come in." I felt a tightening in my stomach that almost paralyzed me, but the door was already opening, and there stood an ascetic figure who received me with a fairly warm greeting: "Dear friend!" He extended a bony hand, which I kissed with respect.

"Good day, Father."

"Good day, Brother Xavier. Come in, sit down." While I sat in a wicker chair, he sat down in a similar one behind a desk. "Let's see if we have another Francis Xavier here!"

He rubbed his hands and smiled both severely and sweetly at the same time. [...]

The priest was tall and austere, with a pale pink complexion and grayish hair abundant for his age; he had an aquiline nose on which metal-framed eyeglasses rested unevenly before vigilant eyes that tended constantly to be fixed on the top of his desk. Under his habit, one could make out a well formed skeleton sparingly covered with flesh. Both the way he spoke Spanish and the descriptive refrain that goes, "long nose and small butt, a sure Basque," readily revealed that Father Master was from the Basque region.[1]

Arrupe's Disk

Pedro quickly identified with his master of novices and with daily life in that old rambling house. Without losing any of his jovial spirit, he used to carve out time to do additional prayer within the novitiate's strict schedule. "Even then he was praying two hours a day. He had a great gift for uniting the natural and the supernatural, joyfulness and religious virtue."[2]

---

1   Xavier de Liédena, *Un espía en Loyola, memorias de un novicio*, a typewritten, unpublished work. The pseudonym of Xavier de Liédena was used by José María Urzainqui, who was a fellow novice of Arrupe; years later, he became a lawyer in the Office of Urban Property of Navarre. His curious memoirs, written for his friends, reflect the atmosphere of the Loyola novitiate at that time and contribute concrete information about the customs and other interesting details that help us know better the novitiate in which Arrupe was formed. See the description of Father Master on 25ff. When Arrupe entered the Society, the provincial of Castilla was Saveriano Azcona. The province of Castilla included the Basque provinces along with Castile, the northeastern regions of Spain, and the Canary Islands. Before entering, Arrupe was examined by Fathers Bianchi, Garmendia, Azcona, and Errandonea (see Margenat, "De Bilbao a Japón [1907–1938]," 80–81). Margenat also provides interesting information about daily life in the novitiate, including extracts from the letters Arrupe wrote when he was general to fellow novices on the occasion of their fiftieth anniversary as Jesuits.

2   Statements given to the author by Jesuits Luis García Calzada, Luis Arbeo, and Manuel López Uralde, who were Arrupe's fellow novices. Other companions who entered between

López Uralde surprised Pedro one day in the chapel; he was reading a book about devotion to the Holy Spirit, which made it evident that he had had some initiation in prayer before arriving at the novitiate.

"Are you praying that way?" asked López Uralde.

"Sure, it's a great way to pray!" answered Arrupe without hesitating.[3]

Arrupe, López Uralde, and another novice, Andrés Arístegui, formed a threesome that got along well together. Once a month, they went together for long walks that they called their "morning strolls," and their souls were especially refreshed on those days. They would set out at sunrise, as the goldfinches were singing and a mist was rising from the lush fields of the valley of Loyola. They made their meditation during the long walk, interrupted only by the timid greeting of some farmer, who in those early hours was beginning his day's toils.

"After Mass," Xavier de Liédena recounts,

> since we knew all the streams in the area, which were numerous, we used to choose one to bathe in. The novices enjoyed the water's caressing coolness and sought out shade under the oaks and the walnut trees. From our bags, we'd take out an abundant lunch, and we'd spend delightful hours in the peace and grace of God, enjoying one another's company.[4]

A frequent topic of Arrupe's conversations was devotion to the Heart of Jesus, a devotion he would preserve and promote all his life, without ever seeking to impose it on others. He composed a work that gained fame as *Arrupe's Disk*, a small booklet that synthesized information about the Heart of Jesus Christ and ways of practicing the devotion. Typed copies of *Arrupe's Disk* circulated from hand to hand in pamphlet form.[5]

May 1926 and the autumn of 1929 were: Ángel Arín, Luís Ameza, Juan Turoricagüena, the three brothers Luis, Carlos and Manuel Reyna, Tirso Arellano, Jesús Ryan, Ignacio Iparraguirre, José Bólleguir, José Iñiguez de Ciriano, Ignacio Baterra, Jesús M.Vélaz, Juna Alfaro, and Enrique Chacón.

3   Testimony of Manuel López Uralde, S.J.

4   Liédena, *Un espía en Loyola*, 163.

5   Of special interest is how *El disco de Arrupe* came to the attention of the author of this book. The author received the following letter, dated July 25, 1986, and signed by Rafael Baquedano, S.J., assistant to the provincial of Venezuela:

> Dear friend Lamet: The very day of his death, Father Germán Azurza, a companion of Father Arrupe, told me what I relate on an attached page. Also he gave me this worn copy of *El disco de Arrupe*. He asked me to send it to you, as I now do with much delight.

The attached page contained the following:

On the morning of July 24, 1986, at 9:30 I spoke for half an hour with Father Germán Azurza, who was suffering from the grippe and general exhaustion in the infirmary of the Colegio San Ignacio of Caracas. Two days before, he had arrived from Punto Fijo on

The Office of "Angel"

During his second year of novitiate, Pedro was assigned by the master to be an "angel," that is, a guide for the newly entering novices. Benjamín de Mendiburo relates his own experience of becoming a novice:

> In the novitiate, I had the privilege of having Brother Arrupe as an *angel*. I entered the novitiate of Loyola with my twin brother, and Father Garmendia, our master, entrusted the two of us to the care of Brother Arrupe. I have a wonderful memory of him from those days. I consider him a true saint. Since Father Master appreciated him greatly, he was *angel* for about twenty of the new novices. When I entered, there were about eighteen of us in first year, and Brother Arrupe was in charge of us all. I can still see him

---

the peninsula of Paraguaná, where he has lived since the year 1970. I went to speak with him because as soon as he arrived he sent a message through the nurse, saying he urgently wanted to talk with me.

He wanted to communicate some things about Father Arrupe. He looked quite exhausted, but he finally said that he had two things to tell me. First, though, he informed me that he had been a fellow novice of Father Arrupe in Loyola and that they had made the month of pilgrimage together.

The first thing was that, when he was named rector of the juniorate in Orduña in the 1940s, he found in his office the notebooks with the juniors' grades from many years back. Since they had never been told their grades, he was curious to know what his own grades had been when he was a junior. And he recalled seeing, since his last name appeared close to Arrupe's in those notebooks, that a professor had written a note with regard to Arrupe: "Great things are to be expected of this brother." He thought that the notebook was from around 1928 or 1929. Father Azurza would have been named rector of the juniorate in 1944 or 1945.

The second thing he told me concerned a booklet called *El disco de Arrupe* [Arrupe's record], which turned out to be a small collection of the things that Arrupe constantly repeated as a scholastic and that consequently became well known; they were things about the Heart of Jesus. For that reason, it was called *Arrupe's Record*.

After speaking to me of these things, Father Azurza mentioned some matters concerning his community in Punto Fino, and then I took leave of him.

In the afternoon of that same day, the twenty-fourth, Father Azurza died suddenly in the infirmary of the Colegio de San Ignacio. Perhaps he had felt his death fast approaching when he called me to tell me these things and to give me *El disco de Arrupe*, so that I might send it to Pedro Miguel Lamet.

Thus far the letter of Rafael Baquedano. The copy of *El disco de Arrupe* that he sent with the letter has the strange aura of a relic. It has a pamphlet format and is bound within a thin gray cover; its pages are yellow with age. It contains four parts: (1) Origin of the Question; (2) Tremendous Importance of the Matter; (3) Reasons for the Difficulties Found in the Practice of This Devotion; and (4) How to Attain Its True Spirit and Experience It.

The contents are a good summary of the books and talks of that time on the Heart of Jesus. Arrupe would always maintain that devotion, though in the course of time he would develop its mystical dimensions and the way he presented to others.

Sanctuary of Loyola in the valley of Azpeitia, where Pedro entered the Jesuit novitiate and studied humanities (1927–31).

in the Saint Stanislaus hallway, completely still in his prayer, concentrated on God. I still seem to hear the blows of the discipline he gave himself just before going to bed. I was also much impressed by how perfectly recollected he was.

We were fellow novices only four months. I remember once, on a Monday when we used to have an exercise of humility, that Arrupe came forward and knelt down before us so that we could tell him his faults. There were more than sixty of us novices, of different ages and backgrounds; some were priests and lawyers, etc. Well, not a single one of us got up to accuse Pedro Arrupe of any fault. The silence was complete.

So Father Garmendia commented: "Clearly he is very clever in concealing his faults!" That was the only time I experienced such a thing in the novitiate, at least as far as I remember.

When I was a novice, Arrupe was the one in charge of directing our gymnastic exercises. He taught us quite well, with much simplicity of demeanor; just his presence instilled in us respect for him. He was also in charge of teaching us manual chores [...].[6]

Another novice Arrupe received into the house was J. Iñiguez de Ciriano, a smiling, enthusiastic, active lad. While still a postulant, he could not enter the regular community dining room, and so he ate with the other recent arrivals in a separate room. On one feast day, the novices who were serving table brought out large trays of tasty desserts. Arrupe walked over to where Ciriano was seated and invited him to enjoy a dessert: "Here, take this."

Ciriano boldly reached out and readily took the piece of cake.

"And now try this."

6   Testimony sent in writing by Benjamín de Mendiburo, S.J., companion of Arrupe, and dated in Tudela, Navarre, July 8, 1986. Arrupe had the job of buyer in the novitiate and later of librarian and custodian of shoes.

"And now this [...]."

Arrupe repeated the invitation seven or eight times, until Ciriano said he could eat no more. Naturally, he was left with the impression that such a wealth of treats was normal in the house. After taking his habit and beginning to eat in the regular dining room of Loyola, adorned as it was with pictures of Jesuit cardinals, Ciriano was greatly surprised during the next feast when he observed how the novices took very small portions of cake, while some passed up dessert completely in a spirit of sacrifice. Ciriano never forgot that smile on Arrupe's face as he kept repeating: "Take this, and now this, and now this other piece."[7] Already Pedro was practicing that difficult feat of being liberal and open with others, and at the same time very demanding of himself.

The well-known tests that Saint Ignatius prescribed for Jesuit novices included a month of Spiritual Exercises, a month of working in the kitchen, a month of hospital work, and a month of pilgrimage. This last was undertaken by groups of three novices, who traveled with knapsacks and nothing more, asking for alms and begging from town to town while they taught Christian doctrine. Such had been the practice of Ignatius himself and his first companions.

Arrupe made his "pilgrimage" with fellow novices Germán Azurza and Rafael Marcaida y Echavarría.[8] Of the three, Arrupe was the "chief," in keeping with the Jesuit tradition of giving responsibility to individuals from the start of their training.

"We walked on foot with our knapsack on our shoulders," recalls Rafael Marcaida:

> With cape and cassock, hat and umbrella, we traveled through the three Basque provinces. The only food we ate was what we received in alms. We spent our nights in parish rectories, hospitals, or shelters. Along the coast, we passed from Motrico to Ondárroa, then through Marquina and Durango until we arrived in Bilbao, having spent the night before in Bedia. Adventures worthy of note began to happen. In Bilbao, on a rainy, cloudy day, the three of us walked together along the Great Way to the Sacred Heart monument. Pedro Arrupe wanted to do this in order to show his "worldly disdain" for his native city. Crossing the estuary, we entered the University of Deusto, where we were received by the "most blessed" Brother [Francisco] Gárate, who with his renowned kindness led us to the chapel and made all the preparations for Holy Mass; it was an unforgettable day.

---

7   Oral testimony of José María Íñiguez de Ciriano, S.J., companion of Arrupe.
8   Both of these men, the above-cited Father Azurza and Father Marcaida, dedicated their lives to strenuous activities in the peninsula of Paraguaná, Venezuela, where the Jesuits established parishes starting in 1936, following in the footsteps of the distinguished Father Feliciano Gastaminza (1945). A special achievement of Azurza was the creation of Aflapane, a project for disabled children, whom he called "exceptional."

From there, we left for Enkarterri, Gordejuela, Balmaseda, Sopuerta, etc., and passing through Amurrio and Orduña, we arrived at Vitoria de Álava. Along the way, we stopped in the scattered villages and the prominent churches, giving catechism lessons and participating in the "flowers for Mary," with Germán Azurza on his harmonica and Arrupe intoning his incomparable solos. We did the same in the sanctuary and monastery of Our Lady of Estíbaliz, patroness of the plateau and the people of the Grand Chancellor López de Ayala. In the last stage of our journey, around Salinas de Léniz, we descended to Guipúzcoa and arrived happily at the Loyola novitiate, where Father Master Garmendia received us just as Saint Ignatius had received his pilgrims.[9]

From Jokes to Mysticism

What was Pedro like at that time? All those who knew him state that he had an admirable way of uniting a sense of commitment with a sense of humor. Xavier de Liédena described his first encounter with this exceptional novice:

During the afternoon walk, which was a long one since we had a free day, I had my first opportunity to get to know a fellow novice. Several times I had taken note of his ascetic, noble figure: he was tall, pale, and well proportioned, and his pronounced features and aquiline nose gave him a truly Ignatian visage. The third novice in the band I knew only because he belonged to the choir; there was nothing exceptional about him except perhaps his beautiful baritone voice.

No sooner had we begun to converse when this previously unfamiliar fellow novice took the lead. I looked on him with the greatest respect since he appeared to be an extraordinary person. But great was my surprise when I saw that he was a completely natural and fun-loving novice; he was witty and clever, and at the same time restrained. Very soon, the three of us were getting along quite well together; we were laughing so hard it was like we had never laughed before. Viewing my ascetical comrade, I said to myself: "This guy is like me." And contradicting completely his austere mien, he told us a couple of jokes that had us rolling with laughter. What a stupendous brother he was! Since we felt confident with one another and since I didn't want to be less open than he was, I drew on my own well-supplied bag of jokes, which had not been used for a good while. I told two jokes about ruffians that made them laugh. My ascetical friend, with great Jesuitical diplomacy,

---

9   From an article by Rafael Marcaida y Echevarría, S.J., companion of Arrupe and Azurza during their pilgrimage experience. The article was published in the journal *La religión* (Caracas, September 9, 1986) with the title "Los tres peregrinos de Loyola (1926–27)" [The three pilgrims of Loyola (1926–27)].

told me: "Brother Xavier, the first was very good—really, really good." With that, I understood that the second was not so good.

We had made a visit to the Blessed Sacrament in a chapel on the Cestona estate. It was a wonderful afternoon and a wonderful walk, I was telling myself.

When we encountered Brother Jaime on the roadway, he greeted us and then said, "Brother Pedro, what was that joke about the dwarfs again?" And our ascetical Brother Pedro told a very funny story about dwarfs, without mentioning Snow White or anything like that. He imitated the different voices of the little dwarfs, uttering guttural or flutelike sounds, as if he were the characters themselves.

When we began the Holy Rosary before arriving at Loyola, as was prescribed at the end of our walks, I observed a notable change in the composure of Brother Pedro. With eyes lowered, he fingered the beads of his rosary and prayed to the Mother of Heaven with a filial devotion that edified me and might have edified even the angels. In that way, I learned, as a good detective, that holiness is not at odds with a healthy joyfulness. Quite correct was the person who said: "A sad saint is a sad excuse for a saint."

When at supper I happened to be sitting in front of Brother Pedro, I laughed at his serious manner; it seemed to me that he was telling the whole community the story of the dwarfs.

The same Xavier de Liédena recounts in his memoir a facet of Arrupe that had already been seen in the Marian congregation in Bilbao: his brilliant imitations of Basque villagers in the novices' Christmas pageants. Arrupe had a marvelous ability to transform his voice into hoarse or nasal tones. Xavier would play the part of Pachicu and Pedro that of Inoshente as they acted out dialogues that Pedro obtained from his old congregation. Using Basque expressions and the broken Spanish spoken in the countryside, they provided spectacular entertainment for their fellow novices.[10]

Pedro would never forget those intense first years of his religious life, and he would evoke them in letters he sent later to his former companions. For example, he wrote to Vicente Ozaeta Uzquiano:

> I remember quite well the first time we met in the Loyola novitiate, that embrace I gave to a young man from Viana, who was arriving to form part of our novice community. I also remember those walks to the fountain of the Pastors, the *Salves* in front of the chapel of Olatz, the comings and goings along the hallways of Loyola on rainy days, [...] into which each of us managed to inject his quota of humor and glee.

---

10   Liédena, *Un espía en Loyola*, 102.

Pedro (fourth from left, second row) with his fellow "juniors" (students of humanities) around 1930.

And he wrote to his friend Ignacio Aranzadi Barandiarán:

Fifty years ago, we met in the Loyola novitiate. Do you remember those Exercises with Father Garmendia, our holy master? Do you remember his questions, [...] "what have I done for Christ [...], what am I doing? [...] and what should I do for Christ?" We were not lacking in good will, but what was to become of our lives? What future did the Lord have prepared for us? Now at this time of jubilee, which is something like a contemplation for attaining love, we have to "recall to mind the blessing received, [...] pondering with great affection how much God our Lord has done for me, and how much he has given me of what he possesses."[11]

Friends in the Lord

One day during his novitiate period, Pedro was told that he had a visitor. When he went down to the entrance, he was surprised by the familiar face he saw: "Enrique!"

---

11   Margenat has selected a number of these anniversary letters, which were published in a private edition by Isidor Sans, S.J., secretary of the Spanish assistancy from 1993 to 1998. "De Bilbao a Japón (1907–1938)," 84ff. The letter addressed to Areitioaurtena in October 1977 states: "It is time to pray to the Father, with a universal spirit, for all those who have accompanied us on our way, for all those who have helped us (beginning with Father Garmendia, our master of novices) or who have hindered us in our path."

It was Enrique Chacón, his companion from the student residence in Madrid.

"How are you doing? When are you getting married?"

"I am not getting married, Pedro. I'm going to enter the Society."

Pedro felt a shiver pass through him.

"It has all been very sudden," said the young man.

"Wait, Enrique! Let's go to the chapel to thank God. Then you can tell me."

After giving thanks in the chapel, Enrique told Pedro how in the course of eight days he had decided everything: to leave his girlfriend, his career in engineering, and his fancy car in order to become a Jesuit. Enrique gave all the credit to the example of his tireless companion Pedro, who had studied at his side and encouraged him to go without pastries in order to help the poor people in the slum.[12]

In November 1928, during Pedro's second year of novitiate, Father Garmendia was diagnosed with stomach cancer. To accompany him to the hospital in San Sebastián, he chose Arrupe, both for his knowledge of medicine and his human qualities. On December 20, Father Master died in the arms of his beloved novice. One month later, Pedro took his first vows and passed to the juniorate.

What had those two years meant for Arrupe? His experience may be surmised from a letter he wrote to a novice master many years later, on December 31, 1973, when he was superior general:

> Perhaps the most difficult part is getting right what it means to be "Master," someone who forms and doesn't just inform; someone who leads without forcing, but also without yielding; someone who of course learns and benefits from his novices, but whose principal service is to benefit them by communicating to them (by contagion) his own way of living. And all that is to be done by combining doctrine, principles, history, norms, experience, and life. It requires balancing and apportioning each element in convenient amounts and intensities, according to the spiritual and human growth of each novice.
>
> To communicate this *forma societatis*, you must have perfectly clear in your own mind the kind of Jesuit that is to be formed there. It is the one defined by Ignacio, Ribadeneira [...]; it is the new man, the ideal of the Exercises (temporal king, two standards, third class of men, third degree of humility, contemplation to attain love) and the formula of the Institute. It is a man completely committed to the Father through a process of assimilation to Jesus Christ as the one who realizes the Father's will and is the salvation of all people. It is a man who, taking on the mind of Christ Jesus (Phil. 2:5), achieves full freedom from all selfishness, thus making himself

---

12   Oral testimony of Enrique Chacón. What makes this story especially romantic is that Enrique's girlfriend remained faithful to him all her life, even though they never saw one another again. She dedicated herself to writing romantic stories and novels that sold very well.

unconditionally available and ready for whatever service to the people is revealed to be best.

And he should seek and carry out that service as part of a team, a group of "friends in the Lord." Therefore, this *forma societatis* also involves a strong sense of solidarity, corresponsibility, communion, and esprit de corps. And finally, it should also involve a strong sense of church (the *Holy Mother Hierarchical Church*), through which and in which we receive the "mission," and for which we practice a mature fidelity, the fruit of our faith in the active presence of Jesus in the human body of the church.

Now, given all this, it is evident that the emphasis has to be placed on creating men of profound spiritual experience (and your great task is precisely here). The novitiate is above all a school of prayer: the prayer of the apostle, the prayer of the man who will devote his whole existence to evangelizing in one form or another. This requires of him an authentic spiritual experience of the One he is announcing; it requires a personal love of the person of Jesus Christ, true God and true man. Without this love, no one can have the third degree of humility, which is the Ignatian prototype of the person in whom the ideal of evangelical charity reaches its highest level.[13]

This was, without a doubt, the experience of Arrupe himself during his two years of novitiate. From the moment he pronounced his vows in 1929, love for the person of Jesus Christ and a life of prayer became two abiding characteristics of the young Arrupe.

An Intuition

After the novitiate, Pedro entered the juniorate and began his study of classics and the humanities, delving deeply into Latin and Greek. Once again, his congeniality gained the confidence of superiors and professors. At the time, the rector of the house was Father Ibero, and the professor of Greek was Father Ignacio Errandonea; both of them quickly became aware that Arrupe had a good head.

"We were studying Sophocles," Luis Arbeo recalls:

When Father Errandonea had to miss some classes, he named a substitute who knew less than we students did. As the substitute's inadequacy became apparent, Brother Arrupe was named professor, and he explained Euripides to us superbly. He was an exceptional companion. He was named beadle, which was a type of liaison between the students and the rector for organizing the juniors' activities. He was the first student to have a private room assigned to him; for that reason, I was able to notice that he got up an hour earlier than I did in order to dedicate two hours to prayer. During vacation

---

13   Pedro Arrupe, *La identidad del jesuita en nuestros tiempos* (Santander: Sal Terrae, 1981), "La formación del noviciado" (December 31, 1973).

in Guetaria, we used to go swimming early, after making our meditation. One day, I stayed in the house while the others were at the beach, and I met up with Arrupe, who was busy cleaning the bathrooms. When I surprised him doing this, he turned to me and said: "Don't say anything." Arrupe had such fine qualities that one day when he had gone on an excursion to Itziar, our spiritual director, Father Leza, took the opportunity to talk to us about the virtues of our beadle. That was something quite extraordinary.[14]

Other companions recall how Arrupe during this stage of training used to speak fervently of Jesus Christ in the "sermons" that were given during meals from the dining room pulpit, as an exercise in rhetoric and preaching. They also praise his qualities as an actor during the Christmas celebrations. They mention how often Pedro spoke of the Heart of Jesus and how he used to dedicate much time to prayer in the chapel.[15]

During that period, Arrupe experienced his first call toward the still distant and mysterious Japan. As he himself recounts it:

I found myself in the first year of juniorate, making headway in the Latin of the classical Roman period and imbibing the never surpassed equilibrium of the Greek world. In the midst of the monotonous repetition of the declensions and the undeniable beauty of the literature, the annual cycle of the eight-day retreat arrived with astronomical punctuality.

Themistocles and Aeschylus, Caesar and Cicero disappeared from the busy schedule of my life as a student, and I sequestered myself with Christ in an ambience removed from the secular world, equidistant from that world and from eternity. Such are the Exercises: a closing of the eyes to what comes from outside in order to continue on earth without contemplating it, and an opening of the eyes to eternal values in order to take possession of them despite the double barrier of time and space. It was in that world of concentrated solitude, forsaking the human and communing with the divine, that I experienced the first sparks of my missionary vocation.

For my eyes as a beginner, there was no doubt in the life of the spirit. God wanted it, and I would reach Japan to work in the same way as Saint Francis Xavier, who had sowed the first Christian seeds in that distant land.

My intuition was not some youthful dream, nor was it the capricious desire of an impulsive will. I still remember with daylight clarity the gesture,

---

14   Testimony given by Luis Arbeo, S.J., to the author. Afterward, at the age of ninety-four, he confessed to Margenat: "In the novitiate, we all saw Pedro the way he was: gifted for perfection, for holiness. We looked upon him as another person, someone who was not at all like us. When he arrived at the novitiate, he had just passed, in December 1926, his final exam in medicine. He had only one more year to finish. He was a saint, first-class, talented; he was handsome and likable. He wasn't like the others; he was a special person."

15   Testimony of Benjamín de Mendiburo, S.J.

The master of novices, Martín de Garmendia, who asked for the company of the young Arrupe in his last moments.

at once natural and supernatural, with which the priest who was giving the Exercises approved of my decision.

For him, the matter was clear, and for me even clearer. [...] A few days later, I wrote to Rome with all the emotion of someone who was betting his whole future on the slim chance of a single letter.

The weeks passed slowly and anxiously for me as I hovered between hope and fear, until one day I received a reply that was laconic, ambiguous, noncommittal—nothing was affirmed or denied.

There was an explicit approval of my desires, but nothing more. About whether they would be realized there was nothing in writing.

Another year and another letter. The same waiting. The same arguments, which for me were obvious, and the same reply, which postponed to the future a resolution that I was hoping to find today.

I remember how, disillusioned and discouraged, I was holding in my hand the second letter I had received from Rome, when I met up with Father Ibero, the rector of Loyola, who was coming down the stone staircase of that holy house. He didn't need to look at me more than once to note my melancholy.

"But what's happening, fellow?" he asked me in a friendly tone.

Without explaining anything, I showed him the letter I was holding, speaking loudly enough to be heard but softly enough not to shatter the intimacy of the moment: "Look, Father."

As it happened, that man of God, with I'm not sure what prophetic gift, smiled and said to me with kind concern: "Don't worry, Perico, you will go to Japan!"

He walked away from me with a measured pace, without suspecting the enormous good he had done for me and the absolute certainty with which I from then on nourished the desire that overwhelmed me.

"Perico, you will go to Japan [...]" was the refrain that resonated like an echo in my soul for ten years.[16]

Thus, the call of the Far East grew stronger in the imagination and sensitive soul of Pedro Arrupe. Beyond the quiet valley of Loyola, there seemed to rise as by enchantment the temples and pagodas, the mysterious gardens of the Japan he had dreamed of when reading the narrations of Xavier. But thought is creative, and ideas must be turned into reality. Whatever might happen, that vocation being molded in Loyola was intimately linked to this new call to the East: it was a challenge that required at once determination and gentleness, intelligence and sensitivity. The almond-shaped eyes of thousands of silent Japanese seemed to pursue Pedro through the dark corners of the noble house of Loyola. And as always, Pedro did not allow himself the luxury of doubting. Meanwhile, the conflict-filled years of the thirties had already begun.

---

16 *Memorias*, 23. Another testimony from those first years of Arrupe's formation comes from Vicente Leza, who in those days was the spiritual father of the juniors and later became superior of Colombia and provincial of Castilla. A fellow novice reported hearing Leza say of Arrupe: "There you have a Saint John Berchmans. I don't think the saint could have done anything more than this one does." Also, in his reports on his visits to Loyola, the provincial, Father Azcona, makes mention of the four novices who were outstanding in every respect: Luis Ameza, Carlos Reyna, Juan Totoricagüena, and Pedro Arrupe.

5. All Is Horizon

Walking jauntily through the sixteenth-century cloister, the students ascended the broad staircase and entered through the colossal gate of ornate Gothic design. The midday sun shed its golden light on the ancient monastery of San Salvador de Oña. Situated halfway between Burgos and Vitoria, on the Santander highway, the formerly Benedictine establishment had been converted into a major seminary of the Society of Jesus. The young men were reviewing some philosophical concepts in Latin, the language used in their classes and examinations:

"Veritas logica est adaequatio intellectus cum re" (Logical truth is the correspondence of the intellect with the thing).

"How is that again?"

The study companion did not understand the phrase just spoken by Arrupe, who had begun his philosophy studies in Oña a few months before, in the fall of 1931, after four years of novitiate and juniorate in Loyola. Like a good Basque, Pedro sometimes spoke rapidly, and when he did so in Latin, he left others confused.

"Sorry, I always speak too fast," said Arrupe with a smile.

Suddenly, the rector appeared at the other end of the hallway, holding a newspaper in his hand and exclaiming: "Just what I was afraid of! The king is leaving!"

Sure enough, a few months later, on April 17, 1931, the newspapers confirmed the rumors. An article in the *ABC* included a letter signed by King Alfonso XIII, which stated among other things:

> The elections held on Sunday reveal to me clearly that I no longer can count on the love of my people. My conscience tells me that this separation will not be definitive because I have always sought to serve Spain and I have labored always in the public interest, even at the most critical moments. […] I am the king of all Spaniards, and I am also a Spaniard. I could easily find the means to maintain my royal prerogatives and effectively combat those who are opposed to me, but I most certainly want to avoid anything that might set our citizens to fight among themselves in a fratricidal civil war. […] I expect to learn what the true and informed expression of the collective conscience will be, but while the nation deliberates, I have decided to suspend the exercise of royal power and take leave of Spain, even while recognizing that the country holds its destiny is in its own hands.

The text of the king's letter was accompanied by a note of the provisional government of the Republic, which gave permission for its publication and declared itself to be "free of all fear of monarchical reactions." What had happened in Spain? What would this new situation mean for that group of Jesuit students in Oña?

The Vow to a Foreign Power

Three days previously, on April 14, 1931, a historical event had taken place in Spain. At seven o'clock in the morning, the Republic was officially proclaimed in Eibar, and masses of people filled the streets of Barcelona, Zaragoza, Oviedo, Gijón, and many other cities. Madrid overflowed with people. By three o'clock in the afternoon, the republican flag was waving over the government post office. At six-thirty, the Revolutionary Committee left the house of Miguel Maura and drove in several vehicles to the Interior Ministry in Puerta del Sol. So great was the enthusiasm of the people that it took an hour and a half for them to reach their destination. Maura and Francisco Largo Caballero were the first ones to approach the building, which also displayed a republican flag. The door was closed, but it soon opened to reveal a squad of the Civil Guard blocking the way. Maura stood in front of them, declared who he was, and stated: "Gentlemen, I am assuming the government of the republic!" The soldiers, as if they had previously rehearsed their response, opened their ranks, formed a double file, and presented arms.[1]

That same night, in the building at Puerta del Sol, the government was established, and Niceto Alcalá-Zamora proceeded to dictate, without the slightest hesitation, the sixteen decrees that would be published the next day in the *Gaceta de Madrid* (Madrid gazette). These decrees legally established the new Spanish political regime.

This was the outcome of a long process that had begun in 1917, when the restorationist movement had stumbled and started its downward spin. The current crisis was due to a variety of economic, social, and political factors that were aggravated during the reign of King Alfonso XIII. Spain's capitalist development was still quite precarious, and the economy remained largely agrarian. A proletarian social movement was just beginning to appear, organizing itself into unions and political parties. The bourgeois restorationist state was only superficially democratic; in reality, it was controlled exclusively by the wealthy. Universal suffrage was so corrupted by a system of party bosses that the parliamentary system had become a farce.

The dictatorship of Primo de Rivera (1923–30) did not produce a durable system, nor did it resolve most of the pressing economic and social problems. A great error was committed by those who thought that, once the dictatorship was eliminated, it would be possible to return painlessly to the parliamentary democracy that had become corrupt. That error cost Alfonso XIII his crown and handed the country over to the Second Republic. Ultimately decisive in the change of government was the serious social conflict, and most concretely the agricultural problem; this would be an important factor in the outbreak of

---

1   Cf. collections of *ABC* and *El sol.*

the civil war. In 1930, the struggles were carried into the streets and fanned by the PSOE (Spanish Socialist Workers' Party), its trade union the UGT (General Union of Workers), and the CNT (National Labor Confederation).

The municipal elections of April 12, 1931 turned out to be a sort of general examination for the whole country: some seventy percent of those on the electoral roles voted. The victory of the socialist–republican bloc signified the nation's clear rejection of the monarchy, and the decision was accepted by most of those in the monarchical government. From his residence, republican leader Maura negotiated the transfer of powers and demanded that the king's departure take place before sunset on April 14.

What happened next would greatly affect the life of Arrupe and his companions. The provisional government was formed, and on June 28 the republican–socialist alliance triumphed in the elections that were held for the constituent assembly. The constitution that resulted was without a doubt the most progressive in Spanish history up to that moment. Among other egregious errors, however, it adopted a principle of blind anticlericalism that would leave Spain seriously divided. The Republic made its first serious blunder even before that, however: on May 11, after Cardinal Pedro Segura y Sáenz issued a fierce pastoral letter, it allowed the senseless torching of religious houses. These incendiary events were partly in response to what many people, not without reason, perceived as the close association between the Catholic Church and the powerful elites in society. Such irrational actions, however, led to the pillaging of a large part of Spain's cultural history and did not help resolve the many problems with which the Second Republic was confronted.

The Jesuits were among the first victims of the volatile situation. Even in the distant region of Oña, the students were reading *El sol* (The sun), which in its October 14 issue featured three stunning headlines:

SPAIN HAS CEASED TO BE CATHOLIC
Agreement Is Reached to Dissolve the Society of Jesus in Spain and to
Nationalize Its Properties.
Divorce Is Approved, and the Category of Illegitimate Children Is Eliminated.

The dissolution of the Jesuits—or more properly, the expulsion from Spain that resulted from it—was the consequence of a quite curious article of the new constitution, no 24, which established a new law for associations of a religious nature. This law prohibited such associations from engaging in economic or teaching activities, and it also prohibited "vows that implied obedience to authorities other than those of the state." It was tantamount to driving the members of the Society of Jesus out of the country.

The news fell like a bombshell at that distant monastery, where some three hundred young Jesuits from all over Spain were studying philosophy. The *exodus* had been anticipated, however, and plans had been made months in advance.

While Pedro was studying in Oña (Burgos), the 1931 decree dissolving the Society of Jesus in Spain obliged him to adopt secular dress and to go into exile in Belgium.

There were so many students at Oña that it was impossible for them to leave Spain all at once. On January 24, 1932, Alejandro Ruiz, a cavalry officer who was quite friendly with the Jesuits, had arrived from Burgos to inform the community that the republican government had decreed the previous night that all houses and properties of the Jesuits were to be abandoned within ten days and that Jesuits could no longer live together in community, but only as dispersed individuals. Since the Jesuit house in Marneffe, Belgium, was not ready to receive two hundred Jesuits all at once, it was decided that the students would travel there in successive expeditions. Meanwhile, some of them were instructed to stay for a time with their families, especially if they were from the Basque provinces; in due course, they would be told when they should travel to Belgium.

The priests who administrated Oña and Eguíbar remained in Spain in order to organize the orderly transfer of the Jesuits, and by the middle of February 1932 the whole of the student body and faculty from Oña was reunited in Marneffe. Also transferred to Belgium was the library, and the story of how that happened is interesting. During the previous year, all the books had been divided up and hidden in the homes of families of Burgos and Vascongadas who were friendly with the Jesuits. Then, in September and October 1931, after the approval of the constitutional article dissolving the Society, the books were transferred to Belgium in successive clandestine trips.

Before proceeding to Marneffe, the Jesuit students from the province of Castile, which then included the Basque country, were instructed to return to their family homes for a short while. Not wanting to waste time during his stay in Bilbao, Arrupe went to live at his old school, the Piarist college, where he made eight days of Spiritual Exercises on his own. Arrupe later recalled this transitional period:

> The time of our expulsion from Spain was certainly a decisive moment. The young Jesuits left for Belgium, and some of us were given two weeks to visit our families. I did not go to my family home, however, but rather sought a room in a religious institution. For two weeks, I studied the volume of the *Monumenta* (the collection of the Society's basic texts) dedicated to the Spiritual Exercises. I had packed it—without asking permission, I remember well!—in the small suitcase we were allowed to carry into exile. This period of reading, prayer, and reflection allowed me to penetrate deeply into the thought and spirituality of Saint Ignatius.

By that time, Arrupe had already had intense moments of experience of God. In Oña, he had one day perceived an interior light by which he seemed to "see everything as new." Another time at Oña, he was walking along a hallway one day when suddenly he heard a voice that said to him: "You will be the first." He turned around and saw nobody. Only in later years did he understand the possibly mystical meaning of that announcement.[2]

Finally, on February 13, 1932, Arrupe lugged his suitcase heavy with books onto the northbound train and waved sadly as it whistled its final goodbyes. He was being expelled from Spain and beginning his first travels as a citizen of the world.

---

2   Regarding his spiritual experience, Arrupe spoke to the author in Rome in July 1983. On the voice he heard, there exist several testimonies, including that of Luis González, S.J., who was told of it personally by Arrupe. On his retreat before going into exile, cf. *Itinéraire*, 62, and the testimony of Arbeo.

A Happy Exile

Northern mists surrounded the hoary chateau, but the laugher of the exiled students could be heard all around the grounds. A tower with a rusty clock stood to one side of the old red-brick building in Marneffe, Belgium, and a beautiful landscape of pines and chestnut trees spread out beyond. The atmosphere in that community of more than two hundred Spanish "invaders" was joyous, even though for a while most of the members were affected by influenza. As was to be expected, Arrupe was quick to put into practice his knowledge of medicine and became a proficient nurse for his companions. The community as a whole had grown to 350 members. Every day, a question arose as to whether there would be enough food for the next day, but they always made out somehow. Arrupe was the beadle for the philosophers, and he took advantage of his post, according to Mendiburo, to occupy the worst room in the house, one that had no window but only a skylight.

"Arrupe at that time was good friends with Uralde and Arístegui," recalls Arbeo:

> He was totally committed to caring for those who came down with the flu, which meant almost everybody. He had energy for everything. In 1932, he studied second-year philosophy with his usual intensity and application. He did two years of philosophy instead of three, since he had already gone to the university and studied the sciences that were then part of the philosophy curriculum. Therefore, without doing regency (the years of teaching after philosophy), he was assigned to study theology in Valkenburg. Only the best students were chosen to go there, the ones being prepared to be future professors. Some of the Spaniards got sent back to Marneffe since the province did not have enough money to pay for their studies. The provincial of Germany, however, allowed Arrupe to stay without having to pay, saying: "We'd even be willing to pay money to have Pedro Arrupe stay here with us." That's why he was the only one who stayed there the whole time.[3]

The year was 1933, and Arrupe himself tells us of his experience:

> God, who wanted to give me a formation much more complete than any I could have dreamed of, sent me to Valkenburg, Holland, so that I could specialize in medical ethics under the guidance of Father [Francisco] Hürth. He placed me with that great Jesuit moralist so that, with my initial professional training, I could delve more deeply into the difficult, elusive problems that involved both medicine and morality: God wanted to make use of that new phase to prepare me better for the missions.

---

3   Testimony of Arbeo.

With that new assignment, I came into contact with the Jesuit province of Lower Germany, which was precisely the one that had founded and sustained the Japanese mission. I was thus able to get to know many of the missionaries who would later go to Japan.

Before the end of my third year of theology, the international medical conference was held in Austria. It was one of the last ones that the civilized world would be able to hold prior to the confusion brought on by the war in 1939. The famous doctor Fernando Enrique of Salamanca, then president of the Saints Cosmas and Damian Doctors' Association, chose me as a representative of Spanish medical science, and much to my amazement I found myself in Vienna alongside some very distinguished international figures.

I sincerely recognize that there were many participants in the congress whose knowledge was backed by many more years of experience than I had. Nonetheless, when I gave two talks on the difficult topics being discussed there, I felt supported by all the reservations of the Catholic morality that I had just studied in theology, under the direction of Fr. Hürth, a world authority on those questions. […]

If anyone were to ask me to sum up my innermost feelings during those days of intellectual give-and-take, I would say something that might sound strange. I was still not a priest. I had not quite finished my medical studies. Thus, when I was asked to undertake the double conference, I was situated midway between the two professions. In front of me was a most distinguished audience, men of the stature of Niedermeyer, Gemelli, Bibot, Allers, Carp. […] They were people of international repute who without hesitation would listen to what I had to say. What a curious contrast![4]

In fact, they listened to Arrupe with great interest. His presentations on "euphonic castration" and the influence of sterilization on race were received with a burst of applause, to which he responded with smiling simplicity and a charm that captivated all who got to know him.

Many years later, Arrupe would confess: "My conferences went over well with my eminent audience. But I must say, I never felt myself to be so small. When the applause broke out, I didn't know what to do with myself. The congratulations I received seemed to me insincere. That success didn't really belong to me."[5]

The young theologian was still in his twenties. He had a penetrating gaze that illuminated his refined countenance and contrasted sharply with the high, East European-style clerical collar he wore.

Almost without being aware of it, Arrupe was treading on dangerous ground. A small party, called the National Socialists, and a certain Adolf Hitler,

---

4   *Itinéraire*, 21.
5   *Itinéraire*, 21.

Pedro (standing with biretta) in the chateau of Marneffe, with some companions; his friend and confidant Jesús Iturrioz is to his left.

whom nobody had heard of ten years before, was in the process of taking control of Germany. The years after the First World War had offered ideal conditions for the rise of a "savior" of the people. A very broad gamut of small nationalist and reactionary groups had facilitated the election victory of Hitler, who was a fanatical patriot, an alienated member of a threatened middle class, and an extreme conservative. Hitler brought together in himself all the necessary ingredients: nationalism, socialism, capitalism, technocracy, authoritarianism, militarism, bureaucracy, and racism. The *Führer* was able to take advantage of Germany's economic chaos and moral anarchy in order to capture the attention of a nation that was insecure, frustrated, and fearful. For that purpose, he targeted some easy scapegoats: Jews, capitalists, foreigners. From the German elections of March 1933 arose the horror called Nazism.

What impact did these events have on young Arrupe? He would never forget, for example, the martyrdom of Alfred Delp, a victim of the Nazis. Delp had studied theology with Arrupe, who later wrote:

> We lived some terrible moments together. I was coming from Spain by way of Belgium and Holland, and meeting up with the Nazi mentality was a tremendous cultural shock—mainly cultural, I must confess. I wasn't so interested in the political questions. At the time, we hardly read the newspapers. It must be remembered that in those days a young Jesuit did not have access to many means of information. Personally, I was less interested in what was

happening than in the way people around me were reacting. I used to like to ask other people what the newspapers were saying, so they would sometimes joke with me: "Don Pedro just arrived from the moon!"[6]

Masses Longer Than Two Hours

The date of Arrupe's ordination to the priesthood was drawing near. The custom was that Jesuits received the sacrament of orders after their third year of theology, when most would be around thirty years of age. Jesús Iturrioz, who had been a novice with Arrupe and had followed him to Marneffe and Valkenburg, recounts how that momentous occasion arrived. At the time, Pedro was going deeper into the theological foundations of devotion to the Heart of Jesus, and he was reflecting on how this devotion was a strategy for the work of redemption: "I don't want to think that after I die the world will go on the same way as if I had never lived," he said. "We are so little, we can do so little, and the work of redemption is so great!"

In a handwritten note from that time, Arrupe wrote: "My ministries and my daily tasks, my work, including that of today, will exceed in fruit (not in the future, but in the present) beyond my hopes […] Lord, expand my heart with hope, as you expanded your own in order to love us!" On November 6, 1933, he gave Iturrioz a prayer to the Heart of Christ, with the title *Magister adest et vocat te* (The master is here, and he's calling you). Arrupe had composed the prayer in August of that year, and the text reveals clearly how unconditional was his commitment to Christ. He revised the text seven years later in Japan, improving perhaps on the pious style of the earlier years. What follows, then, is the definitive formulation:

Jesus, my God, my Redeemer, my Friend, my dearest Friend,
        my darling, my beloved.
Here I come, Lord, to tell you from the depths of my heart
and with the greatest sincerity and affection of which I am capable,
that there is nothing in the world that attracts me,
        but only you, my Jesus.
I do not want the things of the world.
I do not want to console myself with creatures.
I want only to empty myself of everything, even of myself,
        in order to love only you.
For you, Lord, all my heart,
        with all its affection, all its tenderness, all its kindness. […]

Oh Lord! I do not grow tired of repeating to you:
I want nothing but your love and your confidence.

---

6   *Itinéraire*, 25.

I promise you and swear to you, Lord,
  that I will always be attentive to your inspirations
  and will always live as you yourself lived.
Speak to me frequently in the depths of my soul,
  and require much of me.
I swear to you by your Heart to do always what you desire,
  however easy or costly it be.

How can I deny you anything,
  if the only consolation of my heart
  is in waiting for a word to drop from your lips
  so that I may satisfy your desires?
Lord, look at my miserable state, my hardness, my weakness. [...]
Kill me rather than have me deny you anything you want from me.
Lord, by your Mother! Lord, by your souls! Give me this grace [...].[7]

---

7   See for this period: Jesús Iturrioz, "Pedro Arrupe, cincuenta años de sacerdocio," *Mensa-jero* 1149 (Bilbao, July 1986): 23–27. For Arrupe's prayers, see José A. García, ed., *Orar con el padre Arrupe* (Bilbao: Editorial Mensajero, 2007). The first version of the prayer, which is longer than the one cited here, can be found in Ignacio Iglesias, "Aportaciones a su biografía interior," in La Bella, *Pedro Arrupe, general de la Compañía de Jesús*, 991–92. For the shorter version used years later in Japan, see Fernando García Gutiérrez, S.J., *El padre Arrupe en Japón*, 2nd ed. (Seville: Ediciones Guadalquivir, 1992), 87–88.

The first version was written in the 1940s, at the beginning of his missionary life, and was sent to one of his collaborators in Japan. Arrupe would have been about thirty-three years old then. He had just been weeping upon catching sight of his longed-for Japan for the first time, in the port of Yokohama. The text reveals not only his passionate character but also the youthful, fiery, almost crazy love for Jesus Christ that would be the secret and the driving force of his life. It is almost like a love letter:

Jesus, my God, my Redeemer, my Friend, my intimate Friend, my Heart, my Darling: here I come to tell you, from the depths of my heart and with the greatest sincerity and affection of which I am capable, that there is nothing in the world that attracts me except you alone, my Jesus. I do not want the things of the world. I do not want to console myself with creatures. I want only to empty myself and be free of all things in order to love you alone.

For you, Lord, is all my heart with all its affections, all its loves, and all its delights. O Lord, I do not tire of repeating to you: I want nothing but your love and your trust. I swear to you, Lord: I promise to hear all your inspirations and to live your very own life. Speak very frequently in the depths of my soul, and demand much of me, for I swear always to do whatever your heart desires, as easy or as hard as it may be. How can I deny you anything if the only consolation of my heart is waiting for a word to fall from your lips, in order to satisfy your wishes. Lord, behold my misery, my weakness. Kill me before I deny you anything you wish of me. Lord, by your Mother! Lord, by your souls! Give me this grace.

As the years went by, Arrupe's prayers became more sober and profound, but not less ardent or sincere. We see in them his enormous joy and confidence: "I have great

Iturrioz's testimony continues thus:

By November 1935, he was writing to me excitedly: "We have already begun the course on liturgical practice, and concretely the praying of the breviary. This indicates how close ordination is." As July 30, the day of the ordination in Marneffe, was approaching, he was still in Valkenburg but quite anxious to take care of all the details in advance. On May 25, 1936, he wrote me: "I will be very grateful to you if you write me when you learn of the dates for the Exercises for those being ordained. Even if you are not completely certain, but have even a rough idea, I beg you to write and tell me. That will allow me to prepare for my exams at the opportune moment."

In fact, the Exercises were to begin on July 16, the feast of Our Lady of Carmel, and would finish on the feast of St. James. On the twenty-seventh and twenty-eighth, the orders of subdeacon and deacon would be administered and finally, after a day of rest, the priesthood.

Once Father Arrupe was reunited with us, we began the Exercises under the direction of Father [Pedro de] Leturia. […] Despite our distance from Spain, we became aware that important events were taking place there. Father Leturia informed us that civil war had broken out and he stated: "From the way it looks, it will last a good while."

Apart from the tragedy that the civil war was in itself, it also had a painful consequence for us who were soon to be ordained priests: we could not expect that any of our relatives would be able to travel from Spain. Of the forty who were ordained, only one received a visit from his parents: they were from Pamplona, and the father was a magistrate in the courts.

On the evening of the twenty-sixth, the bishop who was to ordain us arrived: it was Ludwig Josef Kerkhofs, bishop of Liège, the diocese that included Marneffe. He had a reputation for holiness.

On the morning of the ordination to the priesthood, the bishop rose early. On arriving in the chapel, he drew close to the tabernacle, very close; kneeling before it, he prayed for more than hour; he was praying for us. He told us so himself, more or less: "As you have seen, before laying my hands on you and praying to the Holy Spirit, I spent an hour before the tabernacle, asking of God that you all be faithful to the priesthood of Christ." On that thirtieth of July, forty of us were ordained priests.[8]

---

confidence in God, for we are in his hands. Things can never turn out badly if one follows the will of God, though one might have to suffer."

8   Iturrioz, "Pedro Arrupe." When Arrupe was ordained deacon, he wrote to Iturrioz:

This is the first letter I write you as a deacon. […] I am overflowing with joy, confusion, gratitude to Our Lord. […] This is something great, so great that I cannot even express it, and perhaps you won't be able to imagine it until the month of July, when the Lord will imprint on your soul the sacramental character of Orders and the same

Delivering discourse at the international medical conference in Vienna (1936), representing Spain.

Holy Spirit will take complete possession of your soul. Now we don't just belong to the church of Christ, we are completely part of it!

I don't know if Father Rector has already told you. God willing, I will be ordained with you in Marneffe. […] Father Provincial is sending me for a couple of months to the novitiate in London, and he proposed to me that I be ordained either in England or in Marneffe, in order to be able to make the best use of the two months. I didn't hesitate at all, […] I chose Marneffe! Look how the Lord has reunited us again. […] We will go up to the altar together, God willing! Clearly the Lord is determined to bring us together again, and you don't know how happy that makes me. I believe that we could work so well together for Christ!

On that day—July 30, 1936—there was a strange blend of emotions, both because of what had happened in the morning, our being sacramentally made "priests of Christ," and because of what was awaiting us the next day. That day, we concentrated on preparing the ritual of the so-called "first Mass." We felt regret at the absence of our families, and we also felt great concern for them; since the start of the civil war, there had been almost no news of what was happening in Spain. In the afternoon, we did some rehearsals of the Mass we would celebrate the next day. We even took some photos, which still help us remember those moments.

On the feast of Saint Ignatius, we had to divide up into groups in order to celebrate the first Mass. In Marneffe, there were a lot of altars for celebrating, but there were forty of us newly ordained. I remember my altar. Years later, I passed by Marneffe and visited what had then been our chapel. There was nothing there that recalled our former stay. There was only an empty space where my altar had been.

Father Pedro de Leturia, whom we admired tremendously for his great knowledge of Saint Ignatius, was the priest who assisted Father Arrupe in his "first Mass."

Father Arrupe, from the first days of his priesthood, began to experience great devotion in very prolonged celebrations of the Mass. Once he invited me to help him: it was to be at one o'clock at night. He perhaps went beyond two hours. It was a contemplative Mass. Insofar as possible, Father Arrupe has continued with this devotion.

I preserve one very special memory: he gave me a "memorial card" with this inscription: "Ask, dearest father Jesus, that the Lord *faciat cor nostrum secundum cor eius* [make our heart to be as his heart is]. Marneffe, first Friday as a priest."

On September 4, Father Arrupe was in Marneffe. That day, which was precisely the anniversary of my entrance into the Society, he gave me an envelope without any address on it. He had written only this: "*Petite et accipietis* [ask and you will receive]. Marneffe, September 4, 1936." Inside, there was a little piece of paper, which I transcribe here just as it was. It was typewritten and had two colors of ink. I highlight what was written in red.

Today we received a good "Mitarbeiter" [collaborator] for our sanctification: the HOLY Spirit [*sic*]. […] Farewell, my dearest Jesús, do not forget me in your prayers. May the Lord make us into holy priests, which today are so necessary for the salvation of the world!

Write at length. Insignificant in Christ, P. Arrupe, S.I.

September 4, 1936, First Friday

Jesus!

Grant to this other Jesus whom you love so much that he become *a great saint and apostle of your Sacred Heart.*

For myself I ask only that: *fiat mihi secundum verbum tuum* [Be it done to me according to your word].

For you: *Adveniat Regnum tuum fiat voluntas tua sicut in caelo et in terra* [Your kingdom come, your will be done on earth as it is in heaven].

Soon Arrupe would begin to absent himself from Marneffe. Among other tasks, he was preparing for his first transoceanic journey.[9]

Arrupe's brilliant performance at the medical congress made the provincial more convinced that the recently ordained Jesuit should receive better preparation and become specialized in medical ethics. Thus it was that one fine day in 1936 Pedro received the laconic telegram: "Immediately prepare trip to United States. Provincial."

That was all, but those few words were enough for Arrupe to obey. Interiorly, he was still certain of one thing: if God wanted to send him to Japan, he would send him, even it was by such a roundabout route that would put him in touch with many diverse languages and cultures.

"The trip did not turn out to be as easy as appeared at first sight," commented Arrupe later,

because at that time the international Olympic Games were coming to an end in Germany, and naturally the spectators were returning to their respective countries. The United States, which fifteen years before had bested England in the aristocratic sport of tourism, had sent a considerable contingent of its citizens to that event. The simultaneous return of all of them caused transportation problems and shortage of space, but at last I managed to find myself sailing toward the Americas.[10]

On the Other Side of the "Puddle"

Arrupe was crossing the Atlantic for the first time, but he would cross great oceans dozens of times later in his life. At first, he thought that, given the shortage of space on the cruise ships, he would be traveling on a freighter, but such was not the case. In a letter dated September 15, 1936, from Antwerp, he told his companion Iturrioz of his disappointment:

I have just now returned from visiting the transatlantic steamship. They have deceived me! They changed everything about. I was hoping to travel on

---

9   Iturrioz, "Pedro Arrupe."

10   *Memorias,* 26.

the *London Corporation* [...], and I find myself on the *Jean Jadot*! Outside, the boat looks like an ordinary merchant ship, but inside [...] it's the last word. The double cabins are stupendous, with two beds (not bunks), running water, electric light, large wardrobe, etc., etc. Well, they have deceived me. I thought I was going to have to sleep on little more than a coil of rope or cable, [...] and I find myself in a very comfortable cabin. The whole crew (and I think the passengers too) are Catholics. I haven't spoken with anybody yet, apart from the steward (who speaks Spanish) and an officer who speaks German. For Mass, I will have no difficulty. I still don't know whether I will say it in the room or in the parlor. That depends on how devout the passengers are, since I will gladly abandon the delight of my long Masses if there are people who want to attend. We leave today at twelve midnight. I will try to say Mass, if I can, at one o'clock so as to start the journey by offering myself to the Lord along with the "holy, pure and immaculate" Victim. We'll soon see what my fellow passengers are like. My cabin mate, they tell me, is a young fellow: I still haven't seen him.[11]

The next letter is dated "on board the *Jean Jadot*, September 22, 1936." Pedro had by then had seven days of "delightful sailing." He returns again to the topic of the change of ship: "Believe me, I have regretted it, since all those plans of traveling almost like Saint Francis Xavier have been frustrated, and I am traveling instead almost like a great lord [...]."

After describing the people on board the ship, including the captain, "an extremely agreeable fellow," and several of the passengers, Arrupe gives news of his own doings:

I forgot to mention a mysterious guy. Quite agreeable. He helps me every day at Mass. He is German. He has lived in Switzerland and is now going to the United States. I don't quite understand him. There is something mysterious about his behavior. [Later in the letter, Pedro seems to indicate that he has cleared up the mystery in a positive way.] I have spent many delightful times with the sailors and the cabin boys in their quarters. We talked a lot about their work, and I've learned a lot. They are good lads, but what dangers they run! [...] Last Sunday, I announced that we would have Mass at nine-thirty in the parlor. I was greatly consoled that four received Communion and that many more people were there than I expected: three officers, several sailors, and the Catholics from among the passengers (the "schismatic" woman also attended). The day before, I heard several confessions; [...] some of them gave me great consolation. [...] Until now, I have not failed to say holy Mass a single day. As I was saying, I have an assistant; that means that, even if I cannot celebrate in pontifical fashion, I have the

---

11   Iturrioz, "Pedro Arrupe."

great consolation of being able to do good for this soul. Starting tomorrow, at least one of the cabin boys will come to receive Communion every day. What a wonderful soul this little sailor has; [...] it makes me ashamed! [...] These days, I find really appropriate the counsel of Saint Paul to become "all things to all people," from the student to the septuagenarian. From playing cards (not for money, of course) to explaining the history of the Schism. [...] One of the most interesting things is the custom of holding meetings after the meals. Everything comes out there. Naturally, the Jesuit is the one who is supposed to know everything. The captain doesn't miss a chance to challenge me, and as a result we have become very good friends—especially since he hasn't been able to beat me in the game of "wolf and dogs" (played on a checkerboard) [...].[12]

Thus did Pedro experience his first transoceanic crossing and his first priestly ministries. The blue Atlantic spoke to him of great expectations and apostolic projects to be undertaken. An incredible horizon opened up before his eyes. He was leaving behind a world in turmoil, with no idea of the political consequences there would be for his own life. In Germany, there was the menacing shadow of the Third Reich. In Spain, the Popular Front had taken shape after the repression of 1934. Military figures such as Emilio Mola, José Enrique Varela, and Francisco Franco, in alliance with right-wing politicians and with the fascist governments of Germany and Italy, had been preparing for an uprising from the beginning of March 1936. On July 18, Spain's bloodiest civil war broke out, and it would pave the way for the longest dictatorship in the country's history. Meanwhile, on the deck of the boat that was carrying him to America, Arrupe contemplated the sea, believing in a Gospel that spoke of the power of love and that placed him clearly on the side of "the little ones."

America Live

From afar, the Statue of Liberty greeted the Spanish Jesuit who at the age of thirty was already becoming a citizen of the world. The skyscrapers of Manhattan stood out in the surrounding smog. The United States of the 1930s was joyously celebrating the "wonderful life" of Frank Capra's films but was also experiencing the sharp pangs of industrialism, portrayed by Chaplin in the movie *Modern Times* (1936). It was the shining America of Franklin D. Roosevelt, who in that year 1936 had just been re-elected president.

Onboard ship, the passengers celebrated the success of the athletes who had participated in the Olympic Games in Berlin, especially the triumph of Jesse Owens, "the Ohio flash." And, of course, great were the expectations of the arriving immigrants in search of a better future. Arrupe's eyes, however, beheld the

---

12   Iturrioz, "Pedro Arrupe."

Ordination to the priesthood in Marneffe, along with forty fellow Jesuits (July 30, 1936).

famous symbol of liberty in a very different way. America was not for him a port of arrival, but only a stop on the way to greater freedom still.

At first, the Jesuit provincial of New York did not make him feel welcome. When Pedro told him his plans, the provincial responded: "Psychiatry? No, no. Whenever Jesuits want to study psychiatry, it is because they themselves need a psychiatrist!"

"Once in America," Arrupe recalled,

I got in touch with the famous Father [Thomas Verner] Moore. He would later become a Carthusian of Miraflores, but then he was still a professor of much reputation at Catholic University in Washington. In addition to the tremendous support I received from that true specialist, I had at my disposition all the materials that had been patiently collected by Father Agostino Gemelli, who with admirable generosity offered them to me unconditionally. It was a wonderful collection of material that was of great interest to me. Thus, by making use of the work already done by someone else, I was able from the start to delve deeper into the subject.

I felt myself at the time like a young boy seated before great teachers. In the eyes of everybody, I was a brazen fellow, and in my enthusiasm for the work I had to do, I even forgot about Japan [...]."[13]

Arrupe did his fourth and final year of theology studies at Saint Mary's College in Kansas. He studied hard, so much so that by August 1937 he found himself exhausted, and the provincial superior decided to send him to the southwestern United States. There, he would find a change of climate and occupation. Thus, after long hours of traveling by train, he found himself in a very different ambience. The bright sunlight and some of the customs of the Southwest reminded him of far-off Spain. He became quite involved in a Hispanic parish that was attended by Jesuit Martínez de Silva, rector of the Montezuma seminary, along with a monsignor and another priest.

"Come with us to see Mexico!" Their invitation was so insistent that Arrupe agreed, and some five of them, riding in a Pontiac, crossed the border heading south. As they drove along, enjoying the landscape and the conversation, the motor suddenly began to make strange sounds. Finding themselves stranded in the middle of the desert—a place with no garages, no hotels, no gas stations—they looked around in dismay.

Taking refuge in a little inn, they waited for a mechanic to come from a nearby town with some parts to repair the car. The five of them were dressed informally, since Mexico had been suffering many years of religious persecution. The food in the inn was typical of the country, seasoned with abundant spices, so that the monsignor abstained every time a dish with pimento or hot pepper appeared, which was almost always.

In order to alleviate his fast, Arrupe asked for some eggs. His companions felt relieved, thinking that at last the poor man had found something he could eat. As soon as he took a bite of the eggs, however, the monsignor raised his hands to his mouth, then to his throat, his chest, and his stomach, and with swollen eyes shouted: "Fire! Fire!"

---

13   *Memorias*, 26.

The recently ordained priests, along with Bishop Ludwig Joseph Kerkhofs (Pedro is fifth from left, last row).

Arrupe and his friends tried their best to contain their laughter. It turned out that the cook, in order to make the eggs tastier, had seasoned them with a mixture of spices that scorched the throat. With a pitcher of water, the monsignor managed to put out the fire.

One night, after his fellow travelers had gone to bed, Pedro struck up a conversation with a respectable-looking young Mexican, and the two of them continued talking for a good while. They spoke of a variety of topics, and although the Mexican did not open himself up much, Arrupe thought he noticed a certain sincerity in the young man's eyes.

After the young man retired, the innkeeper approached Arrupe mysteriously and called out to him from behind, "Don Pedro […]"

Arrupe turned around and said, "What is it?"

"Nothing right now, but just in case."

"Just in case what?"

"Do you know who you were talking with?"

"Well, no."

Pedro looked with curiosity at the innkeeper, who was slowly shaking his head.

"Don't trust appearances."

"Very well, but what is it with that young man?" he asked, now intrigued.

The innkeeper looked around to make sure nobody was watching them. Then he said in a low voice:

You will see. It is not that he is a bad fellow, but during these last three months he has personally killed more than twenty people. Of course, I don't mean to say anything bad about him, but there are some small failings that are worth pointing out. And believe me, it is not just a matter of rumors [...].

Arrupe went to bed wondering about that phrase "small failings." Meanwhile, the little inn came to life, as it did every night, with singing and dancing. Nobody suspected that there were five priests staying there.

Once the car was repaired, they made their way to the capital, where Arrupe spent two weeks enjoying a variety of experiences in his first contact with a country that would remain important for him all his life.

Arrupe would always remember especially his trip to Morelia, where he visited a boarding school with five hundred Spanish students who had been exiled to Mexico without their parents as a result of the Spanish Civil War. Soon after arriving in Morelia, Arrupe met by chance some students who had escaped from the school without permission. The next day, he arranged without difficulty to visit the school. Since he was dressed informally, nobody suspected that he was a Jesuit. Indeed, when they learned that he had studied at the University of Madrid under Professor Negrín, who had since become prime minister of the Spanish Republic, they figured that the disciple would be like the master, and therefore a "communist." This mistaken impression actually helped Arrupe, for the school physician came to his hotel to invite him to visit with the "little Spaniards" in the infirmary. He tried to convince Pedro that their little colony was being supported by the generosity of the Spanish government.

Arrupe visited the infirmary and spoke with the students; he learned that those who did not come from communist families suffered discrimination. At one point, he heard a twelve-year-old boy calling him from one of the beds.

"Are you Spanish?" the boy asked, his voice interrupted by a hiccup. The boy began to cry inconsolably while Pedro tried to soothe him.

"Yes, I am Spanish, but don't cry. What's wrong?"

"I'm sick, and nobody pays me any mind. I've been here six months, and I've lost more than twenty pounds. My stomach hurts a lot, but nobody cares. I want to go back to Spain."

Pedro tenderly passed his hand over the boy's forehead to push back the hair that was falling over his reddened eyes. The boy grabbed his hand hard and asked, "Will you help me return to Spain? Tell me you will. Please, tell me you will! See how much I'm suffering. I don't want to die so far from my mother!"

The boy would not stop crying. Pedro spoke to him for a while and managed to calm him down. He knew that he could do nothing for him, but he lavished smiles and cheerful words on the lad. Finally, he was able to inspire in him a little hope.

As soon as he began to celebrate the Eucharist, Pedro liked to prolong his Masses in contemplative prayer.

"I will do what I can for you," he promised as he left. Meanwhile, the boy held on to his hand as if trying to keep him from leaving.

That was not the only experience the young priest had in that infirmary of exiled children. In another bed, he came upon a little girl whose face was covered with bandages; her skin had been burned by having gasoline poured on it—to get rid of lice!

"Lice?" Arrupe asked, "But couldn't you have just washed them away?"

"What do you mean? I had gone six months without bathing and almost without seeing water. Imagine how I was […]."

A little further on, Pedro met an eighteen-year old girl who had left Spain with her two younger brothers. Her story affected him deeply. During the trip on the ship, she had had to flee the deck several times in order to avoid getting raped. When she finally arrived at the school and thought she was safe, the girl was subjected to ugly insinuations from the staff there. Pedro left the place feeling disheartened.[14]

On returning to Washington, Arrupe again dedicated himself fully to the studies that had been his reason for crossing the Atlantic. He had almost everything ready when he suddenly received another abrupt command: he was to leave off his studies until receiving new instructions. Arrupe immediately sensed that something providential was happening.

---

14   *Memorias*, 25ff. Years later in Rome, while speaking with the author, Arrupe warmly recalled those days in Mexico, a country where he would eventually have many great friends.

The year was 1937: America was at peace, even though the preludes to a terrible war were already unfolding abroad, especially in the country to which Pedro hoped to go as a missionary. In July 1937, Japan, claiming that a group of its soldiers had been fired upon, undertook a war of conquest against its perpetual rival, China. Bolstered by their successful war against the Russians in 1904–5, the Japanese military sectors had conducted a long campaign of political indoctrination within the country and of aggression against their neighbors. After the military succeeded in installing a hardline general, Senjuro Hayashi, as prime minister, the Tokyo government launched an attack against China, alleging that Chiang Kai-shek was yielding to communist pressure. This was the first stage of the strategy that brought the whole Far East under Japanese domination in the course of the Second World War.

On the far side of the ocean, Arrupe was meditating. What might God be asking of him in this abrupt change in his life? He had already become good friends with his American companions. Their good humor fit well with the frankness and joviality of this Basque who was preparing to be a citizen of the world, a world that was tragically beginning to split in two.

6. From Cleveland to Yokohama

"I will do so gladly," Father Francis X. McMenamy said with a smile, as he took leave of Pedro and prepared for his trip to Rome.

McMenamy was the tertian instructor in Cleveland, where Arrupe was assigned after receiving the order to suspend his specialized studies in medical ethics. He spent the 1937–38 academic year in tertianship, the final stage of formation that Saint Ignatius prescribed for all Jesuits. It is a year when the young priests dedicate themselves to deepening their spiritual life and studying the Society's founding documents. The tertian experience, which takes place after the long years of study, includes a thirty-day retreat, in-depth analysis of the Constitutions, pastoral activity, and other revitalizing experiences. For Pedro, it was still another opportunity to kindle his enthusiasm and to commit himself ever more firmly to his ideal.

Despite the intensity of the tertian year, Arrupe could not forget his heart's most cherished dream: to go to Japan. He therefore asked Father McMenamy, who was on his way to Rome, to intercede for him there and to recommend his assignment to Japan. He knew that McMenamy had much influence in the Society: he had twice been provincial and was now about to attend the procurators' congregation being held in Rome.

Pedro waited expectantly for McMenamy to return from the Eternal City. Finally, on June 6, 1938, around eight in the evening, the tertian instructor arrived home. Pedro relates the moment as follows:

> My heart was beating with unusual rapidity. What kind of answer would he bring from Rome? The crossroads of my life appeared now to diverge more than ever: Japan or Spain, missionary in the Far East or scientist in the West. I felt an anxiety that I wanted to call *holy*, but after analyzing it, I saw that it contained much that was human and little that was holy.
>
> Still another sacrifice: waiting until the next morning without asking him about my assignment. I hardly slept. My prayer the following day was a continual repetition of the verse: "Then I said, Lo, I have come to do your will, O God, as it is written in the roll of the book. [...] Here I am, send me." During Mass, I offered myself as I had never done before, I think. I prayed: "I do not flee the work [...] Now I am bound in the Spirit, without knowing what will happen to me there (Acts 20:22). May God live and may the Lord my King live, so that where my Lord is, whether alive or dead, there also will be his servant (2 Samuel 15:21)."
>
> The hour to see the Father Instructor was at nine in the morning. I finished breakfast at seven-thirty [...]; there was still an hour and a half. I went

out to the garden; that morning, I just could not sit quietly in my room. […] I began to recite the office. I think I walked twice all the way around the house. […] I don't know how many times I dropped the holy card I use as a bookmark in the breviary. […]

Suddenly, Father Minister came looking for me. He called out to me since he couldn't catch up with me: "Peter! Mail for you! You are a very important person! A letter from Father General for you!"

I was amazed. What could it be?

I went to the chapel. I didn't really so much open the letter as destroy the envelope. I read: "After considering the matter before God and discussing it with your Father Provincial, I have decided to assign you to the Japan mission."

It would be useless to try to describe what I felt at that moment. To me, the least of all people, was granted this grace of announcing to the gentiles the incalculable riches of Christ. For that reason, I bend my knees before the Father of Our Lord Jesus Christ (Ephesians 3:8, 14).

I tried to calm myself down, and at nine o'clock on the dot I went to the room of Father Instructor. After we greeted one another, I asked him as innocently as possible if he knew anything about my future.

"Nothing," he told me, smiling with that Saxon soul so characteristic of him. "It seems your provincial sees some problems, and Father General still hasn't decided the matter."

"Then I can give you some interesting news," I told him, reflecting his smile at a higher octave and showing him the letter that had just arrived from the Eternal City.

Many years have passed since that time, but I have never forgotten the thrill I experienced upon receiving the news in that sealed envelope or the fierce emotion that invaded me when I read that I had been assigned to Japan.

During those moments of peaceful meditation, which everyone has in life, I have often reflected on the historical process of my vocation. It was not a straight line, much less an arrow hitting the bull's-eye. There were difficulties and obstacles and abrupt orders that appeared contradictory, and all of it seemed to be precisely because God wanted me in Japan.[1]

Arrupe began to see some meaning in the labyrinth of paths that had led him to this point: the obligatory exile from Spain for political reasons gave him contact with Europe; the assignment to Valkenburg led to his being trained in medical ethics; the direct contact with the German Jesuits, who were then in charge of the Japanese mission, gave him a chance to learn the German language; and finally, the

---

1   *Memorias*, 35.

experience of America, the opportunity to practice English, and the acquisition of new medical knowledge prepared him providentially for the future.

In later reflections, Father Arrupe stated that his missionary vocation had not been motivated by an adventuresome or quixotic spirit, even though he was much moved by youthful idealism in those years and throughout his life. Arrupe chose the missionary vocation in keeping with the ecclesial spirit of the epoch, which saw the missions as an important way of realizing the Gospel mandate. Since the time of Benedict XV, the church had experienced a missionary revival that generated many new institutes, publications, and movements. For Arrupe, going to Japan was simply the best way to express his commitment to Jesus Christ in the spirit of discipleship he had learned from the Exercises of Saint Ignatius. But when Pedro asked himself what had really moved him to go to the missions—the work, the souls to be saved, "the greater glory of God," or the desire to live in a more sacrificial way—he answered thus:

> My only motivation for the missions was the will of God. I felt that God was calling me to Japan, and therefore I wanted to go there. I am interiorly convinced that the familiar play on words, "Each thing in its place, and a place for each thing," can modified a little so as to say, "Each person in his place, and a place for each person."[2]

That attitude of following God's will at each moment would the spiritual key to all of Arrupe's life. In current language, it might be understood as living "in the center," being faithful to one's own depths, or remaining authentic whatever the consequences. This is the spirit he reveals in another letter to Iturrioz, dated December 17, 1937, while he was in tertianship:

> Here I am since September 1, spending one of the happiest years of my life, if not the happiest. [...] I have a lot of things to tell you, but the main thing is to ask that you continue praying for me, as you say in your letter. I would like to leave this year having obtained "all the fruit" that the Holy Father proposes that we should get out of this year. Concerning my future, I don't have the least idea. And it doesn't matter [...]; wherever they send me, I will try to be an instrument, as much of an *instrument* as possible, of Jesus Christ. Certainly this life viewed superficially appears complicated; when it is seen in the light of "God and me" or the *guinea pig*, it becomes incredibly simple: loving Jesus Christ with all my heart, identifying myself with him, living his life! When one reflects that our role in this world is to be a collaborator of our elder brother Jesus in the *opus* that *our* Father has given *us*, this life takes on great depth and at the same time becomes one with the life of Jesus, so that one really feels that the phrase *adiutores Dei sumus* [we are

---

2   *Memorias*, 38.

God's helpers] is a sweet reality. Well, dear friend, I wanted to congratulate you, not *lecture you* [...]! It's just that Jesus Christ is so good and so great and so much our brother!

In Maximum-Security Prisons

On June 30, 1938, Arrupe finished his year of tertianship in Cleveland, but he did not leave immediately for Japan. He had to spend two months making the necessary travel arrangements.

Since he did not want to spend that time in idleness, Arrupe sought some pastoral work, which was not difficult to find in New York, a city that had people coming from all over the world. Arrupe decided to get involved in work with Hispanics so that he could practice his new priesthood.

At first, Arrupe gave talks and conferences, which, he himself confessed, "were rather abstruse and ambitious." The talks were politely received, but they were really no more than a cultural event that he hoped would open the door to more intimate pastoral contact with people.

Finally, someone offered him a "less prestigious audience, but one that might respond better": the more than five hundred Spanish-speaking inmates in a maximum-security prison.

Getting access to the prison would not be easy. This was a time of witch-hunts, and everybody, even a priest, could be suspected of being a communist infiltrator. When an Irish friend of Arrupe learned of his desires, however, he offered to solve the problem, and he was a man of his word: within a few days, a telephone call opened the doors of the prison to the young Spanish Jesuit.

The working days in the prison were long and intense. Pedro would celebrate Mass at four in the morning and then be on his way to the prison when the last stars were still visible.

On his first day there, he noticed that the guards were looking at him with misgivings. Even though his passes and documents were in order, they still harbored suspicions.

The pavilions were those typical of American prisons. All the cells, with their doors of steel bars, faced onto a lengthy corridor. At the entrance to each pavilion, a couple of guards were constantly on duty. Next to them was an electronic panel with lights and buttons that controlled the cell doors. The prisoners were rigidly segregated, and security measures were extreme. Most of the inmates had been sentenced for crimes of violence.

The first time Pedro entered into one of those prison hallways, he could sense his pulse beating more rapidly than normal. He felt nervous and almost frightened, though he kept a tranquil exterior. Arrupe explained the reason for his visit to the guard, who looked at him strangely and finally said, "Father, which *lion* should I let out of his cage for you?"

"Give me the list for a moment so that I can choose one," the priest responded.

The guard handed him the list of prisoners, and Arrupe looked rapidly over the names, which were mostly Spanish. Finally, he picked one at random.

"Open cell 279 for me."

The guard looked at the name and muttered: "You have chosen a bad egg. He is one of the worst. Does he know you're going to see him?"

"He knows nothing."

"Hmmm! I don't know how he will receive you."

"Neither do I, but we'll soon find out."

"That's right. Good luck, don't let him bite you."

The guard pressed a button, and the barred door opened. Arrupe entered into the stark cell, and behind him the door slowly swung shut again.

The prisoner stood up and looked at the priest without uttering a word. His look was hard and metallic. Pedro could not tell whether those distant pupils were displaying hatred, rage, defiance, or gratitude, but he stood there firmly, with his hands in his pockets. He stayed on his guard, without knowing what to expect. He seemed to be in control of the situation.

At first, the priest felt even more inhibited than the prisoner. He lifted his heart and prayed that the conversation would at least not be counterproductive. Immediately he felt himself completely at peace and relaxed. Sitting down casually on a cot that was in a corner of the cell and resting his hands next to his knees on a blanket with dark stripes, he rhythmically tapped his foot.

Now it was the prisoner who became anxious. Pedro became aware that things were going his way, so he decided to break the silence: "Are you surprised by my visit?"

"You can imagine I am. I don't think I know you."

"Nor do I know you. But that doesn't matter. We can be friends. I don't think you'll regret that."

"What do you know about me? Why have you come?"

"I know only what I saw on your card. Explaining my reason for coming is more difficult. For the moment, let's just say I'm here to talk with you. Confined as you are in this cell, I don't imagine you mind having someone talk to you."

After they conversed for a while, Pedro took off the scarf he had wrapped around his neck. In doing so, his Roman collar became visible, and the prisoner immediately took note of it: "You're a priest?"

"Yes. Does that bother you?"

"I didn't expect to see a priest around here. We have little to do with you priests," he said with a hint of nostalgia.

The two men entered into serious conversation. The prisoner asked Pedro if it was possible to remake one's life. Pedro spoke to him of the embrace of God, of mercy, of the possibility we all have of starting over again. Then the two of them were silent for a while. When the prisoner opened his mouth again, he was quite choked up. Now he was hooked and needed to pour out his soul. Seeing the wide smile and sincere visage of the priest seated there before him, he knew that his intimate thoughts would never be revealed outside the walls of the cell.

This was the first success Father Arrupe had in the maximum-security prison, and many others followed, born out of his deep-seated conviction that men are not evil but are victims of circumstances and a corrupt society. Pedro firmly believed that every person needs a friend.

Amid curses and obscenities, Arrupe gradually found his way into the heart of those inmates. At times, curious contrasts could be observed, such as that of the Panamanian. He was not a bad fellow, but when something bothered him, he went wild. Once, when Arrupe was visiting his cell, the conversation turned to family matters. When Pedro noted that he seemed comfortable with the topic, he asked him:

"Do you have family?"

"Yes, I still have some family."

"Are you married?"

"Twice. But my two 'ribs' are already in the grave."

He said it in an indifferent, almost brutal tone. Pedro felt a chill run through him. For the sake of saying something, he continued: "Tough luck, no? They died early. Were they very young?"

"Neither of them died. You're mistaken."

"But didn't you tell me [...]?"

"Yes, they are in the grave, but not because they died, but because I killed them. If they were alive, I wouldn't be here. The truth is that I had bad luck. I ended up with two bad women." He burst out laughing. "But now they got what they deserved."

Pedro's eyes bulged. He asked the prisoner whether he had children:

I have two: a boy and a girl, a couple of years apart in age. The two are from the first woman. I got rid of the second one quickly. I couldn't let her stay in the house. Imagine, she was treating the children badly. I had to make her pay for that, and boy, did I make her pay.

The Panamanian spoke of how he enjoyed the little ones: Luisillo, twelve years old, and Rosita, ten.

"If you could just see them!" he gushed.

As he spoke of his children, the Panamanian's eyes became watery. Arrupe took advantage of that. It had been a long while since the man had seen his children. He would be willing to do anything for those kids.

"It was a long time since I'd known what it was to cry, but, believe me, when they took them away from me and brought me here, I cried like a baby. They were all I had, and they took them away from me. Bastards!" The Panamanian spewed curses and strong words that revealed both the hate and the love he was feeling. Pedro let him get everything off his chest.

"Before getting locked up," he continued,

I used to work in a factory that was about a half hour's walk from their house—about ten minutes in trolley. I always used to walk to work, since it saved me the ten cents' fare. It wasn't much money, of course, but it was enough to buy some candy for the kids. There wasn't a single day that I failed to do that, not even on the rainy or snowy days, when the walk seemed very long. My shoes were always worn out, but it was worth it to save those ten cents.

Arrupe discovered in the man a zone of love, and he entered into it in order to free that tormented spirit. The Panamanian was not the only study in contrasts in that prison, but he was a good example of how Pedro was able to make his way into the remote recesses of human psychology, always in hope of discovering a ray of light.

Another day, the guards told him as he was entering:

"Don't bother today. They're not there. They have the day free."

"Free?"

"Yes, they're in the baseball area."

The guard pointed toward an enormous field where the three thousand inmates were playing ball as if they were school kids.

"What a shame. Can I go there to be with them?"

The guard looked at him intently.

"You would dare go in there among those beasts? You'll get a lot of jeering, for sure. But if you want, go ahead."

"Nothing lost in trying. Please tell the guard to let me in."

The guard presented no difficulty though he tried to dissuade Arrupe, especially since he was wearing a Roman collar. Finally, he opened the barred gate and wished him luck.

As locks squeaked shut behind him, Arrupe entered into the den of the "beasts." The English-speaking prisoners did not know him, so their stares went right through him. Pedro kept walking, trying to find a face he knew, and the tension within him built up. Finally he came across someone he knew, and he talked for a while with a few of the prisoners. One of them told Pedro that a Cuban friend wanted to go to confession, but that he was dangerous and prohibited from being alone with anyone else. Pedro told him to call the man. The prisoner said the meeting with the Cuban would have to be clandestine, but Arrupe replied that it would be better to speak with one of the guards. When they finally found a guard, he asked Arrupe, "How did they let you in here?"

"Well, you see, I've come to greet these old friends of mine. The other guards gave me permission to do so, and I didn't want to lose the opportunity."

From that point on, Arrupe maintained two alternating conversations: in English with the guard about American politics, and in Spanish with the Cuban prisoner about God. Finally, in a covert manner, he gave the man absolution. The confession had lasted two and a half hours.

Arrupe then took leave of the guard and went over to where most of the Hispanic prisoners had gathered together. As he drew near, he noticed that they were talking earnestly among themselves—a certain tension filled the air. Suddenly, they formed a compact group in front of him, and one of the prisoners, representing the others, stepped forward to where Pedro was and began to sing a few Spanish and Latin American songs for him.

The prison grounds were suddenly flooded with the nostalgic refrains, accompanied by simple homemade instruments, as some seventy prisoners sang sad laments that pierced the air with the sound of old and distant loves.

Pedro was greatly moved. These outcasts were thanking him for becoming their friend, giving generously of his time, and letting them share their lives with him. Pedro was once again convinced that the first message of the Gospel is simple affection.

When the prisoners finished singing, there was complete silence. Arrupe understood that they were expecting some words from him. In his youthful voice, he thanked them: "I think the best way to respond is to sing you a song of my own."

Pedro recalled his days of singing in the choir during his years of formation, and he thought of the green plains of his homeland, over which he had often heard the sweet sound of his father's powerful baritone voice. Then, putting all his soul into it, he struck up a vibrant *zortziko*, full of tenderness: *Desde que nace el día* [...] (From the moment the day is born).

Into that frigid prison yard, the mellow Basque song went forth as an immense lullaby assuaging all the pain and the untold wounds of those convicts. They gazed at Arrupe with a mixture of nostalgia and wonder.

As the final words of the song sounded, a round of applause filled the grounds. Pedro realized that he had won the day. From that moment on, he never experienced any sign of hostility. Working in that prison, he became convinced that there was no better apostolate than just loving people and being their friend. It was a lesson he would never forget.[3]

Weeping at the Sight of Yokohama

Between his visits to the prison and his pastoral work with other Hispanics, Arrupe's days went by profitably but slowly. New York had become too small for the idealism and the optimism of the young Spanish Jesuit.

When Pedro finally had all his documents in order and his greatest hopes were on the verge of being realized, he realized that he then had the sad duty of saying goodbye to the many people he had come to know. Two farewells

---

3   *Memorias*, 39.

remained especially engraved in his memory. First were the many Hispanics in New York with whom he had established contact soon after arriving from Europe; the whole colony turned out for a joyous party, complete with lively songs and dances. Far more painful for Pedro was his separation from the prisoners. They had minimal resources, but they did their best to wish him well on his journey. Arrupe recalled that moment later:

> When I passed for the last time through the barred doors behind which those poor fellows lived, I felt a terrible oppression in my chest. I suppose that their crimes made their imprisonment necessary, but the justness of the punishment did nothing to diminish the pain I felt since I knew well the tragic stories that gnawed away at those hearts that appeared to most people as hard as granite. And perhaps because I saw those men suffering more than most others, I was sorry to leave them, for the priest's place is always at the side of pain. Those wonderful groups of Hispanics, both in prison and outside, gave me a great deal to think about. That was so much the case that if I had not already felt, for many years, such a clear and decisive vocation for Japan, I might well have made that type of Hispanic ministry my life's apostolate.[4]

When Father Arrupe wrote those words, he did not know how much of his future work would be on behalf of Latin America and the world of the refugees and marginalized people in general.

On September 30, 1938, Arrupe began his journey to Japan. He embarked in Seattle on a ship heading for Yokohama. As the coasts of North America disappeared from the missionary's view, he had the sensation that the ship was moving at a moderate speed, neither speedily nor slowly. When he looked to the horizon, it always appeared quite still. It was only when he looked down at the foamy spray splashing up from the prow that he became aware that the boat was making headway, with only the slightest pitching on the tranquil days. Pedro filled those monotonous hours with his reading, writing, praying, and conversing with other passengers; he never lost an opportunity to share a little of his faith and optimism with others.

Finally, one bright morning, when both sky and sea were an imperturbable blue, the port of Yokohama appeared on the horizon. During the night, they had entered into Tokyo Bay, and as day broke they experienced their first Japanese sunrise:

> My God! What emotion I felt then and there! All the expectations and desires of the preceding ten years descended on me at that moment with a force that took away my breath. Yes, ten years begging to go to Japan, and finally I was anchored at its coasts!

---

4   *Memorias*, 51.

I felt the terrible weakness that accompanies great emotion, and I wept. It was one of the few times that I have done so as an adult. Perhaps it was the second time after the deaths of my parents, because the first time was in that prison where they spoke in Spanish and suffered in English.[5]

His farewell from those poor inmates had also brought tears to his eyes.

As people emerged from their cabins, the boat was rolling strongly, and docking had to be delayed for almost ten hours, even though the docks were not distant. Leaning on the ship's railing and entranced by the first Japanese houses he was seeing, Pedro's soul experienced a moment he would never forget. Many years later, when gravely ill, Arrupe recalled that moment for the author of this book. His hands, deformed by the stroke he had suffered, shuddered still with emotion, and he cried again like a child.[6]

Japan at last, the promised land before his eyes! At that moment, he could hardly think, but he was feeling and praying. He prayed intensely, but with few words, putting all his soul into each of them.

He handed all over to God, and he did so unconditionally, simply asking God to give him a generosity that knew no bounds. He was leaving behind forever not only old Spain, which he had left many years previously, but also Western culture. He was entering into a new world that would require of him a difficult *inculturation*. Even as it revealed to him its fascinating wonders, it would also present him with unsuspected challenges:

I remembered the past that had been mine, and I desired to break with it in order to consecrate myself decisively to a future that until then had not belonged to me: Japan. With an infinite desire of advancement and total commitment, I begged the Lord to keep always alive in me the sacred fire

---

5   *Memorias*, 52.

6   Rome, July 13, 1983. During my long interview with Arrupe, which lasted more than twenty hours, this was the moment when he became most emotional. As he recalled the episodes of his life, he relived them vividly, with great simplicity but also with emotion. In this case, though, he seemed almost mystically transported. When he burst into tears, I held his hand, but he pulled himself together, as if he did not want to be consoled. He let go of my hand, as if to show that his tears were not from sadness, but from spiritual consolation. Then with dreamy eyes he commented: "How nice, how nice!" and he added: "I felt myself to be clearly an instrument of God in Japan. I wasn't interested in anything else. I was alone. Most of the others were Germans." The impression made on him by that recollection was so strong that he felt even more deeply the distress of his helplessness. He confided to me that he felt broken by his infirmity. "I am alone, I am no use for anything. I used to speak seven languages and now I cannot even express myself in Spanish. Everybody treats me with kindness, but I am alone, alone." At the same time, he confessed, "I was always happy," and he recapitulated three important spiritual lights he had thus far had in his life: in Oña, when he had a kind of illumination and "saw everything as new"; in Cleveland, when it seemed that he "was being born again"; and in Yokohama, where he felt himself to be "one with Christ."

of those moments, so that I would always feel strong in the face of whatever sacrifices and heroic acts would be required.[7]

God heard the prayer of Arrupe on that morning in the fall of 1938, for his life in those islands would truly turn out to be as he had hoped. Yokohama was a peak spiritual moment in the life of Arrupe and would be a reference point for his future encounters with God in prayer.

After the first impact wore off and that intense moment of prayer was over, reality reasserted itself. The busy port of Yokohama had in those days some forty concrete wharves on which there was a continuous movement of cargo and passengers. A forest of cranes could be discerned amid the fog and the smoke, as Pedro heard for the first time the syncopated speech of the Japanese dock workers. After passing through the slow process of customs and immigration, Arrupe found himself seated in a train that with Japanese punctuality carried him to the capital city, Tokyo.

Every impression was something new for him, as if emerging out of a strange movie. His eyes took in colors and forms that he knew were going to be the main setting of his life. When boarding the train, he encountered what he thought was a legion of railway workers, all dressed in uniforms: black or navy blue pants, dark jackets, and pointed hat with metal insignia. Only later did he learn that they were university students. It was his first contact with a people that loved collectivity, order, uniforms.

But what most impressed him was his own perception of himself as the foreigner, the one who was different in the middle of a sea of yellow faces, oblique eyes, high cheekbones, imperceptible noses, and close-cropped hair, as was then the custom.

The Japanese face was totally enigmatic for a European. Their opaque gaze seemed to conceal a whole world of ideas and feelings. Their smiles and bows could not be translated easily into Western gestures. The pauses, the serenity, the impenetrability of Japan were displayed before Arrupe's eyes as a wondrous Japanese countenance.

Arrupe was still savoring those first glimpses of Eastern culture when the train whistle blew to indicate their arrival in Tokyo. The great capital already had some six million inhabitants and was the seat of the emperor, who was still venerated as a descendent of divinity. Arrupe, whose eyes had so recently been dazzled by the skyscrapers of Manhattan, was disillusioned as he first looked upon the wooden tenements and noisy streets of Tokyo's crowded slums; it seemed to him a very poor and depressed place. To be sure, this was pre-war Japan. It was not the Japan we know today, with its economic miracle and its status as a world power. The "made in Japan" label would come later. Arrupe was by no means the

---

7   *Memorias*, 52.

first person to be disappointed by the city. The famous missionary Father Aimé Villión was said to have been so distressed by his first years there as a missionary that at one point he returned to the same dock where he had arrived, looking for a boat on which to leave. Eventually, he overcame his depression and stayed, but his desperation was an indication of how the encounter with a completely different world can provoke an instinctive impulse of rejection.

For Arrupe, however, disappointment did not come easily. His eyes quickly became accustomed to the impenetrable faces. His ears began to hear the exotic music of the language. From the start, he sought behind each kimono a way to reach the hidden human heart. At last he was in Japan, and he was already slightly Japanese, at least by virtue of his enthusiasm and good intentions.

Meanwhile, tragedy was already taking shape in other parts of the world. The outbreak of the Second World War had its diplomatic prologue in the Munich Pact. On September 29, 1938, the leaders of Germany, Italy, France, and Great Britain had sealed the fate of an absent nation, Czechoslovakia, by recognizing German sovereignty over the Sudetenland. It was another triumph for Hitler and the National Socialist Party. The tactic for annexation was similar to the one used with Austria, the Rhineland, and the Saar; similar also was the cowardly and conciliatory reaction of Great Britain and France. A little later, when the Reich's appetite turned to Poland, the Second World War broke out. By the final months of 1937, the Berlin–Rome–Tokyo axis had already crystallized, so that Japan was fully implicated in the terrible war. Japan's involvement would deeply affect the life of Arrupe, a young priest who for the moment kept absorbing his fascinating first impressions of the Far East. His great dream, lovingly visualized in his imagination over many years and made spiritually present in long hours of ardent contemplative prayer, had now become a reality.

7. That Incredible Japan

O agari kudasi, said the woman with an indefinable smile that seemed to blend with the almost imperceptible curves of her oblong eyes.

They explained to Pedro that the phrase meant "step up, please," which in Japan is used instead of "come in, please," since the floor in traditional houses was above ground level. Arrupe had removed his shoes and carefully left them in the *genkan*, or stone vestibule; wearing slippers, he had ascended the wooden stairs to the immaculate room, where he saw for the first time a tatami, a straw mat carefully extended in the center of a room free of furniture. The tatami is the space where the Japanese carry on much of their life: eating, sleeping, conversing, and working. The Japanese concept of a dwelling is very economical and versatile. Utensils and other practical items are kept behind sliding doors until the moment they are needed.

That contrived starkness, mixed with an unusual delicacy, fascinated the recent arrival, who was visiting a typical Japanese house for the first time. Even before that visit, though, he had had other experiences.

Arrupe was living at the time in Nagatsuka, on the outskirts of Hiroshima, engaged in one of the toughest tests for a foreigner trying to enter fully into Japanese culture: the study of the language. The language was more than just a way of writing and a mix of very strange sounds: it was a whole new way of conceiving life.

Arrupe dedicated six intense months to this activity, which, given its importance, would ordinarily have required much more time. He later would describe this period as "overwhelmingly monotonous." The greatest difficulty was making the huge leap from Western languages like English, French, German, and Spanish, which have a certain common structure—subject, predicate, complements—to a language that "for any European is a truncated tongue, whose spinal cord of meanings seems to be terribly twisted."

Japanese belongs belong to the Ural-Altaic family of languages of northern Eurasia and has some relationship with Magyar and Finnish. As a spoken language, it is polysyllabic and inflected and thus has no relation to spoken Chinese, which is monosyllabic and uninflected. However, that dissimilarity explains some of its complexity. Before the sixth century, the Japanese had no written language, but they gradually began to use Chinese characters, or ideograms. Most of the characters have two different pronunciations, one purely Japanese and the other sounding like the Chinese symbol, but with the same meaning as the Japanese word. Which of the pronunciations is used normally depends on the context or the type of discourse.

A simple construction of even a few words, "I see Tokyo," can get twisted into a different order, and longer sentences become hopelessly complicated, requiring extraordinary syntactical gymnastics.

Added to that is the difficulty of learning the characters, the *kanjis*, which can require twenty or as many as thirty strokes and can have two, three, or even six or seven different (and frequently unconnected) meanings. Japanese is considered one of the most difficult languages in the world for foreigners, and even for the Japanese themselves it can be difficult.[1]

"To understand the precarious nature of his missionary initiation," writes José María de Vera,

> it is necessary to forget about the careful preparation received by those of us who arrived in Japan after him. Largely due to the importance that Father Arrupe himself gave to preparing new missionaries, we had the benefit of a well-organized language school where we could systematically take the first steps in the lengthy task of learning Japanese. We also were introduced to Japanese history and culture, which helped us deal with the confusion and dismay we felt living in a society build on such different foundations. None of this was available to Father Arrupe when he arrived.[2]

Japan Is Not Like That

Assimilating Eastern culture and relating it to Western Christianity has historically been a difficult task for the hundreds of missionaries who have tried to inculturate themselves in Japan. Pedro experienced much frustration in trying to cross that language barrier, despite his intellectual ability and his excellent study habits.

While passing through that long dark tunnel of language learning, Arrupe was unable to get involved in many pastoral activities. Nonetheless, he was always ready to help out in any kind of work, accompanying others and assisting in any way possible.

On one occasion, Arrupe made preparations for celebrating Mass with Father Hubert Shiffer at the home of one of the Christians. Arrupe thought they

---

1   There exists, for example, a Japanese character that is associated with the idea of birth and growth; it is pronounced *sheng* in modern Chinese, *sho* in its Sino-Japanese form, and in still other ways in colloquial Japanese. Each have different meanings, such as *iku*, live; *umaru*, carry a child; *nama*, raw. There can be as many as ten different pronunciations (see W. Scott Morton, *The Japanese: How They Live and Work* [Tokyo: Tuttle, 1979]).

     Arrupe told the story of some new missionaries who, while walking along the street, stopped in front of a very difficult Japanese character. While they consulted their dictionary, a crowd of people surrounded them, laughing and making commentaries. When at last they figured out the meaning of the character, they understood why the people were laughing: the symbol meant "stopping prohibited."

2   José María de Vera, "Misionero en Japón," in La Bella, *Pedro Arrupe, general de la Compañía de Jesús*, 111–38, here 118.

would be going to the home of a Japanese family; he did not realize that the German Jesuit for a long time had been working with the Koreans who labored on the docks and did other similar work.

When they arrived in the Korean neighborhood, Pedro did not realize that the inhabitants were Asians of a different nationality. With his missionary eyes eager and open, he and his companion walked through the narrow streets toward Fuichi. Finally, they stopped in front of a Japanese-style house that was dilapidated and dirty.

"Is this the place?" asked Arrupe.

"This is it," replied his companion.

They opened a sliding door and said, *Gomen nasai* (Excuse me).

There was no reply to the greeting. Pedro was shocked by the extreme poverty of that house. When they called again, a small door opened. There was only darkness and silence. In the smoky interior, they could make out a group of people who seemed to be waiting uncertainly. Not knowing what to make of the dispirited reception, they opened the windows so the smoke could escape. As the cold air rushed in, they improvised an altar.

"This was my first apostolic contact," Arrupe later confessed, "and when I found myself confronted by such misery and indigence, with people confined in such a small space, my soul sank down to my feet."[3]

Much affected by that depressing ambience, Arrupe spoke to Father Shiffer after the Eucharist and asked him, "Father, is all Japan like this indoors?"

"No, man, no. Japan is not like this either indoors or outdoors."

Pedro sighed in relief. He felt a weight had been lifted from his shoulders. That was not Japan. That was simply a poor and abandoned group of immigrants who, far from their home country, were living in extreme distress. That experience, however, like all those that put him in touch with dire poverty, remained impressed on Arrupe's memory. Curiously, even with the passage of time and after the "Japanese economic miracle," immigrants to Japan from other parts of Asia continued to be second-class citizens, subjected to constant security controls and marginalized by the opulent Japanese society.

Little by little, Pedro deciphered the mysteries of that exotic new world. One very striking discovery for him was the *furo*, the typical Japanese bath. The tub is twice as tall as a European bathtub and half as long, so that one sits in it cross-legged, and the water reaches to the neck. For Westerners, the water, which reaches a temperature of 45 degrees Celsius (113 Fahrenheit), is at first unbearably hot. A whole family bathes in the same tub and with the same water, but they are already perfectly clean before getting in, having previously soaped up and rinsed themselves off. What is sought in the tub is not so much cleanliness as the sedative effect.

---

3   *Memorias*, 59ff.

Arrupe once prepared such a bath for a foreign Jesuit. When he explained to him the norms for using the bath, the foreigner took great offense, claiming that he already knew the norms, having lived for two weeks with a Japanese family. Arrupe was thus surprised when he saw the visitor soaping up after entering the bathtub. When he explained to him the problem, the truth came out: he had been two weeks with the Japanese family without ever having bathed!

In his *Memorias*, Arrupe recounts another amusing anecdote concerning Westerners' ignorance of Japanese customs. It concerned a European family that, exhausted from their long sea journey, went to a typical Japanese hotel after arriving in Yokohama. In their room, the family found only straw mats and very few other furnishings. After searching, they discovered the beds, or futon mattresses, hidden away in the closets. The next day, the steward entered the room and found nobody there. Eventually, he opened the closet doors and found that the different members of the family, instead of pulling the mattresses out into the room, had slept inside the closets.

Hana ga takai desu ne: What a Schnozzle!

The first six months in Japan went by slowly for Pedro. Dancing about his head, like gnats, were hundreds and hundreds of ideograms. Despite his difficulty in speaking and even greater difficulty in understanding others, he made his way to Tokyo.

His first destination in the huge city was a military-style barracks called "the settlement," a social center that during the day was a nursery for the children of workers and in the evening became a night school for adults.

Just as Pedro was about to practice the Japanese rite of removing his shoes before entering the building, several children who were watching him began to laugh. Pedro became nervous, having no idea what the laughter was about. He wondered whether he had practiced the rite incorrectly or had failed to make the proper greetings or to line up his shoes properly.

With his broken Japanese, the priest asked the children why they were laughing. They pointed at the aquiline nose of the Basque Jesuit and exclaimed: *Hana ga takai desu ne* [...], which translated meant "What a schnozzle!" There and then was his true Japanese baptism!

Pedro had endless talks on religious matters with Michel, the Jesuit who directed the social center, and with the university students who came around. He was profoundly impressed by how those young people could sit calmly for hours on their mats, first kneeling and then falling back on their heels, while he himself was writhing in pain, not knowing which hurt more, his knees or his ankles. That style of sitting was a veritable torture for a Westerner whose bones and muscles were already hardened. As time went by, his ears became attuned to those strange sounds, and his legs began to fold without excessive pain.

Suddenly, in a corner of the room would appear Tamura-san, an important figure in the house: she was a widow with three children who cooked for the priests. According to Michel, she lived with one foot on earth and one in heaven, receiving Communion and praying the rosary every day. One morning when breakfast was late, Michel and Pedro waited a good while and then went to look for the cook. In an inner room, they found her absorbed in ecstatic prayer, her head bowed and her hands joined, hardly breathing. She was seated before a magnificent statue of the Buddha.

The two Jesuits were astounded. "But what are you doing, Tamura-san?"

Losing nothing of her beatific peace, Tamura-san turned and answered, "I am praying for my poor husband. He was so good! He gave me this Buddha. Now that he is dead, how can I not pray for him?"

As a devout Catholic, Tamura-san instinctively felt that she should pray to the God of her husband. Little by little, Pedro was beginning to discover the Japanese soul.

But Tamura-san also became a true torturer of Arrupe. Since she never repeated a meal and always asked for his opinion about each one, the newly arrived missionary felt obliged to render her continual praise.

Pedro used to have to brace himself before trying raw fish or the strange condiments she used. One day, he found himself in front of something completely new, a kind of soup called *kombu*; of all the Japanese food, it was, he confessed, the only dish that produced in him real repugnance, despite his spirit of sacrifice.

"Did you like it?" asked Tamura-san.

Pedro rapidly paged through his mental dictionary. "*Omoshirokatta*—interesting, fascinating [...]," he answered.

The cook smiled with satisfaction, but Pedro later regretted he had ever learned that expression: Tamura-san served the dish seven days straight! After about four days, though, the *kombu* began to seem to him even tastier than a consommé.

Gradually, Arrupe found himself more at home in the "settlement," and his time there provided him ample opportunity to practice conversation and enter more deeply into the Japanese spirit.

Curiously, Arrupe's first three apostolic activities in Tokyo coincided with three funerals, the first of which was another new jolt for Arrupe. Accompanied by Brother Francis Xavier Hidezo Masui, he went to a house with many Buddhist images inside. When he asked about the body, he was told that it was "there." Since he could not see it, he insisted: "Where?"

"There."

He saw a small box containing ashes. On top of the box was an immense blade shaped like cross.

"What is that blade?" he asked.

"It is symbolic. Aristocratic families place on the casket an expensive sword, such as the old samurai used, so that the deceased person can defend

"If I had known then how much I would have to suffer, my hands would have trembled when elevating the host." The dedication on the worn photograph reads: "The elevation at the Mass I celebrated on Mount Fuji, the highest point in Japan. P. Arrupe" (August 23, 1939).

himself from the evil spirits. Poor people have to be satisfied with just using a barber's blade."

Pedro soaked it all in without ever losing his good humor. There was the day, for example, when after a funeral he found himself with a Japanese girl who wanted to get married within three days to a boy whom she did not even know, but who was soon leaving to fight in China. That situation made several things clear to Arrupe: that the Japanese never get right to the point, that you must wait patiently for them to communicate what they really want to say, that tradition did not allow young people to choose their marriage partners—and that the war was still going on.

Little by little, Arrupe probed further into the culture. After consecrating the chapel of some religious sisters to the Heart of Jesus, he had the idea of doing something similar with Japanese families. He found that a simple and authentic practice of this devotion sometimes brought family members together in prayer, even if they were Buddhists or Shintoists. At times, it even produced conversions.[4] Arrupe's manner of promoting the devotion always provoked a certain curiosity and interest among the people.

One day, Arrupe was especially impressed by the way a young catechumen was praying. She spent hours in ecstatic prayer, without moving, totally concentrated on the tabernacle and completely indifferent to all around her. The first time he noticed this, Arrupe asked her, "What do you do all this time that you are quiet here before the tabernacle?"

---

4   *Memorias*, 76ff. Arrupe writes: "How often I was able to feel the grace of conversion in those brief moments of devotion that became permanent. Frequently, when I walked barefoot on the tatamis of the houses I went to bless, I found before me sullen faces that revealed resistance. [...] But many of them gradually changed from being passive spectators who could not escape to being fervent catechumens preparing for a baptism that would make them Catholics."

"Nothing."

"What do you mean, nothing? So much time without doing anything?"

The young woman appeared troubled. After a long Japanese silence, she opened her lips: "What do I do, *Shimpu-sama*? Well, I just am here." In this way, she expressed her practice of combining two ways of praying that are really just one: the "being here" of Zen and the "being here" of Christian contemplation.

Another day, Pedro would be impressed by a conversation about the existence of God, or by those youngsters in catechism class who placed their presents for Jesus in a cardboard box with the note: "For your sake, I have made peace with Takeo-san, even though he was the one to blame and I wasn't. To console him, I will take him home as if nothing had happened." Arrupe would never forget that soiled scrap of paper scribbled by a slum kid.

Anyone who knows Japan and the great difficulties in gaining conversions to Christianity will surely be surprised by Pedro's first successes. There was, for example, the family in which the father was opposed to the Catholic faith, though he allowed his wife and his children to practice it. The wife wanted Arrupe to consecrate their house to the Heart of Jesus, but when the day arrived for him to do so, the father was unexpectedly at home. Without any hesitation Arrupe went ahead with the ceremony. Suddenly, the father appeared from behind a curtain and stated boldly: "I want to be baptized."

What was the secret of Arrupe's effectiveness? As he would later explain in numerous homilies, he understood the Heart of Jesus as the center of his own person, of his own deepest being. Years later, he would write:

> In sum, we have here what is most simple and profound in true devotion to the Sacred Heart. Studying that book "written from within and from without," we can learn "the riches of wisdom and knowledge," for it is Christ in whom are hidden "the riches of wisdom and knowledge" (Colossians 2:3). Looking upon and contemplating that crucified one with his pierced side, we will see in him the Son of God "who humbled himself and became obedient unto death, even death on a cross" (Philippians 2:8). Approaching him, we will believe with that faith, which, if it is true, will impel us toward works—works of love, of course, but a love that becomes manifest in love for the brothers and sisters.
>
> If God's love is so great that he gave us his only begotten Son—"God so loved the world that he gave his only Son" (John 3:16)—our response to that love must be complete commitment to Christ and our fellow men and women. "Therefore be imitators of God, as beloved children, and walk in love, as Christ loved us and gave himself up for us, a fragrant offering and sacrifice to God" (Ephesians 5:1). It is for that reason that Pius XII has written that in devotion to the Sacred Heart "is to be found the culmination of all religion and a perfect way of life."

This love for Christ and for our fellow men and women is not only the most perfect expression of Christianity; it also includes what is most characteristic of God's Spirit, for it makes fear disappear: "There is no fear in love, but perfect love casts out fear. [...] He who fears is not perfected in love" (1 John 4:18). It drives away anxiety: "I am writing this to you so that you may not sin; but if anyone does sin, we have an advocate with the Father, Jesus Christ the righteous one" (1 John 2:1). It increases confidence: "And now, brothers, remain in him, so that we may have confidence when he appears" (1 John 2:28); "in this is love perfected in us, that we may have confidence for the day of judgment" (1 John 4:17). It is a source of joy: "These thing I have spoken to you, that my joy may be in you, and that your joy may be full" (John 15:11). It is an expression of peace: "Peace I leave with you, my peace I give you. [...] Let not your hearts be troubled, neither let them be afraid" (John 14:27); it is a promise of victory: "Whatever is born of God overcomes the world; and this is the victory that overcomes the world, our faith" (1 John 5:4).[5]

Such a spiritual life was the secret to young Pedro's energy. He could be seen constantly moving among the settlement barracks, making his first contacts with the Japanese. With his restless and joyful spirit, he appeared to be someone deeply in love, and he was indeed in love with that "inner self" of Christ. From the very start of his work as a missionary, he seemed convinced that the effectiveness of his activity did not depend on him. Wherever he went, he always left a little bit of heart, and since he did not want it to be his own, it was the heart of Jesus Christ he left. That was the secret of a universal spirit that later would burst forth more fully in years to come.

For the moment, though, Pedro limited himself to smiling, carefully bowing his head, and timidly removing his shoes before walking on the tatami. Meanwhile, he worked with determined insistence on improving his Japanese, even if he spoke it with a mix of Spanish, English, and Basque accents. He soon discovered that much more important than what he said was what he really was—just as that young woman who was simply "there" before Jesus had already learned. That work in the settlement barracks was another important element in the experience of a man who in future years would accomplish much in advancing Christian concern for social justice.

---

5   *Una respuesta de fe y amor*, homily given in Rome, 1973. Pedro Arrupe, *En él solo la esperanza* (Bilbao: Mensajero, 1983). This book, with a prologue by Karl Rahner, contains Arrupe's thinking about the Heart of Jesus as it was expressed in his writings during this stage of his life. It also contains some excerpts from *Memorias*, which are useful for knowing the evolution of Arrupe's thought on this topic.

Arms Raised over Fuji-san

Without a doubt, Arrupe's most memorable experience of those first contacts with Japan was the Mass he celebrated on Mount Fuji, situated in the Hakone region, a little more than thirty kilometers from Tokyo. Mount Fuji is something more than a mountain of 3,776 meters; it is the highest peak of Japan and an authentic Mount Olympus for that country. When one for the first time views that white peak standing out against the blue sky, one's soul seems to be flooded with pure mountain air. Someone has written: "It is remarkable not only for its sacred character, but also for its unequaled esthetic value, which has inspired countless poems and paintings." The etymology of its name is uncertain, but it seems to refer to the fire of a volcano. It is known to have erupted eighteen times before 1707, but it has not done so since then. Until the restoration of the Ming dynasty, women were prohibited from ascending Mount Fuji, but today some three hundred thousand pilgrims, men and women, visit annually.

We can imagine what it meant for the young missionary Pedro Arrupe to climb Mount Fuji, or Fuji-san, as the ideogram has it, since it was a mountain consecrated to a female divinity. Forty years later, Arrupe himself would recall this experience:

> I recall quite well the Mass I celebrated on top of the famous Mount Fuji, more than three thousand meters high. I had climbed up there with one of my companions. At that time, the only way to get up there was on foot. The horses did not go above one thousand meters, more or less. It was necessary to reach the peak around four o'clock in the morning in order to be able to catch the superb panorama, because after six o'clock clouds covered the summit and there was no way to see anything.
>
> We arrived on time and celebrated Mass in the midst of an absolute solitude. I had just arrived in Japan, and I was feeling intensely the first impressions made on me by that new world. Within me were stirring a thousand projects for the conversion of Japan. We had climbed Fujiyama precisely to be able to offer to the Eternal Father, from the highest place in all of Japan, the sacrifice of the Immaculate Lamb for the salvation of that great country. The ascent had been exhausting since we were hurrying in order to arrive in time. Several times we called on Abraham and Isaac, recalling how they had ascended the mountain to offer their sacrifice. We reached the peak and marveled before the spectacle of sunrise, which raised our spirits and prepared us for the celebration. I had never celebrated the Eucharist in such conditions. Stretched above us was a pure, majestic blue sky, like the dome of an immense temple, and down below we felt the presence of the Japanese people, composed at the time of eighty million persons who did not know the Savior. Our spirit pierced the sublime dome of the material heaven and was raised to the throne of the divine majesty, the seat of the Trinity,

and I thought I was seeing the celestial Jerusalem. I thought I was seeing Jesus Christ, accompanied by Saint Francis Xavier, the first apostle of Japan, whose hair had turned gray in a few months because of the sufferings he had to undergo. And there now was I, standing before Xavier's Japan, facing an unknown future. If I had known then how much I would have to suffer, my hands would have trembled as I elevated the host![6]

Those raised arms of Arrupe, wearing priestly vestments and painfully lifting the Eucharist on the highest mountain of Japan, were a superb symbol of what his life was going to be. As the rising sun bathed his eyes and the wind rippled his chasuble, Arrupe learned once again the mysterious meaning of his mission. But his heart was greater still than anything that could be caught sight of from the snowy summit of sacred Fujiyama.

---

6   *Itinéraire*, 42.

8. An Exceptional Pastor

On September 1, 1939, that insignificant-appearing man with the ridiculous mustache named Adolf Hitler had begun the Second World War by invading Poland. When Neville Chamberlain resigned as prime minister of Great Britain and was succeeded by Winston Churchill, the British breathed a sigh of relief: "Churchill is back!" With his intelligent gaze and a cigar in his mouth, that stout man suddenly became a key arbiter in one of the century's most critical conflicts. He had tremendous authority in his hands, and he was not troubled by the fact that he had it at one of history's darkest moments. His British composure allowed him to remain serene in the face of every eventuality. He was ready to play hard and win, and when he told his compatriots, "I can only offer you blood, sweat, and tears," they were willing to accept the offer.

Churchill intensified his contacts with the US president, Franklin Roosevelt, who wanted to assist Britain but was held in check by a Congress and a public opinion that favored neutrality. Churchill soon had to concentrate his attention on Dunkirk, where around 350,000 Allied soldiers had been forced into retreat by the German army. On June 25, 1940, the armistice that Germany signed with Marshal Philippe Pétain entered into effect. The German troops broke through the Maginot Line and headed toward Maas and the Channel coast. That same day, they had entered into Paris. The French government was installed in Vichy, and General Charles de Gaulle began the resistance in London. British and German bombers began to darken the skies from Dakar to London. For its part, Japan created a separatist Chinese government in Nanking, under the command of Wang Ching-wei. The whole world was at war.

In mid-1940, Arrupe, after spending eighteen months learning the language and customs of the Japanese, packed his bags and caught a train to Ube, an industrial city near Hiroshima, where the main activity was mineral production. He went there with instructions to continue the work of social acculturation that he had begun in the settlement project of Tokyo. No sooner was he in Ube, however, when he received different instructions. He was told to pack his bags again and proceed directly to Yamaguchi.

In Xavier's Parish

Situated about 140 kilometers from Hiroshima, in a valley surrounded by green mountains, Yamaguchi was a city with a long history. Founded in 1350 by Ouchi Hiroyo, the city had been modeled on the imperial capital, Kyoto, and came to be the second most important city in the country. For Arrupe, however, Yamaguchi had a different significance, for it was there that in 1550 another lord of the region, Ouchi Yoshitaka, gave Xavier permission to use an abandoned Buddhist temple. From that base, Xavier formed an important Christian community, one that would suffer severe persecution starting in 1551, when Xavier left for the Indies.

Arrupe experienced a certain disappointment as he got off the train in that city of thirty thousand inhabitants.[1] Though a "province capital," it was no more than a large town that could be reached only by a secondary train on a narrow railway. Wondering whether he was in the right place, Pedro asked: "Could you tell me what station this is?"

"This is Yamaguchi," they told him.

Pedro could not conceal his disillusionment. At the time, there was no cathedral or sanctuary commemorating Xavier. All he found there was a tiny church and a small house, where the only person who received him was an elderly cook. The other missionary assigned there, Fr. Moisés Domenzáin, was traveling in Spain at the time, so Arrupe found himself quite alone in the place.

There was very little to see in Yamaguchi, but Arrupe discovered a strange friendliness among its people. "It was like a large town," he later wrote,

> and it preserved the patriarchal air and sacred heritage that came from its distinguished history. It was not especially industrial or commercial or war-oriented. Its most distinctive characteristic lay in its aristocratic spirit, which was to be found in certain privileged souls, irrespective of wealth or accomplishment. Yamaguchi had that quality, but it was not easy to see where exactly it came from; all the inhabitants contributed something impalpable out of their own spiritual refinement. Such was the setting that received me and that framed all my activities during the next two years.[2]

Pedro threw himself heart and soul into the work. In the course of that week, he prepared his first homily in Japanese in order to ingratiate himself with the Christian community and overcome the uneasiness that a newly arrived stranger usually provokes.

When Sunday finally arrived, Pedro nervously rang the bell. When the hour for Mass arrived, there were only seven devout elderly women in the church, nobody else. Pedro began vesting himself very slowly, and he drew out the first part of the Mass as long as he could. After reading the Gospel and turning to the people to give his homily, there was still nobody there except those

---

1   Around one thousand kilometers from Tokyo and 141 from Hiroshima, Yamaguchi today has around two hundred thousand inhabitants and a campus of the national university. The Jesuits presently are in charge of the church in Yamaguchi, where a sanctuary in memory of Saint Francis Xavier was built in 1952, along with a museum. On the saint's work in this city, see Pedro Miguel Lamet, *El aventurero de Dios: Francisco de Javier* (Madrid: La Esfera de los Libros, 2006), 654ff.

2   *Memorias*, 89.

seven women, scattered about on the tatamis and seated on their heels. He was tempted to forget about the homily he had worked so hard to prepare—he had even sought help from others for the more difficult terms. Nonetheless, he got a grip on himself and began to speak, asking God to increase that small flock.

After that disappointing start, which for Arrupe was like a baptism of fire, the Christians gradually became more visible. There were not many of them anyway, and they had little time off—the men frequently had to work on Sunday. After a few weeks, Arrupe had managed to make contact with sixty or seventy persons who were the mainstay of his congregation.

In July 1940, when a Spanish business commission visited Japan, official receptions were prepared for the commission members in the principal Japanese cities: Tokyo, Yokohama, Yokosuka, Nikko, Nagoya, Toba, Nara, Osaka, and Kyoto. Since Japan was interested in fostering economic relations with one of the few neutral countries left, the Spaniards received a warm welcome wherever they went.

Father Domenzáin had sent a telegram to Arrupe, instructing him to prepare "a superb reception" for the Spanish delegation in "the land blessed by Xavier's presence." Enthusiastic as always, Pedro moved into action, traveling to Shimonoseki to make arrangements with the tourism office. The people there were astonished that he would want to invite the Spanish authorities to Yamaguchi: "But there's nothing to see there!"

Fortunately, Arrupe had in his wallet a photograph of the monument to Xavier, which he showed to the tourism officials. He then set about preparing a banquet for the commission, as well as lodging in a place not used to receiving foreign visitors. Domenzáin also suggested giving the visitors a marble replica of the monument to Xavier, but that would have cost fifty thousand yen, a large sum in those calamitous times. The civil governor of the city thought that maybe a postcard of Yamaguchi would be enough, but Arrupe convinced him with his invincible smile: the replica would be made.

In the end, all turned out well. The visit of the Spanish commissioners was an excellent occasion for making known the person of Saint Francis Xavier and for educating the people about his mission there. The city government sponsored a program with three talks, which were given by Arrupe, the rector of the university, and a history professor.

It was a difficult challenge for the young missionary and a tough exposure to the reality of Japan. The rector spoke first, on current events, and the history professor followed. He began his speech: "Gentlemen, my task this afternoon is to explain something about the personality of the man named Saint Francis Xavier [...]." At first, all seemed to be going well, but then the professor continued: "Personally, I admire Xavier as a man, as an adventurer, as a restless spirit with great aspirations, but I do not admire him as a fanatical propagandist of religion or as the apostle of an exotic teaching."

Memorial in Yamaguchi for Saint Francis Xavier, first Christian missionary in Japan and a model for Pedro Arrupe.

Arrupe felt quite embarrassed and could hardly maintain his smile. The professor's discourse continued:

> It says much of Xavier that he was able, so long ago and without such primitive navigational means, to cross unknown seas, leaving behind continents and islands, and arrive on our shores as the first ambassador from the West. His heart beat strong with the spirit of adventure and an intrepid heroism that knows no fear. But he came with the cross in one hand and a sword in the other, hiding a suit of armor under a plain missionary cassock. The ideal that was really firing his fanaticism was plain: as is clear from the historical documents, Xavier came with the banner of faith in order to prepare for the occupation of our country, to undermine our nation, and to clear the way for the conquering ships of Spain and Portugal [...].

As the discourse continued in this vein, with all kinds of historical distortions, Arrupe felt his blood boiling with indignation. He considered his dilemma: either to read the speech he had so painstakingly prepared or to refute the professor's statements. As he looked upon his Christian faithful, he felt emboldened.

When his turn came, Pedro commended himself to Xavier and began to speak. As he himself admitted later:

> I began the discourse not knowing how I would proceed and much less how I would finish up. If someone were to ask me today what I actually said, I would be in a predicament; I have only the vague idea that I presented Xavier as the saint whose only goal was to bring happiness to the Japanese and who pursued that goal at great cost, without concern for his own life and welfare. There were moments when I thought that Xavier himself was

speaking through my mouth, as he had spoken four centuries before in that same place.[3]

The incident was a good experience for Arrupe. When the Spanish commission arrived later, there was a public reception, and a young Japanese fellow from the community gave a little discourse in Spanish. The commissioners were even allowed to take a siesta on the tatamis since they were quite exhausted from a month of strenuous travel around Japan.

The Orchestra Man

But days such as those were exceptional. Arrupe was dedicated mainly to the routine work of helping that struggling community to grow, and he used his fertile imagination to make that happen. He was convinced that it was necessary to do something that would energize the people, something that would produce a powerful visual impact. He hit upon the idea of organizing a Western-style procession, which he figured would have about the same impact there as a dragon dance would in the streets of Zaragoza.

Arrupe set to work and put up posters all over Yamaguchi announcing the event. He got Brother José Arregui to build a platform, even though the brother protested in his heavy Basque accent: "How ridiculous: a procession among pagans! How ridiculous!"

One day, Arrupe was working with his sleeves rolled up, spreading a carpet of red sawdust in the garden, and a lovely visitor appeared. She was a teacher from the nearby girls' school, who seemed to want to talk with the priest. Arrupe turned around to attend to her, but when she saw him in that attire, she quickly disappeared.

The procession was a success, attended by people from all corners of Yamaguchi. They crowded into the garden and the small church, and many had to stand outside. Arrupe had achieved the effect he sought: producing an exotic, unforgettable visual impact. Arregui embraced him, weeping with emotion at the success of the event. After all had gone, Pedro took refuge in the chapel for a long while to give thanks.

A few days later, the teacher appeared again. After bowing and smiling graciously, she got to the point: "I would like to learn about the Catholic religion, if that is possible." The conversation left Arrupe puzzled, and the young woman explained that she had decided to take this step after seeing him that day: "I was so impressed to see you so hard at work. I immediately thought: the faith of anyone who works without desire for profit must be very great. So I made up my mind." Fukugawa-san converted to Catholicism because she had seen Arrupe covered in sawdust from head to toe.

---

3   *Memorias*, 91ff.

Another idea that occurred to the young parish priest was inspired by the Japanese government's practice encouraging the people to do gymnastics. Radio Tokyo used to broadcast a special program that was carried by all the stations in the country, urging everybody to take part in oriental gymnastics at six in the morning. To nourish people's devotion, Arrupe's small parish community had the custom of celebrating a daily Mass at six-thirty every morning, but the government-sponsored gymnastic program was interfering.

Arrupe was not deterred. He contacted the person responsible for the radio program in the neighborhood and offered to make the church's gardens available for people to do gymnastics there. That person did not hesitate but exclaimed, "What luck! Just now I was looking for a place to do precisely that!"

Arrupe set one condition: he wanted to add on some movements from Western gymnastics and thus lengthen the Japanese educational program by ten minutes. That was agreed to, and the exercise turned out to be doubly attractive for the neighbors. Each day when the radio program finished its exercises, Pedro would go up on the platform and perform his own set of gymnastics, which the Japanese imitated with all seriousness. He would then recite a prayer of thanksgiving and invite anyone who wished to enter the chapel. At that point, he would put on his vestments and celebrate Mass—never did he have so many people in attendance! For some two weeks, he took advantage of that opportunity in order to tell people the essence of the Gospel message, so that they could freely decide themselves whether to accept it.[4]

Following up on the success of his early morning venture, Arrupe took another step by organizing some Spiritual Exercises according to St Ignatius's method. At first, the effort did not pay off, since that early hour was not a good one. It was one of the few times in the day when a family could get together for a good breakfast. When he changed the time to three-thirty in the morning, he succeeded in gathering together some thirty Christians who wanted to make the Exercises.

"I did it with all my heart," he later recalled:

I understood from the start that I had to live up to the expectations of those courageous people who were willing to get up for three days at three in the morning. They did so faithfully even though they had a whole day's work ahead of them. For me also it was rather hard, since the apostolate in the mission stations takes place mostly at night. During the day, the catechumens and the faithful have to work, so that instructions and devotions had to wait for a later hour. Often I did not finish my instructions until eleven at night, and by three in the morning people were already waiting for me.

---

4   "I worked especially with young people. It was something entirely new, like an experience of God. In those days, I was preaching a very general vision of God. That difficult war period was very important" (declarations of Arrupe to the author in 1983).

My nights were short and my days very long, but would that we were always blessed with such an excess of work!

In this period, Arrupe also took advantage of the Japanese people's love of music, a characteristic that would later motivate the Jesuits to establish music schools. With the help of other Jesuits, he organized a concert in Yamaguchi, announcing that the proceeds would be for the benefit of those incapacitated by the China war. Enlisting the help of Father Ernest Goossens and some German Jesuit students who lived in Hiroshima, the young parish priest managed to sell fifteen hundred tickets. Father Goossens would later be in charge of the Hiroshima Music University.

Such missionary tactics, despite their success and their ability to arouse the people's curiosity, did not really result in conversions. After satisfying their cultural interest and learning more about how Westerners thought, the Japanese would return to their mysterious interior world. Arrupe was aware of this and continually devised new tactics, such as arranging small group discussions. He also continued to organize concerts around the parish. Since the people interested in music would often arrive a half-hour early, Arrupe would take advantage of this time to offer them a cup of tea while he delicately turned the conversation to higher matters.

The Subtle Japanese Soul

Around this time, Arrupe discovered that the most effective way into the Japanese soul was through profound person-to-person relationships.

Such was the case of Nakamura-san, a sixteen-year old girl who was considered the best student in her university. One day, she came to see Arrupe, and after two months of conversations she decided to be baptized.

Making such a request during wartime was not at all easy. Japan was experiencing great tension because of its involvement in the bloody conflict. Throughout the country, foreigners were beginning to be viewed with suspicion, and even with hatred. An ancient imperial pride that considered itself invincible was facing the full force of the enemy's resistance, and the fateful outcome was already being foreshadowed.

Nakamura-san did not renege on her commitment, but after her baptism she felt people at the university acting strangely toward her. A city official's daughter, who was jealous of Nakamura's intellectual ability, insulted her in the middle of class. The professor failed to defend the slighted student since he feared the other girl's father.

After class, Nakamura-san went to see Arrupe and told him, "This morning they insulted me publicly in the university. The professor did not defend me, but he told me that tomorrow, at the start of class, I can defend myself from the calumny. What should I do?"

"Do as you wish. You will know yourself how best to behave."

Feeling very nervous, since honor was a delicate subject for the Japanese, Nakamura-san said, "No, Father, tell me what I should do. I don't even dare to think about it."

Arrupe got up and took a copy of the Gospels from his bookshelf.

"Here you have the life of Christ. Read how he acted in his most difficult moments."

Nakamura-san left, with the book tightly grasped in her hand. Arrupe withdrew to the chapel to beg strength for the girl.

The next day, two friends of Nakamura-san came to visit Arrupe. They excitedly told him:

> It was something unbelievable. Just before class started, the professor had Nakamura-san come up on his platform. The silence was total as she spoke: "I come up here only out of deference to the professor, who wants me to defend myself because of what was said in class yesterday. But I really don't have anything to say. What you heard yesterday is only a small part of my defects. The only thing I desire is that you indicate to me what my other defects are, so that I can correct them." Then, enveloped in a strange peace, she returned to her seat.

Arrupe knew that finding such peace had been very difficult for her. She had not told him anything, but he understood the meaning of the two dark circles under her eyes.[5]

Meanwhile, Arrupe continued his strategy of organizing small concerts. Once, they asked him to sing some Western songs in one of the colleges of Yamaguchi, but he needed someone to accompany him. By chance, the mission superior, Father Hugo (Enomiya) Lassalle, had announced that he would be visiting the city; he was a German who would later become provincial and eventually a Zen master, well known for the courses he gave in the West.[6] Recalling that Las-

---

5   *Memorias*, 113ff. Nakamura-san tragically died in the Hiroshima explosion.

6   Enomiya-Lassalle was of German origin but became a Japanese citizen. This pacifist Jesuit became provincial of Japan and was considered a "teacher" by the Zen masters, that is, one who had attained "illumination." Esteemed as one of the great spiritual figures of our time, he wrote many books about the synthesis of Christianity and Zen and traveled tirelessly around the world giving workshops of initiation to Zen and to *seshin*. He arrived as a missionary in Japan in 1929; after surviving the Hiroshima atomic bomb, he became a defender of intercultural dialogue between Buddhism and Christianity. In 1987, Yamada Kôun Oshi, a Zen master of Kamakura who had had Lasalle as a disciple, stated: "The fact that Catholics can practice Zen is due to Father Lassalle, who was the pioneer who first broke the ice." His basic message is that "true Zen does not contradict Christianity or any religion. It can help any person to advance along his path" (see Ursula Baatz, *H. Enomiya Lassalle, jesuita y maestro zen* [Barcelona: Herder Editorial, 2005], and *H. Enomiya Lassalle: Una vida entre dos mundos; Biografía* [Bilbao: Desclée de Brouwer, 2001]).

salle played the violoncello, Arrupe sent him a message asking him to bring his instrument with him. The messenger could not find the superior, but brought the violoncello anyway. Arrupe placed it under the bed of the guest room.

When Lassalle arrived, Arrupe very diplomatically asked for permission to sing in the college, but stated, "The problem is that I don't have anyone to accompany me. Could you help me out?"

"I'd like to, but I am really out of practice. I would have to rehearse."

"Great, I have the scores right here [...]."

"But I would need a violoncello."

"Don't worry. I'll get you the best one there is in Yamaguchi."

"Impossible. I am used to my own, and there's no time to bring it here."

"The only solution, then," replied Arrupe a bit waggishly, "would be for your violoncello to appear right here as if by magic, no?"

"That's right," answered Lassalle with a laugh.

"Well, if that's the case, then there's no problem." Arrupe then got up, walked over to the bed, and pulled out the instrument that he had hidden beneath it.

Lassalle looked at him dumbfounded and could not refuse his request. The two of them harmonized quite well together, and Pedro's magnificent voice once again drew applause. Ten years later, Catholic nuns would be teaching in that same college.

Almost every day, Arrupe had fresh new ideas for carrying out the difficult mission of evangelizing a people not very receptive to the preaching of Christianity. A favorite tactic was organizing expositions, one of which consisted of

Arrupe with a group of the faithful of his parish in Yamaguchi as the Second World War was beginning (1940).

pictures of the life of Christ displayed in a large department store—it certainly got people talking. Eventually, Yamaguchi established a permanent exposition about Saint Francis Xavier.

The Profound Self of Zen

During this period of Arrupe's life, he had a great interest in inculturation, a concept hardly discussed at the time. Nowadays, many people in the West are interested in Eastern spirituality, and they study Zen, archery, the tea ceremony, or calligraphy. In the 1940s, however, a Western missionary generally went into the field with dogmatic ideas of "the truth" and a consequent rejection of anything that might smack of paganism. By contrast, Arrupe's attitude was both courageous and prophetic.

During his time in Yamaguchi, Arrupe sought to enter deeply into the Japanese mentality and so also into Zen, which was at the cultural heart of this people. He zealously applied himself to studying the Zen practices of interiorization, self-discipline, and encounter with the deeper self. He also sought to become proficient in forms of Zen that go beyond specific movements and rituals in order to seek a higher illumination; these included the tea ceremony, the writing of Japanese characters, the self-defense system called judo, and the practice of archery and fencing.

Westerners frequently confuse Zen with Buddhism or consider Zen to be another religion, but as Paul Arnold writes: "Research has finally convinced us that Zen proceeds from the esoteric Buddhism expounded discreetly by two traditional sects, *tendai-shu* and *shingon-shu*, that are Japanese variations of two schools of Chinese tantrism."[7] However that may be, there is much truth in what was written years later by Lassalle, the Jesuit who accompanied Arrupe with his violoncello:

> From the spirit of Zen are born all these ways of achieving spiritual wholeness and even of reaching oneness with Nature, with the All. These ways require the *mu-ga*, the "not-self" or awakening of self, and they transmit a complete interior balance and peace of soul. [...] For that reason, many Japanese are quite skilled at judging a person's interior spirit by observing his external behavior. Non-Christian Japanese, for example, will judge a Catholic priest's interior discipline by observing his external posture while celebrating Mass, [...] just as one might judge the moral character of an artist on the basis of a work of art.[8]

7   Paul Arnold, *El zen en la tradición japonesa* (Bilbao: Ediciones Mensajero, 1979).

8   Enomiya-Lassalle, *Zen, un camino hacia la propia identidad* (Bilbao: Ediciones Mensajero, 1975) (Spanish version of *Zen weg zur erleuchtung* [Vienna: Herder, 1974]), 69ff., and *Zen y mística cristiana* [Madrid: Ed. Paulinas, 1991]). See also: Heinrich Dumoulin, *La esencia del Zen: Los textos clásicos de los maestros chinos*, ed. Thomas Leary (Barcelona: Kairós,

This connection with the deeper self helps explain the success of many of Arrupe's ventures in Japan. His authenticity, his interior harmony, his simplicity, and his transparency of soul did more to convince his audience than any words or activities.

During these years, Arrupe began to make his daily meditation in the Zen posture, thus practicing a type of cosmic prayer that is beyond all techniques and schools. Arrupe even decided to set up a Zen archery range in Yamaguchi by way of experiment. He wrote of it later:

> Generally shots were taken at a range of twenty-five meters. The bow was made of pieces of bamboo joined under pressure, giving it extraordinary strength and flexibility.
>
> Before using the bow, the archers do something equivalent to tuning a musical instrument before a concert. They solemnly grasp the bow. Slowly, very slowly, they draw it back, as if concentrating on the importance of the act they are going to realize. Then they shoot at a special straw target just a few meters away. After that, they can begin to shoot the regular distance. I asked them to teach me, and they gave me all the instructions they thought necessary.
>
> The instructions were strange. I was expecting them to tell me: "Keep your eyes fixed on the target." Instead, they told me: "Forget about the target, because that is not important at all. Don't worry about whether you will hit it or not. Your only intention should be identifying yourself with it. Then shoot, let the arrow go serenely, and it will reach the target by itself. But if the anxiety produced by your effort stretches your nerves instead of the bowstring, then you certainly will never hit the target.[9]

Arrupe was entering fully into a cultural world that years later would fascinate a great many Westerners. Zen was a matter of searching for the very center of being rather than of struggling for competitive standing. Such was the discovery of the Frenchman who one day, after many months of practicing archery, finally shot his arrow with complete disinterest, and his teacher exclaimed, after bowing reverently: "*It* has scored."

Arrupe was impressed by the district judge, who used to arrive at his archery range promptly at six every morning. After shooting with slow and concentrated

---

1991); *Zen: El camino de la iluminación en el Budismo* (Bilbao: Desclée de Brouwer, 2002); Karlfried Graf Dürckheim, *Hara, Centro vital del hombre* (Bilbao: Mensajero, 1987); *Meditar, ¿cómo y por qué?* (Bilbao: Mensajero, 1989); *Práctica el camino interior* (Bilbao: Mensajero, 1994); Daisetz Teitaro Suzuki, *Budismo zen y psicoanalisis* (Madrid: Fondo de Cultura Económica, 1979); *El ámbito del Zen* (Barcelona Editorial Kairós, 1981); *Vivir el Zen* (Barcelona: Kairós, 1995 [1949]); Yoka Daishi, *El canto del Inmediato Satori* (Barcelona: Kairós, 2001).

9   *Memorias*, 126.

rhythm for an hour, he would proceed to the court and take his seat as president of the tribunal.

As was to be expected, Pedro wanted to become skilled in archery and so sought instruction. After taking all the preliminary steps, he aimed carefully, trying his best not to be obsessed with the idea of hitting the target. When he released the string, the arrow went flying off at an angle and embedded itself in a window to his right. Even after many years, Arrupe laughed when talking about his lack of skill with the bow and arrow.[10] But he did not give up easily. He practiced archery for many months, even as he put ever more pressure on his tense soul in his tireless efforts to transmit his faith.

Arrupe was always coming up with ingenious ideas, such as sponsoring a public talk about vitamins, given by a Catholic doctor from the University of Keijo in Korea. Five minutes before the conference was due to start, however, there were only three persons in the lecture hall. Excusing himself with the doctor, Arrupe rushed into the street in search of people. He had the good luck to meet up with a medical doctor that he had met only once before. He asked her to help out by bringing some friends and students to the conference. Within a half-hour, she had gathered together about two hundred people, among whom was a relative of hers who would later become a Catholic.

Around that time, there occurred something that would happen frequently throughout Arrupe's life. A primary school teacher was attending some talks Arrupe was giving, and she spent hours talking to him about the existence of God. To convince her, Arrupe used all the resources of Scholastic theology, including the five ways of Saint Thomas. One day, the teacher said to Arrupe: "Do you believe, then, that God's existence is necessary?"

Arrupe was uncertain how to answer and finally said, "Then you haven't understood anything?"

> Yes, I have. I could repeat to you word for word everything you have explained to me. But you are a *hotoke* [perfect being], and I have been observing how you live for some months now. I see how convinced you are and how much you have studied the topic in order to be more certain of the truth. But what has convinced me most of all is you yourself.

Arrupe learned a new lesson about the oriental mind: a living reality is more important than any abstract argument.

All the testimonies from this first period in Yamaguchi are in agreement: Arrupe was bold, tireless, and optimistic. He never got discouraged because

---

10   In the interview granted to the author a little before losing the ability to speak, Arrupe laughed as he tried to show me, with his weakened hand, how he practiced archery. He was happy to evoke his failure in the Zen experience since he had failed to hit the target because of his excessive zeal and passion. He finally arrived at the height of detachment without practicing Zen.

conversions were few and far between or because many people attended church for a time and then disappeared back into their traditional practices. According to Father Shogo Hayashi, then a boy but later a convert of Arrupe, "From the Japanese point of view he was rather brash, but he succeeded in getting people together. I don't know if he performed even ten baptisms, but he was admirable. Nothing could discourage him. He was always learning something new. He was indefatigable."[11] Father Takao Moriwaki recounts how he had lived in Kobe until 1940 but moved to Yamaguchi after his father's death. Arrupe received his family in a house near the church that was used for catechism classes. "Father Domenzáin," Moriwaki relates, "had gone to Spain to raise money. Arrupe was alone and was working without stopping, almost without sleeping. He had a lot of appeal for the youngsters. He managed to convince Hayashi and me. He baptized us and now we are Jesuits and professors at the university."[12]

"His missionary methods," explains Robert T. Rush,

> were sometimes quite exceptional. Most extraordinary perhaps were the concerts he used to give, along with other Jesuits who had musical talent— his deep baritone voice combined well with their instrumental accompaniment. In those days of scarce conversions and the many suspicions typical of wartime, he made use of whatever method might help people to know Christ and his church better.[13]

The tragic shadow of warfare kept spreading across the globe and finally fell on Arrupe himself. One day, while he was vesting for Mass in the tiny sacristy, the boots of the military police were heard at the gate of the mission.

---

11   Declarations made to the author by Shogo Hayashi, S.J. in the Jesuit residence of Kobe a little before Hayashi's death in 1987.

12   Declarations made to the author by Takao Moriwaki, S.J., professor at Sophia University in Tokyo.

13   Robert T. Rush, "Pedro Arrupe, misionero: Un corazón tan grande como el mundo," in *Pedro Arrupe: Así lo vieron*, ed. Manuel Alcalá et al. (Santander: Sal Terrae, 1986), 43–65, here 45.

9. Light in the Prison

Churchill got up from the table and crossed the foyer. Visibly worried despite his English dispassion, he took the cigar from his mouth and dialed a phone number. In two or three minutes, President Roosevelt was at the other end of the line.

"Mister President, what is this I hear about Japan?"

"Quite right. They have attacked us at Pearl Harbor. Now we're all aboard the same ship."

The president then exchanged some words with his ambassador in London and gave Churchill a return call. After listening to what the president had to say, the prime minister responded: "Of course, that simplifies matters. May God protect you."

Churchill could not conceal his smile. The United States was taking their side.[1]

On November 26, 1941, a Japanese attack fleet composed of six aircraft carriers supported by cruisers had received orders to assemble in a remote spot near the Kuril Islands, to the north of the Japanese archipelago. The date of the planned attack had already been set by the mastermind of the operation, Admiral Isoroku Yamamoto. The naval formation, under the command of Admiral Chuichi Nagumo, set sail toward the east, staying well north of Hawaii. Moving stealthily amid the storms and fogs of those latitudes, it managed to get to within 275 miles of Pearl Harbor without being detected. At 7:55 a.m. on Sunday, December 7, the first bomb fell from the armada of 360 bombers, escorted by fighter planes. At the time, some ninety-four ships of the US Army were anchored at Pearl Harbor, among which were eight battleships of the Pacific fleet, the primary targets of the Japanese attack. The experienced Japanese pilots swung into action, and by 8:25 a.m. the first waves of dive-bombers and torpedo planes had unleashed their deadly cargo on the unsuspecting naval forces. By ten o'clock, the battle had ended, and the enemy withdrew, leaving behind a fleet reduced to a heap of mangled steel. More than two thousand Americans lost their lives, and another two thousand were wounded. Control of the Pacific had passed into the hands of the Japanese, and "for the moment," as Churchill wrote in his memoirs, "the world's strategic balance underwent a radical change." But something in the wounded American pride was begging for revenge.

With their control over the Pacific assured, the Japanese imperial spirit grew apace, reaching even the small city of Yamaguchi. There, a smiling, unthreatening Jesuit of European appearance was arranging the things that would be necessary for benediction of the Blessed Sacrament. It was six o'clock in the evening of December 8, 1941, feast of the Immaculate Conception.

---

1   Sir Winston Churchill, *Memorias, La segunda guerra mundial*, vol. 3, *La gran alianza* (Barcelona: José Janés, 1950), 865ff.

"International Spy"

"Father Arrupe, three police officers are asking for you." They had orders to search the house.

The few people waiting in church for the liturgical act to begin felt bewildered. Benediction was cancelled. Within an hour, the news had silently spread to all the Catholics of Yamaguchi. At first, there was no way of knowing whether a wave of persecution was about to begin.

The police officers proceeded carefully. They searched every last inch of the property. They even made Arrupe open the tabernacle, at which point he asked them to treat it with respect.

Everything was going well until the police found something that appeared suspicious in one of Arrupe's desk drawers: an enormous bundle of perfectly cataloged letters.

"I had been imprudent enough," Arrupe wrote later,

> to keep all the letters I had received since arriving there. Thus, when they began to look through them, they found some in Japanese and the rest in Spanish, German, English, French, Italian, and even a few in Latin. For them there wasn't the least doubt but that all that polyglot correspondence, totally unintelligible to them, concerned political matters and was evidence of espionage.[2]

The police carefully gathered those documents and took them to their headquarters. They also took Arrupe to the prison.

"Don't be afraid," they assured him. "We are just going to examine these letters to find out what they contain. As soon as your innocence is evident, you will be released."

Pedro rushed to grab his breviary, his shaver, and a dictionary that would allow him to continue his study. With that minimal baggage, he was taken under guard to the central building of the Japanese military police.

As he walked along, Arrupe's mind was racing wildly. What possibly could have brought him to this situation? It was obviously the climate of war in the country. He knew that his public activities had created great sympathy toward him on the part of the people, but also great suspicion on the part of the nationalist groups who controlled the government.

At first, Arrupe was unaware of being observed, but he had become increasingly alarmed at the constant presence of a police officer around the house, always asking him questions. "He was one of those types who never looks you straight in the eye," wrote Arrupe later. "He appeared somewhat effeminate and was forever peaking through the windows. He talked about everything and asked about

---

2   *Memorias*, 142.

everything, from the most insignificant details of ascetics to the complexities of the major political problems—there was nothing left out of his investigation."[3]

Arrupe initially thought that the man was interested in the Christian faith, so he answered his questions with clarity and care. Soon, however, he realized the real reason for the frequent visits and became more evasive with the sleuth. The persistence and the passion with which Arrupe carried out his mission motivated the police to investigate him all the more thoroughly. They could not understand why anyone would work so hard for an invisible God, especially at a time when the Buddhist faith was in decline.

When full-scale war broke out, the military police, thanks to the detailed reports given them by the local police unit, had a complete account of Arrupe's activities.

A Bare Cell

With their prisoner in tow, the soldiers reached the military base.

"The prison no longer exists today," I was told by Mister Yoshizama, who took me personally in his small car to the former site of the prison:

> It was a large, old wooden house that held thirty or forty prisoners. Father Arrupe was a prisoner there for thirty-three days, and they used to throw his food at him, calling out "Spain." The Christians were quite terrified, since professing the faith at the time was viewed as an act of disloyalty. There were no more than a hundred persons in the Catholic community, and they had a bad name given the nationalist climate produced by the war.[4]

Father Arrupe was first led into a spacious cell, some fifteen by twenty-five meters in size. The only thing in the cell was a bare tatami mat, and there was a tangible sensation of cold and loneliness. Judging from some shafts he saw in a corner, Pedro guessed that in times of peace this had been a hall for practicing fencing. He later wrote of his experience:

> It is night. The December sun sets at four in the afternoon and does not rise until fourteen hours later. Without a futon, I curl up in a corner, and I try to fall asleep without worrying too much. God will determine what my fate is to be. It is too cold to get to sleep. I spend the night shivering, with teeth chattering, doing spells of Swiss gymnastics in order to get warm.
>
> The cold light of the sun filters through the large, open windows of the hall. Absolute silence. The hours of waiting pass with painful slowness. My

---

3   *Memorias*, 141.
4   Statements made to the author in Yamaguchi. On a sunny July day, Mister Yoshizama showed me with much enthusiasm where the prison had been. Despite his sober Japanese demeanor, his eyes and his gestures revealed the affection he had for Arrupe and his nostalgia for those years of war that were so difficult for the Christian minority.

hopes of being able to celebrate the Eucharist gradually disappear, since the morning is passing fast and there's no sign that they will release me.

Around eleven o'clock, since nobody could be seen on any side, I looked out one of the windows and called a soldier who was passing by. Our dialogue was brief, but long enough to make it clear to me that I was going to be there a good while.

"Listen! I am waiting here for them to tell me when I can leave to say Mass."

"Well, you'd better ask them to bring you food, because I think this is going to be drawn out."

After two days, the door burst open violently, and about twenty soldiers marched into the hall. They were strong lads from the countryside, without much education. Their entrance smacked of the confidence of an army that knows only triumphs. They put me in a corner and then suspended curtains around me, making me a small room of about two meters on each side, at most. There I was to be kept detained, and the worst of it was that I did not know for how long.

By the third day, I had a sinister-looking beard. Since there was no point in continuing that way, I asked the guard permission to shave. That poor soldier from the countryside was greatly puzzled; he scratched his head and decided that, since he had no authority to grant me such a permission, the appropriate thing would be to put the request in writing. I had no problem with following the laws of protocol, so when he brought me a paper and pen, I asked him to write the petition, since I did not know how to do so myself. He wrote it out quickly, and I only had to sign it.

In all earnestness, he sent the request to his immediate superior for it to be acted upon. And so it happened: several hours later, permission was conceded by the benevolent authorities, for seven o'clock the next morning. Precisely at seven o'clock, two soldiers presented themselves with a large basin overflowing with very hot water. Thanking them, I told them that the next time a tenth as much water would suffice, and I prepared to shave.[5]

Arrupe narrates the odyssey of his shaving experience in great detail. The soldiers took him, with the basin, to a place where there were sinks with running water. He requested a mirror, and they brought him a tiny one, such as might fit in a woman's purse. Even though he told them that that mirror sufficed, they brought him several others, including one that was body-length. At first, the only people observing him were the two soldiers who had brought the basin and two others who had brought the mirror. When he started to shave, however, all those engaged in other tasks gathered around him, nudging one another with

---

5   *Memorias*, 143.

amazement and making gestures of great admiration. The explanation for this was simple: Japanese men have very little beard and shave rarely. Moreover, compared to the slow and careful way the peasant farmers used their blades, Arrupe's agility in shaving was quite a spectacle.

A Prisoner Who Captivates

That same afternoon, an official came to the cell to interrogate Arrupe. Since the cell had no furniture at all, they brought in a table and a chair, along with pen and paper. The official asked Arrupe only for his full name and the names of his parents and siblings. Then, to the prisoner's surprise, the official packed up everything and departed.

Two days later, the same operation was repeated, but now Arrupe did not remain silent. He asked his interrogator to tell him why he was imprisoned.

"Do you want to know all the charges against you?"

"Yes," answered Arrupe with his typical self-assurance.

The officer took a thick folder of papers from his briefcase. At that moment, Arrupe began to feel fear. Could it be that somebody had slandered him?

Sitting at the table, the official read for forty-five minutes straight. The accusations mixed together the political with the religious. When the officer explained that this was the file of his activities before the war broke out, Arrupe understood everything. The reports had come from that sorry character whom the local police had sent to spy on him and who after each interview had written down his suspicions.

At that point, Pedro relaxed, satisfied that it was not one of his own faithful that had betrayed him, and he responded with some irony: "As Christians, we are taught that we should be humble. I have many defects and a very poor view of myself, but I'm not so bad as all that!"

Pedro was left alone again, absorbed in his memories and ruminations. His nervous condition deteriorated as time went by. All kinds of gruesome images flitted through his imagination. Everything was a lie, but how to prove it? Despite his inborn optimism, the future appeared to him very dark indeed.

The presence of the soldiers deprived Arrupe of the tranquility he needed for prayer. He had less room to move around now, but he was given some magazines, which allowed him, with the help of the dictionary, to continue his study of Japanese.

One day, the soldiers were engaged in a strange conversation: Which came first, the water or the cloud? The discussion continued for a good while, and others joined in, but nobody could give an answer. Finally, one of them suggested: "Why don't we ask the foreigner? He is a teacher and should know about this."

The others agreed, and all of them approached Arrupe. The only one who was not involved in the discussion was the guard. The others spoke freely with

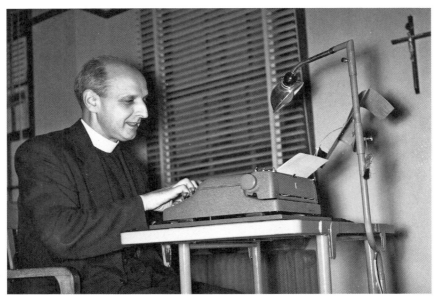

When the police found letters Arrupe had written to missionaries in various languages, he was impris-
oned and accused of being an "international spy" (Yamaguchi, November 1941).

the prisoner, and he took advantage of the occasion to lead the conversation toward more general themes, and by means of them to God.

Arrupe spoke with his customary passion and enthusiasm, and the soldiers listened intently. They were fascinated by what he had to say. From that time on, there was an improvised catechism class each day for the soldiers. The officers in charge had no objections since it did not contravene the prison regulations.

Nobody knows whether that seed fell on good earth. Once again, Arrupe became aware of the enormous abyss that existed between Eastern and Western cultural concepts:

> I was giving them the contents of our theology, and they used their own words and expressions to let me know how they understood what I was saying. There was always some divergence and contradiction, but we strove to bring together continents and contents in order to achieve greater mutual understanding. That work gradually developed into true friendship, though of a strange and rather paradoxical kind.

Finally, one day the prison head approached with a letter that he wanted Arrupe to read.

"Impossible," said the priest, "I can't read it because the characters are written in a style I don't understand."

"It is from my parents," the officer explained:

They are telling me that they have found me a suitable fiancée and all that remains is to fix the date of the wedding. The letter is not so much to ask me what I think, but to inform me. I would really like to decide whom to marry on my own. Teacher, do you think I should marry her? If I am wrong, it will be an error that affects my whole life.

Arrupe did not know the fiancée and was unable to give counsel about the matter, but he appreciated the confidence he had inspired in this man who consulted him on such a personal issue.

Despite these moments of grace, the prison regime was severe. Arrupe was never allowed to leave the prison, except once, when he was taken by two soldiers to a public bath. This was done since bathing, according to Japanese custom, was an obligatory ritual that left a person feeling like someone new, with a changed sensibility.

When they took Pedro from his cell, he thought that the bath would be within the prison building, but such was not the case. They took him out to the street at around four o'clock in the afternoon, the hour when students were leaving the university where Arrupe gave Spanish classes. His appearance was miserable: he was dirty, unshaven, and unkempt. For a man so particular about cleanliness and tidiness, the experience was humiliating. The teacher had to walk among the students looking like a delinquent.

Still, he could not help recalling a Gospel scene: "It didn't take much time, but it was enough to be teach me a little of Christ's suffering when he was twice led from the Roman courtyard to the Jewish one, with his hands cruelly tied."[6]

This was just one of many profound experiences he had during the time he spent in prison: "Many things I learned during that period! The great wisdom of silence and the interior dialogue with 'the guest of my soul.' I think it was the most instructive period of my whole life."[7]

Many years later, after being laid low by a stroke in Rome, Arrupe recalled that time in prison and kept repeating again and again: "How beautiful! How beautiful!" He laid great stress on how that solitude with Christ had been for him a profound mystical experience. "There was nothing in my cell. I was alone with Christ." And he would half-close his tear-filled eyes.[8]

---

6 *Memorias*, 149.

7 *Itinéraire*, 27.

8 Statements made to the author in July 1983. It was one of the most intensely emotional moments of my long conversation with Arrupe about his life. It appeared to be one of the mystical experiences that most deeply marked his whole existence.

Tonight Is Christmas Eve

Christmas Eve arrived. That night, while the city slept, Arrupe stayed awake in silence, feeling an enormous sadness. Reflections on Christmas Eve caused him great pain. As his soul traveled to the small chapel of his parish, he imagined the midnight Mass that he would not be able to celebrate this year. All he could hear was the breathing of the soldiers who were sleeping on the other side of the curtain.

Suddenly, Arrupe was surprised by a strange noise outside one of the windows. It reached him softly, like the quiet murmuring of many voices that did not want to give themselves away. He listened more intently. In prison, any sound is enhanced by anxiety and by the fear arising from the sheer fact of being incarcerated.

Then, over the quiet chatter that reached his ears there flowed the slow, soft strains of a Christmas carol in Japanese, one that Arrupe himself had taught his people. Pedro could not contain his tears, so strong was the contrast between the solidarity of these faithful Christians and the injustice of those holding him prisoner for a false accusation.

After a few minutes, that Christmas melody disappeared into the darkness of the sleeping city. His people had left, leaving Pedro curled up in his silence, but then, all of a sudden, it seemed to him that that primitive cell had all the glory of the manger of Bethlehem.

The days passed by in uncertainty until January 11, when the prison door opened abruptly at midnight, while Arrupe was asleep. The lights were turned on, and the officer in charge appeared, accompanied by several subordinates. They had with them books and papers for undertaking an official interrogation, which Pedro thought would be the final and definitive one. He had no idea that it was going to last thirty-seven hours straight.

Not a detail was neglected. They started with his private life: the hour he rose and went to bed, the praying of the breviary, the customary morning meditation.

All that was quite incomprehensible to them, but Arrupe kept answering their questions carefully, with his usual assurance and confidence.

"During my interrogation, I became aware of the extraordinary impression my answers were causing in them. In their treatment of me, they gradually showed more respect, more puzzlement, and less hostility. They were always courteous, but eventually they began to be quite deferential."[9]

The first part of the interrogation, dedicated to his private life, lasted fourteen hours. The second part concerned the doctrine he was teaching. Arrupe was immediately afraid that they would question him about the thorny issue of the "emperor-god." He later confessed that he began to feel tired and nervous and feared mainly for what might happen to his Christian faithful.

---

9   *Memorias*, 151.

Arrupe singing "Maite" and other zortzikos *with his excellent baritone voice. During his time as parish priest, he used every means at his disposal to attract the Japanese.*

"Explain to me," said the police official, "the first commandment of God's Law."

Pedro lifted his heart to God, asking for help, and he felt a special inspiration.

"Very well. So that you see that I have no problem in treating this topic, I am going to do so in exactly the same way as I do with my catechumens in the church."

The tribunal agreed, and Arrupe explained some basic ideas about God and creation. Then he asked them bluntly: "Do you believe that the emperor is the creator of the world?"

At that time, the emperor was recognized as a "god" who was a descendant of "gods" and a begetter of "gods," but the Japanese term *kami* was very vague in meaning, and it seemed difficult to accept that the emperor had existed for millions of years and had created the world. Arrupe thus put them in a predicament: if they answered "no," they were unfaithful to the emperor; if they answered "yes," they would appear unreasonable.

So they answered, "We don't understand anything about philosophy."

Pedro relished their quandary. Now he was on his own territory. Their confession of ignorance hindered their ability to rebut his teaching. He then dealt with each of them personally, asking them about their own lives, for which they would have to answer to God. This argument left them disturbed, so they changed the topic of conversation and spoke again of politics, social problems, the war. In the end, it was thirty-seven long hours of interrogation.

Finally, a sign of hope that things were going well: the official grabbed his pen and began to write, and Arrupe observed him as he filled the pages with large

Japanese characters. When he had finished writing, the official asked Arrupe: "Do you understand what is written here?"

"No. I haven't been able to read it. The characters are difficult, and they are upside down from where I am sitting."

"Okay, before you sign it, I will read it to you."

Arrupe later wrote:

> There came from his lips the most beautiful first-person confession of faith that had ever been written in my name: "I, Pedro Arrupe [...]." That man had penetrated to the depth of my thinking as a missionary and a priest, thanks to the providential contact I had had earlier with the soldiers. In those previous days, I had managed to find the precise expressions that were needed to make myself understood in a way that they would understand. Thus, during the thirty-seven hours of interrogation I did not give a single answer in which I meant one thing and they understood something else. As I was placing my fingerprint on one of the pages to show that I was in agreement with what was written there, I asked the official if he would allow me to have a copy of that document that so marvelously summed up my beliefs and my activities. He did not grant me that favor.[10]

"It is an official document," he answered in a surly tone. Nevertheless, Pedro surmised that the official felt quite pleased at the appreciation that was implicit in his request for a copy.

A half hour later, Arrupe was called to the office of the commander, who told him that he was being granted his freedom and could leave whenever he wished. First, though, the commander had a long conversation with him. By way of excusing himself, he explained that the reports they had received from the civil authorities had been quite negative; they felt obliged to detain him and search his house as a precautionary measure. He had been imprisoned to allow for an in-depth investigation of his person, his activities, and his beliefs.

"But then why have you held me so long without interrogating me?"

"Because one of the most important elements for judging such cases is the conduct of the accused person. You have submitted to whatever you were told to do without the least objection. You dedicated yourself to your studies and your prayers without protesting, without complaining about anything, without insulting anybody." Arrupe remembered that imprisoned near him there had been a Chinese professor who was constantly insulting people with foul language and complaining in a loud voice.

When Arrupe stood up to take his leave, the commander again asked for pardon: "Of course you know that in times of war people's nerves are on edge and it is easy to fall into errors."

---

10 *Memorias*, 154.

"I already told you not to worry," replied Arrupe:

My statements make it clear that I am dedicated to preaching the Gospel of Jesus and that I have come to Japan to suffer for the Japanese. For a Christian, suffering is not a cause of shame or hatred. Jesus Christ suffered much more than any other human being. A believer has no fear of suffering with him and in the same way he suffered. You are the person who has helped me most in this way. I have no hard feelings toward you. Rather, I feel gratitude to you, as to someone who had done me a great favor.

"I have done you a favor?"

"Yes, you have brought me closer to fulfilling my ideal. You are the man who has made me suffer most for the Japanese."

Those words left an incredible impression on the official. He extended his hand to Arrupe in a European handshake. As he firmly held the priest's hand, he said: "Preach, preach that admirable religion that is yours." Pedro could hardly believe what he was hearing. As he looked into the official's eyes, he noticed they were wet with tears of emotion.

Before leaving the prison, Arrupe went to say goodbye to the soldiers and to take one last look at the improvised cell where he had been kept for more than a month and where he had passed some very difficult moments. He had been treated neither well nor badly—he was just another prisoner. For a foreigner, though, the conditions were trying. In almost any prison in the world, a prisoner can count on a cot, a table, a stool, but Arrupe had only a tatami mat. He had to remain all day stretched on the ground, with no support for his back; his abdomen ached for lack of a bed. For food, he would have preferred bread and water to the fibrous turnips and concentrated soups that made him feel nauseous.

As Arrupe bid farewell to them, the soldiers who had been with him and had heard so many teachings from his lips had a hard time hiding their emotion. Even apart from his friendly attitude, they found something impressive in this foreigner. Arrupe later explained it this way: "They felt an undefined, vague yearning for something they couldn't pin down. They thought they were sad because I was leaving, but such was not the case. It was Christ that was leaving them. Can there be any other explanation for their sadness?"[11]

Returning to the Parish

Besides that profound spiritual experience of "mystical emptiness" he had had, Arrupe took away from the prison other fond memories. For example, one day the officer in charge had reminded him that at six o'clock he had to bow down to render homage to the emperor. Later on, the guard on duty approached Arrupe

---

11 *Memorias*, 156.

and whispered to him: "Don't worry. Just bow as does everybody else at six o'clock, but do it in the direction of your chapel and adore your own God."[12] Arrupe never forgot that shrewd thoughtfulness.

Another time, the soldiers were celebrating with a tasty treat of rice cakes on New Year's Day. Arrupe was in his cell, studying with his dictionary. The soldiers asked Pedro whether anyone would be sending him some food, and when he said no, one of them tossed a rice cake into his cell. As he did so, the soldier uttered a vulgar expression, one used when feeding animals, but Arrupe saw that the man did not intend his words to be mean, and he was grateful for the favor.

Returning to the parish, Arrupe wondered what had happened while he was away. He discovered that the Jesuits had not been standing idly by. Lassalle had contacted Shibata, a chemistry professor in Hiroshima, who was also a ranking graduate of a military academy. The professor traveled to Yamaguchi and spoke with the officers who had detained Arrupe. They did not allow him to speak to Arrupe, but his arguments certainly helped to clear up the case, as did other interventions of friends of the Jesuits in Tokyo. All the same, as Lassalle stated later, "The days that Father Arrupe spent in prison were extremely hard."[13]

For his part, Pedro was fearful about how his conduct and the accusations against him might have affected his Christian faithful and other Jesuits in Japan. In fact, several Christians in Yamaguchi had been visited and interrogated by the police. Among them were Teresa Moriwaki, Arrupe's cook and collaborator and the mother of a man who later became a Jesuit; and Murata-san, a young man of twenty-two who was still a catechumen. They had responded to their interrogators with the decisiveness and integrity that characterizes the Japanese when they are convinced of something. For example, the young man told the police that he would continue to talk with his foreign teacher even if they prohibited it and even if it were to cost him his life.

Pedro felt great relief on leaving the prison. He enjoyed walking again amid the small houses of Yamaguchi with their undulating roofs, and he mixed in freely with the people strolling through the streets. But he hurried his pace, anxious to return to his chapel.

Teresa gave a shout of joy as soon as she saw him approaching. The typical Japanese moderation was nowhere in evidence. Arrupe was back. It was like a vision, an apparition.

On hearing Teresa's shouts, Father Arnold Lademann came out and gave Arrupe a strong embrace. He had been passing through Yamaguchi by chance, but he found himself obliged to stay there in order not to leave that small group of faithful without a pastor.

---

12   *Memorias*, 159.

13   Statements and information provided to the author by Enomiya-Lassalle, S.J. and Klaus Luhmer, S.J.

Years later, when general of the Society, Arrupe greeted German Jesuit Hugo Enomiya-Lassalle, who had been Arrupe's provincial superior in Japan; Enomiya-Lassalle was later recognized as a "Zen master" by the Japanese themselves.

Yoshizama, a Christian from those days who is still alive today, recalls that Arrupe celebrated a Mass of thanksgiving right after his release. In those times of scarcity, the church collections did not reach even two yen, which would be equivalent to two hundred yen today. Teresa confessed that, even before they had arrested Arrupe, the police had tried to persuade her to treat him and feed him badly since he was spying for a foreign power.[14]

Gradually, life returned to the ordinary routines, but Arrupe found that after his incarceration the people's support was even stronger than before. Many military police—he had gotten to know more than twenty of them in prison—used to greet him in the street with a friendly "Arrupe-san, Arrupe-san."[15]

Around that time, Arrupe got to know a young university student named Shogo Hayashi, who was studying Spanish under his guidance. Eventually, the young man wanted to talk about religious topics. He later recounted his meetings with Arrupe:

I didn't know what to talk about with him [Arrupe]. I talked around the problems, but he kept insisting: "You are basically a believer."

"No, I don't think life has any meaning."

"Yes, there is an answer: 'Through him, with him, and in him': God."

14   Testimony of Mister Yoshizama.
15   *Memorias*, 163.

"I don't believe God exists."

Father Arrupe would then review all the arguments for the existence of God. We would spend three hours together that way, and I would end up with a headache.

"I'll come back in March," I told him.

"Keep your promise."

Then he did something that amazed me. He took me to the chapel and said to me: "Pray before God."

"No," I responded.

And he told me, "You do not know God, but neither can you deny him. Pray before God or before something."

That impressed me greatly. In April, I went back to see him. Sometimes, when I went to study with him, he would be asleep, because he went to bed at twelve midnight and got up at four in the morning. He would get up and wash his face in order to perk himself up. When he left the prison, he sent me a telegram telling me to come and be baptized by him. That is when I saw things clearly and got baptized.[16]

In his *Memorias*, Arrupe recognizes that he made a mistake with that young man at first, loading him down with Scholastic arguments:

I managed to forget all the theological arguments, except one. After my earlier failure with him, I was afraid of confusing his understanding further if I kept multiplying the proofs. I insisted only on the miracle of the resurrection, following the logic of Saint Paul. It was a clear line of argument, without buttresses or other props to reinforce it: like the smooth curve of an arch, it allowed the light of truth to pass through its stone arms.

Although I had my doubts, I told him to repeat the prayer of the famous German convert M. K. Kolb. Even when still in doubt as to whether she was Protestant or atheist, she used to repeat this prayer when walking in front of a church: "If you are there, why don't you let me believe? If you are there, let me believe."[17]

Hayashi was baptized by Arrupe on January 18, 1942, along with a fellow student, Takao, the son of Teresa Moriwaki, and four others.[18]

Even as Arrupe's stay in Yamaguchi was coming to an end, life kept on normally. One of the more curious notes of those days was the boisterous presence of the military police, who frequently passed by the parish to "pay a return visit" to their former prisoner and to play ping-pong in the parish halls.

---

16   Statements to the author. Shogo Hayashi became a Jesuit and has held important positions in the Society of Jesus in Japan.

17   *Memorias*, 167.

18   Information supplied to the author by Takao Moriwaki, S.J.

"When the Americans reached Yamaguchi," recounts Arrupe,

and learned that I had been in prison, they wanted to know who had ordered my arrest and why, in order to hold them accountable. But I recalled that handshake with the chief of the military police, when he told me, "Keep preaching that religion!" and I remembered those young soldiers, tough but basically good. So I preferred to keep quiet rather than reveal who they were. That was all in the past, while my being a missionary, an envoy of peace, was something in the present and was completely opposed to any desire for vengeance or excessive justice. I thought it better to pardon, and I am happy that none of those soldiers went to jail because of me.[19]

Lassalle, who at that time was Arrupe's superior, paid a visit to Yamaguchi on March 9, 1942. As the two men were talking, he casually proposed to Arrupe: "How would you like to go to Nagatsuka to be the master of novices?"

"Dear God, Father," replied Arrupe, "I can hardly speak the language and I know little of the psychology of the Japanese."

"Don't worry. Things will work out. The present master needs to be replaced urgently, since he is sick and cannot continue there."

"Well, I will think it over and get back to you soon."

"Yes, it's the best thing. I have already thought it over," he said with a mischievous smile.

Two days later, Arrupe received a telegram instructing him to pack the essentials and travel immediately to Hiroshima. The parish faithful rushed to organize a farewell party, which included songs, speeches, folk dances, and the endless cups of bitter yellow tea that are unavoidable at a Japanese celebration. Arrupe recounts the experience: "When the moment came for me to speak, I got all choked up as I thought of all their kindnesses. At that moment, I became aware of how united we all were, faithful Christians and missionary, and I knew how close were the ties that bound us."[20]

Without delaying, Pedro grabbed his suitcase and was on his way. As he left, he gazed with nostalgia on that green valley where Xavier had started everything centuries before. Arrupe too had had the privilege of preaching the Gospel among these beloved people. He looked back a moment and then hurried his pace. A piece of his heart remained there in Yamaguchi.

---

19 *Memorias*, 168.
20 *Memorias*, 169.

10. The Novice Master

With the humid cold penetrating into his bones, Arrupe put up his coat collar and pedaled hard up the hill as he left behind the rolling green hills of Nagatsuka, his new home on the outskirts of Hiroshima.

Hiroshima was 873 kilometers from Tokyo and 141 kilometers from Yamaguchi. At this time, its four hundred thousand inhabitants would never have dreamed that one day their city would be compared to the phoenix, the fabled bird that emerged from its own ashes, or that its population would exceed a million. Founded centuries before on Hiro Shima (Great island) by Terumoto Mori, who built a castle there, the city in 1942 still preserved its typically Japanese character.[1] Aside from a few cement buildings in its center, Hiroshima, like many others cities in Japan, consisted mostly of small houses built of wood, reeds, mud, and paper. The floors were usually covered with a thin mat of rice straw, famous for its combustible qualities.

Arrupe had just moved into Nagatsuka a few days before. Besides being novice master, he was also appointed as rector of some other small communities made up of young Jesuits studying philosophy and theology. Today, he was bicycling to one of his twice-weekly meetings with Kato-san, his instructor in the tea ceremony, one of the essential "ways" of initiation into Zen. Arrupe's intuition made him eager to learn ever more about Japan and its cultural secrets. His attempts to delve deeper into Japanese culture was marked in those days by minor humiliations. Having already spent two years dedicating an hour a day to the art of drawing Japanese characters, he had learned at least one thing clearly: what was important was not the writing itself but becoming *one* with those forms; it was not so much a matter of doing something useful, but of experiencing vividly the "deeper self."

Arrupe also continued studying the Japanese language, as he wrote to his friend Iturrioz:

> The idea is to have thousands of these characters enter into a brain that is a bit hardened by the years. [...] From morning to night, Japanese and more Japanese. But don't think that it's boring; personally, I have had some very delightful times. The study is really very interesting since the structure of the language and the thought are so different from our own. The only problem is that we have to sit here muzzled because of this difficulty, while we are surrounded by so many millions of people who have never heard of our Jesus Christ. Here you can understand well the ardor and the tears of Xavier.

---

1   See "Breve historia de Hiroshima," in *Japón* (Paris: Hachette Guides Bleus, 1984), 220.

[…] This is a great mystery, but also reality: that our Lord has chosen us to save these souls, us who do not even know how to speak […]; indeed, if ever God *infirma mundi elegit* [chose the weak things of the world] […], it is stupendously true in this case: we are so *infirma* that we cannot even speak.[2]

The Infinite in a Cup of Tea

Kato-san, a Catholic and a professor with a doctorate in the tea ceremony, had agreed to give private classes to Pedro, who kept a folder full of the notes given to him by his teacher. On the first page was written *Wa-Kei-Sei-Jaku*, four terms represented by as many characters, with the meaning of "peace, respect, purity, solitude." These words evoked the ambience and profound meaning of the tea ceremony.

Kato-san received Pedro with a bow and his proverbial smile and then had him sit in the lotus position in a corner of the room. With a slowness that was excruciating for a Westerner, the teacher began the ceremony. The first part consisted in the presentation of the objects of that mysterious rite: the tea pot, the box with its powder, the cups—all kept within a kind of shroud folded in four parts.[3]

The teacher brought in a large pitcher full of cool water and then went to get the box of tea, which he brought in his left hand, while in his right hand he held a cup. The cup contained a small napkin and a bamboo stick to stir the tea in the water. To the right of the pot, he placed the pitcher, behind it the cup with its accessories, and to the right the box of tea.

All those gesture were only the beginning of an endless series of perfectly modulated bows and gestures made with incredible interior discipline. Even the simple act of taking hold of the handleless cup involved a complicated ritual, for one had to hold the cup with the thumb inside and then place the cup with both hands a certain distance in front of one's knees. Just the description of this extraordinary liturgy would fill several pages.

After all those reverences and perfectly measured hand movements and postures, the teacher turned toward Arrupe and with a disconcerting casualness told him: "Now you do what I have done."

"But I don't remember any of it," objected the Jesuit.

"It doesn't matter. Try and see how it turns out."

Pedro made the attempt but accomplished nothing. He could not reproduce that endless series of small gestures and movements. After several frustrating sessions, he told the teacher: "This can't be explained with words. You have to capture it by intuition."

---

2   Letter to Jesús Iturrioz, February 12, 1939, in *Documentos dejados por el P. Iturrioz*, cited by Iglesias, "Aportaciones a su biografía interior," 996.

3   Arnold, *El zen en la tradición japonesa*, 213ff.

Arrupe had the teacher explain to him the movements he was making, and he took careful notes at the same time. In that way, he made notable progress.

Feeling somewhat encouraged, Arrupe asked, "Do you think I will be able to master the ceremony sufficiently in a couple of weeks?"

Kato-san smiled and replied, "If you are constant and make the effort, maybe in three years you will know the essentials."

"Later on," Arrupe wrote,

> I realized he was right. In the tea ceremony, as in any other of the Zen ways, there is a much deeper dimension that gives it its essential meaning. This is hard for a Westerner to understand at first, but it becomes a bit clearer if we compare it, for example, with music: we speak much about performing music and about giving music soul. With a piano, to name a specific instrument, the performance consists in touching the keys, but the soul consists in the spirit or the life that one gives to the piece one is playing.[4]

About the tea ceremony, Arnold has written:

> The *Cha-no-yu* creates harmony by appealing to the five senses: harmony of touch (the cup), harmony of smell (the tea), harmony of sight (the translucent screens), harmony of hearing (the water boiling in the pot). These new harmonies are deliberately roused to the subtlety of an awakened sensibility, and they completely invade one's being, calming the shocks, the struggles, and the worries that normally vex our spirit. At once we recover calmness and refinement, and we are surrounded by perfect accord between our five senses and the world. That is the meaning of the words of Tekuan: The tea ceremony is the feeling of harmony between Heaven and Earth; it is the norm of a world "at peace."[5]

The purity, the harmony, the serenity, and the stimulation of everything and everyone flow together to yield the objective of Zen: "original" human nature, "our true nature," which is beyond all the artifacts of existence.

Arrupe could sense the degree to which this ceremony formed an important part of Japanese culture, even when it was not practiced faithfully. (The same is true of Christian ideals: they are part of the Western cultural heritage, even for those who do not believe.) He also understood that he had to enter deeply into that world if he wanted to transmit a solid spirituality to Japanese youth in his new post as master of novices. Referring to the "ways" of Zen, Arrupe stated years later:

> I was attempting to learn all these things, insofar as a European is capable of doing so. It was a matter of discovering a way of thinking, and nothing is achieved unless one has penetrated into the larger cultural dimension.

---

4   *Memorias*, 172ff.
5   Arnold, *El zen en la tradición japonesa*, 226.

156   PEDRO ARRUPE

My initiation into archery helped me acquire some degree of inculturation by means of Zen. During a time of intense concentration, the archer must identify with the target, so that the target actually *attracts* the arrow and the arrow has no reason for *not* hitting the bull's-eye. Needless to say, my first arrows landed far from the target. Since then, I have always asked myself what is really the benefit of Zen sessions in Western countries, if they last only three days![6]

Arrupe gave himself heart and soul to the practice of the tea ceremony with Kato-san. Later on, in the middle of the cold night, he would return home on his bicycle.

A Novitiate in Times of War

Soon, the people of Nagatsuka grew accustomed to seeing the broad smile of that strange Westerner with his high collar and aquiline nose. He often rode his bicycle through the rice fields that then lay between the city of Hiroshima and the Jesuit novitiate. The novitiate was housed in a single wooden building, built in the Japanese style, with a tower attached. About ten meters from the chapel, there was a small two-story house, also of wood, that was called *dendoba*, that is, "place for teaching doctrine." The novitiate was couched in a fold of a small mountain, at the summit of which was the community cemetery.

The year was 1942, a time when the Germans and the Japanese were expanding their territory through forceful invasion of foreign countries. The Pacific Ocean had become the staging ground for a fierce confrontation between Japan and the United States. Japanese expansion had achieved complete control over more than four hundred million persons and had gained access to a large portion of the world's raw materials. A turning point came, however, with the US triumph in the Coral Sea battle in May 1942—it was the beginning of the end of Japanese hegemony. From that point on, the US armed forces launched major operations against all the Japanese strongholds.

The successive American victories in the archipelagos that had been controlled until then by Japan—Midway, Guadalcanal, New Guinea, to name only the most important—forced the Japanese into a defense posture, very different from the one they had hitherto been maintaining. By the beginning of 1943, the tendency of the war in Asia was similar to what was taking place at the same time in Europe: the Axis forces were in evident and irreversible retreat from the territories they had so swiftly occupied.

The conflict also reached the small property of Nagatsuka, where Arrupe was engaged in a daily struggle to make sure his young brothers had food to eat. The only rations to which there was assured access was rice: 330 grams per

---

person per day. There was no provision for meat, eggs, fish, sugar, or milk—it was a diet of extreme austerity.

One day, as the theology professor was explaining to his young students the treatise *De Trinitate* (On the Trinity), the house administrator (Father Minister) appeared excitedly in the door of the classroom, inviting the students to help unload a truckload of potatoes. Knowing what that meant, they quickly rushed to the task.

Since the few farmers who had been cultivating the novitiate garden were disappearing into the war effort, Arrupe decided to work the land himself, with the help of the students, even though he knew that their spiritual formation and studies would suffer as a result.

Considering the gravity of the situation, the Jesuit superiors decided to transfer the philosophy and theology students to Tokyo, while Arrupe remained in Nagatsuka with the novices. Even then, the struggle to put food on the table was constant.

Without any means of transport or any money to purchase a vehicle, Pedro spent hours on his bicycle, making endless journeys around town in search of food for the novitiate. He also used his bicycle to go to his classes on Japanese literature and to attend the Zen spiritual exercises of *chado* and *shodo*.

The condition of Arrupe's bicycle deteriorated so much that one day he had three flat tires just traveling the six kilometers between the novitiate and Hiroshima, and finding new tires and tubes in those days was an impossible dream. Finally, one day, as he was walking through the garden, he thought of a solution. He saw a long hose that was just the right size. He cut the hose to the size of the bicycle wheel and then filled it with a mixture of earth and straw. That improvised tire was both durable and flexible; it made the bicycle heavier, but also more dependable.

That invention of Arrupe lasted for many kilometers, until the straw gave way and the hose lost its cylindrical form. The tire gradually flattened against the rim, but it lasted a while longer before bursting wide open and spilling out its strange innards.[7]

The effects of the war were felt in other ways. One day, a young fellow, at the recommendation of Father Tanaka, came asking to be baptized. Arrupe considered him well intentioned and gave him some work to do in the garden, but then another Jesuit warned him that the young man might well be a member of the military police. Despite the experience he had had in Yamaguchi, Arrupe did not believe it was so. Moreover, after the fellow had been with Arrupe for six months as a catechumen, everybody was convinced that he was not a spy and in time could well become an excellent Jesuit.

---

7   This recollection made Arrupe laugh heartily many years later, when he was quite sick in Rome in the summer of 1983. This confirms how revelatory the anecdotes are of his personality.

Novice master Arrupe directing a novice in Nagatsuka, on the outskirts of Hiroshima.

Finally, though, the man was recognized for who he was by a Korean postulant who had known him while working in an arms factory, where the Korean had been accused of being a spy. The young fellow was indeed from the military police. Arrupe reacted immediately, calling him to his office and telling him bluntly: "We have discovered that you are not a catechumen, but a member of the military police. You should put an end to this farce immediately."

Arrupe demanded of him documentation giving evidence of his background. Since the young man did not have the documentation, Arrupe with the help of the novices organized a counter-espionage effort that turned out to be rather comical. Taking turns, the novices kept a constant covert watch on the spy and gave Arrupe an account of all his movements. Meanwhile, the fellow wrote up a series of reports, making Arrupe fear that they would be a bundle of falsehoods and that the sad experience of Yamaguchi would be repeated. Fortunately, such was not the case. The spy issued a favorable verdict, and Arrupe avoided the distress of having to tell his superiors that he had again been deceived by the secret police.

Law enforcement officers came to the novitiate on other occasions in order to carry out a series of investigations. They were especially intrigued by the pagoda-styled tower with its three stories, right beside the residence.

"Why have you built the tower?" they asked.

"All Catholic churches have towers. Since we are in Japan, we built it in an oriental style. In other places we would adapt it to the customs of the country."

"Fine, but since you have made it with three stories, it must be for spying on Hiroshima. Or maybe you have a radio transmitter set up there or some other apparatus for sending signals."

"Come with me," said Arrupe, inviting them to follow him. He led them up to a little bluff with an excellent view of the city. (Years later, an image of the Sacred Heart would be set up there.)

"Doesn't it seem absurd to you that, having this marvelous natural lookout, we would build our little tower twenty-five meters lower down in order to spy on people?"

Despite everything, they insisted on searching the tower, where they found only dust and grime.[8]

Profile of a Novice Master

Meanwhile, life in the novitiate proceeded apace. What was Arrupe like at the time? His forehead had grown higher due to baldness, so that he had a greater resemblance to Saint Ignatius of Loyola. He never lost his sense of humor or his amiability, but the responsibility inherent in his new job—forming future Jesuits—made him more radical and demanding with himself.

There are many testimonies about Arrupe in these years:

> I often saw him cleaning the novices' shoes in the entryway during the time of siesta. Quite noteworthy was his poverty and great detachment regarding clothing and personal possessions. He never used to sleep more than five hours, and often only four. Every day without exception I would see him begin the so-called "holy hour" in the novitiate chapel, near the tabernacle. Every morning, he made more than an hour of meditation. I think he had made a promise to visit Jesus in the chapel frequently during the day, for I used to see him go in there more or less every two hours. While praying, which he did while sitting in the Japanese style, he stayed perfectly motionless, with an impressive power of concentration and recollection. His love for Japan was so profound that he would not tolerate in his presence any murmurings or negative comments about the Japanese.

Such are the memories of Alberto Álvarez Lomas, who as a young Jesuit was assigned for his regency to Hiroshima to teach the students Latin.[9]

Álvarez describes other traits of Arrupe's life at the time: "Those of us who worked with him could not keep up with his pace. He never took a siesta, in order to work more. He was very considerate of the guests who came to the house. He especially enjoyed spending time with the Jesuit brothers." Manuel Díez, another Jesuit who taught Latin while Arrupe was master of novices, recalls a special detail: "On the cold days of winter, he used to prepare a little fire so the novices could warm themselves when they came back from their walks."[10]

---

8   *Memorias*, 182ff.

9   Letter written by Alberto Álvarez Lomas, S.J. to the author (from Iwakuni on September 11, 1966).

10   Statements made by Manuel Díez, S.J. to the author (in Tokyo, July 1986).

There is some debate about how demanding Arrupe was with the novices. Díez recalls that he was indeed demanding, but also that the young Japanese in his charge were difficult fellows. The times themselves were difficult because of the war, but the situation was complicated because many of the candidates were returning from the fields of battle, where they had had all kinds of experiences.

"He was severe and rigorous, but at the same time very human," states Katsusuke Seto, a former novice of Arrupe:

> He was known for his creativity. He was very original, always full of ideas. When food was scarce due to the war, he himself would get busy in the kitchen and put together a cake using flour and saccharine. We followed Japanese customs, bathing in the typical way and praying in the Japanese sitting position. He knew his novices well, and sometimes he even asked them to pardon him.[11]

Applying the norms of Ignatius to the Japanese situation, Arrupe devised humble occupations for the novices. One task, for example, was shoveling into a basket the animal excrement left in the streets:

> Wearing Roman collars, we used to follow after the mules. To understand how difficult this was, you have to be aware how much importance the Japanese place on pride and a sense of honor. But we always knew why we were doing such things, and he always used humor to assuage our feelings. Besides, he knew the novices well, and each one in particular. He was a sincere man, not two-faced. For that reason, he was able to deal handily with those who came to him looking for spies in the house.

Teruo Awamoto has memories of Arrupe from when he was a youth:

> I studied catechism with Father Arrupe. I'll never forget him riding his bicycle with his white collar. I knew nothing about Christianity. In fact, when I first saw him on the bicycle, I experienced a very strong sentiment of rejection and hatred. What was that foreigner doing? Since those were times of war, I was thinking, "This fellow is not earning a living, he doesn't seem to have anything to do." One day, though, a friend spoke to me about the Bible. I became interested and went with him to a place where there was to be instruction. What a surprise it was when I met up there with the "guy on the bicycle." From then on, I attended his talks regularly, and I experienced great changes as I listened to him. That year around Christmastime I received baptism, and a little afterward I entered the novitiate.[12]

---

11   Statements made by Katsusuke Seto, S.J. to the author (in Hiroshima, July 1986).
12   Statements made by Teruo Awamoto, S.J. to the author (in Kobe, July 1986). Father Awamoto was the Jesuit provincial of Japan.

Another former novice of Arrupe was Shogo Hayashi, whom we already know from Yamaguchi. He also recalls how strict Arrupe was with himself:

He didn't have a mosquito net and used to sleep on a hard bed. It was difficult to deal with people at that time. Father Arrupe knew it and suffered as a result. His main concern was understanding how best to deal with people. In fact, he tried to treat people individually, as persons, adapting himself to their mentality. One day, he told us novices to clean the cistern, which was a filthy sewer, full of excrement. We took a good bath afterward. Another day, he had the idea of making us follow the horses. I learned of it and was the first to question him: "Isn't that going to be useless?"

He didn't answer me. The sewer work was awful, but he knew quite well whom he was asking to do it. He gave the month-long Exercises extremely well, and for that reason he was also very strict in selecting people. When someone came to see him, we used to pray that the person would enter, but Arrupe would exclaim: "No, pray that he doesn't enter!" But the novices who lasted—and some of them left in tears—were good men. Don Pedro was very kind in his treatment of the Japanese. He knew how far he could go. When people came from outside, we used to tell him: "You stay here. We know how to deal with them." And he had complete trust in us. It was a good novitiate, not run too rigidly. Since he was so creative, he used to make unexpected changes. He would tell us that there was no need to do something that had already been decided beforehand. We used to think: "Tomorrow is a holiday, the feast of the Sacred Heart. We'll be able to take it off." No way! He would send us to fetch water, and precisely on that day the pump would break down. Or he would have us clean the windows of the police station, which had been painted during the war. He was demanding, but on the day we took our vows, his style changed. He would say to us: "You're no longer a novice. From this moment on, you will go elsewhere and you will see other Jesuits, but what you have seen here is the true Society." I will never forget that.[13]

---

13   Statements made by Shogo Hayashi, S.J. to the author (in Kobe, July 1986). About the "Ignatian trials," in Arrupe's novitiate there exists a curious document from that time. In *El siglo de las misiones* 418 (October 1960), Ramón Gaviña, S.J. tells of some of the trials Arrupe thought up:

Two new trials have been implemented: one is collecting rubbish from the streets of the city. They [the novices] leave from the novitiate at ten in the morning with a small cart, brooms, and shovels, and they move around the streets of Hiroshima, cleaning them of all the garbage left by the animals, etc., etc. At twelve o'clock, they have a meal of rice in a park and then return at four in the afternoon, after having carried out a good series of acts of humility.

The other trial is doing manual labor for ten days in some factory. They go to a factory in a neighboring town, where one of those in charge is a Catholic. He is well

Another of the young men that passed through Arrupe's hands was called Joji Yamamoto. His testimony coincides with that of his companions:

> He was very strict and mortified, but he was a good master of novices for those times. He did what needed to be done. At the same time, he showed himself to be incredibly open, as was seen also in the freedom with which he acted when he was general. He was a "Jesuit" in the literal sense of the term, adapting it to the time. And he knew the Japanese character very well.[14]

Another who received his first formation in the Society of Jesus from the firm, kind hand of Arrupe was Makoto Nakai. With a smile, he recalls:

> He was tall and bright, like Mount Fuji. He was in a difficult situation, since Europeans at the time were under suspicion in Japan. The church, Japanese society, the Japanese Society of Jesus were all closely related. Theories are of no use to the Japanese temperament—we need the experience of a living example. Father Arrupe influenced us by his personality. We saw him get up at four-thirty in the morning, and we knew that he was a man of prayer. He studied our customs in depth. We never heard him utter a word against Buddhism.[15]

Yoshimasa Tsuchiya met Arrupe for the first time in the college of Kobe, when he was fifteen years old and about to be baptized. Much affected by Pearl Harbor and the war, he made the Exercises with Arrupe in Nagatsuka in 1942. Arrupe's eyes shone brightly during those five days that he spoke with the young man. He told him of his own vocation, of his adventures in the slums of Madrid, of his moving experience at Lourdes. Tsuchiya for the first time felt a call, and he was so impressed by the experience that he returned to Nagatsuka with some friends in order to spend more time with Arrupe.

Akijiro Oki was a close friend of Tsuchiya who voluntarily joined the navy in March and was assigned to a base near Hiroshima; he later became a Jesuit. Even though he had been exempted from military service while studying at the Jesuits' Sophia University, Tsuchiya had difficulty following his vocation since his father would not give his permission for him to become a Jesuit; he also had problems in extending his exemption from serving in the war. Finally, on March 31, 1942, he entered the novitiate, having had the satisfaction of baptizing his grandmother *in articulo mortis* (at the point of death). There were only three other novices in the novitiate with him, all of whom were drafted to do military

---

instructed about what is to be done and carries out his task well. For example, he told one of them to clean a chimney.

"And how is that done?" asked the novice.

"By getting inside it!" he answered, and one can imagine how he came out!

14   Statements made by Joji Yamamoto, S.J. to the author (in Tokyo, July 1986).

15   Statements made by Makoto Nakai, S.J. to the author (in Tokyo, July 1986).

Jesuit novices meditating in the time of Arrupe; they sat on tatami mats in the chapel of the novitiate of Nagatsuka (1943).

service. One died defending his bishop in Iawa, and another died in Karaff, executed by the Russians. They died as Jesuit novices, so their tombs are at the novitiate, but not their bodies. Tsuchiya recalls:

> On July 5, I received an order to report for military service. I cannot forget the image I have of Arrupe at that time. Even though he was the rector and master, he personally used to go in search of food for us. At times, he walked great distances just to find a little bread. There were other Jesuit students there studying philosophy, three Japanese and three Koreans, but I was the only novice. Despite that, he gave me a talk every day, and each night he gave me points for the next day's meditation. Even though my novitiate was quite strict, I had very close relations with Father Arrupe.
>
> On July 5, when I was going to serve the Mass he celebrated for the community, Arrupe told me: "They are calling you to the army. Take part in this Mass with great fervor." I did that, and at midday I left for Tokyo, with the intention of saying goodbye to my family. I was unable to do so because there were two bombardments that forced me to remain in the university. There they gave me a certificate to show that I had sufficient preparation to be an officer, but my main job was digging ditches to protect us in case the Americans came. It was only after the war that I could return to the novitiate. One of the things that most impressed me about Father Arrupe was that I knew that he trusted me at every moment. Even though he was the master,

he always would ask me: "And is this how they do it in Japan?" He was an extraordinary educator who knew how to make people's self-confidence grow step by step. He formed us carefully and had a great practical sense. He was not authoritarian, but rather always wanted to know what we were feeling, so that at the proper moment he would give clear instructions about what needed to be done.[16]

Years later, Arrupe recalled that difficult stage:

My novices went through a lot, but at the same time they were hard to penetrate. It was necessary to change their concept of God and show them an even greater God. We must remember that before the war in Japan the emperor was god. When they discovered a supreme God, they experienced great amazement. I used to speak individually with each novice for two or three hours at a time just to answer one question, and then two or three hours more for the next question, and so for each one. However, when a young Japanese finally becomes a Jesuit, he is a true Jesuit.[17]

Transmitting a Way of Life

Arrupe put much emphasis on the month-long Exercises and the interior life. For that reason, he maintained fruitful contacts with Buddhist monks, who came to visit the novitiate. He also paid a return visit to a Zen novitiate. He was quite impressed with the temple of Tsuwano and admired the beauty of its monastery, high in the cold reaches of the mountains. He later described his visit:

We entered the hall where the novices were doing their meditation. Seated on the ground, erect as plaster statues, they were facing the wall and had their backs to the passageway. Passing through the midst of them and sternly inspecting them was a monk with a thick cane about seventy centimeters long. The young monks' immobility was impressive.[18]

Arrupe took an interest in every detail: their posture, the way they held their hands, one over the other in their lap, the use of the cane to wake up anyone who became sleepy. When he asked about the spirit of their meditation, the Zen master answered:

The spirit is that of being in a complete void, without thinking of anything. All thought is an obstacle to reaching "illumination" [satori]. Thus the imagination and the intelligence should be in absolute repose. The effort, then, is not to think. Or rather, neither to think nor to make any effort. It is a

---

16   Statements made by Yoshimasa Tsuchiya, S.J. to the author (in Tokyo, July 1986).
17   Statements made by Arrupe to the author (in Rome, July 1983).
18   *Memorias*, 258ff.

Arrupe with a group of novices, several years later.

question of just being without struggle, without violence, without exertion. And for hours on end.

The two masters then spoke about "illumination," a unique and non-transferable experience by which one knows the essence of all things. Arrupe recalled the vision or illumination that Saint Ignatius had at Manresa, near the Cardoner River, when everything appeared new to him.

The monk emphasized:

It really is something magnificent. By means of "illumination," a person attains freedom of soul and complete control over himself and over all the conditions of his life. He ceases to be a slave of situations and interior passions and surmounts all that can cause problems to a person in the course of this life.

The monk also made clear that "illumination" was attained over the course of years, and that not everybody attained it. He spoke to Arrupe about the uselessness of words and ideas: "Zen seeks the experience of the great reality. It aspires to penetrate into life not by way of explanations or concepts acquired by reading or listening, but by way of direct experience."

Arrupe spent several hours at the monastery, which greatly impressed him. In his work as master of novices, he showed his appreciation of Zen spirituality and applied it in his own way. He eagerly studied the Japanese soul in order to learn its ways. What he did not understand at the time was that his own profound experience, more than any concepts he expressed, was the secret of his effectiveness among the Japanese.

Francis A. Jo Hayazoe is a diocesan priest of Hiroshima and pastor of the Peace Cathedral, which was built by the Jesuits after the atomic explosion. He recalls that when he attended catechism classes with Arrupe, there was always present an elderly man who simply watched Arrupe intently for half a year. One day, Arrupe asked the man if he understood well his explanations. The old man did not answer, for he was deaf.

When Arrupe finally managed to communicate with the deaf man, he obtained just one response: "This whole time I have just been looking at your eyes. You do not lie. What you believe is what I believe."

One day, when still young, Hayazoe felt the call of vocation and went to see Arrupe. "I have a problem," he told him.

"What is that?"

"I like girls."

"That's very natural in a man," Arrupe responded.

"From that moment on, I had no more problems," states Hayazoe:

> He was someone very special and communicated something special. I never saw Father Arrupe angry. Many people wanted to talk with him and confess to him. I was impressed by his gentleness, which was very different from the harshness of the Germans. He was tender and sweet. You must keep in mind that the image of a saint for the Japanese is that of a person who is gentle, non-violent.[19]

Manuel García Casado, who was Arrupe's assistant in the Nagatsuka novitiate and also did his tertianship there, recounts the following:

> On November 12, 1951, I left for Hiroshima, and the next day, the feast of Saint Stanislaus Kostka, I officially began my tertianship in the novitiate, starting with a long talk with Father Arrupe. Since the month of Exercises was to begin that same night, Father told me that to receive the points for my meditations I should go to his room fifteen minutes before the time indicated for the novices. I immediately realized that, according to this plan, Father Arrupe would have to give ten talks each day, five for the novices and five for me. Out of consideration for him, I proposed that I attend the talks for the novices, since ten talks a day for a month was going to be an extremely difficult workout for him.
>
> The father agreed to my proposal, and I began attending punctually the meditation points that he was giving to the novices four times a day, plus the talk that was then customary. He used to speak for thirty or forty

---

19   Statements made by Francis A. Jo Hayazoe to the author (in Hiroshima, July 1986).

minutes each time, and he did so seated Japanese-style on a tatami. All of us also remained for that whole time seated on our legs since the Japanese never use chairs.

After ten or fifteen minutes, my legs would begin to hurt because of the forced posture. I felt sharp pins and needles that made me move to a half-squat, shifting from leg to leg, constantly twisting my body until the end of the session. But then, when I tried to get up, that was too much. My legs had gone to sleep, and my pain was such that I could not stand straight for a good while.

Father Arrupe took notice of this, and he called me to his room on the pretext that the material for the novices was not the same as that which was proper for a tertian. Then he made me follow the plan he first proposed, obliging himself to give ten talks each day during the whole month of the Exercises.

As a curious anecdote, I would add that, since he was continually switching from Spanish to Japanese and from Japanese to Spanish, he one day began addressing the novices in Spanish, and he continued speaking thus for a few minutes. It was only the nervous laughter of the novices, who understood not a word of what he was saying, that made him realize his mistake. After humbly begging their pardon, he continued in Japanese as if nothing had happened.[20]

García Casado points out that, besides giving the talks, Arrupe dedicated time to directing each novice personally. If this feat were made known to the English, who place such importance on extraordinary achievements, they certainly would have included him in the *Guinness Book of Records*! "During the month of Exercises and throughout the whole of tertianship," García Casado continues,

I came to understand that Father Arrupe, no matter what topic he began his talks with, often came down to stressing a single point: blind faith and absolute trust in the goodness of God. The expression on his face changed when he spoke of "the incredible faith of Abraham, *in spe contra spem* [hoping against hope]," or when he cited the Pauline text: *In fide vivo Filii Dei, qui dilexit me* [I live by faith in the Son of God, who loved me].

According to García Casado, the secret of Arrupe's strength was his love for the person of Christ, focused especially on his heart. For Arrupe, believing in the love of God gave a focus to one's life and endowed it with ultimate meaning.[21] His interior attitude during those years is reflected in a letter he wrote to his friend Iturrioz:

---

20   Letter from Manuel García Casado to the author.
21   Letter from Manuel García Casado to the author.

Here I find myself completely centered. You will perhaps recall how, when in Valkenburg and Marneffe, we used to dream about [...] those plans of studying morality, medicine, psychiatry, and I don't know what else, and I always introduced a *but*. The fact is that I was interiorly persuaded that such pursuits were not what God wanted of me. Now it is quite the opposite: I do not plan, but I am convinced that I am in the place for which God has destined me. I told you I *don't* plan; and that is not the truth. I plan, but my plans are in another direction; I plan only my trust in Jesus Christ; that is, I plan only one project: throwing myself into the hands of Christ, so that he carries me. I do not see clearly what my way of working here should be, nor will I be able to see it for a while, but I feel interiorly persuaded that the way to convert souls to Christ is through preaching and above all practicing his doctrine and carrying it to its "ultimate consequences." As I understand it, this was the secret of Xavier's success. [...][22]

As we will see later, Arrupe was the spiritual guide not only for the young Jesuits of Nagatsuka, but for many other persons as well. His influence reached far and wide, and after more than forty years many remember him as someone quite exceptional, a man who lived what he preached. It was that simplicity and genuineness that attracted all who knew him during those difficult times of war, when life in Hiroshima was still fairly normal and people were unaware of what was soon to befall them.

It was shortly before the fiery month of August 1945.

---

22   Letter to Jesús Iturrioz, February 12, 1939, in *Documentos dejados por P. Iturrioz*, cited by Iglesias, "Aportaciones a su biografía interior," 996–97.

11. The Bomb

The immobile clock was fixed in his imagination, its hands permanently pointing to the same hour: 8:15. With his head in his hands, he saw his whole life up to that mysterious moment pass before his eyes: from his first recollections of his native Bilbao to this eternal minute that was going to divide his life into two great chapters: before and after the bomb.

In the quiet solitude of the chapel, Arrupe was begging for light: something had to be done! And what first came to his mind was like a movie of the events that had preceded that fateful August 6 of 1945.

Until that moment, the war had been only a vague phantasm. Despite the shortages of food and supplies, the four hundred thousand inhabitants of Hiroshima had been living peacefully in their typical houses of one or two stories, made mostly of wood. The city had only a few large cement edifices rising in its center and dominating the surrounding plain.

Given the military character of the seaport, Arrupe would almost every week see troops arriving or leaving, but for the most part the Americans seemed unconcerned about that particular city. The bombardments were centered on Kure or on the more distant Osaka and Kobe, and Hiroshima heard only the echoes of those continuous barrages.

At first, the inhabitants of Hiroshima had been spending their nights in the caves of the nearby mountains, but after a while they realized that the sirens were only false alarms, and they became convinced that it was not worth their while to leave their houses. The risk of catching a cold in the caves seemed greater than the threats of bombardment.

The Manhattan Project

Far from that tranquil Japanese city, however, men who were still resentful of the Japanese attack on Pearl Harbor were dusting off an old project. They recalled that in 1918 the British physicist Ernest Rutherford had succeeded in splitting the atom and that in 1938 the German chemist Otto Hahn had carried out a decisive experiment: bombarding uranium with neutrons. In the United States, after the outbreak of the war, several scientists had been engaged in pioneering nuclear research, including Leo Szilard, Paul Wigner, and Enrico Fermi, who had been exiled by his country's fascist regime. They received support from professors like James Chadwick and Jacques Allier, who were working in the United Kingdom, Norway, and France. It had been Albert Einstein himself who had warned the US government about the dangers that would ensue if the Germans managed to develop the atomic bomb first.

After the disastrous Japanese attack on Pearl Harbor, the United States decided to undertake the Manhattan Project, whose primary aim was the creation of history's first atomic bomb. The US Army gave top priority to this project and put General Leslie Groves in charge of it. Groves in turn named physicist J. Robert Oppenheimer the project's general coordinator. This brilliant researcher, thirty-eight years of age and possessed of great technical and managerial ability, developed the complex network of efforts that were needed to carry out the project. The raw material was imported from the Belgian Congo: 1,140 tons of uranium-rich mineral sealed in two thousand steel cylinders.

Hundreds of scientists, technicians, and military officers set to work in Los Alamos, New Mexico, most of them having no knowledge of the real goal of the project. With the greatest secrecy and care, they developed the procedures for isolating uranium-235 on an industrial scale. Laboratory tests were carried out at other sites, such as Columbia University, Chicago, and the University of California. At the same time, spies were informing about the advances of the nuclear research in Norway, where the installations were sabotaged by air-transported commandos.

On December 2, 1942, Fermi carried out the decisive experiment that demonstrated the possibility of a chain reaction. It was estimated that within a year it would be possible to have the first atomic bomb ready. By 1944, thanks to the hard work and the considerable funds invested in the project, the process for creating the bomb had been worked out. Still, the bomb was not ready.

The first voice of alarm was sounded at that time by a scientist named Niels Bohr, a Dane who had won the Nobel Prize in physics and had been able to flee from the Nazi occupation of his country and take refuge in the United States. He wrote to President Roosevelt warning him of "the terrible prospect of future competition among nations for such a formidable weapon as the atomic bomb."

Since by that time Germany was retreating from the Russian front and fighting on the Polish borders, there was no justification for using the atomic bomb, but the scientist's cry of alarm did no good. The politicians considered that too much money and energy had been invested in the project not to take advantage of it. By the start of 1945, Germany was clearly defeated and under attack from both east and west. The military operations against Japan were quickly closing in on that country's main islands. Einstein and Szilard, scientists who three years before had helped develop the project, also contacted the American president to try to dissuade him from making use of the bomb. They warned of the possibility of a future arms race that could endanger the whole of humankind.

It was all useless. In July 1945, in the testing grounds of Alamogordo, some 320 kilometers from Los Alamos, a blinding white light illuminated the desert and the surrounding mountains. A refulgent red sphere rose toward the sky, tethered to the ground by a tenuous gray column. The scientists beheld with amazement that first explosion of a bomb that still had the physical appearance of a conventional weapon.

The pace of events quickened. It was suggested to President Harry S. Truman that he first send an ultimatum to Japan. In Potsdam, the Allies agreed to send the Japanese a message that would allow them to maintain the monarchy in exchange for an unconditional surrender. The imperial government, motivated by romantic nationalism, ignored the message, leading the United States to believe that they would not surrender easily.

On July 26, the carcass of the atomic bomb arrived at the island of Tinian aboard the cruiser *Indianapolis*. The same ship was also carrying part of the uranium-235, while the rest that was needed to create a critical mass was traveling on a C-54 aircraft. Commander Carl Spaatz requested an explicit order to launch the bomb, since he rejected the idea of "killing perhaps a hundred thousand people simply on verbal instructions." He wanted an express order from the commander-in-chief, the president himself.

The preferred object was Hiroshima, followed by Kokura and Nagasaki. A B-29 was given the job of flying regularly over the zone to assure the needed visibility. The bomber chosen to launch the atomic bomb was christened with the name *Enola Gay*, the name of the mother of the pilot, Colonel Tibbets. It would be accompanied by two other B-29s. The bomb, some ten feet long and five in diameter, was assembled during the flight by Captain William S. Persons. It was set to explode at six hundred meters above the ground. No one knew what effects an atomic bomb would have at that altitude.[1]

Truman's explicit order finally arrived on August 5.

On August 6, at 1:37 a.m., the three B-29s took off from Tinian, after a prayer by the military chaplain. What happened with Tibbets and the other crew members of the *Enola Gay* we have already seen.[2]

Down below, in the city of Hiroshima, the people were sleeping and all was calm. Well before sunrise, Arrupe rose to pray, as he did every day. People were already accustomed to the dull roar of the motors of the B-29s, which regularly crossed the city's skies. At 7:55 a.m., a second alarm siren indicated that enemy flights were approaching. Once again, a B-29 flew over at a high altitude, and nobody took much notice of it. At 8:10 a.m., the sirens indicated that the danger had passed, and the city's population got ready to return to their daily routines.

---

1   See Raymond Cartier, *La seconde guerre mondiale*, 2 vols. (Paris: Larousse, 1966), 353ff. On the atomic bomb, see also Gar Alperovitz, *Atomic Diplomacy: Hiroshima and Potsdam* (New York: Simon & Schuster, 1965); S. Arrisue, *Memoirs* (Tokyo, 1974); S. Ashi, *A Bomb* (Hiroshima, 1972); John W. Campbell, *The Atomic Story* (New York: H. Holt and Co., 1947); Herbert Feis, *The Atomic Bomb and the End of World War Two* (Princeton: Princeton University Press, 1966); Michihiko Hachiya, *Hiroshima Diary*, 10th ed. (Chapel Hill, NC: University of North Carolina Press, 1985 [1955]); Gordon Thomas and Max Morgan Witts, *Enola Gay* (New York: Stein & Day, 1985 [1977]); and the documented novel of Masuji Ibuse, *Black Rain* (Palo Alto: Kodansha, 1969).

2   See chapter 1 of this book. For the narrative of Commander Tibbets's story, see Thomas and Witts, *Enola Gay*, a worldwide best-seller on the bombing.

Hiroshima after the first atomic bomb explosion in history (August 6, 1945).

Looking down thirty thousand feet from *Enola Gay*, Tibbetts could see the city awakening to a perfectly clear day. Sitting on the seven fingers of the Ota promontories, Hiroshima had no idea of the atomic baptism it was about to receive. At 8:13:30, Tibbets gave the order to the bombardier, Major Ferebee.

The bomb dropped from the hatch of the plane at exactly 8:15:17. Once relieved of the bomb's ten thousand pounds, *Enola Gay* quickly turned and gained altitude. The crew knew that they had only forty seconds to get the plane at least eighteen kilometers away from the explosion. Each crewmember counted for himself: "40 [...], 39 [...], 38 [...]."

An explosion of unbelievable brightness spread across the sky and dazzled the eyes of the aviators, which were protected by welding goggles. Immediately afterward, a giant cloud in the form of a mushroom silhouetted itself against the sky.

Returning home to the United States aboard the cruiser *Augusta*, President Truman was in a bad mood after the Potsdam meeting, which had concluded with a serious disagreement between the United States and the Soviet Union. He walked about the deck waiting for news and listening to the ship's orchestra. He then went to the dining room and sat down for lunch. Soon, one of his aides arrived with a telegram: "Results clear cut successful in all respects. Visible effects greater than any tests [...]." In his memoirs, Truman would describe his reaction as more moderate, but in fact he shouted out gleefully: "Guys, we have sent them a twenty-thousand-ton block of TNT!" The sailors shouted with delight.[3]

---

3   Cartier, *La seconde guerre mondiale*, 353ff.

The *Pika-don*

In Hiroshima, nobody heard any noise at all. A terrible brilliance, like a purplish-white flash of lightning, penetrated everything and was instantly transformed into a colossal firestorm. Trolleys were converted into twisted iron tombs full of scorched cadavers as the temperature reached fifty million degrees. A windstorm blowing at 1,200 kilometers an hour destroyed all walls within a radius of 1,500 meters and broke windows as far away as twelve kilometers. The resulting cyclone lasted for six hours. Hiroshima experienced one of the most tragic events of all human history.

Years later, Arrupe would write of his own experience:

At that moment, the sirens stopped sounding. Hardly five minutes had passed; it was 8:15 when a magnesium flash ripped across the blue sky. I was in my office with another Jesuit. I stood up immediately and went to look out the window. At that moment, a dull, continuous roar, sounding more like a distant waterfall than an exploding bomb, reached us with terrifying force. The whole house shook, the windows shattered, the doors twisted, and the fragile walls of mud and cane broke like cards crushed by a giant hand. That terrible force, which we thought would rip the building from its foundation, threw us to the ground. While we instinctively covered our heads with our hands, a steady rain of destroyed materials fell on our bodies, stretched immobile on the ground.

When that initial earthquake finished, we stood up, each fearful that the other was wounded. Fortunately, we escaped injury, aside from the bruises from the fall. We checked through the entire house. My main concern was the thirty-five young Jesuits who were my responsibility. After I checked the last of the room, I saw that not a single one was wounded.[4]

Right after that, Arrupe ran instinctively out to the garden in search of the bomb, but he found nothing. After surveying the sad spectacle of the shattered residence, he ascended the nearby hill. From there, looking toward the plain in the east, he could see all Hiroshima burning.

Arrupe reconstructed the scene later:

The noise was small, but it was accompanied by a flash that seemed like a magnesium flame. For several moments, something fell rapidly, followed by a column of flames, and it exploded again, this time horribly, at an altitude

---

4   There are several versions of Arrupe's narrative. In his memoirs, *Este Japón increíble*, he gives a full account of his Hiroshima experience, and he gives further information in the later work *Yo viví la bomba atómica*. There are also dozens of journalistic versions published in newspapers and magazines in the form of articles or interviews in which Arrupe synthesizes or contributes further details. For greater clarity, I will continue to cite his memoir (*Memorias*), supplementing it with other sources.

of 570 meters over the city. The violence of this second explosion was indescribable. Red and blue flames shot out in all directions. Then immediately a horrendous thunder and unbearable waves of heat fell upon the city, devastating everything. Whatever could burn burned, and everything made of metal was fused together.

All this was just the first moment of the tragedy. Immediately afterward, a gigantic mountain of clouds swept up into the sky. In the very center of the explosion, there appeared a horrific thunderhead and, with it, a fierce five hundred-mile an hour wind that swept away everything within a six-kilometer radius. Finally, ten minutes later, a sort of black rain fell on the northeastern part of the city.

Not knowing that they had experienced an atomic bomb explosion, the Japanese used their tongue's imitative harmony to designate the phenomenon as *pika-don*. *Pika* was for them the blinding flash, and *don* was the explosive sound that followed.[5]

As did everybody else, Arrupe considered the event incomprehensible. During four years of war, he had seen many bombs and grenades explode, but what had just occurred was something completely different. There had been talk of secret weapons at that time, but he thought that it was no more than wartime propaganda.

As a first impulse, Pedro wanted to rush to the center of the city in order to help those who were injured; he thought especially of the Jesuits who lived in the residence downtown. But it was impossible to make a move since fire was blocking all the roads, and dense black smoke was emerging from the buildings and enveloping the city.

At that point, Arrupe decided to go to the chapel, one of whose walls had collapsed. In the midst of that darkness, Pedro begged for light. It was an eternal instant that would divide his life in two: before the bomb and after the bomb. The clocks of Hiroshima had stopped, but Pedro contemplated a higher, timeless realm, beyond all human events: "Everywhere there was death and destruction, and we were reduced to impotence. And he was there, knowing everything, contemplating everything, and waiting for our offering to take part in the work of rebuilding everything."

An Improvised Hospital

I left the chapel, and my decision was immediate. We would turn the house into a hospital. I remembered that I had studied medicine. It had been years ago, and I never got to practice it, but in those moments I once again became a doctor and a surgeon. I went to rescue my medical kit, and I found it

---

5   *Memorias*, 171ff.

smashed among the ruins. I was able to salvage only a little iodine, a few aspirin, fruit salts, and bicarbonate. But there were more than two hundred thousand victims. Where to begin? Since we had to work without remedies, this reality imposed the kinds of procedures we used. We found ourselves possessing physiques wasted away by an extremely harsh war and the consequent scarcity of food. There was also a history of tuberculosis, which was common to many millions of Japanese, and we had to strengthen them just to increase their ability to convalesce. For that, they needed plenty of food, but we had nothing in our storeroom. Like everybody else, we were living with the scant rations of rice that were supplied to us, and they were so little there was no way to economize.[6]

Arrupe saw clearly that he had to send his young men in search of help.

"Go wherever God guides you," he told them, "and bring whatever food you can find. Don't ask me anything more. The place doesn't matter to me. Borrow, buy, beg! The important thing is that the wounded people, who will be here when you return, will need something to eat as soon as possible."

Nobody spoke a word in reply. And indeed, within a few minutes the wounded people began to appear, like walking ghosts, with their skin torn and their bodies covered with boils and red and violet spots. Their clothes were burnt and ripped to shreds. Arrupe's improvised hospital began to fill up. The first to come were some young women workers, and there followed several children who were crying for their parents. Later there arrived some older women who were greatly distressed—they had only with difficulty been able to escape from the ruins of their collapsed houses. Finally, there was a group of soldiers.

All of them had expressions of horror on their faces, as if they had just escaped from hell. They were trembling with pain and fright, fainting with weakness, writhing on the ground.

Arrupe could hardly attend to them all. He quickly turned the library and the reception area into an infirmary, and the rector's office became an operating room.

The first thing to do was to clean the wounds:

Many wounds resulted from the contusions caused by collapsing buildings. There were fractured bones and many cuts, but not like those made by a sword or a bullet, which leave the edges of the wound clean. Rather, they were made by the pressure of beams or walls falling on a person, ripping apart the muscles' mass and leaving embedded particles of dirt, glass, and wood, as well as splinters of the destroyed bones. Other wounds were clean, like those produced by glass, and so were easier to cure and less prone to infection. What predominated, though, were the burns. One man came

---

6   *Memorias*, 211.

several hours after the explosion, and he had a huge blister that covered his chest, his stomach, and the whole of his back.[7]

When Arrupe asked people how they had got burned that way, the answer was always the same: they had remained inside the collapsing buildings. Afterward, the houses had burst into flames, and they were burned while trying to escape from the ruins.

Such burns were to be expected, but another type was less easily explained. Pedro asked one man: "Tell me how you got burned."

"I didn't get burned, Father."

"Then what happened to you?"

"I don't know. I saw a light, a terrible explosion, and nothing happened to me, but after a half-hour I felt some blisters forming on my skin. After four or five hours, it was a terrible burn that began to fester the next day, and this happened without any fire at all."

"It was very disturbing," wrote Arrupe many years later:

Today, we know that the burns were caused by the infrared radiation, which attacked the tissues and penetrated not only of the epidermis and the endodermis, but also the muscular tissue. That is what gave rise to the festering, which caused so many deaths and so much distress among those of us who were caring for them.[8]

After just four and a half hours, Arrupe had in the house 150 persons, large parts of whose bodies were open wounds. In order to cure the wounds, it was necessary to pierce the blisters.

"What is more," he relates,

the work was difficult. When a blister is caused by the rubbing of a shoe, for example, you can puncture it with a needle and a few drops of water come out. But when a blister covers half the body, piercing it releases more than 150 cubic centimeters of liquid. At first, we were using galvanized pails, but after the third cure, seeing how many more lay ahead, we began to use the pots and basins that we found around the house.

There was frightful suffering and terrible pain that made people writhe like snakes, but not a single complaint could be heard: all suffered in silence. Nobody was shouting or crying. The Japanese people show themselves to be quite superior to Westerners in this regard: they are very

---

7   *Memorias*, 213.

8   It is interesting to compare Arrupe's diagnoses with those of a Japanese physician who also survived the bomb, Dr. Michihiko Hachiya, author of the impressive *Hiroshima Diary* (in the English translation of Warner Wells, M.D.), who met up daily with the strange new disease produced by atomic radiation. His account was written in those tragic days and is full of compassion and tenderness.

stoical and exercise an absolute control over pain, all the more admirable the more horrible the catastrophe.

In the meantime, the religious sisters of the city were also arriving. Their convent had been destroyed, not by the force of the bomb, but by fire. All the nuns emerged unharmed, except for one who had slight burns on her hand.

Arrupe's little hospital was finally filled to overflowing. There was no room for even one more patient, but the terrible spectacle continued. There was a constant procession of wounded filing along the streets and the country roads leading out of the city. It was an uninterrupted flow of half-burned bodies stumbling forward, trying to distance themselves from the scene of desperation as quickly as their legs would permit.

Almost all the automobiles in the city were destroyed by the fire. The suburban railway lacked electrical energy, and its rails were twisted out of shape in any case. Arrupe and his young assistants helped to transport the wounded to the next aid station. There they asked about the best method for treating the burns, but nobody understood what was happening. The doctors confessed that they had never met up with such pathology. Those wounds were not the result of the direct influence of heat and fire. Some type of radiation must have affected the skin tissues and in some cases even reached the bones.

Arrupe continued his work without medicine or bandages, but his basic intuition yielded results. The poor villagers who lived nearby donated generously the food that Arrupe's emissaries requested of them. Arrupe's medical knowledge came up with the correct therapy: nourish well those destroyed bodies in order to invigorate their natural ability for recuperation. So well did the procedures work that only one child, suffering from meningitis caused by an increase in skull pressure, died. The other patients quickly began to recover, and most were completely cured.

A Desert of Ashes

In the early afternoon hours, the Jesuits from Nagatsuka managed to enter the city. As always happens in major fires, an enormous amount of water vapor had been generated, which later condensed, causing torrential rain. As a result, the fires in the upper parts of the ruins were extinguished: "It was five in the afternoon," recounts Arrupe,

> and before our astounded gaze stretched a truly indescribable spectacle. It was a macabre, Dantesque vision beyond all one's imaginings. Before us lay a city completely destroyed. We made our way through its ruins, still full of hot embers. Any misstep on our part could prove fatal.
>
> But more horrible still was the tragic vision of those thousands of wounded and burned people begging for help. I came across one boy who had

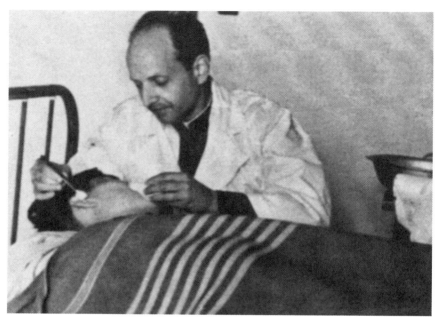

Arrupe practicing medicine in his improvised hospital in Nagatsuka (August 1945).

a piece of glass embedded in the pupil of his left eye and another who had a thick splinter of wood stuck like a dagger between his ribs. With a sob he was shouting: "Please save me, I can't go any farther!" Another fellow was caught between two beams and had his legs completely burned up to the knees.

We kept moving forward, and suddenly we saw coming toward us a young man running frantically and asking for help. Just twenty minutes before, he had heard the voice of his mother, who was buried alive under the ruins of their house. The flames were already consuming her body as the son tried futilely to remove the beams that held her trapped. Even more heart-rending were the cries of the children calling out for their parents. Many other children perished, like the two hundred girls in a college whose roof collapsed, so that not one of them could escape the flames.[9]

Around ten o'clock that night, Arrupe and his companions were finally able to reach the residence of the Jesuits in Hiroshima. All five of the priests there had suffered injuries. Father Shiffer, though he did not seem to be seriously affected, was on the verge of death. He had a head wound, and to stop the bleeding they had wrapped it in a large turban made of newspapers and a shirt. But they had not noticed another wound that Arrupe found behind his ear: a piece of glass had cut a small artery and was causing a steady flow of blood.

---

9   *Memorias*, 215; *Yo viví la bomba atómica*, 209.

Pedro decided to transport him to Nagatsuka. With a piece of rough board and a couple of bamboo poles, he improvised a stretcher. Shiffer grimaced with pain but with a calm Japanese smile said: "Father Arrupe, could you look at my back? I must have something there."

They turned him over and by the light of a torch Arrupe could see that his back was in fact completely peppered with small pieces of glass. Using a shaving blade as a scalpel, Arrupe patiently removed more than fifty fragments. Once this operation was completed, they began the journey toward the novitiate, advancing in the night amid the ruins.

Every hundred meters, they felt the need to stop and rest for a while. During one of those rest periods, Pedro heard some pitiful cries, like those of a person agonizing. Unable to determine where exactly the cries were coming from, he listened more intently and then concluded: "The voice is coming from below us."

The group had in fact stopped on top of a collapsed roof. When they removed some of the tiles, they found an old woman with half her body burned. She had been buried there the whole day and now had little hold on life. Arrupe and the others removed her from there, but she died soon after.

They were to behold many other scenes of horror that night. When they reached the Terma River, the spectacle was terrifying. People had fled from the fires in the city, and taking advantage of the low tide, they crowded along both banks of the river, some removing the bodies of others in order to be able to drink. At midnight, though, the tide had begun to rise again, and many of the wounded, totally exhausted and half submerged in the mud, could not get out. Arrupe recounts: "I will never forget the screams of those who felt the water reaching their necks, with no way of being saved."[10]

Arrupe did not sleep that night, nor would he sleep for many days to come, but an interior strength kept him going in his service to the countless victims of the bomb.

Mass over Hiroshima

Arrupe and his companions finally reached the novitiate around five in the morning. After taking care of the most urgent medical problems, Arrupe prepared to celebrate Mass. As he pronounced again the *Dominus vobiscum* (The Lord be with you), he was overcome by the panorama before him. There in the chapel some fifty sick Japanese had their eyes fixed on him. They could not understand that ceremony, but they beheld a man who had not spared himself for one minute in his efforts to save them. As he passed from one end of the altar to the other to read the Epistle or the Gospel, he had to stoop down and gently move away the children, who were trying to get close. They wanted to get a good view of the foreigner with the strange vestments who was making unusual gestures for them.

---

10   *Yo viví la bomba atómica*, 209.

Many years later, Arrupe recalled that unrepeatable moment:

In reality, the setting for celebrating Mass was not conducive to devotion. The half-destroyed chapel was full of shuddering sick people who were lying next to one another on the ground; they were suffering terribly and writhing in pain. I began the Mass as best I could in the midst of that human mass that had not the slightest idea of what was happening on the altar. I will never forget the horrible impression I had when I turned toward them at the *Dominus vobiscum* and contemplated that spectacle from the altar. I could not utter a word. I was as if paralyzed, with my arms stretched open, beholding that human tragedy—such was the fruit of human science and technological progress, used to destroy humankind. They looked at me with anguish-filled eyes, with desperation, as if they were hoping that some consolation would reach them from the altar. What a terrible scene that was! A few minutes later, the One of whom John the Baptist said, "In the midst of you is one whom you do not know"[11] came down on the altar.

I have never felt again as I felt then the sadness of the unbelievers' incomprehension regarding Jesus Christ. Their Savior was there among them, the one who had given his life for them [...] "but they did not know that he was in the midst of them."[12] I was the only one who knew it. From my lips came spontaneously a prayer for those who had had the savage cruelty to drop the atomic bomb: "Lord, forgive them for they know not what they do," and for those who were lying near me, twisting in pain: "Lord, grant them faith [...], so that they see; give them the strength to put up with the pain." When I raised the host before those wounded, destroyed bodies, a cry rose from my heart: "My Lord and my God, have pity on this flock that has no Shepherd."[13] "So that I may believe in you, Lord, remember that they also have to come to know you."

Torrents of grace no doubt flowed from that host and from that altar. Six months later, when all the patients had recovered and left our house (only two persons died in our care), many of them had been baptized, and all had had the experience of a Christian charity that knows how to understand, help, and console in ways that surpass all human expectation. Such charity had communicated to them a serenity that helped them to smile despite the pain and to pardon even those who had caused their suffering.[14]

After the Mass, Pedro and his companions met together to decide what to do next. Good nutrition to help the body's self-curing powers was helpful, but it was not enough. Fortunately, another providential happening surprised them.

---

11   John 1:26.
12   John 1:26.
13   Matthew 9:39; Matthew 6:34; 1 Timothy 2:4.
14   *Itinéraire*, 44.

A Sack of Boric Acid

At eight o'clock in the morning, an employee of the house, who lived nearby, came to see Arrupe with a sack in his hand and said, "Father, I also would like to help these poor people. Looking about, I found this sack full of some white flakes that look like medicine. Why don't you see if the stuff can be of some use."

The sack contained fifteen kilos of boric acid, which did indeed provide the solution to the problem of hygiene. Cutting up clean sheets and underwear, Arrupe made a large quantity of bandages and undertook a labor that was extremely primitive but yielded excellent results. The cure consisted in placing a piece of cloth over the wound and keeping it moist the whole day with a sterilizing solution of boric acid. In this way, the pain was assuaged, and the wound was kept relatively clean and in contact with the air. The festering from the wounds adhered to the cloth, so that with four or five changes a day, they were able to guarantee hygienic care.

Using this curative process, Arrupe noticed within a week that scar tissue began to form and it kept spreading, with the result that the patients recovered slowly but completely. So effective was the cure that Arrupe observed that in all the cases treated there were no instances when the scars contracted or underwent malignant degeneration.

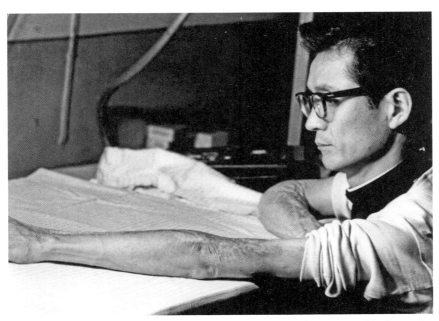

Francis Peter Takezoe Tamotsu suffered radiation burns when he was thirteen years old; after meeting Arrupe, he decided to become a priest.

Arrupe commented further:

After a certain amount of scientific study of the effects of the atomic bomb, a group of doctors from the Atomic Bomb Casualty Center told us they suspected that the atomic bomb had malignant influences on the process of cicatrization. However, we could show them that such was not the case, since among the hundreds of people we had cured there was not a single instance of malignant degeneration. We therefore believed that the keloids were produced not directly by the bomb, but by poor treatment of the wounds.

In fact, those of us who were in Hiroshima and saw the curative procedures that were first used understood perfectly why the wounds, instead of getting better, got worse.

First of all, the shortage of doctors was extreme. Of the 260 there had been in the city, some two hundred perished in the explosion, and many of the remaining sixty were wounded. I found the director of the Red Cross hospital buried under the roof of his house. When we finally got him out, he had six broken bones and was unable to help others.

The bulk of the casualties were cared for by poorly trained nurses or people using home cures. So many times we saw endless lines of a hundred or a 150 injured people, waiting patiently in the street to enter a half-ruined building, where they would be treated by a nurse with a calligraphy brush. She would tincture their wounds with mercurochrome that she had beside her in a can! Naturally, the mercurochrome promoted the destruction of the tissues.

And those were the more professional cures—the domestic ones were much worse. One must always be very careful with home remedies, and all the more so in Japan. They have the idea there, for example, that turnip pulp is good for burn wounds. Since in Hiroshima turnips were plentiful, that cure was used on many burns.

The initial effect was refreshing, but after a half-hour, with the August sun and the puss festering from the wounds, a crust would form that caused unbearable pain. They then tried to remedy this by applying mashed potato, which only increased the crust. Even though this looked like scar tissue, it was clear that there was something soft beneath it. In order to absorb the liquid by osmosis, they would sprinkle the wound with coal dust or ash. Finally, as the pain kept increasing, they tried to relieve it by putting oil on the wound. In sum, this curative process ended up producing an extremely hard crust, black and shiny as newly polished shoes.

Our work, therefore, was to go from house to house where there were injured people and try to convince them that those remedies led to certain death. At the same time, we showed them our simple procedure for curing the wounds. For that reason, during all those first weeks after the bomb, you could count with the fingers of one hand the hours we were able to sleep, because when you know that fifteen minutes of work may mean saving several lives, you can't easily justify taking time off to sleep.[15]

This simple testimony of Arrupe is backed up by the unanimous testimony of others to his heroic behavior during those weeks of crisis. He did not stop for a single instant.[16]

---

15 *Memorias*, 220; *Yo viví la bomba atómica*, 211.

16 The author interviewed more than thirty persons in Hiroshima who had known Arrupe after the bomb was dropped. They were unanimous in affirming that Arrupe's behavior in those days was more than heroic: they were astounded by his endurance and capacity for work, almost without sleeping, as well as by his intuition, efficiency, and ability to solve problems rapidly. Many of those who received medical attention from Arrupe ended up asking to be baptized years later, no doubt captivated by the Christian example of that exceptional man. Nevertheless, as his niece Mariví Gondra stated years later, Arrupe had no desire to exploit his "wonderworking" gifts with the people: "Those would not have been real conversions—even if they had been baptized by the hundreds."

More recent research has revealed new facts about the effects of the atomic bomb: the bomb exploded at an altitude of 580 meters over the Shima Hospital, which was located practically in the center of the city of Hiroshima. The bomb blast had energy equivalent to 12,500 tons of TNT. The enormous ball of fire, similar to a small sun, provoked a type of cyclone when the intense heat came into contact with the surrounding air. Some fifteen percent of the energy released took the form of radioactive energy, some thirty-five percent became caloric energy, and about fifty percent became explosive force.

The result was that between 310,000 and 320,000 civilians and more than forty thousand soldiers were directly affected by the bomb. Some 150,000 persons, including twenty thousand soldiers, died before the end of 1945. About ninety percent of the fatalities occurred in the first two weeks after the explosion.

Of the seventy-six thousand buildings that then existed in Hiroshima, some ninety-two percent were destroyed by the explosion and subsequent fires. The explosive wave covered the whole delta on which the city was built and destroyed about sixty percent of the buildings within five kilometers of the epicenter. Apparently only eight percent of the buildings, mostly in the outlying part of the city, could be restored. The area affected by the bomb covered thirteen square kilometers around the epicenter.

So much is said about Hiroshima that it is often forgotten that on August 9, just three days after this tragedy, the Americans exploded an atomic bomb over Nagasaki. This bomb had nearly twice the destructive power, twenty-two kilotons of TNT. It is estimated that a temperature of three hundred thousand degrees developed within one ten-thousandth of a second after the explosion. As in Hiroshima, the caloric energy caused most of the damage, affecting between 260,000 and 280,000 persons. Despite the greater destructive capacity of the Nagasaki bomb, that the epicenter was near the hills in the northern part of that port city, some distance from the busiest parts of town, partially reduced the destruction wrought by this second bomb (see *Days to Remember: An Account of the Bombings of Hiroshima and Nagasaki*, prepared by the Committee of Japanese Citizens, Hiroshima–Nagasaki [Tokyo: Hiroshima–Nagasaki Publishing Committee, 1981]).

Peace Museums and Peace Parks have been established in both Hiroshima and Nagasaki. These unsettling memorials were created to keep people mindful of both catastrophes. The museum and the park of Hiroshima are located at the epicenter; also preserved

"Give it all you have"

Among the many cases he treated, Arrupe described one in detail:

> I was taking care of wounded people in Nagatsuka when a young married couple came to see me. She was in good health, since she had been outside the city at the moment of the explosion. Her husband, a young man of twenty-two years, was in a sorry state. He could hardly move. Assisted by his wife, who helped him along, he dragged himself toward our house. As he entered the house, he left behind him a trail of pus. Half of his body was covered with sores.
>
> It was the first serious case I was seeing, and I thought to myself that the poor lad had arrived only to die in our midst. He, however, when he saw that I was hesitating, grabbed my hand and said with anguish, "Father, help me!"
>
> His wife took my other hand and explained, "Father, we got married just a month ago. Save my husband!"
>
> I didn't know what to say. On such occasions, a thousand things pass through your head in a single instant. At last, I answered them almost reflexively, "Fine, we'll see what can be done, but […] it's going to be very painful."
>
> He looked straight at me and said, "It's going to be painful? Give it all you have, and I'll put up with it!"
>
> We went ahead, put him on the operating table, which was my desktop, and began to clean his wounds. How that poor young fellow writhed. We had to give him a tough treatment, since the pus had solidified at the bottom of the burns. In the midst of it all, he just kept saying: "Father, go ahead. I'll bear it. Just save me!"
>
> Someone whispered to me, "Wouldn't it be possible to cause him less pain?" But it was impossible. I had to become the torturer of that man if I wanted to save his life. And that's what I was for two and a half hours. When I finished, he was worn out from the suffering, and I was exhausted from the tension I myself had experienced as I crucified him with my treatment.
>
> In Japan the walls are very thin so that sound penetrates them easily. Forgetting that, the injured man, as soon as we disappeared from his sight, discharged upon his poor wife all the anger he had accumulated during those two and a half hours of torment—he piled on the poor thing the worst epithets in the dictionary.
>
> She took it all in. Like a good Japanese woman, she listened to him with a smile. To get back at him, she would light him a cigarette, wipe away his sweat, or give him something to drink. Whenever we saw her, she was sitting

there are the ruins of the building of the Commission for the Promotion of Industry, now called "The Atomic Dome"—its skeletal structure was strong enough to withstand the blast, and it remains today as it was after the explosion.

or kneeling at the side of her husband, always smiling. We never found out when she slept.

After eight months, this couple could finally leave our house. One April morning, I saw them walking down by the garden, laughing, happy, and above all [...] baptized. At that moment, I also felt an interior joy that more than compensated for all the suffering of the previous eight months. If we had not treated that fellow, he would doubtless have died, since he was already showing the first symptoms of poisoning.[17]

Another case that produced a strong impact on Arrupe's soul was that of Nakamura-san, the university student from Yamaguchi who had behaved heroically after being slandered in class for being Christian. This young woman had afterward gone to live in Hiroshima. Immediately after the explosion of the bomb, Arrupe was unable to learn anything about her, but about two weeks later he received news that she had been seriously wounded. Within minutes, he went into the streets of Hiroshima, searching for her in the midst of half-destroyed houses and collapsed buildings. The lack of familiar points of reference made it difficult for him to find his way. After searching for four hours, he was told by some girls, "Right there, sir, just around that corner."

Pedro followed their directions and found a small shed fashioned out of scorched zinc supported on sticks; a wooden wall a half-meter high protected a small inner space. He wanted to enter, but an unbearable stench kept him back. Nakamura-san was stretched out on the ground, with her swollen arms and legs extended. She was suffering from burns all over her body, and pus was dripping from the wounds and seeping into the ground. The scorched flesh revealed little more than bone and skin.

She had been there two weeks, stretched out on a rough board without any medical or hygienic attention. She ate only a little rice given to her by her father, who was also wounded. Her back had turned into a large sore infected with gangrene since she had not been able to change her posture. When he cleaned the burn wound in the hip region, Arrupe found that the muscular mass had wasted away into pus, leaving a cavity the size of a closed fist, in which a nest of worms was breeding.

Overwhelmed, Pedro could not utter a word. Nakamura-san, when she opened her eyes and saw that it was Arrupe attending to her, spoke words he would never forget: *Arrupe shimpu-sama, Goseitai, o motte irasshaimashita ka?* (Father Arrupe, would you bring me Communion?).

Pedro acted quickly and had her brought to Nagatsuka. The procedures needed to cure her were very painful. Fever made the poor woman delirious: she thought she saw a ghost that was trying to choke her. Pedro approached her and

---

17   *Yo viví la bomba atómica*, 212.

A group of investigators from the United States interrogating Arrupe about the effects of the Hiroshima explosion.

calmed her down little by little. When he thought she was asleep, he tried to leave, but she became aware of it and again became agitated. As a result, Pedro decided to stay by her bedside for several nights.

After two months, when it seemed that she was slowly recovering, a heart attack took her life. Her own father took charge of cremating her near the house, but the fire he had built died out halfway through the process, and the father went to call Arrupe. That was the worst part for Pedro: beholding in the middle of the night the cadaver of Nakamura-san, with a grimace of pain on her face and her flesh half melted by the fire.[18]

The cases that Arrupe attended to were countless. He especially recalled many seriously wounded children. When the bomb exploded, the great majority of children were in schools and colleges, since the city had a high level of school attendance. After the explosion, thousands of children found themselves far from their parents, wounded and wandering through the streets, with no one to take care of them.

Arrupe gathered together as many children as he could and dedicated himself to curing them in order to prevent possible infections and fevers. He later wrote of one of these cases:

> We were completely lacking anesthesia, and some of the children were terribly wounded: one of them had his head split open from one side to the other as the result of a tile that fell on him. The lips of the wound were a

---

18   *Memorias*, 222. See also chapter 9 of this book.

centimeter and a half wide; the scalp had separated from the bone and was full of mud and pieces of glass.

The screams of the poor child while he was being treated had the whole house on edge. We had no choice but to tie him with a sheet to a little wagon and take him to the top of the hill beside the house. That place became our operating room: we could work there, and the boy could scream as much as he liked without upsetting everybody else.

It was heart-wrenching to have to perform such cures, but there was a tremendous consolation in being able to return those children to their parents. With the help of the Japanese police, a highly organized body, we were able to get in touch with the families of all the children we had in the house.

Within a few days, people were coming to Nagatsuka from Osaka, Tokyo, and other cities. You can't imagine those scenes of parents meeting up with children they thought had died in the explosion and now were safe and sound, or at least on their way to recovery. Those fathers and mothers, overflowing with emotion, did not know how to express their gratitude. When they threw themselves at our feet, they made us recall those scenes in the Acts of the Apostles when the Jews fell on their knees and adored the apostles as gods.[19]

Radioactive Pathology

In the midst of all those experiences, there was one type of illness that especially worried the former medical student. He found that there were many people who had been in the city at the moment of the explosion and had not suffered any visible wound, but who after a few days had begun to feel weak. Many ended up coming to Arrupe complaining that they were burning up inside and thinking that they had maybe breathed in a poisonous gas. And shortly after that, they died.

The first case came as Arrupe was curing an old man who had two deep wounds in his back. A man introduced himself saying, "Please, come to my house because my son says his throat is hurting him a lot."

Concerned about the very poor health of the old man he was caring for, Arrupe answered: "It is probably just a cold. Give him some aspirin and make him sweat. You will see him get better." But the boy died within two hours. What had happened?

Later, a weeping thirteen-year-old girl came to Arrupe and said: "Look at what is happening to me." Opening her mouth, she showed him two bloody gums. Her whole mouth was full of tiny wounds, and she was suffering from acute inflammation of the throat. Furthermore, when she pulled on her hair, it came out in her hand. In two days, she died.

---

19   *Yo viví la bomba atómica*, 213.

Arrupe compiled data about these symptoms, which included destruction of the hematopoietic organs, the medulla, the spleen, the lymphatic ganglia, and the capillary bulbs. He was actually describing the symptoms of a new disease: radioactive pathology. Once he realized that the illness had been caused by radiation, he was able to save some lives by means of blood transfusions and other measures.

Arrupe would later classify the different effects of the bomb, recognizing that there had been three types of waves: the explosive wave, whose effects were like those of any bomb and reached a radius of six kilometers; the thermal wave, which developed a temperature of ten million degrees and produced infrared radiation capable of destroying tissue; and the radioactive wave, which reached a radius of one and a half kilometers and caused a decrease in red and white globules, hemorrhage in the mouth and throat, spots on the skin, loss of hair, vomiting, and high fever, among other symptoms.

Shadows of Hiroshima

Arrupe argued that the famous shadows of Hiroshima, those human silhouettes that were left on certain walls, were due not to the disintegration but to the incineration of the bodies. The temperature rise in the thermal wave was so instantaneous that the exposed part of any person or object near a wall was incinerated instantly, while the rest of the body or object acted as a shield and so left its silhouette on the wall.

While experiencing all these incredible events, Arrupe suffered a certain sense of isolation. The city of Hiroshima was lacking services of telephone, telegraph, radio, electricity, and railroad, and no help arrived from Tokyo or Osaka until the day after the bomb. Even those who came with assistance were reluctant to enter the city because they feared the effects of the radiation.

Arrupe had himself gone many times into the devastated city in order to help the wounded, but he heard some individuals warning others: "Don't go into the city because there is a gas there that will kill people for sixty years."

Precisely at such moments, Arrupe felt even more motivated to dedicate himself to the sick and the agonizing. There in the city, some fifty thousand cadavers were lying in the streets and in the ruins; if they were not destroyed, they could give rise to a horrible plague. Furthermore, there were a 120,000 injured people who needed attention: "In view of such a situation," wrote Arrupe, "a priest cannot stay away in order to save his life." And he added:

> Naturally, when they tell you that there is a lethal gas in the city, you will decide to enter it only after seeing the real need. But we went in and began to make immense pyramids of cadavers, which we would then sprinkle with gas and incinerate. In that way, the cadavers in the streets disappeared.
>
> In three or four days, however, with the hot August sun and the humid heat, our sense of smell told us that there were still more decaying bodies.

Lifting up collapsed structures, we sometimes found families of five, six, or more persons, crushed beneath their houses. With the help of passersby who were in the vicinity, we would make piles of fifty or sixty cadavers in order to burn them.

When we finally finished that painful work of the first few days, we were totally exhausted. Our fatigue, though, did not make us forget the rumors about the lethal gas, so we asked one another: "How are you feeling?"

And we were all experiencing the same thing. We were tired, but without any symptoms that might cause alarm. That was naturally the case, since the false story about the lethal gas was due simply to people's imaginings, unsettled by the horrendous spectacle of that tragic calvary.[20]

Once the war was over, Arrupe and his students, much to their surprise, were told to leave the house and the city. Since the hostilities had ceased, the reason could not be any suspicion of espionage. Rather, the order of expulsion was due to a certain resentment toward foreigners after the humiliation of defeat. No account was taken of the heroic behavior of that small community or of the great service that had been rendered in that house, which had been converted into a hospital for the casualties left by the bomb.

When given the eviction notice, Arrupe responded shrewdly: "Fine, there are forty-five of us. Tell me where we should go."

The command was issued four times, and each time Arrupe responded that they had no place to which they could move. Finally, four officials came and offered them a hotel beside a lake in Taisaku, a beautiful spot located on high and healthy ground and surrounded by mountains.

The young Jesuits left for that mountainous region, but nobody could get Arrupe to abandon the 150 patients he was still caring for in the house. He was the only doctor, and he did not trust the home remedies of the Japanese. As a result, he stayed in Nagatsuka, along with five other priests.

Within two weeks, the young Jesuits received orders to return to Hiroshima, since there was no danger there. Arrupe ended up quite satisfied with the sequence of events since, without seeking it, he had managed to get a free vacation for the students, who had been of such great assistance to him in attending to the casualties.

Explosion of a New Era

Those days remained firmly engraved in Arrupe's memory, and in his many later trips around the world he recounted his experiences over and over again to the thousands of persons who came to hear the testimony of this "survivor of Hiroshima." Eighteen months after the explosion, five years after, seventeen

---

20   *Yo viví la bomba atómica*, 215.

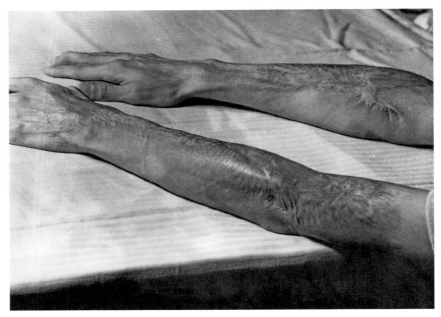

. *The wounds of Father Takezoe Tamotsu, showing clearly the effects of the atomic bomb.*

years after, people still listened to his accounts with lively interest and a shudder. "When something touches the very essence of a person, his conscience, his destiny, it is as if an inseparable hypothesis is realized in him [...] a portent of the possible self-destruction of one who boasts of himself."[21]

When asked what he felt in those moments, Arrupe always answered that the experience was without a doubt a horrible one, but that it was at the same time an experience of war in the midst of ignorance, for no one had had any foreknowledge of "what that solitary B-29 had carefully deposited at five hundred meters up, there in a sky that was tinted with the morning fog of August."

Arrupe later recounted the following:

Incredible as it may seem, I felt a much deeper internal commotion five years later when in Bogotá I saw the movie *Hiroshima*, which was an exact reproduction of that fateful day of August 1945. In an hour and a half, I was able to view on the screen all the tragic, horrifying reality that I had experienced during several months. My eyes tried to protect me by blurring with a curtain of tears. I couldn't bear it. It was just too much for me! Everything I went through in Hiroshima during six months, in a daily reality dosed out minute by minute—it was too much of a dosage to be relived in an hour! It

21   Pedro Arrupe, "A los veinticinco años de la bomba atómica," article published by the newspaper *Avvenire*, Rome, August 6, 1970. Reprinted in Pedro Arrupe, *La iglesia de hoy y del futuro* (Bilbao: Mensajero, 1982), 21.

seemed humiliating! What I had been able to bear in the actual lived reality overcame me in the artifice of the film. My nerves, which I thought were like steel wires, fused together with that emotional discharge.[22]

In reality, as time went by, the bomb became for Arrupe a symbolic explosion ushering in a new era. Many years later, a young Japanese priest named Hasegawa Tadashi visited Arrupe in Rome. Twenty-five years earlier, Arrupe had cured him of the festering sores that had been caused by infrared radiation. The young man had later asked to be baptized, and later still he was ordained a priest and received the gift of a chalice from that "foreign doctor" who had cured the living flesh of his body. Years later, he wrote up the story of his experience of the bomb, his meeting up with Arrupe, and his conversion—it is a spell-binding tale.

The explosion of the atomic bomb was for Arrupe an ambiguous symbol of the times. It expressed at once hope and anguish: "Its sinister light, which can destroy the retina of anyone who looks straight at it, is an illuminating and discriminating power, greater than that of Roentgen."[23] That was only the first of many other incredible explosions that were incubating in the fields of development, hunger, injustice.

Arrupe's voice trembled with emotion when as an old man in the Roman infirmary he recalled those days, but he was also able to exclaim: "How beautiful!

---

22 Arrupe, "A los veinticinco años de la bomba atómica."

23 In the cited article, Arrupe writes: "Another *explosion* is underway today: it is being forged by the death of millions of persons from hunger and a subhuman existence. More than half of humankind is malnourished; the situation of the marginalized populations in the underdeveloped countries becomes more unsustainable by the day":

> The explosive energy that is building up among the marginalized in different regions of the world is nourished by the news and publicity brought to them by radio and television. It is an undeniable reality. The transistor radio today can be a source of instruction, but it can also be a source of explosive energy mightier than atomic power itself. Atomic energy is blind and cannot be controlled easily, but the energy created by the transistor radio is human and therefore intelligent and free; once it is unleashed it is practically uncontrollable.

In this work, Arrupe analyzes topics such as the liberation of the oppressed, development, disarmament, and spiritual energy. He concludes:

> Atomic power takes us into the deepest layers of matter and puts us at the limits of the material universe. It is an impulse toward interiority, seeking the depth of being, of matter; it is a decisive step toward inwardness. When will the day come when human beings, having finally reached down to the ultimate stratum of matter, can discern, as if through a delicate veil, a new, hidden reality within every being, which is the divine reality? And if they then repeat this experience in the very depth of their own beings, they will discover that in the most intimate part of their psyche that same divine reality is alive. For that, we will need a flash of light much more powerful than the one that blinded us in Hiroshima: we will need the light of faith, which illumines without blinding, because it is powerful and dark.

How beautiful! It was something unique!"[24] Amid all those tragic memories, one especially stood out, the clock stopped at 8:15 in the morning:

> No sooner had the tiles, the broken glass, and the beams stopped falling and the deafening noise ceased than I got up from the ground, and I saw before me the clock still hanging on the wall, but unmoving; the pendulum seemed to be stuck. It was eight-fifteen [...]. That silent, paralyzed clock has been a symbol for me. The explosion of the first atomic bomb has become a phenomenon outside history. It is not a memory, but a perpetual experience of something beyond history, something that does not continue with the tick-tock of a clock. The pendulum stopped, and Hiroshima remains burnt into our minds. It has no relation with time: it belongs to a motionless eternity.[25]

---

24   Declarations made by Arrupe to the author of this book. While making them, he confirmed all that is narrated in this chapter, but he also experienced strong emotions. The sorrow provoked by the tragedy was mixed with the instinctive optimism that enabled him to see the positive side of every experience. The atomic bomb helped him discover a future creative explosion in his own life.

25   Arrupe, "A los veinticinco años de la bomba atómica," 21.

12. Condemned to Live

Gathered together around an old radio receiver, Pedro and his companions were listening attentively to a voice rarely heard in public; sounding rather archaic, it was nothing less than "the voice of a god," strange to the ears of the Japanese.

The time was twelve noon on August 15, 1945. The voice was broadcast to the army barracks and reached the loudspeakers in the plazas. It brought tears to the eyes of the soldiers, who remained rigidly at attention, still ready for war.

Nobody knew why the emperor had summoned the people to hear him deliver his address. Many still believed that he was going to call them to make one last heroic sacrifice in the struggle against the enemy. His language was strange, almost unintelligible, but most people understood immediately the essence of his message. The emperor's will was that the hostilities should cease and that the people should accept what seemed incredible: defeat, humiliation, occupation.

Many Japanese rebelled. In many army barracks, the corridors were drenched with the blood of soldiers who committed suicide. Kamikaze pilots plunged their planes into the waters of Tokyo Bay. Many people simply knelt in silence in front of the main entrance of the imperial palace. The aviators at Atsugi air base mutinied and flew their aircraft threateningly over the palace. Admiral Kantaro Suzuki resigned.

The spirit of rebellion, though, was only of a minority, and it contrasted with the obedience of the one hundred million who were condemned to live.[1] "The basic reason for the end of the war was not the atomic bomb," wrote Arrupe,

> but the order of the Japanese emperor, who had been advised to surrender unconditionally, and the people's blind obedience to that order of their Tenno Heika [Imperial Majesty]. This is not really comprehensible to anyone not familiar with the actual situation then and with the true "Japanese soul." The Japanese people would never have given up without that order from the emperor; they would have kept on fighting, defending every inch of their beloved *Yamato* from profanation by the enemy. They would have waged guerrilla warfare as hard as the steel of a Japanese sword; thousands upon thousands would have died; collective suicides would have taken place (remember the forty elders); but Japan most definitely would not have surrendered.[2]

---

1   Cartier, *La seconde guerre mondiale*, 382.

2   Arrupe, "A los veinticinco años de la bomba atómica."

Hirohito Ceases to Be Divine

Knowing the Japanese soul so well, Arrupe was still a perplexed witness of a surrender that could not be compared with others in history, because "in Japan that capitulation to the enemy meant the collapse of a whole tradition and a glorious history."

In Tokyo Bay, with Mount Fuji as a symbolic background, the US naval fleet accepted the surrender. The sensibility of the Japanese was deeply wounded by a photograph in a Tokyo newspaper that showed General Douglas MacArthur in shirtsleeves beside the emperor. In the view of Arrupe, only the voice of that man thought to be a god could have effected such a historical turnabout. The reversal left the Japanese starting from zero, but within twenty-five years it would make them the third strongest economy in the world.

Arrupe also experienced a new stage in his own life after those events. Although he had always been full of energy and eager to serve others, his life could not remain the same after living through that atomic experience. When the occupation forces arrived, Arrupe was surprised that no major conflict arose between the defeated people and the enemy that had cruelly dropped the atomic bomb. The word "war" disappeared from the Japanese language and Japanese politics, to be replaced by "reconstruction."

Arrupe was often invited to celebrate Mass on the US ships anchored at Hiroshima. He was familiar with the American mentality thanks to his stay in the United States, and the occupying troops were very generous in helping the Spanish Jesuit, who was short of supplies for his community. Obtaining supplies for the community was always difficult, but one day a navy captain came to the house to see Arrupe. He was astounded by how little the priest and his young students had in the house, and he promised to send them a good supply of vitamins. A few days later, a car arrived, pulling a trailer full of large, carefully sealed boxes. The driver gave him a card that said: "I have bought the best vitamins there are in the world."

As they were unloading the boxes, one of the novices said, "Father Arrupe, these are rather original vitamins, are they not?" The boxes were actually filled with countless bottles of the best whiskey that there was on the market. Pedro realized immediately that he had a small fortune in front of him. Given the Japanese fondness for alcoholic drinks, that load of boxes would provide the means for the community to survive during the first postwar months. While this anecdote might appear to recount a trivial matter, it remained engraved in Arrupe's memory in the midst of those difficult days.[3]

The degree to which the imperial mentality changed after the war can be ascertained from a document addressed to the Japanese people by Emperor

---

3   *Memorias*, 232ff.

Hirohito and all his ministers on January 1, 1946. After offering an analysis of the long years of war, the document states:

> Above all, as a consequence of such a long war that has ended in defeat, our subjects frequently ask about where we go from here; they are tempted to be impatient and to become deeply discouraged. We are quite concerned that violent systems are becoming more widespread, that the sense of justice is growing weaker, and that disorder is increasing.
>
> Nevertheless, in such circumstances, I find myself alongside all of you, and my only desire is to share with you both your sorrows and your joys and to identify myself with the common interests.
>
> The link that exists between my person and all of you my subjects and that unites us always in mutual confidence and veneration is by no means a reality based only on myth or legend.
>
> However, the idea that the emperor is a god here on earth and the idea that the Japanese people are superior to other peoples and therefore destined to rule the world are conceptions that are based only on pure imagination.[4]

Burning Corpses

Several persons have given testimony about what life in the novitiate was like after the atomic blast. Tsuchiya, the young man who could not enter the Society of Jesus because he was drafted into the army, had an extraordinary encounter after the war ended: the chaplain of the US battleship *Missouri* knelt down before him and advised him: "You promised to become a Jesuit. Do so." Tsuchiya could not do so immediately, but after half a year he presented himself in Nagatsuka, and this was his experience:

> When I arrived in Nagatsuka, I could hardly contain my surprise. Three columns of the house had collapsed because of the bombing, and the roof was leaning. Under that roof, I could see about a hundred wounded people who were still being treated. The novitiate at that time was on the second floor, but the space had actually been turned over to some religious sisters whose house had been destroyed. Father Arrupe was in constant motion. Every day, he left on his bicycle to visit the city and provide medical attention for people who had suffered burns. Sometimes he went to talk with the Australian soldiers who were occupying the city, and he tried to get food and supplies from them.
>
> Everyone knows that Saint Ignatius recommended that Jesuit novices be subjected to a series of tests and trials. At this time, Arrupe organized one trial that was horrifying but unavoidable: every day, a pile of bodies was

---

4   *Yo viví la bomba atómica*, 229.

burned in the garden area. We had to chop wood and make a pyre to burn the corpses.

Little by little, things became more normal. We began to receive more food supplies. The sick people were moved to other places, and the chapel could be used again for church services. We were able to celebrate Christmas Mass there. I remember that Father Arrupe worked at a truly exhausting pace all that time. He hardly had time to sleep. Despite that, he directed the month-long Exercises of Saint Ignatius in their totality, without leaving out a thing.

The next year, sixteen novices entered, many of them coming straight from battle. After the war, there was a kind of spiritual rebirth, and Arrupe had confidence in them. Although not all shared that sentiment of his, I know very well that he trusted me.[5]

On April 16, 1947, Arrupe wrote a letter to his sister Mari, whom he always called "my professor" since it was she who had first taught him to read and write. After reflecting on the efficacy of prayer, he described his work in Nagatsuka:

My work now is tremendously consoling; as you know, these last five years I have been the master of novices here. During the war, we hardly had any novices, but this year there are ten, and two more have been admitted, so that I hope that within a few days we will have "the college of the twelve apostles" (after the resurrection, for I hope that there is no Judas). They are very solid vocations, almost all university graduates, with good qualities. Above all, they are completely determined to become good Jesuits. It is very consoling to live in this setting so different from the world that surrounds us. [...]

There are also many people coming here to make the Exercises. We constantly have people from all over Japan, who come to make a few days' retreat and to treat the *business* of their souls with Our Lord. They include not only Catholics but also non-believers who want to experience the religious ambience and to study the truths of our faith in depth. Above all, students come frequently from very different places, and I believe that all those who have come so far have afterward received baptism.

I send you a photo of our house (the red mark is my room). I also send you a photo taken inside the chapel so that you don't forget to recommend me in your prayers *every* day.

Otherwise, I am quite well. I am able to work as much as time permits. It is really almost impossible to thank the Lord enough for the missionary vocation. In these countries (especially now after the war, with the complete freedom of activity we enjoy), one feels a tangible need for the true faith, and

---

5   Testimony given by Yoshimasa Tsuchiya, S.J. to the author.

at the same time one appreciates the value of our faith and our love for Jesus Christ. We are now at a decisive moment for the church in Japan. Until now, patriotism and the cult of the emperor seemed to substitute for religion. […] Nowadays, the Japanese have realized that without religion there is no solution to the human problem. And that concerns them, […] and so they search, they search. Really, if we had more missionaries here, there would be countless conversions, but there are not enough of us, and the work is slow, despite the advantageous situation. Today, we understand well Saint Francis Xavier's desire to go to the universities in Europe to recruit people to come here to work. It seems to me that many scholars would gladly leave off their studies in order to use their great talents for the conversion of Japan.

In the end, we do not know what the Lord's plans are. The only thing we can do is not place obstacles in the way of his grace. Pray much to the Lord for me, […] for I have a job with much responsibility: the education of these young men and the founding of the Society of Jesus in Japan. If I were a Xavier or a [Joseph] Pignatelli, things would surely go better. But really, if it were not for the blind confidence we must place in Our Lord's power, which can work wonders with such crude instruments, I would certainly despair.[6]

As If All His Time Were for Me

Laypeople who were converted by Arrupe in those years describe him as a man for others. Mrs. Tanimoto, who was his cook, remembers the following:

He got to know me when they fired me from a munitions factory. I was already a Christian, and they fired me from the factory because I was accused of being a spy. I was weeping and he consoled me and offered me the job of cooking in Kure. I was afraid because at the time they were bombing there, and the place was dangerous. He told me: "Don't worry, the Lord will defend you." I had two children in Nagatsuka, so I ended up there with Father Arrupe, and I saw how hard he worked after the atomic bomb. He used to sleep just three hours a day. When he would come back from teaching catechism or from caring for the sick, with his pants all dirty with dust, the food would already be cold. I remember that a novice once came down with appendicitis, and Father Arrupe was going continually to attend to him. I feel a true veneration for that man.[7]

---

6   Letter to his sister María, whom he called his "professor" and who entered the congregation of the Slaves of the Sacred Heart.

7   Testimony given by Tanimoto to the author.

Lay collaborators of Arrupe during his time in Hiroshima. To his left, his secretary Simosako, who helped him translate the texts of Saint Ignatius into Japanese.

Mr. Hashimoto, who got to know Father Arrupe in 1943, recounts the following:

I was the head of the neighborhood youth groups, and I lived near the novitiate. I studied catechism with him. Whenever I saw him smile, my heart filled with joy. He communicated peace. At that time, I was a Buddhist, and we had many discussions about that. He used to receive me in a second-floor room where there was nobody else around—and it was as if all his time was for me. I remember that when Lent began I noticed something different in him, as if he grew thinner and transmitted more peace. Until that time, I had looked on him as a foreigner and felt a certain distrust, but from that moment on I felt a profound veneration for him. It was no doubt Arrupe's personality that moved me to become a convert to Christianity. Since my father died when I was very young, I can say that Arrupe was like a father to me. I even thought of a religious vocation at one point, but then I desisted. I loved Father Arrupe so much that when I decided to get married I took my fiancée to meet him so that he would know her and approve of her.[8]

---

8   Testimony given by Hashimoto to the author.

Another convert, Mr. Kato, comments:

I was interested in learning English, and since Father Arrupe spoke seven languages,[9] I went to see him. He taught me, and at the same time I attended catechism classes. However, I rebelled against the religion because at the time I was preparing to be a kamikaze and wanted to die for the country as a human bomb in a plane. I was practicing with gliders, and Arrupe used to tell me that only God is master of life. Then came the atomic bomb. I was only fifteen hundred meters from where it exploded, and all alone. That is when I went to Arrupe and asked to be baptized. Don't forget that during the war becoming a convert was something very difficult, like opening an iron door.[10]

Books in Japanese

Not content with all the work he was already doing, Pedro continued learning about the ways of Zen and took every opportunity to become more familiar with Japanese culture. At the same time, in those postwar years he began to translate several classics of spirituality into Japanese. In 1949, he published a biography of Xavier and an edition of his letters.[11] The following year, he published *Wakaki sedai ni atau* (Answers for young people), a collection of thirty-five letters addressed to young people, in which he attempted to respond to concerns they had expressed to him. The prologue invites the reader to "read it as if it were written to you personally." The topics treated include prayer, priesthood, matrimony, learning languages, Christ: man or God, faith in our life, vocation, communism and family, students and apostolate, love, and Protestantism. Still later, he published the first edition of his *Kirisutu no Yokogao* (Likeness of Christ)[12]

---

9   English, French, German, Japanese, Italian, Spanish, and a bit of Basque. Arrupe spoke these languages fairly well, though not perfectly or with linguistic brilliance. His liveliness gave him a great ability for communicating with everybody. He mastered English, German, and Japanese.

10   Testimony given by Kato to the author.

11   *Exterior and Interior Evolution of Xavier until He Became a Soldier and Apostle of Jesus Christ.* After recounting Xavier's life story, Arrupe explores his inner history on the basis of his letters, which he presents as a "mirror or his interior life." The letters expound Xavier's idea that, if the plans of Providence are great, then no less great is the suffering they require. The consolation provided by grace is also great. Desires, suffering, consolation: these three elements appear continually throughout the saint's life. Arrupe dwells on Xavier's supernatural interiority and crowns his portrait with themes that are summarized in the section titles: Union with Christ, Action-Contemplation, Life of Prayer, Obedience, Humility, Means, Catholicism, Love, Spiritual Director. "It seems to me that the third part especially is an autobiography of Arrupe himself," states Tomás Eceizabarrena, S.J., a missionary in Japan, quoted by Iglesias, "Aportaciones a su biografía interior," 999.

12   The aim of the work is to interest the reader in the person of Christ. In the prologue, Arrupe states: "Too much is said of the teaching of Jesus, but very little is said of him." Three chapters ("Humanity of Christ," "Virtues and Ideas," and "Divinity of Christ"), divided into twenty

and another curious work, called *The Truth about Communism*.[13] Given Arrupe's later thought and his dialogue with Marxism, this book is remarkable for its ferocious anticommunism, typical of the time. Shortly after that, he undertook an extensive commentary on the Exercises of Saint Ignatius.

By that time, according to Brother Miguel Aguirregomezcorta, Arrupe had taken up residence on the second floor of a *kura*, a type of fireproof concrete house in which the Japanese used to store rice and any valuables they had:

> The only way up to the room was by way of a ladder that was so steep you had to be very careful climbing it. Once Father Bruno Bitter, who was procurator of the Jesuit vice-province, went to Nagatsuka, and when he saw where Arrupe lived, he exclaimed: "There are still idealists in this world!"[14]

The same Brother Aguirregomezcorta asked Arrupe to teach him to drive so that he would not have to depend on others or use only the bicycle. Driving a car, though, was never Arrupe's forte. Several times a week, he nervously took the brother out to practice driving on the road between the house and the tiny playing field. The road was not at all suitable for such practice. On one occasion, Arrupe made a sharp turn that had the car on the point of rolling over. Aguirregomezcorta took advantage of the moment to make a subtle suggestion, which Arrupe understood instantly; he never again tried to emulate the famous racecar driver Juan Manuel Fangio.[15]

---

sections, develop aspects of Christ that seem to result more from Arrupe's contemplation than from academic study. Some of the section titles are: "A Look Overflowing with Love," "A Voice with Authority," "A Man with Affection," "Failure of Jesus Christ," "Realization of the Prophecy," "Eternal Man." See Iglesias, "Aportaciones a su biografía interior," 999.

13   The evolution of Arrupe's thought with regard to Marxism is interesting. For example, it is surprising that a man who was later accused of being "Marxist" by some of his enemies should have written a book in Japanese denouncing communism (*The Truth about Communism*). It is further proof of how Arrupe remained firm in what was essential but could also develop his ideas. This became quite clear later, when he was dealing with the relations between faith and justice and the need for dialogue with the modern world and concretely with Marxism. (It should be noted that when his earlier book was printed in Tokyo, the communists tried to burn down the press, according to Brother Aguirregomezcorta.)

In the library of the novitiate in Nagatsuka, I found the following books published in Japanese by Pedro Arrupe:

The Way of Christ (commentary on the Spiritual Exercises), 5 vols. (Tokyo, 1949–54).
The Dark Night of the Soul: Living Flame of Love (translations of the works of Saint John of the Cross) (Tokyo, 1954 [reprint]).
For You Young Folks (Tokyo, 1950).
Anthology of Saint Francis Xavier (Tokyo, 1949).
Behold This Man (Tokyo, 1952).
Letters of Saint Francis Xavier, 2 vols. (Tokyo, 1949).
Kirisuto no Yokogao [Likeness of Christ], re-edited in Japanese in 2004.

14   *Mis memorias*, handwritten journal of Brother Miguel Aguirregomezcorta, S.J., 6.30, 249.
15   *Mis memorias*, 6.23, 243

The translation work Arrupe did during this period gave him some of his most sustained contact with Japanese women. One of the secretaries who helped him with the task of editing his books was young Simosako; she was tall for a Japanese woman and from the first felt a great fascination for Arrupe.

Simosako had taken refuge in Nagatsuka after the explosion of the atomic bomb. She was Protestant, but as she got to know Arrupe, she experienced him as "a person who really has faith." Thanks to some kimonos that had been rescued from the fire, she had been able to support herself and to buy milk for her seriously injured sister. When the war was over, she began to teach in a girls' school. She relates:

> By then, Arrupe had already begun writing his book on the Spiritual Exercises. One day, he looked me in the eye and asked, "Would you help me?" When he looked at you that way, it was impossible to say no. I was then twenty-three years old. I knew I would have to leave my work at the school and that he could not afford to pay me a wage. But I knew he needed me, so I left everything to help him.
>
> But Arrupe would never get too close to me. He would hand me the pen from a distance. He went to extremes. I remember that on my birthday he asked me, "What do you want me to give you as a gift?" I told him I wanted to ride with him in his jeep. He answered that that could never be.
>
> At times, I thought he was treating me more as a man than as a woman, but at the same time I had never known a man as kind and attractive as Pedro Arrupe. He never got impatient if I was unable to write something. He was very understanding.
>
> Later on, I had to get psychiatric treatment, and I kept a letter from Arrupe that is the best portrait of myself there is. I can truly say that Arrupe is the person I most love in all the world. Three years ago, I went to visit him in Rome, when he was old and sick. At that time, he did look me in the eyes, and he even kissed my hand. He who had always been shy of me as a woman accepted my gifts: a calendar for his table and a *yukata*. At the time, I could not utter a word. I just looked at him. From the first, I knew that I would have to separate myself from him, that what I was feeling within me was impossible.
>
> How to describe Arrupe in those days? With just two words: he was a man of God. Hidden behind the severe appearance as the master of novices was an ardent human being. One had to speak with him only briefly to perceive his great heart. I was very satisfied working with him, but I was not happy. Arrupe knew that I was of a weak constitution and would never marry. I considered that the greatest grace of my life was helping him. I got to know him well. For example, there was something childlike in his personality; he had a certain childish naiveté that made him unaware of many things. I have suffered much. The Society of Jesus helped me when I went to

Tokyo, and there I got psychiatric treatment. Now I am in this hospital with anemia, and they have told me I need a year of repose. I consider myself a disciple of Arrupe. I am like a novice of Father Arrupe who did not get past the first year. The only thing I desire is to die working for the church.[16]

The evidence clearly indicates that this woman, whom the novices called "highest princess" because of her height and in reference to the office of the Blessed Virgin, was deeply in love with Arrupe, who no doubt realized it. This would explain his severe attitude in relating to her; he obviously wanted to dodge her insinuations. Simosako sadly took her own life twenty years after giving these declarations.

Many years later, when he was provincial superior, Arrupe would joke with the Western youths who came to Japan as missionaries, saying: "Be careful with the Japanese women! They are like serpents! They sneak up on you without your being aware of them."

But Simosako was not the only secretary that Arrupe had. A woman named Sakata also helped him from 1950 on, typing up what Arrupe recorded on tape about the life and the letters of Xavier. She recounts:

Before, when I was working in the kitchen, I was impressed by a saying he used to cite from Saint Teresa: "God walks among the pots and pans." He was very kind with everybody and very austere with himself. I was impressed by the fact that he was living in that upstairs room in the inhospitable storage house, in order to make space for others.[17]

---

16   Declarations made to the author. I met Simosako in a hospital for railway workers in Hiroshima when she was already elderly. She was one of those who showed the most enthusiasm when I asked her to speak to me of Arrupe. "I would spend hours talking about him," she assured me as she spoke to me by telephone from her hospital bed. She had white hair and a sweet countenance, and her tall thin body could hardly fit in the bed. A witness to these declarations was the Spanish Jesuit Cristóbal M. Barrionuevo, who served as my interpreter on this occasion and on others as well. Juan Catret, S.J., assistant novice master who had lived with Arrupe in Nagatsuka, told me the following about Simosako: "Yes, Simosako was in love with Father Arrupe, and he knew it. For that reason, he kept his distance and used to speak of Japanese women as subtle serpents." During his final illness in Rome, Arrupe did not usually keep the gifts he received, but rather gave them away to others. Curiously, though, he kept the gifts Simosako gave him and actually used them. I learned from Father Barrionuevo that this lovely Japanese woman committed suicide twenty years after her last meeting with Arrupe; she had been suffering from various psychological problems since her youth.

17   Declarations made by Sakata to the author.

"Where You Never Are"

On November 15, 1949, in a letter to his niece, María Victoria Gondra, Arrupe described his experiences and contacts with young people. Among other things, he wrote:

> Here in Japan we are in an extremely important period. Since the war, there has been a complete change, and enormous new fields have opened up to the apostolate. Losing the war caused much disorientation in people's thinking; all the old ideals that provided spiritual strength to this great people have collapsed. Today, the young people are desirous of knowing the truth. [...] Among the young people of your age, there is also much confusion, since they are experiencing many changes in their ways of thinking and acting, as well as in many aspects of their individual, family, and social lives. As you know, until now Japanese women have not been fully recognized; they were considered to be *second class*. This way of thinking has now changed completely so that women can have completely equality of rights with men. This is certainly an excellent thing though it can be dangerous, especially in a country that is not prepared for such rapid and radical changes.
>
> Right now, because of my work as master of novices, I have very little occasion to work with young people your age. Before, when I was in charge of the church in Yamaguchi, and after that, when I was directing a young people's association in Hiroshima, I was able to appreciate the wonderful qualities of the young Japanese, as well as the excellent education provided by the Japanese spirit and ambience. Now there are some young women who help me with the translation of books into Japanese. They are all Catholics who work with fervor and enthusiasm, and thanks to their help I have been able to publish four books in the last year. If they had not helped me, the task could never have got done.[18]

From Nagatsuka on February 18, 1950, Arrupe wrote another letter to the same niece, in which he thanked his relatives for the help they had given him and described some aspects of Japanese customs and language. On the topic of translation, he wrote:

> As I think I told you the other day, I am writing a few books, and several people are helping me with the task. Among them are four young women who do splendid work. They are truly zealous and desirous of sharing with others the faith they have received. They work so hard that I always have to be forbidding them to stay too late. One of them—of course without my knowing it—went three days without eating anything at breakfast or lunch

---

18 Letter to María Victoria Gondra, November 15, 1949, Gondra–Barandiarán family archive.

in order to be able to finish the work as soon as possible. Then I found out, and I made it clear to her that she shouldn't do that.[19]

Another of Arrupe's collaborators in the numerous translations was a Japanese professor who was suffering from cancer. Arrupe, with his sharp clinical eye, recognized his condition and gradually prepared him for death while he was translating the work of John of the Cross. When his final moment was drawing near, this Japanese intellectual asked Arrupe to read him the *Spiritual Canticle*. He died in peace and with a smile while savoring the immortal poem of the Castilian mystic.[20]

Even though Arrupe's words were direct and explicit, in keeping with his Basque character, there is no doubt that his sensibility was finely attuned to the aesthetic aspects of spirituality, above all through music.

Once he was approached by Kazuo Nakayama, a young man of eighteen who played the piano marvelously. Nakayama was burdened with a mild but persistent sense of shame and by unhappiness that arose from family problems. At the time, Arrupe was organizing one of his concerts, in which he planned to sing two songs, one Japanese—Yamada's *Flower of the Field*—and another German—Franz Schubert's *The Pilgrim*. Looking for someone to accompany him, he remembered his friend Nakayama, who gladly accepted. The two of them agreed to get together to rehearse at six the next evening.

Arrupe saw that Nakayama's agile fingers flew deftly over the keys and that he could play those songs to perfection, even though they were new to him and he had no score. Arrupe always sang well, and his novices were quite aware of the delight he took in singing the *zortzikos* of his native land. In that rehearsal, though, he made a special effort to sing with all his soul, because he had become aware of the musical sensibility of the young pianist. At the end of the rehearsal, both were enthusiastic.

"Father Arrupe," said Nakayama, "would you do me the favor of translating the words for me? I would like to learn the song."

Arrupe sat down next to Nakayama with pencil and paper and began to translate Schubert's *Der Wanderer* from the German:

> *I come down from the mountain*
> *to the mists of the valley.*
> *And while the sea roars,*
> *I go wandering in silence,*
> *seeking joy amid my longings.*
> *Where, oh where are you,*
> *land of the bliss I desire?*

---

19   Letter to María Victoria Gondra, February 18, 1949, Gondra–Barandiarán family archive.
20   Declarations made by Father Arrupe to the author.

How cold the sun is here!
How dry the wilted flowers!
How empty and hollow the words!
How spent the life!
Where, oh where are you,
land of the bliss I desire?

I seek you amid sighs,
land where I left my hopes,
where my roses bloom in your light,
where my friends wander through the hills;
land where my dead will find new life,
where all will speak my tongue.
Where, o where are you,
land of my soul?

And as a fleeting breath of spirit
I hear these words in silence:
"The impalpable joy of your longings
is where you never are!"

After Pedro finished translating the song into Japanese, he passed it to Nakayama, who had been reading it as Pedro was writing. The young man read the words of the song once again and then said with a sad smile, "Why does the same thing happen to all of us?"

"What is it that happens to all of us?" asked Arrupe.

"We go in search of happiness, and it is never where we are. '*The impalpable joy of your longings is where you never are!*'"

Arrupe noticed that Nakayama responded keenly to beautiful art, so he practiced with him another sad song, this one Japanese. The words were as follows:

Beautiful rose of the field,
rose of Ezo.
Without anybody knowing it,
you flourish in splendor.
How gorgeous your colors,
rose of Ezo!

Forest rose,
you still grow in the new air
that God has made for you,
and in your flower, which your stem lifts high,
I divine the love that made you beautiful.

Arrupe sang the song again, putting all the emotional force and richness of meaning that he could into his interpretation of *Flower of the Field*. After a few minutes, he noticed two tears running down the cheeks of the young Nakayama, who was seated at the piano. Arrupe knew then that his young friend had found God in the music. Indeed, it was not long before he asked to be baptized.[21]

Look at the Person, and Then Preach

Not content with all these activities, the tireless Arrupe decided that he should be making use of his medical knowledge and getting to know Japanese doctors. In 1947, at the invitation of Father Kopp, pastor of the parish in the city of Okayama, Arrupe began traveling to that city once a week to give talks in the parish. In those days before high-speed trains were even dreamed of, the train ride lasted four hours each way. In the meetings at the parish, he became friends with a medical student named Egusa, who recalls:

> He met with us from five o'clock to seven, and then he caught the train and spent another four hours returning to Hiroshima. I went with him in the train halfway. I couldn't sit down because the train was usually crowded, but for me it was worthwhile since that way I could spend an hour more with Father Arrupe. We were a rather difficult group of intellectuals, and that was why Father Kopp asked Arrupe to speak to us. He was quite well informed about our culture and the ways of Zen, and he was able to sit on the tatami better than we Japanese. Since he had studied medicine, those of us who were medical students felt especially close to Arrupe, but what impressed me most about him was his knowledge of our Japanese identity. Today, there is much talk of inculturation, but in those days to see a foreigner behave as he did was something new. To teach Johnny you have to know Johnny. There is a Buddhist principle that goes: "Look at the person, then preach."
>
> In Arrupe, we saw above all a person, and that drew us to conversion. But it was not easy, because for our generation Christianity was not something Japanese. In him, though, we saw the profound, serene look of someone for whom life had meaning. For me, Christianity has meant making an important option: as a doctor, I have dedicated myself exclusively to handicapped people since I realize that in this country there is a tendency to hide or to dismiss with a smile persons who are physically or mentally challenged. After my conversion, my mother and my two brothers also embraced the Christian faith, and I married a Catholic girl. We Asians do not act out of logic. When we see someone who really lives something, we feel drawn to that person, and only afterward do we ask why. I hadn't read any biography of a saint, but for two years I was watching Arrupe, and I saw that Arrupe

---

21   *Yo viví la bomba atómica*, 293ff.

The same Simosako visiting the general of the Society when he was sick in Rome. "I have not met a man as lovable and attractive as Arrupe," she said. Suffering from a psychological disorder, she took her own life.

lived out in his own life all that he taught others. He also had a great sensitivity and receptivity for understanding our Japanese culture. It was no wonder that twenty of us young doctors used to meet with him weekly.[22]

Reading the first volume of Arrupe's *Commentary on the Spiritual Exercises of Saint Ignatius*, which he at the time was dictating to Simosako, we appreciate the importance he gave to the Ignatian *magis*, which was also a hallmark of the life of Xavier. It was a "more" that allowed no half-measures:

> When we go along a road, we can move either quickly or slowly; we can run or also, once in a while, stop to rest. But anyone who seeks always and in every way to attain *the magis* does not consider first this means and then another, but decides to choose always, as the only way, what is most conducive to the end. [...] If there are a variety of means, a person will always have to consider and judge that which is the best. [...] He will have to choose the best means. [...] This is the new method that Saint Ignatius teaches us.

For Arrupe, this method was best understood as simply fulfilling the will of God:

> What made Saint Ignatius a saint was not his abandoning an ordinary way of life, or his plunging himself into a pool of cold water to save a sinner, or his letting his hair and nails grow for a long time, or his dressing poorly, or his doing great penances. Sanctity is attained not by difficult means but by

---

22   Declarations made by Dr. Egusa to the author. I am grateful to Dr. Egusa for the special trip he made to Tokyo to speak with me about Arrupe; he spoke of him with great admiration and conviction. I am also grateful for the valuable assistance of Spanish Jesuit Juan Masiá as translator. Father Masiá at present is meeting regularly with the Catholic doctors.

always seeking God's will and seeing what is the best way to put it into practice. This is comprehensible to human reason and a natural way for it. This
is the surest way to reach the state of "being perfect as your Father is perfect."
[…] This is the way, and there is no other!

There is nothing more important than fulfilling the will of God. Sleeping in God is no less meritorious than praying. On the other hand, whatever is done against God's will, as good as the work may appear to human
eyes, diminishes God's glory. For that reason, constantly seeking God's will,
instead of causing us anxiety, will always bring us great peace. […] The
problem is knowing how always to choose the *magis*. […] Choosing *what is
more conducive* does not mean that a person has to be constantly examining
himself and continually stirring up his fervor. That would make life impossible and therefore would never be God's will.[23]

This was no doubt the same radical spirit of commitment that was moving
Arrupe in Hiroshima and that motivated him during his years of formation.
Iglesias, a specialist in spirituality who later worked closely with Arrupe, believes
that Arrupe had by that time already made a special vow of perfection, such as
that practiced by some saints—he alludes to such a vow in his commentary on
the Exercises.[24]

Arrupe's pastoral work continued in this vein, with only minor changes.
In 1949, for example, when Father George Marin was named tertian instructor,
Arrupe moved to the lower house at Nagatsuka and adopted a completely Japanese lifestyle. At the same time, the students of humanities and philosophy were
transferred to Tokyo. Events followed a fairly normal course until 1950, when
Arrupe was elected to represent the Japanese vice-province at the congregation
of procurators, a periodic evaluation meeting in Rome that draws Jesuits from all
over the world. In June, he traveled to Bonn, and in July he met with the superior
general of the Society to give him a report on the situation in Japan.

The general gave him permission to make his first trip around the world in
order to give conferences about his experience in Japan and to raise funds for the

---

23   Pedro Arrupe, *Kirisutu no michi* [The way of Christ], vol. 1, *Principle and Foundation*,
      199–210, cited by Iglesias, "Aportaciones a su biografía interior," 1001–1.

24   In the tradition of Catholic spirituality, the *vow of the most perfect*, as practiced by some
      saints, consists in making a voluntary commitment, out of love of God, to do what one
      believes to be best and most pleasing to God in the present concrete situation. Perfection
      consists principally in charity; concretely, the most perfect act here and now is that which
      the Holy Spirit inspires in the freedom of a person. The more united one is to God by grace
      and charity, the more capable one is of keeping such a vow, the objective of which is to rid
      oneself progressively of self-love, to advance toward greater freedom to love, and to make a
      complete donation of self. By interpreting later texts where Arrupe mentions the vow, Igle-
      sias concludes that Arrupe made the vow as a concretization of the Ignatian *magis* in some
      moment of his formation. See Iglesias, "Aportaciones a su biografía interior," 975ff.

mission. During fourteen months, Arrupe spoke to audiences in America and Europe about how he had experienced the atomic bomb and how the Gospel was being preached on the farthest frontiers. It was clear that the Jesuit general had confidence in him, because he represented Japan again at the procurators' congregation in 1953.

The pace of events picked up when Arrupe was assigned to Tokyo to be temporary substitute for Father Paul Pfister, superior of the vice-province—Japan at the time was not a full-fledged province, but a dependent mission. Pfister had had to travel to Rome to report on a Jesuit who had been detained for supposed misappropriation of funds. Subsequently, Pfister was obliged to go to Switzerland in order to rest.[25]

On March 13, 1954, Pedro wrote to his family:

My dear sisters and little nephew:

Here you have me, all of sudden thrust into a great confusion, but of a most solemn sort! What a change: from the peaceful solitude of the novitiate to this racket of the big city! To make matters worse, since we are going through a difficult situation, I have had a lot of problems to deal with. So I earnestly ask for your prayers.

I have been here since the end of January. Father Provincial became extremely weak during these last months because of the difficulty of the situation, and he was sent to Europe to recuperate. We do not know when he will return.

Everything you can do for the Japanese Missionary Society, that is, for Japan, will be little enough. As I told you, we are passing through difficult times, such as cannot be explained in a letter. We need a lot of prayers.[26]

The letter ends with affectionate allusions to different family members and a curious code word: "I would love to know how much Cata has gotten for each pair of *little balls*." The *little balls* were actually cultivated Japanese pearls, at the time highly valued in Europe. Arrupe was sending them, with no scruples at all, to his sister Catalina as *pious contraband* to obtain funds for an impoverished postwar Japan. On one occasion, he gave a religious sister a box of "caramels" for his family. After passing through customs at the Barajas airport in Madrid and realizing what was in the box, the sister became quite frightened, for the *little balls* in the box were made of something very different from caramel.[27]

As the letter indicates, the Japanese Jesuits were going through some difficult moments. On March 22, 1954, nine days after writing the letter, Arrupe was

25 Information provided by Paul Pfister, S.J., former provincial of Japan and author of the *History of the Society of Jesus in Japan*, published in Japanese.

26 Letter to several members of his family, Gondra–Barandiarán family archive.

27 Testimony of María Luz de la Vega, Spanish collaborator of Pedro Arrupe.

named superior of the Jesuits in Japan: he now had the post of greatest responsi-bility in the vice-province. Thus began Arrupe's *explosion* in governing posts, the first explosive wave on the spiritual plane after his Hiroshima experience. "A new world is beginning to arise," he wrote after the atomic blast, and he found himself having to *row* hard in the very center of the windstorm.

13. Leader of a World in Miniature

The last pigeons of the afternoon were flying among Bernini's robust columns and splashing in the water of the fountains in Saint Peter's Square. On the third floor of a Vatican palace, the pope, with his mystically aristocratic bearing, had just handed a document to the cardinal secretary of state, after carefully signing it with his golden pen. The whole world still had a vivid image of him stretching out his arms in the midst of the ruins of the Second World War.

Directing a penetrating look through the rounded glasses that were perched on his narrow aquiline nose, Pius XII called out: "Have the provincial of the Jesuits of Japan come in."

"Immediately, your Holiness."

"It is an important matter. I was quite impressed by the report we read about the church in Japan. Since the end of the war, we have not had such a propitious moment in the Far East."

The pope had indeed been informed about the change in the emperor's attitude. Hirohito had not only renounced his divine pretensions but on August 15, 1949 the imperial family for the first time in history had attended a Catholic religious service, the pontifical Mass celebrated in Osaka by the pope's legate, Cardinal Norman Gilroy, on the occasion of the fourth centenary of Xavier's arrival in Japan. On that occasion, Prince Takamatsu, the emperor's brother, had cited Xavier as a symbol of reconciliation after the war:

> We Japanese are now firmly determined to follow the footsteps of Saint Francis Xavier. Our nation, with profound feelings of sincere repentance after this terrible war, feels strongly that it should not ally itself with any side in any future war. We therefore ask God to help us in this endeavor of ours.

Conscious of the moment's importance, Pius XII had just addressed a handwritten letter to the superior of the Jesuit mission in Japan. In it, he declared himself "extremely satisfied" after reading the provincial's report on the situation in Japan. And he added: "We are confident that the Society of Jesus, embedded in the Japanese mission since its very beginning, will know how to manage the present situation, which is 'unique in history,' in keeping with its traditional commitment to the defense and the growth of God's kingdom on earth."

He continued:

> Your plan for developing the Catholic University of Tokyo and assuming responsibility for the seminary of that city are incontrovertible proofs that our confidence rests upon a firm rock. [...] With paternal interest, we have watched how the city of Hiroshima has risen from its sad ruins, even though

the labor of reconstruction has often been hampered by the irresistible forces of nature.[1]

Pius XII ended his letter by encouraging the work of the Jesuits and blessing the provincial and the other members of the mission. On Easter Sunday, April 13, 1952, the pope, through the transmitters of Vatican Radio, directly addressed the Japanese people for the first time in history: "For a long time, we have desired to manifest and declare to you the profound and sincere feeling of love that we experience for you."

On November 1 of that same year, seven years after Hiroshima, the first H-bomb burst onto the world scene. This new invention, with a thousand times more destructive power than the atomic bomb, was successfully tested in the Pacific Ocean. The explosion made an entire island disappear and created a crater two kilometers in diameter. The great powers were now engaged in a new style of confrontation: the Cold War.

Learn the Rules of Baseball

It was in this setting that Arrupe took over the reins of the Society of Jesus in Japan on March 22, 1954. His task was not at all easy. That mission had originally depended directly on the general of the Jesuits, but in 1921 it became a mission entrusted to the Jesuit province of Lower Germany. Subsequently, the Spanish provinces of Andalusia and Toledo also collaborated by sending men to help out in the mission.

When Arrupe arrived in Japan, most of the Jesuits there were German, but the mission gradually become more internationalized, so that his task as provincial was like governing a miniature world of many nations. In 1948, the Jesuit students studying Japanese in the language school numbered twenty-four, and they came from twenty-two different provinces around the world. Both Pius XII and the Jesuit general, Jean-Baptiste Janssens, were personally interested in the future of that small but fascinating country.

Many of the young Jesuits who arrived with great enthusiasm were surprised when they asked the new provincial how they could be effective missionaries in Japan, especially among the young. Arrupe used to answer them, "Learn the rules of baseball!" The American sport had been introduced to Japan even before the war, and it became immensely popular from that point on. Arrupe's reply was a clear indication that his being made provincial had not changed his basic character.[2]

---

1   See the complete texts in the documents cited in *Yo viví la bomba atómica*, 25ff.
2   Robert T. Rush, "Pedro Arrupe, misionero: Un corazón tan grande como el mundo," in Alcalá et al., *Pedro Arrupe*, 43–65, here 47.

Consecrating the province to the Heart of Jesus on July 25,[3] Arrupe was aware that, given the calamitous situation in postwar Japan, his most urgent task was raising funds to establish works that would exercise intellectual influence, since these were thought to be most effective for apostolic work in Japan. Such works, however, required large expenditures.

Years later, Arrupe would describe the crucial moment when he was named provincial:

> It was on the feast of Saint Francis Xavier in 1954 when the preceding superior phoned me and asked me to go as soon as possible to Tokyo to take his place. I had not yet received Father General's letter naming me provincial, but he [Father Pfister] was experiencing great difficulties and could not continue: there were calumnies, accusations of being a spy [...]. We had problems with the police, with the press [...] It was a distressing time![4]

"You Have All Eternity to Rest!"

After resolving the most urgent problems, Arrupe undertook a second trip around the world on November 16, 1954. He left Father Karl Reiff as his substitute and spent almost a year traveling, returning on October 16, 1955. He flew

---

3   See García, *El padre Arrupe en Japón*, 89–90. Among other things, this consecration of the Japan mission to the Sacred Heart states: "O Eternal King and Universal Lord! You who chose the weak things of the world to confound the strong, here you have the weakest of missionaries trying to conquer for you this part of the world so difficult that it made even Xavier's hair grow gray." The text calls on the Virgin Mary, Saint Joseph, Saint Ignatius, Xavier, and the martyrs of Japan to insure that, "even when we disappear completely, this mission will be the irrefutable proof of the reality and efficacy of your promises" (also in Garcia, *Orar con el padre Arrupe*, 27–28).

Another text from this period, part of a commentary on the litany to the Sacred Heart written in Hiroshima (1954), reveals Arrupe's fervent spirit of confidence in God:

> Lord, I want to live in your house for endless time. Teach me where your house is. Lord, once I am in your house with you, place me with your Father. The Lord's house is a "house of prayer"; therefore, when I have entered into prayer I feel my heart wounded by the beauty of your Heart, which is the "house of the Lord." I thank you, Lord, for this boundless favor: "The people are nourished by the substance of your house." Therefore, until whatever hour, without a moment of rest, show me your beauty. "Day and night your eyes are upon this temple, upon the place where you wanted your oracle to reside." Scorched thus by the fire of your Heart, I can penetrate into the beauty of the Lord and also show others the riches of that Heart. The passion for your house will consume me. Therefore, without ever leaving your house, "I will dwell in the house of the Lord for years without end." *Cor Iesu, domus Dei et porta coeli, miserere nobis* [Heart of Jesus, house of God, and gate of heaven, have mercy on us].

In Garcia, *Orar con el padre Arrupe*, 29–30.

4   *Itinéraire*, 28.

to San Francisco by way of Manila, and he spoke to the provincial there about founding a college in Hiroshima. He then went to Spain, Italy, France, Germany, and other European countries. Finally, he returned to the United States and visited several countries in Latin America.

During his travels, Arrupe was generally received with much interest and sympathy. He gave spirited conferences and talks that were full of anecdotes, enthusiasm, and humor. As always, he drew on his profound humanism and his charismatic Gospel spirit to explain the challenges presented by Japanese reality. His audiences listened spellbound to his accounts of the atomic bomb, still a fairly recent event.

Arrupe did not arrive unannounced in the countries he visited. He relied on two young Spanish women who helped him prepare the ground and arrange for the meetings. They were María Luz de la Vega and Concha Traver. María Luz has vivid memories of their time together:

> He had an irresistible appeal. He knew clearly what he wanted. I accompanied him on his 1955 journey, and he told me simply: "We must travel around the whole world." He laid down for me three conditions for the trip: that I stay in convents, generally of the Sisters of the Sacred Heart; that I request a diplomatic passport of the Spanish foreign minister, then Martín Artajo, in order to be able to move around more easily; and that I find a companion who knew English. After nine months of traveling, I told him, "Father Arrupe, I'm exhausted." And he answered me with a smile: "You have all eternity to rest!" Later, in 1957, I spent three months in Japan. There I saw firsthand that the needs were truly pressing. As a result of the postwar situation, the Jesuits in Japan did not even have enough to eat. To help him in raising funds, Father Arrupe had obtained a letter from Pius XII, in which the pope made a plea for assistance, above all for the university.[5] For this reason, the leaders of the anti-communist parties sometimes met with Arrupe and seemed to support him, but afterward they did not give him a cent. Batista, for example, did not even receive him. Arrupe was not concerned about how many people were in the audience. He gave the same importance to a conference in the Hilton that was overflowing with influential people as to a small meeting in the nunciature, such as the one where he spoke with only four people. As usual, he hardly took time out to sleep or rest.

> I remember that once in Santo Domingo we had difficulties. I had advised Father López there to prepare the necessary papers for us, and he responded assuring me, "Tomorrow Trujillo will receive us." However, an incredible rumor was making the rounds. In Caracas, they went so far as

---

5   The letter "To Our Beloved Son Pedro Arrupe, Superior of the Vice-province of the Society of Jesus in Japan," was signed by Pius XII and dated January 17, 1955. It praises the work done by the Jesuits and supports the projected expansion of the university.

After being named superior of the vice-province of Japan, Arrupe moved to Tokyo. He was the third to hold the post, serving from 1954 to 1958.

to take away our passports, and Father Arrupe was accused of trafficking in prostitutes! After a while, things were cleared up. They had confused him with some German guy who owned houses of prostitution and had connections with a North American outfit that was then promoting abortion in Japan. Despite all this, Father Arrupe did not lose his calm. I remember how affected he was by the film we were showing about Hiroshima. Once while we were watching it, he broke down; he had somehow lost the defenses he had previously built up in order to experience that with such fortitude.

We did all sorts of things to raise funds. For the sake of the mission, I was selling shawls from Manila, dolls, and gypsy outfits. What was really most important, though, was the establishment of centers to support Japan; these were set up in Chicago, New York, Havana, Santo Domingo, Colombia (Cali and Medellín), and Lima. The benefit from these centers came from the very favorable rate of exchange of dollars into yen. Arrupe also went to the cloistered convents to ask for "spiritual assistance."

One detail especially shows the kind of person he was. In 1955, we were in Havana. On our way back from a conference, he was going into the house that the Society has in the Cuban capital. In front of the doorway, he found a drunken man sprawled on the steps; he was a tall fellow and was blocking the passage. Arrupe bent over and with great respect and delicacy asked his permission to pass. He helped the fellow get up from the ground and treated him with extraordinary tenderness.[6]

---

6   Testimony of María Luz de la Vega. Through her recollections, her personal friendship with Arrupe's family, and her youthful enthusiasm, María Luz has been a great help in gathering much information for this biography.

María Luz was completely committed to the cause, to the point of making her apartment in Madrid a sort of museum and shop for Japanese items. She continues her story:

> There are a thousand anecdotes to tell about Father Arrupe. Perhaps what most impressed me was that his supernatural spirit was not at all in conflict with his great human sensibility. I remember once that a Jesuit had to make a long-distance phone call to Japan, to consult him about some matter. The priest was very excited and began to recite pious ejaculations, but Arrupe cut him short saying, "Get to the point, man, because this call is expensive!"

Conferences of a Friend

Further information about Arrupe's journeys comes from the Colombian Eduardo Briceño, who would later work with Arrupe in Rome:

> I got to know him personally in 1954. [...] I was in Berchmans College in Cali, where I had been assigned a few months previously as rector. Father Arrupe arrived there and stayed about a month. He was full of energy. He had turned forty-six the previous November and wanted to use all the strength he had to do the work the Lord had entrusted to him: promoting the province of Japan, of which he was superior and which, like the whole of that country, had been left devastated after the Second World War. He was idealistic and completely convinced of what he was doing. He felt fully responsible for the challenge that history was presenting to him and the church: Japan was at a crucial juncture. [...]
>
> I have a vivid memory of the impression Father Arrupe made on me from the first moment, an impression that became stronger over the years, until today, thirty years later. He was a visionary, a prophet, an apostle, a mixture of Paul, Xavier, and Ignatius. He was a man deeply convinced of his mission, and he felt viscerally obliged to carry it out without sparing a moment of his own life. Paul's "Woe is me, if I do not preach the Gospel" was something he could repeat with complete authenticity.
>
> He had a resolute faith, and he stood fast on that. That faith impelled him and gave him strength to work without rest. I remember that once we had announced that he was to give a conference in the departmental library. We went there, but only ten or twelve persons showed up. I approached him and said that, if he liked, I could tell the people that because of the small number the conference would be postponed to another occasion. "No," he told me, "these people have come to hear me, and I should oblige them. The Lord will take care of the results." Gradually, more people arrived, and the conference really was quite successful.

Arrupe at Sophia University, where he opened a department of Spanish and faculties of law, physics, and engineering.

His spirit of prayer impressed me especially. Busy as he was with meetings and conferences, he used to arrive back at the college quite late at night. He would go to the dining room and have a glass of milk and a banana that we left for him in the refrigerator, and then he would go to his room. The next day, his light was unfailingly on at four in the morning. "When does this man rest?" I was asking myself. I did not know that from the time of his medical studies in Madrid he had developed the habit of sleeping only four hours. In that way, he had time for everything and especially for prayer, because every day he spent long hours in intimate dialogue with the Lord.

We might suppose that a man engaged in so much activity would have a forceful character and would always move about quickly. But it was quite the contrary with Arrupe. In dealing with people, he was kind, simple, friendly. He never imposed his opinion forcibly. In Cali, Medellín, Lima, Buenos Aires, Havana, Mexico, wherever he stopped on his endless journeys as provincial of Japan, he left behind countless friends who were captivated by his sincere and kindly manner. He showed concern for them and their families. He remembered names with incredible precision, and he stayed in touch with them with great affection.

In this way, the Japan Aid Office was born. There a group of efficient collaborators was able to organize a network of friends who helped make possible the great apostolic projects that Arrupe carried out in that distant province. He was admirable in his attention to detail with each of his friends. With regard to myself, I can say that from the year 1954 until he was elected general I always received from the provincial of Japan a handwritten note of greetings on the feast of Saint Edward. And my case was not exceptional—it was normal with all those whom he considered his benefactors.[7]

In 1955, Arrupe returned to Cali and spent another month there. The situation now was different, because he already knew the territory and the group he had organized had prepared for him a series of activities that kept him constantly busy.

Arrupe himself recalled those journeys in later years, and in one testimony among many he speaks of the impact those apostolic trips had on him:

I began the trips in 1949–50, before becoming provincial. In the first trip, I went one and a half times around the world. After that, there were trips in 1954, 1957, 1961, each of six months' duration. I had more than a thousand opportunities to speak to people about Hiroshima and Japan.

---

7   Letter written by Eduardo Briceño, S.J. to the author (August 30, 1968), and memories published by him in *Noticias de Colombia*, an internal bulletin. Dating also from those days, August 1954, is a letter written to Brother García Torres, who was studying philosophy in Madrid. In the letter, Arrupe discusses devotion to the Heart of Jesus from the Japanese perspective. Perhaps the most original part of the letter is the "idea of the master":

A great force has been exercised in Japan since ancient times by the idea of the master and the idea of the living Way that embodies a doctrine or an ideology. More than the doctrine in itself, the personality of the master who teaches the doctrine is what effectively influences the Japanese. Accordingly, more than any philosophical or theological doctrine, the truth incarnated in the *Magister bonus* has for them the most extraordinary attractiveness.

Cf. "Carta inédita del padre Arrupe sobre el Sagrado Corazón," "III Centenario del *Munus suavissimum*," Secretariado Reina del Cielo, Madrid, 1988.

On the great majority of occasions, I encountered great understanding and generosity, but I also had some curious experiences. In one country that I will leave unnamed, a very wealthy woman of the aristocracy invited me to go to her house after the conference. There, in the presence of friends and journalists, she rather solemnly gave me an envelope. On the way home, I opened it with a certain impatience and found that it contained only a few dollars, but the next morning a prominent photograph of this generous gesture appeared in the newspaper![8]

To help maintain the worldwide network of friends created in the course of Arrupe's journeys, the Society in Japan founded the Jesus Kai Center, an organization that even today carries on personalized correspondence with thousands of people who contribute to the mission in Japan.

One of Arrupe's most immediately useful achievements came from his meeting in Madrid with the minister of foreign affairs, Fernando María Castiella. Arrupe requested Spanish citizenship for seven Hungarian Jesuits who had no passports since they had fled from their country. The Jesuits Béky, Albert Bihari, Horváth, Litvanyi, Edmund Nemes, Peter Nemeshegyi, and a man who later left the Society thus became Spaniards.

In the Place of the Other

The year 1956 marked the fourth centenary of Saint Ignatius's death, and it was celebrated in Japan with an ordination to the priesthood and the creation of a theology faculty. Present on this occasion was Paolo Dezza, an influential Italian Jesuit who would later have a very direct connection with Arrupe. Dezza came to Tokyo empowered by the Vatican to integrate the ecclesiatical faculty into Sophia University, which was run by the Jesuits. He was a man who would intervene several times in Arrupe's later life at the request of the Vatican.[9]

The more or less serious mishaps that distress most people hardly ever bothered Arrupe, who continued his work tirelessly. In 1958, when Hiroshima became a diocese and Japan became an autonomous Jesuit province with Arrupe as superior, his activities only multiplied. He helped to open a college and a school of music in Hiroshima. He created the Saint Francis Xavier Educational Foundation to sponsor student residences in Nikko, Komaba, and Kobe. He strengthened social work projects such as Christmas Villa and the settlement project in Tokyo, where he had had his first direct contact with ordinary Japanese life. He expanded Sophia University, tripling the number of students and opening

---

8   *Itinéraire*, 29.

9   This a curious precedent since in the course of time the elderly Dezza, an intelligent Jesuit of a conservative bent, would be a confessor to two popes, including Paul VI. He would eventually be designated the "papal delegate" of John Paul II for the Society (see chapters 17 and 19).

new faculties of law, physics, and engineering; he also set up there a Spanish department and developed one of the largest language laboratories in the world. He contributed to the construction of a new church dedicated to Saint Francis Xavier in the Yamaguchi parish where he had first labored. He also helped build a church in Kobe and chapels in the mission posts of Bofu, Tokuyama, Matsue, and Iwakuni, and he began building projects in Onoda and Hagi. He opened up ten new mission posts. He built one retreat house, reorganized another, and bought lands for a third.[10]

But what was Arrupe really like in his dealings with his subjects as provincial? We can state that this was his most difficult period as regards human relations, since his office required him to make definitive decisions about the assignments and labors of concrete persons.

Several testimonies agree that he in some ways favored the Germans over the Spaniards. That may be explained by a certain reluctance to allow his place of birth to influence his decisions. As would be clear later in his trips abroad, he maintained the spirit of a citizen of the universe, preferring to indulge foreigners rather than to be perceived as favoring Spaniards in any way.

The Japanese Jesuit Hayashi explains this attitude:

> Yes, I have heard some of the Spaniards say that he was rather harsh with them. I think he was more like Xavier than like Valignano. The next provincial, [Hildebrando] Martini, had a tough time putting order in what Arrupe had done. He was a charismatic man. "Do the work," he seemed to say. "Find the right procedure and do it as you wish." He detested any type of nationalism. Even though he was Basque and loved his native land, he believed strongly that a Jesuit really had no country. He put himself in the place of others, by loving them.[11]

Yamamoto claims that Arrupe was more a charismatic leader than an administrator: "He had great ideas and an extraordinary spiritual impulse, but he needed to have people close at hand who would execute what he thought up."[12]

And Tsuchiya comments:

> He assigned me to study liturgy long before the Second Vatican Council. He sent me to Europe to study with the best specialists. He saw that liturgy was going to be important. He was way ahead of events. Later on, he asked me to help the Japanese bishops with liturgical reform. Arrupe was a man who was always growing and changing. I remember that he was always asking me, "Is this the right way for Japan?"[13]

---

10   Information provided by Fathers Pfister and Maruri.
11   Testimony of Shogo Hayashi, S.J.
12   Testimony of Joji Yamamoto, S.J.
13   Testimony of Yoshimasa Tscuhiya, S.J.

Arrupe with the king and queen of Belgium, Baudoin and Fabioli, at the monument to the martyrs of Nagasaki (January 29, 1964). The monument was erected by Arrupe on June 10, 1962.

Arrupe's style of governance was characterized by close human contact, as Rush writes:

> One of Pedro Arrupe's favorite tasks as provincial of Japan was his annual visit to the communities. He had to visit each house of the province, interview each member personally, and then give an evaluation of the state of the community's religious life and its apostolate, both to the community members and to the superior general in Rome.
>
> It was on the occasion of one of his visits to the language school in Yokosuka, more than thirty years ago, that I had a chance to meet Pedro Arrupe personally. The provincial made an excellent impression on the community. Although we all had the custom of rising at five in the morning, he rose earlier, even when the schedule of the day before had been exhausting. He seemed never to get tired.
>
> During the personal interviews, Pedro Arrupe acted as if nothing else in the world existed for him. He consoled, he encouraged, he asked about family and work, and he discussed plans for the future. And above all, both in those interviews and in the exhortation he gave at the end of his visit, he urged us to love the Japanese people and to desire to make Christ known to them. We were all impressed by his sincere cordiality, his personal holiness, and his apostolic zeal.
>
> It was during his time as provincial that the Japanese province of the Society experienced exceptional growth.[14]

---

14   Rush, "Pedro Arrupe, misionero," 48.

Ángel Setoáin, a Basque Jesuit from Navarre, believes that Arrupe

was an extreme optimist. He believed in people too much. He did not want
to bruise the broken reed or expel any Jesuit, no matter how many problems
he had. He was excessive in his respect for persons, even in extreme situations. And he never lost his sense of humor. When examining the construction of a college that was designed by the Germans and looked like a bunker,
he asked with a smile, "How's the flour factory going?"[15]

The German Jesuit Klaus Luhmer insists that Arrupe

was very austere with himself and kind with everybody. He never spoke
behind anyone's back. He was clear, humble, spiritual, and he knew how to
be demanding. If I have to mention something negative, I would add that his
knowledge of people was not very good. At times, he was naïve and did not
choose people well. He believed too much in people's goodness, so that at
times he suffered disappointment. He was too sincere and simple.[16]

But even in those days one could hear the constantly repeated affirmation
that in the course of the years would spread beyond the borders of Japan and be
heard from Jesuits around the world: each one of them could say, "I am a friend
of Arrupe."

The Hill of the Martyrs

Perhaps Arrupe's greatest work as provincial, or at least the one he cherished
most, was the monument to the martyrs of Nagasaki.

The story began in 1958, when Arrupe traveled to that beautiful coastal city
that had also been devastated by an atomic bomb, with the intention of founding a
Jesuit house there. To that end, he conversed with Archbishop Paul Aijiro Yamaguchi and offered to have the Society assume responsibility for a parish or a college in
the diocese. The archbishop then invited him to take a ride around the city.

Because of its critical location as a port, Nagasaki was for many years the
principal point of contact between Japan and the rest of the world. Its wooded
hills rose gently from the sea and the blue bay, where in ancient times pirates,

---

15   Testimony of Ángel Setoáin, S.J.
16   Testimony of Klaus Luhmer, S.J. In a long letter to the author, Mariano Peñuela, S.J. insists
     on a controversial aspect of Arrupe's term as provincial superior: at that time, Arrupe was
     very demanding, had very high standards, and supposed that other Jesuits had reached
     his own level of spirituality. But Peñuela's letter is also full of admiration and gratitude.
     He recalls, for example, that in his travels abroad Arrupe sought out the families of the
     Jesuits who were in Japan and spent long hours telling them about "their children." That's
     what he did with Peñuela's "old lady" in Cordoba, Spain. The letter concludes: "I come to
     an end. I thought I was going to criticize Arrupe, but it just doesn't come out. My heart
     betrays me. He is a great man and has taught me too many good things."

merchants, and missionaries had come ashore. The archbishop took the provincial to the top of one of those hills, from which they contemplated Nagasaki, without doubt one of the most luminous cities of Japan and the whole Far East.

In the sixteenth century, with the impulse of Portuguese, Spanish, Dutch, and Chinese merchants, the city's economy was thriving on trade with China, Korea, India, the Philippines, Southeast Asia, and the South Pacific. In 1587, Toyotomi Hideyoshi had made Nagasaki his base of operations, with the aim of conquering the island of Kyushu.

At that time, there were already a good number of Europeans in the city, and missionaries had successfully introduced there the Christian faith. The Jesuits were converting many people, but their success provoked the hostility of the Japanese authorities, who unleashed a wave of persecution. They accused the Jesuits of collaborating with Spanish designs to conquer Japan.

The archbishop took Arrupe to the hill where on February 5, 1597 twenty-six Christians had been crucified by order of Hideyoshi. As the two men looked out on what was then only a barren esplanade, they recalled that cold winter morning of 1597 when twenty-six crosses were erected facing the sea. Executed on them were six Franciscans, three Jesuits, and fifteen Japanese laypeople. Except for the Franciscans, all were Japanese. The three Jesuits were named Paul Miki, John Soan, and James (Diego) Kisai. Executed along with them were two Japanese Christians who had received the priests into their homes on their way to Nagasaki. They were all canonized by Pius IX in 1862. It is curious that the Franciscans and the Jesuits, who in those days differed sharply over methods of evangelization, were brothers in martyrdom.[17]

After recalling those events, the archbishop returned to the present and commented: "We have plans to erect a monument; a committee for preserving the holy place has already been organized."

In a low voice, as if speaking to himself, Arrupe said: "Perhaps something could be done with regard to the martyrs."

Archbishop Yamaguchi made no response, and Arrupe thought that perhaps he did not agree with his suggestion. The next day, however, when Arrupe was

---

17 See Diego R. Yuki, S.J. (Japanese name of Diego Pacheco, S.J.), "Nagasaki: La colina de los mártires," *Missionalia hispanica* 17 (1961): 229–45; William V. Bangert, *Historia de la Compañía de Jesús* (Santander: Editorial sal Terrae, 1981), 197ff.; and Paul Pfister, S.J., "San Pablo Miki y sus compañeros," in *Semblanzas espirituales de los santos y beatos de la Compañía de Jesús* (Madrid: Eapsa, 1974), 67–71.

From a strictly historical viewpoint, this martyrdom would be an ominous precedent. After recovering to an extent, the Jesuits were definitively expelled from Japan on January 27, 1614, when Hideyoshi ordered the expulsion of all missionaries and demanded that all Japanese Christians return to the Buddhist faith. Suddenly, a community of three hundred thousand Christians was left without pastors. Even today, in the towns near Nagasaki, communities can be found that have, in their own way, preserved the Christian faith, combined with syncretistic practices.

Placing the first stone for a residence hall for students of Sophia University in Tokyo (1955).

taking leave of the archbishop to return to Tokyo, the archbishop said to him: "The mayor, Tsutomu Tagawa, approves of your idea."

"What idea?"

"That the Society of Jesus take charge of building the monument. I have spoken with him, and he is all in favor."

Arrupe was caught by surprise. He had not been thinking of that, nor could he make such a quick decision, but the archbishop would not yield. The prelate also cherished the idea of creating a historical museum that would be a kind of living catechesis, with a small residence alongside.

As always, once Arrupe saw something clearly, his enthusiasm grew. So after carefully studying the plans drawn up by architect Kenji Imai, he undertook the task of raising funds. Once again, María Luz in Spain offered to lend a hand, and others helped as well.

At first, the archbishop did not want a church to be built, but he later gave in to the insistence of the Mexican bishops and agreed to the construction of the church of Saint Philip. Arrupe also thought of building a retreat house and a student center on the site, and Propaganda Fide gave economic assistance, specifically for the retreat house. The Jesuit superior in Nagasaki at the time was Arrupe's former fellow medical student, López Uralde, but the provincial later assigned Andalusian Jesuit Diego Pacheco to take charge of the work.[18] López

18   Information provided by Diego R. Yuki, S.J., who accompanied the author in Nagasaki and provided him with many materials and documents.

Uralde recounts how he himself was persuaded by Arrupe in Bilbao to go to Japan, even though he was too old to learn Japanese, and he speaks of how determined Arrupe was to have this work built, even though it meant an incredible economic expenditure.

The date for inaugurating the monument happened to coincide with the centenary of the canonization of the twenty-six saints (June 8, 1862). On June 10, 1962, which was the feast of Pentecost, the inauguration was presided over by Bishop Alonso Manuel Escalante, who came with a group of Mexican pilgrims. From Spain, there came the auxiliary bishop of Madrid, Bishop José María García Lahiguera, and the sub-secretary of justice, Ricardo Oreja Elósegui. The monument was designed by Kenji Imai, professor of the University of Waseda and disciple of the brilliant Catalonian architect Antoni Gaudí. Its attractive and exotic style was both traditional and avant-garde, and it contrasted with the Buddhas and shrines on the nearby hillside. That same day, twenty-two men retraced on foot the path of the martyrs.

Arrupe later wrote a long letter to his brother Jesuits in Japan, beginning with a quote from a letter that Jesuit Francisco Calderón wrote as he beheld the site of the martyrs' crosses: "We still have before our eyes, here from the ship where I write this letter, this holy procession of bodies, which are still fixed to their crosses, even though thirty-six years have passed since they were crucified."

Calling for authenticity in translating the Christian faith into the realities of life, Arrupe wrote:

> This is the fundamental problem of our evangelizing work. Is our main testimony really the testimony of our lives? Let us think about this in prayer. The veracity and the effectiveness of our apostolic efforts will depend on the answer we give to this question. What would it matter if we had works that excelled "in appearance," but were run by mediocre spirits? There is so much danger of intoxication in this century of appearances and propaganda!

Arrupe was pronouncing such words in the 1960s. The world had changed much since he had been named provincial eight years before. The so-called Japanese miracle had already blossomed. Now the problem in Japan was not scarcity but superabundance. In his letter, after insisting on the importance of the "testimony of our lives," the provincial dedicated several paragraphs to the "most advanced nation in the East":

> Japan has become home to all the Western ideologies, whose hybrid products are a skepticism and a relativism that penetrate everything. Japan believes that it is sufficient unto itself. As a result, our presence is tolerated rather than appreciated, and our influence is severely hindered and limited. Given the present economic prosperity and technological advances, both state and private institutions excel to such an extent that our trying to compete with

them requires an effort that seems disproportionate, compared to what is required in other countries. If we add to all that the sensitivity and reserve that characterize the Japanese soul, we can understand why our work appears to proceed at a disturbingly slow pace.

Further on in the letter, Arrupe referred to the difficulties arising from the international character of the Jesuit communities, since the members were often deprived of the relaxation that comes from sharing a common language and tradition. He also mentioned how some Jesuits, unable to speak Japanese well, might feel that their best qualities "remained hidden in anonymity during their whole life." The solution, suggested Arrupe, was to realize that one is an instrument of God and a witness of Jesus Christ.

On the day the monument was inaugurated, Arrupe addressed the authorities and the public gathered on the hill of the martyrs. After the customary expressions of gratitude, he concluded with the following words, which in their references to the Cold War and to pacifism are well in advance of the sensibility of the time:

> It is said that this monument is made of rock and bronze, but there is also a lively spirit of love breathing within it. This monument is a document that bears witness to love and communicates a message of peace to the world. Diverse parts of the globe are still divided by hatreds and by the Cold War, but the fervor of all those who unite around this symbol of love assures us that humanity will never again suffer the effects of such a great tragedy.

"On the day of the inauguration," recalls Pacheco,

> both the museum and the church were still unfinished, for lack of funds. Father Arrupe continued to support the project unfailingly, and he visited Nagasaki frequently. He used to travel in the night train, even though during those years his lumbago made it difficult for him to sleep in the berths. When, a year after the inauguration, our superior, Father Uralde, had an auto accident and I had to substitute for him, I had the opportunity to discuss with Father Arrupe many matters related to Nagasaki. The difficulties and the problems that kept arising during his last years as provincial prevented him from promoting the work as much as he wanted to, but his interest never diminished. Even from Rome, he continued to encourage us and to show his enthusiasm.[19]

---

19   Testimony of Diego R. Yuki, S.J.

Accused in Rome

It is difficult to describe succinctly the work that a provincial superior does in a religious order, since much of the activity involves intimate human relations and the complex task of providing leadership. One of Arrupe's secretaries during this period, José María Maruri, describes him thus:

> I read in some newspaper, I think in Bilbao, that Father Arrupe is neither tall nor short, neither fat nor thin, neither big nor small. As regards his physical appearance, the description is correct. Even so, in his idealism of spirit he has gigantic stature and tremendous breadth. And I confess frankly: it is difficult to keep up with him when he sets the pace, for he moves rapidly, with little doubt or hesitation. He had a very clear vision of the Jesuits' supranational destiny in Japan. He considered Japan to be a pioneer mission that broke with all the old patterns. He was the ideal man for this work, for he seemed to have been born for every challenge. His ability to adapt to circumstances was prodigious. Not only was he able to do many things well, but he moved quite naturally from one thing to another in a matter of minutes, without giving evidence of even the slightest psychological distress.[20]

What were Arrupe's inner feelings and experiences during those years? Even though he was involved in quite varied activities, we do not possess many of his own personal reflections from this time, since as superior he had many confidential communications that had to be kept secret.

Arrupe wrote regularly to his family in Bilbao, or he sent them information by means of his collaborators. One of his letters reveals that his sisters were experiencing economic hardship. A little before the inauguration of the Nagasaki monument, he wrote the following letter to his cousin Fernando Gondra and his wife Emilia, who enjoyed an excellent social position:

> Dear Fernando and Emilia,
>
> I received Fernando's letter on the twelfth, and I want to send you some lines of greetings and gratitude.
>
> From what you tell me, I can see how difficult the times are in Spain. But today I especially want to thank you for the "assistance" Cata tells me she has received from you. She did not tell me what or how, but to judge from the letters I have received these last months, it seems that they were in serious problems. Everything is always going well and there are no problems (!), but between the lines I can see that something is bothering them very much these days.
>
> For that reason, I want especially to thank you for everything you can do to help them. The sacrifice they made when I became a Jesuit was really

---

20   Testimony of J. M. Maruri, S.J.

Spanish ambassador Antonio Villaciero awarding the Cross of Isabel the Catholic to Arrupe for his work as a missionary, on the occasion of the fiftieth anniversary of the Jesuits' return to Japan (Tokyo, December 3, 1958).

very great, but they did so with a generosity of spirit for which I will never be able to thank them enough. On the other hand, the heavy cross they have with Joaquín has made their situation even more difficult. I really feel bad about it.

But the Lord will surely help them.

We continue here more or less the same. I hope that some groups are encouraged to come on the occasion of the centenary of the canonization of the martyrs of Nagasaki. I hope Mariví and Guillermo come as well! How would it be if Emilia and Fernando were to accompany them?

Greetings to all the members of the family. More and more we find ourselves more connected with those *above*. Little by little, so many loved ones are leaving us [...] When will our turn come?

Yours gratefully in the Lord, Pedro.[21]

In other letters that Arrupe wrote to Fernando and Mariví, there are affectionate references to his sisters: "If you see the little ladies of Marqués de Puerto, [tell them] that their brother, even though he has ever less hair to comb, is quite

---

21   Statements of Mother María Arrupe, religious of the Slaves of the Sacred Heart, to the newspaper *Ya*, May 26, 1988. Cf. Gondra–Barandiarán family archive. Her sister Margarita, who was married to Joaquín Sautu, had a son who was developmentally disabled.

The Japan vice-province, with missionaries from diverse places and speaking different languages, gave Arrupe an international outlook.

well." In a letter written in 1964, he refers to his contacts with the king and queen of Belgium, Fabiola and Baudoin, and with Prince Juan Carlos and Princess Sofía of Spain, with whom he had long been friends. Other heads of state with whom Arrupe had dealings in these years, apart from Pius XII and John XXIII, were President Carlos Delgado Chalbaud of Venezuela, President Arturo Frondizi of Argentina, President Manuel Prado of Peru, Chancellor Konrad Adenauer of the German Federal Republic, and General Franco of Spain. On July 10, 1958, Franco conceded to Arrupe the Commendation of the Order of Isabel La Católica. As he was leaving the ceremony in which he was decorated by the Spanish ambassador in Tokyo, Antonio Villacieros, Arrupe commented: "Can I sell it? Commendation, commendation—what I need is that they *commend me!*" When he made his final journey abroad as provincial in 1962, the Japanese government commended to him several matters of public welfare.

What comes out clearly in all the testimony about Arrupe is that what he lacked most was *time*. His sister María, who was a Slave of the Sacred Heart nun, wrote of him: "He likes it when we write to him, but he, because of his many occupations, does not write to us as much as we would like. His letters are always very short, and he promises that he will write at greater length later, but that long letter never arrives."

Behind some of the texts we have quoted, however, there seems be a certain melancholy that does not fit well with the optimistic and cheerful spirit that Pedro usually displayed. What was really happening? We can understand this better by examining later events. A man with the courage, farsightedness, and mental acuity of Arrupe is not always comprehended, especially within institutions that hold strictly to traditional ways.

"There were some," explains Rush, "who felt that things were moving too quickly, that there was too much expansion, too many new ideas."[22]

The malcontents seemed to be mainly among the rather inflexible second Jesuit generation of Germans, and, as usually happens in such cases, they took their complaints to Rome. The superior general of the Jesuits at the time, Janssens, appointed an official visitor to prepare a report on the situation in Japan, and especially on the performance of Arrupe as provincial. The person named as visitor in 1964 was Father George Kester, a Dutchman who had formerly been provincial of Indonesia.

The visitation lasted two years, during which Kester conducted a thorough investigation, always assisted by the humble and kind cooperation of the provincial Arrupe. The provincial himself gave no indication of feeling hurt, but those closest to him knew that the visitation was a humiliation that caused Pedro tremendous suffering. What the visitor never imagined was that, when he finished preparing his final report, he would have to hand it over to no one less than the new superior general of the Society of Jesus: Pedro Arrupe!

Later on, Arrupe would recall that circumstance with a smile and a lament: "Poor Father Kester!"

Since then, there has been no other official visitor in the Society of Jesus.

---

22   Rush, "Pedro Arrupe, misionero," 50. Curiously, this incomprehension came from Germans, who, as we have seen, were treated by Arrupe with special interest and even predilection.

14. General for a Council

It was an unforgettable morning in Rome. At eight o'clock on October 11, 1962, the vast plaza of Saint Peter was already the scene of a celebration that would be recorded forever in the annals of history. Among the white miters of 2,540 bishops, who were proceeding six abreast from the apostolic palace to the steps of Saint Peter's Basilica, there could be made out here and there the heads of the oriental prelates, dressed all in black. Bishops of every race and background had been called together for the inauguration of the Second Vatican Council.

When the First Vatican Council was held in the nineteenth century, the seven hundred council fathers came mainly from Europe. This time only thirty-seven percent were Europeans, while thirty-three percent came from the Americas and the remaining thirty percent came from Africa, Asia, Australia, and Oceania. Among them were 855 missionary bishops. For the first time in history, the whole globe was truly represented in an ecumenical council. And also, for the first time in the history of the church, forty representatives of non-Catholic Christian communities attended as observers at the opening of the council. They were considered guests of honor "in the Father's house," in the words of Pope John XXIII.

A "Transitional" Pope

Once the council fathers were installed in the immense benches that stretched the full length of Saint Peter's Basilica, the papal retinue entered. From a chair born aloft through the plaza, John XXIII smiled with the tenderness of a universal grandfather. What really had happened in the lucid mind and heart of that man for him to take such a decisive step? Born eighty-one years before to a farming family of Sotto il Monte, in the diocese of Bergamo, that good priest, simple but cultured, had arrived at the chair of Peter on October 28, 1958 with the aim, as he said himself, of being more a pastor than a high priest or supreme pontiff. The press had spoken a bit precipitously of "a transitional pope." His gestures touched the whole world deeply. He smiled paternally not only on the inmates of Regina Coeli prison, when he made a quite unexpected visit, but also on unbelievers, on the separated brethren, on non-Christian confessions, on the countries behind the Iron Curtain, and on the working-class districts of Rome. "I am one of you," he used to say quite naturally and without the least pretense—because in fact he was.

That stout, affectionate man appeared straightforward, far removed from the mysterious aristocratic air of his predecessor. As he would confess later to a group of Venetians, the idea of convoking a council had been with him from the very first weeks of his pontificate. He made the announcement on January 25, 1959, stating that the purpose of the council was "the consolidation of the Catholic faith, the renewal of Christian customs, and the adaptation of ecclesiastical life to the present times."

Upon entering the basilica, the pope left behind his chair and its bearers and walked between the rows of bishops stretched along the length of the transformed nave of the council hall. The opening ceremony lasted about four and a half hours. It was impressive to contemplate the elderly pope begging illumination from the Holy Spirit during the Mass and then kneeling to make a profession of faith before the whole assembly. In his inaugural discourse, John XXIII stressed that he had not convoked the council "to discuss primarily certain key points of doctrine," which were already well known, but to delve deeper into them and bring them up to date, as the times required. He insisted also on the serious pastoral obligations of the new assembly, saying: "The Spouse of Christ should have recourse today much more to the remedy of charity than to the arms of severity." He called the council a "fraternal meeting of bishops" and encouraged the council fathers to debate in complete freedom. For that reason, he did not enter the council hall during the general sessions and attended only the last session of the council's first stage.

That day marked the beginning of a process whose eventual results would have been difficult to foresee. Even though certain sectors of the Roman curia had prepared documents designed to guide the council along conservative lines, the assembly decided to make important changes and to take a far more pastoral orientation. The schema of Cardinal Alfredo Ottaviani, *The Sources of Revelation*, was rejected in its totality by the council fathers, and John XXIII personally took the side of the progressive majority. The church had never up to that moment shown itself so desirous of understanding the world and dialoguing with it. The frank exchange among those prelates coming from all over the world, the urgent concerns arriving from all corners of the globe, and the presence of non-Catholic observers made for a tremendous explosion of modernity within the church.

For that reason, when on June 3, 1963 John XXIII closed his eyes for the last time, the entire world wept, from the cabdrivers in the city of Rome to the distant hillside farmers in Latin America. With his unique style, more pastoral than dogmatic, the "charismatic pope" of the twentieth century disappeared from our view. A little before his death, he was heard to utter: *Ut unum sint!* (May they be one!).

On June 19, 1963, the cardinals in conclave elected his successor, Giovanni Battista Montini, son of a lawyer and a journalist of Brescia, and a man who brought to the office both the prudence of a long diplomatic career and intellectual acumen that knew how to question. Would the council be suspended? Denying rumors that were appearing in the columns of some newspapers,

Paul VI fixed September 29 of that year as the date for the reopening of the council sessions.[1]

Among the council fathers who were becoming known about Rome, there was one who would most definitely affect the life of Arrupe: Karol Wojtyła, the archbishop of Kraków. According to theologian Giulio Girardi, an expert in the Christian–Marxist dialogue, Wojtyła and the other Polish bishops "had a concept of the council very different from that of most bishops." For the more progressive European church, the most important thing was opening up "dialogue with the modern world," after so many centuries of estrangement, but for Wojtyła the most important thing was getting ready "to combat the world and above all Marxism." Many of the theologians and bishops—above all the French and the Germans, who were very influential in the council—considered atheism to be a sort of "criticism of the church and its abuses of power," but for the Polish bishops atheism was above all "the great obstacle for the formation of a new Christendom." Wojtyła insisted on his personalist philosophy, according to which the atheist is an isolated individual and the Christian faith, far from causing alienation, is humanly liberating in the deepest sense.[2] Mieczyslaw Malinski, in his reports on the council, takes note of a certain isolation of Wojtyła himself, who felt he was not understood. Nor did the future pope understand certain progressive postures of the Central Europeans, as he confessed to his friend Malinski while they ate together at a Roman pizzeria. Later on, as pope, Wojtyła warned in his book *Crossing the Threshold of Hope* about the danger of what he called tendentious interpretations of the council.[3]

Thousands of miles away, a man with a broad forehead and determined air, surrounded by smiling faces and gentle eyes, was especially excited as he heard of the events in Rome. Accustomed as he was to dealing on a daily basis with people from very different parts of the world, he had great sensitivity for the present and a clear vision of the future. Arrupe was a man of the council even before the council convened.

---

1   See H. [Hubert] Jedin and K. [Konrad] Repgen, *Manual de Historia de la Iglesia*, vol. 9 (Barcelona: Herder, 1984); G. [Gastón] Castella, *Historia de los papas*, vol. 3 (Madrid: Espasa-Calpe, 1970); *Documentos del Vaticano II* (Madrid: BAC, 1985); Giovanni Caprile, *Il Concilio Vaticano II: Cronache del Concilio Vaticano II*, 4 vols. (Rome: Ed. "La civiltà cattolica," 1965–68); Y. [Yves] Congar, *El concilio día a día* (Madrid: Estela, 1963), and *Diario del concilio*, 3 vols. (Barcelona: Estela, 1967); José Luis Martín Descalzo, *Un periodista en el concilio*, 4 vols. (Madrid: Propaganda Popular Católica, 1963–66), and *El concilio de Juan y Pablo* (Madrid: La Editorial Católica, 1966); Rocco Caporale, *Vaticano II: El último de los concilios* (Barcelona: Nova Terra, 1966); Casiano Floristán and Juan-José Tamayo, *El Vaticano II, veinte años después* (Madrid: Cristiandad, 1985); Santiago Madrigal, *Vaticano II: Remembranza y actualización* (Santander: Editorial Sal Terrae, 2002).
2   *Acta Synodalia*, 4, 3, 660–63. On everything related to John Paul II, see my work *Juan Pablo II, hombre y Papa* (Madrid: Espasa Calpe, 2005), 105ff.
3   *Cruzando el umbral de la esperanza* (Barcelona: Plaza-Janés, 1994), 165.

Wearing a cloak and just elected general of the Society of Jesus (May 25, 1965), Arrupe receives his first instructions from the secretary of the general congregation, Pedro Abellán.

Precisely in those days Arrupe was completing a quarter-century of missionary work in Japan. "In these twenty-five years," he wrote,

> the mission of Japan has been transformed in such a way that we hardly dare believe our eyes. How different is the situation now compared to those pre-war years, when we moved about with extreme caution, trying to carry out a precarious apostolate, when we suffered extreme material need and were completely misunderstood by the people!

With these lines, he evoked the war, the atomic bomb, and the new works that were just emerging. He concluded his message with an exhortation: "Help me to give thanks to God on this day, with the certainty that your prayer strengthens me and all the missionaries who are still full of great new plans for the future."[4]

But for Arrupe himself the future would mean another qualitative leap in his life, one for which his past journeys, experiences, contacts, and responsibilities had been preparing him well.

---

4   Letter of Arrupe on the occasion of his twenty-fifth anniversary in Japan (September 17, 1963).

A Prophetic Toast

On October 5, 1964, Father Janssens, superior general of the Society of Jesus, died in Rome. The machinery of the order's Constitutions swung quickly into gear. John L. Swain, the vicar general named by the deceased Janssens, convoked General Congregation 31, the "Jesuit parliament" that would choose another successor to Saint Ignatius of Loyola.

Because of the changes being decreed by the council, Janssens had decided, even before his death, to call a general congregation once the conciliar deliberations were finished. Its aim would be to study the inevitable adaptation that would be required of the Society in view of the church's new needs. Much preparatory work had already been done by special commissions, and the convocation awaited only the propitious moment.

Swain had consulted with Pope Paul VI about the matter and had initially decided to convoke the congregation for Easter of 1965, even if the council were still underway. However, the death of the superior general changed the course of events. During the first months of 1965, each province of the Society held its own provincial congregation, at which they elected two delegates or "electors," who along with the provincial superiors would represent the Jesuits of that region at the general congregation in Rome.

Arrupe did not arrive in Rome as just another provincial or elector. His many trips around the world and his knowledge and leadership of the small world that was the Jesuit mission in Japan—a concentration of two hundred Jesuits from twenty-nine nations—made him an exceptional participant with a unique perspective.

"During my final year as provincial," he confessed,

I had reflected and discussed much with some of my companions in Japan about what we used to call the "limit situation" of the Society. We had talked a lot, and when I arrived at GC 31, I told myself: "This is what must be done: we must make the Society understand the situation in which it finds itself in the world." My basic aim was to ask: What must the Society do? [...] Because the changes in the world were pressing.[5]

In that year of 1965, the Society of Jesus had 36,038 members working in more than a hundred countries around the world and organized into eleven assistancies with eighty-four provinces and vice-provinces. The Jesuits ran more than 4,600 colleges, 618 parishes, sixty-four universities, thirty-eight seminaries, and fifty-seven social centers. More than thirty members of the order were bishops or cardinals.[6] The Society was at the zenith of its influence and prestige in civil society and the church; it had a vigorous intellectual and educational

5   *Itinéraire*, 32.
6   See *Atlas geographicus Societatis Iesu, editio separata ex annuario Societatis Iesu 1964–1965*.

apostolate, but also worked extensively in communications and social development. At the same time, the Society was experiencing in its ranks a certain unease and discontent that would later, with the post-conciliar crisis, spill over into many other sectors of the church. In a conference marking the twentieth anniversary of Vatican II, Father Yves Congar argued that the council had earnestly attempted to respond to the first manifestations of the crisis, which only increased as the years went by. He spoke of a "sociocultural change whose breadth, radicality, rapidity, and cosmic character had no equivalent in any other period of history."[7]

Profound changes were taking place in philosophical thought and the human sciences; secularization and the myth of progress were extending their influence; there was a crisis of the church's magisterium, as well as a crisis of models at the level of politics, family, culture, and the labor movement. The turmoil of the times was reflected in the 2,021 postulates or petitions that arrived from all the provinces of the Society for the congregation's consideration. These postulates constituted "a great cry for change"; they expressed a desire of many Jesuits that the Society, while preserving its original core, would change some of the elements until then considered *substantive*, with the approval of the Holy See. The postulates also revealed, according to Valero, many problems and crises, and they made plain "the urgent need for the Society to renew its own self-conception and to undertake a thoroughgoing adaptation to the emerging apostolic needs of the world that it is called to serve."[8]

With such ideas in his head, Arrupe flew to Rome, where rumors were already circulating that he might be a possible candidate for general. At the same time, some Jesuits in Japan were sending information to Rome with the hope of preventing Arrupe's election.

The Spanish Jesuit Juan G. Ruiz de Medina commented to Arrupe a little before he left: "Well, you won't stay there in Rome, will you?"

To which Arrupe responded, "Wow! Don't worry, there's no danger of that!"[9]

Pedro made a stop in Taipei, Taiwan, where many of the Spanish Jesuits who had been expelled from communist China were working. Some of them had been companions of Arrupe during studies, and when he met with them, they toasted the "new general"—a prophetic gesture.

Pedro took all such suggestions lightly. In a letter written from Tokyo to a Colombian Jesuit on March 10, 1965, he commented:

---

7   Yves Congar, *Le Concile Vatican II: Son église, peuple de Dieu et corps du Christ* (Paris: Beauchesne, 1984), 69. On this point see Gianni La Bella, "La crisis del cambio," in La Bella, *Pedro Arrupe, general de la Compañía de Jesús*, 811–41, here 841.

8   Urbano Valero, "Al frente de la Compañía: La Congregación 31," in La Bella, *Pedro Arrupe, general de la Compañía de Jesús*, 139–71, here 151.

9   Testimony of Juan G. Ruiz de Medina, S.J.

I write these lines with one foot in the stirrup, before leaving for Rome. In a few moments, I leave for the airport. [...] Do not forget me in your prayers. After the general congregation *I don't know by which route I will return to Japan*, but if I can, I will certainly pass through Cali to greet all of you. Here we continue as always. I hate to leave Japan, though it will only be for a few months. There is so much to do![10]

General Congregation 31 did not begin until the month of May. Arrupe dedicated the two prior months to working with a select group of Jesuits, the Preparatory Commission summoned by the vicar general, Swain, to prepare for the meeting. One of the things that Arrupe sorely missed in the Roman curia, the Jesuit headquarters, was a telex and other modern instruments of communication, which he had become accustomed to using in his offices in Japan. "My work here is totally different from the work in Japan," he wrote on April 25:

Here I see only papers, documents, etc. As you know, the general congregation begins on May 7. [...] I don't want to write at length, but just one counsel: have only one ideal in life, loving Jesus Christ with all your soul. Let that be the fixed idea of your existence.[11]

Despite his hopes, Pedro would not be returning to Japan or passing through Colombia anytime soon.

The congregation began on the appointed date, with some 224 Jesuits assembled in Rome, of whom 125 were Europeans (thirty of them residing in mission countries), forty-five were North Americans, thirty were Latin Americans, and the rest were from other continents. Their average age was fifty-two. Paul VI received the assembled fathers amid great expectations on the part of the international press. Because of their influence and polemical history, the Jesuits always attracted the notice of journalists. Speculating about what Paul VI would say in his initial discourse, several newspaper editorials claimed that he would oppose the "Jesuit revolutionaries," would condemn the "evolutionist religion of Father Teilhard de Chardin," and would seriously warn the Society to avoid "dissension among its members."

However, the audiences the Jesuits had with the pope did not follow that path. Paul VI addressed them with great affection: "You have come to Rome and have assembled to choose a successor to superior general Jean-Baptiste Janssens. [...] Consider the matter, therefore, with sound criteria, and deliberate every aspect with the balanced judgment and wise prudence, in order to reach a desirable result."

---

10   Letter to a Colombian Jesuit, from the journal *Jesuitas*, no. 21, published by the Western Colombian province.
11   Letter to a Colombian Jesuit, from the journal *Jesuitas*, no. 21.

The pope referred to "the glorious annals of your history" and warned that the new general "should take special care to prevent your symphony from emitting discordant sounds." He even stated: "The church recognizes that you are her most devoted sons. She loves you and honors you in a special way, and I would even dare to say she reveres you." Later in the discourse, Paul VI invited the Jesuits to work hard in the struggle against atheism in all its forms and in all parts of the world.

That same afternoon, a Jesuit commented to Arrupe about an "interrogatorium" that the electors had received to guide their election: "They have given us a questionnaire, as if the ninth part of the Constitutions that Saint Ignatius dedicates to the portrait of the general were not enough. Of one thing we can be sure: the new general will not have the same defects as the preceding one." Arrupe did not seem to be much influenced by such comments, but he was seen visiting the chapel frequently in those days.

The election of the general was preceded by an intense and unexpected debate about the length of the general's term. The discussion lasted three plenary sessions, a total of nine hours, during which the possibility of changing the post's lifetime character was considered. It was decided to make no change until after the election of the superior general. The assembled Jesuits then proceeded to swear that they would elect the person they considered most suitable to fill the post. They took time to share ideas among themselves about the qualities desirable in the future general, in accord with the questionnaire that had been handed out:

> According to the questionnaire distributed at the beginning of the first day, the ideal superior general would be a person capable of combining tradition and progress wisely and effectively; he would preserve what must never be lost, namely the basic values of the Society's spiritual patrimony, and he would foster the innovation needed to adapt the Society to the new situation of the world and the church, in keeping with the pronouncements and decrees of Vatican II. The desired general, therefore, would be a person capable of carrying out what was the universal intention, already described, of General Congregation 31.[12]

On May 22, the election took place. At 6:25 a.m. that day, the 218 assembled fathers celebrated the Eucharist, presided over by Vicar General Swain and twelve other Jesuits. Immediately afterward, the *Oratio de eligendo praeposito* (Prayer for the superior general to be elected) was recited. A little before the election, Maurice Giuliani, director of the French journal *Christus*, gave an exhortation:

> We need a general who will always keep the Society connected to the world, to which it must effectively bring the word of salvation. It is not enough that our general be concerned with continuing and prolonging works born

---

12   Valero, "Al frente de la Compañía," 167.

of local needs; he must also fix his vision on the universal good and help us as companions of Jesus to embrace the entire world and to cooperate in the redemption of our era.

At 9:19 a.m., voting began.

The secretary of the congregation, Father Pedro Abellán, addressed the vicar general: "Father, in the name of Jesus, cast your vote." The vicar general rose, genuflected before the cross, blessed himself, and read the oath written on the back of the ballot: "In all reverence, I invoke Jesus Christ, whose wisdom is eternal, as my witness that I John Swain will choose and name as superior general of the Society the person whom I believe to be the most fitting to hold this post." Immediately afterward, the electors were called by Swain to come before the crucifix, which was placed beside the ballot box. "In the name of Jesus, cast your votes." At 10:44 a.m., the first scrutiny of ballots was finished, with no decisive result, for no one had attained the absolute majority needed: 110 votes out of 218. According to information leaked later, Dezza (the Italian ex-rector of the Gregorian University, who had visited Japan) and Swain (the Canadian vicar general and right-hand man of the previous general) had received about forty votes each. Two new figures appeared to have received more than fifty votes: the Canadian Roderick MacKenzie (rector of the Pontifical Biblical Institute) and Arrupe. All of them were still far from the absolute majority required. At 11:20 a.m., a second balloting took place, in which Dezza and Swain lost votes, and Arrupe obtained seventy-eight. At 11:40, in a third balloting, Arrupe attained 110 votes, an absolute majority. His name sounded in the hall: *Praepositus Generalis Societatis Iesu electus est Reverendus Pater Petrus Arrupe* (Reverend Father Pedro Arrupe has been elected superior general of the Society of Jesus).

What had happened? Quite simply, what had been expected. Arrupe's name won out, although, as we saw, not from the start. The commission that had drawn up a list of possible candidates had named at least ten other Jesuits ahead of Arrupe. In any case, the election had basically just one purpose: to choose as the new general someone who was at once loved, respected, and invested with an undeniable prophetic aura. He had to be a man of the moment, possessed of the true Ignatian spirit, knowledge of the Institute, experience of the Society, leadership ability, and a pronounced sensitivity for the modern world.

After three minutes, the secretary of the congregation, Abellán, proclaimed the election of Arrupe as superior general of the Society of Jesus. According to the Constitutions, he could not refuse the post. His name was communicated to the public a half-hour later, after the postulator general, Father Paolo Molinari, had informed the pope about the election and received his approval. Until that moment, the two hundred-plus electors had been limited to a diet of bread and water, in accord with the astute foresight of Saint Ignatius, who had had much experience of very long conclaves.

Shortly after being elected general, Arrupe meets with the coadjutor brothers of the Jesuit curia.

One of those present writes:

From the very start, the figure of the provincial of Japan appeared to be one of the likely candidates. The day of the election I was behind him in the hall and a little to one side. I could see him perfectly. He was serene, and when his name reached the number of votes required, he stayed tranquil, waiting for Father Vicar to proclaim the result. Once this was done, he simply stood up and went to the center of the hall to receive greetings from all the electors.[13]

---

13   Testimony of Eduardo Briceño, S.J. in a letter to the author (July 30, 1988). According to Valero, Arrupe's possible defects were also to be taken into account:

> In the exchanges that took place before the election, it was necessary to evaluate with special attention his capacity for governance, in the light of his disputed performance as provincial of Japan and various weaknesses attributed to him. It is well known that the other two representatives from the Japanese province clearly manifested some of Arrupe's limitations in government as they saw them: excessive idealism, a fanciful and ingenuous character, little organization, many plans but lack of a plan, little attention to following up on the concrete day-to-day realities. But it was necessary to understand that these possible limitations, perhaps more evident because of the provincial's special situation at that time, did not cancel out the positive qualities already mentioned; they were limitations that could be compensated with the help of the assistants and counsellors the GC would give him.

Valero, "Al frente de la Compañía," 172–73.

In his simplicity and surprise, Arrupe did no more than ask, "And now what do I do?"

Father José Oñate, who was beside him, answered, "Now, Father, for the last time in your life, you obey."

Oñate did not realize what he was saying. Outside the hall, the Jesuits of the curia were anxious with expectation. When Molinari left with the sealed envelope, they realized: "We have a general." But who was it? In thirty-five minutes, they would know. Arrupe went to a nearby room to put on the *mantello* (a simple cape formerly used by clerics). There he found himself alone with the Jesuit who had made the skeptical comments about the questionnaire. Arrupe embraced him with emotion, saying, "What a cross, Father!"

Arrupe turned down the cup of tea they had prepared for him. If for a short while he seemed troubled by the turn of events, after a few moments he reappeared in the assembly hall confident and smiling.

The *Te Deum* resounded in the hall, and outside the teletypes of the principal international news agencies communicated the news to the whole world: the new "black pope" was a man with the short, resonant name "Arrupe."

That same afternoon, the brother sacristan asked the new general: "Father, what time do you wish to celebrate Mass?"

"Early, very early."

"Does six-thirty seem a good hour to you?"

"Please, brother, I don't want to break up the morning […]."[14]

On the Front Pages

The newspapers and broadcast media of the whole world took up the news the next day: *The New York Times, Le monde, The Times, Frankfurter Allgemeine Zeitung, Il corriere della sera, ABC, El espectador, La libre belgique, Ya.* Hundreds more, especially in Latin America, stressed the attributes of the newly elected general: student of medicine in Madrid, a Basque with broad experience, eyewitness of Hiroshima, world traveler.

The *New York Times* gave a curious diagnosis:

He is a man with white hair and an ascetic figure; he is known for various qualities, not all spiritual. In Vatican circles he is considered a skilled, suitable administrator. Although the Spanish Jesuits are by tradition conservative, Father Arrupe is considered liberal and could be compared with the deceased John XXIII.

---

14   Valero, "Al frente de la Compañía," 172–73. And from the same witnesses already cited.

The new general pledges his obedience to Paul VI and asks to be photographed kneeling at his feet. "I know that I have thirty-six thousand soldiers at my orders," the pope told him.

After giving other biographical details, the New York daily added:

> Many of the students who used to meet with him in Hiroshima recall him as a clear and challenging exponent of Christian philosophy. In Campion House (Manhattan), he is remembered as the young, cheerful priest who in the summer of 1938 lived on the fifth floor there. He had a beautiful baritone voice and was often asked to sing at the community's religious services. He used to rehearse in his room, and it is said that his neighbor complained only once.

Le figaro of Paris considered Arrupe's election to be of "great importance" for the church and stressed in its headline: "He is said to be very open and at the same time faithful to the spiritual traditions." The newspaper judged his work in Japan to be "cutting edge" and thought he would inject a youthful spirit into the order; it also noted the significance of his disappointment at not finding a telex in the Roman curia. Some reactions were less enthusiastic, such as those of *La nazione*, *The Times*, and *L'unità*, the organ of the Italian Communist Party, which classified him as a "centrist," situated between the innovationist and traditionalist sectors of the church that had come to the fore in the council.

Radio Moscow, at 8 p.m. on the same day, May 22, broadcast the following information for the Russian people:

> Unusual Roman election. More than two hundred delegates representing thirty-five thousand Jesuits around the world today elected the general of

their order, the "black pope," as he is popularly called. The former black pope died last October. The new Father General of the order will be the twenty-eighth after the founder of the Society of Jesus, Saint Ignatius of Loyola. In order to avoid overlong proceedings and debates, the delegates consumed only bread and water.

The next day, Radio Moscow included the name of the newly elected general and added: "Common opinion has it that the new general hopes to help the Jesuit order recover some of its former power. He even seems to be striving to be a new Saint Ignatius."

In Spain, the newspaper *Ya* interviewed two of Arrupe's sisters, and in Bilbao *La gaceta del norte* gave generous coverage that featured photos of Arrupe as a child dressed in a sailor suit, the record of his school grades, and recollections of his life in Bilbao.[15] An eighty-three-year old Piarist priest, Father Felipe Díaz, a former professor of Arrupe, sent a telegram to Rome: "At my age of eighty-three, I feel much satisfaction in seeing a student of mine as the Jesuit general." As a tribute to his former college professors, Arrupe celebrated one of his first Masses as general in the Roman chapel that had originally been the room of Saint Joseph Calasanz, founder of the Piarists. On that occasion, he expressed his gratitude to the Piarist general and the members of that order and told anecdotes about his years studying in the college.

Telegrams arrived from politicians, cardinals, presidents, and other heads of state. Many were interesting, but some were quite prophetic, mentioning how Arrupe would be carrying "a heavy, burdensome cross" and would be "facing problems greater than those of the Counter-Reformation." Another message called him "eminence," a title reserved to cardinals. Telegrams even arrived from the president of Tokyo's International Tobacco Association, from the congregation of Madrid garbage collectors, and from the Bilbao Anti-alcoholic Association. Perhaps the most moving one of all came from a sick man who wrote: "On my sickbed, I have received two of the greatest satisfactions of my life: one was being ministered to by Father Arrupe in moments that were critical for me, and the other was hearing he was named general."

What no newspaper or journal could report was what was happening in Pedro's heart in those moments. Swirling around in his imagination were many memories of past experiences and prayerful illuminations: the Bilbao of his childhood, the scruffy kids of the Madrid slums, and that strange voice he heard in a corridor of Loyola that now appeared prophetic: "You will be the first." And of course there were memories of Japan, his tears in the port of Yokohama, his imprisonment in Yamaguchi, the Hiroshima bomb. More than anything, though, he would be overwhelmed in these moments by thoughts

---

15   Cf. newspapers of that date.

of the responsibility that now was his. Knowing only too well part 10 of the Jesuit Constitutions, in which Ignatius describes the sterling qualities required of the superior general of the Society, he would have felt his own inadequacy intensely. He now found himself at the head of thirty-six thousand men at a crucial moment, when crisis seemed to be looming on all sides, brought on by the onrush of modernity, the advance of secularization, the decrease in vocations, and the era of *aggiornamento*.

In previous decades, many Jesuits had become famous for their profound explorations of the world and of the church's interior life. There were thinkers like Émile Mersch, Sebastiaan Tromp, and Henri de Lubac; there were philosophers and theologians like Joseph Maréchal, Pierre Rousselot, Pierre Scheuer, Karl Rahner, Bernard Lonergan, Jean Daniélou, Claude Mondésert, and Josef Jungmann.

With the development of nuclear energy and the exploration of space, these were years when the influence of scientific studies was expanding rapidly, but there was also intellectual unrest and anxiety. French Jesuit Pierre Teilhard de Chardin expressed his fear that humanity might lose all sense of meaning and find itself disoriented and trapped in a corner from which there was no escape. Many expressed their admiration for Teilhard's evolutionary optimism, which posited a world process that found its climax in Christ, true God and true Man.

In these same years, US Jesuit John Courtney Murray was credited with being a principal architect of the "Declaration on Religious Liberty," one of the great documents of Vatican II. Two other Jesuits, Gustave Weigel and Cardinal Augustin Bea, were receiving generous praise from non-Catholics for their ecumenical labors. Many sociologists were studying economic development based on the "Christian solidarity" promoted by Jesuits Heinrich Pesch, Gustav Gundlach, and Oswald von Nell-Breuning. These are only a few of the names that were making the Society of Jesus highly esteemed in intellectual circles.

Arrupe would have responsibility as well for a Society with a far-flung educational system. A third of all Jesuits, some 11,500, were teaching more than 1,250,000 students in some 4,672 institutions. Almost a fifth of all Jesuits were working in mission lands, principally in the Third World. The order also ran publications (some quite prestigious, such as *La civiltà Católica* and *Etúdes*), radio stations (like Vatican Radio), and astronomical observatories (Specola Vaticana). Jesuits held chairs in non-Catholic universities and labored in a great variety of occupations, ranging from artists and cinematographers to worker priests. The newsweekly *Time* went so far as to compare the Society with General Motors.[16] Some fifty-eight Jesuits were council fathers at Vatican II, and many others attended the council as experts and had a decisive influence on the resulting documents.

---

16   William V. Bangert, *Historia de la Compañía de Jesús* (Santander: Editorial Sal terrae, 1981).

In his first allocution to the general congregation, Arrupe started off with the words of a prophet:

> "Ah, Lord God, behold, I do not know how to speak" (Jeremiah 1:6). These words express well my present feeling of smallness. Nonetheless, it is evident that God's will has done this: that is my only consolation, the only thing that lifts my spirit: "Be not afraid, for I am with you" (Jeremiah 1:8). God has chosen me by means of you, and he will grant me the grace to carry out this great work that he has placed in my weak hands. I have never before felt so intimately those words of the Lord: "Without me you can do nothing" (John 15:5).

In his talk, Arrupe asked especially that his companions "go out to meet the demands of young people, which are also the demands of our times," even when they cannot be easily formulated. He also exhorted them "to know what it means to *do battle under the standard of the cross* and to strive to make our way of life effective in the concrete conditions of the twentieth century."[17]

In Defense of Teilhard

Though he had already appeared briefly before the cameras of the Italian network RAI, Arrupe held his first formal news conference on May 24. His style was novel for a Jesuit general, and his cheerful dynamism won journalists over from the start. His declarations were striking: "Dialogue consists in knowing how to listen. Dialogue can take place only in a setting of mutual respect, where people are speaking the same language." He stressed how the Society's work was based on dialogue, both in the missions and in the scientific apostolate: "In regard to atheism, our position is not one of simple opposition, but of dialogue, in order to help the atheists surmount the obstacles that prevent them from discovering and knowing God."

In this press conference, which was held in the offices of *La civiltà Cattolica* and moderated by the paper's Jesuit director, Roberto Tucci, Arrupe stated: "The atheists need to be treated gently, as the Japanese treat the cherry blossom. We must discern in the soul of each atheist the moral, social, intellectual, philosophical, economic, and other reasons that have led them to adopt their position."

When a journalist asked the new general his opinion about the "progressives," Arrupe responded:

> If by progressive you mean those who struggle against the great social injustices that exist in all parts of the world, and especially in the developing countries, then we agree with them, in line with the social doctrine contained in the great encyclicals. We cannot ignore the inequalities that exist in

---

17   General Congregation 31, documents 17–19.

the cities and in the rural areas, where the workers who feed our people are dying for lack of solidarity.

In those days, there was certain to be a question about the polemical Teilhard de Chardin, the Jesuit anthropologist who had been unable to publish his works during his lifetime. The journalists pointed out the contradiction between the 1962 Vatican warning against the French Jesuit and the esteem in which he was held by many Catholic thinkers.

Arrupe answered carefully, saying that Teilhard's work was voluminous and that his thought was very difficult to grasp with precision; he explained many of his books were not meant for publication and that he was not "professionally a philosopher or a theologian." He went on to say, however:

> It is necessary to state that the positive elements in Father Teilhard de Chardin's work far outweigh the negative elements, and it is to those elements we must study and discuss. His vision of the world has a very beneficial influence in scientific circles, both Christian and non-Christian. Father Teilhard is one of the great masters of contemporary thought, and the success he is finding today should not surprise us. In reality, he has made a magnificent attempt to reconcile the world of science and the world of faith.

After pointing out how in Teilhard's work and spirituality all things flowed together in Christ, Arrupe concluded that "we must recognize the richness of Father Teilhard's message for our time. [...] It is completely in line with the apostolate of the Society of Jesus." One can imagine how these words were received by the international press, especially the French. Arrupe had passed a favorable judgment on one of the century's most intuitive prophets, despite his many detractors.

The new general's frankness and openness produced a great impact. One foreign correspondent commented to a colleague: "He is one of the most impressive men I have seen. Now I know why they chose him."[18]

Face to Face with the Pope

The encounter with the representatives of the press had been a success, but on May 31 Arrupe had a more exigent interview. At noon, he was to be received by Paul VI.

After inviting him to be seated, the pope told him that he should speak in Spanish and that he would answer in Italian, but the conversation was eventually carried on in French. The pope said, "I know that the Society is at my disposition, that I have thirty-six thousand soldiers at my orders."

"That is precisely what I wanted to tell your Holiness: the Society is completely at your command. Just give the order, Your Holiness, for obedience is the essence of the Society."

---

18   Cf. newspapers of that date.

"Yes, I am going to use the Society, but not abuse it. I wish to ask some sacrifices of it."

"What are they?" asked Father Arrupe. "We are ready to comply."

"I will tell you once the council is finished."

"And with respect to the struggle against atheism," continued Arrupe, "which your Holiness recommended to the general congregation, does your Holiness have any concrete suggestion to make to us?"

"Yes, I have something more to say, but I will do so also after the council."

"Is there anything else?"

"Yes," replied the pope,

I want the Society to become involved in the formation of laypeople, so that they can fill the positions that correspond to them, according to the dispositions of the council. Such formation is quite necessary; otherwise we will run into dangers. But I have complete confidence in the work of the Society.[19]

Arrupe left the meeting feeling optimistic. On June 7, he gave a report to the general congregation on his meeting with Paul VI, saying that it had provided him "great light for my generalate." He stated that the Ignatian spirit of obedience

should be the key for our supernatural mentality and for the effectiveness of our work for the Kingdom of Christ. I believe that the confidence and the conviction with which the Holy Father spoke to me about the Society's faithfulness should be considered a new call for us to serve the Holy See. In other words, it is like the voice of Christ, who wants the Society to show itself faithful and docile to his vicar on earth in these very difficult moments for the church. Such docility is a source of supernatural prudence that will help us develop the most effective strategy possible and practice the Ignatian mobility that is so necessary for our times.

Arrupe went on to stress that the present circumstances, which were "similar to those in the time of Saint Ignatius," needed to be studied, using the means offered by modern science and technology, but always under the orientation of the supreme pontiff, so that Jesuits might submit themselves in complete obedience. He then told his brothers how he had wanted to have a photo taken of himself on his knees before the pope:

At the end of the audience, the supreme pontiff invited me to stand next to him for the photographs. The first one shows the two of us under the image of Christ, and the pontiff indicated to the photographer that he should capture that image above us. The second photo, at the express desire of the

---

19   Exact words repeated by Arrupe himself.

First press conference as general: "If by progressives you mean people who are concerned about justice, then we are with them."

supreme pontiff, shows Paul VI blessing me as I kneel at his feet. I have afterward thought of these photos as symbolic of our future work. There you see the place of the superior general and of the Society: under the image of Christ with his vicar. That is the attitude of the sons of Ignatius: kneeling humbly at the feet of the pontiff, placing themselves in his hands, because whatever proceeds from those hands will be a blessing for us.[20]

After speaking with the press and the pope, Arrupe wanted to speak at length with his own brothers, the Jesuits assembled in the congregation, who wanted to know more about his proposals for the future.

Arrupe's guiding principle was the same as that of Saint Ignatius: "The more universal, the more divine." He explained to his companions what he considered the most universal problems of the day and the actions that needed to be taken to resolve them:

The most universal problems exist on different levels:

a. On the *ideological* level, for example, are found atheism, Marxism, ecumenism, and the problems of social and international justice.
b. On the *cultural* level, there are the cultural evolution of the West, the East, Africa; there are also the progress and the cultural evolution of the human sciences and of anthropological concepts.

20   *Acta congregationis generalis*, 35.

c. Above all, on the *political* level there are important phenomena such as the unification of Europe, Africa, and other regions; the existence and activity of organisms such as the United Nations, UNESCO, etc.; different realignments, such as the Common Market, the Association for the Defense of Civil Rights, and others. According to the council, our objectives will be attained more easily if the faithful themselves, and of course the Jesuits, become aware of their responsibility as humans and as Christians and make an effort to develop a true concern for cooperation, first in their immediate surroundings, but also at the international level.

Both the church and the Society should focus their attention on these problems and seek to help resolve them.

In the exercise of our diverse works and ministries, we should keep in mind certain universal criteria. For the solution of these problems, we will need some flexibility in apostolic action and also in institutional structures. For example, we need theological, philosophical, and scientific studies and publications that attempt to study these problems and find a solution for them in the modern ideological context. The borders of provinces or nations should not be allowed to limit this kind of undertaking, since our work has a universal character. For this purpose, we need cooperation, which consists in coordinating works and persons for the sake of concerted action at a higher level.

Education and pedagogical methods should be restructured in accord with present-day demands and possibilities and should include:

- the educational apostolate in schools of different levels, in which we propose clear principles and orient the students accordingly;
- the social communications media, such as radio and television;
- the social apostolate, through education and action in different centers;
- mutual cooperation in working with laypeople, as for example in the apostolate of the press.

For all this, Arrupe insisted on the need for flexible structures. The divisions among provinces could impede efforts to undertake a common labor: "Adaptation must take place in the structures, the works, the men, the mentalities. It is not an easy job! We should think of the type of transformation that in the world of industry is called *reconversion.*"

While Arrupe saw the need to effect changes to respond to these new and urgent priorities, he recommended that the changes be carried out in a mature and reflective fashion so as to avoid disorder and waste of energy:

We must proceed organically. We don't want to put things off till later. We don't want to remain idle, "waiting for the waters to move." But out of

respect for the real situation of people, we should proceed with full knowledge of the situation and always with the necessary resources at hand [...].[21]

Arrupe's plans were brilliant but presented many challenges. They presup-
posed a new direction and a change of mentality that would inevitably meet up
with obstacles.

In a reception held on June 12 in the Spanish embassy, Arrupe stated frankly:
"Yes, I am Spanish, and I feel deeply the impact that my election has had on our
country. But as a Jesuit I am a Spaniard committed to a universal mission, which
is the only true way to be Spanish."

The first session of the general congregation finished on July 15, 1965, and a
second session was planned for September 1966. One of the principal decisions
of that first session had been the confirmation of the lifelong term of the general,
but with new dispositions that would affect Arrupe's term in office. As we have
seen, provision was made for the resignation of the superior general when he
became incapable of performing the job because of sickness, advanced age, or a
notable diminution of strength. At the same time, some changes were made in
the structure of the order's governance, such as the creation of a general council
made up of the general's four assistants; they would both represent the whole
Society before the general and be his closest consultants for general problems.
The assistants chosen by the congregation were the Italian Dezza, the Canadian
Swain (former vicar general), the American Vincent O'Keefe, and the Hungarian
Andrew Varga. At the same time, regional assistants were appointed to attend to
the concrete needs of the eleven geographical areas into which the Jesuit provinces were divided. The congregation also approved decrees on the mass media
and atheism. Father Oñate became Arrupe's private secretary.

When the first part of the Jesuit parliament ended, Paul VI received Arrupe
again in a private audience, along with his assistants. After expressing gratitude
for the Society's work, he made four significant recommendations, which can
be summed up in Arrupe's own words: (1) we must be faithful to ourselves, to
our Institute, and to our laws and Constitutions; (2) we must keep in mind the
well-known recommendation that Jesuits should "be as they are, or not be," so
that the *aggiornamento*, as necessary as it is, in no way prejudices the fundamental spirit and laws of the Institute; (3) we must harmonize this fidelity to
the Institute with the adaptations required by the modern apostolate, since the
Society must live and work in today's world; and (4) we must be faithful to the
church and the Apostolic See.[22]

---

21   See documents of General Congregation 31. Cited also in *Itinéraire*, 33.
22   *Carta a toda la Compañía sobre la Congregación General 31*, July 31, 1965, *Acta Romana*
     S.I. 14 (1961–66): 643–48.

Faith for the Year 2000

Changes were immediately evident in the Jesuit headquarters in Rome. The Arrupe era revealed something of his character. The long, solemn dining room tables of monastic origin were replaced with small five-person tables; the furniture in the general's office was rearranged to allow for more relaxed conversation; and Arrupe arranged to have installed in his room a small bar so that he could treat his guests to refreshments. The whole house became infused with the cordiality, simplicity, joyfulness, and industriousness of the new general.

Arrupe did not change personally. He continued to get up before the chickens and to work until late at night. He continued to dedicate long hours to prayer, and for that purpose he remodeled a room near his office in the oriental style. Arrupe would sit Japanese style in that carpeted chapel for his meditations and periods of reflection.

Arrupe's agenda as general afforded little free time. He was endlessly busy with correspondence, interviews, committee sessions, speeches, talks, and meetings with distinguished personages. Never far distant were the journalists, who became fascinated with the statements of the new general, who was lively, quick with his answers, possessed of a clear vision, and devoid of the fear typical of many high-ranking clerics. He was interviewed, for example, for the Italian journal *Epoca* by Domenico Agasso, who asked him what the faith would be like in the year 2000. Arrupe answered by referring to young people:

> We see them now restless and unsteady. Their contact with the world during this period of transition and change manifests itself in very different ways, but they all possess much dynamism and great sincerity. At times, they appear hostile to religion, but in reality they object only to the formalisms and external trappings of the faith.

He then recalled Hiroshima and how the Japanese people were able to reconstruct their country. After the bomb, he noted, 170 new religions appeared in Japan.

The journalist then asked him another question: "Will Father Arrupe maintain his optimism, even after coming from a Japan that was so slow in accepting Christianity?" The general's answer was lucid:

> The Christian element has been given to all people, whether they believe or don't believe, whether they follow one religion or another, or none at all. This element is present today even in the wayward and in criminals, in their desire for truth, for goodness, for happiness. All of us need a great deal of insight in order to discover this element everywhere, seeking it in the depths of people's souls and leading people toward those values of truth, goodness, and happiness. Our best collaborators are living there within every soul, in those chosen values. We must therefore become very familiar with the ideologies that influence them, but we must always look first to the person,

who is distinct from any ideology and who can always be reached through understanding, friendship, and charity.

Thus we follow the path of love, the path of love's triumph among people through understanding. True understanding is reached by the path of peace, which brings people together and allows them to understand one another. It is therefore clear that we must work hard in order to establish this basic condition of peace. In order for this great factor of peace to be established, we must seek justice, not only among classes but also among peoples, eliminating the differences between rich countries and countries that are starving.

This eloquent response reveals in succinct fashion the essential elements of Arrupe's worldview: faith in human beings, in every person, whether believer or not; an attitude of dialogue; the need for love; and consequently, a commitment to justice and peace. Arrupe's faith is transformed above all into optimism: "Yes, I have complete confidence in the seed that God has sown in men and women."[23]

The cardinals and bishops present in Rome for the council invited Arrupe to meals, or they were invited by him. Brother Roger Schütz of Taizé, accompanied by other non-Catholic observers at the council, also came to talk with the new general, and he would maintain a warm friendship with him all his life.

Before the year ended, Arrupe also had a chance to speak in the council hall. When his name was announced by the president on September 20, a murmur was heard from the more than two thousand council fathers. Though Arrupe's intervention was scheduled for an hour when the bishops usually took refreshments, their curiosity made them remain expectantly in their places, and silence reigned. At the time, the council fathers were debating the famous "schema 13" on "the church and the modern world."

Arrupe's most notable talk took place, however, on September 27, two days after the pope had received him in a private audience. Speaking on the topic of atheism, the general stated:

> The schema on the church in the modern world is praiseworthy for its attempt to find solutions to the problems of today, but I fear that such solutions still remain too much on the intellectual level, especially what is mentioned in number 19 on atheism, no doubt against the intention of the authors. This is a defect of which we are often guilty: [we believe that] the church possesses the truth, the principles, and the arguments, but does it communicate all this to the world in a truly effective way?

After analyzing the failures in communication, Arrupe stated that "atheism is not primarily or exclusively a philosophical problem; it is an experiential one." He continued:

---

23   Magazine *Época* (August 22, 1965). Reproduced in many other journals around the world by correspondents stationed in Rome.

The most radical way to cure the ills that nowadays proceed from atheism and naturalism is the construction of a Christian society, one that is not separated from the world or situated in a ghetto, but exists in the midst of the world. Such a society should be imbued and enlivened above all by a communitarian Christian spirit. Breathing in such an atmosphere, modern men and women will more readily become Christian, or at least religious. Without such an atmosphere, we will convert a few people to Christianity, but we will then quickly lose them to a world that is not Christian or even religious.[24]

Arrupe's speech found favor among many attending the council and was echoed in several later speeches by the assembled bishops. But there was also a conservative wing in the council chamber, led by Marcel Lefebvre, who at the time was superior general of the Missionaries of the Holy Spirit but who years later would become a dissident and schismatic bishop. Those who believed that Paul VI's commission to the Jesuits to fight atheism should take the form of a fierce anti-Marxist crusade felt defrauded. At the same time, Arrupe's speech was met with incomprehension on the part of other sectors as well. The prestigious theologian Yves Congar termed the speech "horrible" in his *Council Diary*: "It seemed to me horrible: he is preaching a great mobilization against atheism, as an army under the orders of the pope."[25] The German weekly *Der Spiegel* subsequently dedicated a cover story to the Jesuits.[26]

On October 10, Arrupe intervened again in the council, this time on a topic dear to him: missionary activity, its deficiencies and its needs. This speech did not please the conservatives either since he advocated inculturation of the faith rather than transculturation. The new general's broad experience as a missionary aroused so much interest that he would later be requested to give a conference on the topic in the Vatican press office. There he dared to state the following:

---

24   In Pedro Arrupe, *La iglesia de hoy y del futuro* (Santander: Sal Terrae, 1982), 125. This interview was not well understood in some sectors. Concretely, it was criticized in the United States since the "struggle against atheism" seemed to contradict the famous "dialogue" that was also promoted by Paul VI. Arrupe was happy to clarify this point in statements made to the German weekly *Der Spiegel* and the French journal *Réalités* (December 1965), where he stated:

> Our struggle must always respect the person of the atheist, because even if error can be absolute on the theoretical level, it cannot be so on the concrete level. Absolute error never becomes totally concrete in human beings. Since that is the case, there is always something to be appreciated in what the atheists tell us.

In this interview, he also expressed esteem for Zen and oriental mysticism: "I am very sensitive to the human values that I have discovered in Japan: self-control, the delicacy of souls, courtesy, fidelity to country, respect for the law, concern for the family, love of children."

25   Yves Congar, *Mon journal du concile* (Paris: Cerf, 2002), 2:409.

26   *Der Spiegel*, October 27, 1965.

In its universality, the church encounters very diverse cultures, and these provide it with the occasion to detach itself from forms and expressions that it has sometimes thought to be definitive and necessary. The selfsame message must become completely Latin, completely Oriental, completely Chinese or Japanese, etc., without any one culture imposing itself on another, not even in announcing the Gospel.[27]

To be sure, the spirit of Vatican II greatly influenced the activity of the new Superior General of the Jesuits. As Santiago Madrigal has observed,

Vatican II oriented and nourished Arrupe's deepest intentions and his style of theological reflection, as he sought to be true to the theological reach of the maxim cited above: "following in the wake of the Second Vatican Council." *This is not a rhetorical formula that can be reduced to more or less trite and random citations from* council texts for the sake of illustrating topics treated in a conference. Rather, [...] it provided the main focus of Arrupe's thought, which was in perfect agreement with the specific theological method underlying *Gaudium et spes*, the pastoral constitution on the church's task in the world of today.[28]

Many newspapers carried Arrupe's words on their front pages, but in Spain there was particular interest in the rather exceptional meeting that took place between Arrupe and Josemaría Escrivá.

With the Founder of Opus Dei

The meeting took place on October 10, 1965, the feast of Saint Francis Borgia, when Escrivá visited Arrupe, returning a visit Arrupe had paid to him on September 12. The two priests concelebrated and conversed; they had photos taken of themselves together on the terrace of the Jesuit curia, near Saint Peter's Basilica. Arrupe and Escrivá appear together in a photo with basilica's dome in the background. They were accompanied by Álvaro del Portillo, who would succeed Escrivá as president of Opus Dei. From that moment on, Arrupe tried to get closer to the founder of Opus Dei, but his numerous attempts did not always meet with success.[29] His efforts were aimed at smoothing over the persistent tensions and dissensions between Jesuits and members of Opus Dei. Despite the rebuffs, Arrupe never uttered a word of criticism about Escrivá or his institute. At the most, he might make a joke, but always in good humor. Once he was asked, "Father Arrupe, how are your relations with Monsignor Escrivá?"

---

27   Typewritten text.
28   Santiago Madrigal, "Su sentido de iglesia siguiendo la estela del Vaticano II," in La Bella, *Pedro Arrupe, general de la Compañía de Jesús*, 635–67, here 661.
29   See newspapers of that date.

Arrupe with Josemaría Escrivá de Balaguer, founder of Opus Dei, on the roof of the Jesuit curia.

He responded, "Fine, though he must like me less now, because before he used to give me two kisses, and now he gives me just one."

Before the end of that eventful year 1965, Arrupe would be involved in countless other activities. For example, the day after the council ended, he wrote to all the Jesuit provincials, instructing them to begin a sociological survey of the whole order and to develop apostolic strategies in keeping with the council.

On December 19, Arrupe made his first major trip as general, which his secretary described in a letter to Fernando Gondra and his spouse, Emilia:

Our Father General has made his first intercontinental journey. Today, he is in Beirut, and tomorrow he will be in Cairo, on his way to Addis Ababa early on the twenty-fifth. Before Beirut, he visited Damascus and Baghdad. He is planning to visit all our African missions in Zambia, Rhodesia, Congo, Cameroon, and Chad. The final leg will be from Tripoli to Rome, and we will have him back in the house on January 14. This little trip is going to be a workout for him since there is a lot of territory to cover in such a short time, but you know that he is not afraid of such workouts. The vitamins arrived well, Emilia. He received them and is already using them. I think that they help him a lot, even if he doesn't put on weight. I hope that after this journey is over he will have a more relaxed program. The pace he was keeping during the council was frightful, but the fruit reaped from his interviews has also been very consoling.[30]

---

30   Letter of Arrupe's secretary, Father Oñate, to Fernando Gondra and wife (December 23, 1968).

The Novitiate of a General

Arrupe displayed an attitude of great simplicity during this first trip. In Lebanon, he told the Jesuits that he had gone there to learn from them and that he did not want to do what he had seen so many new arrivals do in Japan: after two weeks there, they were experts on the country. He wanted to get to know people and get to be known by them. He kept repeating humorously, "I am in my novitiate as a general." He discussed his ideas concerning atheism, the need for adaptation, and the challenges of the future, but what most impressed his audiences was the tone of his talks. One report on his trip stated:

> He left everybody, both young and old, charmed and very encouraged, perhaps because he was seen to be very Jesuit, capable of rethinking practically about everything in the light of a few fundamental principles and without prejudices. He was free in his thinking about how to adapt the means to the ends.

The next day, in his visit to Syria, Arrupe had to cross a mountain range in a helicopter that had been put at his disposal by the Lebanese government. He was supposed to land in the agricultural center that the Jesuits had set up on the wastelands of Tanali Ksara, but fog prevented the aircraft from landing at the site; as a result, it had to fly to the observatory the Society ran, which was five kilometers distant from Ksara. From there, the party traveled by land to the farm. Arrupe later joked with the brother who was in charge of the farm: "Of course, since you haven't left a patch of land uncultivated, we couldn't find any place to land."

Arrupe had interviews with countless people: the Melkite patriarch Cardinal Maximos IV Saigh, representatives of the Syrian Orthodox and Greek Orthodox patriarchates in Antioch, the Muslim Grand Mufti, the president of the republic, several ministers of government, and many other less notable persons. Arrupe was, by all accounts, quite charming in his formal and informal talks with Jesuits. He told jokes and stories about Brother Gárate, the saintly porter of Deusto (Bilbao), whom he as a young man had known personally. In Iraq, more impressive than his many meetings with dignitaries and his visits to the university and schools was his encounter with an elderly coadjutor brother. The brother lived in a language-learning school situated a thousand meters above sea level; for reasons of health and the difference in air pressure, he could not leave the place, so Arrupe made a special journey there for the sole purpose of visiting him.[31]

The journey continued to Ethiopia, Nairobi, Lusaka (Zambia), the Congo, Cameroon, and Tripoli. In statements made later to Radio Bilbao, Arrupe expressed satisfaction with his eighteen thousand-kilometer journey. Asked about his contacts with political leaders, he responded: "These leaders see that we

---

31   Information of Miguel de Epalza (December 19–24, 1968).

are not involved in politics, but that we work for the people and for their cultural and religious development." Taking advantage of the microphones, Arrupe sent greetings to all the inhabitants of Bilbao and saluted the patroness of his native city, the Virgin of Begoña.[32]

From the very first, however, despite the importance of the journeys and the contacts, the general's attitude made one thing quite clear: persons were more important than works. Human beings had priority over institutions. In his extended hand, his sincere look, and his ready smile, Jesuits could sense not only the authority of a superior but the affectionate closeness of a brother and a friend. Every Jesuit who came into contact with him in any part of the world could state with a strange interior certainty: "Father Arrupe really likes me."

He had hardly been in the job eight months.

"Here You Have Me"

What was happening meanwhile in Arrupe's interior depths? We need to go back to the summer of 1965 to know something of that. As we have seen, on July 17 of that year he had his second audience with the pope, accompanied by his general assistants. On July 24, he joined the community of the curia, who had gone for their traditional vacation to the house at "Villa Cavalleti," near Frascati. On July 31, he interrupted his vacation to preside at the Eucharist on the feast of Saint Ignatius in the Gesù Church, where the founder's remains are venerated. That same day, he made a very typical and memorable gesture: he went out of his way to congratulate the brother who was the cook for the curia, Ignacio Urcola, on his name day. On August 1, he returned to "Villa Cavalletti" to begin ten days of Spiritual Exercises, the first retreat he was making as general of the Society.

Iglesias has published and annotated the rich text of the retreat notes that Arrupe made during those days.[33] They were written down in a school notebook of fifty-two lined pages (thirty-two by twenty-one centimeters), in cramped text that gave evidence of having been written rapidly, as if by someone whose heart was running faster than his hand.

These notes on the Exercises reveal a man who felt himself chosen by God for a great mission and who was trying to express his inner turmoil in the face of his new responsibility. I refer the reader to the study and the annotations of Father Iglesias for a full understanding of this interesting text. Its central focus is what Arrupe calls "serving in mission" by following Jesus, which means that a Jesuit "reproduces his traits" and undertakes a "worldwide action" or "worldwide planning," for which he must first know the modern world in depth.

---

32   Cf. the Bilbao daily *El correo español: El pueblo vasco* (January 18, 1968).

33   Pedro Arrupe, *Aquí me tienes, Señor: Apuntes de sus Ejercicios espirituales (1965)* (Bilbao: Mensajero, 2002). Iglesias has expanded on this spiritual process in "Aportaciones a su biografía interior," 975–1019.

During a session of Vatican II, Arrupe chats with eminent theologians Karl Rahner and Henri de Lubac.

Arrupe was ahead of his times and saw himself as a global missionary who needed a Trinitarian inspiration. He affirmed the need for working on social structures, for choosing ministries suitable for the present time, for bringing about internal reform, and above all for "being absolutely committed to persons" in order to "keep the Society in shape." All of this would mean for him personal abnegation, poverty, humility, work, generosity, much study, austerity—in a word: a lifestyle in accord with the Gospel.

These notes deserve the serious study of specialists, but what most interests us here is how they reveal facets and traits of Arrupe himself. They reveal a generous heart in the Ignatian manner, a heart open to the "whole universe," to the church, to the pope. They reveal an authentic missionary, a man of intense prayer, a man united to God not for himself but for the sake of others and especially for Jesuits. Thus, without intending to do so, he spelled out in these notes what he would actually become in the years ahead: "The general is the chief, but he is the head and the father. He is governor and administrator; thence follow friendliness, affection, fatherly frankness, clarity, determination, firmness [...], understanding, kindness, warmth, and love."

Arrupe felt that God was asking a great sacrifice of him: God wanted him to become a "servant," a "little one" in the Gospel sense—only in this way would he be endowed with "an extraordinary strength." These dense notes also confirm the already mentioned thesis that Arrupe during his formation years had made a "vow of perfection" to God, a voluntary commitment to seek God's will and to do it, always choosing what was most conducive to that end. "Now I must observe it with great care, for my preparation for hearing, seeing, and being an instrument of the Lord will depend on that."[34]

Iglesias states that there are Jesuits who have personally seen the document of Arrupe's vow of perfection. In a handwritten letter that Nicolás Verástegui, sub-secretary of the Society of Jesus, sent to Iglesias, he mentions that he collected Arrupe's personal belongings after he had fallen seriously ill, and he adds:

> In a small drawer of the pre-dieu, next to the door to his office, I found, among other things, a monochrome postcard with the image of the Lord (I think it was the Sacred Heart), printed in a dark greenish tone; on the back, he had written down the formula of his vow of perfection. I have the impression that at that time I concluded that it was made during, or at the end of, his tertianship. Now, twenty-three years later, I cannot be more concrete.[35]

It appears, therefore, that the original text still exists, but for the moment its precise location is unknown.

In the swift, diminutive handwriting of Arrupe's retreat notes, his particular devotion to the Heart of Jesus and the Eucharist reappears:

> Real presence of Christ, my friend, my great chief, but at the same time my most intimate confidant. The work is of both of us: he communicates to me his plans, his desires; my job is to collaborate *externally* in his plans, which he must carry out internally with his grace. What a magnificent work he is placing in my hands; it requires a complete union of hearts, an absolute identification: Always with him! He will never leave me! I must show him confidence and fidelity, never separate myself from him. But the root is in the *amor amicitiae* [love of friendship], in feeling like the other self of Jesus

---

34 Iglesias notes:

> These two pages (25–26) should be interpreted as a formulation of the Third Kind of Humility, in accord with the interior dynamic that Arrupe experienced on the morning of August 6. Can this personal intimation be confirmed *ab exteris* [by external evidence] with the historical fact, frequently mentioned by members of the Jesuit curia in Rome, that Arrupe went to confession every day with Father Dezza?

> As we shall see, Dezza will be an antagonist of Arrupe in the most dramatic crisis of his life (Arrupe, *Aquí me tienes, Señor*).

35 Iglesias, "Aportaciones a su biografía interior," 985–86n19. In this profound chapter, Iglesias analyzes Arrupe's spiritual trajectory in light of his retreat notes and compares his evangelical radicalism with that of Ignatius of Loyola, who in the *Spiritual Exercises* speaks of "considering, according to all reason and justice, what I ought to offer the Divine Majesty." On Arrupe's discernment, see Ignacio Iglesias, "Una aportación del testimonio y del magisterio de Pedro Arrupe: El discernimiento espiritual," in *Testigos del siglo XX: Maestros del siglo XXI*, ed. María Teresa Alonso Baquer et al., XIII Simposio de Historia de la Iglesia en España y América, Academia de Historia Eclesiástica, Sevilla, April 8, 2002 (Córdoba: Publicaciones Obra Social y Cultural CajaSur, 2003), 243–63.

Christ. With a most profound humility, but also with tremendous joy and happiness. I am always with him! Always waiting on his words and desires! What a joyous life! Thanks, my God. Here you have me, Lord!

Still another fragment that is valuable for understanding the motivating force of Arrupe's whole life was what Arrupe calls "Jesus Christ and I: the unique personal relationship":

> That personal love has a very important aspect of exclusivity or uniqueness. After all is said and done, all that remains is Jesus Christ. Everything else— collaboration, personal esteem, and even sincere love—is found to be something contingent, limited, temporal, variable. The only thing that remains always and everywhere, the only thing that must orient and help me always, even in the most difficult circumstances and in the most painful cases of incomprehension, is the love of that unique friend who is Jesus Christ. That does not discount other friendships or other truly charitable relationships based on sincerity and esteem on the part of human beings. But life is such, people are such, and one's own personal difficulties are such, that one can count always and in all circumstances only on Jesus Christ.
>
> This idea is of immense value. We must be theoretically and practically convinced of it. Jesus is my true, perfect, perpetual friend. I must give myself over to him, and from him must I receive friendship, support, direction. But also his intimacy, rest, conversation, advice, comfort […].; the place is before the sanctuary: Jesus Christ can never leave me. I am always with him. Lord, may I never leave you, *et numquam me a Te separare permittas* [and never let me be separated from you].

These words are all the more impressive when we know all that happened subsequently, events that will provoke a situation not unlike that of Christ himself: "I will strike the shepherd and the flock will scatter." These retreat notes constitute in fact a kind of spiritual anticipation of all that Arrupe would experience as general, and they provide a synthetic vision of his profound communication with God, his closeness to the world to which he dedicates his mission, and his affectionate and deeply human character. Much evidence for all these traits is found throughout these retreat notes, which Iglesias has published under the very Arrupian title: *Aquí me tienes, Señor*—Here you have me, Lord.

15. The Contentious Sixties

The decade of the sixties will be remembered in future times as years of alarm and surprise; it was an epoch that engendered tremendous cultural and political changes in which we find ourselves still embroiled. Simply recounting some of the events of that decade can give us an idea of the worldwide upheaval that brought about an authentic "future shock."

While Brasília, a symbol of the city of the future, was being born, another city, Berlin, was being divided by an impassable wall. Hardly had the decade begun when seventeen African countries were obtaining their independence. In 1961, Yuri Gagarin became the first human being to venture into outer space in a capsule named Vostok 3KA. Down below, people continued to war among themselves. Algeria, battered by a new kind of guerrilla warfare, devised a new system for undermining the established powers, which would later become the cancer of international terrorism.

In the year 1962, the Cuban missile crisis unmasked the truth behind the arms race, while Fidel Castro celebrated his first success in the Bay of Pigs. At the same time that the ideals of John F. Kennedy were suffering their first onslaughts, the United States and the rest of the world were mourning the death of Marilyn Monroe, a star who suffered an infirmity that was becoming ever more prevalent in the opulence of the great cities: loneliness. An internal crisis of values also took the life, in Dallas, of the thirty-fifth president of the United States, killed by an almost phantom assassin, behind whom was hidden a more powerful hand: the corruption of the system itself. Nothing could be the same after Kennedy's death, just as no artistic sensibility could be the same after four unknown lads, calling themselves the Beatles, emerged in Liverpool, armed with guitars, and revolutionized the world of music.

Such events led up to 1964, when Khrushchev's decade in power began and brought with it a thawing of Stalinism in the Soviet Union. Japan was now boasting of its economic miracle, and the whole world was becoming a global village, thanks to ever speedier and cheaper telecommunications. Young people, however, were increasingly disillusioned with such a bourgeois society and dreamed of escaping from an overly complicated world. First there was the beat generation, then the rockers, and finally, with the fullness of the sixties, the flowering of the hippies. The contrasts between progress and distress at the global level became accentuated. Technology and consumerism penetrated into First World homes, while hunger devastated the Third World. There was no place for dreamers like Che Guevara and Martin Luther King, but there was abundant opportunity for military regimes in Africa and Latin America, for lightning conflicts like the Six-Day War, for US bombardment of countries in Southeast Asia, for an uncontrolled space race, and for the crushing of the Prague Spring by around six hundred thousand Warsaw Pact soldiers. As a consequence, the students in Paris got fed up and invaded the streets; they raised barricades such as had not been seen since the time of the Commune; they plastered the walls with slogans that were half provocation and half hilarity. Finally, the situation exploded in the month of May, shaking a weary society out of its terminal boredom and portending the downfall of industrial society. "All power to the imagination"; "be realistic: ask for the impossible"; "the revolution is the orgasm of history"; "do what you like"—such were the slogans that decorated the walls of the City of Lights, reflecting a supercharged consciousness on all sides. It was on young people such as these that the police finally fell on October 2, 1968, spilling blood on the Plaza of the Three Cultures in Mexico.

This was the remarkable setting within which the first years of Arrupe's generalate were to unfold. By the time the sessions of Vatican II came to an end in 1965, the world was seeing a new face of the church. Given the involution that has taken place since then, it is important to remember that the council's focus was mainly pastoral: it communicated to people a new vision of the church's inner life, it established new contacts with non-Catholic Christians, and it forged a fresh way of relating to the realities of the modern world.

An Era of "Protest"

The council redefined the church in terms of being "the people of God" rather than just a simple juridical society: all Catholics, and not just the hierarchy, have responsibility for the church's life. This new vision of the church was less pyramidal and authoritarian and more fraternal and communitarian. Thanks to the greater stress on human and democratic values within the church, more importance was given to episcopal conferences and the practice of collegiality. The Synod of Rome was created as a council of bishops to advise the pope, and priest councils and pastoral councils were formed in the dioceses. The liturgy was reformed to bring it closer to the people, and the Mass was celebrated in the vernacular. The church passed from being a sectarian institution to one that fully recognized the autonomy of human realities. It made its own "the joys, the hopes, the sorrows, and the anxieties" of all peoples, and it committed itself firmly to human rights and the struggle for justice. This shift did not take place painlessly. The worldwide social crisis soon made itself felt in the church in a series of internal crises: of obedience, of vocations, of priestly identity, of family life, and of sexuality. People felt a new freedom and were more prone to protest. A new world was bursting forth.

In the midst of this confusing turmoil, Arrupe refused to lose hope and kept moving forward, as he once had amid the rubble of a devastated Hiroshima. As La Bella has written:

The decrees of GC 31 and the tough, laborious, often excruciating post-conciliar adaptation were for the order much more than an *aggiornamento*. No other religious order or Catholic organization experienced in those years so radical and profound a metamorphosis as the Society of Jesus. So much was this the case that many who specialize in the order's history, such as Manuel Revuelta González, Jean Lacouture, and Jean-Claude Dhôtel, view this important moment as one that brought about a decisive conversion in the institution. With Arrupe's election and the process begun by GC 31, they argue, there came into being a third, "renewed" Society, very different from the "restored" Society of 1814 and much more faithful to the original intuitions of the "old" Society.[1]

After returning from his trip to Africa, Arrupe visited France in 1966. In Paris, a cultural bellwether of Europe, not a few Jesuits presented problems of obedience, and others were deeply involved in politics or the worker-priest movement.

Addressing Jesuits in the chapel of Montmartre, where Ignatius and his companions had pronounced their first vows, Arrupe spoke in his direct and lively style:

> This apostolate has no limits other than those of the entire world, which is called to be the church of Jesus Christ. I do not fear to tell you this, you who live in Paris in a society so rich in cultural exchanges and stimulating ideas, you who have such a great responsibility to a world suffering from war, hunger, and poverty. And you will not be surprised to hear it from me, the general superior of an order committed by Saint Ignatius to the universality of the church's mission. As poor as you may be, you are extremely rich in natural and spiritual goods. May the light of Christ help you open your eyes to the immensity of human misery so that you may offer some remedy, either by prayer or by action. God is found in the whole of life. God is always communicated. God is working for the salvation of the whole world.[2]

On April 19, 1966, Arrupe became the first Jesuit general to travel to the United States, where, accompanied by Father O'Keefe, he kept up an exhausting pace, insisting as always on having direct contact with the many Jesuit communities. The press, which had been critical of his speech on atheism at the council,[3] produced abundant commentary on the homily that he gave at the

---

1   La Bella, "La crisis del cambio," 884–85. Cf. Manuel Revuelta González, "La Compañía de Jesús renovada (1965–2003)," in *Los jesuitas en España y en el mundo hispánico*, ed. Teófanes Egido (Madrid: Marcial Pons; Fundación Carolina, Centro de Estudios Hispánicos e Iberoamericanos, 2004), 399–445.

2   Cf. *Loyola* (1966), a journal for friends and benefactors of the Loyola province (Basque Country).

3   Cf. *El correo español: El pueblo vasco* and *La gaceta del norte*, April 6, 1966.

Church of Saint Ignatius in New York. There, Arrupe pointed out that a great many Catholics were wary of the "new world" that had descended on them so rapidly and unexpectedly:

> They believe that in this world machines have supplanted human beings, liberty has replaced law, and doubt has banished certainty. Even the church finds itself in such a state of ferment and internal renewal that the ordinary Catholic feels confused, while the sophisticated Catholic adopts a very critical spirit. But it is not this new world that I am afraid of. What worries me, rather, is that we Jesuits will have little or nothing to offer it, little or nothing to say to it or do for it, so as to justify our existence as Jesuits. I fear that we will repeat yesterday's answers to deal with tomorrow's problems; that we will speak in such a way that people don't understand us; that we will use a language that does not reach directly to people's hearts. If we do that, then perhaps we will speak more and more, but only to ourselves; nobody else will listen to us, because nobody will understand what we are trying to say.[4]

Speaking at Fordham University on the topic of the council and human rights, Arrupe aroused much enthusiasm in the audience.[5] In his speech, he touched on liberty, dialogue, and the church's esteem for human values:

> Modern men and women have focused their attention on the dignity of the human person, and they have devoted centuries to understanding better what that dignity requires: new rights and a new awareness of personal responsibility. The church responds to this favorably with a growing appreciation of human autonomy and also of human responsibility.[6]

---

4   Due to the sharp criticisms emanating from the press office of the US bishops, both the secular and the religious press in the United States were overwhelmingly negative in reporting about Arrupe's speech on atheism. *Time* quoted an anonymous Jesuit professor in Rome: "I think his speech was naïve. [...] It was the discourse of a man who does not understand the situation. His language was that of the old papal bulls that spoke of putting oneself under the standard of Christ. Of course, if it's taken seriously, it's absurd."
    The American commentator on the council, Francis X. Murphy, using the pseudonym Xavier Rynne, wrote that Arrupe's "detailed suggestions for combating modern atheism seem rather to be taken from a page of [...] Opus Dei. Not so much because Arrupe recommends a concrete plan for combating atheism, but because he unfortunately expresses himself in military terms." According to the *New York Times*, "Arrupe's statement was a surprise [...] Among Americans in Rome there were murmurs about McCarthyism" (see James F. X. Pratt, "Pedro Arrupe, catalizador de la reforma de los Estados Unidos," in La Bella, *Pedro Arrupe, general de la Compañía de Jesús*, 585–620, here 588ff.).
5   The *New York Herald Tribune* called the visit historic, and the *New York Times* published a photo of the general of the Jesuits on its front page. The visit to the United States lasted two weeks.
6   Cf. *Loyola* 1966.

Arrupe views a map of Jesuit works in the United States during his first trip to that country (April 1966). His assistant and close collaborator, Vincent O'Keefe is third from left.

Arrupe did not rest for a minute during his trip. When boarding a magnificent plane lent to him by a company to travel around the country, he exclaimed: "Amazing! If Xavier, who had to travel to the Far East on sailing ships, could only see this contraption!"

In Saint Louis, a journalist asked him, "Will there some day be an American pope?"

"I haven't the slightest idea," responded Arrupe.

"How about an American general of the Jesuits?"

"I see no reason why not [...]."[7]

The "American way of life" was something already familiar to Arrupe, who knew quite well how to move about in US society. At one point, when asked about Father Daniel Berrigan, an anti-war Jesuit who had been imprisoned for burning draft records and was at the time exiled in Central America, Arrupe answered: "We respect individual cases; therefore we should also respect authority. It is necessary to study each personal case in depth in order to understand it. This is a local case that I have not studied enough to be able to understand it completely."

In the same press conference, Arrupe reminded journalists that "God has not died; rather he is quite alive." He insisted that "the church is the same; only the appearances change, not what is essential." And he stressed that the Society of Jesus could not respond to today's questions with yesterday's answers.

---

7   *St. Louis Review* 26 (April 15, 1966).

Shedding Light on *Aggiornamento*

Much of Arrupe's time was naturally taken up also with the ordinary governance of the Society, out of Jesuit headquarters on Borgo Santo Spirito in Rome. In all the interviews and meetings he had with his closest collaborators and with provincials from all over the world, one theme stood out especially during the year 1966: preparation for the second session of GC 31, which was to be held from September 8 to November 17 of that year.

In a letter to his niece Mariví and his nephew Guillermo, Arrupe wrote:

> We continue in this life around here, busy in a great many things, in the midst of a troubled world with so many problems. I hope that the Lord will enlighten us to take the measures needed at this moment when everything needs renewing. Wouldn't you be interested in taking a trip to Rome? It gets very hot around here, though; it can't be compared with the breezes of Abra.[8]

There arrived in Rome for the general congregation hundreds of postulates that had been previously examined by the provincial congregations; they represented the concerns of the whole order. The task of *aggiornamento* that prevailed after the council influenced the work of the commissions into which the 225 delegates were divided.

The Society's governance, its apostolic activities, its intellectual formation, its spiritual life, its internal structure, and its place in the present-day church were the main topics debated in the second session of the Jesuit parliament. The congregation's decisions were guided by the encyclical *Ecclesiae sanctae*, in which Paul VI asked religious orders to treat the topic of "adaptation and renewal" of religious life in their chapter meetings. The decrees of GC 31 expressed a new appreciation of the legacy of Saint Ignatius and the importance of adapting it to the present day. One interesting change was that the Society's six thousand coadjutor brothers, who were not priests, could now hold certain posts in the order that were formerly reserved to priests, especially posts of an administrative nature. Collaboration with laypeople and a posture decidedly in favor of ecumenism were among the issues that the mass media highlighted.[9] Arrupe intervened in the congregation no fewer than twenty times, exercising strong personal leadership while encouraging and stimulating the delegates to appraise the crises of the day in a realistic manner.[10]

---

8   Gondra File. Rome, August 4, 1988. In a handwritten note, Arrupe added: "To Cata and my other little sisters, my greetings."

9   Cf. *Documentos de la Congregación General XXXI* (Zaragoza: Hechos y Dichos, 1966), "Discurso del Padre General" (May 24, 1966), 17.

10   Valero writes:

> In this sense, it can be said that Arrupe exercised clear leadership in the GC, both in planning how it dealt with issues and in helping the delegates to deliberate well

At the start of this second session of the Jesuit assembly, Arrupe gave the delegates a "secret" talk, in which he sketched out the image of itself the Society was projecting to the world, an image that the pope thought was in need of "serious adjustments." It seems that the pope did not want to speak about this in public in order to avoid distortion on the part of the press; he therefore communicated it to the general, who in turn undertook to transmit it confidentially to his companions. Valero gives a summary of this secret three-page communication. It contained a warning about "five dangers," later referred to as "evils," which Paul VI felt were affecting the Society: carelessness about the spiritual life, neglect of discipline, lack of vigilance on the part of superiors, problems with obedience, and a certain secular mentality and lack of knowledge and appreciation of the religious life, especially among the younger men. The document ended with some considerations about the pernicious effects of these ills on the Society and the church and the need to remedy them in strict union with the Apostolic See. The text, which apparently was written in an objective style for the general's own use, also made reference to the Society's publications and advised that their function should be that of declaring and promulgating the church's doctrine rather than criticizing the church.[11] Perhaps the pope was unaware that the general congregation, in its "Account of Defects," had been more severe and even ruthless in its own self-diagnosis and in its analysis of the causes and remedies of

---

and keep up their spirits in difficult moments. In some cases, when he considered it convenient, he also contributed his own opinion on issues being treated, even while expressly refraining from influencing the result of the debates. Among his interventions linked to special moments, apart from the three conferences or points for meditation he offered freely to the delegates during the triduum preceding the second period of sessions, were his allocutions after his election and his first audience with the pope, his allocution at the opening of the second period of sessions, another one on the progress and situation of the GC at the end of the first month of this second period (to all of which we have already referred), and finally the one pronounced on the occasion of its closure (to which we will refer later when dealing with the GC's result).

Valero, "Al frente de la Compañía," 190ff.).

11   By a pure stroke of fortune, I have been able to find among the *Documenta varia GC 31* a three and a half page document with the title "Excerpta ex allocutione Patris Generalis in sessione plenaria Congregationis Generalis die 20 septembris habita," with a note on the top of the first page "Ad usum stricte personalem." There can be no doubt that this is the allocution we are commenting on or that, from the style of the text, it is at least a full summary of it, if not its complete reproduction (apart from its motive and plan of which there is no trace), which is what I personally consider more probable. We therefore have at least the substantial content of the papal message to the GC transmitted through Arrupe.

Valero, "Al frente de la Compañía," 199ff.

those defects.[12] In any case, the debates about obedience were very lively; in fact, the American representatives reportedly threatened to leave the assembly hall at one point.

But all this was only a prelude to what the media would highlight in the discourse the pope gave at the end of the congregation's labors. Regarding that speech, the French weekly *L'express* had a headline that read, "The Pope Pulls the Jesuits' Ears,"[13] and many other newspapers had captions along the same line. What had happened? The news agencies, relying on a truncated text distributed by the Vatican press office, had supplied to the media only one side of the discourse, namely the harsh questions that Paul VI had addressed to the Jesuits. Pronounced in the setting of the Sistine Chapel, a place that according to the pope was "sacred and tremendous for its beauty, its power, and especially for the meaning of its images," the questions were certainly dramatic:

> Do you, sons of St. Ignatius, soldiers of the Society of Jesus, want even today and tomorrow and always to be what you have been from your foundation right up to the present, for the service of the Catholic Church and of this Apostolic See? Does the church, does the successor of Saint Peter think that the Society of Jesus is still their special and most faithful militia?

Paul VI then referred to "certain reports and rumors that have come to our attention about your Society," certain deviations that have pained the pope.

The discourse as a whole, however, was really quite laudatory of the Society of Jesus. The pope reaffirmed his confidence in the Jesuits and concluded: "The church needs your help, and she is happy and proud to receive it from the sincere and dedicated sons that you are. Yes it is time, most beloved sons: Go forth in faith and ardor. Christ chooses you, the church sends you, and the pope blesses you."[14]

Even so, Arrupe felt a need to clarify things and so wrote a letter to the whole Society on September 3, in which he stated:

> Those of us who were present could not help but be inwardly moved, not only by the contents but also by the sincere, simple, paternal way in which the pope spoke to us. With his tone of confidence he made quite clear to us his concern

---

12   "Such detriments were certainly not more serious than the *Deputatio ad detrimenta* would suggest to the GC a few days later, more straightforwardly as mentioned above, and already substantially known to the delegates" (Valero, "Al frente de la Compañía," 200ff.).

13   *L'express*, November 28–December 4, 1966 refers to the negative reports that were reaching the Vatican. The columnist concluded his article with this paragraph: "The question is the following: the crisis of the church from 1953 to 1955 was preceded by a Roman attack directed against Father de Lubac and the Jesuits. It was the first sign of a harder line. Is history repeating itself? Is the reprimand of today not a sign that in the Vatican prudence is taking the place of boldness?"

14   *Documentos de la Congregación General XXXI*, "Documentos, discurso de Pablo VI a los padres congregados," November 16, 1966.

for the Society; he revealed to us how concerned he has been about certain reports about the Society's condition and how much dismay and pain they have caused him. He mentioned ideologies and defects, which, if they were widespread, would undermine the Society's basic nature—ideologies such as historicism on the level of ideas and secularism on the level of practice.

The general added that the pope was in fact feeling renewed confidence in the Society; he recognized that those dangers existed, but they were often exaggerated.[15]

How had the pope come to have such a negative image of the Society? Certain conservative sectors of the order had been busy. On August 16 and 17, 1996, the ancient house of Loyola had been the site of an international congress on the Spiritual Exercises, originally promoted by Janssens. Swain, Arrupe's first general assistant and vicar, presided over the congress in the general's name. Arrupe had in fact written a letter to his family asking them to receive his special envoy and to accompany him to Bilbao. Taking advantage of free time at the congress, about thirty of the Jesuits present met together with some of the delegates who would be attending the next session of GC 31 in order to discuss with them their gloomy view of the Society's future. Concerned about what they considered a serious deficiency in governance, they wrote a joint communiqué that stated, among other things: "Many Spanish Jesuits continue to be faithful to the true meaning of their vocation and are ready for any sacrifice so that the Society *may once again become fully* what it has gloriously been and must always be."[16]

The accusation could not have been more direct, and it was being made virtually in the presence of Arrupe's delegate. When these representatives of "reaction" were accused of having failed to act in accord with the Society's norms for such cases, they responded that this situation was so exceptional that they had resorted to the method of "assembly," which was certainly a very post-conciliar idea.

Their document was certainly not the only one that reached the Vatican. Some Italian Jesuits close to the curia were also thinking and moving along the same lines. Arrupe was aware of this, but in his magnanimous and respectful way he refused to remove anyone from his post.

In November 1966, Arrupe held a well-attended press conference in the Vatican, where he explained with great care and in several languages the preparations underway for the general congregation and the work that would be done there. The Vatican daily, *L'osservatore romano*, noted the next day that at the press conference Arrupe had received a prolonged ovation, something quite unusual for a journalistic event of that type. The many questions about Paul VI's speech to the Jesuits were answered by the general with incredible agility, as he situated the pope's thoughts within a fuller context.

---

15 *Acta Romana Societatis Iesu* (1961–66): 757–60.

16 Manuel Alcalá, "Gozo y martirio en España," in Alcalá et al., *Pedro Arrupe*, 65–101, here 78.

Second session of General Congregation 31, presided over by Arrupe. He began by quoting Jeremiah,
"Ah, Domine Deus! *I don't know how to speak."*

In a letter to his family, Arrupe made the following comments about the
effect of the pope's discourse on him:

> You no doubt have already heard the racket made by the press, especially
> the foreign press, about the speech the Holy Father gave at the end of our
> general congregation. It seems to me that the storm is blowing over, but we'll
> see how long it lasts! The general congregation was for all of us a great grace
> of God. Now it is our job (and especially mine) to put into practice all that
> was decided there. As you can see, the matter is not simple, but with God's
> help everything will move forward![17]

In reporting on Arrupe's press conference, the *New York Times* stressed
that the general had admitted that some Jesuits had possibly committed errors,
and it cited verbatim a statement that attracted worldwide attention: "I do not
wish to defend any mistake that we Jesuits might make, but the greatest mistake would be to be so overcome by a *fear* of committing errors that we simply
paralyze our work."[18]

The secretary of state of the Holy See, alarmed by the flood of protests,
requested more information from the order. The Jesuits responded with a note
dated March 11, 1968, in which it recognized that

> there exist quite noticeable internal problems: a sharp division between the
> more tenacious traditionalists and the progressives. [...] The small minority
> of conservatives refuses to accept almost any innovation and expresses
> very harsh sentiments toward the present-day Society, and sometimes even

---

17   Letter to his cousin Fernando Gondra, Rome, December 21, 1966. Gondra File.
18   *New York Times*, November 25, 1966.

toward the church and the Holy See. They write letters and memoranda to the civil and ecclesiastical authorities, they circulate mimeographed pages, and they anonymously publish injurious articles.[19]

Dissatisfied with this response, the secretary of state ordered an investigation in Spain, in which several bishops would be involved, as we will see later.

Meanwhile, "Don Pedro," as they were already affectionately calling him in the curia, was settling down to work. In some incisive observations regarding obedience, he recommended that there be greater closeness between superior and subject, "in friendly conversation, as brothers among brothers"; that there be more dialogue between superiors and the governed; that there be a greater "sense of mutual responsibility for the common good, with the one who commands delegating his functions as one who trusts in others"; and that there be respect for the person of the subject and a spiritual communication that is open and sincere.

There were those who malevolently asked whether this was the same Society as the one founded by Saint Ignatius, or rather some kind of modern democracy. Arrupe was not thinking along those lines at all, however, as will become clear below.

The Letter on Latin America

That busy year 1966 was not to end without other new decisions that would provoke consternation. Arrupe understood clearly that the spirit of the council had to be applied to the Society, and he was already giving serious thought to the great evangelical theme of social justice, which was to be a source of much conflict during his generalate. Recalling the excruciating poverty of the slums he had visited in his student days, the postwar misery of Japan, and his extensive trips around Latin America, Arrupe knew that social injustice and lack of solidarity were urgent challenges for people of faith.

In view of this, Arrupe decided to address a letter to Latin American Jesuits in order to stir their consciences and make them aware of how little was being done in the area of social justice. Dated December 12, the feast of the Virgin of Guadalupe, the letter stated:

> The Society is in fact not effectively oriented toward an apostolate on behalf of social justice. Following a strategy justified basically by historical conditions, it has always been more dedicated to exercising an impact on the influential social classes and the formation of their leaders; it has not exercised much influence on the evolving factors that are today bringing about social transformation.

---

19   La Bella, "La crisis del cambio," 884–85.

Arrupe went on to state that social consciousness was "sadly lacking, even in those who have positions of great responsibility" in the order. Concern for justice required Jesuits to review the Society's works in terms of their social function, "because it is conceivable that certain colleges—whether because of their exclusive clientele or their system of financing—raise serious questions about their reason for existing or their need for a radical transformation." The letter was strong and challenging. It called for the courage to make decisions; it declared that the Society was at the service of all people, but with a preference for the very poorest; it asked that discussion of these matters not be demagogical or offensive, but at the same time that no one be surprised if the truth did not please everybody. Speaking the truth was bound to bring problems, but Jesuits needed to find all their strength in Christ. To that end, he asked Jesuits to practice an austere life of witness, reminding them that social justice was not satisfied with almsgiving; rather, it required that all people be given the opportunity to develop themselves fully. He asked whether the wealthier classes attending Jesuit schools were not being confirmed in their class prejudices, and he ended by saying:

> My hope is that, if the Society of Jesus in Latin America and throughout world reacts with true love of neighbor and struggles for a more just and equitable social order—both in distribution of goods and in responsible participation in social, economic, and political life—then God our Lord will mercifully pardon our omissions and the scandals we have possibly caused. For love covers over a multitude of sins.[20]

It was a revolutionary call, not well received by all, since it questioned the existence of many traditional activities, above all the elite colleges. Some of these were eventually closed down. What was perhaps most novel and courageous in this text, however, was the public recognition that Jesuits also commit sins.

The letter, dubbed "Father Arrupe's encyclical" by a French newspaper, caused anxiety among the more conservative Jesuits, who were already beginning to perceive Arrupe as having the ears of a "Marxist wolf." Statements were

---

20   "El apostolado social en América Latina," in Arrupe, *La iglesia de hoy y del futuro*, 281.

> Though based on the encyclical *Mater et Magistra* of John XXIII (May 15, 1961), Father Arrupe's doctrine, resumed in this way, had become, like the pontifical doctrine itself, the target of opposed interpretations in the various mass media and also in the Society. The situation gave rise to attitudes that degenerated into radicalism, dividing the clergy and Christians of different countries and within the Society itself, so that individuals and communities were classified as being "left wing" or "right wing." This confrontation showed itself during the Second Conference of Latin American Bishops in 1968 in the Colombian city of Medellín, at which Father Arrupe was present.

Alberto Gutierrez, "Arrupe y América Latina," in La Bella, *Pedro Arrupe, general de la Compañía de Jesús*, 399–426, here 408).

Pope Paul VI receives the assembled Jesuits in the Sistine chapel and tells them: "The church needs your help" (November 16, 1966).

appearing in print such as: "Following that path will be the ruin of the Jesuits; their concerns about temporal affairs will definitely sink them."

José María de Llanos, the well-known Spanish Jesuit who years before had left the center of Madrid in order to live in a poor slum dwelling, came to the defense of the "scandal of Arrupe" in an article he wrote for the newspaper *Ya*. He argued that since the church has a certain temporal mission, that mission must be carried out from below, and it requires a change of mentality.[21] José María Pemán, the conservative monarchist writer and poet, less suspect of being leftist than Llanos, wrote an essay for the newspaper *ABC*, in which he compared Arrupe with Paul VI, both of whom he said had a "birdlike profile":

> I see them engaged in responsible and resolute dialogue, as two sharp saws applied to the same toughened, impenitent stalk of vicious old vegetation. [...] What is truly sad to see is the delight with which some people—from among those who have surely murmured a thousand times about the class bias of the colleges or the preference for such types—murmur now about Father Arrupe's letter, adopting a papal traditionalism stricter than the pope's own; they speak of the letter as a revolutionary manifesto, a call to class struggle, a dissimulated form of Marxism. It is totally absurd to implicate in such decadent aspects of our Western world that missionary general who has emerged from so many years of humble work in Japan, after being

---

21   Diario *Ya*, Madrid, March 11, 1967.

an eyewitness in Hiroshima of the first atomic bomb. If he is now trying to counter the nuclear bomb of hate and war with his bomb of fraternity and love, it is simply a logical step in his path away from indifference and lack of commitment.

He applied to Arrupe a phrase of François Mauriac: "The world will be saved only by a few people who are fully in the world, but who are nothing like the world."[22]

The reactions cited here come from the first months of 1967. In a letter written to his family on February 23, Arrupe commented:

> I see from Mariví's letter that the *private* letter I wrote to the provincials of Latin America has been published everywhere (today there is no longer anything secret!). It has also been interpreted by some people in a demagogic sense that it just doesn't have: it is simply an application of the encyclical *Mater et magistra* to our Latin American provinces. [...] In the end, we see that the Lord disposes things in *his* manner, which at times is painful for us, but no doubt is best.[23]

An analysis of the handwriting of this personal letter would no doubt reveal the blend of enthusiasm, optimism, naturalness, and balance in Arrupe's character. His main reason for writing this letter to his cousin Fernando was a matter that was quite disagreeable for Arrupe. In the stormy atmosphere of protest that prevailed at the time, some persons, including certain Jesuits, had attacked Fernando, who was a mining engineer, an influential person in Bilbao, and president of Vasconia, S.A. A major strike was called against this business, and several Jesuits participated actively in the strike. It was thus a very distressing situation for Arrupe. The letter states:

> Dear Fernando:
>
> Finally I have decided to write you a few lines. Mariví's last letter has motivated me to break the silence that has in a way been forced on me by the deep pain I have felt at the events that have occurred recently and that have caused you to suffer so profoundly. You can believe me when I say that these events have also touched a very sensitive fiber of my own soul because of my affection for you and because I realize that some of my own brothers are to be found among those who have offended you.
>
> I understand your situation, Fernando, and I want you to feel me closer to you than ever. If I have not made my affection plain to you before, it has been for fear of not knowing how to do so in the proper way, and so I have increased your pain.

---

22   *ABC*, Madrid, March 31, 1967.
23   Letter to his cousin Fernando Gondra, February 23, 1967.

During his first visit to India, Arrupe visited 1,830 Jesuits in the course of twenty-five days (January 1967).

You no doubt have been quite offended by the fact that among those who have attacked you there are some of our people. You can imagine how much that has pained me. [...] I have tried to receive this test from the Lord as a cross that is not at all small. [...] He will know why he has allowed it. I hope that from all this torment you also find great benefits. In situations like this one, it is difficult to see how God's hand allows it, but there is no doubt that the way of Christ is one of humiliation and the Cross. This is his incontrovertible sign! As regards the part that some Jesuits have had in this, you surely know that many others have strongly deplored their action. They have discreetly made this known to me by means of other parties.[24]

This text is a good example of how Arrupe preserved his cordial human spirit in the midst of the vicissitudes of his weighty institutional responsibility. In the end, neither rumors nor sufferings could frighten him or hold him back. In March

---

24   Letter to his cousin Fernando Gondra, February 23, 1967.

1967, he named as provincial of France Jean-Yves Calvez, a forty-year-old Jesuit who in his sociopolitical studies had specialized in the thought of Karl Marx.[25]

Trip to India

During 1967, Arrupe made his fourth and fifth major journeys as general. On January 6, he set off on a twenty-five day trip to visit India and Sri Lanka, where 2,830 Jesuits were working, of whom 1,780 were natives of those countries. Arrupe traveled the length and breadth of India, which encompasses three million square kilometers and then had 490 million inhabitants. His purpose was to encourage the already flourishing work of missionaries who were dedicated to direct pastoral work, education, and inculturation. Wearing garlands and local garb, he traveled endless kilometers in caravans of cars, jeeps, and motorcycles, as well as in trains and planes. As always, what was most important for him was direct contact with people: Arrupe knew how to listen, how to understand, how to smile.

Reflecting on this journey afterward, he wrote:

> India obviously suffers from hunger, but the solution appears no less obvious, since the land is fertile and water is abundant. It is necessary to instruct and educate the people, and work must be done in that regard. The agrarian revolution is coming soon, and there has been no less progress in industry, principally in the area of Calcutta–Ranchi–Jamshedpur, which have plenty of iron, coal, and magnesium.[26]

With regard to the work of the Jesuits, as always his vision was toward the future and the need to adapt to the times.

In his second 1967 journey, from April 21 to May 13, the general visited Alaska, Canada, and the United States. In the middle of a fierce snowstorm that brought extremely low temperatures even for those arctic latitudes, Arrupe visited the legendary Father Segundo Llorente, who commented, "For us Alaskans, Father Arrupe's visit was like a lightning flash." While in the northern climes, the general also conversed with Eskimos and Native Americans, visited Expo 67 in Canada, and joined in pleasant conversation with his brother Jesuits, for whom he sang *Boga, boga, marinero* (Row, sailor, row). Arrupe's visits always left behind the tangible fruit of renewed enthusiasm and idealism among his fellow Jesuits;

---

25   Calvez was born in Saint-Brieuc, Brittany, and served as director of the journal *Études*, consultor to the Holy See, expert at Vatican II, member of the Centre Sèvres in Paris, provincial, and assistant to Arrupe for fourteen years. Among other works he authored are *Le père Arrupe: L'église après le concile* (Paris: Cerf, 1997); *Foi et justice: La dimensión sociale de l'évangélisation* (Paris: Desclée de Brouwer, 1985). His most emblematic work was *La pensée de Karl Marx* (Paris: Éditions du Seuil, 2006).

26   *Loyola* 1967. On Arrupe's role in India, see Rudolf C. Heredia, "Arrupe y la India," in La Bella, *Pedro Arrupe, general de la Compañía de Jesús*, 563– 83, here 563ff.

he communicated a sense of optimism and joy in difficult moments. One person who saw him on this trip revealed Arrupe's secret: "Thanks to a special charism, he is present to others as somehow inferior, as if he were a servant and wanted to learn instead of teach; he acts as if he were an intimate friend who has been away for a long time."[27]

Against Racism in the United States

On returning to Rome, Arrupe was again busy with the normal governance of the Society, rejuvenating the curia, reorganizing some provinces, and launching an in-depth sociological survey to assess the real state of the order he was governing. Before the year ended, however, Arrupe was preparing another strong declaration, in the form of a letter addressed to American Jesuits on racial segregation.

Stressing the urgency of finding a solution to the racial crisis in the United States, the letter points out that, although race and poverty are not necessarily aspects of the same problem, they cannot be considered separately. Further, human attitudes are even more important than laws for resolving the racial problem, which affects not only African Americans but also Hispanics, Native Americans, and immigrants.

In the letter, the general exhorted Jesuits to work closely with racial minorities, and he proposed the following measures: studying the problem in depth, training young people for this work, promoting vocations of blacks, integrating schools and other institutions, contracting firms that obeyed the new anti-discrimination laws, creating Jesuit residences in black neighborhoods, and naming a permanent Jesuit director in each province for the interracial apostolate.

Arrupe's words were, as always, clear and direct:

Although past and present achievements in the interracial apostolate must be duly recognized, it continues to be true that the Society of Jesus has not committed its human and financial resources to this apostolate to the degree to which the blacks need our service. The unsatisfactory social performance of our houses of formation, parishes, retreat houses, schools, and universities can be seen to be the result of our past failure to preach, teach, and practice sufficiently the Christian truths of interracial justice and charity, in conformity with our Jesuit vocation.[28]

---

27 *Loyola* 1967. Cf. Pratt, "Pedro Arrupe, catalizador de la reforma de los Estados Unidos," 588ff.

28 "La crisis racial en Estados Unidos," November 1, 1967, in Arrupe, *La iglesia de hoy y del futuro*, 291ff. The volume of *Acta Romana* where the letter on racism was published also has the letter Arrupe wrote on February 10, 1976 to Father John Markoe of the Wisconsin province on his fiftieth anniversary of religious life. Arrupe stressed that Markoe was one of the few American Jesuits who had carried on an apostolate with African Americans, something he did for many years in Omaha, Nebraska:

This bomb exploded throughout the world. The international press commented that the letter was applicable not only to North Americans. Some journalists were already beginning to call Arrupe a "prophet of our time,"

> because he does not have the bitterness of the old prophets, because he shouts in the middle of the church, because he not only destroys but also plants; he not only criticizes but also praises, stimulates, and motivates; he not only demands but also defends; he not only condemns but also offers solutions and sows ideas and initiatives.[29]

Two other important events for Arrupe in 1967 were his participation in the Synod of Bishops and his election as president of the Union of Superiors General, a post to which he would be re-elected five successive times, until August 1980.[30] Designed to serve as a consultative body that institutionalized episcopal collegiality around the pope, the Synod of Bishops was meeting for the first time. Arrupe gave a talk there titled "Present in the Church," in which he analyzed the need for close spiritual collaboration and mutual confidence between the hierarchy and religious institutes. He also spoke of the existence of tensions between the pastoral planning and the charism of each institute. He ended his talk commenting on the Ignatian maxim of "the more universal being the more divine." Arrupe would be invited to future synods, where his interventions were even more important.[31]

Thus 1967 gave way to 1968, the year of student convulsions and revolutions. In all parts of the world, philosophers, theologians, and other thinkers were asking questions about the new culture that was coming to birth and about the meaning of God for such a changing world, in which the old values were gone and people found themselves caught up in flux and instability. After the Prague Spring, religious persecution increased in Europe, while in Latin America the so-called popular church was beginning to blossom.

In February 1968, as a way of addressing such concerns and of responding to the mandate of Paul VI to "struggle against atheism," Arrupe helped establish

---

> Your lifetime work for blacks was pioneering, and I must also mention your brother in the same context. You were one of the relatively small group of Catholics who understood clearly the urgent demands of charity and justice in this sector of American life and who compensated, as much as any small group could, for the neglect of their Catholic colleagues. The love which so many grateful friends have shown you over the years and the solidarity they still experience are a small measure of the love that the Heart of our Lord has for you.

See Pratt, "Pedro Arrupe, catalizador de la reforma de los Estados Unidos," 601ff.

29 Juan Arias in the daily *Pueblo*, Madrid, November 7, 1967.

30 See Manuel Alcalá, "Pedro Arrupe y la vida religiosa en el posconcilio," in La Bella, *Pedro Arrupe, general de la Compañía de Jesús*, 672–709, here 672ff.

31 Alcalá, "Pedro Arrupe y la vida," 680–81ff.

Arrupe lighting a candle at the sepulcher of Saint Francis Xavier (Goa, January 12, 1967).

in Spain the Institute of Faith and Secularity as a place for studying and reflecting on unbelief. At the institute, believers and agnostics could talk together, and committed Christians could sit down with politicians, intellectuals, and theologians in order to dialogue about the meaning of God in a world undergoing profound transformations.

Writing to the first director of that institute, Alfonso Álvarez Bolado, Arrupe insisted on the need to unite forces with laypeople and to seek assistance from them:

> Every good Christian must be ready to view his neighbor in the best light rather than condemn him. [...] This readiness to listen to one's neighbor and learn from him should go together with what Saint Ignatius, using Pauline language, called "discernment of spirits." In this way will the dialogue be sincere, fruitful, and revealing.[32]

---

32 On the dialogue with cultures, see Jean-Yves Calvez, "Diálogo, cultura, evangelio," in La Bella, *Pedro Arrupe, general de la Compañía de Jesús*, 805–28, here 805ff.

In Dom Hélder's Brazil

As we have seen, however, Europe was not Arrupe's main concern. In April 1968, he undertook another important trip to Latin America, this time to Brazil.

Working in the northeast of that country, in the midst of terrible poverty and injustice, was a diminutive bishop with a worn cassock and a kindly visage. His house had been ransacked several times, and his personal secretary had been murdered. Called the "red bishop," Hélder Câmara was a man who felt very close to Arrupe in spirit. At that time, Brazil, a country almost equal in size to all of Europe, was preparing the ground for the famous base communities and for what would soon be called "liberation theology."

On his arrival in the airport, Arrupe spoke of the country's immense potential. He spent a whole month in Brazil, including a week during which he met with the Latin American provincials for a time of study and reflection. In order to clarify his thought in people's minds, he wrote, jointly with the provincials, a second important letter to all the Jesuits of Latin America.

The letter began by mentioning the situation of injustice that prevailed on the continent: "The urban and rural populations grow at an accelerated rate. The indigenous populations encounter de facto racial segregation. Both those who reject the profoundly innovative transformations that are needed and those who despair of any peaceful solutions are engaged in a dialectic of violence." The joint letter stated that, since the present epoch was "a moment in the history of salvation, […] we propose to give absolute priority to this problem [of social injustice] in our apostolic activity. Furthermore, we wish to conceive the whole of our apostolate in function of this problem." For this purpose, the provincials declared that they were ready to work with anybody, "irrespective of ideology or regimen, for the sake of a more just, more free, and more peaceful society."

Conscious of the thoroughgoing renewal required by this commitment, the provincials recognized that "a certain rupture is necessary with some of our past attitudes," and they stated that they wished to avoid "any attitude of isolationism or domination": "We wish to adopt an attitude of service to the church and to society and to reject the image of power that is frequently attributed to us."

The key word, "liberation," now appears:

> In all our activity, our goal should be the liberation of people from any form of servitude that oppresses them. We want all our efforts to contribute to the construction of a society in which the people participate with full rights of equality and liberty—and not only political rights, but also cultural and religious ones.

The letter called for a renunciation of bourgeois attitudes and of special relations "with the privileged classes." Aware that there would inevitably be strong reactions to such statements, the provincials stressed: "We will not provoke such reactions by following political lines, but we will continue to preach the Gospel of the poor, whatever reactions may come." They committed themselves to "bold transformations that radically renew structures." At the same time, the letter rejected violent attitudes that were "inspired by frustration and hatred, and not by conscientious reflection and Christian love."

The document went on to propose concrete measures, such as orienting the apostolate "toward the countless and growing masses of abandoned people," "developing and improving the educational works that help promote the impoverished masses," bearing witness to poverty in our lifestyle, motivating students to be socially concerned, and helping them break free of the individualism that education can breed. Finally, the provincials recognized that such renewal can only take place over a period of time.[33]

This letter of the Latin American Jesuit provincials spread quickly to the teletypes, and it was given wide publicity in the mass media. Meanwhile, Arrupe made good use of his time in Brazil, visiting some twenty cities. In his press conferences, he deftly handled reporters' questions about possible frictions with the hierarchy, stating that "they are a natural consequence of the reforms proposed by the council."

One journalist asked: "You are the first black pope to visit Latin America. How do you like being called the black pope?"

Arrupe answered with a smile: "You're partly correct and partly wrong, because my clothing is black. What is lacking is the other part: being pope!"

Many of Arrupe's answers to the journalists' questions touched on some of his favorite themes such as *aggiornamento*, the intrinsic value of human nature,

---

33 *Loyola* 1968. The Spanish press gave plenty of space to this letter. (See, for example, *ABC*, June 6, 1968.) It is worthwhile recalling what Arrupe was also demanding within the order, even if it had much less effect on public opinion. On April 14, 1968, he addressed a letter to Jesuits on internal problems related to "poverty, work, and common life." He agreed that economic arrangements could not treated the same way they were in the times of Ignatius. How was it possible, he asked, to remain faithful to the original spirit of poverty and at the same time manage important educational establishments? How was it possible to invest in scientific research, earn a living in non-religious employment, publish books and journals, and create training centers, without giving in to the attractions of profit and financial gain sought for own sake? Arrupe recalled the principle of the community of goods (see Arrupe, *La identidad del jesuita*, 139):

> Clear evidence that the proposals contained in the Rio letter would not stop at mere theory has been the tremendous development in Latin America, especially after the Rio letter, of the popular education movement "Fe y Alegría," a pioneering institution founded in Venezuela in 1954 by Father José María Vélaz and today established in almost all the nations on the continent. The movement is dedicated to providing integral education to children from the poor districts of our cities, "arriving there where the asphalt doesn't reach."

Gutierrez, "Arrupe y América Latina," 408.

the vitality and idealism of young people, atheism, and the defense of Father Teilhard de Chardin. Of Teilhard, he said that "his message is being read by people who would never have read a religious work, as is the case with many university students and professors in Japan." With regard to atheists, he insisted on his belief that "many seek happiness and find solutions to life that presuppose the existence of God. They are in fact seeking God, even without knowing it."

Some commentators pointed out the keen prophetic instinct of this successor of Saint Ignatius in visiting Brazil precisely at this moment. It was being said in those days that Paul VI had urged Dom Câmara, the bishop of Olinda-Recife, to launch a campaign of active non-violence, along the lines of Martin Luther King. Around that same time, eighteen bishops, meeting in the northeast state of Bahia, demanded "profound reforms in social, economic, political, and religious structures," while in São Paulo five hundred priests and Protestant pastors were denouncing the terrible exploitation of the people.

On such trips, Arrupe did not limit himself to contacts with government officials or Jesuits. Arrupe provided an eloquent personal testimony of how he experienced Brazil:

> Some years ago, when I was visiting a province of Jesuits in Latin America, I was invited to celebrate in a *favela*, one of the poorest parts of that region. Some hundred thousand people lived there in the middle of mud since this neighborhood was built in a depression that flooded every time it rained. [...]
>
> The Mass took place in a kind of poorly built shed with no doors, so that dogs and cats entered freely. The Eucharist began with hymns, which were accompanied by a guitarist who was not exactly a virtuoso. Even so, the overall effect for me was marvelous. One hymn kept repeating: "To love means to give oneself [...]! How beautiful it is to live in order to love, and how great it is to have in order to give!"
>
> As the hymn progressed, I felt myself choking up. I had to make a real effort to continue the Mass. Those people, who seemed to have nothing, were ready to give of themselves in order to communicate joy and happiness to others. When at the consecration I lifted up the host, I perceived, in the middle of a great silence, the joy of the Lord who finds himself among those who love. As Jesus says: "I have been sent to preach the Good News to the poor," and "Blessed are the poor" [...]
>
> As I gave out Communion, I looked closely at those faces, which were rough, hard, burnt by the sun; there were tears running down like pearls. They had just met up with Jesus, who was their only consolation. My hands were trembling.
>
> My homily was short. It was mostly a dialogue. They told me things that are not usually heard during important discourses; they were simple

things, but profound and sublime from a human point of view. One elderly woman said to me: "You are the superior of the fathers, right? Well then, sir, a million thanks, because you Jesuits have given us this great treasure that we need and we didn't have before: the Mass." A young man spoke up in public: "Father, I want you to know that we are very grateful, because these fathers have taught us to love our enemies. A week ago, I had gotten a knife to kill a companion I hated, but after listening to the father preach the Gospel, instead of killing that companion, I bought an ice cream and gave it to him."

Finally, a heavyset fellow, whose tough appearance almost scared me, told me: "Come to my house. I have a gift for you." I was doubtful as to whether I should accept his offer, but the Jesuit who was with me said, "Go ahead, Father, they're good people." So I went with him to his house, which was a dilapidated hovel, and he invited me to sit down on a rickety chair. From where I was sitting, I could contemplate the sunset. The big guy said to me: "Look, sir, how beautiful!" We stayed there in silence for a few minutes, and then the sun disappeared. The man exclaimed: "I didn't know how to thank you for all that the fathers do for us. I have nothing to give you, but I thought you would like to see the sunset. Didn't you like it? Adios!" And he shook my hand. As I was going, I thought: "It is not easy to find a heart like that." I was just leaving the lane when a poorly dressed woman came up to me, kissed my hand, looked at me, and said in an emotional tone: "Father, pray for me and my children. I also heard that beautiful Mass you just said. I have to return to my house, but I have nothing to give my children. [...] Pray for me: he will help us." And she disappeared in a rush toward her house.

What things I learned in that Mass among the poor! How different it was from the grand receptions organized by the powerful people of this world![34]

The trip was a great success. On his way back to Rome, Arrupe stopped briefly in Puerto Rico and spent an hour and a half in the Barajas airport in Madrid. There he conversed with reporters about unbelief and the need for authentic intellectuals to reflect on the present moment and especially on the Third World.

Recalling a question he had been asked in Puerto Rico, Arrupe stated that "when human promotion, correctly understood, is naturally imbued with charity, it has apostolic value of the first order and is a perfecting of the work of redemption."[35]

---

34 *Itinéraire*, 45. For his declarations in Brazil, see, for example, *La gaceta del norte*, Bilbao, April 16, 17, and 28, 1968.

35 Declarations in Barajas airport, Madrid. Cf. *ABC*, May 21, 1968.

Arrupe in Alaska, where he visited the legendary missionary Segundo Llorente, well known in Spain for his letters (April 21–27, 1967).

Speaking on May 21, 1968, Arrupe focused on the problems of young people:

In these days, a great effervescence is evident. Young people truly feel this, and they sense their future. And this is universal, all around the world. […] Whatever political machinations there may be behind this, there is no doubt that young people are pronouncing an emphatic "No!" to a social order they do not approve of. And this is the great problem that the leaders of today's world, both political and non-political, have to consider. That is why these youngsters have a great need of people who know how to think with complete openness and energy and boldness and who can formulate the real problems and try to solve them.

Arrupe related how he at one point came upon a students' strike in a university run by the Jesuits in Recife, Brazil. His response was to enter into dialogue with the assembled students. When they told him that they wanted to have more representation in order to demand their rights, he agreed that they should have such representation. After a round of applause, the students told Arrupe that the university was "the dictatorship of the dictatorship," to which Arrupe responded firmly: "That is not true. Don't insult my sons, who wish to do everything that is within their power."

"But they have raised the tuition, and we can't pay," protested the students.

"University education is a public service, and the state should help," Arrupe proposed. His open, direct, and simple style captivated the students, and the dialogue gradually became more sincere and serene.[36]

New Winds at Medellín

That summer, Paul VI traveled to Medellín to participate in the Second Conference of the Latin American Bishops (CELAM). This conference was to be a major historical event, since it marked the first time that the Latin American church took a bold stand on crucial issues such as poverty, justice, development, and the use of violence in extreme situations. Arrupe was part of the papal party and also represented religious institutes at the conference. He sat beside Dom Câmara, as Arrupe later recalled: "We became very friendly."[37]

The CELAM conference adopted positions very close to those of these two prophetic figures, though there were strong tensions in the assembly. For example, three experts, including a Chilean Jesuit named Arroyo, prevented Câmara and Arrupe from attending certain deliberations. Despite these maneuvers, most of the bishops at the Medellín conference were clearly and decisively in favor of social justice; they saw a need for urgent solutions to the continent's problems, and they spoke without fear of using strong language. The Bolivian bishops, for example, spoke harshly of militarism, the selfishness of the privileged classes, and the corruption of many politicians. Bishop Eduardo Pironio spoke of the urgent need to elaborate a "theology of underdevelopment." One document, approved by vote of 125 to five, stated that the "the church is peaceful, but not pacifist"; it condemned violence, but it considered that it might be justified in certain conditions of tyrannical oppression that was imposed "not only by an individual but also by structures"; the document also claimed that the actual situation in the continent was such as "to incite people to use violence." There followed a series of concrete proposals: the church had to bear witness concerning poverty; education was not be considered the privilege of a few; governments should promote development and transform social structures; priests should defend the poor and the weak. In summing up, the document concluded that peace was not possible without social justice.[38]

Arrupe felt all the more confirmed in his convictions after returning from Medellín. He wrote a letter to the Spanish Jesuits, urging them to strengthen their

---

36 Declarations in Barajas airport, Madrid. Cf. *ABC*, May 21, 1968.

37 Statement of Arrupe to the author, in Rome, August 1981.

38 See the journal *Vida nueva* 643 (September 14, 1968). "Father Arrupe's contribution to the Medellín Conference was especially meaningful in the elaboration of document 12 on religious life in Latin America. It was particularly relevant in putting into practice the inspiring teaching of Vatican II in several documents, but especially in the decree *Perfectae caritatis* on the renovation of religious life adapted to modern times" (Gutierrez, "Arrupe y América Latina," 414ff.).

*After landing in Porto Alegre, Brazil: "A certain rupture with some attitudes of our past is necessary"
(April 1968).*

commitment with the countries of Latin America,[39] and he spoke to the superiors general of the religious orders about the style of pastoral work on that continent.[40]

Tensions in the Vatican

New problems, however, were waiting for Arrupe when he returned to Rome. Many Jesuits around the world were finding it difficult to accept the profound changes in mentality that were being proposed. The curia was being flooded with letters of protest from the more conservative elements. Even if Arrupe's thought was at the time accepted and even shared by many in the Vatican, there was strong disapproval of the protests of some of the more progressive Jesuits and of their negative reactions concerning certain decisions of the hierarchy. The Holy See was especially bothered by certain commentaries on the encyclical *Humanae vitae*, which forbade contraceptive methods of birth control. Several Jesuits came out against the encyclical in various journals and public statements. The papal

---

39   "A los padres y hermanos de la asistencia de España: De la necesidad de una ayuda mayor y planificada a América Latina."

40   Talk given by Arrupe, as president of the Union of Superiors General, to the Council of the Pontifical Commission for Latin America: "Los religiosos frente a los problemas de América Latina," June 18, 1969; Pedro Arrupe, *Ante un mundo en cambio* (Madrid: Eapsa, 1972), 145ff.

document had in fact caused turmoil in the church, and not a few priests were in conscience advising people to follow a line different from that proposed by the encyclical. Arrupe felt obliged to write a letter to all Jesuits (August 15, 1968) asking them to practice an obedience that was filial, prompt, decided, open, and creative: "I don't claim that it will be easy or comfortable." At the same time, he recognized that some Jesuits, given their expertise, might have reservations concerning the encyclical. He affirmed that obedience did not require that people stop thinking, and he urged Jesuits to seek out the real meaning of that papal directive in collaboration with the human science research centers. Even in this obligatory document of reprimand, the Arrupe spirit was manifest in various ways. After stating that "the difficult times are those of the Society itself," he affirmed: "I am certain that I will be understood by all of you. Those of you who have a problem of conscience with regards to the encyclical should be assured that for that very reason I have you very present in my spirit and in my prayer."[41]

Speaking for the Vatican secretary of state, the influential bishop Giovanni Benelli wrote a letter to Arrupe thanking him for his reaffirmation of *Humanae vitae*: "The Holy Father is thankful and delights to see that his sons are also adhering to the Chair of Peter in this matter." Another letter, signed by Paul VI himself, expressed gratitude for the volume containing the documents of General Congregation 31, which Arrupe had sent to him.

---

41   *Acta Romana* 15 (1967–72): 318, 329; and in Arrupe, *La identidad del jesuita*, 314–16. *Ya*, Madrid, August 31, 1968. Paul VI's promulgation of *Humanae vitae* was not an easy matter for Arrupe. The pope himself, as the *Acta Apostolicae Sedis* attests, gave a talk six days after publishing the encyclical, in which he affirmed that paragraph no. 7 was more important than the much-cited no. 14, about the openness of each and every act to procreation. Two years earlier, the pope, commenting on the results that were still awaited from the commission on problems of birth control, had told a group of Italian women: "The magisterium of the church cannot propose moral norms except when it is certain that it is interpreting God's will; but in order to have such certainty the church cannot prescind from research or from answering the many questions put to it from all parts of the world—it is a long, difficult work" (AAS, 58, 1966, 218–19). The pope later decided not to take into account the recommendation of the consultative commission. According to John Marshall, a member of the papal commission from the start, four theologians of the minority group (Professors John C. Ford, Marcelino Zalba, Jan Visser, and Stanislas de Lestapis) admitted that they could not demonstrate the intrinsic evil of contraception; they therefore based their decision on their fear of the possible consequences of a change, both for authority and for sexual morality (J. Marshall, in a letter to *The Times*, August 3, 1968, cited by Leo Pyle, *Pope and Pill* [London: Darton, Longman & Todd, 1968], 83–85). For two excellent articles on how *Humanae vitae* has harmed rather than strengthened the authority of the papal magisterium, see Richard A. McCormick, "Moral Theology 1940–1989," *Theological Studies* 50 (1989): 3–24, and Lisa Sowle Cahill, "Catholic Sexual Ethics and the Dignity of the Person: A Double Message," *Theological Studies* 50 (1989): 120–50. For reactions, see Manuel Cuyás, "En torno a la *Humanae vitae*," in *Selecciones de libros: Actualidad bibliográfica de filosofía y teología; Boletines, libros, notas* (Barcelona: Facultades de Filosofía y Teología San Francisco de Borja, 1969), 10–46, 239–390.

With the cooks at the college in Florianópolis, Brazil (May 4, 1968).

Another affair that caused difficulties for Arrupe was the case of the Basque terrorist Iñaki Sarasketa. He was a member of ETA and was to be executed by the government of General Franco. When Arrupe sent a telegram to Franco asking for clemency and suspension of the execution, his gesture was interpreted by some newspapers as political interference. Given his universal vocation, Arrupe was not intruding into the politics of the Basque conflict; he was simply requesting clemency to save a human life that was to be eliminated by the power of the state. On another occasion, significantly, Arrupe refused to receive in Rome a delegation of ETA members who wanted to meet with him.

Outwardly, Arrupe never stopped smiling. He was always encouraging and supporting people with his imperturbable optimism, but inwardly he was suffering. He confessed as much to his cousin Fernando:

First of all, I don't know why, but I feel myself ever more closely united to you. I feel you very close to me, helping me with your prayers and your understanding. You don't know how much this encourages and comforts me. Your integrity and presence of mind in the midst of difficulties has been for me a good lesson, and you have also taught me the most dignified way to face up to the vicissitudes and adversities of the times.

After thanking Fernando Gondra for his kindness toward his sisters, Arrupe added:

You can imagine how my life is. The times we are living in bring surprises of every sort. I don't know if I will end up being surprised by absolutely nothing, which I certainly hope does not happen. Lack of sensitivity saves us pain, but it also dulls the reflections that are needed to combat evil. Thanks be to God, I feel myself well supported by my collaborators; that is an inestimable grace in these times, which often seem to be unreal. Both of you play a large part in this grace, since you sustain me with your prayers and your intimate understanding![42]

In addition to all these surprises and concerns, the following year would produce another strong commotion in the Society of Jesus and among many others. In April 1969, after making a trip to the East, the pope received the superior general and his assistants, along with a group of Jesuits who were participating in a course on religious governance. After affirming that the order was a "distinguished body," the pope once again manifested his basic concern: "What happens with you will in a way affect what happens with the entire Catholic family, whether it prospers as we hope it will or whether it eventually declines." The pope then described the post-conciliar era and made another call for the Jesuits to help the church: "Come to its assistance in this time of need; show us once again, in this dangerous but exciting historical circumstance, what the sons of Saint Ignatius are capable of doing."[43]

Within twenty-four hours of this speech, there was a shocking bit of news: one of the regional assistants, Mario Schönenberger, a forty-year-old Swiss, was leaving the Society of Jesus. He had been responsible for the assistancy of Germany, which included Germany, Austria, Hungary, Switzerland, and the Baltic states. He was asking to leave the order but to continue working as a priest. His leaving occurred at a delicate moment, since other prominent Jesuits were leaving as well, such as Father Alfons Hermans, the provincial of Holland, and Fathers Oosterhuis and Van der Stapa, who worked at the university parish in Amsterdam. The polemical Dutch Pastoral Council was already flourishing in those days.

Arrupe responded to the crisis by sending a letter that manifested his habitual respect for the personal decisions of the men. He was patient, as always, with the two university chaplains who were about to leave the order. Without passing judgment on what had happened in the parish, since that pertained more to the hierarchy, he wrote:

Do not fear that your apostolic dynamism and creativity will be impeded. The general has the task of leading the order toward the future. [...] I wish to add only that this healthy dynamism will be possible only if we lead an intense life of prayer and Christ truly lives within us.[44]

---

42   Letter to Fernando Gondra, Rome, February 20, 1968.

43   *La gaceta del norte*, Bilbao, April 22, 1969. In the same edition, information is given about Father Schönenberger's departure from the Society.

44   With regard to the Netherlands, polarization there did not affect only the Jesuits. The famous "Pastoral Council of the Ecclesiastical Province of the Netherlands" reported a crisis of the whole Catholic Church in that country. The Roman Curia considered the situation explosive. It felt that the discussions on new forms of ministry, celibacy, and the "democratization" of the church were very dangerous for the

On a plane with the pope, who invited him on a papal flight to Colombia to participate in the Second Conference of the Latin American Bishops (CELAM) in Medellín. "With Paul VI I had all the confidence in the world."

The tumultuous sixties did not diminish Arrupe's hope and optimism. In 1969, he made bold to travel behind the Iron Curtain, to Czechoslovakia and Poland. There, he spoke with the famous cardinal Stefan Wyszyński about an eventual visit of Paul VI to Poland. He also spent four days visiting England and Scotland.

That same year, Arrupe wrote a letter to all Jesuits about the "preservation and renewal" of the Society of Jesus on the occasion of the 429th anniversary of the order's approval by the pope. In this letter, which was published

universal Church. For this reason, it decided to organize a special synod in Rome to reply to the questions posed by the Dutch Catholics. The polarization had greatly affected religious institutions and parishes.

   Arrupe did not underestimate the seriousness of a conflict that had become collective in the years 1967–1970, with repercussions that went beyond the frontiers of that country. In dealing with the situation, he showed his capacity for clear and speedy decision: some Jesuits, among them Huub Oosterhuis, a very well-known and especially gifted religious poet, were expelled from the Society, while other more traditional Jesuits left the country to work in German parishes. Later, the Dutch province failed to regain its balance: all its colleges (except that of Delft), the theological faculty of Maastricht, and many other houses were closed. From then on, the province lost much of its apostolic drive.

Jan Kerkhofs, "Arrupe y Europa," in La Bella, *Pedro Arrupe, general de la Compañía de Jesús*, 503–28, here 511. Cf. *La gaceta del norte*, April 9, 1969.

in *L'osservatore romano*,[45] he speaks of the order's extraordinary dynamism. He acknowledges that there might be abuses, "but good will prevails"; he mentions the problem of Jesuits leaving and the decline in vocations, and he analyzes the mixture of "chaff and wheat" that exists in the process of *aggiornamento*. At the same time, he criticized do-nothing policies and urged Jesuits not to let themselves "be carried away by the torrent of uncontrolled events or *faits accomplis*." "Conscious of its apostolic mission," he continued,

> the Society tries to anticipate the future by analyzing present circumstances, and it prepares for the future with modifications and changes, which, though bold and far-reaching, do not in the least alter what is essential; they are changes that become necessary in order to give our apostolic work greater supernatural efficacy.

He mentions two errors explicitly: being open to the world without a corresponding openness to Christ, and promoting attitudes and practices of a monastic character that are now outmoded and obsolete. He ends the letter: "Without closing our eyes to the importance and the complexity of the present moment, let us meet the challenge of present-day circumstances and make every effort, while being completely committed to Christ, to 'serve God and the church under the Roman pontiff.'"

With this stamp of bold dynamism and serene poise, Arrupe arrived at the end of the turbulent sixties. Even though the young rebels of May 1968 had returned to their classrooms, the sea was still stormy. In Cuba, the dream of the fallen Che Guevara had given way to Castro's enthusiastic support for armed intervention. And Bernadette Devlin was denouncing in London the outrages of the English in Northern Ireland. A US astronaut placed on the moon, next to the first human footprint there, a plaque with the inscription: "Here men from the planet Earth first set foot upon the Moon, July 1969 AD. We came in peace for all humankind." Meanwhile, in Africa and Latin America millions of human beings were suffering the excruciating drama of hunger. And in the small chapel next to his office, in the silence of dawn, Arrupe sat, legs folded oriental-style, and prayed.

---

45 *L'osservatore romano*, Spanish edition, December 14, 1969. In declarations made on television in the Federal Republic of Germany, Arrupe stated: "The Society of Jesus finds itself not in a moment of crisis, but in one of adaptation." Referring to one of Arrupe's own phrases, "We want Jesuits who think," one reporter asked the general: "But it turns out that the men who think sometimes prepare for the revolution, is it not so?" Arrupe responded, "There are many people who do not think; there are few who think. Therefore the best service the Society can offer the church is to provide it with people who think. That is not revolution, but evolution. What we want is an organic, dynamic, positive evolution, and for that it is necessary to have people who think creatively."

16. In the Crater of a Volcano

"And when is he thinking of coming to Spain?" The question was repeated over and over again. Five years had passed since his election, and Arrupe had made only one short stopover in Spain, on his way to the Americas. Why had he still not visited his native land?

Arrupe never renounced his roots, but in his youth he had experienced expulsion from the Spanish Republic, and during the Second World War he had suffered imprisonment because of Japanese xenophobia. His extensive travel to many parts of the world in later years makes it easy to appreciate how he felt himself called to a universal vocation, beyond all national boundaries. In his conversations and speeches, he made clear that his spirit was global, the polar opposite of any type of chauvinism. During his years as provincial in Japan, the Spanish Jesuits there were never given special favors. Once he was elected general of the Society of Jesus, he made clear his intention not to return to his home country until he had traveled to many other parts of the globe, in fulfillment of the mandate given him by GC 31: to have direct contact with Jesuits worldwide. He later confessed:

> I have made only one and a half trips to Spain in my generalate. It was a country I knew well, and as a Spaniard I didn't want to favor it. I felt it more urgent to have contact with Jesuits in lands I did not know, including Africa, Asia, and Oceania. Thus, in my first three years as general I was able to get a good view of the whole situation.

Conservative Reaction

The situation in Spain was actually becoming quite tense. In the political arena, the first inklings of future change were becoming visible. The dictator, General Franco, was beginning to feel his age and had taken certain precautionary measures. On July 22, 1969, in a plenary session of the legislature, he had with all solemnity designated Prince Juan Carlos of Bourbon as his successor. On October 29 of the same year, he appointed a new cabinet, which was notable for its homogeneity. Of a total of nineteen ministers, eleven had a technocratic orientation and belonged to or were sympathizers of Opus Dei. On the ecclesiastical level, the implementation of Vatican II was creating strong tensions between most of the bishops and a small minority, which from the time of the council had not been hiding its sympathies for men like Lefèbvre, the bishop who would later become schismatic. This minority included men such as Laureano Castán (bishop of Sigüenza), Ángel Temiño (Orense), Abilio del Campo (Calahorra), Félix Ervit, OMI (Ifni), Demetrio Mansilla (Ciudad Rodrigo), and José López

Ortiz (Tuy)—this last had sought unsuccessfully to have the council explicitly condemn communism.

The election of an obviously pro-conciliar candidate like Arrupe did not sit well with the more reactionary sectors in Spain, which still flourished under the protection of the Franco regime. The more progressive parts of the Spanish church were beginning to detach themselves from the government and to become fully conscious of the important role the church had in promoting civil liberties. This development became especially manifest in the decade of the seventies, with government censorship of homilies, the attacks on Cardinal Tarancón, the controversy around Bishop Antonio Añoveros, and other cases.

Given this situation, it is not surprising that Arrupe's declarations and decisions incited the fury of these minority groups.[1] On March 18, 1970, the seven Jesuit provincials of Spain united together to present to the general their resignation from their posts. They intended their resignation to be a protest against the Holy See's decision to consult the Spanish Bishops' Conference about the appropriateness of creating an "autonomous province" of Jesuits of the "strict observance"—for some wags, this group was known as the "discalced Jesuits." Most of the Spanish bishops had given a green light to this project, but the provincials were totally opposed to it, since it would split the Society in two in Spain and possibly in the world. They had therefore decided to resign to make their position clear.

The origins of the crisis went back two years. On November 11, 1968, the provincial of the Jesuit province of Toledo, Luis González, who resided in Madrid, had received an alarming phone call from the nuncio, Luigi Dadaglio, a friend of the Jesuits who was disliked by the Spanish government because of his practice of naming auxiliary bishops independently of the concordat protocols. At the pope's request, the Vatican diplomat was seeking detailed information about the activities of Jesuits in Madrid. In December, the president of the Bishops' Conference, Casimiro Morcillo, and his secretary, José Guerra Campos, traveled to Rome to speak with Paul VI about the Jesuits, among other matters. Upon returning to Madrid, Morcillo wrote a letter to Arrupe in which he deplored the activities of certain Jesuits in his diocese; he also mentioned the "spontaneous and bitter" comments about the Society he had heard from the lips of Paul VI. He added that the pope had asked him "what might be done to remedy that crisis." Naturally disturbed, but without losing his calm, Arrupe phoned the provincial of Madrid and told him to seek an immediate interview with the archbishop in order to understand the meaning of those expressions.

When the disaffected Jesuits heard about the controversy, they held a meeting in Madrid on January 9, 1969, this time with the provincial's permission.

---

1   On the crisis of the Society in Spain, see Alcalá, "Gozo y martirio en España."

The eighteen veteran Jesuits[2] who attended the *informal* meeting centered their debate on the order's problems in Spain, the crisis of governance, and possible solutions to the crisis. From this meeting emerged the idea of a "personal province." Arrupe reacted to this suggestion with perfect serenity. The conservatives, who called themselves Vera Societas, the "True Society," were irritated by the general's silence and undertook a press campaign using pseudonyms. Among other things, they publicly asked the Vatican to send an "apostolic visitor" for the Society in Spain. On May 29, the secretary of state sought the opinion of Cardinal Tarancón, who was then archbishop of Toledo and primate of Spain. Don Vicente responded, in a letter of June 6, that the problem was not exclusive to the Society, but was more general, affecting other religious orders and the secular clergy as well. In fact, he stated, the radicalization was affecting students and young people in Spain at all levels. Tarancón was clear in his opposition to any division in the order, as he later stated: "I persuaded Paul VI not to take any measure aimed at dividing the Jesuits."[3]

After more meetings and confrontations, the Spanish bishops, under the leadership of Morcillo, held their twenty-second plenary assembly in Madrid. The atmosphere was tense because of the famous "Burgos trial,"[4] and because of the delicate situation of the church in the Basque Country. During the assembly, the bishops were requested, quite apart from the proposed agenda, to offer their opinions, for the pope's sake, about "the possibility of creating in Spain a special province for those Jesuits who wished to continue in the Society with the same observance that had always been the norm in the country." The bishops were subsequently consulted about the "personal province" that had been requested by the "faithful" Jesuits, thirty-two of whom had submitted ample documentation denouncing the "revolutionary Marxist climate of the worker-priest mission," "politicization," the lack of "spiritual depth," "doctrinal uncertainties," "infidelity to the hierarchy in Jesuit journals," "disrespect for bishops," and so on. Forty-nine of the bishops voted in favor of the division, eighteen voted against, and five abstained. On January 27, 1970, Archbishop Morcillo wrote a letter to Arrupe stating that the "personal province" appeared to be a painful remedy, but it was practically inevitable.[5] He then encouraged the general to make bold,

---

2   Among others: Jesús Solano, Eustaquio Guerrero, José Caballero, José Antonio de Aldama, Eduardo Fernández Regatillo, Manuel Foyaca, José Ramón Bidagor, and Jesús Muño. In general, they were highly educated Jesuit superiors and professors of theology or canon law (see La Bella, "La crisis del cambio," 886).

3   Statement of Cardinal Vicente Enrique y Tarancón to the author. Cf. Vicente Cárcel Ortí, *Pablo VI y España: Fidelidad, renovación y crisis (1963–1978)* (Madrid: Biblioteca Autores Cristianos, 1997), 629.

4   The Burgos trial of September 1970 sentenced six ETA members to death, but Franco commuted the death sentences after strong international criticism and pressure.

5   Alcalá, "Gozo y martirio en España," 86.

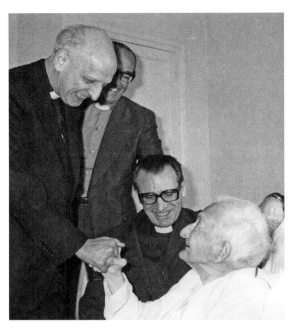

On a trip to Spain, Arrupe greets Father Quiroga, who was then the oldest Jesuit in the infirmary of Alcalá de Henares (September 9, 1974).

rapid decisions. Other bishops, such as Cardinal Tarancón, were totally opposed to the project.

In reality, neither the pope, nor the nuncio Dadaglio, a friend of the Society, nor any other Vatican body had asked that the Spanish bishops be consulted in this regard.[6] The dubious decision had originated with Morcillo, who was pressured by the group of the "True Society." For their part, these dissident Jesuits had written letters asking for authorization to create residences and novitiates that were autonomous and independent of the rest of the order. The main instigators of this campaign were Jesús Solano, ex-rector of Comillas, and Cándido Gaviña, regional assistant for Latin America (and later Arrupe's personal secretary), both of whom adhered to the conservative Italian line of Dezza, confessor to Paul VI.

Thus the year 1970 began with somber notes for Arrupe, and it was indeed a difficult year. Provincial congregations had been convoked throughout the world to review his style of governance. Arrupe himself had already planned to make an official visit to Spain. At the urging of the Spanish provincials, he wrote to Cardinal Jean Villot on March 13, 1970, asking him for trustworthy information about what had actually happened. Exactly two days later, the Spanish provincials met at Alcalá de Henares (Madrid) and decided to present their resignations to the general and to advise the pope of the matter. They felt that the bishops' initiative had ruptured the relations of unity and confidence that had previously existed between the hierarchy and Jesuit leadership in Spain, so that they could no longer serve credibly as provincials.[7] Anxious to prevent the creation of the

6   The Jesuit José María Martín Patino was a confidant of Tarancón; he became pro-vicar of
     Madrid and a leading figure in the Spanish political transition. It was he who informed the
     cardinal that the bishops had acted on their own, without the authorization of the Holy See.
7   The joint letters addressed to Paul VI and to Arrupe were signed by Valero, provincial of
     Spain; Alejandro Muñoz Priego, provincial of Andalusia; Mariano Madurga, provincial

commission proposed by Villot, Arrupe asked for an urgent audience with the pope, and he was granted same for March 21. That audience and a response from Cardinal Villot resulted in a clarification of the situation. Even though Arrupe kept a respectful silence, this news traveled quickly to Spain through clandestine channels. The essence of Villot's response was that the Holy See did not intend to interfere in Jesuit governance and that the general could make his own decisions, although he was advised to govern prudently and decisively. Villot did issue a warning, however, about a decline of discipline and doctrinal rectitude; he advised the "faithful" Jesuits to follow the directions of their superiors, even at personal sacrifice; and he insisted that Jesuits should be free to communicate directly with the Holy See, while avoiding unofficial news leaks.

On March 29, 1970, Arrupe wrote a marvelous letter to the Spanish provincials, in which he refused to accept their resignations "because he knew in whom he had placed his trust." Without reproaching anybody in the least, he expressed his desire to govern the Society effectively, prudently, and decisively, as the pope himself had recommended. He went on to encourage everyone to continue in their efforts toward unity, and he deplored the news leaks, though he recommended that the collective humiliation caused by them be assumed in the true Ignatian spirit.[8]

Tension was also evident in the provincial congregations in Spain, which were held at the end of March and beginning of April. A majority of the congregations determined that a new general congregation was not necessary, which meant a vote of confidence in Arrupe. The same conclusion was reached in the other provincial congregations held that year around the world and in the procurators' congregation, which met in Rome from September 27 to October 6.

The Conquest of Spain

At the same time, many people were suggesting in various ways that Arrupe should visit his home country as soon as possible. Among them was Fernando Gondra, who in 1968 had written his beloved cousin a long letter describing the situation through which Spain was passing, especially the Basque Country and the more progressive sectors of the church, and expressing his concern about the turn these developments were taking. In this letter, he also mentioned how good it would be for Arrupe to come to Spain "to silence the rumors that impute a political motive to your absence from your native land, interpreting it as intentional, for the purpose of avoiding certain confrontations."[9]

---

of Aragon; Gutiérrez Semprún, provincial of Castilla; Iglesias, provincial of Leon; Oñate, provincial of Loyola; Enric Rifá, provincial of Tarragona; and Luis Sanz Criado, provincial of Toledo (March 18, 1970, in APS).

8   Letters of Villot to Arrupe and to Valero, March 27, 1970. Letter of Arrupe to the provincials of Spain, March 29, 1970, in APS.

9   Letter of Fernando Gondra to Pedro Arrupe, Bilbao, August 10, 1968. Gondra File.

When Arrupe had been elected general, the Spanish government received the news respectfully, but it did not approve of his ideas; it had especially objected to his petition of clemency for a Basque prisoner condemned to death. Despite these tensions, Arrupe had a very close friendship with the Spanish ambassador to the Holy See, Antonio Garrigues. Always a great admirer of Arrupe, Garrigues later said, "He was simply delightful. We talked together frequently about everything, and we used to dine together in Villa Cavalletti,[10] the Jesuits' country residence outside of Rome."

Before traveling to Spain, Arrupe visited Cardinal Villot to receive instructions. In the course of the conversation, three days before his departure, he learned that the pope thought that his letter of March 27 to the Jesuits in Spain had not adequately addressed the grave concerns the pontiff had spoken to him about in the audience of March 20. According to Arrupe's own notes of the meeting, which convey his pain, he assured the pope once again that that letter was only the first step "of all the things I have proposed to do in order to respond to the desires of the Holy See."[11]

Finally, on the sunny spring morning of May 2, 1970, a DC-9 of Alitalia carried the general to the Madrid airport. A smiling, tranquil Arrupe descended from the plane and greeted the Jesuits waiting for him as if nothing special was happening. One newspaper headline that day read: "Father Arrupe Arrives Today in Spain: A Visit at a Time of Crisis in the Society of Jesus." Most of the newspapers quoted the declarations that Arrupe had previously made to the weekly journal *Vida nueva*.[12] In that interview, the general anticipated his meeting with the Spanish Jesuits by stating some things quite clearly: "My main concern is of a general nature, namely that the Society of Jesus remain faithful to its tradition and at the same time adapt to the present-day world. [...] In Spain, just as in other countries, such adaptation is a slow process with repercussions for the future."

In these declarations to *Vida nueva*, Arrupe also addressed the matter of the "personal province" requested by those of the "strict observance":

> There has in fact been a request in that regard. The problem has perhaps arisen because of a difference of mentalities. Some people believe that they could perhaps in that way follow more faithfully the spirit of Saint Ignatius in the present moment. [...] My own opinion is that such a procedure can by no means resolve the problem; rather, there is a need to move in the other direction, trying to restore a sense of union. By strengthening charity and obedience we can arrive at a true solution.

---

10   Statement given by Antonio Garrigues to the author.
11   Letter of Arrupe to Paul VI, May 1, 1970, in *Minute Curia Romana (1968–1970)*, in ARSI.
12   See "Padre Arrupe: Toda la verdad sobre la Compañía de Jesús," *Vida nueva* 727 (April 25, 1970): 603ff. Cf. also Spanish newspapers on these dates.

In the same interview, Arrupe revealed that, in a private conversation he had had with Paul VI, the pope had recognized that such division in the Society was not a solution to the problem.

Arrupe also addressed the matter of political involvement. He did not hesitate to affirm that he was convinced that religious devotion without social commitment was a form of alienation and demonstrated a lack of charity, given the unjust conditions in the world of today.

Arrupe's trip to Spain lasted for seventeen intense days; they were full of personal and group contacts with Jesuits, with the press, and with a series of Spanish dignitaries. He traveled to twenty-one cities. All the drama and intrigue described above seemed to dissipate before the smile and the extended hand of Arrupe, who dealt with everyone in a very familiar, personal way. One outstanding detail of the visit was the special trip he made to see Father Llanos, who had been Arrupe's companion in the Marian congregation during his student years; Llanos was living in a poor slum of Madrid called Pozo del Tío Raimundo.

In an action that had political overtones, a few of the progressive Jesuits boycotted the meetings Arrupe held in Valencia, Barcelona, Seville, and Madrid. They were protesting his plans to visit General Franco. Some of the "faithful" Jesuits also kept their distance from Arrupe's visitation, refusing to attend concelebrated Masses and maintaining an audible silence during the meetings and conversations.

During the meeting with Franco, which lasted sixty-five minutes, Arrupe took advantage of the opportunity to denounce cases in which the police used torture. Franco asked him: "Do you have some proof of such cases?"

Arrupe answered: "I have seen the backs of some young men who were tortured."[13] Franco remained silent and then spoke of the dangers of communism for Western civilization.

Arrupe also met with Prince Juan Carlos and Sofía, whom he had known from his time in Japan and who later would become the reigning monarchs. He also met with the four Spanish cardinals and with twelve local bishops. Significantly, on that trip he was not able to meet with Morcillo, archbishop of Madrid.

At no time did Arrupe lose his serenity and equanimity. As always, while others came to the end of the long days exhausted and tense, Arrupe knew how to pace himself by taking a quick snooze in a car or a plane, so that he always maintained a spirit of hopefulness, optimism, and joviality.

Someone once asked him: "How do you get time to pray amid such hustle and bustle?"

He answered simply: "It's a question of priorities."

---

13   Alcalá, "Gozo y martirio en España," 95ff.

His declarations during those seventeen days appeared in a volume entitled *Escala en España* (Stopover in Spain).[14] The themes found in these discourses and talks are in keeping with his usual way of thinking. He made no effort to steer clear of controversial topics such as political commitment, tensions between theology and the magisterium, social justice, the crisis of faith, the future of young people, the schools for rich people, hunger in the Third World, and the need for a prophetic stance.

Arrupe was always straightforward and cordial with the conservative Jesuits, even though some of them were claiming that, given the present situation, "the extinction of the order would be justified." The general uttered not a word of reproach. What is more, he was graceful enough not to cite Cardinal Villot's letter, even though he knew that it had been leaked in Spain. Some of his opponents conceded that Arrupe had managed to "put them in their place." In the course of time, many of the most recalcitrant Jesuits, while remaining critical of Arrupe's style of governance, came to appreciate his formidable moral and Christian authority.

Upon returning to Rome, Arrupe sent a detailed report of his visit to the Vatican secretary of state. His view of the trip was positive and optimistic.[15] A few days later, he had a meeting in Rome with the provincial superiors of Spain for the purpose of carrying out a more thorough evaluation of that critical visit. When Paul VI received the group on June 17, he cordially exhorted them to maintain the fundamental lines of the Ignatian charism and to seek brotherhood and unity among all their members. One Jesuit who attended that private audience, Manuel Gutiérrez Semprún, claims that the pope, after a brief greeting, put aside the official text of his discourse and offered some words of apology for what had happened with the letter to the nuncio. He said that he had not intended such a thing, and he deplored it. He assured them that he still maintained his confidence

---

14   Pedro Arrupe, *Escala en España* (Madrid: Apostolado de la Prensa, 1971). As evidence of the delicacy with which Arrupe personally treated these ordeals of veteran Jesuits, Facundo Jiménez, S.J. provided the author with a letter from Arrupe (November 30, 1967) that impressed him greatly:

> Dear Father Jiménez: Being somewhat relieved of the work of these last weeks, I personally wish to thank you for your sincere letter of October 5, in which you open your heart to me as a son and express your distress at the defects you presently see in the Society. God will surely reward you well for the life of prayer and sacrifice that you offer for the renewal of our Society. Keep on doing so, without failing to encourage unlimited confidence in the Heart of Jesus, which knows how to bring good out of the evils that afflict us and even out of our own faults and sins. Would that all those who are pained for the state of the Society imitated you [...].

15   His long note reads in part: "The visit has been quite positive and has engendered new confidence within the order and in the Spanish hierarchy." *Informe privado sobre el viaje del Padre General a España (2 al 19 de mayo de 1970)*, annex of the letter of Arrupe to Jean-Marie Villot, June 13, 1970, in Public Administration.

in the Jesuits. Having made those statements in all simplicity and sincerity, he again took up the papers of his discourse and read them. Recounts Semprún:

> This attitude on the pope's part left us impressed. Still, we were sorry that he did not take advantage of the occasion to ask us what was actually happening and what our opinion was. In effect, despite his affirmations of confidence, there was something of a barrier that prevented an exchange of information. It was rather difficult to understand.[16]

In this way, the idea of a "personal province" was laid to rest, even though, as would be seen later, there remained deeper problems relating to the post-conciliar crisis that would continue to trouble the Society and the church.

The Creative Explosion

The "Spanish bomb" came close to dividing the Society of Jesus, but in the end it never exploded. Arrupe went through this trying situation exactly twenty-five years after the Hiroshima explosion. He recalled this event in an article published in the newspaper *Avvenire*[17] on August 6, 1970:

> That immense, fateful mushroom cloud, which remained hanging in the serene blue sky of Hiroshima, while the whole city, as far as my eyes could see, was burning like a furnace, is for me today like a symbol of other kinds

---

16   Statement of Gutiérrez Semprún to the author. The improvised words of the pope were these:

> First, we will speak from the heart; then we will read another speech. We are happy to be able to be here with the fathers of the Society, who are a treasure for the church. […] If it has ever appeared that the Holy See has pronounced words that could have wounded the sensibility of some, know that the Holy See requires much of the Society, and that these high expectations are not a sign of distrust or ill-will, but rather of love. Much is required of those who are loved, of sons, of friends, of collaborators. The influence of the Society extends to all the church; it radiates to Latin America and from the south pole to the north. This is a great responsibility for you all; have confidence in yourselves, have confidence in the Society, in your Society; be faithful to Saint Ignatius. Renew yourselves, yes, as a tree renews itself in the spring, and be ever faithful to the spirit of the Society; a tree that does not renew itself every year is a dead tree.

Audience of His Holiness with the Fathers Provincial of Spain and Portugal, June 17, 1970, in APS.

17   *Avvenire*, Milan, June 6, 1970; and in Arrupe, *La iglesia de hoy y del futuro*, 21. On September 10, 1970, Arrupe also spoke at the Katholikentag in Trier, Germany, where he made a succinct presentation of the church's problematic situation and its future possibilities. The last words of this speech are impressive: "I continue to believe completely today what I said at that time: 'Perhaps never had the Lord been so close to us, since never had we been so certain.'" *La iglesia de hoy y del futuro*, 35.

of explosions, which are much more dangerous since they are rooted, not in physical forces, but in the human spirit itself.

The explosions that most seriously worried Arrupe were those of unbelief, of injustice, of violence. He was also concerned, of course, about the problems of young people. In March 1971, he wrote an audacious letter on the role of religious men and women in modern-day education, in which he dared to cite an iconic Latin American figure:

> When he came across a malnourished child with a swollen belly, crying out with hunger, Che Guevara used to ask himself in anguish: "Why do these things have to happen?" This question, this cry, is nothing more than a muffled echo of that terrible cry that cleaved the air of Calvary: "My God, my God, why have you forsaken me?"

In the same letter, Arrupe sketched out a new conception of fraternal love: "As individuals and as members of a community, we now realize more clearly that love should be oriented toward liberating the creative forces in others that can lead them to true liberation. Love foments autonomous development." Published in *L'osservatore romano*,[18] this letter was criticized by some, but it is a true testimony to Arrupe's extraordinary interest in the education of young people. His speeches to the alumni of Jesuit schools always overflowed with a contagious enthusiasm; they have been published in a volume called *Hombres para los demás* (Men for others).[19]

In the year 1971, Arrupe undertook several more invigorating journeys. In March, he had the great consolation of returning to his beloved Japan. Tokyo, Yamaguchi, Hiroshima, Nagasaki, and Kobe were all visited by the former missionary who was now an esteemed world leader. The general also traveled to other countries of the Far East, renewing contacts with the Jesuits of Thailand, Taiwan, Indonesia, Hong Kong, Australia, Korea, Oceania, and South Vietnam.

One small detail shows how Arrupe, in the midst of such dizzying activity, never lost his sensitivity or his warm, personal touch. Jesuit José María Ortiz-Villajos recounts this anecdote about the general's visit to Vietnam:

> The day Father Arrupe was to take the plane to return to Rome, a good number of us Jesuits accompanied him to the Saigon airport. As we were walking from the airport parking lot to the terminal, I for a moment felt alone and lost in the midst of that large and lively group; even though I kept walking in the same direction, I separated myself a little from the group. Immediately, Father Arrupe, who had been walking and talking with the father superior

---

18   *L'osservatore romano*, March 21, 1971.

19   Pedro Arrupe, *Hombres para los demás* (Barcelona: Diáfora, 1983). This book contains the texts of all the speeches that Arrupe addressed to former students of the Society of Jesus.

of the Vietnam mission, took leave of him and came to my side. In a friendly way, he took me by the shoulders, looked at me, and smiled. I don't recall what we spoke of, nor do I think it was anything important, but his gesture, his look, his attitude, his style [...] made me feel *at home*.[20]

From April 30 to May 10, Arrupe visited the United States again. On this occasion, he spoke with U Thant, secretary general of the UN, and offered the services of the Society of Jesus to help solve some of the problems of development; concretely, he proposed creating "a center concerned with questions of peace, justice, and development."[21] U Thant responded that this first visit of a Jesuit general to the UN was a "significant event in the joint efforts" for peace, and he added: "The members of your Society are especially well suited for meeting the spiritual and intellectual needs of our time. A spirit of internationalism has characterized the Society of Jesus for four centuries." The secretary general praised the efforts of specific Jesuits who were collaborating with the UN, and he stated: "The world has finally become the concern of everybody. We may be reaching the time when the unity of our planet, our space, our oceans, and our resources finally bring about the unity of all people."

Arrupe had many other visits and meetings in the United States, but the most unusual one was his visit to Father Berrigan, who was in prison in Danbury, Connecticut. The pacifist Jesuit was a poet and dramatist who later played a secondary role in the famous film *The Mission* (1986). In 1968, he, along with others, had burned some draft cards in Maryland to protest the war in Vietnam. After several months of clandestine existence, he was arrested in August 1970 by members of the FBI and sentenced to jail.

The general said that "while traveling through the northeast part of the United States, I wanted to visit him, since he couldn't come to visit me." Without getting involved in US politics, Arrupe stated that his visit to the imprisoned Jesuit was to provide "brother-to-brother consolation." Recalling that he himself had once been a prisoner, he commented that priests should oppose violence and that they needed to fulfill a prophetic role, both decisively and prudently. He insisted on defending the "good reputation" of this Jesuit, and he commented: "I found Father Berrigan in good health and in good humor. I thank all those who have made this visit possible."[22]

---

20   Letter of José María Ortiz-Villajos to the author, Morazán, Honduras, September 14, 1986.

21   *Información S.J.* 2 (May 25, 1971); *St. Louis Post-Dispatch*, May 5, 1971. See also the long interview given to the Jesuit weekly magazine *America* (August 7, 1971).

22   *Información S.J.*, "El padre General en Estados Unidos" (from several news sources); *St. Louis Post-Dispatch*, May 6, 1971, "The Jesuits and the U.N.: Common Ideals"; newspaper *Pueblo*, report of J. M. Carrascal, Madrid, May 5, 1971; newspaper *Ya*, "Cordial entrevista del padre Arrupe con el secretario general de la ONU," Madrid, May 5, 1971.

Curiously, Arrupe's visit coincided with the appointment of a Catholic priest, the Jesuit John McLaughlin, as a personal advisor to President Richard Nixon. The pluralism characteristic of the order was on full display. Later on, Arrupe would write several letters clarifying the conditions for Jesuits to become politically involved, insisting that they remain free of all party politics and electioneering.

Seated Japanese-style, Arrupe polishes the shoes of a shoeshine boy in Quito, Ecuador, after receiving from him his "Working Boy" identification card (May 1971).

Decorated as a Shoeshine Boy

After leaving the United States, Arrupe traveled to Panama and Ecuador and then dedicated five days to a meeting attended by all the provincials of Latin America. While he was flying from San Francisco to Panama, a man seated beside him asked: "Are you a Jesuit?"

"Yes, sir."

"Is that so? Then you must have read the last statements of Father Arrupe. He's a strange type, I'd say revolutionary. [...] What do you think of Father Arrupe?"

With only the slightest smile, Arrupe answered simply: "Arrupe and I are fully in agreement, as if we were the same person."

During the rest of the trip, the man became more intrigued. When the plane stopped in Guatemala, about thirty persons came forward to greet that strange priest, and in Panama reporters and photographers appeared. The man was dumbfounded when he realized that he had asked Father Arrupe his opinion about Father Arrupe![23]

The general reached Panama without much strength of voice. He admitted that the previous day, in the United States, he had spoken non-stop from eight in the morning until one o'clock at night. In Ecuador, he was treated to the high praise of the president of the republic, a former student of the Jesuits. The president wanted to confer on him the country's most distinguished medal, but Arrupe politely turned down the honor. In Quito, however, he agreed to receive another curious decoration, a card that identified him as a "Working Boy." The young fellow who gave it to him first read the Rules of the Association: "The card will be taken away from associates who use profane words. It can also be taken away for improper behavior in the center, in the plazas, and in the streets [...]." And the boy impishly added: "Or in Rome."

The general listened carefully to the rules, and the next day, when he received a visit from one of the boys, as a sign that he had committed himself to obeying the rules, he took off his jacket, sat on the floor Japanese-style, and polished the boy's shoes. The boy was so impressed that he got down on his knees and did the same for Arrupe.[24]

One reporter, observing Arrupe's thin physique and recalling that he was a Hiroshima survivor, wrote in a Guayaquil newspaper: "Although there is no clear evidence of radioactive symptoms in his organism, his lean physique and extreme paleness make one suspect he has an incurable illness."

When another reporter raised the perennial topic of priests getting involved in politics, Arrupe answered: "The priest's obligation is to teach the Gospel doctrine and to form the people's conscience according to the Gospel message, so

---

23   *Información S.J.* 3 (July 16, 1971).
24   *Información S.J.* 3 (July 16, 1971): 2.

that they can discern clearly and participate actively in the process of liberation, but the priest should not take up the banner of political struggles."[25]

Arrupe flew in a military helicopter over the poor neighborhoods of Guayaquil, which were being built out over the water. The Society had a parish in one of the neighborhoods, and Fe y Alegría had social projects in another.[26] Arrupe was amazed at the extreme contrasts between those wretched slums and the nearby residential areas where the wealthy lived.

The provincials' meeting was to take place in Lima, Peru, but a problem arose that overshadowed it. In Lima, some ten thousand homeless people had occupied the grounds of the Jesuit school, La Inmaculada. Bishop Luís Bambarén, the Jesuit auxiliary bishop of Lima, was supporting the protesters and had been arrested. The Peruvian ambassador in Ecuador asked Arrupe not to change the site of the provincials' meeting, which therefore took place as planned. Within three days, the minister of the interior had resigned, and the government offered the squatters new lands.

At the Lima meeting, the Rio de Janeiro letter issued by the Latin American provincials was further discussed. The socioeconomic perspective of that famous letter now needed to be complemented by considering the new liberation theology that was being elaborated. The Lima meeting ratified the Rio document, stressed the importance of spiritual renewal, and committed Jesuits to the "search for the total liberation, of ourselves and others, from spiritual and material conditions (including those of class) that prevent Latin Americans from fully realizing themselves as children of God."[27]

During that year 1971, Arrupe spent relatively little time in Rome. In August, he visited Ireland, where he gave an important speech to the Fourth International Congress of Jesuit Ecumenists. That same month, he attended another congress of former students of Jesuit schools, held in Liège, Belgium.

The trip that had the most impact on public opinion, however, was Arrupe's stopover in Moscow, when he was returning to the Far East. There was speculation over whether that trip to Russia had some hidden significance, perhaps as part of Vatican diplomacy, but Arrupe stated clearly that the reason was simply that he wanted to pay a return visit to Nicodemus, the metropolitan of Leningrad. Arrupe spent almost a week, from August 27 to September 1, in Leningrad and Moscow, where he established many contacts, primarily of a religious

---

25   See the newspapers *Ya, Pueblo, Informaciones.*

26   Fe y Alegría is a federation of national organizations that offer educational opportunities to the poorest sectors of society, along with teacher training, in nineteen countries of South America and Africa.

27   See "Al habla con el padre Arrupe: Rueda de prensa después de su viaje a Lima," *Hechos y dichos* 8–9 (1971): 25ff. See also "Problemas en que pensar," interview with *Noticias Aliadas* of Lima, May 2, 1971, in which he explains his attitude toward atheism, Marxism, socialism, liberation in Latin America, etc., in *La iglesia de hoy y del futuro,* 51.

nature, including a visit to the patriarch Pimen, the "mystery man" of the Russian Orthodox Church. In Leningrad, he attended the Orthodox celebration of the Assumption of the Virgin, and he visited the famous fortress-monastery of Zagorsk (Sergiev Posad), where he was the guest of honor at the opening of the academic theology course, though no public mention was ever made of his presence there. Years later, when asked, "Were you on some concrete mission for the Vatican?" Arrupe answered: "I wish I had been!"[28]

Commentators noted that Arrupe was the first superior of a religious order to visit the Soviet Union and recalled that the Jesuits had long been interested in things Russian, as could be seen in the Russicum College, the Oriental Institute, and the department of Russian studies at the Gregorian—all under Jesuit supervision in Rome. On this trip, Arrupe was accompanied by his assistant for Asia, Herbert Dargan, and by Miguel Arranz, a Jesuit expert in Russian culture and professor of oriental liturgy in Rome. Arranz had given the Spiritual Exercises to the patriarch, who was very interested in Ignatian spirituality; he has also written about the friendship between Nicodemus and Arrupe, who met together several times. Arranz recounts details of the trip:

> On August 26, 1971, we left Brussels, where Father General had attended a congress of former students, and we headed to Moscow in a chilly Aeroflot plane that was covered with hammers and sickles, part of the price that had to be paid. Accompanying Father General was Father Herbert Dargan, the regional assistant for East Asia. We landed in Moscow, and as always two giant uniformed guards with imposing machine guns were waiting at the foot of the stairway. Father Arrupe hardly took notice, and apparently Father Dargan didn't either. For my part, I was worried, and more so when we were in the office of the immigration police and I didn't see the Orthodox priest that usually came to welcome me. In what kind of a mess had I gotten the superior general of the Society of Jesus? Outside, however, our designated companion was awaiting us, the archimandrite Chrysostom Martyshkin, who is now the Orthodox metropolitan in Vilnius.
>
> At midnight, we left Moscow aboard the "Red Star" train and arrived in Leningrad at eight in the morning. We were going to attend the solemn celebration of the feast of the Dormition of the Mother of God according to the Julian calendar, which would be the feast of the Transition in the Spanish liturgy or that of the Assumption in the Roman. August 28 corresponded to August 15 in the Roman calendar.

---

28 *Información S.J.* 8 (November 19, 1971). See extract of the diary of Father Herbert Dargan, regional assistant for East Asia. See also *Vida nueva* 1971, Madrid, "El padre Arrupe, embajador volante del Vaticano," and newspapers for that date.

The trip in the sleeping car occasioned a little anecdote. Father Arrupe and I were sleeping in one compartment, and in the adjoining compartment were sleeping Father Dargan and the interpreter [Pavel] Kutepov, son of the famous White Army general who was kidnapped in Paris by the Soviets after the war and taken to Moscow to be executed; Kutepov was now on his way back from Stalin's prison camps.

I was awoken early by Arrupe's struggling with the door of the cabin. "They have shut us in," he said smiling; he tried the door, and it wouldn't open. I sat up, worried, but when I turned the latch to the other position, the door opened. The two of us let out a laugh of relief.

The celebration lasted three days: Dormition, funerals of the Virgin (following the pattern of Holy Saturday), and Assumption. There was a vigil every afternoon and a Mass every morning, each lasting a minimum of three hours. We accompanied the metropolitan in a solemn automobile procession to the respective churches of each station. Inside the sanctuary, Arrupe was captivated by the unceasing, elaborate evolutions of the numerous clergy, without showing either curiosity or fatigue. His presence was edifying in its prayerful immobility, which made him seem to be one more figure in that huge cohort of saints in the frescoes, who, more than decorating the walls, seemed to be participating in the ceremonies.

In that dense, incense-laden setting, where all were moving in the calculated precision of the complex Byzantine rites to the breathtaking chords of the choral music, Father Arrupe was quite at home. He was one more member of that "heaven on earth." On one of those days, we visited the house of a priest who was son of a priest and father of priests, and later grandfather of priests; no sooner had Father Arrupe left than he said, "He is a prophet!"

For his part, Father Arrupe told me as we were leaving, "What spirituality in a married man!"

During the next synod, in which the topic of married ministers was discussed—some say with a certain displeasure on Paul VI's part—Father General was favorable to the petitions of some bishops in this regard. But it was the vision of those Russian clerics, persecuted and beleaguered by an overwhelming atheism, with their tangible and lively faith, that made Father Arrupe's silent presence (he was not given a chance to speak in public) so manifestly edifying. None of those who came into contact with Father Arrupe in those days ever forgot him.

We visited the beautiful city on the fragile delta of the Neva River. In the fortress of Saints Peter and Paul, the pantheon of the czars, we prostrated ourselves before the tomb of the benefactress of the Society, Catherine II, and while kneeling, we gave her thanks. Beneath her statue in a public park, we took several photographs of ourselves. One of them, with just the three of us Jesuits, became the object of curious commentaries. On the frieze below the statue were named the collaborators and favorites of the czarina: [Grigory] Orlov, [Grigory] Potemkin, and others. Below that were we, "the new favorites of the czarina."

In our visit to the onetime "anti-religious" museum, now restored again to being the cathedral of the Virgin of Kazan, the director who accompanied us wanted to eliminate from our itinerary one hall that I knew contained some anti-Jesuit caricatures, a heritage of the French encyclopedists. I insisted, assuring her that we were not going to be offended. Arrupe's Homeric smile calmed her down. However, an infrared photograph behind us included Jesuits in a torture scene from the Inquisition; I had already criticized it to the director since it showed Dominicans wearing Franciscan cinctures. Later on, the photo appeared in a popular anti-religious book on the Paraguay missions, called *Kingdoms of This World*.

In our visits around the city, always in luxurious Chayka sedans, the sarcastic interpreter kept lecturing us about the many myths of the country. In front of the cruiser *Aurora*, which fought on the side of the 1917 revolution, his interpretation of the famous November 7 shelling of the Winter Palace, which neither signaled the revolution nor had any other effect, was delightful. His serene prudence was extraordinary. We spoke a lot in the hurried Spanish of the people of Madrid, and I don't think any tape recording would have been able to catch it. In that country, everything was recorded, and still is.

We went everywhere in habits. On September 1, we attended, in habits, cloaks, and birettas, the inauguration of the school year of the Moscow Theological Academy in Zagorsk. We were welcomed as guests of honor, but Arrupe was still not allowed to speak. He did not get that chance until two years later, when he visited the country for the second time.

Every year from 1969 to 1979 I went to Russia for several months to teach in the Theological Academy of Leningrad, and Father Arrupe always wanted to see me for an hour whenever I was going or coming. At times, he was concerned about the risks I might be running, and he even asked me if I was not afraid. He informed himself, in the kindest way possible, of all that I had done and all that I planned to do. Sometimes he would forbid me something, but in general he was fully conscious that the mission had its risks, and he had confidence in me.

He showed the greatest confidence when, on ending his first trip and leaving for Japan, he gave me the mission of going to Istanbul to meet with the patriarch Athenagoras, in order to assure him that the

With his four sisters at their home in Bilbao. From left to right: Isabel, María, Catalina, and Margarita.

Society was not making any deals with the Russian church behind the back of the patriarch of Constantinople. Thus it was that, in the name of Father General, I found myself embraced by a giant with a white beard that enveloped me, while the prophetic hierarch told me in broken Spanish, "Just one chalice! Just one chalice! You theologians have separated the churches. Now you must reunite them!"[29]

Arranz also recounts a human trait very typical of Arrupe:

At the beginning of September 1971, we left to bid farewell to Father Arrupe in the Sheremetyevo airport in Moscow, where he would begin his flight to Tokyo with Father Dargan. I wanted to shake his hand respectfully, but he told me: "But in this country everybody has kissed me as much as they want. Let me kiss you also, man!"[30]

The Synod on Justice

The last major event of 1971 was the Bishops' Synod, whose main themes were ministerial priesthood and justice. Father Arrupe had been re-elected as president of the Union of Superiors General, which included 220 orders and

---

29   Miguel Arranz, "Contactos con la Iglesia Ortodoxa rusa," in La Bella, *Pedro Arrupe, general de la Compañía de Jesús*, 620–35, here 629ff.

30   Arranz, "Contactos con la Iglesia Ortodoxa rusa," 633.

congregations with a total membership of three hundred thousand religious around the world. Representing the union, Arrupe intervened three times in the synod, giving two speeches on priesthood and one on the church's contribution to the establishment of justice. In the talk on justice, he pleaded for rapid, effective, constructive, courageous, and universal action on the part of the church. He called for the formation of new men and women who would be authentic "agents of social change," "persons interiorly free, committed to service, fully developed, and gifted with a sense of the universal; persons who know how to read the signs of the times and are capable of serving humankind in responsible ways."[31]

However, the topic that most preoccupied the press during the synod was priestly celibacy. When Arrupe commented that "young people are tired of documents and declarations," he was asked: "Doesn't it seem to you, Father General, that some leaders in the church are not very much in contact with reality and that they have a pre-conciliar mentality in the way they apply Vatican II?"

"That follows naturally," replied Arrupe:

> They give the impression of making concessions reluctantly; there seems to be a defensive attitude that tries to maintain distances. In reality, the way to avoid having to be defensive is to take the initiative and maintain an open posture. There is a noticeable lack of contact with the young people of today.

When asked whether the church should denounce specific injustices and structures imposed by unjust governments, he answered: "I believe that that is the duty of the local church, which should denounce any evident injustice. It also seems to me that the universal hierarchy should express solidarity when there are well-documented injustices in some country."[32]

In one of his synod speeches, Arrupe defended Paul VI, stating that "no one can do, or in fact has done, more for justice than he has." At the same time, he pointed out that the pope had less influence in some countries because of the way his person and his doctrine were presented. Despite such clear statements by Arrupe, the press manipulated them and insisted on presenting the distorted image of Paul VI that was found in some places.[33]

On December 3, 1971, Arrupe sent a message to the alumni of Jesuit schools who were meeting in Mexico at the Sixth Inter-American Congress on Education

---

31 The synod interventions of Arrupe were: "The vital problem of the priest in his ministry," "The ministerial priesthood of religious," "The contribution of the church to the establishment of justice," "In collaboration with the diocesan clergy," in *La iglesia de hoy y del futuro*, 303, 481, 485, 627; and in *Nuestra vida consagrada* (Madrid: Apostolado de la prensa, 1972), 81.

32 "Impresiones sobre el Sínodo de Obispos," interview with the Jesuit press office, in *Información S.J.* 9 (November 30, 1971).

33 "Father Arrupe regrets the way the figure of Holy Father has been deformed in some news reports as a result of criticisms," *ABC*, Madrid, February 11, 1972.

and Poverty. In this message, he stated clearly that education, especially that of the destitute and the marginalized, was the responsibility of the whole of society, and he encouraged the former students to be "the voice of those who have no voice." He added:

> If the wealthy members of Latin American society do not make a joint effort with the governments of their different countries to resolve the grave educational problems that exist, then they will only be fostering an irremediable climate of moral, religious, social, and political crisis. Any Christians who ignore the serious educational inequalities that exist today have forgotten the true meaning of the call that the Gospel makes to their conscience.[34]

God Is Joyful

In the midst of all this hectic activity, Arrupe still had time for governing the order and for writing personally to members of his family, concerned as he was about the health of some of them:

> I am now quite aware that, after suffering so much and becoming so debilitated, Marga will have great difficulty in being cured of this sickness. We are in God's hands, ready to accept whatever his divine providence decides for us, even though at a human level it pains us to be continually seeing our dearest relatives leaving us.[35]

In another letter, he spoke of his three sisters, María, Catalina, and Isabel, and he thanked his cousin Emilia, the wife of Fernando, for her readiness to help them prepare for a trip to Rome, which they would undertake on July 8. He sent them a photo of a young man with long hair, seated in a low chair, and he wrote beneath it: "The superior general of the Society of Jesus waiting for July 8 *in the chair*."[36]

After Christmas, Arrupe wrote a letter to his cousin Fernando, thanking him for calling to mind the absent family members (namely himself and his sister María, the nun) when all the family got together at the Gondra home in Bilbao on Christmas Eve: "As you say, one never knows what the new year will bring in circumstances like these, but we can always be sure that God's constant aid and his loving, if at times inscrutable, providence will never fail us." The letter also contained an insight about Bishop Antonio Añoveros, who had just been

---

34   "The Schools of the Society, Open to All," message of Father General to the Sixth Inter-American Congress of Former Students of the Society of Jesus, Mexico City, December 10, 1971.

35   Letter to Fernando Gondra, Rome, January 29, 1971. Gondra File.

36   Undated card, with a drawing enclosed. Out of a cuckoo clock pops, not a little bird, but a fricasseed chicken, which a diner receives at his table by means of a spring. It also includes photos with the following written on the back: "Basilica of Saint Peter, seen from our terrace" and "The three windows of my room and office," March 5, 1971. Gondra File.

named bishop of Bilbao and who would later have serious conflicts with the government, to the point of being expelled from Spain. Arrupe wrote: "I trust that Bishop Añoveros will be able to unite the spirits of the people in Bilbao, never an easy task, given our illustrious Basque lineage! He is an excellent bishop, and I have no doubt he will know how to do what is right."[37]

Another humorous note: a small community in Barcelona, conscious of the criticisms being voiced against Arrupe, sent him an anthology of religious jokes that had been edited by journalist José Luis Martín Descalzo under the title *Dios es alegre* (God is joyful). Arrupe personally answered this group of young Jesuits of the "Bovila" community, telling them, "I have found this very refreshing in the midst of all the work and the problems that are never lacking. I will continue to enjoy the book in the less busy moments of my day." He even included two jokes in his letter. One was a drawing by May Rink, which shows Arrupe seated before a very complicated computer and asking it, "Computer, tell me what I must do to save the Society." The next panel shows a hand coming out of the contraption and offering Arrupe a rope tied in a hangman's knot. The other was a cartoon by Ryan that had been published in the *Catholic Herald*: Arrupe is pictured completely surrounded by tall, heavy-set Soviet thugs, whom he is telling, "Gentlemen, I really appreciate your interest [...], but I am quite capable of taking care of myself."[38]

It would be tiresome and repetitive to recount all the journeys Arrupe made and all the documents he wrote during the following years. His ideas and his attitudes kept taking on new concrete forms, according to the circumstances. For example, in 1972 he drew a magnificent sketch of the ideal religious superior, based on his ideas regarding dialogue, simplicity, service, and respect for persons. At the Fourth Pan-African Symposium, he spoke on the future of mission, pointing out that "future shock" would give Africa a healthy shaking up; he also stressed the need for foreign missionaries to know when they should leave Africa, so that the continent can become ever more independent.[39] At Fordham Univer-

---

37   Letter to Fernando Gondra, Rome, January 14, 1972. Gondra File.

38   Letter to Father Estanislao Balanzó, S.J., October 11, 1971, provided by Jordi Ginestà I. Fabre, S.J. in a letter written to the author on June 29, 1986. Ginestà notes:

> You can easily imagine our surprise at receiving an unexpected response in the form of a personal letter from Father Arrupe. For those of us who did not have the good fortune of dealing with him at those levels, that meant a valuable memory of his profound humanism, so full of sympathy and kind simplicity. Afterward, I became superior of our community, and when I was assigned to another, I wanted to keep this letter as an exceptional souvenir.

39   "África desea cada día más ser ella misma," report of Pedro M. Lamet in *Vida nueva*, 1972, 1382–83. On Arrupe's trip to the African continent, see Simon-Pierre Metena M'nteba, "Arrupe y África," in La Bella, *Pedro Arrupe, general de la Compañía de Jesús*, 356–70, here 356ff.

sity in the United States, he analyzed the problems of secondary and university education.[40] He held a series of meetings with superiors in Nice, Rome, Mexico, Goa, and other places, and he made an extended visit to the Jesuits in Germany.

During his trip to Mexico, an incident occurred that captures Arrupe well. The government of that country assigned him two groups of bodyguards. Arrupe won them over to such a degree that on the last night one of the officers asked him for permission to bring his "mama" to meet him so that he could bless her. Sure enough, as he was leaving at five in the morning, the officer appeared, accompanied by his very aged mother. The two of them, mother and son, knelt down to receive his blessing, and Arrupe was radiant with joy as he gave it to them.[41]

In 1972, it became clear that another meeting of the Jesuit "parliament" was going to be necessary. Previously, in April 1971, the general had written: "In many places, people are feeling the need to take a pause, in order to carry out an evaluation and to situate ourselves, precisely as Jesuits, in the post-conciliar world." On April 22, 1972, Arrupe communicated to the whole Society that Pope Paul VI had blessed the decision to convoke a general congregation, which would begin at the end of 1974 or beginning of 1975.

Fire at Discretion

The year 1973 was also a stormy one. The first months brought the "Díez-Alegría case." A professor of ethics at the Gregorian University in Rome, José María Díez-Alegría was already controversial because of his conferences on social themes in Spain and some of the talks he had given in Italy. He was, for example, in favor of allowing civil divorce. He had also written a book of personal testimony called *I Believe in Hope*, part of a collection of short works in which outstanding polemical persons of the Spanish church made a sort of autobiographical confession of faith. Suddenly, it was announced that Díez-Alegría had been removed from his teaching position and ordered to return to Spain for two years. There had already been a long dialogue going on between Arrupe and Díez-Alegría, and the professor had conscientiously objected to the censoring of the book since it was of a completely personal nature. Using his knowledge of ethics, he based his arguments on the principle that the church does not have

---

40   "The Jesuits and Secondary and Higher Education," conference given at Fordham, December 10–11, 1972, and in St. Peter's College, in *Información S.J.* 17 (December 1, 1972). See also "La figura del superior religioso actual," conference given in the "Approdo Romano" to curial bishops and professors and superiors of academic centers in Rome, *Documentación S.J.* 15 (May 4, 1972), and in *Nuestra vida consagrada*, 87. In 1972, Arrupe also gave a brilliant talk at the priests' retreat in Foligno: "Frente a un mundo incrédulo, acción pastoral." He there recalled one of his favorite maxims, citing E. Barrotin: "Contemporary man pays more attention to the witness than to the teacher," in *La iglesia de hoy y del futuro*, 149.

41   Manuel Acevez Araiza, S.J., *P. Arrupe: Tres ensayos y un anecdotario* (México: Jus, 1989), 102.

authority in matters of conscience: *De internis necque ecclesia* (On interior matters [of conscience], not even the church [can judge]). In his book, Díez-Alegría is quite controversial, denying papal infallibility, accusing the hierarchy of blessing the doctrine of private property, and openly discussing his own sexual tensions and the non-sinfulness of masturbation. The burning question, however, was his basic refusal to subject his work to any censorship at all.

Given Arrupe's style and his incredible respect for people, it can be understood how much he suffered with this case. On the one hand, he wanted to be faithful to the Holy See and its institutions; on the other, he respected the conscientious decision of a mature Jesuit, who was also a personal friend. Seventy-two students at the university came out in support of the professor. The Canadian Jesuit Jean Gregoire, who was then a graduate student, told *Newsweek*: "We agree with his personal testimony of faith, and we think he should remain in the university. There are many people around the Pope who are misinterpreting his ideas. Personally, I believe he thinks differently."[42]

Díez-Alegría felt obliged to leave the Society of Jesus for not abiding by the customary norms. To be sure, if he had not explicitly refused to have his book censored, it would hardly have been noticed or would simply have been subject to criticism and commentary. However, he wanted to make a public gesture. Even though pressured directly by the pope, Arrupe was still magnanimous. Since Díez-Alegría wanted to continue to work as a priest, Arrupe wrote a letter allowing him to "live in perpetuity" in houses of the Society of Jesus, and so he did. Though not officially a Jesuit, Díez-Alegría lived as one, first in the Pozo del Tío Raimundo barrio with Llanos, and then in a residence of the Society in Madrid. In that way, he could exercise his priesthood, continue to work as a writer and lecturer, and above all speak freely:

> I told myself: for once in my life I am going to write everything that I feel. Arrupe did all he could to rescue my status with the order, but he could not override the norms of the Holy See. At every moment, he behaved with me as a true brother and a gentleman.[43]

Tensions also arose around other issues, especially publications, such as Études, the prestigious journal of the French Jesuits, known for its serious articles

---

42 "Heat on the Jesuits," *Newsweek*, March 5, 1973, 52.

43 Declarations made by Díez-Alegría to the author. After the first editions of this biography were published, the exceptional human quality and the significance of Father Díez-Alegría for the church moved me to write a biography of him as well; it included a detailed description of his theological and personal evolution and his dramatic dialogue with Arrupe. In my opinion, Díez-Alegría had to make his legitimate and difficult conscientious objection without being able to perceive the incredible complexity of tensions and difficulties with which the general of the Society was then besieged (see Pedro Miguel Lamet, *Díez Alegría, un jesuita sin papeles* [Madrid: Temas de Hoy, 2005]).

and commentary on current events. The journal was regularly read by Paul VI, whose collaborators reported that he frequently kept it on his night table. At one point, however, the journal published an article by Bruno Ribes that described situations in which abortion might be allowed and speculated about when exactly an embryo becomes a person. Across the Channel, Peter Hebblethwaite, director of the English Jesuit journal *The Month*, wrote an article in the *Sunday Observer*, in which he attacked the excessive power of the pope's right-hand man, the substitute secretary of state Archbishop Benelli. Such dissident voices were not heard gladly in the Vatican. Though it was never believed that the pope would dare dismiss Arrupe as superior general, many observers were wary of the power of the more conservative wing of the Society, which was still asking for more rigorous discipline for the "pope's soldiers."

Of all the trips Arrupe took in 1973, two occasioned considerable comment, one to Spain and the other to Latin America. The first trip was to Valencia in July for the 110th European Congress of Former Jesuit Students, which was attended by some seven hundred alumni. The main subject of discussion was the one treated in the most recent bishops' synod: social justice. Before the congress, a survey had been done among four thousand alumni, and the results were published a few days before the congress convened. The setting chosen for the event was significant in itself: it was not the Jesuit college in downtown Valencia but the technical schools of San José, whose student body consisted of fifteen hundred workers. The speakers at the congress were Ramón Echarren, Father José María Castillo, and Arrupe. The general readily responded to many questions relevant to his coming visit to countries such as Argentina, Chile, Cuba, and Paraguay, but the long speech he gave at the end of the congress was what provoked the strongest reactions. He dramatically described what he considered to be the Goliath of the contemporary world: a selfish, permissive, consumerist society. And he proposed that the alumni strive for the highest ideals, such as a simpler lifestyle, less personal gain from a society built on the backs of the poor, collaboration with all who were trying to transform society, and the use of influential positions to help the most disadvantaged. [44]

While Arrupe's bold comments were well received by broad sectors of public opinion, they were not appreciated by all the alumni, many of whom belonged to wealthy families of high social standing. The congress was followed by well-publicized criticisms and resignations. Despite the controversy, Cardinal Villot, Vatican secretary of state, wrote to Arrupe in the pope's name, thanking him for the text of the Valencia address and affirming that his call for justice was based on the Gospel message. Such praise must be placed in context, though,

---

44   "La promoción de la justicia y la formación en las asociaciones," speech given in Valencia, July 1, 1973; and "Preguntas y respuestas," Arrupe in dialogue with the young people in Valencia, July 31, 1973. Cf. Arrupe, *Hombres para los demás*, 127ff.

Arrupe with members of his family on a visit to Rome: his nephew Guillermo Barandiarán with his wife Mariví Gondra; Emilia Oraá, mother of Mariví; Arrupe's sister María; his favorite cousin Fernando Gondra; and his personal secretary, Cándido Gaviña.

since Villot was still highly critical of the positions of some Jesuits, especially those who had published articles in the field of morality that were not in accord with the Holy See's views. Earlier in the year, Villot and Arrupe had met together, along with Benelli and the Vatican secretary for public affairs, Agostino Casaroli. During this meeting, Arrupe regretted the lack of "an atmosphere of constructive dialogue"; rather, he had "the impression that the reports received were given credence too readily; that is, the informers were accorded more authority and credibility than the explanations" given by Arrupe himself. He complained that the Vatican paid more attention to one-sided tales and rumors about Jesuits than to what official contacts had to say, and he asked that the accusations be clearly and openly formulated. Villot responded with thirteen pages of the usual criticisms, which could be summed up with the phrase: "Lack of responsible authority." This meant that Arrupe was not taking effective measures to deal with the dissident journals, the excessively permissive formation of young Jesuits, criticisms of *Humanae vitae*, or such particular details as the time of night when the students at the Gregorian were coming home.[45]

From Valencia, Arrupe traveled through Brazil and Argentina and arrived in Asunción, Paraguay, on August 2. It had already been reported in the press there that the dictator Alfredo Stroessner, during his visit to Rome, had requested and obtained a secret interview with Arrupe. In that interview, Stroessner had

45   La Bella, "La crisis del cambio," 904–5.

stressed his government's favorable disposition toward the church. Arrupe had quickly replied that if he was so well disposed, he should give permission for three expelled Jesuits (Fathers José Antonio Caravias, Vicente Barreto, and Francisco de Paula Oliva) to return to the country. Stroessner immediately changed the topic of conversation. Arrupe repeated his request three times and received no answer from the dictator. That same afternoon, Arrupe telephoned Paraguay to guard against the possibility of negative publicity disseminated by the censored press in that country. Indeed, the next day the Paraguayan press gave a distorted version of the interview, stating that it had taken place at Arrupe's initiative and omitting any mention of what was discussed.

Arrupe's first item of business in Asunción was therefore to make it abundantly clear, in an address given in the auditorium of the Catholic University, that his efforts to have the expelled Jesuits return to Paraguay had not been looked upon favorably by President Stroessner. The next day, *La tribuna* gave significant headlines to Arrupe's speech.

On August 7 at 5 p.m., Arrupe concelebrated a Mass at San Ignacio de Guazú, one of the former reductions in Paraguay. He was accompanied by hundreds of small farmers of the area and by the priests who worked with them. The liturgy was in the Guaraní language, for which Arrupe had a simultaneous translator. The homily was carried on in dialogue with the farmers, one of whom declared, "I spent three months in prison for belonging to the agrarian leagues,[46] and they tortured me." Another stated, "I haven't been imprisoned, but I would be ready to give my life before renouncing my ideals of liberation."

That hour-and-a-half liturgy had a profound impact on the general. Several of the priests who concelebrated had been threatened by Stroessner with expulsion. The day after the Mass, the police tried to identify the farmers who had spoken during it, in order to take reprisals. Arrupe's visit ended with another impressive ceremony, which took place in another of the ancient Jesuit reductions, just over the border in Argentina. During the celebration, Arrupe received the solemn profession and final incorporation into the order of two of the priests who had been expelled by Stroessner. Their only crime had been working with the small farmers in the agrarian leagues.[47]

On his way back to Rome, Arrupe visited Argentina, Chile, Mexico, Canada, and Cuba. In this last country, he established contact with the government of Castro, but the climate was still tense and difficult. Perhaps the greatest impact on public opinion came when *Time* magazine dedicated a cover story to him on April 23,

---

46   The agrarian leagues are associations of small farmers that work for land reform and improvement of conditions in the countryside.

47   "Arrupe asked Stroessner to allow the return of the expelled Jesuits"; see *Vida nueva*, 1973, 16, 17. See also the extended interview with Ricardo Sanchis and Javier de Juan at Vatican Radio, where Arrupe treated questions related to violence, Marxism, liberation, and Latin America's most pressing problems.

1973. Titled "The Jesuits: Catholicism's Troubled Front Line,"[48] the article reported that the Society of Jesus was a "diverse and disconcerting fraternity." It stated that an ideological division existed between conservative and liberal Jesuits but that the latter predominated, and it summed up the challenge for the general:

> One of the most serious dichotomies that Arrupe will have to try to resolve is between those who patrol the corridors of power, still hoping to influence the conscience of the king, and those who have chosen to work for the only solution they consider effective: radical change in society.

The article continued: "The Jesuits are settling down somewhat these days, recovering from the traumatic departures from their ranks and the impressive changes in the order, but it is still not at all clear whether the Society of Jesus is on the edge—or in the eye—of the hurricane." The article asked whether one of the objectives of the next general congregation would be putting an end to the confusion and division that existed in the ranks. It offered an evaluation of Arrupe's performance as general, noting that many Jesuits accused him of being a poor administrator:

> The conservatives claim that his permissive governance has weakened the order, and sometimes the liberals think that his most daring innovation was having an automatic Pepsi machine installed in the curia. In the midst of it all, Arrupe acts with a profound serenity that his supporters find saintly and his critics find irritating.

The article concluded with a theological evaluation of Arrupe's way of proceeding.

During these years, the whole world was a volcano. In the United States, President Nixon was obliged to admit to the "Watergate" scandal. A Chilean general named Augusto Pinochet entered the Palacio de la Moneda, where President Salvador Allende had been killed with a machine gun in his hands. In Madrid, President Carrero Blanco was torn apart by a car bomb just as he was leaving Mass at a Jesuit church. The automobile in which he died landed in the courtyard of the residence of professed Jesuits nearby. Vietnam, Israel, Ethiopia, Thailand, and Greece were all passing through tragic chapters of violence. It was not by chance that the movie *The Exorcist* (1973) was attracting the attention of a weary world: the protagonists of the film were Jesuits from Georgetown University in Washington, DC, and one of the actors was actually a priest of the Society.

The world's worst fiends, however—injustice, marginalization, greed, violence, the pride of the mighty—had an appearance less horrifying than that of the exorcized demon, but they were closer at hand. The times were therefore ready for the "great collective option." As Arrupe realized in his long hours of meditation and silence, something else was being required of him.

---

48   "The Jesuits: Catholicism's Troubled Front Line," *Time*, April 23, 1973, 40

17. The Great Option

In the warm afternoon, the ochre color takes on a golden transparency, as if the gold dust of an ancient icon was flowing down from the domes, facades, and crenellations. Visible from the ample terrace atop the headquarters of the Society of Jesus are the peeling walls and the varied forest of towers and steeples of a thousand styles that lend a colorful air to the historical panorama that flows like the Tiber itself. To the right, toward the ancient Rome of the Coliseum and the forums, there is a labyrinth of vaults, pinnacles, and rooftops. Straight ahead in the distance, the bulk of the Castello Sant'Angelo, where at the pope's orders a general of the Jesuits, Father Lorenzo Ricci, was imprisoned, is bathed in the honey color of the Mediterranean afternoon. To the left, toward the setting sun, the dome of Saint Peter's, like a huge half-orange dominating everything, emerges from the colonnade of Bernini with a size that surprises. It is so close that one has the sensation of being almost able to reach out and touch it. On the third floor of the Vatican palaces a light is already turned on in one window, that of the pope. It seems to be keeping watch against the approaching night.

Beneath the broad rooftop terrace swarms an international community composed of more than a hundred persons from all over the world. With their variety of faces—Asian, African, Nordic, Latin, Caucasian—they are the members of the curia of the Society of Jesus, ranging from the counselors of Father General to the most obscure clerks. They work in fifteen offices and secretariats, receiving and answering thousands of letters. Also working there are a variety of Jesuit experts and activists in a broad range of areas—theology, communications, spirituality, education—all under the direct orders of Father General.

A General's Agenda

It was seven o'clock, and night was descending on Rome. Arrupe was bent over his desk, reading his correspondence. He had been up since four in the morning, at which hour, after making his bed and ordering his room, he withdrew to his tiny chapel and, seated oriental style, gave himself over to prayer. There also, at six in the morning, he celebrated the Eucharist.[1] Arrupe once described this chapel in a diary of his intimate thoughts:

> A mini-cathedral! Just six meters by four in size. A little chapel that was prepared at the death of Father Janssens, my predecessor, for the new general [...] whoever he might be! Providence disposed that I be chosen. I give thanks for whoever had the idea: he could not have interpreted better the

---

1   Schedule provided to author by Arrupe himself.

thought of this new general. The one who planned this little chapel perhaps wanted to provide for the new general a more comfortable and private space, so that he could celebrate Mass without being bothered and could visit the Blessed Sacrament without having to leave his quarters. Perhaps it was not expected that that small space was going to be the source of incalculable force and dynamism for the whole Society, a place of inspiration, consolation, strength [...] a place just to be! Or that it was going to be the space for the most active idleness, where by doing nothing everything gets done! [...] Like the idle Mary, who drank in the words of the Master, much more active than Martha her sister! Or that it was going to be the place where my gaze crossed with the Master's [...] where so much is learned in silence.

The general would always, every day, have the Lord just a room away, the same Lord who could enter through the closed doors of the cenacle, who made himself present in the midst of his disciples, who would make himself present in so many conversations and meetings in my office.

They call it the general's private chapel. It is a cathedral and a sanctuary, Tabor and Gethsemane, Bethlehem and Golgotha, Manresa and La Storta! Always the same, always different. If only its walls could talk! Four walls that enclose an altar, a tabernacle, a crucifix, an icon of Mary, a Japanese cushion, a Japanese picture, and a lamp. Nothing more is needed [...] That is all: a victim, a sacrificial table, the *vexillum crucis*, a Mother, a burning flame that consumes itself slowly as it gives off light and heat, and love expressed in a pair of Japanese characters: God–love [...]

In this cathedral is celebrated the most important act of all our daily life: the Mass. Christ is the true high priest, the Word become human. Only the divine can be contained in what is tiny and yet exceed the bounds of the universe [...].

United to Jesus Christ, I as priest carry with me also the whole body of the Society. The walls of this little chapel seem to want to crack open. The tiny altar seems to turn into the "sublime altar" of heaven (canon 1), where the prayers of all the members of the Society reach the Father, "by means of your Angel." My altar is like "the altar of gold placed before the throne" mentioned in the Apocalypse (Revelation 8:3).[2]

He continues this way, commenting on his Eucharist over the universe, this man who carried on his shoulders the responsibility for twenty-seven thousand Jesuits throughout the world, as if the responsibility were his alone.

Not content with this type of spirituality, at 6:45 each morning Arrupe would go to the community chapel to attend Mass along with the brothers. At 7:30, after a frugal breakfast—he ate "like a little bird"—he would read the newspapers,

---

2   Pedro Arrupe, "La misa en mi catedral," in *Él solo, la esperanza*, confidential notes, 59.

though he confessed: "I didn't have much time; I mainly read the headlines and the main stories." From 7:45 to 9:00, he dedicated himself to personal study, mainly theological and other serious subjects. At 9 o'clock, Father Louis Laurendeau, the secretary general of the order, would enter his office to attend to the most urgent business. A half-hour later, Arrupe would hold his regular meeting with the regional assistants, who were responsible for large geographic areas.

After reading a little and receiving Jesuits and other visitors from all over the world who wanted to see him, Arrupe would join the community for some short prayers. At one o'clock, he would go to the dining room and sit down along with the rest of the community at one of the five-person tables. On some days, certain visitors and guests might be designated to join Arrupe for the meal. As always, he would be in a wonderful mood, telling jokes and recounting anecdotes of his life and his trips. On his plate was about a tenth of what would be a normal serving. A Jesuit sitting beside him would comment, or at least think: "He neither sleeps nor eats. What does Father General live on?"

After eating, Arrupe would go up to the community recreation room for ten minutes and enjoy the company of his brothers, displaying the cordiality and friendliness, part Latin and part American, that was so characteristic of him. He rarely watched television, though once in a while he might catch some newscast of RAI.

At four o'clock, another meeting with his general counselors. If need be, a mid-afternoon coffee with some other visitor. And so the afternoon would progress, revising speeches and receiving people until the buffet-style supper at 7:45. Life was not much different for him on Sundays, though perhaps he had more time to read and receive visitors. He was continually receiving visits from church figures and even politicians of diverse tendencies.[3] "But for me," he would later confess, "the most important thing was always being with Jesuits." When asked if he had some hobby in his life, he answered: "My hobby has always been dealing with people." Even on his major trips, he had practically no interest in monuments and other sights. His only passion was to get to know more human beings and know them better, not in the abstract, but personally and individually.[4]

Now, as the first artificial lights played with the shadows in the twisting Roman roadways, steeped in ancient histories of princes and cardinals, Arrupe continued working until the late hours of the night. Some interior force, like a

---

3   Statements made to the author.

4   Without a doubt, in all the Society's history, Arrupe is the superior general who has most cultivated friendship. Many friends for life resulted from his international trips as provincial of Japan, his innumerable personal contacts as general, and the many interviews people had with him. And those friends always received their Christmas greetings or some other personal acknowledgment. That is why Arrupe received continual visits from hundreds of persons who knew him or were interested in knowing him.

light, was visible in his gaze; it was a magnetic aura that kept this charismatic leader ever tireless, jovial, and serene.

Rumors of Resignation and Other Campaigns

Arrupe's working days were centered on his favorite task, what he claimed was the most important one of his generalate: preparing for the general congregation. He had actually convoked it on September 8, 1973, with a letter that explained: "The principal reason for this convocation is the need to seek, define, and make effective the type of service that the Society should render to the church in this time of rapid change in the world, so that we can respond to the challenges the world presents to us."[5] The date set for the start of congregation was December 1, 1974. Arrupe noted that the world was undergoing tremendous mutations and that there was a great need to reflect on them and "to make decisions that exceed the powers of the superior general." His letter also pointed out the existence of "certain deviations" in the Society.

Even before this letter, however, a great deal of groundwork had already been done. The preparations for this congregation would be the most thorough in the history of the Society. After the meeting of the procurators' congregation in 1970, Arrupe decided to set up a preparatory commission composed of six members of very diverse backgrounds. The commission worked almost three years, preparing the topics that would be treated in the general congregation.[6] Arrupe also arranged for the provincial congregations to be held before 1974, so that the postulates from them could arrive in time and be properly organized for study. Numerous surveys, reflections, deliberations, and communal discernments were carried out at all levels of the Society during those three years.

The Holy See received news of the convocation of the general congregation with a certain wariness, as shown in a letter of Cardinal Villot: "Since he [the pope] is aware of some of the current expressions of the orientation and the

---

5   Pedro Arrupe, "Carta convocando la Congregación general 32," *Acta Romana S.I. (AR)* 16 (1973): 126–27. In a letter to his cousins Emilia and Fernando (January 22, 1974), Arrupe wrote: "Thanks for your best wishes for me and the Society: in this year of preparation for the general congregation I especially need and count on your continual prayers, for I am sure that this congregation can be of great importance for the Society in the present moment." In another letter (May 6, 1974), which expresses concern for Emilia's fragile health, he states that he would be spending more time in Rome that year "since I have to keep close tabs on the preparation for the general congregation." And he insisted: "Don't forget this intention in your prayers." In still another letter (August 17, 1974), he shows interest again in the health of his cousin Fernando's wife and states: "For sure, she will also offer some of her pains and discomforts to the Lord for me and my responsibility in the Society. I hope she does!"

6   The preparatory commission was made up of the Frenchman Calvez, the Indian Parmananda Divarkar, the North American Walter Farrell, the German Juan G. Gerhartz, the Brazilian Luciano Mendes de Almeida, and the Spaniard Tomás Zamarriego.

state of the Society, he judges the convocation opportune, and he desires […] on behalf of all a generous and faithful recovery of the Ignatian ideal." The letter also asked that all the different tendencies in the order be present in the congregation, including therefore "those who call for fidelity to the proper spirit and mission of the Society in a more traditional form."[7] A later letter, however, clarified that this desire did not imply any intervention in the Society's Constitutions: "In no way did we mean to suggest any change in the present norms for the selection of the delegates to the general congregation."[8] As we saw in the previous chapter, during 1973 Villot and Arrupe exchanged several letters about the situation of the Society and the way it should be governed.[9]

The pope, for his part, handwrote a personal letter to Arrupe, expressing

> our desire, and even more our will, that the Society adapt its life and its apostolate to the situations and needs of these times in such a way that there be clear confirmation of its nature as a religious, apostolic, sacerdotal order, united by a special bond of love and service to the Roman pontiff, as established in the Formula of the Institute or the fundamental rule of the same Society.

He insisted that this was "a crucial moment for the order."[10]

While the general found himself busy with such affairs, another press campaign was launched against him. His latest visits to Spain and Latin America had aroused criticism of his activities. A Spanish publication had gone so far as to denounce his speech to Jesuit alumni in Valencia as an exercise in "impertinence, careless demagogic discourse, and countless confusions" and advised him: "In America, speak as little as possible." Arrupe's visit to Cuba also caused perplexity in many, especially after he declared to the Agence France-Presse: "Six days are really too few, but at least I was able to admire the dedication with which the Cuban church has undertaken a serious theological and apostolic reflection on the profound social changes that the country has experienced."[11]

Some Latin American newspapers reacted immediately. The Cuban refugees in the United States saw in this attitude a "suspicious maneuver" on the part of the Jesuits, based on judgments that were mistaken and intolerable. An article published in the *Diario de las Américas* of Miami criticized Arrupe for concealing his motives for visiting Cuba and accused the church and the pope of

---

7   Jean-Marie Villot, *Sensus Summi Pontificis relate ad propositum indicendi Congregationem Generalem, AR*, 15, 1972, 827–28.

8   Villot, *Sensus Summi Pontificis relate ad propositum indicendi Congregationem Generalem, AR*, 15, 1972, 828n1.

9   See Alfonso Álvarez Bolado, "La Congregación General 32," in La Bella, *Pedro Arrupe, general de la Compañía de Jesús*, 251–350, here 254ff.

10   "Litterae autographae S. Pontificis relatae ad futuram congregationem generalem," *AR*, 16, 1973, 15–26. The document was published in Latin, English, French, and Spanish

11   Dispatch of the Agence France-Presse, quoted in several bulletins of the Jesuit press office.

contradicting themselves: they declared Marxism and Christianity to be incompatible, but to further their own interests they praised the Cuban situation, which "degrades the whole people and deprives them of freedom." *O estado de Sâo Paulo*, a Brazilian daily with a very large circulation, accused Arrupe of "Jesuitry." In its edition of September 9, a commentator wrote that the Society of Jesus, which had been given the mission of "fighting atheism," had rather opted for a dialogue with atheists that was "very similar to capitulation." Socialism had executed ten thousand Cubans, placed another ninety thousand in concentration camps, and caused six hundred thousand to go into exile, but Arrupe "did not mention any of these aspects of the Cuban regime."

Back in Italy, Arrupe read these commentaries, as well as those in the European press, without losing his sense of humor. In the prestigious daily of Milan, *Il corriere della sera*, Fabrizio de Santi wrote that Arrupe was doing nothing less than "riding a tiger," but he correctly interpreted the declarations that Arrupe had made to France-Presse: critics had accused him of "unconditional approval of the Castro regime, when actually he had limited himself to praising the church's efforts to understand the new reality of the country." Speaking on Vatican Radio, Arrupe had the good taste and intelligence to refrain from attacking the press; he even thanked them for their interest and their accuracy in reproducing his words. He added that the press had helped him to reach a larger public, one that would never have known of him otherwise.

Another aspect of this hurtful campaign was the spreading of rumors about Arrupe's imminent resignation and the publication of various anonymous articles. On September 5, 1973, the newspaper *Il tempo* of Rome headlined what was supposed to be a "Revolutionary Initiative of Father Arrupe: Resignation of the 'Black Pope' for the First Time in History." On October 7, 1974, the French weekly *Le point*, of conservative bent, dedicated nine lines to the same topic under the heading "Opposition to the 'Black Pope.'" It reported that Arrupe would resign during the general congregation because of the strong opposition from conservative elements of the Society and the lack of support from Paul VI.

Televisión Española, which tended to turn the speculations of the foreign press into hard news, made the rumor into a certainty in the evening newscast of October 7 but then had to retract the next day. The US weekly *National Review* went even further in its October 11 edition. Not only did it make Arrupe's resignation a certainty but the author of a long article, Farley Clinton, assured readers that "well-informed sources" were convinced that the successor of Paul VI would suppress the Society of Jesus: "We more or less take it for granted" were reportedly the words of Benelli's secretary.[12]

At the same time, there was a rising tide of letters and anonymous commentaries, manifesting their disagreement with the way the Society was being governed and asking for the general's resignation. These protests, claiming loyalty to the Constitutions and the Holy See, proliferated in the form of mimeographed pamphlets or articles published in the conservative press, above all in Spain. Another protest emerged during a congress on the Spiritual Exercises that was held in Loyola in 1974 and attended by some two hundred retreat directors from all over the world. This time, Arrupe himself was present, having made a quick trip to Spain just for the occasion. At the congress, he acquitted himself with his proverbial elegance and returned immediately to Rome after short stops in Granada and Lisbon. One Jesuit of the "True Society" had left in his napkin box at Loyola an anonymous insult: "One Basque founded the Society of Jesus; another one is destroying it." Several traditionalist Jesuits continued their clandestine activities, principally in Spain and Argentina. Calling themselves "Jesuits in Fidelity," they included Fathers José Antonio de Aldama, Solano, Eustaquio Guerrero, and Manuel Parente; their goal was to confront Arrupe directly and demand his resignation. The eccentric Jesuit Nicolás Puyadas, using the pseudonym Javier Pignatelli, went so far as to publish early in 1974 a curious book called *The Truth about the Society of Jesus*, in which he attempted to defame Arrupe. At the Loyola congress, a pamphlet was circulated that summarized the contents of

---

12   See the cited newspapers. In a letter to his family (October 15, 1974), Arrupe again shows concern for Emilia's health and then says: "On December 1 the general congregation will begin. It will be an arduous task, but I trust in the Lord that it will be very beneficial for the Society and for the church itself. I count on your prayers and your sacrifices, especially those of good Emilia." He added: "I don't know if you will see on television an erroneous news story they put out about me—it has no basis in truth. They promised they would correct the error, and I suppose they will, since they innocently trusted in a French publication without checking out the facts." An article published in the journal *Fuerza nueva* with the title "Chequeo al padre Arrupe," presented an interview with three anonymous Catalonian Jesuits, who stated that Arrupe was incapable of governing the Society, oblivious to its ruin, deaf to the Pope's warnings, etc.

the book and accused the general of having manipulated the election process, of not having informed Jesuits about the pope's posture with regard to the Society, of seeking to secularize the order, and of not having followed a canonically valid process in preparing for the general congregation. These actions were basically reverberations resulting from the trauma caused in the conservative sectors of the church by the *aggiornamento* brought on by the council. Their aim, as always happens in moments of important change, was to stop history in its tracks. However, the immense majority of the Jesuits were on Arrupe's side and made this clear in a variety of documents and manifestations of support.

In February 1974, the Spanish provincials felt obliged to write a letter condemning the anonymous articles. The Society's press office at the same time put out a communiqué stating that "it is absolutely true that Father Arrupe has no intention of resigning when the general congregation meets in December. He personally reaffirmed, in a press conference in Loyola, that his post, by decision of the congregation, continues to be for life."

Arrupe felt interiorly free enough to treat explicitly the questions raised by the press and public opinion, and in so doing he showed extraordinary comprehension of the work of the communicator. He admitted that the church could at times have reasons for maintaining a certain reserve, but he added, "in general, it is better to avoid secrecy." He pointed out the need for criticism:

> Communicating only what is positive and good guarantees that credibility will quickly be lost. Fear of criticism is always harmful, since it leads us to conceal possible errors or culpable limitations. Sincere authenticity is not only the best ground for credibility; it is the best way to avoid the need to adopt a defensive attitude which tends to deny defects and even tries to defend them.[13]

Without wishing to do so, Arrupe seemed to be speaking about himself, but that was the way he generally treated the mass media. What is more, he dared to state:

> It is true that the church has suffered much from the prejudices and distortions to which public opinion has frequently been prone. Nevertheless, we must ask ourselves whether at times we have not given cause, at least in part, for such prejudices and distortions, given the limitations we have imposed on ourselves and some of the attitudes we have adopted with regard to the free flow of information.

---

13   See *Documentación S.J.* 26 (May 5, 1974). Arrupe's other interventions in the 1974 synod were: "The Contemporary World and Its Challenge to the Missionary Church," "Global Experience of Evangelization," and "Evangelization and Human Development," in *La iglesia de hoy y del futuro*, 207ff.

In the midst of the press onslaught and during the months prior to the congregation, another Synod of Bishops took place, taking as its theme "evangelization in the contemporary world."

The Pope Asks Questions

Given these circumstances, there was obviously much anticipation of General Congregation 32. Those familiar with Arrupe's character and the long preparation that had taken place were sincerely hopeful that there would be a profound repositioning of the Society in the light of the signs of the times. Shortly before the congregation began, theologian Karl Rahner, a German Jesuit, had commented that developments in the church

> presented themselves suddenly, with all the peculiarities and dangers that accompany the indispensable changes that need to be adopted with all due speed. But such change is necessary if the church does not wish to continue to be a church only of the rural sector and the petit-bourgeois, typical of the old Europe, with a continually diminishing body of faithful members.

According to Rahner, change in the church, once the idea is accepted, presents the difficulty that it is no longer possible to use "the nice maps from headquarters, with all the routes clearly indicated." Arrupe personally considered the general congregation to be extremely important. Two days after being elected general, he had commented: "I would prefer five interviews with reporters of all languages to having to present myself before the general congregation. If I could at least have at my side Father Abellán [...]."

Nine days before the great event was to take place, Paul VI granted another private audience to the general of the Jesuits. According to Arrupe's own account, they discussed the issues that might affect the essence of the Institute, and the pope told him that he wanted time to reflect before responding.[14]

On December 1, 1974, the 237 participants, representing sixty-eight provinces and twenty-two vice-provinces of the Society, arrived in Rome. The image they offered was not of a standardized army, uniformed in black. They wore

---

14   I gave the pope a document that presented a short compendium of the postulates received and indicated certain ones that might at some point affect the Formula of the Institute. I told the Holy Father that the general congregation would need a long time and great serenity to be able to judge the possibility of reconciling some of these propositions with the essence of the Institute; in each case, it would have to determine the advantages or disadvantages of attempting such a modification. I spoke with the Holy Father briefly about these points, and he told me that, with regard to the concession of the fourth vow to those who were not priests, he wanted more time to consider the matter.

Communication of Arrupe to the assembled fathers on December 16, 1974, *Acta CG 32*, actio 11, 51.

jerseys of different colors, Roman collars, cassocks, jackets and ties, and they came from all over the world. In contrast to former times, these Jesuits treated one another with great familiarity, often using first names. On December 2, Arrupe read some verses from scripture, and the hymn *Veni Creator* was sung. In the church of the Gesù, next to the sepulcher of Saint Ignatius and the preserved arm of Saint Francis Xavier, the general reminded the assembled brethren, as an encouragement to be humble as they began their work, how Xavier had "had to limit himself to waving his biretta to attract the attention of the Japanese who were walking through the streets, inviting them to hear the sermon of Brother Fernández, not his own."[15]

The next day, which was precisely the feast of Francis Xavier, the first missionary to Japan, Paul VI received the assembly in a papal audience. Speaking of a "decisive moment" and considering himself "the supreme superior of the Society," the pope first asked, "Where are you coming from?" before giving a synthetic history of the order's origins. He then asked the question, "Who are you?" and supplied his own answer by making it clear that they were "a religious, apostolic, sacerdotal order, united to the Roman pontiff by a special bond." Continuing with his questions, the pope asked, "Then, why do you doubt?" and directly attacked "the systematic doubt, the desire for change, the independence, and the individualism" that was to be found among Jesuits. Paul VI acknowledged that there existed in the order "a strong state of uncertainty, or even more, a strong and fundamental questioning of your very identity," and he made reference to some "clouds" that he claimed were overshadowing the trajectory of the Jesuits. The pope's final question, "Where are you going?" was therefore answered with much subtlety. Adaptation was needed, yes, but adaptation that was "just, healthy, balanced." He warned the assembled brethren of another danger—"the phenomenon of novelty for its own sake." After reflecting on the depth of discernment that was needed, the pope added: "We believe that it is not asking you too much, and we expressly desire, that the congregation delve deeply into the 'essential elements' [*essentialia*] of the Jesuit vocation and proclaim them again, so that all your brothers can fully recognize themselves."[16]

Paul VI stressed again the confidence he had in the Society, and the tone of his discourse showed how important an institution he considered it to be. At the same time, his many questions revealed that he was looking for satisfactory answers.

Álvarez Bolado, one of the delegates, commented:

Anyone who compared the pope's allocution with the three instructions Arrupe gave at the start would notice a sharp contrast. The pope appeared to be saying: the experiments are finished; get back to the essentials; be careful

---

15   "Congregación General XXXII," *Razón y fe* (Madrid, 1975): 279.
16   "Congregación General XXXII," 239.

of novelties. Arrupe, on the other hand, with the tremendously profound spirituality of his allocutions, showed us the need to confront the challenges of the future. The two lines of thought did not exactly coincide, and I dared to tell him so. He answered me, "Don't believe it. There's not that much difference."[17]

The Holy See Calls for a Stop

From that moment on, General Congregation 32 became the supreme authority of the Society, though all bear witness that the general exercised important spiritual leadership during the whole assembly. Arrupe's only privilege would be having two votes in the balloting, which for the second time would be done electronically. About twenty Jesuits took care of the simultaneous translation.

Among other internal matters, GC 32[18] treated two controversial and challenging topics that greatly affected Arrupe both personally and publicly: grades and the so-called "decree 4."

On December 3, the same day as the pope's allocution, Cardinal Villot had written a letter to Arrupe that made explicit mention of the question of grades. To understand this matter, it is necessary to go back to the Constitutions written by Saint Ignatius, who, in accord with the pyramidal and monarchic mentality of his time, organized the Society as an army or "light cavalry" of the church. The order's "general staff" consisted of the "professed of four vows," who made, in addition to the usual religious vows, a special fourth vow of obedience to the pope in regard to missions. This is not a universal vow of obedience to the pope, but one concerning the apostolic missions that the pope wishes to be undertaken. Only a select minority of Jesuits, chosen for their sound spirituality and intellectual formation, became professed fathers. In the original idea of Saint Ignatius, the Society consisted only of this group of "reformed priests." Later he allowed two other grades. The second was that of the so-called "spiritual coadjutors," who were non-professed Jesuit priests, and the third was that of the "temporal coadjutors," who were non-ordained Jesuit brothers. The relationship with the order differed according to the grades. Being a "professed of four vows," for

---

17 Statement of Alfonso Álvarez Bolado, S.J. to the author.

18 See Álvarez Bolado, "La Congregación General 32," 254ff.; John W. Padberg, *Together as a Companionship: A History of the Thirty-First, Thirty-Second, and Thirty-Third General Congregations of the Society of Jesus* (St. Louis, MO: Institute of Jesuit Sources,1994); Bartolomeo Sorge, "32 Congregazione Generale della Compagnia di Gesù: La preparazione e le atesse I y II," *La civiltà Cattolica* (1974): 424–34, 526–39. Sorge, "Postfazione: Il post-Concilio della Compagnia de Gesù," in Jean-Yves Calvez, *Padre Arrupe: La Chiesa dopo il Vaticano II* (Milan: Paoline Editoriale Libri, 1998), 223–69. Sorge, "Arrupe, Pedro," in *Diccionario histórico de la Compañía de Jesús: Biográfico–temático II*, ed. Charles E. O'Neill and Joaquín María Domínguez (Rome: Institutum Historicum, S.I., 2005), 1697–705.

example, made dismissal from the Society more difficult and made the subject eligible for posts of greater responsibility.

This division into grades grated with the mentality of many twentieth-century Jesuits, who were inspired by a more democratic vision and by evangelical ideals of equality and justice. Moreover, general practice had begun to treat all Jesuits equally, and the idea that there were first- and second-class Jesuits was effectively disappearing. For that reason, many of the postulates that had arrived in Rome from the provinces expressed the desire that the question of grades be reviewed. Thirty-six of the provincial congregations had asked that the fourth vow be extended even to the brothers.[19]

In this context, Villot's letter reminded Arrupe that the pope felt that "such an innovation, after due consideration, seems to present grave difficulties, and these would prevent the Holy See from giving the necessary approval." The letter did not forbid treatment of the topic; it stated only that such a change would not be approved by the pope. The Italian Jesuits, more familiar with the subtle language of the Holy See, understood quickly what that meant: "Let the matter not be treated."

Nevertheless, the assembled Jesuits insisted on treating it. With a majority of votes (187 in favor versus forty-three against), they decided that there was still room for "representation" in the Ignatian spirit, according to the norm: "A subject always has the option of representing his reasons for not obeying an order, before the superior gives his final decision." They would therefore discuss whether it was fitting to submit to the pope's consideration the reasons that moved them to reassess this basic feature of the Society, in accord with the times.

In a meeting Arrupe had with the Spanish Jesuits, a comment was made about the need to deal with the Holy See "diplomatically." One person stated: "The Gospel says that we must be simple as doves, but also prudent as serpents."

Arrupe took on a serious aspect, quite unusual for him, and answered: "Well, I prefer to continue being simple as a dove." And he added firmly: "The Society is governed by the general, not by the cardinals."[20] In so saying, Arrupe was not stating anything new. He was limiting himself to applying what canon law lays down concerning an exempt order.

In this case, however, since a general congregation was in session, the decision was no longer Arrupe's; it was in the hands of that supreme organism of governance of the Society. At the same time, the assembly was receiving frequent warnings regarding the topic from Villot. On February 20, after further

---

19   Some 1,020 postulates were sent to the general congregation. Of the eighty-five provincial congregations, thirty-seven expressed a desire that the fourth vow be extended, as did four of the fifteen task-forces that had elaborated the preparatory material for the congregation (see Sorge, "Postfazione," 251n41).

20   Witnessed by Gutiérrez Semprúm, S.J. per his letter to the author, Montevideo, June 10, 1988.

proceedings of the congregation that would perplex the non-specialized reader,[21] Arrupe went to the Vatican to get a better idea of what the pope expected of the assembly and at the same time to assure the pope of the assembly's sentiments of fidelity and affection. Arrupe proceeded to the interview along with one of his assistants, but the monsignors in the antechamber indicated that he should enter to see the pope alone. During the meeting, Paul VI was, it seems, extremely severe, serious, and brusque. Accompanied by Cardinal Benelli, the pope simply said to Arrupe: "Sit down and write what Cardinal Benelli dictates to you."

Arrupe did so. The dictation consisted of a stern admonition. The Holy Father was troubled and pained because the Society was not responding as he wished. As custodian of the founding essence of the Society, he had decided not to allow any extension of the fourth vow, though he had no objections to the Society's otherwise adapting itself to the times. He considered the fourth vow an essential point of the Formula of the Institute. According to Arrupe, the pope requested that "we be faithful to ourselves." Paul VI was surprised that it was not understood from the start that he wished to exclude all debate concerning the matter, and he referred to his letter of February 15. In the course of the conversation, the general realized that the congregation had erred in treating the matter of the fourth vow.

One of the harshest paragraphs dictated to Arrupe by Cardinal Benelli read thus: "It is sad that the fourth vow has been discussed and that there has been an exploratory vote in the assembly, against the express will of the Holy Father (letter of December 3, 1974), which was confirmed again by his own petition." The statement continues, repeating the accusation made already by the secretary of state in his letter of January 23:

> In this way, the assembled fathers were deprived of an indispensable element for expressing their opinion objectively, according to the criteria of their own conscience. Thus the Holy See is obliged to undertake an epistolary correspondence that is quite disagreeable. And it does not appear that the truth of the matter has been re-established in the minds of all the assembled fathers.[22]

Thus, the Jesuits were commanded to obey and not to treat the matter of grades in any way.

When he left the papal premises, Arrupe's eyes were filled with tears.[23] According to witnesses of this historic moment, when he returned to the assembly hall, he had a terribly haggard appearance. He immediately assembled the delegates and communicated to them the will of the pope. The substance of the audience coincided with the contents of the personal letter that Paul VI would later send to the

---

21 See Álvarez Bolado, "La Congregación General 32," 254ff.

22 Álvarez Bolado, "La Congregación General 32," 322.

23 Information confirmed personally to the author by Arrupe.

general, after receiving the report requested of Arrupe on this question of grades. The letter stated quite clearly: "Therefore we repeat again, with all due respect, to you and the assembled fathers: 'No innovation may be introduced with respect to the fourth vow.'" With regard to the labors of GC 32, the letter repeated the questions about how much confidence the pope should have in the Jesuits and how congenial were the order's relations with the hierarchy. In a word, the pope wanted to know, "Where are you going?" and he insisted that the future decisions of the Society would have a great effect on all the other religious families.[24]

Apparently related to the whole question of the vows was the fear that the Society might in the future come to include laypeople as members and become a sort of secular institute, thus ceasing to be a clearly sacerdotal order. A revealing piece of information in this regard is an article that appeared shortly before the congregation in *La civiltá cattolica*, the Jesuit journal that reflected Vatican thinking. The article, thought by some to be inspired from above, presented the abolition of grades as "part of a plan of the left wing of the Society to transform it into a secular institute, composed indiscriminately of priests and laypeople."[25]

In the midst of this tension, one Italian Jesuit rose in the assembly and exclaimed: "Don't you see that it has been an error to treat this topic? We had already said so and repeated it a thousand times."

With a very serious mien, Arrupe intervened vigorously, saying: "Excuse me, Father, but here we have very qualified people: theologians, philosophers, writers, persons of much virtue, who decided to proceed this way. We must respect their reasons."[26]

Arrupe then invited the members of the congregation to celebrate the Eucharist, during which he gave a homily on "obeying with joy." With incredible self-control, he had in a matter of minutes surmounted the ordeal. He was again joyful and optimistic and was communicating faith to others by his attitude and his words.

One of those in attendance recounts:

I believe that the main reason for the misunderstanding with the Vatican regarding the matter of grades was Arrupe's firm belief that the congregation had authority over him and was free, and that he should not pressure it. The pope thought that by simply suggesting it to the general, the general would persuade the assembly not to treat the matter, as seems to have been the tradition with earlier popes and generals.[27]

---

24   Personal letter of the pope to the general congregation (February 15, 1975). Cf. this document and the letter of Villot (December 3, 1974) in "Congregación General XXXII," *Razón y fe* (Madrid, 1975): 261, 263.

25   Brian Daley, S.J., "Identifying Jesuits," *The Month* 236 (May 1975): 146–51, here 146ff.

26   Statement of Alfonso Álvarez Bolado, S.J. to the author.

27   Letter previously cited of Gutiérrez Semprún.

Years later, Arrupe clarified the matter: "We are not 'papists' in the old understanding of the term. We do not form another 'Swiss Guard' for the pope [...]; no, no. We owe him complete loyalty. We have a special spirit of fidelity to the Roman pontiff." Speaking of those tense days, he said:

We had thought—and even voted—that the matter was open and that the members of the congregation could exchange opinions about it. For the Holy Father, however, it was a fundamental point of our Institute that could not be changed in any way. After I had an audience with the sovereign pontiff and communicated his decisive view to the fathers, all of them accepted it without the least bit of discussion. For me, that was one of the most beautiful examples of total obedience in the Society, and I must confess that I have great admiration for this congregation.[28]

Later still, when he was quite ill, Arrupe confessed to the author of this book:

That day when the pope called me was very hard, believe me, very hard. Terrible! Father O'Keefe went with me, and they would not let him enter. The pope ordered me to write. I wanted to speak, but he would not let me. I held back my tears and wrote. When I left, I broke into tears. I could not comprehend that attitude, for interiorly I saw things clearly. It was very beautiful how the fathers of the congregation reacted. Within a few minutes, I was already quite calm."[29]

The former director of *La civiltà Cattolica*, Bartolomeo Sorge, believes that one of the most exalted pages of Arrupe's whole generalate was the discourse he delivered at that moment to the assembly:

We find ourselves in a unique situation, one from which we can hope to reap great fruits and which can lead us to purification by the Spirit, to greater union with God, to more profound love of the Holy Father, and to a closer bonding with the church. We feel very acutely our limitations and sorrows—because we failed to understand what we needed to understand. We have not considered the totality of the extent and profundity of the Holy Father's directives, which are of great importance for the renewal of the Society. Although it does not appear that we can attribute this to a lack of goodwill, we have perhaps lacked real spiritual discernment in not listening to what God is saying to us through his vicar. Let us make an effort to see here the hand of God. Here is the way and the trail of the Spirit! Just as previously God led the people of Israel by means of warnings, in order to prevent deviations and lead them to the Promised

---

28   *Itinéraire*, 129.
29   Statements to the author by Arrupe.

Land, we too need a real purification. God himself questions us through his vicar, a watchful father.[30]

Despite this pledge of fidelity, the Italian press went so far in those days as to speak of the "disobedience of the Jesuits"

"Did you sleep that night," I asked Arrupe many years later:

Yes, of course. I have always slept. I have never lost my peace. I have a tranquil conscience. I don't know if I may have made a mistake. God knows, and in heaven it will be seen, but I always did what I thought I should do before God, what appeared to be my obligation.[31]

The Option for Social Justice

The second great topic of the general congregation was the option the Society of Jesus made for social justice. Whoever has studied Arrupe's life in all its stages knows the extent to which commitment to the poor, the dispossessed, and the marginalized was an integral part of his human and Christian development.

In 1973, Arrupe confessed to sensing that his life was moving in a different direction: "That year, I saw clearly that something completely new was beginning. I was interiorly certain. I didn't have the least doubt that I had to travel by a new road. What a beautiful experience it was!" In speaking of this intimate matter, he put his hand on his chest and continued: "I told this to the procurators who met in Rome, and they agreed to convoke the general congregation. The Jesuits had to come to terms with something new."

When asked if this was the option for social justice, Arrupe answered: "Yes and no. The idea was still budding." He then added enthusiastically: "It was something precious!"[32] This was, then, another crucial and even mystical theme in Arrupe's life story.

After long debate,[33] GC 32 issued a decree that would not be an idle docu-

---

30   Álvarez Bolado, "La Congregación General 32," 326; Sorge, "Postfazione," 255n51.
31   Statements to the author by Arrupe.
32   Statements to the author by Arrupe.
33   Reading the *acta* that summarize the last two sessions, it is difficult to avoid the emotion produced by the splendid manifestation of spirit. The debate over the report came to a close when the moderator proposed this motion: recognizing all the observations made, it seemed good to the assembly to commit the final editing of the report, in the name of the congregation, to Father General and his general assistants, who could count on everyone for help and support. The argument made by someone who spoke against the motion is significant, stressing "the desire of the general congregation to assume, in this case, full responsibility." Father General abstained from voting, but the motion proposed by the moderator obtained a comfortable majority.

Álvarez Bolado, "La Congregación General 32," 297ff.

Arrupe enjoyed visiting groups of children on his frequent trips to developing countries: "Some die of hunger, others for excess of cholesterol."

ment in the Society's future. Titled "Our Mission Today: The Service of Faith and the Promotion of Justice," the decree had a style of language that was new, different, closer to the modern sensibility. "Decree 4," as it came to be known, could be summed up in "two phrases": "The mission of the Society of Jesus today is the service of faith, of which the promotion of justice is an absolute requirement."

After lively discussion and the elaboration of three successive versions, the congregation wanted to stress the importance of faith as the basis for this great option for justice. The decree explicitly stated:

> We must bear in mind that our efforts to promote justice and human freedom on the social and structural level, necessary though they are, are not sufficient of themselves. Injustice must be attacked at its roots, which are in the human heart, by transforming those attitudes and habits which beget injustice and foster the structures of oppression.

Father Calvez, a specialist in this area and a close collaborator of Arrupe, later wrote that GC 32 had made the commitment to justice in response to many postulates arriving from all over the world:

> It is especially necessary to repeat that the novelty of decree 4 is not so much in the statements about the service of faith, but almost exclusively in the statements about the promotion of justice. This was the topic that received the greatest development. And that was the reason for some of the strong expressions that were used. Right from the beginning, it could be foreseen that this aspect would later attract much attention and would produce a powerful impact.

The many amendments proposed did not prevent the final vote from being very close to unanimous.[34]

Despite this strong support, Cardinal Villot months later addressed another letter to the general, in which he complained that "along with statements that deserve every consideration, there are others that cause a certain perplexity and, in their formulation, might be interpreted incorrectly." Villot suggested five additions to the decrees. The longest of them referred to decree 4 and stated that "in the order of temporal things human development and social progress should not be exalted excessively, so as to cause harm to the essential significance that the

---

34   "Congregación General XXXII," *Razón y fe* (Madrid, 1975): 59. See also the historical introduction of Álvarez Bolado and the chapter cited above. For a detailed analysis of the genesis of decree 4 and a study of its evolution, its reception, and its parallels with other church documents, see Jean-Yves Calvez, *Fe y justicia: La dimensión social de la evangelización* (Santander: Sal Terrae, 1985). On the topic of justice in the life and work of Arrupe, see Eduardo Martín Clemens, "Pedro Arrupe: Testigo creíble de la justicia" (thesis for the licentiate in the Gregorian Pontifical University, Madrid, 1989); Matías García, "Arrupe y la justicia," in La Bella, *Pedro Arrupe, general de la Compañía de Jesús*, 753–91, here 753.

church grants to evangelization, that is, to announcing the whole of the Gospel."[35]

It would not be proper to view this important assembly only in terms of the debates on grades and justice. GC 32 also published brilliant decrees on Jesuit identity, fidelity to the magisterium and the supreme pontiff, formation, union of hearts and minds, poverty, and internal governance. Decree 2 states that a Jesuit is one who "engages, under the standard of the cross, in the crucial struggle of our time: the struggle for faith and the struggle for justice that it includes." Arrupe gave two other significant allocutions during the congregation. One was on the state of the Society, in which he analyzed quite frankly the existing problems, among which he mentioned the doctrinal deviations of the journals, the decline in vocations, the formation of young Jesuits, and relations with the hierarchy.[36] The other was the homily he gave at the closing Mass, concelebrated with more solemnity than usual in the Basilica of Saint Peter, beside the chair of the Fisherman. There, among many other things, he stated:

> We can say that the Society leaves this general congregation more conscious of its limitations, more knowledgeable of the needs of the world and the church, inflamed by a desire for unity, more perfectly committed to obedience, more sacerdotal, possessed of more realistic vision of the apostolate, and finally more ready to hear and obey Christ's voice, whether it comes directly from him, is manifested through obedience, or is communicated to us indirectly, that is, through the human family that suffers affliction and awaits its salvation and liberation, which it will not find except in Christ.[37]

As the Jesuits finished their labors on March 7, 1975, the pope once again addressed them, and this time he was brief. In an audience granted to the general and his four assistants, he limited himself to expressing again his appreciation of the Society, "so closely bound to us and certainly so beloved," and to explaining why he had imposed his authority on the congregation. He also commented on how the assembled fathers "understood in good spirit the force and the significance of our indications and accepted them with obedient will."[38] In this audience, the pope gave the Jesuits a crucifix that had belonged to the Jesuit saint Robert Bellarmine.

The mass media immediately sniffed out the wrangling that had taken place during the assembly. Representatives of the international press had followed the proceedings with great interest, and they understood that there had been

---

35   "Carta del secretario de Estado al padre General" (May 2, 1975).

36   Discourse on the state of the Society, "Congregación General XXXII," *Razón y fe* (Madrid, 1975): 337.

37   Homily in Saint Peter's, "Congregación General XXXII," *Razón y fe* (Madrid, 1975): 335, and "Final Allocution to the Congregation (March 7, 1975)," *Razón y fe* (Madrid, 1975): 361.

38   "Allocution of Paul VI before Father General and the General Assistants" *Razón y fe* (March 7, 1975): 267.

tensions, although many of the details we have recounted here were not made public until later. A sample of the reporting at the time could be seen in two French journals, *Le figaro* and *Le monde*. The first, under the headline "Paul VI and the Jesuits: An Exemplary Conflict," reported that "the congregation of the Jesuits ended without being able to respond to the questions posed by many members of the Society and with a certain sense of dissatisfaction." The article referred to a communiqué broadcast by Vatican Radio, which had advised that the prudent *aggiornamento* desired by Paul VI should not lead to "hazardous experiments" and even less to "radical innovations." The *Le figaro* commentator, Joseph Vandrisse, considered language to be a key problem: "It is quite clear that Paul VI and the congregation do not speak the same language." He also saw a problem regarding "information": "Father Arrupe had the courage to refer, in his speech of January 2, to difficulties between the Society and the Holy See, and especially with the secretary of state. To sum up, who is informing the pope, and how is he being informed?" Vandrisse insisted that the Jesuits had not criticized or at any moment called into doubt the role of the Apostolic See. Censuring the climate of adulation and fear, he considered the fact that the congregation had called certain things into question to be "a sign of health." He concluded: "Paradoxically, the unity of the Society around Father Arrupe and its union with the pope may emerge reinforced."[39]

In an earlier article, "Paul VI and the Jesuits: A Difficult Dialogue," Vandrisse made an interesting observation:

> At base, Paul VI and Father Arrupe have different ways of viewing life, tradition, and the council. They have profound esteem for one another, but their temperaments are opposed. While one man is more anxious, though also a prophet for his times, and speaks of "maintaining" things, the other is more optimistic, though traditionalist on certain points; he cites C. P. Snow, who invites us to "wear the future on our sleeves." During the congregation, this difference made for a conflictive situation. Paul VI made clear his preferences and then, in mid-February, his discontent. The assembly nevertheless deliberated and declared what it thought it had the duty to declare. Afterward, it referred the question to the pope. The Jesuits have gone through this crucifying experience with faith.

Le monde was harsher. In an article titled "The Jesuits: In Guarded Freedom," it stated that Arrupe's press conference had been disappointing in its attempt to minimize the problems with the Holy See; it considered Arrupe disingenuous in his enthusiastic talk about "the great interest with which the pope has followed our deliberations and his manifest attitude of wanting to help us with his instructions." The special correspondent of *Le monde* added: "'Jesuitry' is not

---

39   *Le figaro*, Paris, March 11, 1975.

the forte of this peaceful general of ascetical mien, who responds passionately to the most impertinent questions. But whatever his opinions, his ideas concerning obedience and union with the pope are difficult for a non-Jesuit to understand." Robert Solé, writing for *Le monde*, considered the question of "theological liberty in the church" to be more serious than the problem of grades. He interpreted Paul VI's readiness to intervene in the Society's affairs whenever he judged it to be "useful for the Society and the church" as a form of "regulated liberty."[40]

What is beyond discussion in this whole story is that Arrupe never cast doubts on the obedience due the pope by the fourth vow, which he considered a "principle and foundation of the Society of Jesus." Affirming that "the Holy Father is the supreme superior of the Society," he was utterly sincere when he said: "The pope represents Jesus Christ: we must love him, we must defend him, we must study and apply his doctrine."

At the same time, Arrupe qualified his statements:

This certainly does not mean that we do not have the duty of "representation," as Saint Ignatius taught. [...] Our obedience is not passive; we have the availability of free persons. What is certain, however, is that we Jesuits, once the representations have been made, practice an evangelical obedience; it is Jesus Christ who, through his vicar and the superiors of the Society, sends us: that is a fundamental apostolic dimension. Everything is involved here: Trinitarian love, fidelity to Jesus Christ, love for the church, discernment, availability and mobility, loyalty; such is the Ignatian conception.[41]

Concerning this difficult year 1975 there is an especially interesting testimony. Years before, in 1968, Father Víctor Codina wrote an article for the journal *Manresa*, in which he analyzed the "dark night" that Saint Ignatius experienced in his relations with Paul IV. After the article was published, he sent a copy to Arrupe. At the time, he received no response, but he was greatly surprised when, seven years later, he received the following personal letter:

Rome, March 28, 1975
Dear Father Codina: P.C.

You will no doubt be surprised to receive this letter from me. [...] Perhaps you will be even more surprised at the reason for it.

Maybe you remember an article that you wrote in *Manresa* several years ago (in 1968, to be precise) and a copy of which you were kind enough to send me with the inscription: "To Father General, that it may bring him consolation in his dark nights. Affectionately."

Well, I think I have a duty to tell you that even then it was a consolation, but that during the general congregation I reread it and it consoled me

---

40 *Le monde*, Paris, March 14, 1975.
41 *Itinéraire*, 128.

greatly in the "dark night"—I don't know if it was as dark as Saint Ignatius's, but it was certainly "dark."

I feel obliged, therefore, to tell you as much and to thank you for the article, so that you may see that your effort in writing the article and your kindness in sending it to me have had a good effect, at least "brightening the dark night" of Father General.

I am sure that all this will produce good effects for the Society. It has been, as the fathers of the GC stated, a "unique experience."

Thank you, then, dear Father Codina. May the Lord reward you in love. Pray for your "consoled brother" in Christ.

—Pedro Arrupe, S.J.[42]

The importance of the decisions taken in 1975 in Rome would become manifest in later years in the countless options made by Jesuits, in the martyrdom of more than ninety Jesuits killed while working for justice, and in the activities of Jesuits with refugees, poor farmers, and socially marginalized people. Because of its ecclesiastical and social consequences, GC 32 was perhaps the most important and decisive step among those taken during the whole of Arrupe's life.

---

42   Victor Codina, "La noche oscura del P. Arrupe: Una carta autógrafa inédita," *Manresa* 62 (April/June 1990): 165–72.

18. Profile of an Eagle

The light filtering through the office window splashed across Arrupe's forehead and bald scalp and, against the dark background of books, brought out even more his aquiline profile. In a corner of the room, the Murcian painter José María Falgas was swiftly moving his pencil, capturing in rapid glances the soul that emanated from the striking features of the model.

"Will my nose fit in the picture?" Arrupe asked with a smile.

Falgas knew he did not have much time. Arrupe was a restless man, too busy to pose long hours in front of a portrait artist. He would have to take advantage of a general meeting to complete the details.

"I painted Father Arrupe," he declared later,

> motivated only by the desire to put the face of authenticity into a picture. This human condition is so rare, so scarce, that I consider it something I am ceaselessly seeking to discover. I do so because I think it signifies the order that establishes truth, and on such a structure rises the poetry of artistic creation. [...] I have found in the face of Father Arrupe such a trace, left by a life spent doing the greatest work a man can do. For me, this trace is so attractive that it turns wrinkles into youthful lines of force and communicates to the eyes that profound expression of an inward gaze. The hair is white, perhaps because white is the color of light.[1]

Another painter, Adolf Meister, S.J., more expressionist than classical, painted Arrupe's face in daring oil colors, in such a way that joy seems to float over the nerves and wrinkles, which are bathed in light. His eyes are full of tenderness and fade into their sockets as into deep wells, while his open, friendly hand points to a book that shows an abstract representation of the Hiroshima disaster. On the facing page appears the statement: "I lived through the atomic bomb." The painting has an interesting similarity to Alonso Sánchez Coello's portrait of another universal Basque, Ignatius, in his later years.

Another picture that became known around the world was an acrylic painting that appeared on the cover of *Time* magazine. Showing a lively face, youthful and smiling, it served as a lure for the feature story, "The Jesuits: Catholicism's Troubled Front Line." The newsweekly also offered an interview with Wilton Winn, who became a great admirer and close friend of Arrupe.

The publication of that cover picture gave rise to an anecdote that delighted the general. It happened that that edition of the magazine came out around the same time that painter Pablo Picasso died. When two women approached a kiosk in Rome to buy some magazines, one of them took a copy of *Time*, looked closely

---

1 Testimony of painter José María Falgas

at the smiling visage of Arrupe, and commented in a disappointed tone: "But it doesn't look anything like Picasso at all!"[2]

Such were some of the depictions of Arrupe's physical appearance in the last decade of his active life. Juan Lorente gives a poetic description of the image that emerges from these paintings and photographs:

> Like an eagle on the topmost ridge of a cliff, you watch the world and keep your unmoving eye fixed on it. You have thrust your head forward to drink everything in and keep the image safe in your regard. Others drown in the perplexing reality. You know how to enter it and leave it, how to embrace it without drowning, love it without becoming disillusioned. Your lips do not yield. There they are, quite firm, without a frown of disappointment or twinge of fear. They are simply closed, preferring to listen, keep still, and wait. You know the what and the where. You probe the how.
>
> Like a watchdog seated on the doorstep, neither inside nor outside, simply present in everything. No voice, no wind is strange to you. You lean forward to listen and, tilting your head, you are quick to ask, "Did you say something? Do you need something?" You do not look, you encompass all the light. You meditate, you retain. At any moment, you might jump, explode into urgent action. There is no prey that can escape you. Pacific goalkeeper now, you can move an army any day, and many will be happy to follow after you, as you inhale the intuitively perceived Spirit.
>
> Your forehead shines forth like a snow-covered mountain. Over the winds and the storms, over all the abysses and shadows soars imperturbably the incorruptible peak of your erudite light. If there is something of rock in you, it is because you communicate security. The mountain is not frightened of the abyss. You possess the eminence of one who never sinks. And come what may, you will know how to raise your head to the light, and there will always be a bit of blue in the black lake of your eyes.
>
> Today I have seen you, and I have begun to understand you, missionary of all futures, messenger of hope, eagle, watchdog and mountain, protagonist of all except yourself.[3]

Because of the personal attractiveness that shone through Arrupe's physical appearance, many Jesuits around the world, especially the younger ones, kept a photo of him in their rooms, and if possible an autographed one. Consequently, when he visited communities, he sometimes was obliged, with half a smile dancing on his fine lips, to sign hundreds of photos, as if he were an actor or a famous singer being hunted down by autograph seekers.

---

2   Anecdote narrated by Vincent O'Keefe, S.J.

3   Text of Juan Lorente, S.J. during the presentation in Madrid of Falgas's portrait and of Arrupe's book, *En un mundo en cambio*.

Before the Cameras of RAI

At this point in our story, the reader will have his own personal image of Pedro Arrupe. But perhaps we should retreat a bit from the frenzy of events and the plethora of anecdotes that portray the life of our central character and enter into the daily life of those years when he was general. In this way, we can give a fuller human portrait of the man, before moving on with the story.

What was Arrupe experiencing interiorly, even as he was being buffeted by setbacks and difficulties?

The cameras of RAI were captivated by him—there was something about that man. On January 26, 1975, the program *Incontri* was being transmitted live on Channel 1, Italy's national television network. The powerful spotlights did not seem to disturb the simplicity and spontaneous style of the person being interviewed, as he answered in Italian the questions of the Spanish reporter, Juan Arias:

> Who is this man who gets up at dawn every morning, the one we have seen praying on a straw mat, oriental style, the one who lives with another 120 Jesuits just a few steps from the Vatican and who celebrates Mass alone, like the pope, in his private chapel?[4]

Arrupe did not hesitate for a moment:

> I think I am the last person who should be asked that question, because we already know that nobody is a good judge of his own character. I can say of myself that I am just another poor human being, but I think I am good-willed, and I try to work for the church and the Society as well as I can. I always try to do what seems to me best, which is what God always wants. Naturally, virtue is usually in the mean, and for that reason those of us who take the middle course are bound to receive criticisms, both from the right and the left. And that is also why I do not know exactly who I am.

In the course of the interview, nevertheless, Arrupe's lively personality once again bubbled forth as he gave voice to his many experiences, his childhood memories, the atomic bomb, and his belief that he was "nothing"—"neither Spanish nor Japanese, but universal." He answered the perennial questions about the legendary power of the Jesuits, the problems with the Holy See, the increase in men leaving the order; he spoke of his conception of happiness, which he identified with "tranquility of conscience"; he talked of the Spiritual Exercises, which, far from being a form of brainwashing, were "aimed at helping each person find himself and in himself find God."

The reporter than asked him: "Imagine you meet up with a worker who labors on an assembly line. How would you speak to him of God?"

---

4   Interview for RAI, "An Hour with Father Arrupe" (September 26, 1975), transcribed in *Hambre de pan y de evangelio* (Santander: Sal Terrae, 1978), 7.

"I would speak to him in a simple way," replied Arrupe:

That is, I would try to help him
understand and become aware of
how God is in the depth of his soul.
As Saint Augustine would say: God
is more deeply within him than
he is himself. I would tell him that
his monotonous work is precisely
where he can find God; we see this,
for example, in the contemplative
orders. Religious men and women
do simple agricultural labors, and
now also they do technical jobs and
handicraft projects that are sim-
ilarly oriented. You can find God
more easily in simple labor, where
you can maintain a spiritual disposition, than you can in the middle of
the noise of the city.

Portrait by Murcian painter José María Falgas:
"Will my nose fit in the frame?" joked Arrupe.

"But don't you think you are too optimistic?"

Maybe what I just said makes me look that way, but I believe that, when we
see things as they are and we recognize we are in God's hands and that God
is omnipotent even when things might appear to go badly for a time, then
they will never be able to go really badly as long as we follow God and let
ourselves be helped by divine providence. That is my optimism, an optimism based on faith in God and faith in my brothers and sisters.

On another occasion, Arrupe recalled the words of Teilhard de Chardin:
"The world will belong to those who place the greatest hope in it." He also frequently quoted Abraham, who "hoped against all hope," but he distinguished
that from utopian hope, "because Christian hope begins right now":

It is not something for the future, an eschatological good; it is here in the
present. And its fullness is found in charity toward all people: it has a present, social dimension that leads to mutual love among people. That is what
Saint Paul was telling the first communities and what he bore witness to in
his own life.[5]

---

5   *Intinéraire*, 111.

Jesus Christ Is All

Picking up on the reference to God, the RAI reporter took another tack: "That word 'God' has given rise to many images in the course of history. They are images of God that seem to be especially for the use and the benefit of the powerful, to make sure the slaves don't rebel. But who is that God for Father Arrupe?"

As the producer of the television program focused the camera on Arrupe and the red light on the camera went on, the general's face lit up:

> For me, God is everything, right? For me, God is everything. Therefore, I would not know how to describe the face of God. I don't even imagine him having a face, but God is something that completely fills my life and appears in the physiognomy of Jesus Christ—of course in the Jesus Christ hidden in the Eucharist, and also in my brothers and other people, who are God's image. So I think that sums it all up for me. Who is God for you? The answer is quite simple: everything.

Later in the interview, Arrupe expanded on this response, saying that Jesus Christ was the motor of his life:

> He was my ideal from the time I entered the Society. He was and continues to be my way; he was and is always my strength. I don't think it necessary to give much explanation of what this means: remove Jesus Christ from my life and everything collapses. It would be like a body that had its skeleton, its heart, and its head removed.

Arrupe concentrated this Christocentric interiority in the image of the Sacred Heart, devotion to which he first learned in the novitiate and would cherish and preserve until the end. During his generalate, however, he spoke much of Jesus Christ and not so much of the Heart of Christ. He explained:

> There is a reason for that, which we might call pastoral, especially with regard to the Society. A few years ago, certain emotional reactions and allergies became evident with regard to the expression "Sacred Heart"; they had their origin partly in devotional exaggerations and manifestations. Because of that, I have felt it necessary to let some time pass, during which this emotional charge, which is understandable but in a way not very rational, dissipates.

By "heart," Arrupe understood "center" or "source"; for him, it was an *ur-Wort*, a primeval word full of meaning.[6]

For this reason, in 1972 Arrupe decided to change the formula of consecration of the Society to the Heart of Jesus; the old formula had been used since the time when Father Pieter Jan Beckx was superior general (1872). To this end,

---

6   *Intinéraire*, 49.

he asked fellow Jesuits Friedrich Schwendimann and Solano to prepare a new formula, of which thirty thousand copies were printed and distributed. Later on, while making his Spiritual Exercises, Arrupe called Father Luis González one day after supper and told him that Father Giuliani had offered to take him to La Storta. This was the chapel on the outskirts of Rome where Ignatius, after praying to Mary "to place him with her Son," saw clearly that "God the Father was placing him with Christ" and that Christ told him: "I want you to serve us." During his visit to the chapel, while he was at prayer, Arrupe had the idea of writing then and there the new formula of consecration. The austere, profound text he elaborated at that moment succeeds well in conceiving the commitment of the modern-day Jesuit as a prolongation of the grace and illumination received by Ignatius at La Storta.[7]

We have already quoted some texts expressing Arrupe's passionate love for Jesus Christ, taken from the notes he wrote while making the Exercises soon after his election as superior general. Another revealing text is the following:

> Personal love for Jesus Christ (for the members of the Society) is absolutely necessary and is the basis for identification with him; that is, for being

---

7   Statements of Luis González, S.J. The complete text of the consecration reads as follows:

> O Eternal Father: While Ignatius was praying in the chapel of La Storta, you wished with singular favor to accept the petition that he had long made to you through the intercession of Our Lady: "To be placed with your Son." You also assured him that you would be his support when you told him: "I will be with you." You manifested your desire that Jesus, bearer of the Cross, admit him as his servant, a desire that Jesus accepted as he addressed Ignatius with these unforgettable words: "I want you to serve us." We for our part, who are successors to that band of men who were the first *companions of Jesus*, repeat the same prayer: to be placed with your Son and to serve "under the insignia of the Cross," on which Jesus is nailed by obedience, with his side pierced and his heart open as a sign of his love for you and all humanity. We renew the consecration of the Society to the Heart of Jesus, and we promise you the greatest fidelity, asking your grace to continue serving you and your Son in the same spirit and with the same fervor as Ignatius and his companions. By the intercession of the Virgin Mary, who received the prayer of Ignatius, and before the Cross on which Jesus gives us the treasures of his open heart, we tell you today, through him and in him, from the depths of our being: Take, Lord, and receive all my liberty, my memory, my understanding, and my entire will, all that I have and possess. You have given all to me. To you, O Lord, I return it. All is yours, dispose of it wholly according to your will. Give me your love and your grace, for this is sufficient for me.

"New Consecration of the Society to the Sacred Heart," June 9, 1972, in Arrupe, *La identidad del jesuita*, 594.

Maurice Giuliani studied the genesis of this text and has published the draft version with the original corrections. It was the fruit of various readings and ten pilgrimages to the chapel of La Storta (Giuliani, "Génesis de un texto: Plegaria al Padre Eterno," Dossier Pedro Arrupe, *Manresa* 62 [April/June 1990]: 195–98, here 195ff.).

possessed by his grace in such a way that his thoughts are my thoughts and his love is mine. [...] Arriving at such identification is the ideal and the secret of true sanctification and of true performance of my role as general, since I am only his rational instrument; I am not just a secondary subordinate (in the human sense), but a true instrument that should not act unless moved by the principal agent. What joy and happiness to reach that far!"[8]

Possessed by a Mission

Father Briceño, the regional assistant for northern Latin America and superior of the curia community, gave the following definition of Arrupe's manner during these years: "The impression he gave was always the same: a man possessed by a mission to which he wanted to devote every single second of his life; but at the same time a simple, serene man, full of kindness and extraordinarily respectful of the opinion of others." To corroborate the first quality, Briceño mentioned Arrupe's overloaded work schedule, but he added:

> It should also be noted that he never took any days off for vacation. If he sometimes went to "Villa Cavalletti" in Grottaferrata, he carried on there with his same work routine. Once, I went to spend a few days at "Villasimius," a beach house of the Society near Cagliari. There I found myself with companions from the different houses in Rome, and I got a truly agreeable rest. When I returned to the curia, I told Father Arrupe that he should do the same, since it would do much to help him rest [...]. "No," he answered me, "I don't need rest. If I went to Villasimius, I wouldn't know what to do." What is interesting is that such a work pace never made him nervous or exhausted. He might have serious concerns to deal with, but his temperament always remained calm. He was always ready to encourage anyone who felt disappointed, to enjoy a joke or to tell one.
>
> How is such extraordinary equanimity to be explained? He used to say that his rest was the *furo*, the Japanese bath that he used to take every day in very hot water after eating. Of course, that was a wonderful aid, but I have often thought that his serenity was grounded partly in his admirable psychological balance and partly in the intense spiritual life that made him rest completely in God. That was the beach to which he retreated with his fatigue and his concerns, and there he invariably found peace.[9]

An American Jesuit visiting Rome, upon observing Arrupe's intense work pace, insisted, as did many others, that he take a rest and go out with him one night to a pizzeria. Arrupe answered: "But don't you see that everybody would recognize me?"

---

8   Arrupe, *Aquí me tienes, Señor*, 95.
9   Statements of Eduardo Briceño, S.J.

"Remove Jesus Christ from my life, and everything would collapse."
Arrupe praying while sitting Japanese-style in his private chapel, which
he called his "mini-cathedral."

"Well, put on a wig."

To which Arrupe replied, "How about if I put it on my nose?"[10]

Father Pedro Ferrer Pi, who was then rector of the University of Deusto, recounts that on August 6, 1975, Paul VI received a group of rectors of the Society's universities and treated them to an especially affectionate allocution. He also displayed special warmth toward Arrupe, which contrasted with the tension that had been felt some months before, at the time of GC 32. Later that day, Arrupe was radiant with joy and did something he had not done before during his ten years in Rome: he accompanied the rectors to a performance of *Aida* in the open-air theater in Termas de Caracalla. During the intermission, he told

---

10   Narrated by Luis González, S.J.

Ferrer Pi that the last performance of an opera he had seen had been just before entering the Society, and that it had been precisely *Aida*. Almost fifty years had passed since then![11]

Father Arranz, in his account of the journey he made with Arrupe to Russia, describes the general's extraordinary ability to recoup energy:

> Once, we attended a long service, during which we were standing for hours at a time, and we went afterward to an official meal where Arrupe, faced with a thousand exotic delicacies, practiced his customary "scandalous" frugality. After all that, he looked exhausted. As soon as we were in the car, he would tell us, "Now just leave me alone for a quarter of an hour." He would then go into a sort of trance, which was not quite sleep. In a while, he would come out of it, as if he had just slept for a whole night; he was fully awake and aware of everything he was told.[12]

Father Ignasi Salvat also relates:

> In November 1978, I was participating in a meeting or "school" for the new Spanish-speaking provincials. It was a time when group dynamics was very popular, and of course we did several of them in the nearly three weeks that we spent in the Eternal City. I had the good luck of being in the same group with Father Arrupe. I remember that one of the dynamics consisted in commenting among the members of the group about what their real schedules were like, and then comparing that real schedule with the ideal schedule that each one thought he should keep in order to lead a life that was spiritually profound and psychologically sound.
>
> When it was Arrupe's turn to explain the life he led, he commented with great simplicity: "I have no freedom of choice. All my hours are dedicated to the Society." And we figured that all his hours meant from four-thirty in the morning until eleven or twelve at night. And it also meant that his schedule began with three hours completely dedicated to the Lord, in prayer and the Eucharist.[13]

There is still another fact about Arrupe that has received little comment but is quite revealing. At the beginning of his term as superior general, in order to comply with his ideal of a church of the poor and an option for the most disadvantaged, he considered the possibility of leaving the curia and living in a small apartment in a working-class neighborhood or in the poor neighborhood nearby called Trastevere. However, he abandoned the idea after consulting others about it; among the

---

11   Statement of Pedro Ferrer Pi, S.J.
12   Arranz, "Arrupe y la Iglesia Ortodoxa rusa," 633.
13   Ignacio Salvat, "Lo que permanece," in *Pedro Arrupe: Memoria siempre viva*, ed. Norberto Alcover (Bilbao: Mensajero, 2002), 191–218, 198.

reasons he gave was that he wanted to have more time for work and not have to spend time traveling back and forth.[14] Prayer occupied the prime time in his overall commitment; he stole long hours from sleep in order to be able to celebrate his own Mass and then attend that of the coadjutor brothers, which was in the community chapel in the afternoon. "I don't call him a 'man of God,'" wrote Francisco Ivern, his counselor and close collaborator for eleven years,

> just because of the quantity or duration of his prayers. I call him that above all because he was always thinking in terms of God and God's reign. God was what was absolute in his life. All the rest was relative. His long prayers were both a source and an expression of his familiarity with God and of his profound religious experience, which was manifest in many other forms. [...] He was a man of God, not simply because he prayed, but because he always thought, spoke, and acted from a divine perspective.[15]

Details with Soul

About Arrupe's considerateness and humorous traits there are hundreds of anecdotes, of which the following are just a sampling.

When Arrupe was visiting two Jesuit communities located on Greek islands, he discovered that the superior of one of them liked to hunt during his hours of recreation. He learned also that certain Spanish shotguns were highly prized by the man, so after returning to Rome he phoned some friends in Bilbao and asked them to get such a gun and send it as a gift to his Greek friend.[16] The whole thing was quite surprising: that a superior should make a gift to a subject, and that the gift be a shotgun—something out of the ordinary! The person who told the anecdote could not at the time remember the name of the Greek Jesuit, but the author of these pages heard from Father Makros Macronitis, the recipient of the gift of the gun, after he had found a copy of the fifth edition of this book at an airport. He confirmed to me the curious anecdote and gave further details.[17]

Besides confirming the story, Macronitis related how he had played a joke on Arrupe that brought out the general's very human character and at the same time displayed his naïve trustfulness. During a visit to Athens, while Arrupe was

---

14   Statement of Igano M. Ganzo, S.J.
15   Francisco Ivern, "El hombre que yo conocí," in La Bella, *Pedro Arrupe, general de la Compañía de Jesús*, 1037–51, here 1051.
16   Statement of Fernando Suárez, S.J.
17   Letter written to the author by Makros Macronitis, S.J. (January 15, 1991). Father Macronitis invited me later to visit him in his old residence, in a valley on the Greek island of Tinos. There he showed me the shotgun that Arrupe, in an unusual gesture for a religious superior, had given him as a gift.

walking toward the Acropolis with his assistant Father Giuliani and the provincial, I began to sigh deeply and said to Father General: "Father, I have serious problems with my vocation. I am ashamed of it, but I can't go on. I am desperate." Father General looked quite concerned. The two other priests looked at me suspiciously, because they knew me well. For a few more minutes, I kept up an appearance of being forlorn and discouraged, without coming clean. Father Arrupe told me, "But speak, dear Father, cheer up." Then, sighing tragically from the depth of my heart, I said, "Father, I am madly in love with Brigitte Bardot, but she doesn't love me, and I am in despair." Father Arrupe replied, "Father, tell me what I can do for you." Then everybody burst out laughing. I never would have joked that way with another Father General, say with [Włodzimierz] Ledóchowski, who would have sent me to Alaska. But with Father Arrupe it was another matter. In an instant, I had experienced the greatness of his spirit, his humor, his humanity.

When Arrupe had the shotgun sent to this Greek Jesuit from the finest gun store in Spain, he placed only one condition on the gift: "Careful: just for killing little birds, never Jesuits!"[18]

Arrupe did something similar for a Jesuit brother at the curia who was learning to do enamel work. On his birthday, he ordered the special kind of oven that is required for this type of handiwork.

Giuliana Panchetti, an Italian laywoman, was Arrupe's secretary for his post as president of the Union of Superiors General, a position to which he was always re-elected. Giuliana recalls many considerate gestures of Arrupe that moved her greatly, such as when he sent her a cake with candles on her birthday.[19]

A Spanish brother named Luis Tomás, who was working in the American city of Detroit, created a unique portrait of Arrupe based on one of his photos. To do so, he had spent long hours at a typewriter, using nothing but simple typed letters. As Arrupe was shaking hands with each of the Jesuits in the community, he came to the brother, who offered him the picture as a gift. Arrupe inscribed his signature on it and said, "Many thanks, brother. Keep it for yourself. I don't want to deprive you of this work of art."[20]

Arrupe's friendship and his kindness were not restricted to certain kinds of person or to people of a certain ideology. It is interesting to note that he counted financiers and aristocrats among his friends, men like Tony Saez de Mantagut and Javier Benjumea of Spain. Benjumea was a consultant for important societies, such as Abengoa, Domecq, and Groupe Pallas; he was also Arrupe's economic advisor and was collaborating with the professional schools created by the Jesuits of Andalusia (SAFA). According to Benjumea, Arrupe was "charming, and also

---

18   Letter written to the author by Makros Macronitis, S.J. (January 15, 1991).

19   Statement of Giuliana Panchetti.

20   Statement of Luis Tomás, S.J.

a statesman as regards his breadth of ideas and his intuitive way of getting the jump on everything. He used to receive me and my daughters at any moment, even when we gave no warning."[21]

Arrupe believed in people almost excessively. Some insisted that the province of Japan had lost many Jesuit scholastics because Arrupe as provincial had been too trusting of them and had sent them abroad without the human and spiritual support they needed. There were also commentaries about how Arrupe knew more about the Díez-Alegría case than he revealed, even though false interpretations were being made in that regard. He never tried to defend himself from such accusations.

When the Pontifical University of Comillas moved from Santander to Madrid, Arrupe gave full authority in the matter to the Spanish provincial. The task was very complex because there were overlapping jurisdictions, opposed interests, contrary currents, and all the turmoil typical of the post-conciliar period. The general thus assisted, respected, and empowered his local delegate as much as possible.

Briceño says that when the provincials had difficulties, Arrupe suffered along with them and was always close to them:

> On one occasion, when Father General was writing a letter to a provincial, he added in his own handwriting a phrase that the provincial took badly. The provincial wrote back expressing his pain, suggesting that the phrase had no doubt been written by some secretary. When Arrupe checked the draft written in his own hand, he wrote the provincial another letter, affirming that it was he who had written the famous phrase and asking pardon for having hurt him. When I saw this new letter, I was speechless. Father General was asking pardon for a matter in which he had not had the least desire to offend.

"Father Arrupe's respect for his subordinates," Briceño continues,

> was something that always impressed me. He treated me in ways that I will never be able to forget. On a certain occasion, Father General was thinking of calling to Rome a Jesuit of the northern Latin American assistancy, to have him undertake a delicate job. He asked me about it, and my first reaction was negative. I was thinking that that man was needed in his province. Father General, while still showing his enthusiasm for the solution he had found, said to me, "Good, if you think so, we'll look for someone else." I kept thinking about the matter and in two or three days I spoke again to Father General. "Father," I said, "I have been thinking of that case and I think that we can find a good way to replace that father, so that he can come to Rome for a time." "Very well. If you are in agreement, we will call him."

---

21   Statement of Javier Benjumea.

Briceño mentions another personal case:

When it came to naming me superior of the curia, Father General came to my room along with Father Laurendeau, the secretary of the Society. He said with a smile: "I have been thinking of naming you superior of the curia. Poor you! Don't tell me no!" Naturally, I answered: "Father General, how can I tell you no? Do as you wish." So we looked for a date when the nomination would become effective. That job gave me the opportunity once again to experience Father General's considerate nature. He never interfered in the governance of the house. He always supported my decisions, and he always took part in community activities with genuine interest.[22]

Just Another Guy

On the occasion of anniversaries or other celebrations, Jesuits all over the world would receive letters from Arrupe expressing affection, praise, and encouragement. He had an extraordinary memory in this regard. When traveling through Belgium once, he remembered that a father working there had served several years in the curia. Arrupe found time to look him up and telephone him personally.

In 1977, while I was in Turin, Arrupe had Iglesias, his Spanish assistant, call me to ask a favor. He needed a journalist to translate his ideas into radio language for a program on the "Seven Words of Christ," which was to be distributed to the whole Latin American continent. After hearing Arrupe's own ideas and receiving his personal instructions, I elaborated a draft text that he corrected with exquisite delicacy. Once the definitive script was ready, we went to the studios of Vatican Radio, where he was to record the program. He asked me to sit down beside him facing the microphone, and he told me: "Please correct me without hesitation. At times, I speak too rapidly."

And so I did, making several suggestions about the colloquial tone used on the radio, the use of pauses, an intimate quality of voice, and so on. He accepted the suggestions quite readily. The recording turned out very warm and direct, done in a youthful voice that nobody would have thought belonged to a sixty-year-old man. As we were leaving, I walked with him to Borgo Santo Spirito. When we reached the curia, he turned toward me, put his hand on my shoulder, and with a charming smile and great simplicity said: "Forgive me for adorning myself with other people's pens!" Those words were not a compliment, but simply gave evidence of his marvelous authenticity and warmth.

The well-known liberation theologian and Basque Jesuit Jon Sobrino had a similar experience. Interested in liberation theology, Arrupe asked Sobrino to come to Rome from El Salvador to give him some theology classes. For a time, he received daily lessons from Sobrino. Finally, with great simplicity he exclaimed: "Now, now I understand."

---

22   Statement of Eduardo Briceño, S.J.

Sobrino also recounts: "I was much impressed by the humility with which he asked me about other topics: 'Tell me, Father, what do you think of eternity?' They were moving encounters that I will not forget."[23]

Calvez, Arrupe's advisor on justice matters, also recounts:

Once, when I was one of his general assistants, I went on a trip to Paris. On returning to Rome, I told him about the success of the "new philosophy" there, due mainly to publicity about it, but also to its significance. I had brought back the books of [André] Glucksmann, [Guy] Lardreau, Bernard-Henri Lévy, etc. Father Arrupe wanted to have a look at them. Certainly he read parts of them, and we spoke of them. What interest and attention, I thought.

Another time, Enrique Berlinguer, the seductive secretary general who directed the destiny of the Italian Communist Party toward truly new goals, had spoken about "austerity of life." Father Arrupe was struck by the idea: he recognized in it his own conception of a civilization of sobriety, fraternity, attention to the poor.

Calvez mentions another trait revealing Arrupe's understanding of the immediate future:

I went with him to visit an elderly Jesuit, a great servant of the Society, whose death was imminent. As we were leaving, he said to me, "There you see how we are all destined to diminish." Life and death were for him tangible things. Always present. Years later, when I was accompanying him in the hospital after his cerebral thrombosis, I remembered that, and one night, since I was rereading Teilhard de Chardin's *Divine Milieu*, I read some phrases to him. I think they were these: "Our capacity for diminishment is our true passivity. [...] In a way, in order to penetrate into ourselves definitively, God must dig into us, empty us out, make a hollow space for himself." For him, an avid reader of Teilhard, that was one of the certainties by which he lived.[24]

Arrupe always traveled as a poor man, even on long journeys, with his small handbag containing the bare essentials. The same could be said of the austerity of his private quarters. And as regards gifts, Ivern recounts the following:

He used to give away everything people gave him—not only the things they gave him as general, which were customarily kept, exhibited, or stored in the curia, but even more personal objects given to him by friends or fellow Jesuits who hoped he would make good use of them. Occasionally, this was a source of confusion for those giving the gifts, but it was even more so for

---

23   Statement of Jon Sobrino, S.J.
24   Calvez, *Fe y justicia*, 83.

"He never refused to meet with Jesuits, and he talked to them with a great sense of humor" (Vincent O'Keefe).

those to whom he then gave them. I remember how one day, when I was in his office, some Jesuits brought him a handsome Basque beret. He very graciously thanked them for it and held it in his hands several seconds, playing with it. But almost immediately after that, he placed it on my head saying: "I think it's just right for you." The donors did not seem too happy about that, and I, observing their expression, thanked them for it but returned it to them with some excuse, though I must confess I would like to have kept it.

One of my final acts as general counselor was to accompany Arrupe, at the beginning of 1979, to the Latin American Bishops' Conference in Puebla, Mexico. At the end of the conference, we bade one another farewell, since I was not returning to Rome but going on to Brazil, the country to which I was newly assigned. He embraced me, wept, put his hand in his pocket, and gave me, as a parting memento, the gold fountain pen that he had just received as a present. I have never used it, but I have kept it to this very day.

In his frequent journeys by airplane, he always booked a seat in "tourist class," but often he was accommodated in "first class" as a courtesy. This allowed him to rest better, and having more space, he could prepare more easily for his next engagements, whether by reading letters, studying, or revising his talks. He never took advantage of special treatment or the privileges offered to "first-class" passengers, especially as regards food and drink. He always maintained his Spartan regime.[25]

With regard to his great capacity for working late and his frugality in eating, Arrupe used to say of himself: "I am able to sleep at any moment, or I can be hungry enough to eat."

"No wonder," Father Antonio García Evangelista used to comment in Japan, "since he neither eats nor sleeps!"

And drink? Once in a while he had a little wine at meals, but almost never strong liquors. He might take a few drops of Spanish brandy or Italian sambuca, as a sign of solidarity when they were offered to him on special occasions or during informal social gatherings with his collaborators or visitors. Occasionally he did so in order to get close to certain persons.

Father Luis Urbez, a specialist in mass media who had just finished his studies in Italian cinematography, once asked Arrupe what he thought about apostolic work in the world of films and other media. Arrupe answered: "It is not we superiors who are to say what must be done. You know the subject well. Tell me what I should do." On another occasion, Urbez was participating in an international meeting in Rome. Since he did not know English, he was amazed that the general himself served as his simultaneous translator. Since the dialogue at the meeting was free and the atmosphere was post-conciliar, the participants were

---

25   Ivern, "El hombre que yo conocí," 1042.

quite unrestrained in their speech. Arrupe kept translating with extraordinary fidelity for his companion, even the more colorful language. At one point, Urbez himself, referring to a journal the Society published in Spain, made a harsh criticism, which Arrupe translated into English. He then smiled and said to Urbez: "You shoot real bullets, eh?" His English translation was perfect.

After this meeting, Arrupe and Urbez met up again in the café, with a bottle of Spanish cognac in front of them. Urbez invited the general to join him. Arrupe told him that he did not usually drink, but that he would have a glass with him. Luis asked him what he thought of the work Jesuits were doing in the world of cinema and what they should be doing concretely. Arrupe again answered: "It is you experts, who know about these matters, who ought to tell us superiors what we must do." That night, they continued the conversation in the general's room, and on the table of the superior general of the Society of Jesus was something unusual: a bottle of Veterano.[26]

Though he never smoked himself, Arrupe used to keep cigarettes in his room for the sake of guests. In this regard, there is another anecdote, about a meeting of the superiors general of all the orders during one of their gatherings in Rome. Several of the superiors had gotten together in the room of one of them to have a drink. Arrupe appeared with the face of a rebellious child and with one hand in the pocket of his habit, where he had a glass. As he entered, he laughed and said: "Here, I bring my dentures glass!"[27]

Particularly valuable is the testimony of Father Aimé Duval, the famous French singer whose records were very popular in the fifties. With his motorcycle and guitar, he traveled the world singing ballads that were full of poetry and evangelical spirit. Only later did the world learn of Duval's personal tragedy. This French Jesuit of exquisite sensibility, now deceased, suffered from alcoholism. After long years of struggle, he confronted it and overcame it. A little later, using the pseudonym Lucien, he wrote *L'enfant qui jouait avec la lune* (The boy who played with the moon), a fascinating book on his spiritual experience; it has helped many people free themselves from the tyranny of alcohol. The book contains not only sincere confessions but also strong criticisms of the lack of sympathy that characterized many institutions and many persons. Quite different, though, is what Duval says of Arrupe:

> I don't wish to say that the people of Alcoholics Anonymous are the only ones acceptable. I know hundreds of people who are better than we are. Naudin, for example, did not have to pass through alcohol to understand easily what we have confessed with great difficulty: that man is great and his dimensions tend to the infinite. And Father Arrupe, my great Jesuit chief who was superior in Tokyo for a long time, knows the world as do few others.

---

26   Statement of Luis Urbez, S.J.
27   Statement of Giuliana Panchetti.

Arrupe in India (July 1980). "Faith must continually dialogue with all cultures. Faith purifies and enriches culture, and culture enriches and purifies faith."

He also had no need of alcohol. But it is noticeable that he always stays near the "Burning Bush," listening to unheard-of Truths.[28]

We have already seen something of the direct and friendly style Arrupe used on his trips. Father O'Keefe sums up this trait as follows:

He used to visit all the communities he could, and he always spoke when he had the opportunity. That meant a long series of meetings and talks from early in the morning till late at night. He found it very hard to turn down a petition of his brother Jesuits, and only his amazing energy and resistance made all that possible. Don Pedro acted as if he didn't accept the fact that the day has only twenty-four hours.

He usually transmitted very concrete messages to men who were working in very different areas—young or middle-aged, sick or elderly. [...] He had a great influence on the young men, and he always told them that they were expected to have an experience of obedience. He said that it was something essential for the effective apostolate of a Jesuit in whatever place he might find himself. With those in charge of the formation and education of young Jesuits, he always insisted that they should teach the exercise of obedience as part of the program for integrating the intellectual and the apostolic during formation.

---

28   Aime Duval [Lucien], S.J., *El niño que jugaba con la luna* (Santander: Sal Terrae, 1984).

Along with the serious sessions during those visits, there were other more relaxed and festive moments, where Don Pedro's marvelous sense of humor was on display. He loved to represent with words and gestures certain attitudes and postures that are typically Jesuit, and he enjoyed getting guffaws from his audience. He also enjoyed singing, and he had a substantial repertory, ranging from the traditional Ignatian hymn *Fundador* (which strictly speaking should be sung with the accompaniment of a band) to classical German songs, which he sang with an excellent baritone voice. Many people were surprised that his singing voice was so different from his talking voice. With one assistant he would sing a duet in Japanese, and with another a Negro spiritual, which he humorously claimed was his "own story": "Nobody knows the troubles I've seen [...]"

A wonderful characteristic of Father Arrupe was his enormous capacity to pay attention to individuals, to such an extent that he sometimes paid no heed to buildings or landscapes or anything else. [...] There is one anecdote that illustrates perfectly what I mean: when he was visiting the Jesuit houses in Egypt, during a trip to the Middle East, the great pyramids suddenly appeared on the horizon. One of his assistants could not repress an exclamation of amazement. Father Arrupe stopped speaking, looked up for a moment toward where the other was indicating, nodded with his head, and then immediately turned back to his conversation about the apostolic tasks and problems of the Jesuits in Egypt.[29]

Arrupe extended this friendly manner to everybody, including those who did not exactly view him favorably; even his severest critics were received cordially at his table when they visited the curia. He knew perfectly well who his potential enemies were, but he seemed not to be concerned about them. He was kind even to persons he had to reprimand severely. Forgiveness was part of his nature; he knew nothing of rancor:[30]

Children felt comfortable around him, and they were not intimidated by his office, his aristocratic bearing, or his black cassock. Years ago, when I was in Rome, some friends of mine from Canada came to visit me, and Father Arrupe found time to receive them and entertain them. The youngest daughter of the family, Julie, a child at the time, was so impressed by Arrupe's gentle, friendly manner that after the meeting she exclaimed spontaneously: "He's a beautiful man." Often the truth appears in the mouth of the innocent, because he was in reality a charming man.[31]

---

29   Vincent O'Keefe, "Pedro Arrupe, apóstol de la palabra," in Alcalá et al., *Pedro Arrupe*, 111ff.

30   Ivern, "El hombre que yo conocí," 1043.

31   Ivern, "El hombre que yo conocí," 1044.

Concerning Arrupe's language and rapid speech, O'Keefe recalls that his fluency in speaking many tongues sometimes made him introduce words borrowed from another language. Thus, when he wanted to express the word "level," he always used the French term *niveau*. In 1966, during his first visit as superior general to the United States, he was explaining to a large group of reporters how Pope Paul VI had asked the Jesuits to undertake certain fields of work. "The Holy Father," he said, "has asked us to work valiantly on behalf of [...]," and he pronounced a word that sounded like "communism." Everybody stood agape and could hardly believe their ears. "Yes," he continued, "we have to stand out in the defense of [...]," and again he said the same word. Before the reporters could rush out to the telephones, however, one of Arrupe's assistants intervened, saying, "I should clarify, for those of you who are at the back of the hall, that the word that Father General has spoken is 'ecumenism,'" and he spelled the word out carefully. Arrupe quickly added, "Of course, that is exactly the word," but then, once again, he pronounced the word just as he had before![32]

Brother Pedro García, Arrupe's driver and amanuensis for many years, drove him on the trips that were closer to home, in Rome and its environs. He recalls:

> If he didn't have to speak with someone else, he always sat up front beside me. And when he wanted to take advantage of the time to pray, he would first ask my permission. I don't remember even once when he didn't do so. Frequently, while in the car, he would discuss sensitive matters with other persons. He never told me that I should keep things secret. He simply trusted. He did the same with correspondence. He often came to my room to get it, and he would tell me: "Please correct my Spanish style, with complete liberty." I believe that much will be discovered about Arrupe when there is access to the files and his "drafts," the annotations he made to the letters written by his assistants and substitutes. He infused all his letters with humaneness, affection, and a spirit of faith. But perhaps the most important experience I had with Father Arrupe was the day that Father Schönenberger, the regional assistant for Germany, left the Society. It was a very serious moment, the first time in history that an assistant was leaving the order. He had just informed Father Arrupe, and a few minutes later I took Arrupe someplace in the car. There was something special about him. Not only was he not annoyed or worried but he transmitted a supernatural faith and peace. I don't know how to express what I felt, but I can say that at the hour of my death I will remember that first half hour.[33]

Arrupe's simple manner was the subject of many other anecdotes. As regards his extraordinary physical resemblance to Saint Ignatius, O'Keefe recounts that

---

32   O'Keefe, "Pedro Arrupe, apóstol de la palabra," 111ff.
33   Statement of Pedro García, S.J.

Arrupe in Zagorsk, near Moscow (September 1, 1971). "The silent presence of Father Arrupe in the USSR was manifestly edifying and eloquent" (Miguel Arranz).

Arrupe liked to spend the three days before the feast of Saint Ignatius in the quarters where the founder had lived and died: the famous "chambers" that are still preserved in the residence beside the church of the Gesù. He used to do so, he said, "with the hope that something will rub off on me."

One day, while Arrupe was praying in this Ignatian space, an American Jesuit came with some friends to celebrate Mass in the chapel there. When Arrupe promptly helped him prepare what he needed and ended up serving him at the Mass, the clueless American thought he was a coadjutor brother. As Arrupe was stealing away afterward, the Jesuit asked him, "Brother, allow me a question: have you ever been told that you look like Saint Ignatius? What is your name?"

Arrupe murmured, "Arrupe."

"Excuse me, I didn't hear you well."

"Arrupe!" said Don Pedro, raising his voice.

"Holy Mother!" exclaimed the oblivious American, hoping the earth would swallow him up.

Of course, Arrupe's resemblance to Saint Ignatius was not only in his physical appearance.[34] "How is it that this father who is so important can at the same time be so impressive and so humble, so *mfumu* [boss] and so close to everybody?" Such was the astonished question of an African cook during one of Arrupe's visits to the African continent. The answer is simple: because he had a heart full of love, one capable of being moved by all that is human, and especially the human![35]

---

34   Vincent O'Keefe, "En las huellas de San Ignacio," *Testimonio* 130 (March/April 1992): 18.
35   M'nteba, "Arrupe y África," 379.

Last One Out, Turn Out the Lights!

The many departures of Jesuits from the Society and the alarming decline in vocations were of course topics that came up in all the conversations of those times. To explain these phenomena in his interviews, Arrupe mentioned the well-known post-conciliar crisis, the more general social crisis, or the great changes that the world itself was going through. But Arrupe preferred to use words other than "crisis" because, he said,

> we are most definitely living in a moment of adaptation to new circum-stances. [...] I don't know how long the situation will last, but certainly it will last long. Perhaps the Society will diminish in numbers for a certain time, because today the life of a priest, and specifically the vocation of Jesu-its, is more difficult than before.

These words are from Arrupe's interview before the cameras of RAI in 1975. Some six thousand Jesuits had left the order by that time.

Arrupe felt an extraordinary respect for the decisions that each person made in good conscience. At one point, there was the extreme case of two superiors gen-eral of religious congregations resigning from the priesthood in quick succession. Giuliana, the secretary of the Union of Superiors General, entered Arrupe's office quite concerned, thinking that she was going to upset him, since he was president of the union. Arrupe responded quickly: "Don't worry, Giuliana. It's very simple: now we have to love them more." Giuliana herself, despite being a very indepen-dent and even somewhat anticlerical woman, finally decided to enter the Merce-darians of Berriz, confessing: "I owe my vocation to Father Arrupe."[36]

Once, while driving through Rome's chaotic traffic, Margaret Hebblethwaite, wife of the well-known British ex-Jesuit Peter Hebblethwaite, collided with a small car. When she got out of her vehicle to see what damage had been done, she was amazed to discover that she had collided with nothing less than the car of the superior general of the Society of Jesus. Feeling quite upset, Margaret approached Arrupe and extended her hand, saying: "Look, I am Margaret Heb-blethwaite, the wife of an ex-Jesuit. I love the Society very much. I have made the Spiritual Exercises many times, and I also direct retreats and give the Exercises in personalized form."

Arrupe smiled and returned her greeting: "How wonderful it is to meet a new member of the Society of Jesus!"[37]

When the topic of departures came up in chance conversations, Arrupe always changed paths. Someone once said to him: "At this rate, we'll have nobody left."

Arrupe answered: "Last one out, turn out the lights!"

---

36   Statement of Giuliana Panchetti.
37   Narrated by Peter Hebblethwaite.

Pedro Basterrechea, who had been his companion in the Marian congregation of Madrid, when Arrupe was studying medicine, was quite scandalized by the calamities that he attributed to Vatican II. In a confidential conversation with Arrupe, he recounted one by one to the general the terrible things that had happened after the council. Arrupe listened to him impassively. When Basterrechea finished, Arrupe simply asked him: "Do you think, Perico, that all those evils have come from Vatican II?"

"Sure, I think so," answered Basterrechea, feeling somewhat uneasy.

"Well," concluded Arrupe, "since the Holy Spirit has been the one who messed everything up, then he will fix things again."[38]

This interior liberty of Arrupe was evident from another anecdote about a 1976 meeting of the editors of Jesuit journals in Europe. The story is told by Raymond Bréchet, who was then chief editor of the Swiss journal *Choisir*. The editors were commenting on the denunciations that were arriving in the Vatican and in the Jesuit curia about one or another journal or editor. Discussion centered especially on the polemical Swiss journal *Orientierung*.

Arrupe addressed the editors' problems of conscience, telling them: "Let's suppose you have written an article that you have researched in depth, and that you have even had the article reviewed and checked by one of your brothers. Good: you have reached a final version. And then you begin to receive criticism from various sides, even from your brothers. You are not understood. Your superiors do not understand you. They are in clear disagreement with your orientation. Even," said Arrupe as he pointed toward the Vatican,

> those from above disagree, and they make it known to you. What is to be done then? Well, sit down before Jesus Christ, in your house chapel. Place yourself before Christ abandoned in Gethsemane. Leave everything there, your person, your things, everything. And then you will feel *free*, totally free.

Bréchet recalls: "Arrupe pronounced the word 'free' with such full tones that one realized that he himself had had such an experience of interior liberty many times."[39]

Father Albert Longchamp, the director of the journal *Choisir*, tells of how his publication on several occasions had had problems with the archbishop of Freiberg for printing a talk given by the Dominican Father Stefan Pfürtner about questions of sexual morality. Longchamp had been called to Rome because of this. Arrupe spoke to him for a half-hour without mentioning the controversial topic. The general then asked him to attend a meeting of Jesuits who were working in communications media. The meeting was set for a Saturday when Longchamp was supposed to preside at a wedding. Arrupe told him that he would

---

38   Narrated by Pedro Ferrer Pi, S.J., who heard it from Pedro Basterrechea.
39   Statement of Raymond Brechet, S.J.

still have time, after the wedding, to catch a train to Geneva and then a plane to Rome. When he reached Rome, he found that the general assistant for Germany was himself there to receive him in the airport.

At one meeting, the Jesuit editors treated the sensitive matter of the publication in *Choisir* of an article on Opus Dei titled "Opus Dei: A Church within the Church?" Pierre Emonet, a Swiss Jesuit who spent many years living in Spain, had been asked to write about the movement with all due respect and accuracy. After the article was published, however, the leaders of Opus complained to the journal's director that it was an "offense against charity." The German assistant subsequently called Longchamp and showed him a letter that the Vatican secretary of state, Cardinal Casaroli, had written to Arrupe, asking the general to order Longchamp to cease all discussion of Opus Dei in *Choisir*, because such discussion "was offending against the church's charity." Immediately recognizing the expression, Longchamp knew that the crisis had resulted from a report originating in the nunciature of Bern, where Opus Dei members had influence. Longchamp notes that this case was "the only time when Father Arrupe took heed of a denunciation of this type, because of its gravity." Arrupe was generally extremely respectful of freedom of expression, of information, and of thought in the Society's journals, as long as there was no scandal or harm done to persons or institutions.[40]

Arrupe's respect for the work of journalists was also evident with regard to the Spanish Catholic weekly *Vida nueva*, which was known in the post-council period for its openness and frankness. When the magazine published controversial news about Jesuits, there was never any censure or complaint from Arrupe; in fact, several Jesuits wrote for the journal. When *Vida nueva* broke the story about Opus Dei's wanting to become a personal prelature, as actually happened years later, the leaders of Opus, concerned that such news would frustrate their hopes in this regard, met with various members of the hierarchy in Rome and Spain in order to get them to take action against the weekly. Arrupe requested reports about the performance of the Jesuit who at the time was the editor-in-chief of *Vida nueva*. Although there was pressure to remove the editor from his post because of his role in publishing such stories, Arrupe once again respected press freedom and did not remove him.[41]

When Arrupe considered it necessary to create a press office for the Society, he appointed as director Jean-Claude Dietsch, who has since published the oft-cited book *Itinéraire d'un Jesuit* (1982). Arrupe told Dietsch that as head of the press office he had the right to attend all the important meetings in the curia:

> I would not have created a press office without giving its director the necessary means for knowing what was happening daily in the Society. You

---

40   Statement of Albert Longchamp, S.J.
41   At that time, the editor-in-chief of *Vida nueva* was the author of this book.

are expected to have the boldness and the prudence that are required to do good reporting about the activities of our order. [...] It is not for me to be in agreement or disagreement with what you publish. [...] Since you are schooled in the Exercises, you must decide what is suitable and what is not. Your work is by no means easy, and I personally know what the consequences can be. Just remember the sensationalist headlines announcing the return of Jesuits to China, using some phrases of mine from a press conference! Well, fine! We run those risks.[42]

Many journalists admired Arrupe as a "newsmaker" and an ideal person to interview. Several cameramen of Italian television became his personal friends and called him regularly by phone, simply because of the way he greeted them and took an interest in them.

This attitude of respect and freedom extended also to political opinions. The Catalonian Jesuit Miguel Batllori, a historian, relates meeting one day with the eminent Spanish politician and statesman José María de Areilza, shortly before the death of General Franco. Areilza asked him: "Has Father Arrupe given the Jesuits instructions for what will happen afterward, as have other 'religious institutes'?" (He was referring to Opus Dei.)

"None at all," answered Batllori. "Father Arrupe leaves us free to think for ourselves."

Areilza, who like Arrupe was from Bilbao, smiled and said: "Very good! My compatriot is clearly intelligent."[43]

We have already seen how some Jesuits, above all the older ones, were highly critical of Arrupe's style of governing. When the general was visiting a Jesuit residence in Guadalajara, Mexico, the members of the community naughtily tried to get an elderly priest to tell Arrupe what he usually said about him. The old priest blushed deeply and excused himself. Finally, though, he was persuaded to state his ideas about the progress of the Society with the different generals: "Saint Ignatius founded a *company*; Acquaviva, an *army*; Roothaan, a *military camp*; Ledóchowski, a *concentration camp*; and Arrupe said 'Break ranks!'"[44] Arrupe laughed heartily at these jokes of which he himself was the butt, thus demonstrating the wonderful sense of humor that comes with being able to laugh at oneself.

Arrupe's attitude of respect, openness, and tolerance might lead one to the false conclusion that he did not require Jesuits to have a religious spirit, but nothing could be more false. His respect for persons did not prevent him from proposing lofty objectives. His speeches on religious life were read with great interest by members of other religious orders, and his writings on the interior and exterior life of Jesuits fill several volumes. He wrote letters on poverty, prayer,

---

42   *Itinéraire*, 119.
43   Narrated by Miguel Batllori, S.J.
44   Narrated by Luis González, S.J.

simple lifestyle, community life, discernment, obedience, priesthood, mission, the rules, the Spiritual Exercises, availability, the novitiate, the vows, vocations, the saints of the Society, the Ignatian charism, and so on and so forth. They fill hundreds of pages of profound Ignatian reflection and lofty spirituality. However, a proper analysis of Arrupe's thought on religious life is beyond the scope of this biography; that must be left to specialized works. I simply want to point out what is always the central focus of his writings: fidelity to what is essential in the Ignatian charism, the vital importance of the spiritual life and discernment, and an earnest desire to respond to the challenge of the times.[45]

But many readers may ask this question: Was Arrupe totally lacking in defects? Our narrative has mentioned certain aspects of his character that might be considered defects. A negative aspect of his optimism and idealism could have been a certain naiveté, which of course had its own simplicity and charm. His unlimited confidence in people made him want to believe that all Jesuits were striving for the same ideal as he, with the result that he would give them responsibilities that were more than they could handle. The reverse side of his charismatic and prophetic impulse might have been a certain deficiency in the practical sense and the institutional instinct that some thought every superior should possess. Some critics would have preferred him to be more authoritarian. Others criticized him for his tendency to favor the Germans when he was provincial in Japan or for the weakness he showed toward North Americans when he was general. Others thought that he was too yielding with certain powerful figures, such as Jesuits in the curia who exercised influence in the Vatican. He was also criticized for not being skilled in teaching Jesuits how to put into practice some of his own insights, such as "community discernment." Other Jesuits, such as Luis S. Martínez, believed that

> the only fault of Father Arrupe was that he thought and felt that other Jesuits were like him. That was the reason for his absolute confidence in each and every one of his sons, a confidence that he never withdrew, even if we defrauded him in some way. Father Arrupe could not conceive that there were men who were Jesuits in name only, half-hearted Jesuits. We were all—we all had to be—the way Ignatius of Loyola dreamed we would be and the way his son and successor Pedro Arrupe tried to be and in fact succeeded in being.[46]

It is customarily said that no man can hide his defects from his closest associates. In this regard, we have the testimony of one of Arrupe's personal secretaries,

---

45   Cf. the three books that contain a large selection of Arrupe's texts on religious life: *La identidad del jesuita*; *La vida religiosa ante un reto histórico* (Santander: Sal Terrae, 1978); and *Nuestra vida consagrada*. See also Ignacio Ellacuría, "Pedro Arrupe, renovador de la vida religiosa," in Alcalá et al., *Pedro Arrupe*, 141–72, here 141, and Alcalá, "Arrupe y la vida religiosa en el posconcilio," 669ff.

46   Statement of Luis S. Martínez, S.J.

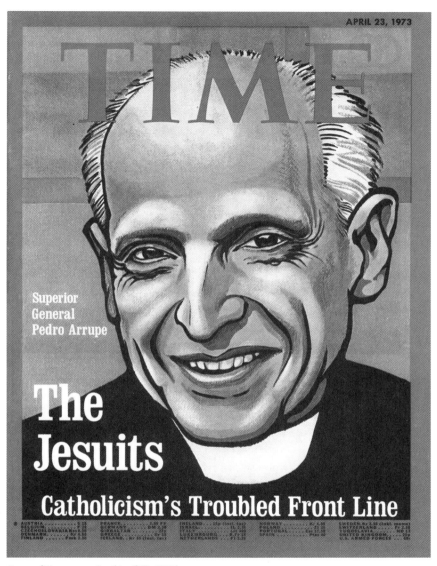

APRIL 23, 1973

TIME

Superior
General
Pedro Arrupe

The
Jesuits

Catholicism's Troubled Front Line

Cover of Time *magazine (April 23, 1973).*

Father Gaviña, who used to say that "he found no defects in Father Arrupe." This statement would be impressive, except that the Jesuit who uttered it, an outstanding representative of the order's conservative wing, was already betraying Arrupe by handing over presumably confidential information to the Vatican. Though the general had removed Gaviña from his position as assistant for Latin America, he showed great confidence in him in naming him his secretary.

Some members of the hierarchy also felt honored to be friends of Arrupe. Besides the already mentioned Dom Hélder Câmara, there was the bishop of Cuernavaca, Sergio Méndez Arceo; the Argentine cardinal and president of several Vatican dicasteries, Eduardo Pironio; and the archbishop of Madrid and president of the Spanish Bishops' Conference, Cardinal Vicente Enrique y Tarancón, who often repeated that "Father Arrupe is one of the most exceptional persons that I have met in my life."[47]

In 1999, the highly acclaimed Spanish National Radio program "Fin de siglo" (Turn of the century), wanting to dedicate a special segment to Arrupe, searched through its sound archives. They found a great variety of interesting declarations in Arrupe's own voice, as well as statements of his contemporaries; these were collected and edited for the program. Outstanding among the testimonies was that of the lucid cardinal of the post-Franco transition, Enrique y Tarancón:

> Father Arrupe, who was a prophet, was exceptionally charismatic; he could intuit the future. Consequently he was way ahead of many others, who could not keep up with him because they could not maintain his pace. For that reason, he was not only a man of his time but a man who tried to prepare his companions for the future, for that third millennium in which the waters will become calmer and they are able to carry out the labors entrusted to them.[48]

The opinion in Roman ecclesiastical circles, as Spanish Jesuit Elías Royón explains, was that Arrupe, despite his undoubted personal holiness, was less than outstanding in his ability to govern. He was criticized for his naiveté, idealism, lack of force, and excessive optimism. "One thing is certain, however," continues Royón: "Father Arrupe was aware that governance in religious life could not continue to be exercised as if the Second Vatican Council had never taken place." After analyzing in depth the documentation and Arrupe's activities, Royón concludes that Arrupe did in fact govern the Society effectively: "He gave instructions, encouraged people, corrected abuses, clarified ideas, pointed out apostolic priorities, proposed challenges, warned of future threats." Arrupe's style of governance was clearly Ignatian, spiritual, and apostolic; it broadened discernment to a community context; it was open to history and the signs of the times; it had clear priorities and encouraged an esprit de corps; it sought an exercise of obedience marked by a spirit of dialogue and careful attention to concrete persons. In sum, Arrupe practiced what he called the "new art of commanding and obeying" out of "creative fidelity"; it was based on a return to the sources in the light of the council.[49]

---

47   Statement of Cardinal Vicente Enrique y Tarancón to the author. The same statement is found in various published interviews.

48   Program "Fin de Siglo" (Sound Archive of Spanish National Radio), first broadcast on Good Friday, 1999.

49   Cf. Elías Royón, "Su modo de gobernar," in La Bella, *Pedro Arrupe, general de la Compañía de Jesús*, 711–51, here 713ff.

Arrupe in Madrid with the author of this book (1970).

In this regard, a curious fact was revealed to this author by García Casado, a Jesuit who had been Arrupe's assistant in the novitiate in Hiroshima and had also been a tertian under Arrupe's direction there. Arrupe once told him, "Thanks to you I have passed through all the stages that are possible in the Society, from novice to general." When García Casado went to visit Arrupe in Rome in 1967, while the post-council crisis was at its peak, the general spoke to him of the confusion and disorientation that reigned among the clergy and Jesuits and of his fear that the situation might also spread to the faithful. "He then slightly changed the angle of his smile and, as if trying to discern a horizon through the window, said to me: 'What am I to do if I write letters to the whole Society and some Jesuits don't even read them?'"[50]

Golden Jubilee

We find ourselves now, as our story moves forward, in the first years after GC 32. On January 15, 1977, Arrupe celebrated his golden jubilee, fifty years of being a Jesuit. On that day in 1927, he had presented himself at the Loyola novitiate without the proper documents but full of enthusiasm. When recalling those times, Arrupe used to say with emotion that every personal history has a thread

---

50   Letter of Manuel García Casado to the author. "Father Arrupe was tertian instructor just once, and with only one tertian, who was I, starting on November 13, 1951." Tertianship is the year that Jesuits, once they have finished their studies, dedicate to renewing their spirit before their definitive incorporation into the Society.

running through it, and each history is original and different: "When we hear these personal histories," he comments,

> we perceive that something is left unsaid in all of them because it cannot be spoken: it is a personal secret that even the person himself cannot fully perceive. This part of our story that is hidden or half-hidden, even to ourselves, is the most truly interesting part, because it is what is most intimate, profound, and personal. It is the close correlation between God, who is love and who loves each person in a different way, and the person, who in the depth of his being gives a unique response, for there will be no other response like it in all of history. It is the secret of the marvelous Trinitarian love that irrupts, when it so desires, into the life of each person in a way that is unexpected, inexpressible, irrational, irresistible, but at the same time marvelous and decisive.

Arrupe recognized the hand of God in all the decisive tugs, "radical turns," or even "reversals":

> My vocation to the Society of Jesus in the middle of medical studies that so interested me, and before finishing the courses; my vocation to Japan (a mission for which even God's call felt no inclination), which superiors denied me for ten years, while they prepared me to be one day a morals professor; my presence in the city over which exploded the first atomic bomb; my election as general of the Society—these have been quite unexpected and brusque events, but they have at the same time borne the *mark* of God so clearly that I have really considered them, and I still consider them, as those *irruptions* whereby God's loving providence is pleased to manifest its presence and absolute dominion over each of us.

Faced with this process, Arrupe reacts with wonder and gratitude, and he recognizes himself in three figures that symbolize his spirit: the first is Abraham, into whose life God irrupted:

> This was the sensation of my first years living in the Society [...], when I went to Japan [...], and above all when I was elected general. But it became even more radical, bringing with it a profound uncertainty that was burdened with responsibilities; it meant relinquishing a whole series of attitudes, practices, concepts, and priorities that had to be left behind, according to the council, in order to enter into others that were more amorphous, still to be clarified and defined; it meant leaving a world of security created in the course of the age-old traditions of the church and the Society, in order to enter on a road that led to a world still *in fieri*, a world unfamiliar to us, but one to which God was calling us by the council.
>
> For me, that figure of Abraham was always a source of profound inspiration. "Where is the Society going?" they would ask me; my answer was

Flying over the slums of Guatemala City (1971). "Europe cannot conceive its development independently of the less favored countries."

always: "Where God takes it." It was like saying: "I don't know, but I do know one thing, that God is taking us somewhere: we are traveling safely, we are traveling with the church that is guided by the Holy Spirit." I know that God is taking us to a new earth, the promised land, his own land. He knows where it is; our job is simply to follow him.

Since difficulties would not be lacking along the way, Arrupe evoked a second patron or model: the apostle Paul and the confidence he expressed in phrases such as: "Not I, but the grace of God in me" (1 Cor. 15:10). And the third model on whom Arrupe calls is Saint Francis Xavier, for whom "the true source of apostolic energy is confidence in God." Arrupe ends his declaration by affirming his confidence in his three loves: for the Society, incarnated as concrete persons and as an institution and instrument of the apostolate; for the church of Christ, through which the Spirit circulates; and for Jesus Christ himself, the great love of Arrupe's life, as he repeated hundreds of times.[51]

On May 2, 1978, Arrupe's sister, Mother María Arrupe, Slave of the Sacred Heart, celebrated her golden jubilee in religious life. As a personal gift, brother Pedro recorded a tape cassette, which was played during the festivities honoring María in the community the sisters had in La Moraleja (Madrid). The tape, recorded in a warm, youthful-sounding voice, contains not only interesting biographical data but also veiled mystical confessions. A transcription follows:

---

51   Arrupe, *La identidad del jesuita*, 535.

María, how I would love to have been with you today! I feel bad and am really sorry that I am not there in La Moraleja, but what do you want me to tell you? […] I have no remorse. It's one of those pains that life and above all religious life carries with it. I don't feel any sensation of culpability. […] But that doesn't mean I am not sorry—and very sorry!

[…] Some months ago, I celebrated my own fifty years of religious life in the Society. As you see, I am older than you. Life has changed things around! You, my professor and teacher in the days of Astarloa, now are younger than I am. That does not mean that you are not more mature in the spiritual life and religious experience than I am, who, after fifty years of being a Jesuit and seventy years of living, still find myself like a child, like an immature kid before God. But immature as I am, I have great desires to be transplanted to the best of lands, Heaven, in order to mature once and for all […] the once and for all of eternity.

While I was thinking of your fifty years of religious life and my own, so many memories have come to mind, so many things: the figure of my "professor" in papa's office, who, across the large drawing table, always standing, managed to put my little eight-year-old head through that torrent of different subjects contained in the textbooks. There was no other way: "Either I learned or I wouldn't go out to play," like Marga and Isa (and I would sit in the chair in the middle).

That teacher was relentless. But she was the one responsible for the countless scholarships that Uncle Pedrito de los Gondritas won, due more to the constancy of the teacher than to the brilliance of that little head that once wanted to test its consistency by banging itself against a lamppost in front of the Augustinians. There followed a swollen nose, which then began to grow longer!

Another image of María occurs to me: the one of her seated under the wall clock in the dining room at quarter to nine every day, with a cup of hot chocolate and a piece of bread before her. While hiding herself behind *El noticiero Bilbaíno* (News of Bilbao), she spent more than half an hour pretending she was reading, when actually she was eating that succulent breakfast of two cups of chocolate.

And with that feasting, it is no wonder that your weakness reached such a point that you ran the risk of losing your sight, so much so that papa had to write to me in Madrid, when I was already at San Carlos: "Look, Pedro, María is quite sick. But what most shames me is people saying that my daughter is dying of hunger!"

But you did not die. Rather, a little more than a year after I entered the Society at Loyola, you also appeared at Loyola and entered the novitiate of the Slaves. If that wasn't a first-class miracle, then it certainly was a second-class one! (I don't know if you even weighed thirty-five kilograms.)

It was difficult to understand how with such poor health you could be admitted as a religious.

But the Lord has his ways, and he it was who chose you, even though you did not appear to be eligible; and he knows what he is doing and whom he is choosing. [...] He certainly made no mistake, right?

Our lives, which until then were so united geographically, became completely separated. Salamanca and Tokyo are a good distance apart, are they not? But you wrote to me frequently, even when I did not answer you. I'm sorry! "Pedro, I always have you very present with me in my watches before the Blessed Sacrament." And I felt the effects of that in Yamaguchi (in the prison), in Hiroshima (the atomic bomb), in Tokyo (during my provincialate). [...] And later, in the hall of the Society's General Congregation 31, when I heard those words: *Praepositus Generalis Societatis Iesu electus est Reverendus Pater Petrus Arrupe* [...]. That is when I really needed your prayers. Mamma mia! That's when everything came down on top of me! But the Lord, to whom you always prayed with such insistence, once again did wonders: I was spiritually more blind than you were physically so for not eating, and with less spiritual weight than your thirty-five material kilograms, but he chose the last, *infirma mundi* [the weak things of the world], this time *infirmissimus* [the very weakest], and he again worked a miracle like that of curing lepers or raising the dead [...]; "your student" felt that he had to accept that cross since he could count on the graces that you would win for him while his job lasted.

For that reason, here in Rome I have also been feeling you very close: your arthrosis, your fractured femur, your lumbago [...], things that are very prosaic and painful, but that for me were a mine of graces. Yes, Mari, the more you suffered the closer you were, not only to the crucified and Eucharistic Lord but also to this poor Pedro, who was in need of your pains and troubles. You in the porter's lodge and the bed; I in what the world considers the limelight, but which in fact is a cross, different in appearance from the cross of lumbago or a fractured femur, but at base the same cross, the cross of Jesus.

And so we keep on hauling, right? But we do so gracefully, at least in your case. For my part, I slip up once in a while, feeling that this is too great a weight. But just a room away I have the Lord exposed in your monstrance, in a Lilliputian chapel, which for me is greater than any cathedral, a true source of ultra-atomic energy. And so the haul is almost effortless, because he is the one who is hauling.

All right, Mari. I hope you have a stupendous, joyful, and deeply felt golden jubilee feast. May you remember one by one the greatest graces you have received during your life, which externally may appear not only hidden but even monotonous. It is a life in which you will discover an interior landscape that is varied and sublime; it is a landscape that only you and Jesus know and that you will never be able to explain to others. No matter how hard you try, you won't find words to say what you want to explain. Maybe you can say it as Saint John of the Cross did:

> *I knew not where I stood,*
> *Great things I understood;*
> *I'll not say what I felt,*
> *But I was as if not knowing,*
> *And yet transcending all knowledge.*

I would have so many other things to say to you, but I don't want to distract you since you have many things to attend to. I end with the verse of Saint John of the Cross that I think sums up very well what I would like to say:

> *Love has done such work*
> *After I got to know him,*
> *That, whether there is good or evil in me,*
> *He makes it taste all the same*
> *And transforms the soul into himself:*
> *And thus, in his delicious flame,*
> *Which I am feeling within me,*
> *He captures, without leaving anything,*
> *And all of me is consumed.*

Many thanks, María. And to all the community I send my warmest greetings and gratitude for this beautiful feast they have prepared for you. Till another time![52]

That is the heartfelt message that Pedro recorded for his sister María.

Perhaps one of the best syntheses of Arrupe's personality is the one traced by García Casado, who was a tertian and then the assistant novice master in Hiroshima. He recounts how, when he traveled to Rome in 1967, he found the general very busy. By chance, he met him in the doorway of the curia along with two assistants. To Manuel's surprise, Arrupe, as soon as he saw him, called out to him with his sonorous voice and said: "Welcome to Rome, my lone tertian!" That afternoon, he was told that Arrupe had found a spot in his busy agenda and would meet with him:

> He received me in the same room where Saint Ignatius had lived so many years. As I entered, he got up from his desk and, pointing to an easy chair, invited me to be seated, while he smiled and greeted me affectionately. He

---

52   Transcription of the tape cassette sent to Mother María Arrupe by her brother Peter on the occasion of her fiftieth anniversary of religious life.

Celebration of Arrupe's "golden anniversary" as a Jesuit in the Roman church of the Gesù (January 15, 1977).

began to speak to me with the same affability and simplicity, as if we were still in the novitiate of Nagatsuka.

I quickly saw that he was still observing things and people with the same soft eyes as ever. They were the eyes of one who, after focusing them a long while on something vital, draws them back gladly again to behold a friend. They were the eyes, I imagine, that Jesus would have if one day, after the tabernacle door was suddenly opened, his sacred visage were to shine out in human form, to look smilingly at a friendly heart [...].[53]

---

53   Letter of Manuel García Casado to the author.

Such, in broad strokes, was the human profile of Arrupe in his years as superior general, the "profile of an eagle." Perhaps what in the end is most important is that that profile, that silhouette, gave off an aura of energy, and even more, of love. In all parts of the world today, there are people who keep repeating, "He was my friend," and they display a photograph, an autograph, or a letter brimming with attention, respect, and affection. This is especially unusual when the man was a superior. Arrupe's keen sensibility and intuition, developed through many years of meditation and concentration, could discern whenever somebody was in need of a friendly gesture. Sometimes, when he perceived that someone was dispirited, he did not simply extend his hand in a conventional greeting; rather, he unexpectedly grasped the other person's hand and pressed it between his own, as a particular sign of support and warmth. After all, it is well known that personal respect and kindness bear more fruit than do all the writings, institutional declarations, and commands from above. For all these reasons, Arrupe will not pass into history simply as a superior general of the Society of Jesus; he will be remembered as something more important: as a great man who has dignified the human race.

19. The Resignation

The oppressively warm summer calm of Sunday, August 6, 1978 was suddenly shattered by surprising news: "Paul VI has died." During his last years, the pope's heart had been worn out by a series of ailments: progressive arthrosis, bronchitis, flus, pulmonary edema, and operations on his prostate and kidney. He died after a brief agony, during the Roman vacation period, as if not wanting to bother anybody. His physical pain had been aggravated in his latter years by the inner spiritual suffering that came from the great seriousness with which he, despite his age, took his responsibility for guiding the church during the post-conciliar tempests. Still full of faith and interior strength, but with less energy and with the doubts characteristic of an intellectual—they called him "Pope Hamlet"—Paul VI died beset by infirmity, but not defeated. Known as the "Pope of Peace" and the "Pope of Dialogue," he was until that time the pope who had traveled most outside the Vatican, the one who had given the most ecumenical embraces, the one who, after John XXIII threw open the windows to let in the fresh air of the council, had opened the doors as well. His final ten years, slower paced of necessity, had erased some of the memories of the first ten, during which he proved himself a faithful executor of the conciliar commitments.

On that August 6, however, with the death of Paul VI, there began a period of seventy-five days that would shake up the church.[1]

The Posthumous Discourse of John Paul I

On August 25, while the cardinals of the church were enclosed in the conclave that would elect the new pope, a curious entity in the United States called the Committee for the Responsible Election of the Pope, led by sociologist Andrew M. Greeley, was making some original claims: that the new pope should have the ability to address not only Catholics but the whole world, that he should be a just man, and that he should know how to smile. Great theologians—among them Hans Küng, Yves Congar, Marie-Dominique Chenu, and Gustavo Gutiér-rez—were for their part asking that the successor of Paul VI be a man open to the world, a guide who trusted people outside the church, a brother in collegiality, an ecumenical mediator, an authentic Christian.

A tumultuous ovation broke out in Saint Peter's Square on Saturday, August 26, after the proclamation: *Habemus papam* (We have a new pope). A swarm of

---

1   See Pedro Miguel Lamet, reports from Rome in the weekly magazine *Vida nueva*, collected in the book, *Del papa Montini al papa Wojtyla (Los setenta y cinco días que estreme-cieron a la iglesia)* (Bilbao: Mensajero, 1979); see also Lamet, *Juan Pablo II, hombre y papa* (Madrid: Espasa Calpe, 2005).

telephone lines, television cameras, and microphones were soon transmitting the news to the world: the new pope was the patriarch of Venice, Albino Luciani, who took a name that combined the names of his two predecessors: John and Paul. And behold, a miracle: he was a pope who knew how to smile. The next day, he appeared before two hundred thousand people congregated in Saint Peter's Square. He was known to be a good pastor and a teacher who liked to write intimate letters to Saint Teresa and Pinocchio.

But the pope's smile lasted only a short while. On the morning of September 29, the world awoke to incredible news: John Paul I had died only thirty-four days after being elected pope. There was much speculation about the causes of his death. The most plausible thesis is that he was overcome by an obscure heart condition and, perhaps even more, by the aversion his simple, evangelical soul felt at assuming the heavy responsibility laid on him. Naturally, some of the speculation implicated the Jesuits in the tragedy. It was said that the pope had died right after preparing a discourse he planned to address to members of the Society; it was about a matter he had reportedly discussed with Cardinal Villot. He may not have had the discourse in his hands the night he suffered the attack, but the document was in fact on his table and was due to be read before members of the Society of Jesus.[2]

Before the pope's death, Arrupe had taken part in the Eucharistic Congress in Philadelphia, along with Câmara and Mother Teresa of Calcutta, with whom he symbolically shared a loaf of bread. At the congress, he gave a speech on "hunger for bread and the Gospel,"[3] in which he stated that

> the Eucharistic community of the first Christians was above all a community of love. It treated people not as instruments simply to be utilized, but as persons who are loved for themselves and whom it is a joy to serve. This same spirit of love should characterize and inspire all our actions on behalf of justice.

He had also addressed the 1977 Synod of Bishops on catechetics, arguing that the church needed to reach out to people and not wait for people to come to it; he also insisted once again on inculturation.[4] At the same time, decree 4 of GC 32 was being progressively implemented around the world. In those days when El Salvador was witnessing terrible violence and bitter conflicts between church and state, Arrupe and thirteen Latin American provincials wrote:

---

2   Lamet, *Del papa Montini al papa Wojtyla*, 163.

3   In *Hambre de pan y de evangelio*, 39.

4   Cf. "Catechetics and Inculturation" and "Marxism and Catechetics," Arrupe's interventions in the 1977 synod. On Marxism, he states: "It is impossible to ignore Marxism; it is necessary to refer to it explicitly, starting from a certain level of intellectual development. Silence would mean that Christian catechetics is incapable of taking a position with respect to one of the most important options being offered to people today." See Arrupe, *La iglesia de hoy y del futuro*, 235, 241.

Out of fidelity to the Gospel of Jesus, we wish to make a simple but firm statement affirming our solidarity with our brothers who are being persecuted for supporting peasant organizations. Along with them, we proclaim our belief as a seed of change. We reaffirm our rejection of repressive and subversive violence. We want to express our joy at seeing how seriously these brothers have accepted the call to undertake the crucial struggle of our time, the service of faith and the promotion of justice.[5]

In statements made to the newspaper *Avvenire* on his fiftieth anniversary as a Jesuit, Arrupe came out against two extremes: apathy and irresponsible activism:

Several provinces have made serious efforts to evaluate the more traditional works, with the aim of freeing men up for apostolic work among the poor. Programs of this type are numerous in Asia, Africa, and Latin America, but they exist also in Europe, North America, and in the more industrialized nations generally.[6]

At the same time, Jesuits were beginning to be imprisoned and killed. One was arrested in India for protesting against obligatory sterilization. In Mozambique, the Jesuits had lost everything. After July 1977, no Jesuit could live in Vietnam. Shortly before that, three Jesuits had been killed in Rhodesia. Arrupe also stated in the interview: "We are also losing many of our major benefactors because in our schools we are teaching their children the social precepts of the Gospel. They accuse us of being leftist radicals when we are simply quoting the encyclicals *Populorum progressio, Octogesima adveniens*, and *Mater et magistra*."

It was the beginning of a true calvary, which would eventually leave scores of Jesuits martyred for the defense of the faith and the promotion of justice. Those who gave their lives in the years 1977–81 included men like Desmond Donovan, John Conway, Francis Louis Martinsek, Rutilio Grande, Luis Espinal, Godofredo Alingal, Carlos Pérez Alonso, João Bosco Burnier, and Alfredo Pérez Lobato. Eight years later, on November 16, 1989, an unprecedented massacre would cause the world to shudder. Some forty armed men wearing uniforms of the Salvadoran army invaded the residence of the Jesuits of the Central American University (UCA) in San Salvador. They dragged six Jesuits, their housekeeper, and the housekeeper's sixteen-year-old daughter out into the garden and killed them. Their names appeared the next day in the news media around the world. They were the university rector, Ignacio Ellacuría; the vice-rector, Ignacio Martín-Baró; the professors Segundo Montes, Amando López, Juan Ramón Moreno Pardo, and Joaquín López y López; the housekeeper, Elba; and her daughter, Celina. The Jesuits had previously been threatened by the Salvadoran oligarchy simply for taking the side of the poor in the struggle for a more peaceful and just country.

---

5   *Vida nueva*, Madrid, 1977, 1845.
6   Newspaper *Avvenire*, Milan, January 15, 1977.

A subsequent investigation proved that the perpetrators did in fact belong to the army and that they had taken advantage of the confusion provoked by ongoing battles against guerrillas in the city to murder the Jesuits in cold blood.

The prime target of their assault rifles was Ellacuría, fifty-nine years of age, favored disciple of the Spanish philosopher Xavier Zubiri and a strong proponent of liberation theology. Ellacuría had become a key figure in the country's search for peace since he had contacts with the guerrillas of the FMLN and was recognized as a skilled negotiator by the Salvadoran government. A native of Bilbao, like Arrupe, Ellacuría had made a decisive contribution toward convincing Arrupe that it was necessary for the Jesuits to take a radical posture regarding faith and justice in Central America. He went so far as to claim that the general embodied an ideal of religious life in Latin America that was oriented toward "integral liberation" of the people. On a journey he made to Madrid shortly before he was killed, Ellacuría discussed with the present author some of these same propositions, which would in a way cost Arrupe his own life.

The martyrdom of these six Jesuits, who were close collaborators of other martyrs such as Rutilio Grande and Óscar Romero, along with that of Elba and Celina, gave rise to a great many testimonies and commentaries. Except for a few dissident voices, these testimonies coincided in their support for the great option that years earlier had been promoted by the main character of this story.[7] At the time of Grande's death in 1977, Arrupe had written:

> These are the Jesuits that the world and the church need today: men impelled by the love of Christ, who serve their brothers without distinction of race or class; men who know how to identify with those who suffer and live with them to the point of giving their lives to help them; brave men who know how to defend human rights, to the point of sacrificing their life if it be necessary.[8]

Decree 4 had been generally well received by Jesuits around the world. Many social research centers became more actively involved in concrete projects, such as helping impoverished rural communities. Small Jesuit communities were established in poor neighborhoods and the slums surrounding the great metropolises. Sensitivity to justice issues was introduced slowly but gradually in the educational institutions and other ministries, such as giving the Spiritual Exercises. When the "procurators" from the various provinces met in Rome in 1978, Arrupe told them that the new social consciousness was "one of the greatest changes presently taking place in the Society. [...] We are witnessing the gradual disappearance of the fear that some groups initially had." In a series

---

7   See Roberto Martialay, *Comunidad en sangre* (Bilbao: Mensajero, 1983); Lamet, *Del papa Montini al papa Wojtyla*, 331. For the complete list, see "Jesuitas muertos violentamente en misión," in La Bella, *Pedro Arrupe, general de la Compañía de Jesús*, appendix, 1061.

8   Pedro Arrupe, "Carta con ocasión de la muerte violenta del P. Rutilio Grande," March 19, 1977.

of internal letters, Arrupe dealt carefully with possible deviations, warning that excessive stress on socioeconomic factors, unnecessary political involvement, or Marxism could detract from the faith dimension of Jesuit work.[9]

Paul VI had received Arrupe in audience for the last time on May 18, 1978. That day, the general no doubt spoke especially of the preparations for the CELAM conference, which was to be held in Puebla, Mexico, in October. The atmosphere of the audience was described as cordial, and the clouds that had been hovering over the relations between the Jesuits and the Vatican since 1966 seemed to be dissipating.

Arrupe warmly recalled the bonds that united Paul VI with the Jesuits:

> He always showed great esteem for the Society and maintained great confidence in it, even when he felt a certain fear, which he expressed clearly, of our having erred or faltered in his mission. His great desire was that the Society remain faithful. And it is true that at various moments we gave him good reasons for disquiet. His solicitude, and even at times his anxiety, were not only personal—because of his many ties with the Jesuits—but also ecclesiastical. He told me several times: the Society's influence is enormous, and its experience is bound to have important consequences for the whole of religious life and the entire church. I found myself as before a father who wants his son to behave well. After meeting with him, I always felt enthusiasm, even the times that he was scolding me! Our relations were very cordial.[10]

But precisely at that moment, Paul VI died. One of the first items on the agenda of the newly elected John Paul I was an audience with the procurators' congregation of the Jesuits; it was scheduled for September 30. As we have seen, on the morning of the twenty-ninth the whole world woke up to the shocking news of the death of the "Smiling Pope."

Less than forty-eight hours after being elected, John Paul I sent a personal letter to the general, in which he thanked the Society for wishing him well. He was to die, however, before he could address another text to the Jesuits, this one written in harsher language. In this document, which was not made known until December 8, 1978, the pope recalled how his predecessor, Paul VI, "had loved the Society of Jesus so much and had done so much, prayed so much, and suffered so much for the Society." He then made some recommendations that had the appearance of a reprimand: "Do not allow the teaching and the publications of Jesuits to become a source of confusion and disorientation. [...] Naturally, that means that the doctrine taught in the institutions and faculties where young

---

9   Calvez, *Fe y justicia*, 63ff. In the final allocution to this procurators' congregation, on October 5, 1978, Arrupe spoke about the challenges facing the Society. He was of the opinion that the order was advancing too slowly and too cautiously.

10   *Itinéraire*, 131.

people are formed should be solid and safe." Furthermore, Jesuits should not "involve themselves in trying to solve economic problems" that pertain to the laity, not priests; they should maintain discipline and an intense interior life.[11] In reality, this undelivered speech of John Paul I added nothing new to the recommendations of Paul VI. Moreover, it contained many words of sympathy and affection for the Society, and it stated clearly that the pope placed great hope in the order, recalling the words that Marcellus II, another pope with a very brief reign, had addressed to Saint Ignatius: "Recruit the men and train the combatants, and we will use them."

Pre-conclave Discussion

Cardinals from all over the world assembled in Rome for the pre-conclave. The moment was extremely difficult. Arrupe asked Cardinal Villot for information about the deceased pope's allocution, the contents of which were still unknown. Villot answered that he could not comply with his request: such a decision would be made by the next pope or by the assembled cardinals. When Arrupe then insisted that the pre-conclave deliberate on the matter, the cardinals dedicated two days to discussing the Society of Jesus.

Villot felt obliged to distribute the posthumous discourse to the cardinal electors, many of whom already had their own complaints about the Jesuits. During the pontificate of Paul VI, many bishops and papal nuncios had lodged bitter criticisms of certain activities of the Jesuits, as well as of Jesuit publications they judged to be too progressive or irreverent toward the Roman magisterium. Some of them had reproached the superior general for not reining in his troops. The cardinals also had in their hands photocopies of an interview given by O'Keefe, an assistant of Arrupe who was considered to be the second most important man in the Society. This interview, published in the Dutch magazine *De Tijd*, contained three explosive proposals for the new pope: reviewing the prohibition of artificial methods of birth control, allowing women to be ordained priests, and accepting the ordination of married men. Evidently, O'Keefe's actual declarations had been much more nuanced. Some of the cardinals were, of course, strong defenders of the Society. Among those attending the pre-conclave was the cardinal of Kraków, Karol Wojtyła, for whom this was a new experience. As a result, he felt a certain malaise, as he confirmed in audiences he held with bishops after he was elected pope.[12]

---

11   See *Información S.J.* (1978): 198. In May of the same year, Arrupe wrote an important letter in which he gathered together his theses on "inculturation."

12   See Giancarlo Zizola, *La restaurazione di papa Wojtyla* (Rome: Laterza, 1985); Alain Woodrow, *Los jesuitas* (Barcelona: Planeta, 1984).

The Surprise of the New Pope

On October 15, in the middle of a mild Roman autumn, hundreds of thousands of people congregated on Saint Peter's Square. By six o'clock, night had already fallen. Bright floodlights from the Braccio di Carlo Magno, with their powerful beams aimed toward the Janiculum, bathed the plaza in light. The whole world was awaiting the wisp of white smoke. The first indication that there was a new pope was given by some nuns, probably the cooks, who came out onto the balconies of the conclave. Vatican Radio informed about the nuns' appearance, and about a light being turned on. When the white smoke finally appeared, there were loud cries and ovations. Within a few minutes, the new pope appeared on the balcony. He smiled, yes; but it was a different smile, one that seemed to emerge from pain. And his first gesture was unusual. In contrast to earlier pontiffs, he placed his hands firmly on the balustrade, in a clear demonstration of assertion and leadership.

The church had just elected a Polish pope, Karol Wojtyła, who would take the name of John Paul II. Amid the general sense of surprise, various interpretations of the election were quickly forthcoming. The director of the Spanish edition of *L'osservatore romano*, who was accompanying Cardinal Alfonso López Trujillo, then secretary of the Latin American Bishops' Conference, declared to Spanish National Radio: "This is the end of the dialogue with Marxism." Others insisted: "He is man of dialogue, respectful and open; he is no Wyszy ski."[13] A member of Opus Dei commented: "The other day, he had supper with Álvaro del Portillo," who was then president of that organization. But the predominant reaction was one of astonishment. Many months would have to pass before clear conjectures could be made about the line of action of the first non-Italian pope in centuries. His initial trip to Poland would throw much light on his style: he was open to the world and modern in his ways; he wanted to rechannel Vatican II toward greater concern for doctrine and better internal discipline.[14]

Unlike his immediate predecessors, Wojtyła had not studied with the Jesuits. Even though he had earlier wanted to study at the Gregorian, he eventually presented his thesis at the Angelicum, the Roman university of the Dominicans. Some Vatican pundits claimed that his ideas about religious life, especially at the beginning of his pontificate, favored the conventual and monastic forms that predated Saint Ignatius of Loyola more than they did the ideal of "contemplatives in action," religious men and women prophetically immersed in the active life.

---

13 Polish cardinal Stefan Wyszyński was well known for his heroic and principled stand against Nazism and communism.

14 See Pedro Miguel Lamet, "Y ocurrió lo increíble," reports on these dates in *Vida nueva*, collected in Lamet, *Del papa Montini al papa Wojtyla*, 135, and Lamet, *Juan Pablo II, hombre y papa*, 171ff.

Four days later, on October 19, Arrupe wrote a letter to his cousin Fernando, in which he expressed concern for the health of his sisters:

Today, your letter of October 3 reached me, in which you recount in detail the visit you made to my sister María in La Moraleja. Many thanks for that thoughtful deed and for the vivid impressions you give me of how you found María. It is clear that her physical weakness is increasing, although her spirit remains firm and she has the energy to deal with her failing body.

I understand that Catalina is also unable to move around much: a couple of days ago, I greeted her by phone, and she told me that she notices her eyesight is diminishing. It is the law of life, which little by little renders us less capable of responding to the difficulties that old age presents. At the same time, we must still thank God for the many blessings of every sort he has showered on our family. [...]

Now you have seen how much change has occurred in Rome in these recent months and what a great surprise this last conclave has given us in the person of His Holiness John Paul II. I have no doubt it will be for the good of the church.

Next Sunday, we will see the royal couple again and the delegation that is coming from Spain for the ceremony in Saint Peter's. That will give me another occasion to ask the Lord to bless that Spanish land and the efforts it is making to achieve a well-balanced democracy.[15]

Among Arrupe's achievements in 1978 must be included his visit to Hungary, the first ever made by a general of the order to that Central European land. The press saw the trip as proof of the esteem in which Arrupe was held in socialist countries. In Hungary, he was able to meet with some sixty Jesuits, who were gathering together for the first time ever, after many years of silence, prison, and dispersion. Arrupe's amiability helped to facilitate communication between the authorities and the bishops; as always, in the dialogue with Marxism he insisted more on what united people than on what separated them.

Arrupe's reputation and leadership continually increased in certain sectors, to such a point that people began to fear for his life. That same year, 1978, when returning from one of his trips and landing in the Fiumicino airport, three automobiles raced to the staircase on which Arrupe was descending from the plane. In a question of seconds, twelve policemen with machine guns got out of the cars. One of them approached the general and said, "Father Arrupe, we have confiscated a list of attacks planned by the Red Brigades. You are among those at the head of the list. We have received orders to escort you."

Arrupe smiled and joked with one of his assistants: "Don't give them even ten liras for me!" For several months, the police accompanied Arrupe in his

---

15   Letter to Fernando Gondra (October 19, 1979).

Arrupe in his first audience with Pope John Paul II (Rome, November 12, 1978).

movements about Rome and kept watch at the entrance of Borgo Santo Spirito. His bodyguards ended up becoming good friends with him.

In another letter to his family, dated January 17, 1979, Arrupe thanked them for the news about their Christmas celebration and expressed concern about the violence in the Basque Country: "It is clear that the proximity of the elections can contribute to a more tense situation." He then added:

On December 11, I had my first private audience with the Holy Father, a man of great personality who very quickly informs himself about the different situations of persons and institutions. He was quite kind in every way, and at the end he gave me a special blessing for the Society. I sent Catalina some photos of that meeting. I enclose here one that catches the moment when the pope was about to give me his blessing.

This photo is one in which Arrupe, dressed in a cloak and kneeling down, is receiving the blessing of John Paul II; copies were also sent to all the houses of the Society. The letter continues:

> You know that I leave on the twenty-fifth for Mexico. I have been invited to participate in the Third Latin American Bishops' Conference, and since the event seems to me very important, I have accepted. I will be in Mexico until the middle of February. I ask your prayers especially for this trip and that Puebla meeting.[16]

Good News in Puebla

The Puebla conference got underway on January 28, and it lasted until February 13. Some four hundred persons, 346 attending the assembly and fifty-four assistants, gathered together to carry forward the torch that Medellín had set alight. Once again, a spirit of dialogue, freedom, and hard work reigned in this meeting, amid the inevitable tensions. Puebla imparted an intense experience of fraternity, but it was not easy going, due to the very diverse tendencies, including some that sought to reverse the process started in Medellín. However, no such reversal took place. The final document, more than three hundred pages long, revealed the existence of three theologies in Latin America: traditional, developmentalist, and liberationist. The Puebla conference broadcasted a new message of hope to the crucified continent, but avoided the easy temptation of indiscriminate condemnation. While it did condemn Marxist collectivism, it also castigated capitalist liberalism and the doctrine of national security. It condemned guerrilla violence, but it also condemned the institutionalized violence exercised by the powerful. There was also a welcome valorization of indigenous cultures and a strong defense of prophetic denunciation. Few clear references were made to more polemical and less essential topics, such as celibacy.

In this hopeful and vibrant ambience, a press conference by Arrupe was naturally anticipated with great interest. Reporters were attracted by his famously charismatic personality, but they had also been roused by a story that was making the rounds. Colombian cardinal López Trujillo, who was then secretary of the Bishops' Conference and would soon be elected president, had earlier spoken to a reporter of the Mexican daily *Uno más uno*. Since the reporter was lacking a cassette for his tape recorder, he had asked the archbishop to lend him one. The prelate gave him one that he had lying on his desk. The reporter was greatly surprised later on, when he played the tape back, to find on the reverse

---

16   See also the letter of January 2, 1980 to Fernando, Mariví, and Guillermo.

side a recording of a personal letter of López Trujillo to his friend Luciano Cabral Duarte, the archbishop of Aracajú (Brazil), who was president of CELAM'S Social Action Department. When the reporter made the contents of the letter known to persons attending the Puebla conference, a great commotion ensued. The cardinal's letter urged Cabral to use his influence at the conference; it issued strong criticisms of the Brazilian theologian Leonardo Boff and suggested ways to deal with him; and it spoke of his own efforts to get Rome to name "hard-line" bishops in Latin America. But the most interesting part of the letter was the concern the cardinal expressed about the choice of the delegates at Puebla: "In this case also, because of pressure from others, Father Arrupe was invited. This causes serious doubt."

Cardinal López Trujillo told the Spanish press agency EFE that the letter was bogus: "Let them show the letter with my signature. People are trying to cause problems. It's a kind of warfare [...]." When he threatened to sue the reporter, the reporter promised to demonstrate the authenticity of the letter, since he had proof of it in his possession, namely the tape with the voice of López Trujillo. The cardinal spoke with Arrupe, assuring him that it was false. Don Pedro replied: "Fine, we know how things are," but he did not believe the denial. The cardinal finally admitted that the letter was his, but claimed that it was only a draft that he later revised.[17]

That contretemps took place on February 1. On February 9, Arrupe held his press conference, which was described by a journalist who was present, Bernardino M. Hernando:

> With great simplicity, humor, and humility, but with firmness, and I repeat, much humor, Father Arrupe won the sympathy and devotion of the majority of us reporters who attended his exceptional press conference at noon today. He did not evade a single question, though not all of them were answered to our complete satisfaction—especially the final ones, perhaps because of his fatigue. He began by making some reflections about the identity and the activity of the Jesuits, stating that "in other times, we may have committed sins of pride, but today we are following a line of humility and of commitment with the poor, or at least we are trying to do so." His main point, logically, concerned the present situation in El Salvador and the many accusations being made against the Jesuits there, especially the declarations of Bishop [Pedro Arnoldo] Aparicio, who blames the Jesuits for what is happening there. "Those accusations are being made by many people, and I cannot accept them; I simply cannot accept them. I am quite familiar with what the Jesuits are doing in El Salvador, and I am convinced that they are doing good work for the sake of justice. We have possibly committed some errors,

17   Bernardino M. Hernando, *Los pasillos de Puebla* (Madrid: PPC, 1979), "La carta bomba de López Trujillo," 115.

but in general what they are doing is good. When they were threatened in July and were told that they would be killed if they did not leave, I told them to stay. The Society is not intimidated by threats. [Loud applause] Father César Jerez, the provincial of Central America, has been here two days, and we have had long talks. We are against the violence, but we are not afraid. They have killed seven of our men in Rhodesia, four in Beirut, and they have expelled us from Iraq. [...] When they ask me where the Society has problems, I answer by asking: Where don't we have them?"

All the questions were submitted in writing, and even though someone who had submitted a question did not appear, Arrupe was interested in having it asked because "it is short," he said, "and I want to answer it." It was about a letter that John Paul II had supposedly written, condemning many attitudes and persons of the Society. "I don't want to be impolite, but I personally have not received that letter," he answered with a smile, and we all laughed a little. Suddenly, a certain person named Sánchez got up on the platform—they tell me he is from the ultra-right *El heraldo de México*—and asked that the question he submitted be read. The question was long and drawn out, and its reading was interrupted several times by whistles and displays of disapproval by the crowd, but it basically asked what the general of the Society of Jesus was doing to condemn Mexican Jesuits Luis del Valle, Alfonso Castillo, Enrique Maza, Porfirio Miranda, and two other men who were not Jesuits. At this point, Father Arrupe left us all amazed by his clarity, energy, and humor. "You are acting as general of the Society, Mister Sánchez. I always claim that I was elected general because of some distraction on the part of the Holy Spirit, but I try to do the best I can. When I see an error, I call people to account, but I do so personally, not in front of television cameras. It is always possible to make general accusations, such as those you have made, but there is nothing concrete there. Tell me concrete things and I will take the necessary measures. But I cannot accept the accusations you are making. [...] I can deny, and I do deny, that the Society is teaching heretical doctrines, because that would weigh heavily on my conscience. I do not accept that." [Loud applause] "As regards the accusation of Marxism, let us distinguish 'Marxist analysis of reality'—which like all doctrines, from Buddhism to whatever you want, can have partial truths that may be useful—and Marxism as a global ideology opposed to Christian spirituality. [...] Here at Puebla there are now some 120 Jesuit sociologists, theologians, and others—I spoke with them some days ago, and I can assure you that it was the happiest moment of my stay in Puebla. There are bishops who consult with them, even though they are not part of the conference, and I myself consult with them. So as regards a 'parallel Puebla,' there is nothing of the sort. That is a false accusation they have raised against us." And we applauded strongly—though not all, of course.

Father Arrupe was extremely nuanced and prudent in speaking about violence, and he made clear his opposition to it. He cited, however, the words of Paul VI in Bogotá about extreme situations, in which Catholics involved in armed violence must take responsibility for their drastic posture with all its consequences. [...] Arrupe also spoke of the feminist movements, recommending that they be hardworking, patient, and "elegant" in their attitudes. He observed that "an institution like the church changes slowly, but I think it is already becoming aware that women should have more say [...]."

As regards the pros and cons of events in Latin America during the past ten years, he pointed to "signs of vitality": catechetics, popular religiosity, the increase in vocations, and insertion among the people; he also indicated some "pastoral failures" regarding the evangelization of intellectuals and political leaders, and the application of the spirit of the council to the traditional families of Latin America.

I conclude—though it was not the final question—by indicating that Arrupe said he was happy to be here and that his invitation came through a letter of Cardinal [Sebastiano] Baggio, who got along well with López Trujillo—about all the rest, he knew nothing. He was concise and prudent, he refrained from negative statements, and he had little hierarchical pomp about him. Nobody could expect Arrupe to "tell stories"—if indeed he had any to tell—and his replies were sufficient. Despite a certain exhaustion that came through in his last statements, the general impression he gave was: This Arrupe is a great fellow! "He's a Spaniard, isn't he?" a Canadian asked me. Well, yes, Spanish. But even so![18]

Thus far the lucid chronicle of Hernando, who also recounts an anecdote that reveals Arrupe's sense of humor. The reporter had not been able to get the complete, rather voluminous text of the final document of Puebla. Since he was returning to Europe on the same plane as Arrupe, he asked the general if he had a copy of the text. Arrupe answered: "Yes, and I'll gladly let you have it. Ah, but take an aspirin also!"

After returning from Puebla, Arrupe passed through Madrid. He went to La Moraleja and celebrated Mass for his sister María, who was seriously ill. From there, he phoned Bilbao to converse with his other sister, Catalina. Once back in Rome, he wrote a letter to his cousin Fernando on February 23, in which he commented:

Certainly, the experience of Puebla has been very interesting, and I think it will be very beneficial for the Latin American church and, by extension, for the whole church. In Mexico, I had a press conference touching on the

---

18   Hernando, *Los pasillos de Puebla*, 199ff. The complete text of the press conference is in *Mensaje*, Santiago de Chile, June 1979.

points that most interested the reporters; it was very well attended and there were a lot of questions. If something gets published, I will send you a copy.

What turned out very well was the Holy Father's visit to Mexico: we don't know how he was able to endure those long days of intense work; on thirty-five occasions, speaking a tongue relatively new for him, he addressed crowds that were almost always huge. They have already published a little book with all the discourses, but it was just a provisional edition, for the occasion. Once they put out a good Spanish edition, I will send you a copy (surely they will soon publish those speeches of the pope there in Spain as well).

I don't remember which photos I sent you, so I send you now a couple more: on the back, they have the dates when they were taken.

I am happy to hear the good news about Catalina, and she tells me she is very grateful to all of you for the way you took care of her during her illness.

With the elections there, God willing, things will calm down, and the new government will be able to deal with the economic and social problems. Above all, it will be able to keep at bay or entirely suppress the terrorism, which is the modern plague of our Western countries.[19]

The Cry of the Refugees

Puebla had a great impact on Arrupe. On November 5, 1979, he wrote a letter to the provincials of Latin America for a meeting they had in Lima. As a "basic idea," he took the following phrase from the Puebla document: "The fundamental mission of the church consists in evangelizing in the here and now with a view to the future." He states in the letter that Latin Americans possess a profound faith that must be "defended, educated, and purified." He insists that, in view of the continent's grievous injustices and inequalities, the preferential option for the poor is a necessity, even though care should be taken that Jesuits not make the economic and political aspects of this option their primary concern.[20]

One afternoon, just before Christmas that year, during an informal conversation with his assistants, mention was made of the dramatic news arriving from Southeast Asia about the "boat people," refugees who were embarking on fragile boats and traveling through the seas of that region without finding any place to land. At one point, Arrupe's eyes lit up: feeling the first call from the refugees, he thought the Society needed to respond immediately to that challenge. The next morning, he sent telegrams to about twenty provincials in the Far East and India, as well as to others in Europe and North America. A few months later, he commented:

The response was really remarkable. We immediately received offers of aid in the form of persons, material, and all types of resources. We also received

---

19   Letter to Fernando Gondra (February 23, 1979).
20   Y. Calvez, *Fe y justicia*, 83.

foodstuffs, medicines, and money. In several countries, efforts were made to use the mass media to influence the respective governments and private institutions that were capable of intervening. Different persons offered themselves both for pastoral work and for organizing work among the refugees.

That was the starting point. The Jesuits began to work intensively in the refugee camps of Thailand, Cambodia, Indonesia, the Philippines, sub-Saharan Africa, and Central America. In the years since then, the Jesuit Refugee Service has extended its work to ten regions of the world that have been most affected by war, famine, and economic distress; it currently has projects in more than fifty countries.

The Resignation

Meanwhile, relations with the Holy See continued to be difficult. John Paul II had not only made his own the document that John Paul I had intended to address to the Jesuits, but on September 22, 1979, he received a group of provincials with the stern words:

> Be faithful to the laws of your Institute, especially as regards austerity of religious and community life, and do not yield to secularizing tendencies. Maintain a profound sense of interior and exterior discipline, and be orthodox in your doctrine. Be fully faithful to the supreme magisterium of the church and the Roman pontiff [...]; and exercise the apostolate that is proper to an order of priests, solicitous for the sacerdotal character of your activity, even in the most varied and difficult of apostolic endeavors.

Though he did not show it, Arrupe was deeply affected by the pope's comments, which only added to his worries. He wrote a letter to the provincials on October 19, asking them to reflect on the pope's comments and to make an examination of conscience concerning the deviations indicated: "All should conform themselves to the pope's desires." He even pointed out the need for explicit self-criticism: "We must conclude that what we have done is insufficient."[21] This was only one of several letters he wrote urging fidelity to the church's magisterium. He addressed a letter, for example, to the US provincials about an ordination ceremony during which a protest asking for the ordination of women was staged: "Although I personally am in favor of legitimate research and theological reflection, I am convinced that protests carried out during an ordination ceremony, or in relation to such a ceremony or any other type of liturgical act, are not a part of such research or reflection."[22] Another case involved the controversy around the book published by US Jesuit John J. McNeill, *The Church and the Homosexual*. Published in 1976, the book was condemned in 1977 by the

21 *Acta Romana S.I.* 17, 3, 641–43; *Información S.J.* 164 (1979): 262–65.
22 Arrupe, *La identidad del jesuita*, 647, 649.

Audience with John Paul II, in which Arrupe was accompanied by the general secretary of the order, Louis Laurendeau.

Congregation for the Doctrine of the Faith for defending "a moral opinion contrary to the traditional and current teaching of the church." McNeill claimed that it was necessary to accord fair treatment to homosexuals in the church, and he unabashedly confessed that he himself had homosexual tendencies, though he evidently did not act on them because of his religious option. The controversy revived when the Italian version of the book was published, something McNeill could not prevent since he had signed a contract with the publisher that allowed the translation rights to be sold abroad. Arrupe was firm in expressing "his profound disapproval of the publication of the book in Italy, without authorization of the church or the author."

At the same time, people around the world were reading with great interest a document that would later be considered a precious part of Arrupe's testament. It was the conference he gave on January 18, 1980, on "our way of proceeding."[23] Analyzing in depth "how our way of proceeding has evolved," it is an excellent study of the way Jesuit identity has adapted to the changing times.

As a result of the pope's September 22 discourse, Arrupe began to feel tempted by an idea: "If the pope does not like my style of governance, then I should resign." At the beginning of 1980, however, a new dimension was added to the panorama. Although the pope disapproved of certain deviations of the Society, he nevertheless decided to name a Jesuit to be archbishop of one of the most important

23   Arrupe, *La identidad del jesuita*, 49.

dioceses of Italy, Milan, where Montini had previously presided. Named to that post was Father Carlo Maria Martini, renowned biblical scholar, rector of the Gregorian, and formerly rector of the Biblical Institute in Rome. His appointment as archbishop effectively removed from the stage one of the most likely candidates to succeed Arrupe as superior general. The nomination caused Arrupe to postpone and shorten his trip to the East, as he wrote to Fernando Gondra:

> I was planning to leave on January 1 for Thailand, India, and Nepal, and to return to Rome on January 21, but the recent nomination of Father Carlo M. Martini, S.J., as archbishop of Milan requires that I stay in Rome to attend his ordination as bishop on the Epiphany. I will leave for India (shortening my itinerary) on the eighth. I commend to you this intention.[24]

During his visit to India, Arrupe appeared to have the same enthusiasm as always, but his emotion seemed to be somehow more spiritualized and detached. He began the trip with a visit to Nobili College, the largest house of formation for Jesuits in the world. The rector, Father Robert Cutinha, had written Arrupe a letter asking him to come, and Arrupe was pleased to do so, answering in English, "I say yes!" The students naturally gave him a spectacular reception. Cutinha recalls with great emotion the Mass the two of them said side by side at the end of the visit:

> He wanted me to preside! And of course I asked him to give me his blessing. [...] Arrupe summed up in himself the Ignatian *magis* with his life, and by living the *magis* he achieved what was "magical": he left a mark on the Society that has made him one of the greatest in its history.[25]

Arrupe also addressed the seminarians of Mangalore. When the rector began by recounting something of Arrupe's life story and elevating him to the skies, Arrupe replied in English:

> I don't recognize myself in the image you have presented of Father Arrupe. I don't feel myself to be a great leader. I feel like a poor man who—I'm not sure how to say it—has been elected general of the Society of Jesus. I try to do the best I can, but I am very conscious of my defects and weaknesses.

He expressed his joy at the seminary's work and gave thanks for it, since training young men for the priesthood was one of the Society's most important ministries:

> It is important for me to hear this, because you will frequently read in the newspapers and magazines that the Society of Jesus, and especially its general, are Marxists who are destroying the church. As someone expressed

---

24 Letter to Fernando Gondra (January 2, 1980).
25 Letter of Robert Cutinha, S.J. to the present author, sent from the Jesuit Refugee Service, Jor Bagh, Delhi, India (October 30, 1986).

it concisely and frankly: "One Basque founded the Society, and another Basque is finishing it off!" Well, you already know what some people think of Father Arrupe.

Then, without defending himself further against accusations, he talked about the work of the seminary, its function in India, and the life of the seminarians:

If you ask me what should be the basic attitude of a seminarian, I would tell you: knowing Christ and becoming a good friend of Christ during these years of training. That way you have everything in your hands! Then you will go about, and you will talk, and the people will say: "Ah, this priest is different! What he says is what he lives!" Then you will have credibility. Because one of the problems in the world today is lack of credibility. Too many words! Too many organizations! But not enough realities. Then you will be men in truth [...]

He spoke to them also of inculturation, which was so important in India, and he explained it carefully:

But please, don't forget that inculturation today does not mean closing yourself off to something; it does not mean enclosing yourself in a culture and becoming introverted. That is suicide. Today a culture must be open to learning, because there is no culture that is perfect, no culture that has all the truth. Each culture must learn by assimilating other values, without destroying its own. So this is delicate work. Besides, today the world is becoming universal. We must be open to the universality of values, while at the same time preserving our own authentic values as much as possible. That is, we must integrate those other values into our own culture.[26]

Shortly after returning from India, Arrupe received sad news. On March 20, 1980, his sister María, his "professor," died. During the days before her death, he was kept constantly informed about his sister's health through telephone contact with Madrid:

Through news received from La Moraleja and from our fathers in Madrid, I have learned that the funeral service for Mother María went quite well and was very consoling. Poor María—she had to suffer so much almost her

---

26 Transcription of a taped recording, published in the bulletin of Saint Joseph Seminary, Mangalore, India. The material was provided to the author by Richard Sequeira, S.J. Its spontaneity and impromptu nature make it one of Arrupe's most beautiful texts, though it is practically unknown. He gave another talk with young people in Assisi in 1977, "The Project of Today's Youth" In 1980, he wrote an article in English that was published in the United States in 1981 with the title "The Heart of Christ, Center of the Christian Mystery and Key to the Universe"; in it, he cites, among other things, Teilhard de Chardin and his theory of Christ as the "Omega point." See Arrupe, *En él solo la esperanza*, 83.

whole life because of her fragile health, but especially in these last years, when she became quite disabled. The Lord will now take account of these sufferings in order to reward her more. I have also learned that Catalina and Isabel, thanks to you, arrived well and were able to accompany their sister in this final hour of her funeral and burial.

Arrupe did not himself travel to Madrid. He loved his family, but at the same time he was detached from it and totally dedicated to his universal work.[27]

Among the speeches made by Arrupe in 1980, two stand out especially. One, delivered at a meeting with Jesuits who were "worker-priests," considered such work to be very proper for the Society in those times, though he put certain conditions on it.[28] The other was a brilliant speech at the Synod of Bishops, whose main theme was the family. Given on September 30 and titled "Our Pastoral Approach to Families in Difficulty," the talk maintained Catholic principles but stressed the importance of realism, understanding, and humaneness in dealing with de facto situations:

> This capacity for "human closeness" and "sympathetic participation" with families in difficulties and the prudent "ability to wait" have always characterized the pastoral actions of the great apostles. They help us to understand that pastoral care is essentially a question of "maturity" and "art," which are the equivalents of clarity of principles and Christian wisdom, respectively.[29]

This was the last synod in which he would be able to participate.

Though the theme of social justice was doubtless the one that caused most conflicts and problems for Arrupe, analysis of his synod presentations and his many other speeches reveals that justice was not his only, or even his principal, theme. His greatest passion was faith, and his greatest concern was the problem of unbelief. This passion and this concern nurtured his tremendous openness to the world and to all topics concerning humankind. On February 8, 1980, he gave an inspiring conference in Rome on "the Trinitarian inspiration of the Ignatian charism," in which he formulated the following prayer:

> The more I feel your inaccessible greatness, the more I feel my own smallness and nothingness, but as I go deeper and deeper into the abyss of that nothingness, I find you at the very bottom of my being, *intimior intimo meo* [more intimate than my most interior self], loving me, creating me, [...] working for me, for my sake, with me, in a mysterious communion of love.[30]

---

27   Letter to Fernando Gondra, Rome (March 27, 1980).

28   "With the Representatives of the Workers' Mission," in Arrupe, *La identidad del jesuita*, 193. See also *La croix*, Paris, September 2, 1980.

29   "Nuestro acercamiento pastoral a las familias en dificultad," in Arrupe, *La iglesia de hoy y del futuro*, 489.

30   *Acta Romana S.I.*, 18, 1, 67–114; and J.A. Garcia, *Orar con el padre Arrupe*, 37–41.

By that time, Arrupe had already made the first consultations about his resignation. Since GC 31 had made it possible for a superior general to present his resignation, despite the lifetime nature of the office, Arrupe was obliged to consult the assistants and the provincials "about the adequacy and the gravity of the reasons for his resignation."[31]

The reason officially proposed was Arrupe's "advanced age," but given the situation, nobody could believe that reason. Arrupe at the time was seventy-three years of age, and he was as healthy as ever. In an audience with John Paul II on January 3, 1980, the pope had declined to specify what plans he had for the Society. Arrupe must have sensed a lack of confidence in the pope's attitude. At first, his closest assistants—the Frenchman Calvez, the Indian Parmananda Divarkar, the Irishman Cecil McGarry, and the American O'Keefe—were opposed to his resignation, but Arrupe insisted. After a week of "spiritual discernment," the assistants ceded. Then came the second part of the procedure: consulting the provincials, who had to indicate their will by a secret ballot. Of sixty-two provincials, fifty-eight responded that the reasons Arrupe gave for resigning were "sufficient." All of this provided Arrupe great consolation, as he confessed to his closest advisors. Juridically, however, the general congregation had the last word. It was therefore necessary to call one.

At that point, Arrupe decided to communicate his decision to the pope, not because he was obliged to do so, but "because of the special bonds by which the Society is linked to him." It was not a question of presenting his resignation to the pontiff, but of informing him of the process that was being initiated in conformity with the Society's internal legislation. Since the pope was not in the habit of receiving Arrupe frequently, he tried to make himself heard through a Jesuit bishop who was making his *ad limina* visit to Rome in those days. Nothing resulted from that overture. He then tried to make contact with prelates close to the pope through a Polish Jesuit: "I have extreme need to see the pope. It is a question of conscience." The pope finally granted him an audience, just as Arrupe was about to fly to Paris, on May 30, 1980. He was accompanied to the door of the papal chamber by his assistant O'Keefe, who remained waiting outside, and he was allowed only ten minutes to explain his intentions. The pope was surprised by what Arrupe told him and interrupted him twice with questions. He then asked the general to halt the initiative. The pope's first question was: "What can I do in this process?" Arrupe answered: "Whatever you wish, because you are our superior." John Paul II commented: "Good." The pope posed a second, more incisive, question at the end of the interview: "Do you think the Society will obey me?" The general answered: "Of course, Your Holiness." He repeated: "Good."

---

31 Decree 41 of GC 31. This decree says nothing about informing the pope of the decision to resign, but it does state that "Father General's resigning from his post is not effective if it is not approved by the Society meeting together in the general congregation."

And that was where it ended. Standing up, John Paul II simply told Arrupe to await his answer. Arrupe's own personal notes mention that the pope seemed worried: "You leave, but I remain here. What am I to do with the Society?" The pope appeared to be concerned about the accusations being made against the order, and he had undertaken his own international investigation. Arrupe waited thirteen days without receiving any further information, and it seemed like an eternity. Finally, a personal letter arrived from the pope, in which he ordered the general to suspend the project of calling the general congregation since he did not "consider it opportune for the good of the church or of the Society." He would speak to Arrupe about it later. It seems that the pope was awaiting more information before making his final decision.[32]

Many were surprised that the pope had asked the general to postpone the convocation of the general congregation; some even speculated that John Paul was at the time seriously considering the suppression of the Society of Jesus, as Clement XIV had done two centuries before, but there is no documentary evidence or basis for this thesis.

In any case, Arrupe continued to manifest his great devotion to the pope. In one of his letters to Fernando Gondra, written in May 1980, he expresses his admiration for John Paul II:

> This year rains have spoiled several of the public audiences the pope gives on Wednesdays. The reason is that so many people come to hear him that no covered locale is big enough to contain the multitude, which has oscillated between thirty and fifty thousand in each audience. But the pope is not deterred by the rain and fearlessly holds fast to the programmed event. Only once, when there was a persistent downpour, did he decide to end the audience after only a few minutes, with an Our Father and the apostolic benediction.[33]

Arrupe was so devoted to the pope that every Sunday, early in the afternoon, he would go down to the corner of Borgo Santo Spirito, where the papal entourage passed weekly on its way to visit the Roman parishes. Arrupe would smile and wave to the pope, though he never received a wave in return.[34] This practice of Arrupe was often observed by his assistant for Spain, Iglesias, who recalls how the general used to ask Brother Tomás Redín, the porter, to advise him as soon as he noticed that the pope was about to pass by.

---

32   See Chinnappan Amalraj, S.J., "Those Painful, Traumatic Moments: Exclusive Interview with Father Vincent O'Keefe," *JIVAN* (*News and Views of Jesuits in India*) (November–December 2003): 25–27; Manuel Alcalá, "La dimisión de Arrupe," in La Bella, *Pedro Arrupe, general de la Compañía de Jesús*, 913–56, here 920–21; Zizola, *La restaurazione di papa Wojtyla*, 107.

33   Letter to Fernando Gondra, Rome (May 3, 1980).

34   Information confirmed in its details by Arrupe himself: he responded "it is true" to my question when I interviewed him in the curia infirmary (July 1983).

So Arrupe used to go down quickly to wave to the pope from the sidewalk, in the middle of the people there. It lasted just a second, no more. I accompanied him many times, along with others, but I know that on some occasions he was alone or just with Brother Redín. One day, when I was returning with him on the elevator, I dared to ask, half-jokingly, why he went down every Sunday. He did not like my remark. He lowered his eyes and went straight to his room. No doubt, my remark hurt him; certainly his silence taught me a lesson.[35]

Meanwhile, life continued on. From May 13 to 17, Arrupe traveled to Cuba, where he had an interview with Fidel Castro, a former student of Belén College, which had belonged to the Jesuits but was expropriated by the government. Arrupe asked Castro to grant visas to some Jesuit missionaries. On the seventeenth, he traveled to the United States, where he visited several provinces. On June 22, the Jesuit priest Joseph of Anchieta, the apostle of Brazil, was solemnly beatified in Saint Peter's. On the twenty-third, Arrupe traveled to Verdú, where celebrations were underway for the fourth centenary of the birth of Saint Peter Claver, the "slave of the black slaves."[36]

In Manresa, near Barcelona, Arrupe had a meeting with the Spanish provincials and then went to visit his sisters, as he later wrote: "You'll understand what a delight it was for me to see Cata and Isabel, since it was the first time we were able to get together since the death of our sister María." He then traveled to Lisbon by car, since the Portuguese airline was experiencing a strike. Back in Rome, he worked with his assistants, who were preparing the provincial congregations, which needed to be held before convoking the general congregation. Finally, on June 30, just before Arrupe was to leave for Brazil, the pope's definitive decision arrived: "Calling the general congregation now would not be for the good of the Society or the church. Neither should there be any convocation of the provincial congregations or the superiors' meetings that were foreseen."[37] Arrupe wanted to prevent the notice from being made public, but leaks to the Italian and Spanish

---

35   Ignacio Iglesias, "El padre Arrupe que voy conociendo," conference given on December 23, 2006 in Villagarcía de Campos, Valladolid, Spain, published by *Castilla jesuitas*, February 2007, 23.

36   In his homily in Barcelona, Arrupe analyzed what it meant to be "slave of the slaves," as Peter Claver defined himself, and he mentioned the violent deaths recently suffered by Archbishop Romero and Luis Espinal. The Verdú event included the presentation of two biographies, one in Catalonian and one in Spanish, both by the author of this book (see Pedro Miguel Lamet, *Un cristiano protesta* [Barcelona: Biblograf, 1980]). I had given Arrupe a copy the day before. The next day, he told me with a smile: "I read it." "All of it?" I asked him. "Yes, of course," he told me in all simplicity. "And thanks for your work!" He had spent almost the whole night reading the biography. Despite all that, he participated with·great vitality and energy in the events in Verdú, the birthplace of the Catalonian saint.

37   *Acta Romana, S.I.* 18, 1, 224.

press were inevitable. The explanatory note sent out by the Society's press office arrived too late.[38]

Premonition of the Test

Two months earlier, Arrupe had made his Spiritual Exercises, during which he discussed his prayer life with Father Luis González, director of the Center for Ignatian Spirituality in Rome. Luis's testimony is of immense value:

> In August 1980, one year before he fell ill, he called me by phone in Madrid, where I was spending a few days before returning to Rome. He told me he was thinking of doing his Exercises around that time and wanted me to accompany him if I could, because he had often recommended the personally directed Exercises to others, but had never done them himself.
>
> Though I tried to decline, since I did not think it necessary, I immediately set out. When I arrived in Rome, he had already started the night before. After supper every day, he would come up to my room and tell me, with admirable sincerity and simplicity, how it had gone for him during the day. He would ask me for advice, and we would agree on the matter for the next day's meditation.
>
> On August 30, since I was very impressed by the conversation we were having, I went to my room and wrote the following lines: "In the evening, conversations with Father Arrupe, he speaks to me of his great consolation when making the three colloquies of the Two Standards and offering himself unconditionally to Christ through the hands of Mary. Great peace. He finds it difficult to *practice introspection* in order to analyze possible deceptions. [He feels] inner consolation in his desire to identify with the sentiments of Jesus Christ and to share in his humiliations. It would be a great merit if he could participate in Christ's abandonment on the cross. He fears nothing. He is ready for everything. He experienced great light, with no possibility of doubt, when he offered his resignation to the consultors. And greater consolation when he saw that it was accepted by the Society. He feels God wants

---

38   The Society's press notice appeared only after the news had already been reported around the world. It said:

> Rev. Fr. Arrupe some months ago took the first steps toward resigning from his post as superior general of the Society, because of his advancing age and all that that supposed, in accordance with the procedures foreseen in the Society of Jesus. His Holiness John Paul II, in consideration of the greater good of the church and the Society, subsequently asked him to suspend the process that had already begun. Father Arrupe received the Holy Father's decision with sentiments of filial availability. This information has been communicated today to all the members of the Society of Jesus.

Press Office of the Society of Jesus, August 1, 1980.

Arrupe and Vincent O'Keefe, in one of the few audiences with John Paul II. "The pope spoke very little with me."

something of him. But he does not know what. He feels ready to obey whatever the Holy Father decides. He recalls the times when he was a philosophy student in Oña, when on leaving the church he felt God telling him: 'You will be first.' He did not know what it meant. He thought he understood it when they made him general. He offers himself in the hands of Mary as a victim on behalf of the Society and the church. With great joy."

Thus far my notes for that day. I recall, though, that the next to last day of the Exercises he revealed his anxiety to me. It was a terrible desolation, such as he had never felt before. He was especially feeling rebellious before the prospect of humiliation. Nevertheless, the last day he calmed down and recovered his habitual calm. But he made it clear to me that he had never before experienced such an intense sorrow and pain. I have always asked myself whether the Lord was showing him the future that awaited him.[39]

This precious testimony of González would indeed be prophetic. It is a document of great value, for it reveals what Arrupe was feeling inwardly in those critical moments. Something of that also became evident in his external behavior.

That same month of August, Arrupe was interviewed for twenty minutes by Antenne 2, the second largest French television network. Among many other

---

39   Information provided to the author by Luis González, S.J., former provincial of Toledo, personal friend of Arrupe, and director of the Ignatian Spirituality Center. He later published the information in an article: "El padre Arrupe que yo conocí," *Razón y fe* (Madrid, 1991): 294–300.

things, the journalist asked Arrupe whether it was true that the pope had once ordered a superior general of the Society of Jesus to be jailed. "Yes," Arrupe responded, "it was Father Ricci, whom they imprisoned here very close to us, in Rome, in the Castel Sant'Angelo."[40] When he was asked about his own relations with the Holy Father, he was clear:

> Well, quite simply, we are always at his service. He is our superior. That is one of the characteristics of our Society since the times of Saint Ignatius, who said that the fourth vow that we Jesuits take, which consists in accepting any mission that the pope wants to entrust to us, constitutes the fundamental principle of the Society's existence.

"So, you say that the vow of obedience to the pope is essential. Yet the pope is, at the same time, both a person and an institution."

"We take the vow of obedience to the Holy Father as the vicar of Christ on earth."

"Yes, but he has a government, and the Society also has its own government. Can it happen that these two governments do not share the same ideas or do not agree with each other?"

> Well, of course. In such a case, we would clearly submit ourselves to the desire and decision of the Holy Father, or else we would represent to him the difficulties we have. That is an old practice, one that allows a Jesuit to 'represent' the reasons that make it difficult for him to fulfill a mission. But in the end the superior's will must always prevail, even when it is contrary to the objections. [...] Saint Ignatius was always very respectful with individuals of the Society and with their opinions. That is why he allowed them to represent their personal reasons.

Arrupe appeared to be speaking of his own case; his words were describing his own future situation.

The French television interviewer continued: "Dominating this room of yours is a picture of Saint Ignatius, and it seems a blend of strangeness and maliciousness. How do you view it?"

"I look at that picture almost every day, and it seems to be saying to me: 'Hey, Pedro, what have you done today for our Society?' [...] And I am conscious that I have to be able to give a response."

"At the present moment, are you optimistic about the propagation of the faith, and if so, for what reasons?"

Arrupe smiled as he replied:

> Yes, I am optimistic, and I will tell you why: because God works over the long haul. Our horizon is very limited. For example, for me, an old crock, life

---

40 Lorenzo Ricci was superior general of the Jesuits when the order was suppressed by the pope in 1773; he was imprisoned in the Castel Sant'Angelo.

is very short. If we look at the history of Christianity, it is extremely impressive, but if we put it in the timescale used by anthropologists and archeologists, life on earth might be 2,300,000,000 years old. On that scale, the history of the Christian religion, measured on a ruler of 2.3 meters, would not reach even the last two millimeters. Despite all the difficulties, the persecutions, the contradictions, the church always advances. For that reason, I am optimistic about the faith advancing, but it will be at a pace that only the Lord can know.[41]

Arrupe's words were broadcast through the stratosphere and reached into the homes of French television viewers. But something more was reaching them: a youthful face that was seventy-three years old, a look that was still brilliant and profound, a bright smile that gave no hint of the deep pain he was feeling: "God works over the long haul"—and amid difficulties and persecutions. In the short haul, however, God had already introduced him into his passion, which was only beginning. "The dark night" was drawing close. There awaited him a long, profound, and terrible calvary.

On November 9, Arrupe would set off on still another journey: India, Ceylon (Sri Lanka), Singapore, and Bangkok. He would spend two days in Madras and eight days in Kuala Lumpur for a meeting of the provincials of East Asia. On November 17, he wrote a letter from Rome to his nieces and nephews, thanking them for their best wishes on his seventy-third birthday. The letter has special value for what it suggests:

> I had you especially in mind that day, as I recalled the long trajectory of my seventy-three years and offered thanks to God for having given me such a good Christian family; I prayed for each and every one of you, so that the Lord may keep you always in good spiritual and bodily health. That day, I also spoke with my sisters by phone, so I felt myself to be closely accompanied by all of you. In Rome, life goes on as usual. I have not yet had the audience that I am hoping to have with the Holy Father, so that I can learn what his thoughts are about my plan to resign from my post and leave it in younger hands. I count a great deal on your prayers, because I need them now in a special way. I send warm greetings to the three of you, and I remember you with great affection. Pedro.[42]

Given his propensity for intense and effective activity, his feeling tied hand and foot this way, unable to move either forward or backward, became an excruciating experience.

---

41   Declarations made to ORTF (Antenne 2), reproduced by *El correo de Andalucía*, August 31, 1980.
42   Letter to Barandiarán-Gondra (Mariví, Fernando, Guillermo), Rome (November 17, 1980).

20. Silence Speaks

Suddenly, no one knows how, the clock stopped. That white sphere, like the one in Hiroshima, no longer had moving hands. Something strange had taken place in his weary brain. Arrupe's hand would not respond. From his lips came only disconnected English phrases. After the uncertain time in the hospital, there was that infirmary room suspended in the air, waiting for eternity.

The interviews, the letters, the trips, the decisions, the hectic days full of activity, the tensions with the Holy See, the meetings with heads of state, cardinals, superiors general, the visits with important cultural and political figures— even astronauts had come to see him. All that stopped. All was empty space. All was whiteness, like that infirmary wall before him.

On the right side of the room was a metal bed painted white and covered with a simple white sheet, and beside that a night table and a small bare stand with a few books on it. On the left was the wall, also white. In front, another white wall, adorned only by a conventional picture of Saint Ignatius and another of Saint Francis Xavier with his chest uncovered, his heart inflamed, and his radiant face lifted upward.

Arrupe had his back to the window, through which poured bright sunlight. His appearance was skeletal and transparent, with an uncanny resemblance to the death-mask of Ignatius. His fine skin had taken on a color between pale pink and violet, and his eyelids had become more pronounced, as if they were protecting him from the world and turning him completely toward his interior realm. The thrombosis had paralyzed his right side and slightly twisted his lip, but not so as to disfigure him. He was hemiplegic and prostrate, but not defeated. Quite visible still was the drive that came from deep in his soul and kept him constantly vigilant.

No longer was there any schedule to keep; there were no meetings with assistants, no traveling here and there, no governance, no assignments, no letters to dictate. The clock had stopped. The only sound was silence.

What had happened to the superior general of the Society of Jesus?

The Last Letters

Like any year, 1981 began with a rush of activities. On February 6, Arrupe delivered a scholarly paper, "Rooted and Founded in Charity,"[1] at the Ignatian Spirituality Center in Rome. This study, along with his previous conferences on "our way of proceeding" and "the Trinitarian inspiration of the Ignatian charism,"

---

1   "Arraigados y cimentados en la caridad," in Arrupe, *La iglesia de hoy y del futuro*, 727; and "Inspiración trinitaria del carisma ignaciano," in Arrupe, *La identidad del jesuita*, 391.

completed a trilogy of essays on the spirituality that gave rise to the Society and maintained it.

At the beginning of 1981, there was also some controversy about a letter Arrupe had written the previous December, in which he responded to many questions about "Marxist analysis." He wanted to dialogue with those who thought that it was possible to distinguish between the social analysis of Marxism and its ideology, with the idea of making use of the former and prescinding from the latter. In the letter, he wrote:

> It seems to me that in analyzing society we can accept a certain number of methodological viewpoints that more or less arise from Marxist analysis, provided we do not grant them an exclusive character. Examples of this are the consideration of economic factors and property structures [...]; sensitivity to the exploitation of entire social classes; consideration of the role played by class struggle in history (at least in many societies); consideration of the ideologies that may be used to disguise certain interests and even injustices.

But Arrupe also expressed some hesitation: "Nevertheless, in practice the adoption of 'Marxist analysis' rarely means adopting only a method or a 'focus'; it generally means also accepting the substance of the explanations given by Marx about the reality of his time." Among the particularly unacceptable elements pointed out by Arrupe were dialectical materialism, the interpretation of class struggle, and the Marxist concept of history. At the same time, Arrupe was just as firmly opposed to those who wished to take advantage of such reservations about Marxism in order to reject or to catalog as "communist" the mission to which the Society had pledged itself, namely "the commitment to justice and the cause of the poor, the defense by exploited people of their own rights, and all just causes." He asked: "Have we not frequently noticed forms of anti-communism that are nothing but means for covering up injustice?" He also warned against another line of thought "surreptitiously spread" among Christians: "The social analyses that are usually practiced in the liberal world imply an individualistic and materialist worldview, which is equally opposed to Christian attitudes and values."[2] In this twofold criticism, Arrupe was in a way anticipating the posture of John Paul II in his social encyclicals, which call into question both Marxist collectivism and extreme capitalism.

As Ivern points out:

> Arrupe's critical position with regard to liberal capitalism, which in a way places him in an intermediate position between Marxism and economic liberalism, is quite pertinent and relevant in our day. Arrupe must have rejoiced there in heaven when he heard about the letter on "Neoliberalism

---

2   "El análisis marxista," *Acta Romana S.I.* 18 (1980–83): 331–38; and in *La iglesia de hoy y del futuro,* 151ff.

in Latin America," which the Jesuit provincials of that continent wrote and made public in Mexico City in 1996.[3]

Although the context was very different, the reasons that gave rise to this letter were very similar to those that had moved Arrupe to write his letter on Marxist analysis more than sixteen years before. Both Arrupe's 1980 letter and the 1996 letter of the provincials mention two elements that are required in any analysis in order to avoid a priori suppositions that would prejudice objectivity. One element is being able to identify and assess scientifically the serious limitations of those social, economic, and political systems, such as Marxism in its day and neoliberalism today, which aspire to exercise hegemony and are often inspired by principles and values that Christian faith cannot accept in their entirety. A second element indicated in both letters is the importance of being able to discern and to utilize the positive elements that may be found even in philosophies and ideologies that are seriously flawed.[4]

Arrupe's readiness to dialogue with Marxists was bound to bother certain sectors, especially those that did not view him with much sympathy, not to mention those that disliked him intensely. As was its custom, the press reacted with distorted readings of a text that was nuanced, but quite clear in its meaning and intent.

Meanwhile, Pedro was concerned for his sister Catalina, who was gravely ill. On April 16, he wrote to his other sister:

> Dear Isabel, I received your card on March 26, in which you tell me about Cata's state of health. I am sorry that she has had this new crisis so that she is experiencing moments of anxiety and her memory is confused. No doubt that is the result of her age; you will have to have much patience during this time, until she improves a bit, if God grants us that. I pray to God much for you both: for Cata, so that God restore her to health and the full use of her faculties; and for you, so that he help you to be patient and strong in these difficult moments. I am very close to you in my prayer.[5]

Arrupe wrote again to his two sisters on April 29, by which time Cata's health was a little better; she was getting out of bed to do some exercise and spoke of her deceased sister María. Arrupe told of visits he received from family friends:

---

3   The letter on neoliberalism in Latin America, published in *Promotio iustitiae* 67, no. 2 (May 1997): 43. Arrupe's judgment regarding neoliberalism in this letter is as severe as his earlier judgment regarding Marxism. The letter states that the economic and political behavior inspired by the neoliberal economic system reflects "the limits of a culture inspired by a conception of the human person and society that is foreign to the values of the Gospel."

4   Francisco Ivern, "La carta sobre el análisis marxista," in La Bella, *Pedro Arrupe, general de la Compañía de Jesús*, 837.

5   Letter to his sister Isabel (April 16, 1981). Gondra–Barandiarán Archive.

"They have even brought me *Santiaguitos*." These caramel candies from his native land—along with chocolates—were known to be one of the minor "weaknesses" of Arrupe, though he always promptly shared them with everybody else.

Arrupe also mentioned an important meeting in this letter:

> On April 13, I had another audience with the pope, who was very friendly and kind, as always. We talked for a long while about the Society, and the pope expressed his desire that we continue such discussion in our next conversation. He is very interested in everything about the Society.[6]

The general panorama was not all that bright, however, and the impatient, energetic Pedro Arrupe was discouraged by the obstructions being placed in the order's path. A half-year had passed since his previous meeting with the pope. With all his heart, he wanted to be able to clarify matters in new conversations with John Paul II, who at the time was quite concerned with Poland. That country was in great turmoil due to the *coup d'état* aimed at avoiding a Soviet invasion, but there was also the promising emergence of the Solidarity workers' movement. Another meeting between Arrupe and Wojtyła finally took place on January 17, 1981. On this occasion, the general could speak at length with the pope and explain in depth his reasons for wanting to resign. Still, the meeting was tense. Arrupe knew from different sources that the pontiff had been gathering confidential information about the Jesuits through the nuncios. He asked Arrupe who would possibly succeed him, but the general said he did not know who that might be. The conversation ended inconclusively, since the pope did not reveal any concrete plan for the order and proposed yet another meeting with Arrupe. Arrupe drew one clear conclusion from the conversation, however: the pope had plans to name his own delegate to guide the future general congregation. This plan naturally unsettled Arrupe, since it was suspected that a non-Jesuit would be named to that post.

The following information, provided by Manuel Alcalá,[7] has been supplemented by reports of the Spanish Jesuit Arturo Martín Menoyo, who accompanied John Paul II on his first apostolic visit to the Philippines, Guam, and Japan. In the land of the rising sun, a key figure turned out to be the Jesuit provincial, Giuseppe Pittau, a man skilled in Italian diplomacy. When the pope paid an unplanned visit to the Jesuits' Sophia University, he was impressed with Pittau's friendliness and effectiveness. On the trip back to Rome, Cardinal Casaroli separated himself from the papal party in order to look after some affairs in Hong Kong having to do with the so-called "Patriotic Church" of China. Accompanying him as translator was the above-mentioned Martín Menoyo, who at Arrupe's insistence questioned Casaroli about the pope's plans concerning the Society;

---

6   Letter to his two sisters (April 29, 1981). Gondra–Barandiarán Archive.
7   Statement of Robert Rush to the author. See also Alcalá, "La dimisión de Arrupe," 927–28.

Menoyo also mentioned to the cardinal possible problems that might arise from naming a non-Jesuit as papal delegate. Casaroli apparently understood the situation quite well; he told Menoyo to be calm and to assure the general that he also should be calm.[8]

Meanwhile, John Paul II continued to gather information about the Jesuits from diverse sources, including several outstanding members of the Society itself, such as Carlo Maria Martini, archbishop of Milan; Sorge, to whom he showed the voluminous report on the order; Molinari, the Society's postulator of canonization causes; and Dezza, the former confessor of Paul VI and a key figure in the drama.

What was the pope's fear? It seems that, besides what he considered to be the order's deviations, he was especially concerned about who would be Arrupe's successor. Would it be the liberal American, O'Keefe, whose declarations had so alarmed people during the pre-conclave? Or would they choose Calvez, the specialist in Marxism, who was thought to have redacted the general's recent letter and whose analysis would not sit well with the anti-Marxist stance of Wojtyła? A third candidate, Molinari, was more acceptable in the Vatican, but he seemed to have fewer possibilities of being elected since he was clearly among those who dissented from Arrupe's policies. For the moment, the pope preferred not to say anything, convinced that the best approach was his unnerving silence, just waiting for conflicts to break out—that was the approach that had worked best for him in Poland when dealing with the communist leaders.[9]

But Providence had its own plans. On May 13, just after embracing a child in Saint Peter's Square and blessing the pilgrims from his white popemobile, John Paul was struck by a bullet fired by Ali A ca. He fell wounded into the arms of his secretary Stanislaw Dziwisz and was quickly taken to the Gemelli Polyclinic. Two weeks later, on the twenty-eighth, while still in the hospital, the pope was grieved at the news of the death of his great friend, Cardinal Stefan Wyszy ski. The pope's recovery was prolonged and required him to return to the hospital from the Vatican because of an infection; he had to undergo three operations, and the subsequent rest required in Castel Gandolfo interrupted the papal agenda until well into the month of August.[10]

Arrupe wrote again to his sister Isabel, expressing his concern for the worsening health of Cata:

> You can imagine how we felt here about the assault on the person of the Holy Father. I was in Villa Cavalletti, outside of Rome, in a meeting with the major superiors of Africa, but I came back to Rome immediately and went to the Gemelli Polyclinic, where the pope is, to find out about his health

---

8   Alcalá, "La dimisión de Arrupe," 928.

9   Alcalá, "La dimisión de Arrupe," 927–29.

10   See Lamet, *Juan Pablo II, hombre y papa*, 229ff.

and recovery. Thank God, he is recovering from the wounds he suffered and from the operation they performed on him. Pray to God for him and for the church.

He added an anecdote with a human touch:

The day before yesterday, I was with Bishop [Luis María de] Larrea, your own bishop. Very kind and friendly. We talked about the *botxo*. He told me that his father had been born in Siete Calles (I thought it was in La Pelota) and that he was baptized in Santiago (like me!). Isa, tell Cata how much I remember her and commend her to God. Both of you do the same for me. With much affection. Yours, Pedro.[11]

In the same letter, Arrupe also mentioned his upcoming journeys. In early June, he went to Ireland and Holland for about five days. From June 26 to July 6, he went to Africa for a meeting with bishops and superiors general about the work of evangelization. At that meeting, Arrupe showed special interest in the refugee question, since Africa had some ten million persons who were fleeing war and famine. He encouraged Jesuits to work with refugees and attend to their needs; he even recommended that they leave aside the more sacramental tasks if necessary. He wrote to his family: "It has been a rich experience. It is an attempt at common action (coordinating the pastoral action of bishops and religious), and it is turning out quite positively. Let us hope that there is the same or similar joint action on other continents." He also noted that he spent the day of his patron saint in Cameroon.

The last two letters Arrupe wrote to his family were addressed to Isabel, one on July 9 and the other on July 23. In both, he announced that the trip would begin on the twenty-fifth: "I leave again for the Philippines, where I will spend about twelve days. There is going to be a commemoration of the fourth centenary of the arrival of the Jesuits in those islands. I ask you to pray much for this intention. I will return to Rome on August 7."

In the same letter, Arrupe asked for prayers for the pope:

Thank you for the news you give me about Cata: I continue to pray to God for her health; tell her that, and tell her that I am asking that she also offer something of her work and suffering for me and for the Society, besides praying also for the Holy Father, so that he recovers completely.

He added a delicate touch for his sister Isabel: "It is well that you continue to go out for a while each afternoon to attend Mass and get a little rest, and that you can sleep peacefully with the help of the Servant of Jesus."[12]

---

11   Letter to Isabel Arrupe (May 19, 1981), Gondra–Barandiarán Archive.
12   Letter to Isabel Arrupe (May 9 and August 23, 1981), Gondra–Barandiarán Archive.

The Swan Song

Arrupe arrived in the Philippines on the afternoon of July 25. He had considered the possibility of making a stopover in Japan, but he reluctantly decided not to do so, in order to concentrate on the Philippines. On the plane, he spoke with Rush, his assistant for Asia, about the possibility of his returning to Japan as a missionary if the general congregation finally accepted his resignation.

Arrupe during his last visit to the Philippines, where he sang at a banquet for two hundred Jesuits. Despite his usual joyful spirit, he was clearly exhausted (August 1981).

"But what am I going to do at seventy-three years of age?" he wondered.

Rush reassured him that he could do much in Japan, above all with the young people. Then, referring to the respect the Japanese have for the elderly, he added: "In any case, Father Arrupe, seventy-three years is just the right age for a prime minister in Japan, right?"

Arrupe laughed heartily, and Rush saw that he was happy.[13] In the Philippines, Arrupe preached in fourteen celebrations, addressed twenty-seven different groups, and participated in another twenty-six meetings during his stay, which also included hundreds of miles of flights in private and commercial planes. One of the principal acts was a conference Arrupe gave at an academic meeting held at the Ateneo of Manila, where he promoted inculturation and interdisciplinary research, and where he once again turned down an honorary

---

13   For his last trip to the Far East, see the account of Rush in *Pedro Arrupe: Así lo vieron*, 54ff.

doctorate. He also gave a homily commemorating the four hundred years that the Jesuits had been present in the islands, and he attended a banquet organized by Cardinal Jaime Lachica Sin, to whom he offered the Society's support. He personally visited and talked with the 380 Jesuits working in the Philippines, including forty members of the China province, who were ministering among the Chinese who lived there.

An unforgettable event was the banquet held on July 31, the feast of Saint Ignatius, with more than two hundred Jesuits from the Philippines and other parts of Asia in attendance. No special program had been prepared, but Arrupe, with complete spontaneity, rose to direct his fellow Basques in the singing of a lively song from their homeland: *Boga, boga.* He then intoned a solo in his still melodious baritone voice. Other songs followed, and the feast concluded with a chanting of the *Salve Regina,* directed by Arrupe himself. The archbishop of Canton, Dominic Tang, who had spent twenty-two years as a prisoner in China, had been invited to the celebration of the fourth centenary, and he expressed the feelings of many, even of those who had not had his experience of prison, when he said: "In thirty years I have not had such a great experience."

Despite the extreme heat and the exhausting program, Arrupe felt relaxed and at home among the friendly Filipinos. Late each night, he would meet together with Rush to plan the next day. He always appeared happy and content. He felt no embarrassment in receiving the garlands of flowers and endless tributes of musical bands, choral groups, students, parents, teachers, Jesuits. Nevertheless, there are photos of this trip in which he appears to be quite exhausted.

On August 5, Arrupe finally departed from the Philippines, leaving behind him much enthusiasm and warmth. He had only one more stop to make: he wanted to bolster his Jesuit brothers engaged in the new mission to the refugees, a charge he himself had commended to the Society in his letter of November 14, 1980. He thus took a TAI International flight to Bangkok, seated between Rush and the Spaniard Iker X. Villanueva.[14] According to Villanueva, when the stewardess asked Arrupe if he would like some champagne, he said with a smile: "I prefer orange juice." Rush took a whiskey, and Villanueva the champagne. They conversed for a while about the problems of Thailand and had their meal together. Arrupe then took a little nap, saying, as was his custom: "I am going to do my duty for the Society."

On the sixth, Arrupe met with the Jesuits who were working in the large refugee camps of Thailand, desolate stretches of land that were fenced off, closely guarded, and even at times bombarded by the Thai authorities. The camps were

---

14   For his stay in Thailand, see the letter to the author of Iker X. Villanueva, who at that time was master of novices in The Seven Fountains, Chiang Mai, Thailand (May 5, 1987). The letter ends with this description of Arrupe: "In my humble opinion as master of three and a half novices, he is one of the greatest generals the Society has had."

packed with hundreds of thousands of Vietnamese, Laotians, and Cambodians who were without a country, without a future, without a hope. Among the volunteers sent by international organizations were the Jesuits, who sought to help those distressed people or simply *to be with them* and to experience their loneliness and their poverty. Curiously, that day was the anniversary of the "hourless day" of Hiroshima.

Those who attended the meeting had the impression that Arrupe not only was interested in concrete matters but was also thinking of more universal projects. The Jesuits there presented their problems to him with frankness; they were especially troubled by their difficult relations with the local church. The archbishop of Bangkok, Michael Michai Kitbunchu, had made known his reservations about the Jesuits who were working in refugee ministries. Arrupe allowed everybody to speak, and at the end he made a prophetic declaration:

> Please don't lose heart. I will tell you something, and don't forget it. Pray, pray a lot. These problems are not resolved through human efforts. I am telling you something that I would like to stress. It is really a message for the whole Society, perhaps my swan song. We usually pray at the beginning and at the end of meetings. Stupendous! We are good Christians! But, if in our longer meetings, say those lasting three days, we were to dedicate a half-day to praying about our eventual conclusions or decisions, then we would obtain, despite all our different perspectives, more lights and more diverse syntheses than we would ever be able to find in books or debates. What we are dealing with now is a classic example: if we are on the front lines of a new apostolate of the Society, then we need to be illuminated by the Holy Spirit.[15]

The talk, which was given in the hesitant and not too orthodox English that characterized Arrupe's improvisations, left a powerful impact on those who were there. Villanueva comments: "As he moved through his text, the style was ever more his own: he had an infinite number of things to say from his heart and only one mouth to express them."

The next day, Villanueva drove Arrupe and Rush to meet with Cardinal Michai. As they traveled in the community's Volkswagen Beetle through the sticky Bangkok heat in mid-afternoon and without air-conditioning, Arrupe commented that they had to "catch" not only what the cardinal actually said but "what he would like to tell them." Upon arriving, they first visited the cathedral, where Arrupe explained: "Yes, we are going to ask the Spirit to help us understand what the cardinal 'wants to tell us.'"

The archbishop was in fact quite congenial and at the same time diplomatic. He expressed his gratitude to the Jesuits, but also expressed his unhappiness with

---

15 "Talk Given by Father Arrupe during the Meeting of Jesuits in Thailand on Their Refugee Apostolate" (August 6, 1981). Transcription of a recorded tape.

some of the activities and positions of those working in the refugee camps. He thought that the Jesuits, "moved by zeal, but ignorant of the delicate internal relations among the different groups involved," had created in the local church situations that were difficult and disagreeable. Arrupe listened attentively and tried to explain certain concrete cases. The talk turned out to be frank and friendly.

As they left, while they were walking through the garden toward the car, Arrupe gave Villanueva an elbow and said to him: "We didn't need the Spirit very much to understand what the cardinal meant to say, did we?"

They concluded that a coordinator was needed for the Jesuit mission, especially with a view to improving communication with the local church. They then went to visit Bishop Yves-Georges-René Ramousse, the former apostolic vicar of Phnom Penh, Cambodia. On the way Arrupe asked Villanueva: "What are you going to do with Vichai?" He was referring to a Thai scholastic who was about to begin his theology studies.

"Well, I don't know. We are waiting for a visa from New Delhi, if there are no further difficulties."

"Send him to Rome, to the Gesù," Arrupe rapidly responded.

"But this is already August."

"It doesn't matter. I'll take care of it myself!"

Thus did Vichai, the second Thai to become a Jesuit, receive his assignment from Arrupe in the streets of Bangkok. This was the last assignment Arrupe would make. In Rome, the superiors at the Gesù had to invent an extra room in order to accommodate the young Asian. It was just one more example of Arrupe's swift, intuitive style.

That day ended with a Eucharistic concelebration followed by a supper, during which all the events of the trip were discussed. When some Jesuits insisted that the work with the refugees should be independent of the bishops, Arrupe disagreed: "We have come to serve and collaborate with the local church."

At the airport, Arrupe looked exhausted. The eleven-hour flight to Rome on the Boeing 727 went normally, and Arrupe was able to sleep. When he woke up, he had some breakfast, and Rush asked him if he wanted to see the movie they were showing. Arrupe answered that it wasn't worthwhile paying for the earphones. When Rush told him they were free, Arrupe took them. The movie was the Australian film *Breaker Morant* (1980), about the British repression of the Boers in South Africa. He liked the movie, though he commented that the "Australian" was rather difficult to understand.

Later on, Arrupe said, "I have a bad headache. I will try to sleep."

The Great Test

A little later, about 5:30 in the morning, the plane landed in the Fiumicino airport. There, Arrupe tried to grab his suitcase, but his hand would not respond.

Paralyzed by a thrombosis, Arrupe spent nine years in the infirmary of the curia, where he suffered his "dark night" in peace and silence.

"I'll take it," Rush told him. Waiting for them were the Spanish brother, Luis García, and the Canadian priest, Laurendeau, general secretary of the Society. Arrupe gave them a friendly greeting in English, which surprised them. They got in the car, Laurendeau up front with Brother García, who was driving, and Arrupe and Rush in the back seat. They talked about how hot it was. Then Arrupe began to utter unconnected words, and the three other Jesuits decided: "Quick! Let's get him to the hospital!"

Arrupe, who was conscious, consented. Brother Luis accelerated the car in order to cover as quickly as possible the thirty-two kilometers that separated them from the Salvator Mundi hospital, where they arrived just before 7 a.m.[16] The medical personnel gave Arrupe oxygen without delay. A rapid examination turned up a clear diagnosis: cerebral thrombosis. The test done later with the computerized thermographic scan confirmed this diagnosis and determined that the cause was an embolism that had originated in the left carotid artery. With the general's full consent and at his request, Father O'Keefe administered to him the sacrament of the sick that same day, August 8.

On June 26, Arrupe had written in a personal letter:

As the years go by, it is necessary to take better care of one's health. I myself am planning to spend part of the month of August resting a little; starting July 25 (when I leave for the Philippines), I will leave the normal administration of affairs in the hands of Father O'Keefe.

---

16   Statement of Robert T. Rush to the author.

The trip to the Far East had allowed him very little in the way of vacation, and now his illness would deny him the opportunity to put into practice the sound advice he had given himself. Now there would be neither work nor rest. The clock had stopped again.

On August 10, in the presence of his assistants and the secretary Laurendeau, Arrupe with hesitant speech designated O'Keefe as vicar general for the duration of his illness. The Constitutions of the Society of Jesus (no. 786) allow the naming of a vicar general when the superior general has lost the use of reason, has become totally incapacitated, or "has contracted an incurable illness and is so sick that he cannot attend to the affairs of his office."

Robert White, a neurosurgeon from the United States, confirmed the diagnosis of his Italian colleagues. According to the doctors, it was necessary to wait two months before arriving at a more certain verdict. During the month that Arrupe remained in the clinic, Mass was celebrated daily in his room. He followed the liturgy quite consciously and did so also with other prayers, such as the rosary and the divine office.

On August 20, Arrupe, still in the clinic, received a visit from Cardinal Casaroli, who had sent his car beforehand to pick up O'Keefe. The cardinal had with him a personal letter from the pope, originally written in Polish. During the visit, which lasted fifteen minutes, Casaroli asked O'Keefe to read the pope's letter aloud to the sick man. Arrupe wept several times, unable to respond to the words of praise offered by the cardinal—he only said, *Non posso parlare* (I cannot talk). The interview ended with O'Keefe asking the cardinal to bless the general.[17]

The text of the letter the pope addressed to Arrupe is as follows:

Most Reverend Superior General of the Society of Jesus:

The news of your illness has caused me to be gravely concerned. Now the latest information foresees that you will be able to leave the clinic in the next few weeks, and so you will find yourself more or less in the same situation of convalescence as myself, here in Castel Gandolfo, after three months of hospitalization.

During this time, I have prayed constantly for the intentions of the Society, offering to God my daily sufferings for this intention. Recently I have added a very special intention for you.

In reality, I cannot forget all the things we have discussed in our conversations together, especially in the most recent ones. We have a responsibility before God: a common responsibility and also a responsibility proper to each of us, you and me.

During my own illness, I have always been comforted by the profound conviction that the infirmity itself, more than anything else, will serve to set the course desired by God and our Lord Jesus Christ.

17   Alcalá, "La dimisión de Arrupe," 934.

I am certain that you also will find in your illness a similar light.

I conclude by expressing to you my desire for every grace and, at the same time, my sincere hope that the Holy Spirit will help us carry forward, in the way God wishes us, the cause that God has entrusted to our human weakness.

With my apostolic blessing.

Castel Gandolfo, August 27, 1981

JOHANNES PAULUS PP. II[18]

As they drove through the streets of Rome on the way back to the Vatican, Casaroli made it quite clear to the vicar O'Keefe that the pope did not want the general congregation to be called and that he was thinking of a provisional arrangement for the order. Judging by Casaroli's tone and diplomatic language, O'Keefe understood that his being named vicar, though constitutionally correct, had been questioned in curial circles, no doubt because they did not approve of his character.

On September 5, Arrupe was transferred to the Jesuit curia and accommodated in the austere infirmary; his simple room was similar to the ones occupied by other sick and elderly Jesuits. He subsequently experienced a slow process of recovery. The main difficulty he had was in moving his right hand and articulating words, especially complete phrases; he had also lost his memory of proper names. He still understood all the languages he had learned, but could express himself only in Spanish, and that rather poorly. He began to take small steps in the course of intense sessions of physical and speech therapy. On August 26, O'Keefe sent a letter to the whole Society informing about the general's health and about the telegrams received from John Paul II and Cardinal Casaroli.

Meanwhile, things were moving forward in the Vatican. On October 6, the council of the general assistants met with O'Keefe, who had written to the provincials on October 3 about the possibility of calling a general congregation to choose a successor to Arrupe in accord with the Constitutions, given the irreversible nature of the general's illness. He added that he was keeping Arrupe informed and that Cardinal Casaroli was aware of what "the Institute of the Society prescribes for such cases."[19]

That same day, October 6, while O'Keefe was meeting with the general assistants, the brother who was porter of the house received a telephone call announcing that Cardinal Casaroli would come at twelve noon bearing a message from the pope and that he should be taken to Arrupe's room. The cardinal did not ask to speak with any other Jesuit in authority. Despite this, O'Keefe received the cardinal at the door, accompanied him to the elevator, and led him to the room of the sick general. Casaroli courteously asked the vicar general to leave the room, since he wished to be alone with Arrupe. The visit lasted only a few minutes, and

18   *Acta Romana S.I.* 18, 2, 397.
19   *Acta Romana S.I.* 18, 2, 617–18.

Visit of Mother Teresa of Calcutta.

without saying a word, Casaroli made his way to the door and left. When O'Keefe returned to Arrupe's room, he found the pope's letter lying on a small table. The general was weeping.

Brother Rafael Bandera, who acted as nurse for Arrupe, later revealed that he had refused to leave the room when Casaroli asked him to; he alleged that he could not leave an incapacitated sick man alone. Arrupe at first seemed happy that the cardinal was interested in the state of his health, but his joy was cut short when the pope's letter was read to him.

What did that letter say? After sympathizing with the general's pain and distress, the pope referred to the matter of Arrupe's resignation and to his own desire to prepare the general congregation more carefully together "with you,"[20]

---

20   Manuel Alcalá reports:

> Apparently, the first papal plan had been to decree *special powers for Arrupe and to appoint Giuseppe Pittau*, the provincial of Japan, *as his extraordinary assistant.* Both men would convoke, preside over, and guide the congregation, according to the pope's own instructions. News of this plan, subtly alluded to in the papal letter, as will be seen, was published in the newspaper *ABC* of Madrid by José L. Martín Descalzo, in a column titled "Wave of calumnies," with the purpose of countering the press campaign against the order. The journalist had been well informed by Cardinal Vicente E. Tarancón, who in turn had been informed by the acting secretary of state, Eduardo Martínez Somalo. The papal decree was to have been published soon after Arrupe's return to Rome from his trip to Asia on August 8, 1981. Because the thrombosis of Arrupe frustrated this plan just before it was to be put into effect, the pope decided it was no longer opportune to put the matter off and so had recourse to a *second plan*, which would center on Paolo Dezza.

Alcalá, "La dimisión de Arrupe," 936.

something that had not been possible because of his long stay in the hospital. He went on:

> Therefore, after long reflection and prayer, I have decided to confide the task to a delegate of my own choosing, who will represent me more directly within the Society, will attend to the preparation of the general congregation, which should be called at an opportune moment, and will jointly, in my name, have supervision of the Society's governance until the election of the new superior general.
>
> To that end, I name as my delegate to the Society of Jesus Father Paolo Dezza, in view of his long experience of living and governing in the Society, and at the same time I propose that he be assisted by Father Joseph [*sic*] Pittau, whom I met in Japan and found to be a diligent superior of that religious province. His function will be to help the delegate in the exercise of his functions and to substitute for him when he is absent or in some way impeded. More particulars about the functions of the delegate and his coadjutor will be indicated in a complementary document.
>
> I trust that the Society of Jesus will be able to recognize in these decisions a sign of my affectionate regard for your person and of my sincere benevolence toward the whole Society, for I earnestly desire that its greater good redound to the benefit of the whole church, in which the same Society carries out such a broad and diverse ministry.

He ended the letter with a desire of "copious graces for you and all the Society of Jesus."[21]

In this way, John Paul II, using his sovereign authority, interrupted the constitutional process of the order and named Father Dezza as his "personal delegate" with plenary powers. Since Dezza was already eighty years old, he was assigned a coadjutor, Pittau, who until then had been provincial of Japan.

When he left the infirmary, Casaroli was not sure whether the sick man had understood the letter. When O'Keefe went to the general's room, however, he found him weeping and asking to be taken to the infirmary chapel. In his personal memoir, still unpublished, the infirmarian Bandera states:

> It was a very difficult moment, but Don Pedro demonstrated what he had been and what he was. After the cardinal read him the letter (both of them were nervous), Don Pedro did not understand much. He asked me to read it to him again, after the cardinal had left with Father O'Keefe. He wanted to know it all, more peacefully. Then, when I finished, as if by an interior impulse or a call of the Spirit, he said to me: "Take me to Father Dezza." And I answered him: "No, you are the general; Father Dezza will come here." And

---

21   *Acta Romana S.I.* 18, 2, 399–403.

so it was. I tried to tell him something, I don't remember exactly what, but I do remember that he answered: "God wants it so; may his will be done." I noticed in his face, after Father O'Keefe left, a sort of transformation; I heard him saying: "God has his ways. He is great." About thirty minutes went by (I think he was suffering greatly), and then his face and his eyes became again as they always were: he smiled with serenity and a profound peace.[22]

Some informants claim that a parallel letter addressed to Dezza contained a series of additional dispositions, such as not making the change public and not accepting the resignation of any major or minor superiors—"superiors are to be obliged under holy obedience to remain in their posts." There was uncertainty about this final point. The pope also advised his delegate to go about preparing for a new general congregation.

Although the news was not supposed to be released to the press until October 31, there was no way to stop the leaks. The media offered biographical sketches of Dezza and Pittau. Regarding the former, they stressed his advanced age, the fact that he was nearly blind, and his ideological stance within the Society. In the general congregation of 1965, he had supposedly been the one whom the conservatives wanted to be superior general. He had also been the confessor of two popes and was especially close to Paul VI. He maintained close contact with the office of the Vatican secretary of state. Although at the time he was officially retired, Arrupe never removed him from responsible positions in the curia; he was the general's "admonitor," the person who was supposed to point out Arrupe's defects. Feeling overwhelmed by his nomination to be the papal delegate, Dezza made a vain appeal to be excused from it.

Pittau's case was different. Born in Sardinia in 1928, he was made rector of Sophia University in Tokyo in 1975 and subsequently became provincial of Japan. John Paul II met him during his trip to Japan in 1981 and, as we have indicated, was quite impressed by the Jesuit, who had served as his interpreter and guide. The pope also discovered there in Japan new dimensions of the Society of Jesus, such as its university work, which he had never before seen up close.

The news of the nominations fell like a bombshell. Public opinion considered the papal maneuver to be "unprecedented" and compared it to the suppression

---

22 *Diario inédito y autógrafo del Hermano Rafael Bandera* [Unpublished personal diary of Brother Rafael Bandera], Archivo Histórico S.I, Andalusia province, OpNN A2 (twenty-three handwritten folios, some of them typed out in Rome, March 17, 1991; others that appear to be hurriedly taken notes). Bandera was born in Malaga on October 20, 1936, entered the Society as a coadjutor brother at the age of nineteen (December 14, 1955), and made his final vows on February 2, 1967. He was the infirmarian of the curia from 1968 to 1992 and then returned to his province of Andalusia. The Little Sisters of Mary Immaculate subsequently took charge of the infirmary. Bandera died suddenly in Malaga on May 27, 1995 of a massive heart attack. He was the uncle of the famous actor Antonio Banderas, who for artistic reasons added the "s" to his surname.

of the order in the time of Clement XIV. Others recalled the reaction of Clement XIII when the French government asked him to name a special vicar for the Jesuits in France: the pope refused to do so, uttering the famous phrase: *Sint ut sunt aut non sint* (Let them be as they are, or let them not be).

The first reactions within the Society were naturally of dismay. What had happened? The decision was not difficult to understand for those who had followed the progressive build-up of tensions and who had read the statements of Paul VI and John Paul. On the one hand, the conservative wing kept up its pressure. On the other, the Jesuit archbishop Martini of Milan and the Carmelite archbishop Anastasio Ballestrero of Turin were said to have interceded with the pope, trying to dissuade him from taking the measure, or at least trying to ensure that the "delegate" was a Jesuit and not someone from outside the order. It was also said that the Spanish prelate who was acting secretary of state, Eduardo Martínez Somalo, had had decisive influence in the process, as he would later have also in controversial dispositions regarding other religious orders, such as the Franciscans and the Discalced Carmelites.

Some of the mass media were interpreting the Vatican measures as a discrediting of Arrupe's policies. For example, the British weekly *The Tablet* went so far as to call the measures a "brutal insult" to one of the holiest and most beloved Jesuit generals since the time of Ignatius. In the Federal Republic of Germany, a group of eighteen Jesuits, among them the great theologian Karl Rahner, addressed a letter of protest to the pope, which included statements such as the following: "Even after much prayer and meditation, we have not found it easy to recognize 'the finger of God' in this administrative measure, for our faith and the experience of history teach us that the highest authority of the church is not immune to error." For the provincial of the French Jesuits, Henri Madelin, the decision was a "test of our faith," but he insisted that

> what is happening right now is outside the normal functioning of the law by which we are governed. Does not our law already foresee the legitimacy of the Father General's resignation, the expression of our communities' lives through provincial and general congregations, and the general's naming of a vicar when he unexpectedly suffers from incapacity for a time?

Nevertheless, Madelin recommended to his own subjects that they remain calm:

> I am profoundly convinced that the Society will be judged in the eyes of many by the kind of discretion we practice in response to what is happening, by the way we undergo the test that is proposed, and by the degree of unity that we are able to maintain.[23]

---

23 See newspapers of that date and photocopies of the cited letters. The letter of Karl Rahner and the eighteen Jesuits is found in *Il regno attualitá* 2 (1982): 8–11. See also Woodrow, *Los jesuitas*, and Zizola, *La restaurazione di papa Wojtyla*.

Arrupe with Brother Roger Schutz, prior of the ecumenical community of Taizé, and a group of youths from the community.

Similar letters were written by the North American provincials, who asked Dezza for clarification of juridical matters. The elderly delegate answered that the measures affected only the central government of the Society, the postponement of the general congregation, and the functioning of the delegate and his vicar. The authority of other provincial and local superiors was to continue as before.

The provincial of Spain at the time was Iglesias, formerly the assistant for Spain, the country where sentiment against Arrupe was strongest. Iglesias exhorted the Jesuits there to abide by the papal decision "in a spirit of faith and obedience" and to give the testimony that was expected of them. At the same time, he prohibited all commentaries and appearances of any sort that would affect public opinion.[24]

Meanwhile, the acting secretary of state, Martínez Somalo, had confidentially transmitted news of the decision to the Spanish cardinals Marcelo González of Toledo and Vicente Enrique y Tarancón of Madrid, insisting with the latter that the pope's letter had been a *capolavoro* (masterpiece). González was delighted that "at last the Society was being called to task," but Tarancón responded: "It's by no means a *capolavoro*."[25]

History gives evidence that the Society, despite its detractors, once again obeyed in a mature fashion—the response was adult, reasoned, and loyal. Even the papal delegate's assistant, Father Pittau, would later comment on the Jesuits' response:

---

24 *Información S.J.* 76 (1981): 182.
25 Letter of Cardinal Tarancón to the author. See also Alcalá, "La dimisión de Arrupe," 940.

These last months have been for the Society a time of very deep spiritual experience. The pope's intervention has been an exceptional act. The naming of the delegate and an assistant delegate was unprecedented in the 450 years of the Society's history. I can state with pride that the Jesuits have received this intervention of the Holy Father graciously. There has been talk of defections of Jesuits and of resignations of provincials and superiors who refuse to serve under this extraordinary regime. Nothing of the sort has taken place. I can assure you of that, because I read all the letters that arrive from all over the world: there has not been a single request to leave the Society that was motivated by the Holy Father's intervention. No provincial superior has asked to resign from his post [...].

Naturally, that does not mean that all have applauded this intervention. Many have been profoundly hurt by it, many have asked why it happened, and many have seen it as an opportunity for reflecting more deeply on our apostolate and our vocation, but the attitudes we have been able to observe have basically been reactions of filial obedience, Ignatian obedience. [...] After reading all these letters, I can say that the behavior of Jesuits has been dictated by faith and the spirit of obedience, but also by the profound desire and the hope that the Society's governance will return quickly to its normal functioning, and that the general congregation and the election of the general will take place as soon as possible.[26]

Diary of a Sick Man

Meanwhile, Arrupe kept up his struggle to recover the use of his faculties. In the first days of December, he was again visited by American neurosurgeon Dr. White, who consulted with two Italian colleagues, Emmanuel Occhipinti and Nick Musacchio, who was Arrupe's primary physician. Some improvement was noticed, and surgery did not seem indicated, even though a Doppler scan detected an occlusion in the left internal carotid artery. Arrupe was walking with difficulty and put great effort into his exercises, though at times he felt discouraged and frustrated. He could move about holding on to the arm of Bandera, the exuberant brother infirmarian from Malaga, who spoke a halting mixture of Andalusian Spanish and Italian.

During this period, Bandera was impressed by Arrupe's "joy and internal serenity, which flowed out of him effortlessly." The infirmarian's journal goes into detail:

When I used to go into his room just to look at him and spend a few minutes beside him, my whole inner being became peaceful. God had given him that charism: giving peace and spreading it by his great faith and love of Christ

---

26   *Información S.J.*

and the Society. [...] He felt humbled in the depths of his being when I had to wash him, change him, etc. [...] I used to watch him out of the corner of my eye; I would sing and talk to him in the most natural way possible. He would look at me and smile with such serenity as if to say: "Continue, for God wants it so." In the first years, that is, starting in December 1981, the two of us prayed the rosary together. After the thrombosis, he couldn't speak clearly, just uncoordinated words, but he said the Ave Marias and the Our Fathers well, and his face used to change. You could see he had a great devotion to Mary. We always prayed the rosary together, every day until 1985.

Don Pedro was easy to take care of; he did not get impatient with anything. Eating was martyrdom for him; he allowed himself to be fed like a small child. Whatever I did for him, he would smile and look at me intensely. Often, I used to provoke him by saying: "Don Pedro, do you feel like flying to heaven?" He would look at me as if I were someone who could help him fly there and would tell me, "Yes, yes," with great joy. [...] When he heard about someone in the community or elsewhere dying, he would fall into a great silence and would shed small tears; I felt helpless. All I dared to do was ask him: "Are you envious?" And as always, his expression would change and with great certitude he would tell me, "Yes, yes."

Another of Don Pedro's virtues, which for me verges on perfection, was his great devotion to the church and the Society. Whenever an article I knew he would enjoy came out in some journal, I would read it to him. He used to cry with such peace that he moved me with his tenderness, all the more so if I read him something about Jesuits in different parts of the world. His joy would be such that he would not even blink. I believe that he was thinking of those distant countries he used to visit, where Jesuits were working.

In the evening, at 6:15, I said vespers with him. It was another moment when his face was transformed. I felt great devotion, sometimes even with tears. God was there, and I could feel it. When I would begin the Magnificat, I'd feel that something was happening to him: he breathed more strongly, his heart was really beating. I used to say this prayer with him until the week before he died. It was a wonderful experience. What grace the Lord has given me!

My happiest moments of staying with him were when I felt some sadness for my faults or my misunderstandings. Then I would sit on the floor and place my head on his knees, and after a few minutes I would lift up my head and look at him. I felt that something had happened in me, because my whole interior being was changed; and he would look at me with such affection, even as he placed his left hand on my head and smiled at me. [...] (That was until the end of 1986.) [...]

Another experience I had, one shared by Father [Antonio] Egaña, occurred in November of 1981. Don Pedro had (what seemed to me) a vision like the one on the Cardoner, as our holy Father Ignatius had.[27] Don Pedro was crying; it was not like other times he wept, from depression, no; it was a crying and a laughing from consolation. He was saying clearly: "God, Mary, the Mother of God wants it so." This lasted almost an hour. I could not resist, but was affected by it and cried along with him; that was when I called Father Egaña. He stayed with him, and I left them alone.

Father Egaña confirmed for me what I was already thinking. He had seen clearly his situation, his cross; in a word, he fully accepted the Lord's will: it was an interior motion that made him see clearly.[28]

Some members of the curia wondered whether such an experience had not been an effect of the medicines, but there was no doubt about the mystical spirit of peace and acceptance with which Arrupe lived out his long illness.

On November 14, 1981, his seventy-fourth birthday, Arrupe attended a festive celebration in the recreation room and heard a recital of songs sung by a group of young Jesuits. The party was very enjoyable and included a telegram with best wishes from the pope. The infirmarian recalls it in this way:

I took him there in a wheelchair; he felt happy and lively, as if he weren't sick. What is more, he let them dress him in a beautiful black silk kimono. As they were putting it on him, he said to me, "We're going to make them laugh with this outfit," and he himself laughed heartily. He was in the hall with all the community after the meal and had some of his birthday cake. The photos are worth seeing.

The next day, when he no longer had the kimono on, the young people from the Gesù came to see him. How Don Pedro enjoyed that! That night, he felt very happy: "These are the Jesuits of tomorrow." In those words, I captured something of his inner being, something I can't explain.

I can also say that for Don Pedro the holy Mass was like the air he breathed; it was everything for him. On the night of December 24, 1981, he told me that he wanted to go down to the church; he wanted to concelebrate with *his* community. I tried to dissuade him, but I could not (God rewarded me afterward). Around 11:30, I woke him up, and I prepared him with an alb and a stole. We went down to the church; he was praying in silence in his customary way, something he always kept up during his long illness: he was in deep recollection, with his head inclined to the left. At the moment of consecration, he raised an arm as concelebrant, but he couldn't keep it up, it kept going down. The smile he gave me made me weep. It will not be easy to

---

27 Bandera is referring to the illumination that the saint received in 1522 beside the Cardoner River in Manresa, when, as Ignatius relates in his so-called autobiography, he experienced "an illumination so great, that everything appeared new to him."

28 Bandera, *Diario inédito y autógrafo*.

Private visit of the Spanish royal family to the embassy near the Holy See (April 8, 1983).

forget. It was an exhausting night, but he felt spiritually charged by it. God was with him, and he had been with his community.

All the Masses were like that. He appeared to be beyond himself—some thought he was sleeping, but no, it was not so. Rather, his recollection was such that he was not aware of what was happening around him. At the moment of Communion, however, Don Pedro would raise his head; he was there awaiting his Lord. That was how it was every day, except the eleven days just before his death.

Was there some defect, some weakness in the man? The infirmarian confesses that he could find only one: "His taste for chocolate, around four in the afternoon. I used to say to him, 'Do you want a glass of water?' 'No,' he replied. 'Do you want some chocolate?' 'Yes,' he responded. 'Well, then, drink the glass of water.' And he would." And there is the amusing anecdote:

Don Pedro was a great believer, which is to say he believed wholeheartedly in all that had to do with the church, but did not believe so much in other things (I mean unimportant things). For example, once a brother came from Japan who claimed to have the gift of healing. Well, he wanted to lay his hands on Don Pedro. So there you have this brother, quite happy and content, carrying out his role in all seriousness. And there was Don Pedro, with his head to one side, dying of laughter. I had to leave the room. I couldn't take it, watching the efforts of that brother and the warmth that Don Pedro showed him, even though highly amused.

Bandera also tells of Arrupe's reaction on one occasion when the brother made a mistake:

> He never complained about the food. Everything was going well. I remember that once I made a mistake and put salt in his milk instead of sugar. When I gave him the first sip, his wide open eyes told me clearly: "How bitter this milk is!" And we had a good laugh.

We have already seen that Arrupe never kept any gifts for himself, and that trait persisted even in sickness, as Bandera makes clear:

> Even in the infirmary, his generosity was constantly making him give away everything he had. One episode was like one of the "little flowers" of Saint Francis: Brother Luis Sánchez, of the Loyola province, came to Rome to substitute for Brother [José Luis] Ruiz during vacation; he brought along for Father Arrupe a canary and a package of asparagus from San Adrián, Navarre. Father Arrupe liked the canary and had fun with it. When the brother left after a few days, he gave the canary away to a brother in the house. And I could never get him to eat the asparagus. He asked me to give it as a gift to the physical therapist.

During the meeting of the Union of Superiors General, which was held in Rome on November 28, the pope made mention of Arrupe, who was still president, and he also congratulated Father Dezza, who had just turned eighty. Both Dezza and Pittau met frequently with John Paul II, who was now very intent on receiving news of the Society firsthand; he authorized a meeting of provincials for the following year. On December 3, the feast of Saint Francis Xavier, Arrupe wanted to go in his wheelchair to the celebration of the fiftieth anniversary of the Historical Institute, which was located in the building next to the residence of Jesuit writers. Meanwhile, the doctors allowed him to receive visits from friends and well-wishers, whom he greeted with his left hand and a forced smile.

On the last day of the year, the pope had the custom of visiting the Jesuits' church of the Gesù and meeting with the city government of Rome, but that day John Paul II wanted also to visit Arrupe personally. He had previously informed Dezza and Pittau of this wish in one of the audiences.

The fragility and emotion with which Arrupe greeted the pope has been forever immortalized in a photograph. Father General—which he still was nominally—received the pope with these words: "Holy Father, I renew to you my obedience and the obedience of the Society of Jesus." The pope responded: "Father General, sustain me with your prayers and your sufferings."

Bandera recounts:

> I can give testimony that for Father Arrupe it was a marvelous encounter. The pope spoke little, saying only (I was present in the room): "What we

have talked about cannot be mentioned." I believe that Don Pedro's look said it all: "I am the same, the one who has obeyed you and continues to obey, the one who loves you and whom you have made extremely happy with your visit."

But that was not all. The Holy Father John Paul II ate with the community. Father Arrupe did not agree to return to his bed until the pope had left our house. Thus he asked me (it was 9:15) to take him down to the entrance; he wanted to thank the pope personally for the visit. The Holy Father told him jokingly: "At this hour, a sick man should be in bed." That night, Don Pedro slept as he had never slept since August 7, 1981. I had a hard time waking him up.

After his visit to the general curia, which was relaxed and informal and included an exchange of gifts, John Paul II commented: "Just as I have been quite edified by the Society for some weeks now, so also I feel edified by this meeting today."[29] After this visit, Arrupe decided to dictate a text to be read in the next meeting of the provincials.

Meanwhile, the governance of the papal delegate was characterized at every moment by his prudence and moderation. Far from giving the Society a 180-degree turn, Dezza convoked the superiors and listened to them. On February 23, 1982, the eighty-six Jesuit provincials met at Villa Cavalletti, where they enjoyed an experience of dialogue and freedom as they discussed the general state of the Society. The text that Arrupe wanted to address to them was read during the meeting. In it, the superior general affirmed that he was happy and content, that he felt that the pope loved the Society, and that for him the Holy Father's decisions and desires were an expression of the voice of God. He stated that the interpreters of those desires were Fathers Dezza and Pittau, in whom he had full confidence. And he ended with these words:

> I repeated to the Holy Father that I love the Society and that I offer my life and my silence for it, content and convinced that this is the path by which God leads me. It is the only thing I can do to help the Society progress in seeking to follow God's will as closely as possible. This is my role. And my desire is that in the Society there be a great spirit of unity, and that the Society be ever more intimately bonded to the church.[30]

On February 27, the Pope, having had supper the night before with the delegate and his assistant, received the Jesuit provincials in the Vatican. With intense emotion, he told them: "This situation, undoubtedly unusual and exceptional, has required an intervention, a *test* that has been accepted by the members of the order in a truly Ignatian spirit." He urged the Society to continue in the

---

29   Bandera, *Diario inédito y autógrafo.*
30   *Acta Romana S.I.* 18, 3, 788.

Arrupe's nephew and niece, José Ramón de Arrupe and Miren Karmele Aizpuru, at the infirmary in Rome (May 22, 1983).

"diverse forms of its traditional apostolate, which still preserve their value," and he asked for increased interest in the initiatives especially recommended by Vatican II: ecumenism, the problem of atheism, and a deepening of dialogue with non-Christian religions. With regard to the promotion of justice, the pope insisted on the properly sacerdotal aspect of this commitment; it was to be carried out through service "that is not that of a doctor, a social worker, a politician, or a union organizer." He spoke of the need for integral formation and for "soundness and purity of doctrine," and he recalled the bond that unites the Society with the Roman pontiff and that extends also to the college of bishops and the departments of the Roman curia. (Some interpreted these words as an extension of the fourth vow to the whole hierarchy.) He ended his talk by giving permission for the convocation of the general congregation,

> which not only should give the Society a new superior general, as our venerated Father Arrupe has for some time desired, but should also give the whole Society a fresh impulse for carrying out its mission with a renewed spirit, in line with the hopes of the church and the world.[31]

With these words, the pope returned to the idea of his predecessors, that the Society is a touchstone of the church's vitality.

But this is a story from which Arrupe was now rather removed. His more ordinary reality was that of profound solitude, emptiness, the mystery of a life that appeared to be truncated. And we should recognize the reality without disguising the facts: Arrupe's final decision as superior general of the Society, which was to resign and designate a vicar, had been invalidated by the pope, who had

---

31   Discourse of John Paul II (February 27, 1983). *Acta Romana S.J.* 18, 3, 721–35.

intervened in the order's constitutional process by naming as his own delegate for the Society a man who did not share Arrupe's ideas. Even though Dezza and Pittau acted in admirable fashion, Arrupe was receiving the hardest blow of his life: it was the *kenosis*, the emptying, the reduction to nothingness, both physically and spiritually.

Despite all this, Arrupe was conscious that he continued to be general. Accordingly, during a Eucharist celebrated just before the meeting of the provincials with the pope in 1982, he sought to communicate with them as best he could, using signed notes. The occasion was the seventeenth anniversary of his election on May 27, 1965. In a homily read by Pittau, Arrupe stated:

> In this declining moment of my life, I feel closer to the Lord whom I have served. I leave all my deficiencies in the infinite mercy of his heart, feeling assured of his understanding and love. In the long hours of my forced inactivity, I am able to contemplate unhurriedly my past and my present. I thus strive to cooperate with divine grace in the process of constant purification and conversion that I have repeatedly recommended to the Society.

He recalled for his sons his last two apostolic commendations, which he left as testaments: refugees and young people, especially those addicted to drugs.[32]

From that time on, Arrupe's world was reduced to his infirmary room. Bandera, who closely controlled visits, wrote this in his diary:

> Normally, when someone asked to see him, the first thing I did was ask if they knew him; I did not want them visiting Father Arrupe just out of curiosity. So sometimes I refused. [...] Well, the father, I noticed, made a great effort to smile, and he looked very intensely at people—he gave me the impression that he was trying to guess whether the visit was sincere or simply out of curiosity. Afterward, he would shut his eyes, because he suffered much from this type of visit. He felt most happy when the visitors were Jesuits, especially when they came from far away and it had been a long time since they had seen one another. That was a great joy for Don Pedro, a party.

Confidences of a Sick Man

Conscious of Arrupe's difficulties in expressing himself and his problematic recovery, I asked superiors in July 1983 for permission to go to Rome and converse with him, with the aim of finishing my long cherished project of writing this biography. The papal delegate allowed me to interview the sick Pedro in order to collect information for the present book. At the same time, I was asked not to make myself very visible in Rome, lest my work appear to be supporting Arrupe's line just as his successor was about to be elected. I began my interviews

---

32   *Información S.J.* 180 (1982): 114–16.

with Arrupe on July 11, and for twenty days I visited him whenever his health permitted: one hour a day and sometimes two, when he requested. Most of the information I obtained in these meetings is incorporated into this biography. I have also included some impressions recorded in my diary[33] that help to situate Arrupe in this difficult moment of his life. Also, since circumstances have changed since the book's first edition, I here include certain details that it did not seem prudent to publish at that time.

In a prior interview, Pittau warned me that Arrupe was a sick man, so that his declarations needed to be understood in the light of the depressed state in which he naturally found himself. My impression was that Pittau was worried by what Arrupe might tell me. Furthermore, it was not easy to deal at first with his primary caretaker, Brother Bandera, who from the infirmary corridor would sharply tell me: "No!" From that moment, I knew that if I was able to "seduce" the brother, I had my work half done. Bandera told me that Arrupe was suffering a lot, that he could not defend himself, and that in 1981 he had a sort of vision, which was mentioned above.

But Arrupe was enduring great pain, but otherwise he was the same as ever: sweet, slight, at peace. There was light in his eyes and strength in his personality, just as always. In that first interview, on July 11, he told me about the illumination he had had in Oña, the time when he felt that "everything was new," so that he wrote to his superiors: "The Lord has given me a bright light."

My main difficulty was in trying to understand his speech. To remember proper names, he had to make an enormous effort and use circumlocutions. When unable to pronounce particular names, he chose special names for some of his closest associates. He called O'Keefe "Jesus." Every once in a while, he would become sad and say: "It is very difficult, very difficult."

I tried my best to create an agreeable atmosphere. I would tell him: "Father, you remind me of Saint Peter Claver in his final days, when he was at the mercy of a slave in Cartagena." When I reminded him that he still transmitted joy and that in time people would understand him, he replied: "Yes, but difficult, very difficult." That first night, I noted down:

> Outside was the garden. But now the garden is no longer his. He lives without freedom, in the hands of a kind but despotic nurse, who likes to appear in the photos and who, to his credit, is aware that the most important thing in his life is this episode of being Father Arrupe's nurse.

Early the next day, July 12, I interviewed O'Keefe, who received me while a reporter from *Paris Match* was taking photos of him. Hanging on the wall were a

---

33 Since the circumstances have changed since 1989, when I was unable to publish some of the details of these interviews, I now include parts of my diary that I left out then (Pedro Miguel Lamet, "Diario autógrafo" [unpublished diary, Rome, 1983]).

stuffed monkey and a poster of Charlie Chaplin's *The Kid* (1921). We discussed what might be the most convenient moment to publish the book. O'Keefe found the Holy See's attitude incomprehensible, especially the fact that Casaroli and Martínez Somalo had not even come to visit Arrupe. He also mentioned that they had marginalized Arrupe during a concelebration at Vatican Radio and that Casaroli had said to him in the Gesù: "Everything turns out very strange." O'Keefe felt that Bandera was assuming too much authority, though he also agreed that Arrupe should not be available for declarations to the press.

In my second interview with Arrupe, I found him happier. Little by little, the preparation for these encounters and the memories of his youth brought joy to the emptiness and silence that he was experiencing. We recalled the years of Bilbao, his parents, his medical studies in Madrid, his vocation. He became excited when speaking of the Virgin and his love for Mary. He insisted to me: "Enrique Chacón knows everything." He had fond memories of his old friend and fellow housemate in Madrid, who would later become a Jesuit also.

On July 13, I found Arrupe very communicative and alert. I had the sensation that he enjoyed remembering the old times. Even so, he sometimes found it difficult to express himself; he was grateful when I would recount his life on the basis of his own memories. He would then smile and exclaim quite clearly: "Very good, very good." We dedicated the day to his formation years in Loyola, Oña, Marneffe, and Valkenburg. He spoke with special emotion of his first Mass and the very long time he spent celebrating each Mass after that: two, three, even four hours. He told how, from five o'clock in the morning on, he would also hear the Masses of the others from the choir loft. He confided: "The Mass and prayer are the same thing for me." He also told me that for him the most fascinating thing was the human heart and that "there was no difference between the spiritual and the human." We then recalled his experience in prison and his arrival in Yokohama. In telling of that, his eyes became dreamy and he wept. Then, as if losing himself in time, he cried out: "Very beautiful, very beautiful. I was alone. Most of them were Germans."

The impact of this communication was so strong that he was overcome again by the melancholy of a sick person lost in emptiness: "I am alone, terrible, terrible; I am no use at all. I used to speak five languages, and now I cannot express myself in Spanish. Everybody treats me kindly, but in my depths I am alone, alone." And he repeated: "Terrible, terrible!" He confided to me: "I was always a happy man, I was always content"; in Oña, he saw everything as new; in Cleveland, it was like a new birth; and Japan was for him a great grace, where he felt himself to be "one with Jesus Christ."

At night, oppressed by Rome's heavy heat, I conversed with Brother Juan Martos Vera, the assistant infirmarian, a quiet and simple man. He told me that he had never heard from Arrupe's lips even the slightest criticism of the pope. He commented that Bandera might be exaggerating in the matter of the vision, since that day Arrupe had just been injected with barium contrast. He also blamed Bandera for the departure of a nun who was helping them and whom Arrupe liked a lot. But he concluded, "From a medical viewpoint, he has stabilized. He is a man of God."

The next day, July 14, we spoke about Japan, his experiences of inculturation, and his work in Yamaguchi. Don Pedro laughed like a boy as he evoked that epoch that was so creative for him: the gymnasium in Yamaguchi, his experience with Zen, and his practice of archery. To try to show where his arrows ended up, he made an effort with his bad hand and laughed with delight. He told of concrete experiences, such as those recounted in earlier chapters. In speaking of the prison, he repeated with wistful eyes: "Very beautiful, very beautiful." And he added: "The war period was very important. The Japanese see the person; they value the person more than theories." What is important for them is knowing that "that person is a friend." I asked him what the Japanese experience had done for his prayer. Was his prayer active or passive? He answered: "Everything at once, everything." There were moments when he forgot about his illness and, delighted by his memories, laughed like a little kid.

In fact, on July 15 I had evidence that my conversations with him were somehow serving as a kind of therapy for his infirmity. He spoke to me of his novices: "They were patient, but at the same time impenetrable. It was necessary to undo the concept of God they had, in order to lead them to a greater God. When they discovered him, they felt great amazement." I asked him if his contact with Zen had helped him to deal with the trials he would later experience in governing the Society, and he answered: "Very much, very much. It is a self-control that requires years of practice."

Afterward, we spoke of the explosion of Hiroshima. He got excited recalling the two hundred-pound Jesuit who was thrown from a window into a hallway by the bomb's expansive wave. Once in a while, he expressed regret at not being able to communicate better. I told him that when he got excited about something he spoke much better, and I made him aware that he was getting better at mentioning some proper names. We laughingly recalled how he created a bike tire from a hose and how he was accustomed to rising before the roosters. He told me that he had already said Mass before the bomb exploded. As I was leaving, he told me to take not one but two pieces of candy from the tray by his door.

On July 16, I found him more downcast. He was very moved by his memories of specific persons who had been affected by the bomb blast. He repeated over and over: "It was something unique! How beautiful, Father!" But it was clear that he was very interested in speaking of more recent years: "Here alone with God, alone, alone [...], everything broken, everything useless!" I told him that many people from around the world considered him a prophet of our time and admired him greatly. He would then smile and with pained detachment exclaim: "I see everything clearly."

Arrupe with his nurse, Rafael Bandera, paying a Christmas visit to the Astalli immigrant center in Rome (December 27, 1982).

"You mean now? Have you had some illumination in your sickness?"

"Yes, everything is clear. I see a new world. To serve God. Everything for the Lord."

"And before, in difficult times also?"

"Yes, I was convinced. I felt that a light was guiding me. We have suffered much."

I reminded him of some of the difficult moments in the Society's relations with the Holy See, and his attitude was a mix of simplicity and enlightened spirit; he was like one who is wise and perfectly conscious of the situation. He confessed that Paul VI had a better understanding of the Society, though he had also made the general suffer. He said that John Paul II did not look him in the eyes, as can be seen in the photos. When I reminded him of the times that he used to go down to the entrance of the curia to greet the pope, who did not return his greeting, he confirmed the fact, but he did so with a gesture of great delicacy and simplicity and without the least resentment. That night, I wrote in my diary:

> I cannot doubt that he is a saint. I am conversing with a saint, an enlightened man who is living out his calvary. Today he told me that those who never understood him now come to see him and are "very kind," but he said he knows perfectly well what they are thinking. "I have always spoken with everybody." I feel that this has been a very important conversation, that he is experiencing a solitude permeated by light, and that God is acting through him.

At the end of the page, I wondered when these lines might get published.

The next day, Sunday, July 17, we continued to talk about his period as superior general. I gave him my pad so that he could write down some dates with his left hand, but he had great difficulty in doing so. We spoke of his program of governance after being elected, of his first letters, of his vision of "communal discernment." He told me, "That is old now; it is already something accepted. It is what Saint Ignatius would do today." When asked what should be the preferred ministries of Jesuits, he insisted on the refugees and the world of those affected by drugs. Since he could not find the appropriate expression for the latter, he managed to express it by making a gesture of smoking and letting his head drop down.

Arrupe then placed his hand on his chest and referred to the great option of GC 34: "My feeling was: today something completely new is beginning. I was sure of it. I had not the least doubt. A new era was starting up, a new value. What a beautiful thing!" I commented on how the option for justice was mentioned in many of his speeches and letters and how he, even during the council, had spoken about dialogue with the world. "Yes," he said, "and at that time many of the council fathers were saying: 'What nonsense!' But I felt free. I knew: 'It is of God.' Now everybody agrees with it." He smiled, as if feeling great spiritual pleasure, and added: "We were beginning something that would have great consequences."

When I brought up the topic of his way of governing the Jesuits and his great respect for the person, he commented: "I can command in only one way. I am not authoritarian. I would explain things to people, and they would have to decide."

Arrupe laughed when I mentioned that some persons considered him "Marxist," and we recalled those who had died for faith and justice, above all in Latin America. At the mention of Archbishop Romero, he said: "A very good friend, a very good friend of mine." I then reminded him that, whenever he was convinced of something, he had a powerful influence on people. With impressive simplicity and firmness, he answered: "Yes, that is true."

At that moment, a young Japanese woman arrived to visit Arrupe. She seemed to be made of porcelain. His eyes turned into a smile, in a curious sort of oriental sympathy. He understood perfectly what she was telling him in Japanese, but he could not speak it. For that reason, I had to serve as an interpreter from Spanish to English, so that she would understand his answers. He gave her a gift and would not let her kiss his hand; rather he kissed hers.

On July 18, while I was on my way to the infirmary, I came upon Father Pittau, who thanked me for the way I was helping Arrupe with these interviews—for the first time in quite a while, Pedro was manifesting a desire again to go out somewhere.

During the conversation that day, Arrupe insisted on the need for dialogue between superior and subject so that they could know one another better. To that end, he explained, it is very important to know how to engage in dialogue; each person's way is very different. Every person has problems and at first does not want to deal with them. The superior–subject relationship is a process that little by little sheds light. We then spoke of the decrease in vocations and the growth of small communities, which in his opinion should be diverse. We spoke also of the importance of prayer, which he defined as "the path to find the truths of one's own life. There are many paths, but all are the same thing in different forms. The most important thing in life is communicating with God." Here he was referring to a homily he had given on the Sacred Heart.

We went on to discuss the schools and the many changes they had under-gone and still had to carry out. We recalled the strong adverse reactions he had met in Valencia, about which he commented firmly, but with a smile: "The reac-tions against me didn't bother me. Much has been achieved, above all in the Third World countries, where the Catholics are a minority but have a multiply-ing effect." He then spoke of the Ignatian *magis*, his favorite word, and the radi-cality of the Spiritual Exercises: "Yes, because everything is there."

At that moment, Rush, his former Asia assistant, appeared; it was Rush who was traveling with him on the day he suffered the thrombosis. Arrupe arranged for me to have an interview with him and spoke of him warmly: "This father is very good and knows a lot." I witnessed once again how lavish he was with affec-tion for everybody.

Since he did not have a speech therapy class that afternoon, Arrupe asked me to return to see him. He then spoke about the Union of Superiors General, over which he had presided for many years:

> We did a lot of things together until last year. It has been a very important labor. We have witnessed marvelous things during these years of change. Despite the difficulties, religious life has been taking form. Cardinal Piro-nio has worked quite well and quite closely with us. We were conscious of a close relationship, and we were in agreement on everything. We used to meet every six months, study a problem, and then meet together with Piro-nio. There are some splendid persons among the major superiors. The most important thing was the adaptation to the council, and that has already been achieved. The meetings were marvelous. John Paul II does not know much about active religious life. He had no experience of it and does not know it well. Today, there are no difficulties between the orders and the congrega-tions; there is a perfect union.

Then, to indicate that he wanted to speak of Central America, since he could not articulate the name, Arrupe asked me for pen and paper to draw a map of North America, and he indicated the lower part. "It is admirable how they have dealt with the difficulties in Central America," he said. He thought that the ques-tion of the priests in the Nicaraguan government was a "delicate matter."

We then spoke of Opus Dei, and he smiled. "I have always got along well with Monsignor Escrivá and Don Álvaro del Portillo. The latter wrote me a letter.

Arrupe with the archbishop of Milan, Jesuit Carlo Maria Martini, who had just been named cardinal (February 2, 1983).

At the beginning, I had several meetings with Escrivá," he said, but he did not want to tell me anything more.

I kept asking him insistently, "Were they serious meetings?"

"Yes, they were serious. I think I succeeded in communicating with him."

"Is it true that on some occasions he would not receive you?"

"I don't know, I don't remember. Once, he told me that he thought that little by little the difficult relationship between Opus and the Jesuits was passing. He thought we were at a better moment."

"What do you think of the 'personal prelature'?"

"It is something new, but it is not exactly what they were looking for at first. It is equivalent to the exemption that a religious order has."

We dedicated our discussion of July 19 to his activities as superior general, which have been amply described in this book, and I asked him what his principal hobby was. "Dealing with people," he replied. I told him that he was an avid student of psychology and knew much about human beings, and he laughed.

After being named general, Arrupe decided to visit the countries that were less known to him, especially in Africa, Asia, and Oceania. He practiced a governing style based on personal relations and immediate contact, which was complemented by his overall perspective from Rome. He said that he was especially interested in Latin America and had made only one and a half journeys to Spain: "I knew the country well, and as a Spaniard I didn't want to favor it." I joked about how his concept of patriotism is rather different from that of the Polish pope, and he laughed again.

At one point, my frayed watchband broke, and Arrupe told me with great interest: "You have to ask for another one." Our conversation was interrupted several times. The nurse, Brother Bandera, entered several times, appearing very nervous. Arrupe dispatched him with some kind words. Then the provincial of the Philippines arrived, asking for his blessing. Arrupe gave it and then took the provincial's hands and kissed them. He seemed happy.

On July 20, Bandera tried to scare me off at first, but I soon regained his confidence. I found Arrupe with a great desire to talk, but he asked me to excuse him since he was going to take a little walk along the corridor with the nurse and then receive a visit from some nuns. When he returned, we talked again of Latin America, an area he had gotten to know well over many years, from the time when he traveled there as provincial of Japan. He mentioned Fe y Alegría, the great social work carried out by the Jesuits there. As regards Jesuit involvement in politics, he did not want to make a global judgment, saying simply that "it depends on the concrete situation in which they live." Violence was not justifiable, he said, except perhaps in very particular extreme cases; Jesuits should rather promote constructive dialogue. He considered that Medellín "had done much good, was more forceful and original than Puebla, and had taken some very positive steps." With regard to the Puebla conference, he reminded me that Cardinal Pironio had defended him against the accusations of López Trujillo, but that he had personally been reluctant to defend himself in his press conference. He recalled with much enthusiasm that encounter with reporters: "I always wanted to get along well with everybody," he said. He said that at Medellín he always associated with Câmara; he felt that Méndez Arceo was also very good in his own way, but with many difficulties.

That afternoon, Arrupe attended a celebration with a group of Japanese in the small chapel of the curia. The visitors displayed a great capacity for concentration, which endowed the rite with an air of deep recollection. Pittau presided and preached nicely in Japanese; tears came to his eyes when he spoke of Arrupe. At the end, Arrupe said a few words in Spanish. The whole time he was blushing with emotion. Mr. and Mrs. Moriwaki, children of friends of his, were celebrating their wedding anniversary, and a nun was renewing her vows. Arrupe said that he could hardly speak, but he was very thankful for their presence. The situation was painful, very emotional, full of contrasts.[34]

On July 21, Rome was aflame with heat. We spoke about his ideas regarding mission and inculturation: "The concept of mission has changed, but our principles must be clear. It is necessary to present the Gospel with all its force, but adapting the formulation according to country and culture. The Japanese, for example, can only be approached on a one-to-one basis." He thought that China was still impenetrable. His visits to Russia, mentioned earlier, could only be a question of presence. He felt passionate about Africa for its energy and its newness.

Unexpectedly, Bandera called me on Arrupe's behalf in the afternoon: since he had no class, he wanted to converse again. We began by speaking of the Virgin Mary, and his face glowed: "Very beautiful!" he exclaimed. He recalled the death of his mother and how they used to pray together as a family; they had special devotions in the month of May, and every Saturday they offered something to Mary—it could be any small sacrifice, for example, dessert. He recalled the congregation of the "Luises" in Madrid, with Chacón, Llanos, Ayala. He said that his preferred devotion was to Our Lady of La Strada. Saturdays were always his favorite days for dedicating more time to prayer. "And now, still more?" I asked him, and he laughed. He recalled how during the novitiate a short Marian anecdote was read aloud each Saturday:

> Mary is very united to Jesus, is one single thing with Him. In Japan I used to speak of Mary only with the more initiated. My love for Mary continues the same as ever. Now I have more time to pray. I pray the rosary five or six times a day. The Virgin is very important for Jesuits.

We ran through his favorite saints: Teresa; John of the Cross, whom he had translated into Japanese; and of course Ignatius and Xavier.

Arrupe named the three contemporary Jesuit authors he read most: Rahner, de Lubac, and Teilhard de Chardin. He pointed to a book on his table: a biography of Teilhard in images. He also told me that he had numerous books of humor in his library.

---

34 Also mentioned in the above cited *Diario inédito y autógrafo del Hermano Rafael Bandera*: "The Mass was very emotional. [...] I wondered about the meaning of those profound looks and the great respect on both sides. I can also add that it will not easily be forgotten."

The Roman heat was unbearable. Arrupe noticed that my shirt was sticking to me. As I was leaving, he touched my back and called out affectionately: "Poor man!"

Indeed, the heat of the city was becoming more stifling by the day. The temperature did not go below 30 degrees Centigrade, and the humidity was oppressive, which no doubt especially affected a sick man like Don Pedro. On July 22, we continued our conversation, concentrating on his relations with the popes. He insisted: "I have always done what I thought I should do before God." He repeated that he felt great confidence in relating with Paul VI, with whom he did not show the least reserve; the relations were quite normal, especially toward the end. "With Cardinal Villot, it was more difficult, but Paul VI loved the Society and read our journals. He was an intellectual, very interested in culture. But Benelli made some very tough interventions. He was a typical Vatican diplomat." Suddenly his face lit up, and he confided to me how he felt during the difficult meeting he had had with the pope in the course of GC 32. He said he had held back his tears as he wrote the text dictated to him, but he broke down weeping as soon as he was outside:

> I could not comprehend that attitude, for interiorly I saw things clearly. The next day, I addressed the fathers of the congregation. It was a precious thing. I told them: "Look, I have this letter from the pope. Does anyone have anything to say?" Nobody raised a hand. I then invited the fathers to concelebrate a Mass, and I preached to them on the joy of obeying. In a few minutes, I was calm.

When I left Arrupe that day, after he had confided so much to me, I went to kiss his hand, and he pressed mine all the more. At several moments, he might have cried had I not distracted him with jokes. And he stipulated: "You will have to see how much of all this is publishable."

On July 23, we touched on the topic of atheism. He was most concerned about "practical atheists." He recalled that Severo Ochoa, the Nobel Prize winner who was his professor in Madrid, had declared himself a non-believer. "He has progressed a lot," he said. Indeed, Ochoa had visited Arrupe during his illness and had expressed his admiration for him; even this "non-believer" wanted to kneel down to receive the blessing of his friend Pedro. Brother Bandera relates the encounter thus:

> It was an occasion of joy when on October 6, 1981, the Nobel Prize winner Severo Ochoa came to visit. He called him "Peru." Don Pedro was smiling and felt very happy; he was even more so when at the end of the visit Ochoa, along with his wife, asked him for his blessing. It was quite wondrous to behold how Don Pedro, grasping his right hand with his left, gave them his blessing; his face irradiated peace.

Arrupe, seated between Paolo Dezza and Rafael Bandera, presenting his resignation as general at GC 33; the delegates gave him a prolonged ovation (September 3, 1983).

Arrupe was so moved by that visit that he later asked Bandera to call the Vatican to get information about the congress in which Professor Ochoa was participating, since Arrupe "desired his conversion."[35]

As with the topic of atheism, Arrupe believed that dialogue was very necessary regarding theological censorship:

> I speak to [the theologians] with simplicity, expressing the way I feel, but I never try to convince them or force them. It is difficult to get a clear picture of the situation in the church. The attitude of silencing or severely censoring is harmful. I have got along very well with the theologians, for example, with Karl Rahner. They can be requested to insist on the forms or to change their styles. But in the present situation silence is imposed, as happened with Teilhard and de Lubac. You have to obey and have faith.

He put his finger on his lips to indicate that it was necessary to keep quiet, and he signaled over his shoulder with his thumb, toward Saint Peter's Square.

In the afternoon, a photographer came by from *Paris Match*. Like an actor, Arrupe pretended to be speaking fluently, in order to appear natural before the camera, but his words were not intelligible. Later, he tried to explain to me the story of another doctor friend of his. His words became more confused. Finally, he pointed to the book of his memoirs, and I realized that he was referring to his time in Japan.

---

35   *Diario inédito y autógrafo del Hermano Rafael Bandera.*

The next day, Sunday, July 24, with the humidity reaching ninety percent in Rome, I found him depressed. He was feeling regretful that the interviews were coming to an end, but he was very interested in knowing when this book would appear. Looking over the catalog of the curia personnel, he pointed out to me persons who could give more information. But then his sadness returned: "I am no use for anything." Reading the names of his collaborators in the catalog had depressed him. Now everything was stopped, frozen: "I have only one more month of being general." Once again, there appeared the sick and limited man, the absurdity, the anxiety, his Gethsemane prayer.

On July 25, the feast of Saint James, Arrupe had still not emerged from his sadness. During our conversation, a barber came to give him a shave. His face was contracted with his suffering. I asked him if he felt pain somewhere, and he told me, "The leg and almost everything." The topic of our conversation, the last five years, was especially important, but he spoke with great difficulty, his voice broken and fading. I tried to encourage him but achieved little. Fortunately, he called me back in the afternoon. Bandera had increased his medication, and I was able to round off some valuable information about this very sensitive, simple, and holy man.

The discourse of John Paul I, never delivered because of his sudden death, was described by Arrupe as "severe": "When John Paul II was elected, he received me and asked me about the Society, but in a very general way. He was already worried and had many doubts." He then recounted the process of his proposed resignation and explained that this was not accepted by the pope: "'I don't see the reason for it,' he told me. 'I will have to study it.' Then he gave me no response. After that, he received me twice for twenty minutes. He spoke very little with me."

Concerning his thrombosis, Arrupe recalled only that during the flight he had had a headache. He told me that I should ask Rush for more information about this matter. Regarding his own life, he said that I should ask other Spaniards, such as Iglesias, who was his regional assistant, and Luis González, who knew of his interior sentiments. Seeing him so dejected, I made bold to tell him: "You are a swell guy." He laughed. Then he told me that the naming of Dezza and Pittau was something incomprehensible, that Pittau was coming from Japan and "knew nothing about anything" and that Dezza was visiting him for one minute every three days and telling him nothing.

Many other people were visiting Arrupe, giving him reading and writing lessons and commenting on current events. He was also given speech therapy and physical therapy by Italian specialists. According to Bandera, Arrupe was not exerting himself too much in all this:

I think he suffered whenever the doctors visited him. Since he had studied medicine, he was convinced that he would not get well; as a result, these visits were in a way bothersome. But he always kept a smile on his lips, and those deep eyes spoke unconditional acceptance of what they told him. He was living obedience.[36]

Arrupe declared to me: "I have wanted only to speak the truth frankly to every person, as I saw it before God. I believe deeply in dialogue. But then you keep the secret, and they betray you; the others don't tell the whole truth." He felt perplexed by the situation. He had no clear vision of the juridical questions that were to be considered by the general congregation, and so with a smile he said of himself: "Poor man!" Trying to cheer him up, I commented that many young Jesuits had his portrait in their room. I told him I was trying to write a beautiful book and that this biography would surely help many people. "And who knows," I said, "maybe some day they'll make a movie about you, since your life has been very cinematographic—although it would be difficult to find an actor with a nose like yours!" He burst out laughing and exclaimed, "Man, that is the least important thing!"

Arrupe told me to request some copies of his books in Spain, since he had no copies there in Rome. I noticed that he sensed that I was going to leave him. He told me: "We'll see you tomorrow." I saw that, given what was possible, he had achieved a total sincerity. I mentioned this that night in front of the Pantheon while speaking to Jesús Gómez Fragoso, a Mexican Jesuit historian. He told me: "He is suffering for something great that God is preparing for the Society. Imagine, a man who has loved so much feels all alone; a man who has traveled so much is now immobile." I replied: "Of course there are differences, but he reminds me of Saint Peter Claver at the end of his days, enslaved by the same persons he freed." As we parted, Gómez Fragoso told me: "Make a copy of your diary, so that it doesn't get lost. It may become an essential item for historians."

On July 26, my last day in Rome, I spent time interviewing again Rush and O'Keefe. Rush gave me more details about the final trip to the East and then added: "Yes, I believe that Arrupe is a true man of God and has mystical gifts. It is incredible that he still understands the letters read to him in German and Japanese, but one must be aware that he is psychologically a distressed man."

In the company of Rush, I paid a last visit to Arrupe. He was just finishing his reading lesson, and he looked sad. He asked whether the two of us had had a chance to converse together. As he talked that day, he closed his eyes. He spoke with great effort, out of faith:

> It is necessary to suffer and to offer it up. That is life. God is beyond everything. Always joy in the Lord. My life is being with God. We have to see God in everything. I don't understand this. But it must be from God, from his providence [...]. It is something very special. For me very good. But for the Society? It must be something of God. Once in a while, I feel a very special force.

---

36 *Diario inédito y autógrafo del Hermano Rafael Bandera.*

He confirmed that he had felt an illumination during his illness, when he was in the hospital. Closing his eyes, he turned away and took his rosary:

> This: much, much, much. Until when? I don't know. I hope, I hope. For me nothing, nothing, nothing. [He said this very expressively and with tragic intensity.] Above, the triune God. Then, the Heart of the Lord, and this poor soul. The Lord gives me his light. I want to give all to the Lord. Everything is very difficult. It is what God allows. Something special that he has sent us in very rapid fashion. Blessed is he. May the men be blessed. [By "men," he meant Jesuits.] But it is tremendous, tremendous.

He said this with force, putting great stress on the "r."

I spoke to Arrupe of John of the Cross, whom he appreciated greatly, and of his Japanese translation of the saint's works. I also reminded him of the professor who had helped him with the translation and who, on returning from the doctor one day, had told Arrupe: "I am going to die soon." Arrupe recalled: "It was a most beautiful thing. I was with him, and we recited together the *Spiritual Canticle*. And that was how he died."

When Arrupe spoke again of his emptiness, I told him that all his life had been an act of love and that we loved him and admired him much. I asked him not to be sad and told him that I did not want to leave with that taste in my mouth. At that moment, instinctively, he flashed an immense smile, that famous Arrupe smile, and he said brightly, "Okay, now I am happy. See how quickly?"

In the course of the conversation, the nurse came in, exuberant as always, speaking his blend of Andalusian and Italian. In a loud voice, as if outdoors, he declared: "Well, Father, I have already made the purchases: 260,000 liras! Too much money, no?"

When the brother had left, Arrupe smiled with intelligence and understanding: he was above it all. When Bandera returned later to take him for a walk, I asked Arrupe for his blessing and knelt down. He closed his eyes and, grasping his paralyzed right hand with his left, he traced a crooked cross in the air. As I kissed his hand, he took mine and kissed it in return. He told me: "Thank you, thank you." I then requested, as a gift for my mother, a commemorative medal of his generalate, the one where he is seen receiving the pope's blessing. He pointed to the cupboard, indicating to the infirmarian that he should get me one of better quality. He then asked me to write this biography quickly. I explained to him that I still had to go to Japan and talk to many persons, but that before doing so I would pass through Switzerland to see his dear friend, the Swiss Jesuit Ludwig Kaufmann, the rebellious old journalist with the heart of a Boy Scout. Arrupe laughed with delight, saying "Give him my best." Then the brother took him for his walk, step by step along the corridor, to assist in his recovery. Don Pedro accompanied me to the stairs. There I kissed his hand again, and he repeated the gesture with me. As I went up the stairs, I could not hold back my tears.

With the new superior general, Peter-Hans Kolvenback (center), and papal delegate Paolo Dezza (right) (September 3, 1983).

These are my notes from July 1983. I have desire to reproduce them in all their freshness in order to transmit the authentic state of soul of Pedro Arrupe when he was sick. I have not tried to sweeten anything. Removing the human tragedy and psychological distress from his interior struggle would be to desecrate this final monumental gesture of his life.

The Farewell of a General

A few days later, on September 2, the general congregation convened to elect Arrupe's successor. After a press conference in which Pittau defended the struggle for justice in Latin America, the pope made an unusual gesture: he went himself personally to inaugurate the labors of the general congregation. Three times John Paul II approached Arrupe: to give him the peace, to give him Communion, and to say goodbye to him. In his homily, he affirmed his affection for the Society, not without insisting once again on the "orientations and recommendations" of his two predecessors, which "retain all their value and which you should keep present before you during the labors of the general congregation."

In the afternoon of the next day, General Congregation 33, composed of 220 Jesuits from all over the world, rendered homage to Arrupe. Led forward on the arms of his two nurses, he seemed to be weightless, a frail old man almost floating through the air with his legs swinging. He showed pain as he descended the stairs. There were reporters, television cameras, photographers. Dezza left the hall to receive him, and Arrupe made his entrance.

Inside the assembly hall, Arrupe was greeted with thunderous applause, like a prolonged rumble. For the last time, with great effort, he mounted the steps of the dais, and for the last time he sat in the place of honor. With sober clarity, Dezza summed up the virtues of Pedro Arrupe; he praised his spirit of sacrifice and his attitude of resignation in the face of the incomprehensible. Dezza also told a curious anecdote: after the death of Paul VI, he was given the book that the pope used to use to prepare for confession; in the pages of that book, Dezza discovered a letter written by Arrupe, which the pope had apparently used for his prayers and meditations.

After Dezza spoke, the provincial of Spain, Iglesias, read Arrupe's statement. The general began his parting allocution with these words: "Dear Fathers: How I would have loved to find myself in better condition as I meet now with all of you! But as you see, I cannot even talk to you directly. The general assistants have understood what I want to tell you all." Even without saying it explicitly, Arrupe was affirming his strong faith:

> More than ever, I find myself in the hands of God. This is what I have wanted all my life from my youth. And that is also the only thing I continue to desire now. But now there is a difference: the initiative is entirely with God. I assure you that it is a profound spiritual experience to know and feel myself in God's hands.

He then gave thanks for the eighteen years he had spent as superior general, affirming that he "had tried his best to respond to God, knowing that he gave me everything for the Society." His only ambition was to serve the Lord. It was possible that he had been deficient in many ways, "but the fact is that there has been much progress." One example of progress was "the attitude of loyalty and filial obedience that has been shown to the church and the Holy Father, particularly in these recent years."

After expressing his personal gratitude to his assistants and counselors, in particular O'Keefe, whose explicit mention was very significant, and to Fathers Dezza and Pittau for "their loving response to the church and the Society in the exceptional charge they received from the Holy Father," he addressed all his brother Jesuits with a message that has become a sort of testament:

> My message today is that we be at the disposition of the Lord. I pray that God be always the center, that we listen to him, that we constantly see what we can do in his greater service, and that we carry it out as well and as lovingly as possible, detached from everything. I pray that we have a very personal sense of God.
>
> To each one of you in particular, I would love to say *so many things*. [...] I want to tell those of you who are young to seek God's presence and your own sanctification, which is the best preparation for the future. Dedicate

yourselves to God's will. Keep yourselves attentive to the world's many needs. Think of the millions of people who do not know God or who act as if they did not know him. All are called to know and serve God. How great is our mission: bringing knowledge and love of Christ to all!

To those of you who are my own age, I recommend that you be open: learn what must be done now and do it well.

I want also to tell my beloved brothers *so many things* and with much affection. I want to remind the whole Society of the great importance of the brothers. They help us greatly to center our vocation on God [...].

I am full of hope as I see how the Society serves Christ, the only Lord, and the church, under the Roman pontiff, the vicar of Christ on earth. I pray that the Society may continue in this way and that the Lord may bless it with many excellent vocations of priests and brothers. I offer to the Lord, in what life remains to me, my prayers and the sufferings arising from my illness. Personally, the only thing I desire is to repeat from the depth of my soul: "Take, Lord, and receive [...]"[37]

Arrupe concluded his allocution with this prayer that Ignatius proposes in his famous "Contemplation to Attain Love of God." A few more items were read, and then Arrupe was given a photograph of the pope, which bore the laudatory text that John Paul had penned the day before: "To Father Arrupe, whom I am delighted to greet here present with us. I recognize how widely acknowledged he is for having governed the Society by his example, his prayer, and his suffering." Enveloped in a great ovation, Arrupe kissed the pope's autograph. Everyone stood up, and Arrupe, standing as well, kissed the hand of Dezza. The Arrupe era had come to an end.

On the arm of his nurse, Arrupe walked through the hall. The walls resounded with the longest and most emotional ovation ever received by a general of the Society of Jesus.

The next day, September 4, another event took place in Arrupe's favorite chapel, La Storta, where Saint Ignatius had heard those decisive words: "I will be propitious to you in Rome." The cameras were waiting when three buses filled with Jesuits, including Arrupe, arrived. The feeble but famous sick man was the center of attention. For the mass media, he was the leading figure in the liturgy.

---

37 Allocution of Arrupe's resignation, *Información S.J.*, CG 33, vol. 2. For this general congregation, see internal bulletins and *Vida nueva* 1391ff. This weekly journal published an editorial titled, "Thanks, Father Arrupe," which stated:

> He is a general of the Society who, despite his detractors, never neglected spiritual concerns or religious observance. This is shown clearly by the fact that the papal delegate, during his period of governance, has not made any substantial modifications, simply because all the truly decisive measures in this regard were already implemented thanks to the concern and commitment of Father Arrupe.

After the scriptural readings, done in several languages, the superior of the curia, Father José Luis Fernández Castañeda, read "the last homily of Father Arrupe." The beautiful text was his *Nunc dimittis*, evoking old Simeon's "for my eyes have seen my Savior," and recalling that in his life he had passed through "difficulties great and small, but always strengthened with the help of God, the God in whose hands I feel myself to be now more than ever, the God who has taken possession of me." The whole homily was centered on the mysterious plans of God, the importance of taking up the cross and following Jesus, and the symbolism of that chapel that Arrupe himself had wanted to restore.[38]

On September 13, 1983, a successor to Arrupe was elected. The pundits had forecast that the election would fall to a "papal candidate." Many observers thought that it would be Pittau himself, given the qualities he possessed. Of the 220 electors, some 154 were participating in an election for the first time. There were eighty-five delegates from the countries of the South and thirty-four from the United States, which was the largest delegation. Their average age was fifty-one and a half. Given the situation, it was thought improbable that one of Arrupe's close collaborators would be elected. On the first ballot and with a clear majority Peter Hans Kolvenbach was elected. A Dutchman from Druten, born in 1928, Kolvenbach had been superior in Lebanon from 1974 to 1981. Arrupe had summoned him in 1981, just before his thrombosis, to direct the Pontifical Oriental Institute in Rome. Considered a talented linguist, Kolvenbach had lived through difficult experiences of war and privation in Lebanon. He was a man of dialogue, prudence, and interior profundity; he also had a sense of humor. The general congregation, defending its freedom and juridical autonomy, elected a man who would guarantee continuity with Arrupe and at the same time seek harmony and understanding with the Holy See. Indeed, the new general, during his twenty-five years in office, did just that.

After being elected, Kolvenbach turned to Arrupe and embraced him, saying: "I will no longer call you Father General, but I will continue to call you Father."

When the pope learned of the election, he was not surprised. Several days earlier, he had told a confidant, "You'll see, they won't elect Pittau."[39]

The last journey of Arrupe—"his final act of love," Bandera called it—was his visit to the refugees of Via degli Castelli and Via Aurelia. The nurse wrote in his journal:

> I could feel how he was vibrating both interiorly and exteriorly. He wanted to talk, but since he could not, he made such an effort that those who did not know him would have thought that he was not sick at all; it was only his hand that didn't move. During the visit, I was able to appreciate his great humility, peace, joy, patience, and above all how he is a man for everybody, especially during the celebration of the holy Mass.

---

38   Cf. GC 33.
39   Alcalá, "La dimisión de Arrupe," 952.

A Light in the Emptiness

The rest of Arrupe's life can be summed up in a single word, "silence." His unadorned infirmary room was occasionally illuminated by some memory of the past, such as the old photograph that was sent from Bilbao by his sisters, with the beloved face of his father, Don Marcelino. He would take the photo in his left hand and kiss it tenderly, while seeming to hear, "Peru, Peruchi." Then he would cry out, referring to his father: *Simpático, simpático.*

Arrupe also received the news that his two remaining sisters, Cata and Isabel, had died piously between 1983 and 1984. At times, when the brother infirmarian urged him to stretch out his arm or move his hand, he would respond, "I can't, Catalina," as if he had become once again that little boy playing in the streets of Bilbao under the watchful eyes of his older sisters. At Christmas and on the feast of Saint Peter, he would receive a flood of greeting cards.[40]

Arrupe's eyes lit up whenever Kolvenbach visited him or when dear old friends came by. One day, Mother Teresa of Calcutta[41] visited, her lined visage shining with tenderness for the outcasts she loved; as she sat by Arrupe's beside, the faces of both of them harmonized in a soundless chord. Something similar occurred when Arrupe received a visit from Brother Roger Schutz of Taizé, a good friend of his. Roger "sang for him with the other brothers who were with him, and they prayed. Don Pedro seemed to be transported."[42]

A "biblical scene" was what Bandera called the meeting between Arrupe and the eminent Jesuit theologian Henri de Lubac on February 3, 1983, just after de Lubac had been named cardinal by John Paul II. "That old man—[de Lubac] was eighty-six—on his knees before Father Arrupe, wanting to kiss his hand. Don Pedro did not want him to. Finally they ended up in a strong embrace." An interesting detail: since the elderly theologian did not have money for the expenses of the unexpected cardinalate, Arrupe sent for the treasurer of the Society and asked for three thousand dollars. Then he had Bandera walk him step by step to the room where the old cardinal was staying, and he personally gave him the money. De Lubac thanked him, saying, "With this, I will be able to fix up my office in Paris."[43]

Arrupe also received a visit from Sargent Shriver and his wife Eunice Kennedy Shriver, who brought along their five children. Their son Bobby was at the

---

40   Brother Bandera. Testimonies of secretaries and amanuenses.

41   December 13, 1981. According to Brother Bandera, she visited Arrupe several times: "Don Pedro became enthusiastic listening to this holy woman speak. I felt vibrations between the two of them" (*Diario inédito y autógrafo del Hermano Rafael Bandera*). The photograph in which Arrupe and Teresa of Calcutta appear together became famous around the world.

42   March 26, 1982, *Diario inédito y autógrafo del Hermano Rafael Bandera*.

43   February 3, 1983, *Diario inédito y autógrafo del Hermano Rafael Bandera*.

John Paul II visiting the ailing general of the Jesuits. "I feel edified by this meeting today," said the pope (December 31, 1981).

time trying to help resolve the Central American conflicts. When Arrupe indicated his solidarity with the cause, the young man told him enthusiastically in Spanish: "We Christians have much love for you."[44]

---

44   December 26, 1982, *Diario inédito y autógrafo del Hermano Rafael Bandera.*

On many other occasions, Arrupe was visited by Jesuit companions from all over the world. Joseph Cocucci, S.J., of Cambridge, Massachusetts, went to see him a couple of times and tells with emotion of how, since he did not know Spanish, he made use of his knowledge of Italian and French to understand him. With one knee on the floor and holding Arrupe's hand, Cocucci repeated in English what he thought he heard him say. If he was correct, Arrupe would say "Sí, sí"; if Cocucci understood incorrectly, then Arrupe would laugh and kiss his hand. "The time went by so rapidly!" comments Cocucci; "it was like being together with a very dear uncle or grandfather."[45]

The letters and visitors that arrived from Japan were especially meaningful for Arrupe since that was his true spiritual homeland. One of the letters was from his former secretary Simosako, the "most high princess"; she was the young woman who had helped him with his writings and translations in Hiroshima. Another letter, translated by Rush and read at the time of the general's resignation, reads as follows:

Dear admired and beloved Father Arrupe:

I will never forget that historic day, thirty-eight years ago, when the atomic bomb was dropped on Hiroshima. Right now, I am reading with great interest the story you wrote a few months after that for *Catholic Digest*. And I am perfectly aware of the need to keep praying for true peace, which alone will guarantee that such a tragedy never happens again.

Today I received a letter from Professor Kanzawa, in which he refers to his meeting with you in Rome. He has left me deeply moved. How are you doing? I pray for you always, trusting in the loving providence of the Heart of Jesus.

Thirty-eight years ago, on August 6, the atomic bomb fell on Hiroshima.

Thirty-eight years ago, on August 9, the atomic bomb fell on Nagasaki.

Thirty-eight years ago, on August 15, Japan surrendered.

These successive tragedies brought me to the edge of despair. It was in April 1946 that I, after returning from Shanghai to Hiroshima, and not knowing what to do or where to go, had the good luck of meeting Mister Matsuda, a Catholic, who took me one Sunday to the novitiate in Nagatsuka and introduced me to you.

At that moment, my desperation turned into hope, and my darkness into light; my heart filled with courage, hope, and joy. My encounter with you meant my true encounter with the Lord Jesus.

Since then, my heart is aflame in love and prayer. When I think of you, I feel strengthened by the love of the Heart of Jesus.

It will soon be the feast of the Assumption. With great longing to reach our heavenly homeland, I pray for you with gratitude.

---

45   Letter written to the author by Joseph Cocucci, S.J.

The letter was signed by Francis Peter Takezoe Tamotsu.[46]

In October 1983, during one of Arrupe's relapses, Alcalá recounts that he was attending the Bishops' Synod, where he was doing simultaneous translation. As he left the hall, the pope's secretary gave him a message for Dezza and asked him about Arrupe's health. When Alcalá returned to the house, he went to visit Arrupe, who appeared quite unconscious in those days, and whispered into his right ear: "The pope's secretary asked me about your health." Don Pedro reacted vigorously and asked clearly: "What did the pope say?"[47] Everyone there was surprised by the alert attitude of this man who had seemed to be asleep.

In the summer of 1984, Jesuit historian Ignacio Echániz, aware that Arrupe's state of health was declining, made efforts to alleviate his distress. Each morning, he went to see him and spent a half-hour reading to him. First he read Gustavo Gutiérrez's *We Drink from Our Own Wells* (1984) and then a book by Leonardo Boff. "I remember," writes Echániz,

> that in a certain passage the author compared the Vatican with the Soviet Union. At first, it struck Arrupe as humorous, and he let out a laugh. But this was only at first, because when the author insisted on the idea and developed the comparison, Don Pedro showed his clear displeasure.[48]

Echániz concelebrated Mass with Arrupe each morning in the small infirmary chapel, assisted by Bandera as sacristan and lector. Arrupe followed the Eucharist with devotion, and his eyes lit up as he gave the peace.[49] At the end of November 1985, he suffered another relapse. There seemed to be internal complications, which were thought to be possibly a tumor or cancer, and he became ever less mobile, giving the impression he was about to die. The superior of the house, Bernard Hall, anointed him on November 29 at 7:30 in the evening. "Without any doubt," stated a neurological report of Dr. White, "he has reached the stage where he has only a minimum perception of reality and his surroundings."[50] This would later be contradicted by his Italian colleagues, who

---

46   *Pedro Arrupe: Así lo vieron*, 62.

47   Alcalá, "La dimisión de Arrupe," 953.

48   Ignacio Echániz, "Si el grano de trigo [...]," in La Bella, *Pedro Arrupe, general de la Compañía de Jesús*, 958–72, here 963.

49   Echániz, "Si el grano de trigo [...]," 964.

50   "In February, Dr. White's report would be contrasted with—contradicted by?—the report given by another neurologist, Dr. Occhipinti. The editor of *Noticias y comentarios* appeared apologetic in presenting to its readers, 'just five months later,' a new medical bulletin." Occhipinti began his report by presenting his credentials, as it were. Whereas Dr. White's visits had been sporadic and a bit superficial, Occhipinti had been following Arrupe "without interruption since August 1981, paying periodic visits as the doctor in charge." Occhipinti admitted that his patient possessed a very limited and fragile ability to relate, but he stated that Arrupe's mental conditions allowed him to remain in contact with the persons who attended to him and who visited him. He concluded: "The

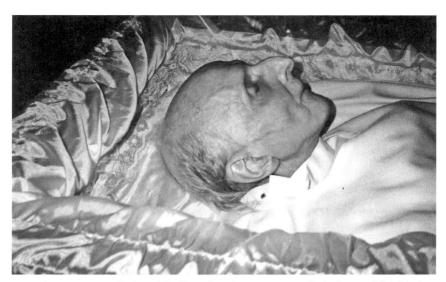

Arrupe lying in state. His final words had been: "For the present, Amen; for the future, Alleluia" (February 7, 1991).

had more contact with the sick man; they believed that Arrupe still maintained a certain capacity for perception and communication. In those days, cardinals and bishops from all over the world were convening in Rome for another synod, one that aroused special interest since its aim was to review and "redirect" the Second Vatican Council. A great many reporters flooded into Rome, and all were asking for Arrupe. As he lay in the middle of the dimly lit room, his face was hardly visible, but it still glowed, perhaps because of fever. With slow and labored breathing, slightly parted lips, closed eyes, and head leaning to the right, he had the appearance of a Christ of Mantegna. People were talking of his death, which at that moment might have had a very special resonance and significance. In Rome, the shop windows were adorned with poinsettias, mistletoe, silver stars, lavish gifts, and *panettone*. In Saint Peter's Square, beside the obelisk, a crèche was being built. And Arrupe, alone in his silence, was holding on, and would hold on several years more.

On July 30, 1986, Arrupe celebrated fifty years of priesthood in his sickbed and wept as the Eucharist was celebrated in his room. Those present sang the Basque hymn *Agur, Jesusen Ama* (Hail, Mother of Jesus), redolent with memories, and Arrupe enjoyed the attention and affection of his niece Mariví, his nephew José Ramón, and his faithful collaborator María Luz, all of whom went often to Rome to visit him.

---

evolution of his cerebro-vascular insufficiency is in accord with his present clinical situation; it cannot be said that a multi-infartual encephalopathy is evolving toward a state of dementia" (Echániz, "Si el grano de trigo […]," 965).

Gabriele Ferrari, the superior general of the Xaverians, went to see Arrupe on October 8, 1986, because he knew how much Arrupe appreciated the visits of those who had worked with him in the Union of Superiors General. Ferrari recounts:

> Father Pittau went with me. Father Arrupe was not sitting today next to the window or wearing his Jesuit attire; rather he was seated in an easy chair in a darker part of the room, near the bed. Dressed in white and almost diaphanous, he was lost in the brightness and blended into the color of his pajamas. He has become extremely thin and was leaning toward the right. In his left hand, he had a little rubber ball that he was squeezing nervously and automatically. He appeared to be quite distant.

Pittau introduced Ferrari to the sick man, explaining that he had come to visit him:

> Pittau said he noticed a smile on his lips, but I really saw very little myself. I saw that he looked at me, but he is no longer the Arrupe of former times. I approached to look him in the eyes, and I had to stoop down to do so. Pittau tried to tell him that his "grandson" was here and was about to leave for Hong Kong and Japan, with the intention of doing something for China. It is clear that he was following what was said to him, and I noticed his effort to express something; I also saw huge, heavy tears forming in his eyes. This was the first time I was seeing this man in this state. I instinctively recalled what he had always told me in our meetings: "It's tremendous!" The trial he is suffering must be terrible; he is conscious of his situation of humiliation, since he is aware of all that happened at the end of his period as superior general. At times, when I think of him, I recall Christ crucified calling out to the Father: "Why have you abandoned me?"

Pittau reminded Ferrari of how much Arrupe had done for the Society, and Ferrari commented on how much he had done for religious life generally: "Without him, the map of religious life would be configured in a very different way today."[51]

Arrupe's eightieth birthday was November 14, 1987, and it was celebrated as well as possible, given the circumstances—a bouquet of flowers from his physical therapist, visits from young Jesuit students, and lively songs. There were also numerous telegrams: from cardinals, from the Sant'Egidio community, and an especially emotional one from Taizé.[52]

---

51   "Incontro con Pedro Arrupe SJ. Roma, Borgo Santo Spirito, 8 ottobre 1986," typewritten text of Gabriele Ferrari, SX.

52   Brother Roger's note states:

> On this his eightieth birthday, the Taizé community praises the Lord for the exceptional witness that our beloved Father Arrupe has been for us. With his dedicated life, he has opened up paths of communion for the church of our time. In his

María Victoria Gondra Oráa, his niece Mariví, wrote in 1987:

The long years of sickness have slowly undermined his strength. [...] However, his brain remains awake as on the first day, almost heightened at certain moments, able to capture with lively attention the minutest detail of a conversation he finds interesting. [...] It might be said that, once the crisis of Christmas 1985 was over, two parallel lives intersected in the interior of this man: his physical capacity has slowly declined, while a creative space has grown, with an energy that progresses toward other worlds, far beyond the point that we material beings can control.[53]

In those years, I traveled to Rome a couple of times for professional reasons. Once, when I visited Arrupe, I told him that I had had to interrupt temporarily the work on this book because, when Father Rubio was beatified, they gave me the task of writing a biography of this man known as the "apostle of Madrid." Arrupe smiled with a sweet and intelligent look, as if conceding the scant importance that should be given to him by comparison. On the second visit, even though he was quite prostrate, he recognized me and tried to speak in a nervous, unintelligible babble. He listened as I described my journeys around Japan and the Basque country, in search of people who could offer recollections of him. He could hardly respond.

To the extent that he could, Arrupe had asked people to write me letters or to call me by phone when he thought they could provide me some additional information. On one occasion, he had even sent a letter to his speech therapist, Mariano Ballester, asking him to write to me, and he insisted on signing the letter personally with his halting script. By that time, he was capable only of an occasional "Sí," which was firm and grateful. He was not dead, but neither was he fully alive; still, he was present, entire, vigilant, with an aura of light and force that filled the room with electricity. I was not surprised to learn that for some time, on a weekly basis, a group of Protestants had been coming to visit him; they would light a candle and simply pray or sing in his presence. This was the case, for example of the Olbrishes, a family of evangelicals; from the day of his stroke until his death, they brought him flowers every Saturday and sweets and chocolates at Christmas and Easter and on his birthday. They did not want to bother him; they simply said: "Father, make no effort; with your eyes we understand everything." Then the sick man would enter into a great peace and bestow on them a smile that would last until they left.[54]

---

infirmity, he is living the paschal mystery with Jesus and showing us the path of Christian holiness. With warm greetings, Brother Roger.

Gujarat Jesuit Samachar [News of Gujarat province], December 1987.

53   Article of María Victoria Gondra in *El correo español: El pueblo vasco*, February 13, 1987.

54   See *Diario inédito y autógrafo del Hermano Rafael Bandera*.

On November 16, 1989, a platoon of soldiers of the Salvadoran army slaughtered Father Ellacuría in the residence of the Jesuit university. Killed with him were his Jesuit companions Ignacio Martín Baró, Segundo Montes, Armando López, Juan Ramón Moreno, and Joaquín López y López. Other victims of the same massacre were Elba Julia Ramos, who cooked for the fathers, and her sixteen-year old daughter, Celina. Brother Bandera notes in his journal:

> When I gave him the news of the martyrdom of Ellacuría and his companions, I did not want to tell him the whole truth, only about Ellacuría. I waited a while, to see how he would react. He kept his eyes fixed on the ceiling (he was in bed) for about five minutes; then two great tears fell from his eyes, and he said: "They are with the Lord."[55]

Thus did Pedro Arrupe fade away: his body was exhausted, but he still possessed a strange inner force. In this regard, we may recall the words that Arrupe had written to bring to an end his long interview with Jean-Claude Dietsch:

> Biographies are always incomplete portraits. In many cases, they lack the light hidden in the deepest part of ourselves, the light that would radically transform our image if it became manifest. But that light cannot be communicated. It has no value if it ceases to be hidden.
>
> The true biography can be written only before the Lord. He alone can correct it and supplement it with the many precious elements that escape even our own eyes. Before the Lord—that is to say, as Saint John of the Cross describes it: "In the happy night, / In secret, when none saw me, / Nor I beheld aught, / Without light or guide, / save that which burned in my heart."
>
> Someone wrote—I don't know where—that the most interesting biography is that which is written "without ink." The same could be said of my own. Remember especially the words of Saint Paul to the Corinthians: "You are a letter of Christ, written [...] not with ink, but by the Spirit of the living God."

Arrupe then added that his own life could be summed up in the words, "Thy will be done":

> That doesn't mean that I consider my life to be particularly extraordinary. What is extraordinary is that, even though I have often failed to orient my life as I should have, the Lord has continued to make possible his plan in my regard. He wants us the way we are, and he has loved me as I am. The miracle of life resides in that love that foresees, disposes, helps, sustains, and reveals the marvels that are seen in all that exists, as if they were ours—when in reality they are his. Here once again is found the great difficulty of tracing a border between the divine and the human.

---

55   *Diario inédito y autógrafo del Hermano Rafael Bandera.*

Reviewing the stages of my life, with their concrete details and external manifestations, I have reached the same conclusion: what is most important and decisive in a life, what is most fully characteristic of it, is incommunicable. This is so either because it is a matter of intimate experiences that cannot be translated into words, or because these experiences have a very personal, interior value and therefore remain in the dark, which is precisely where they have their value.

In this text, written in 1981, Arrupe wonders about the mystery of the last years of his life, "in which I will not be able to dictate my thoughts." Yes, it is a mystery, he says, but it is certain that the end will arrive "when one least expects—like a thief." And that was the way he looked on death:

This death, which is feared so much, is in reality for me one of the most awaited events, an event that gives meaning to my life. Death can be considered as the end of life and also as the threshold of eternity; in each of these aspects, I find consolation. On the one hand, the end of life is always the end of *a* life, a life that is nothing more than a path that crosses a desert to draw close to eternity, a path at times difficult, a path on which the weight of the years grows greater as one's strength fails. On the other hand, since death is also the threshold of eternity, it means entering into that eternity that is at once unknown and anticipated; it means reunion with the Lord and eternal familiarity with him. [...]

Eternity, immortality, beatific vision, perfect happiness [...].; all is new, nothing is unknown. Is death a leap into nothingness? Certainly not. It is throwing oneself into the arms of the Lord, it is hearing the invitation that is undeserved but truly extended: "Come, good and faithful servant, enter into the joy of your Lord." It is attaining the end of hope and faith in order to live in eternal and infinite charity. What will heaven be like? It is impossible to imagine it. "Eye has not seen, nor ear heard [...]." I hope that it will be a *consummatum est*, "all is finished," the final Amen of my life, the first Alleluia of my eternity. *Fiat, fiat.* Pedro Arrupe.[56]

Arrupe wrote that in June 1981, a few days before leaving on the journey from which he would return gravely ill. Those words were echoed in a phrase captured later by his speech therapist Ballester. One day just before bedtime, Arrupe was read several talks he had previously given, and he responded to them in his halting speech: "For the present, Amen [...]; for the future, Alleluia!" It was like a mystical synthesis of his whole life.[57]

---

56   *Itinéraire*, 139ff.
57   Mariano Ballester, "Recuerdo del P. Arrupe y el A.O.," *Oración y servicio* 4 (October–December 1991): 297–302.

Concelebrants at Arrupe's funeral Mass in the church of the Gesù in Rome. From left to right: Cardinal
Martínez Somalo, Cardinal Martini, Peter-Hans Kolvenbach, Damian Byrne (master general of the
Dominicans), and Vincent O'Keefe (February 9, 1991).

Echániz, who attended to him in his final moments, recalls the details of
Arrupe's death. His condition began to worsen on January 25, 1991, and he soon
fell into a coma. At 9:15 p.m., he again received the anointing of the sick. From
that point on, he received no further nourishment:

> With the small forces left to him, he waged the long, hard battle of his agony,
> and never did that word embody more its original meaning of "struggle."
> Each day we thought was going to be his last—he could not go on. Death
> could have come upon him at any moment, for he was suffering frequent
> epileptic-type attacks, a side-effect of the cerebral thrombosis, which
> affected the respiratory system and left him unable to breathe for long peri-
> ods. His heart kept overcoming all the crises, one after another.[58]

Arrupe's illness had lasted ten years; now the coma was going to last ten inter-
minable days. The nurse and the doctors decided to allow the sickness to run its
course and not give him any medicine to combat the coma. A Jesuit from South
Africa who had done medical studies wondered aloud about the decision: Why
not give Arrupe one of the indicated medicines? His suggestion was not accepted.

On Sunday the twenty-seventh, Kolvenbach informed the Vatican and
requested an apostolic benediction for the sick man. The answer came

---

58   Echániz, typewritten report; and "Si el grano de trigo [...]," 967ff.

immediately by means of a telegram sent at twelve noon the same day and signed by the pro-secretary of state, Archbishop Angelo Sodano. Around seven o'clock that evening, the pope's private secretary, Stanisław Dziwisz, phoned the Jesuit curia to announce that the pope would visit the moribund Arrupe to give him his personal blessing. The Holy Father arrived at 7:25 p.m.; he prayed in silence for a while and then recited, along with those present, the *Alma Redemptoris Mater* (Loving Mother of the Savior). The visit lasted about a quarter of an hour.

When he was advised of what was happening, O'Keefe flew from New York to be at the side of his dear friend during those final hours.

A week later, Echániz, who had been Arrupe's chaplain the last six years, decided to remain at his bedside and pray with him, in case he was still able to capture something in his subconscious. As Echániz himself recounts the vigil:

> Freed from my usual occupations, I was able to stay by the sick man's side from Sunday, February 3, onward. Arrupe appeared to have entered into his death agony. Twice that same day, once in the morning and again in the afternoon, I recited to him the prayers from the ritual before death, except the one that says: *Leave, Christian soul.* That day and the next, having finished all the prayers of the ritual, I had recourse to the Ignatian prayer book, reciting the *Soul of Christ*, the *Take, Lord, and Receive*, and above all the prayer we read in Saint Ignatius's spiritual diary, a document Arrupe had helped to rediscover. That Ignatian prayer seemed especially appropriate in those circumstances: *Eternal Father, confirm me; Eternal Son, confirm me* [...]. I also whispered to him some words of encouragement. Recalling the words of Saint John of the Cross, I told him, "Don Pedro, at the end of life we will be examined regarding love. And you have loved much! You have been able to suffer much because you have loved much." When I pronounced these words, Brother Bandera, who was on the other side of the bed, broke down in sobs.[59]

But still the end had not come. Dr. Musacchio, who had been visiting Arrupe faithfully at eight o'clock every Sunday for the ten years of his sickness, saw him on the afternoon of Monday, February 4. After examining him, the doctor stated: *Siamo alla fine* (We are at the end). Believing that he would die that same evening or night, he promised to return around eight o'clock the next morning to write up the death certificate.

Arrupe would still last another twenty-four hours. From 2 a.m. to 5 a.m., Echániz sang softly into his ear motets, hymns, and sequences from the *Liber usualis*. Don Pedro kept breathing and struggled persistently. By eleven o'clock on the morning of Tuesday the fifth, death seemed imminent, and Brother Bandera sent for Father General, who arrived in a few minutes. Others came as well, until

---

59 Echániz, "Si el grano de trigo [...]," 969.

the room was full. At 11:15, Arrupe stopped breathing. A long minute passed, and then he breathed a couple of times more and stopped again, long enough to make us think he had expired. "Now he's gone," said Bandera.

The Jesuits recited the prayer *Saints of God, Come Forth to Meet Him*. Hardly was the prayer finished when this man whom they thought was dead began to breathe again, but convulsively and spasmodically, throwing his head back at each gasp for breath. The eyewitness Echániz comments:

> It was a heartrending scene that lasted a whole hour, from 11:30 to 12:30. He had suffered an epileptic attack, as was later explained to us, and his heart had reacted with beats that resembled the "gallop of a runaway horse," according to Bandera, who was completely astounded after examining him. Little by little, his breathing became more relaxed, but it still was like gasping.

Arrupe died later in the afternoon. The final words were spoken by his chaplain, Echániz, who wove together texts of Saint Paul: "Don Pedro, you have struggled bravely; you have attained the goal; you have manifested your faith. It only remains for you to receive your well-deserved crown. Good and faithful servant, enter into the joy of your Lord." And Echániz comments: "I confess that at that moment, seeing that I was attending him in his death, I felt as if I were representing the Society. I pronounced those words as if I were the spokesman of the whole Society, giving him thanks and taking leave of him in its name."[60]

At 7:30, Arrupe stopped breathing in the presence of Father General, who had returned to his bedside. His heart stopped at 7:45. The Jesuits intoned *Hail to the Virgin of La Storta*, asking for Arrupe the grace that Saint Ignatius had asked of her, that "she place him with her Son," forever. His sickness and his agony had been long and drawn out, quite the opposite of what he would have desired. "I would like to die on the frontlines and, if possible, causing the least possible trouble for others. If our Lord wants to take me away suddenly, I'll be delighted."

Finally, after ten years of waiting, at 7:45 p.m. on February 5, 1991, anniversary of the Nagasaki martyrs, his spiritualized body yielded, and Arrupe departed for the long-awaited reunion with his Lord. Until a few weeks before, he had been able to maintain fleeting moments of lucidity, but his body, weakened by prostration and long illness, could stand no more. The unconscious Arrupe could not say goodbye—the last word he pronounced in life had been "Amen" ("so be it").

With its translucent paleness and its features resembling those of Saint Ignatius, Arrupe's cadaver irradiated peace. It was laid out in the curia chapel, and past it filed cardinals, bishops, priests, religious, and laypeople. Among them were the Italian president, Francesco Cossiga, and the prime minister Giulio Andreotti. A flood of telegrams arrived. On February 6 and 7, the community celebrated the Eucharist *corpore insepulto* (with the body present), and on the

---

60   Echániz, "Si el grano de trigo […]," 969.

seventh Kolvenbach presided at a prayer vigil that was open to the public; among those in attendance was José Ramón, Arrupe's nephew from Bilbao.

The death of Arrupe caused a profound commotion around the world. The pope praised the deceased superior general for "his profound piety, his zeal for the church, and his generous and patient acceptance of the divine will in his sufferings." For his part, the Jesuit general Kolvenbach characterized Arrupe as a person endowed with "radiant optimism that was nourished by profound faith." He stated that Arrupe had earnestly addressed the crucial problem of resolving for the Society the latent tension between two basic directives of the Second Vatican Council: return to the original sources and adaptation to the new times. Meanwhile, flowers and telegrams from all over the world had filled to overflowing the general headquarters in Rome.

As was his life, so was Arrupe's funeral: a manifestation of simplicity and affection. Prime Minister Andreotti commented that it would have been necessary to go back to the funerals of Ignatius, Philip Neri, John XXIII, or Pius XII "to witness such a fervent participation of the people, where everyone was conscious of experiencing another of the eternal city's moments of glory." Andreotti spoke of Arrupe "triumphing in death":

> Yes, because the Christians of Rome celebrate the death of their saints as a triumph or an ascension to glory. What I have experienced in these days since the death of Father Arrupe has reminded me of so many of the marvelous pages of Rome's history, from its martyrs to its saints, such as the deaths of Gregory the Great or Saint Philip Neri and his dear friend, Saint Ignatius: there has been the same participation of the people and the same lively awareness of being before a saint who has left a wake for the future of humanity.

The ceremony on February 9 began with the words of the master general of the Dominicans, Damian Byrne, who presided at the funeral, following a traditional agreement between the two orders:

> We join together here to celebrate the entrance into the Father's house of one of the most excellent men of our time, Pedro Arrupe, a grace of God for our time, an example of generosity, enthusiasm, fraternal love, and justice; he showed us how to open up new ways for humankind.

On either side of the altar were the pope's representative, Cardinal Martínez Somalo, and the Jesuit cardinal Martini, archbishop of Milan. Some 350 priests concelebrated the Eucharist.

In his homily, Kolvenbach depicted with emotion and vibrancy the qualities of Arrupe's *Magnificat*:

> Neither misunderstandings nor criticisms stood in the way of his passion for justice or service to the poor, not even when false interpretations of his

directives gave rise to abuses. Nobody has ever been able to criticize the generosity that inspired all his efforts. Whenever they asked him, "Where is the
Society going?" Arrupe answered with disarming simplicity: "Where God is
taking it." He enjoyed an absolute and joyous confidence in the Lord, and
he knew the meaning of hope before the Crucified One who was burdened
with a terrible cross that broke his body but never his spirit.

After so many years of restless silence about the controversial sick man,
now everyone united in praising him. Before giving the final blessing, Cardinal
Martínez Somalo read a statement testifying to the pope's

> esteem and unwavering confidence in the Society and in this man who was, as
> the Constitutions wanted him to be, full of great goodness and love in order to
> undertake great things for God's service. [...] Our thanks go to Father Arrupe
> for his openness to the desires of the Church and to the needs of a world that
> is lacking God's presence and yet longing for justice in truth and love.[61]

When the blessing was finished, young Jesuits lifted the coffin onto their
shoulders, and the hymn *In paradisum* (Into paradise) was intoned. Immediately
there exploded in the church a long, enthusiastic applause, which continued all
along the streets. As a brilliant sky and splendid sun cloaked in bright colors the
ochre tones of the ancient eternal city, the funeral coach carried Arrupe through
the streets of Rome toward the mausoleum in the Verano cemetery, where so
many Jesuits, famous and unknown, were laid to rest.

A little more than a year later, the pope made the elderly Dezza a cardinal, no
doubt as a way of thanking him for his service during the days when Arrupe was
marginalized by the Holy See. The man who had been assistant to the papal delegate in that exceptional situation, Pittau, was also rewarded, in his case by being
elevated to archbishop and made secretary of the Congregation for Catholic
Education. Cardinal Dezza died in 1999. In 2002, Archbishop Pittau returned to
Japan, where he worked as a simple missionary and parish priest until his death
in 2014. Such are the contrasts and mysteries of a Rome that is long accustomed
to both holiness and intrigues.

From the moment of Arrupe's death, the Society wanted to transfer his
remains to the church of the Gesù, the resting place of Ignatius, Xavier, and other
generals of the Society. To that end, a sepulcher was prepared alongside an altar
in the right nave, marked with a medallion with Arrupe's effigy.

At first, it was thought that the transfer of the remains from the Verano
cemetery would take place in 1995 during GC 34, an event that brought together
once again Jesuit representatives from all over the world. It is said that the transfer
was not done then because the necessary permission of Rome's city government

---

61   *Documentación S.J.* (1991).

PETRVS ARRVPE S.J

XIV NOV. MCMVII - V FEB. MCMXCI

PRAEPOSITVS GENERALIS SOCIETATIS JESV

MCMLXV - MCMLXXXIII

Gravestone on the tomb of Arrupe in the Gesù. His remains were transferred there from Rome's Campo Verano cemetery on November 14, 1997, six years after his death.

was lacking, due to the ever inept and notoriously corrupt Italian bureaucracy. However, it was also obvious that the staff of the Jesuit curia wanted to avoid the massive public display that would have been involved in a solemn transfer through the streets of Rome of the man who had been a renowned leader and renovator of the consecrated life—especially while the same pontiff who had sidelined him was reigning.

Many months went by before the permission arrived. Finally Arrupe's remains were discreetly transferred in June 1997, without advising all the Jesuit provincials.

The transfer was not commemorated until November 14 of that year, the day that would have been Arrupe's ninetieth birthday; it was also the feast day of the Jesuit saint Pignatelli. Even this festivity was arranged without any publicity; officially, it was to be no more than a family party. The only one who was informed of the project was the Spanish cardinal Martínez Somalo, who was protector of the church of the Gesù and, as we know, quite familiar with the problems of the deceased superior general. The civil and ecclesiastical authorities of Rome were not invited. Several Jesuit bishops concelebrated the Mass since they happened to be present in Rome for the special assembly of the synod on the Americas. Most of the rest of the 130 concelebrants were members of the order who resided in Rome; one of the few exceptions was O'Keefe, who had been Arrupe's close collaborator and who traveled expressly from Washington, DC for the event.

Kolvenbach gave a short homily, tracing a careful and measured parallel with Pignatelli. This Jesuit from Aragon had served as a bridge between the

"Father Arrupe dared to abandon customs and habits in order to expose the Society, by means of spiritual discernment, to what God wanted it to be: the mission of Christ in the heart of our world," said Kolvenbach at the funeral (February 9, 1991).

Society that was suppressed in 1773 and the one restored in 1814, while for his part Arrupe had renewed religious life in accord with the directives of Vatican II. Both superior generals had suffered greatly in their labors.

The new general went on:

> Father Arrupe was tested in his love of the church. His efforts to renew the Society in accord with the dynamic pace of Vatican II were met with the incomprehension of some and even with painful interventions by the church, which he loved with an Ignatian heart. Both men, Saint Joseph Pignatelli and Pedro Arrupe, entered into the mystery of God's will, which demands sacrifices for the life of the church and which sometimes imposes the duty of suffering with loving humility at the hands of the church [...].

Kolvenbach drew further parallels between the two figures, stating that Arrupe "dared to abandon old customs and habits in order to expose the Society, through spiritual discernment, to what God desired of it for Christ's mission in the heart of our world."

It might well be said that Arrupe continues to be, even now in the twenty-first century, a sign of contradiction. For certain sectors of the church, he is still a holy "pest," and some would see him as a prophet who needs to be muzzled.

Quite revealing in this regard are Cardinal Tarancón's declarations, as they were heard on Spanish National Radio:

> In the church, anyone can commit errors. Everyone thinks they are acting correctly and fulfilling God's will. But I believe that Father Arrupe could see in the pope's actions [his intervention in the order's governance], which were no doubt done with right intentions, something abnormal for the Society's life. In any case, the example given by Father Arrupe and the whole Jesuit order on that occasion was marvelous, so much so that the very pope who did that, John Paul II, had to recognize after the first meeting of the provincials that he had been extraordinarily edified by the posture taken by the Jesuits. Nobody was expecting it of them. Still, Father Arrupe suffered, and he suffered all the more because now the intervention was not against him, but against someone else, the vicar—it was against the Society—and that was perhaps what most hurt him in that circumstance.[62]

Tarancón, who happened to have been born the same year as Arrupe, went on to suggest the presence of pressure groups in the church, though he did so in his typically subtle and wisely political language:

> As regards authority, especially very high authority, the desire to take advantage of it is something common to everybody, including pressure groups. It is something very human and understandable. But the Holy Spirit still rules the destiny of the church, despite all our human foibles. Father Arrupe afterward was much admired by the pope and the secretary of state because they saw that he was an exceptional man who always acted with noble intentions. For that reason, the pope has been considerate of him and has gone to visit him several times, to show that he truly was an extraordinary man in the church. Father Arrupe, who was a prophet, was exceptionally charismatic; he could intuit the future. He was therefore way ahead of many others who did not follow him because they could not keep up with his pace. That is why he was not only a man of his time but one who prepared his companions for the future, for the third millennium, when the waters will be calmer and people will be able to carry out the work entrusted to them.[63]

Superior General Nicolás and Pope Francis

John Paul II, beloved by many, died on April 2, 2005, and his successor Benedict XVI was elected pope on April 19. It was to the latter that Father General Kolvenbach submitted his resignation in 2008, having turned eighty. Shortly before

---

62   *Documentación S.J.* (1997)
63   Program *Fin de siglo* (Sound Archive of Spanish National Radio). First broadcast on Good Friday, 1999.

that, in November 2007, Kolvenbach gave a conference held at the University of Deusto to commemorate the centenary of Arrupe's birth. Calling his predecessor "a faithful witness of the Second Vatican Council," he stated:

> Some people might call him a "utopian dreamer," others might refer to him as a 'mystic and prophet" for our times, and still others might recognize him as one who has done many new things, in the spirit of the Lord who declares,

Jorge Mario Bergoglio, S.J., at a liturgy celebrated in Buenos Aires in the presence of Arrupe (1960s).

"Behold, I make all things new" (Rev. 21:5). This is what most characterizes the figure and the message of Father Pedro Arrupe.

Perhaps the most telling passage of Kolvenbach's talk is his explanation of Arrupe's option for justice as a consequence of his faith:

> While Pope John Paul II states that struggling for justice against unjust structures is not enough and that such struggle must be at the service of charity and be conditioned by charity, Father Arrupe took what I would consider a more nuanced position in stressing that not all charity is per se authentic. That is, charity can be false and merely apparent; it can even be a camouflaged injustice when, apart from the law, it concedes to persons by benevolence what is due those persons in justice. Concretely, giving charity should not be a sly sort of subterfuge to avoid doing justice to others.[64]

---

64   "Father Pedro Arrupe, Prophet of Conciliar Renewal," Conference of Peter-Hans Kolvenbach, S.J. University of Deusto, Bilbao, November 13, 2007.

Pope Francis praying before the tomb of Arrupe after celebrating Mass on the feast of Saint Ignatius in the Gesù. The pope twice caressed the image of the deceased general (July 31, 2013).

However, the changes that most help us toward a new understanding of Arrupe came with the election of Father Adolfo Nicolás as superior general of the Society on January 19, 2008, and especially with the arrival in the Apostolic See of Pope Francis on March 13, 2013.

The lives of Pedro and Adolfo coincide in many points. The latter was born in Villamuriel de Cerrato, Palencia, Spain on April 29, 1936. Like Arrupe, he spent all his apostolic life in Asia, starting in 1971 after completing his doctoral studies in Rome. Like Arrupe, Nicolás was a polyglot and served as provincial of Japan. Like Arrupe, he took part in many projects involving dialogue, inculturation, and social ministry; he was especially committed to immigrants, both in Tokyo and in Manila. Before being elected superior general, Nicolás served as president of the Conference of Provincials of East Asia and Oceania. His great esteem for Arrupe is evident in many of his letters and addresses, and it is expressed also in the prologue with which he honored this biography.

Toward the end of 2012, Nicolás consulted Anton Witwer, S.J., who as postulator general expedites the processes for beatifying and canonizing Jesuits, concerning the procedures to be followed with regard to Arrupe. The secretary of the Society subsequently took the first steps to gather testimonies in all the provinces and "to consider fairly the motives that exist, for and against [beatification], taking into account the pastoral good of the whole church. Moreover, we must verify above all the authenticity of his widespread reputation for holiness."[65] As I

---

65   Letter of Anton Witwer, S.J. in reply to Father General, Rome, November 17, 2011.

Two Jesuits, both admirers of Arrupe: Superior General Adolfo Nicolás and Pope Francis (March 2013).

believe the many testimonies in this book show, this should not be an especially difficult task.

What Arrupe could never have imagined was that a Jesuit would become pope, the first in the history of the church. With the surprising but admirable resignation of Benedict XVI, the conclave of cardinals elected Jorge Mario Bergoglio, archbishop of Buenos Aires, as the successor to Peter's Chair. Born in Buenos Aires on December 17, 1936, Bergoglio had been master of novices and provincial of the Argentine province of Jesuits. By taking the name of Francis for his pontificate, he showed that he wanted to draw close to today's world in all goodness and simplicity, without in any way renouncing Ignatian spirituality and his deep Jesuit formation. His ready smile and his optimism, his gestures of humility and austerity, his pronouncements in favor of the poor and oppressed, his openness to dialogue, his ecumenism and willingness to talk with non-believers, his exhortations to work on the peripheries, his concern for women in the church, his denunciation of unrestrained capitalism, his love of justice—do not all these qualities find a clear precedent in the figure of Pedro Arrupe? Not only did the new pope twice caress the effigy of Arrupe at his tomb in the Gesù[66] but he has expressly declared his appreciation for the man who had been his superior general and who personally helped him, as various testimonies make clear, to liberate from Argentine prisons some of those being persecuted during the dictatorship of Jorge Rafael Videla. Another example of the pope's appreciation for Arrupe was his visit to the Astalli refugee center in Rome.[67]

---

66   Feast of Saint Ignatius, July 31, 2013.
67   In the Astalli refugee center, Pope Francis stated:

> It is wonderful that in this work on behalf of refugees there are, along with the Jesuits, men and women—Christians, people of other religions, and even non-believers— united for the sake of the common good, which for us Christians is an expression of the love of the Father in Christ Jesus. Saint Ignatius of Loyola wanted there to be

Since some of Arrupe's detractors are still alive, the path toward his beatification will require time and patience, but new doors are now being opened up and hope is growing. In any case, Arrupe does not have to ascend to the altars to continue being a model and a motivating force for men and women today.

Even before his death, Arrupe's name was honored by being bestowed on university chairs, schools, spirituality centers, and even an academy for political formation in southern Italy. During 2007, the centenary year of his birth, many conferences, expositions, homages, and celebrations were organized around the world. In his native Bilbao, a statue of Arrupe was erected on a public road, and a footbridge over the Nervión River was christened with his name.

Arrupe's labor has been beautifully summed up by Jesuit theologian Sobrino in an inscription that could serve as his epitaph: "To Pedro Arrupe, who has helped the Society to be a little more Jesus." We might add another, perhaps more universal, tribute: "Here lies a man who, by being so human, had a heart that was much larger than the world in which he lived. And even though that world was still not quite ready to understand him completely, it could not resist the beautiful but risky temptation to love him."

---

space to receive the poor in the residence he had in Rome. In 1981, Father Arrupe founded the Jesuit Refugee Service, and he wanted its Roman offices to be located in such spaces, in the heart of the city. I think now of that spiritual leave-taking of Father Arrupe in Thailand, right there at a refugee center [...] "Serve, accompany, defend": these three words define the program of work of the Jesuits and their collaborators [Rome, September 29, 2013].

Epilogue: Prophet of the Twenty-First Century

The biographical nature of this book has not allowed us to study in depth specific aspects of Arrupe's multifaceted personality. I have already mentioned, in the prologue and the notes, several works that analyze his thought and spirituality. Even though the whole course of his life, as we have seen, makes clear the prophetic nature of his intuitions, his decisions, and his intellectual achievements, I think it worthwhile to elaborate further on this important quality of his life, even if only briefly.

The ideas and proposals Arrupe put forward are more relevant than ever to the problems and the challenges of the new millennium. It was perhaps because he was so far ahead of his time that this successor of Ignatius of Loyola was misunderstood by some of his contemporaries and even by the church hierarchy. He loved to repeat: "We cannot respond to today's problems with yesterday's solutions." Unable to resign himself to allowing the church and the Jesuits to be immobilized by supposedly "orthodox" ideas, he refused to let them take refuge in a winter retreat and thus abandon the arena of dialogue with the modern world and contemporary culture. He wanted apostles who "had the future in the marrow of their bones."[1]

It is interesting to observe how many of the ideas of this charismatic superior general of the Society continue to make demands on us even today. In recent decades, many people have become increasingly disenchanted with the technological culture, the injustice of globalization, and the notion that "there is no alternative." Arrupe spoke of the "immense spiritual vacuum of our day, which neither technical progress nor materialist ideology can satisfy." He perceived the frustrations of a purely consumerist "welfare" society; he understood the plight of those who long for freedom only to find that their dream evanesces "when they behold people totally divided, envious, and distrustful of one another; and when they discover that the community that was supposed to be their principal source of strength and security threatens to absorb them and deprive them of everything, even their freedom and their personal identity."[2] For evidence of this, we need simply examine the near-absolute power of some of the multinational media conglomerates.

---

1   Interview given to the magazine *Mensaje*, 1973.

2   "The Church, Bearer of the Hopes of Men and Women," conference at the Congress of Jesuit Alumni of Europe, in Padua, August 28, 1977, in *La iglesia de hoy y del futuro*, 87–98.

With the Future in the Marrow of Our Bones

The protagonist of this book saw culture as a human ideal, as "the harmonious unfolding of the whole person and of every person." He recognized, however, that a powerful cultural crisis was on the horizon. He perceived how during the 1960s we became involved in a radical process of change that was too rapid and "was not occurring in a homogeneous, straightforward way, but amid strong tensions and conflicts."[3] He beheld a world experiencing the consequences of colossal disorder: "Wealth, instead of being used to satisfy the basic necessities of the majority of the population, is frequently misspent and squandered."[4] After analyzing the enormous expenditures on armaments and wars, this privileged eyewitness of the atomic bomb argued that true peace could never be attained "simply by changing the structures and institutions if the people living in them remain unchanged."[5] Nowadays we are beginning to observe the kind of such personal change Arrupe saw as necessary. We see it in the explosive demand for solidarity and the call for global revolution; we see it in the international aid organizations that Arrupe considered to be of capital importance for transforming the world. His diagnosis was correct:

> The results obtained from international conferences are so scanty that they oblige us to ask ourselves whether certain urgent and important measures, measures that are quite logical and desirable, are being thwarted by certain people because they are not politically desirable. The basic message of these international meetings is quite evident: there are differences of emphasis, but all these meetings are saying the same thing. They are telling us very clearly and with increasingly solid factual evidence:
>
> - that our world is sick,
> - that drastic measures are needed to cure it, and
> - that a new international order is required.
>
> I am not an economist, and so I cannot defend the merits of one or another concrete measure. But you don't have to be an economist to see that behind the complex technical language there is a naked human reality. Two-thirds of the human beings on the planet do not have enough food, housing, clothing, or education. And they have little possibility of attaining these basic rights until a fundamentally new order is established; only then will they have hope. Nor does one have to be an economist to understand that this fundamentally new order pertains not only to relations among

---

3   Conference given at the Katholikentag, in *La iglesia de hoy y del futuro*, 43.

4   "Fe y justicia: Una tarea para los cristianos de Europa," in *Hambre de pan y de evangelio*, 41.

5   "Fe y justicia: Una tarea para los cristianos de Europa," in *Hambre de pan y de evangelio*, 42–44.

nations but also to the chronically unjust relations within nations. Any community, whether global or national, that allows a tiny group of its members to control a major portion of its wealth, while most people are left in a situation of dire deprivation, is badly in need of radical reform.[6]

The Woes of the Third World

Of great concern to Arrupe was the distressing situation of the Third World, which he believed was caused by the world's gross inequalities. He made clear his views in a 1976 speech:

> I confess it openly: in the last ten years, since I took over the direction of the order, I have gone through a learning process. To be sure, I had lived for twenty-seven years outside Europe, in Japan, [...] but Japanese civilization, forged by the modern industrial economy, has much in common with Europe. Now, however, in these last ten years, I have discovered, though personal contacts and much dialogue, the desperate situation of the Third World in all its breadth: the world of India, the Arab nations, and the countries of Africa and Latin America.
>
> I have experienced the poverty and the hunger of those lands. I won't bore you with statistics, which we hear so often that they no longer have any effect on us. Direct contact with starving people has been decisive for me. I have met poor people not only individually but in groups, en masse, in entire countries. I have been overwhelmed by how abandoned and hopeless they are. Many people experience temporary poverty, but permanent poverty is something else: it becomes incrusted in the soul and the flesh and can destroy all self-confidence. And we should not forget this: there is a profound mistrust and a deep-seated suspicion in those people, which lead them to think that the industrialized countries are the ones basically responsible for their misery and for the great difficulty they have in escaping from it.[7]

Arrupe made a similar exposition in a talk he gave at the Pauluskirche in Frankfurt, Germany:

> At the end of that conference, a reporter asked me: "Father Arrupe, don't you think you exaggerated matters a bit in your speech?" After leaving Philadelphia, I had traveled to Honduras, Guatemala, Venezuela [...], and I was constantly asked what I had told people in the USA. The television coverage had presented the images of the great processions and the evening celebration in the stadium, but the world's hungry people were not evident there. Then I visited my Jesuit brothers who were living in simple quarters in the

---

6   "Fe y justicia: Una tarea para los cristianos de Europa," in *Hambre de pan y de evangelio*, 70.
7   "Fe y justicia: Una tarea para los cristianos de Europa," in *Hambre de pan y de evangelio*, 70.

midst of the poor. I celebrated the Eucharist in the improvised churches of the slums, and I shared the bread of life with the outcasts caught in the grip of hunger.

After the celebration of Mass, many would come to talk with me; one of them was a mother of eight children. I will never forget her face, marked by hunger and suffering. She told me: "Father General, I have nothing to give my children. Pray for me so that God will send us bread."

At that moment, I understood more clearly than ever that I had not exaggerated either in Philadelphia or in any other place where I had spoken of hunger in the world. Perhaps you will now understand why this most recent experience came to mind when I was thinking of what I should say here in Frankfurt on this solemn occasion.[8]

Young People and Native Cultures

Today more than ever, we admire Arrupe's genuine appreciation of the indigenous and mestizo cultures: "I have discovered the richness of this Third World: the richness of authentic human culture, emerging out of the poverty and misery. I have experienced the natural energy and unspoiled spiritual vitality of these people."[9]

As he contemplated young people in all their busy comings and goings, Arrupe manifested a strong, optimistic faith in the future they would build. He opposed "conventional formalism, mere etiquette, pure form" and favored instead "simplicity, naturalness, spontaneity and solidarity." He discovered in young people an impatient idealism, a generosity that took the form of service, an authenticity untainted by hypocrisy. Young people were sensitive to others, especially the most disadvantaged, and they manifested a spirit of universality in a world that was growing ever smaller. Arrupe could see these qualities even in those days when there was still no internet, no information explosion, no digital platforms or mobile phones. This universal spirit of youth touched something deep in Arrupe; it made him feel like a "citizen of the world." As he stated in an interview with RAI: "I feel universal. In fact, our role consists in working with everybody, and so I try to have the biggest heart possible. I try to understand everybody."

Nevertheless, Arrupe also accused young people—and time has proved him right—of sometimes yielding to "superficiality and sensationalism." He stated: "We live in an essentially sensory civilization, dominated by images and strong perceptions. [...] One sometimes notices a certain psychological weakness in the new generations." He commented on "a contradiction that can occasionally be observed in [young people]: the contrast between their good desires and the

---

8   "Fe y justicia: Una tarea para los cristianos de Europa," in *Hambre de pan y de evangelio*, 70–71.

9   "Fe y justicia: Una tarea para los cristianos de Europa," in *Hambre de pan y de evangelio*, 71.

maturity needed to carry them out."[10] He foresaw the advent of what would be called "weak thought."

Arrupe was convinced that the society of the future had to be a "frugal society"; judicious use of resources was absolutely necessary "for the material and social survival of the human race." He condemned wastefulness and defended a politics of austerity. He made declarations that might well appear as part of an essay in any serious journal today:

> Egocentric, egotistic consumers who are obsessed by the idea of having rather than by the idea of being are slaves of needs that they themselves create; they are never satisfied and always envious; their only rule of conduct is the accumulation of benefits. To them are opposed the persons who serve, those who aspire not to possess more but to be better, to develop their ability to serve others in solidarity, and to be content with what is most essential.[11]

Commitment of Blood

For Arrupe the struggle for faith-based justice required "action in many fields: political, social, and economic. Public opinion must be mobilized, the barriers of prejudice and indifference must be broken down, and politicians and legislators must be pressured to act." Such a stance, he knew, would often bring with it suffering:

> There will be times when our commitment to justice in the world will cost us dearly and will require personal or corporate sacrifices in different degrees. At such times, we can draw inspiration from the first Christians, who had to suffer for their faith and who considered it an honor to do so in the name of Jesus. We can also be encouraged by the sight of so many men and women and children throughout the world who at this very moment are suffering for the cause of justice. Some are in prisons or concentration camps, not accused of any crime or falsely accused; some are living in slavery or servitude; and some are being tortured or driven into exile. Many of them know that we are here today, and they look to us with hope. Let we not fail them! May our churches and the organizations to which we belong become fearless defenders of rights and of justice, no matter what it may cost us in material, political, or any other terms.[12]

10 "El modo nuestro de proceder," in *La identidad del jesuita*, 69ff.

11 "Nuestro servicio para el mundo de hoy," conference given at the Third Congress of Religious of North and South America, Montreal, November 21, 1977. In *La iglesia de hoy y del futuro*, 408.

12 Words pronounced at the Eucharistic Congress of Philadelphia, 1976, published in *Hambre de pan y de evangelio*.

In a 1977 interview with the newspaper *Avvenire*, Arrupe commented on the human cost and the suffering that even then were evident, after the expulsion of Jesuits from Paraguay and the martyrdom of Father Burnier: "I fear that in the future we will find ourselves obliged to pay similar costs, not only in these and other Latin American countries, but wherever Jesuits struggle for the service of faith and the promotion of justice." Here also, as we have seen, history has proved the general right: there have so far been ninety-nine Jesuit martyrs; fourteen were killed while he was still in office.

The prophet Arrupe anticipated future developments, such as the flourishing of non-governmental organizations, the increase in international volunteers and cooperation, and the movement for dedicating 0.7 percent of GDP to foreign assistance. He foresaw the resistance against the heavy debt burden laid on poor nations and the vigorous protests of the anti-globalization movements. "Some people die of starvation," he reflected, "and others from excess of cholesterol. Hunger is the natural child of injustice, an injustice the rich countries can eliminate. But let us say it plainly: they do not want to."[13]

Women, Europe, the Church

Arrupe was prophetic also regarding the situation of women. In a well-attended press conference held in Puebla, Mexico, he declared that the participation of women in church matters would come, but that patience was needed—his remark provoked laughter among the reporters. What is interesting is that GC 34 allowed for women to become presidents of Jesuit universities.[14] For his part, Pope Francis has insisted on the need for women to take an active part in the church's decision-making.

My hope is that in the pages of this book the reader will have discovered how this witness of the twentieth century and prophet of the twenty-first became progressively more mature and more Christian in his commitment to our world, especially as regards xenophobia, spirituality, religious life, and a humanism without borders. He was at the forefront of the church's efforts at "inculturation," for he understood that evangelization could no longer use Western cultural molds to introduce the faith to other cultures; rather, it had to recreate or reconceive the faith from within the depths of those cultures:

> Cultural values are not absolute. A culture that is enclosed within itself becomes impoverished, languishes, and dies. If faith remains enclosed within a particular culture, it suffers the same limitations. Faith should maintain a continuous dialogue with all cultures. Faith and culture emulate

---

13   Program "Fin de siglo" (1999).
14   Decree 14, GC 34.

one another mutually; faith purifies and enriches culture, and culture enriches and purifies faith.[15]

For Arrupe, a true humanism without borders was incumbent also on the European Union, which became an economic union with the euro and is now on its way to becoming more united politically. Nevertheless, Europe seems to have closed itself off in its own ambiguous version of a welfare state. Reacting to this parochialism, Arrupe dreamed of

> a humanism open to the entire world. [...] To the extent that Europe expands its possibilities as it becomes more unified, it should also increase its concern for others by distributing its wealth. It should do so in a spirit of dialogue, with respect for the values of other countries, and with the conviction that it has as much to receive as it has to give. Europe should not conceive its development independently of those countries that are less privileged or less developed. Perhaps we can influence our governments so that they fully recognize their responsibility in this regard. We frequently hear about the explosive situation in the Third World, but do we Europeans ask ourselves whether we are not partly responsible for this situation?[16]

These words certainly strike us today as we contemplate the inexorable phenomenon of massive migration.

Regarding the church, Arrupe believed profoundly in the need to respect pluralism:

> Pluralism in the expression of faith is not a necessary evil; it a good to which we must aspire. [...] True communion is achieved "through the uniqueness of human nature and the unity of spirit in every lively effort." The Holy Spirit brings about the humanly impossible desire (which is also our deepest human longing) for radical unity in the most radical diversity.[17]

Arrupe held that democratic principles, which are today so valued in society but neglected in the church, are not foreign to the Gospel:

> Today, there is a crisis of obedience and authority, but that makes the active participation of people very necessary. And this is quite in line with Saint Ignatius. Nowadays we are moving toward a kind of co-responsibility in the way superiors make decisions. In the Society Saint Ignatius founded, there are many democratic elements in the way decisions are made.[18]

---

15 "Catequesis e inculturatión," intervention in the synod of 1977.
16 Congress of Jesuit alumni, in Liège, Belgium, 1979.
17 Allocution at the synod of 1977.
18 He was referring to the practice of "representation to the superior," which is contemplated in the Constitutions of Saint Ignatius (Spanish National Radio, "Fin de siglo").

Arrupe had so much respect for the freedom of his subjects and his companions that he tried to learn from them, even as he was tremendously demanding of himself. For this and for other reasons, he was accused of secularizing the Society. His answer was always the same: "I would say not that the Society is becoming secularized, but that it is adapting apostolically to a world which is becoming secularized. This produces transformations that always have apostolic import."[19] Nowadays the accusations of critics are just the opposite: they claim that the church, for fear of the effects of secularization, has lost contact with the world and is unable to dialogue with secular culture.

The same may be said about Arrupe's attitude with regard to unbelief and atheism. He was at first misunderstood because he used the phrase "fight against atheism," which comes directly from the mandate given to the Society by Paul VI, but he understood the task more in terms of understanding, respect, and dialogue. He was convinced that it was important to know why so many people were rejecting the God of the Bible. The great task for Christians was to make manifest "the true face of God." It would therefore be necessary, he said,

> to recognize that the manner in which Christians have sometimes presented God has made atheists believe that God is against human beings or that adoration and love of God means the death and destruction of lofty human values, such as freedom, responsibility, reason, love, and solidarity among humans. It must also be stated vigorously that that way of presenting God is untrue and unjust because it falsifies the Christian revelation.[20]

Arrupe believed strongly that the disciples of Ignatius should be committed to ecumenical dialogue. For him, ecumenism was "not only a particular apostolic work but a dimension of the entire mission of the church and therefore of every apostolate." Citing Paul VI and the decree of Vatican II entitled "The Missionary Action of the Church," he called for Jesuits to be aware that "the disunity of Christians is without doubt for many people an obstacle in the way of faith." He therefore saw the need "for us to renew ourselves radically in this spirit; to practice what we preach to others—reform, cooperation, and dialogue—so that Christians become so united among themselves that the world will truly believe." On another occasion, he said: "The church does not exist to preserve itself in some kind of 'splendid isolation,' but to preach the Gospel to the world. Christians do not seek unity for their own convenience, but in order to carry out more fully the church's mission according to the will of Christ."

The world since Arrupe's days continues to be a world in flux, shot through with impermanence. Christians inevitably feel the dialectical tension involved in developing their personality to the maximum for the purpose of serving others

---

19   Spanish National Radio, "Fin de siglo."
20   See Calvez, *Fe y justicia*, 155–56.

and dedicating themselves wholeheartedly to the good of others. As inhabitants of a fast-evolving world, their attitudes differ markedly from those of people living in a relatively static society. These latter value stability and perseverance, they find self-criticism difficult, and they view change with suspicion. The former, in contrast, accept the transitory nature of things, they appreciate and practice self-criticism, they seek out creativity, and they know how to adapt quickly, progressively, and wisely, thus avoiding so-called future shock. That, according to Arrupe, is what is required today of Christians "who have the future in the marrow of their bones."[21]

The Ultimate Secret

Today more than ever, the key to the enduring force and relevance of Arrupe's message is its authenticity. If I had to synthesize his life in just one of the thousand anecdotes I have heard in researching this biography, I would choose the one he told about his experience catechizing adults as a missionary in Japan. He related that during the classes an old Japanese man would watch him intensely; for six months, the man said not a word either for or against the instructor. Arrupe was puzzled and finally dared to ask him: "What do you think of my explanations?" The man replied: "I cannot give an opinion because I have heard nothing. I am completely deaf. However, for me it is sufficient just to look into your eyes. You do not lie. What you believe, I believe also." Arrupe truly lived out and irradiated what he preached. He was convinced that evangelizing involves *being* more than speaking.

Arrupe's ultimate secret was a profound faith and spirituality, and these kept him always hopeful: "They say that I am optimistic, and I think I am. It seems to me a grace of God at this time to have an optimistic temperament. The reason for this optimism is that I have great confidence in God; we are in his hands."[22] Arrupe's confidence was accompanied by his charming simplicity and humility: "I am a poor human who tries to spoil God's work as little as possible."[23] He had no fear of insecurity: "I continue to reaffirm completely today what I said then: 'Perhaps the Lord had never been so close to us because we had never been so insecure.'"[24]

With this concluding section of the biography I have sought only to show how valid Arrupe's ideas continue to be, over one hundred years since his birth.[25]

---

21. Interview, *Mensaje*, 1973.
22. Spanish National Radio, "Fin de siglo."
23. Spanish National Radio, "Fin de siglo" (taken also from other declarations to Spanish television).
24. Statement made at the Katholikentag in 1970 and also the year before during a Mass celebrated in a Latin American barrio.
25. To go deeper into Arrupe's thought, see Jean-Yves Calvez, *El padre Arrupe: Profeta de la iglesia del concilio* (Bilbao: Mensajero, 1998).

Far more convincing, of course, and far more moving than these lines is what came before, his very life, because words may move, but examples attract.

The simple facts should show every reader, whatever his or her beliefs, that Arrupe was a man who saw beyond the circumstances of his time; he was, in the words of Cardinal Tarancón, "an exceptionally charismatic prophet who intuited the future."

Many people have asked me what Arrupe's preferred scriptural phrases were. It is not difficult to imagine them, but we already have a selection that he himself made, which is in reality a self-portrait:

- SIMPLICITY: "Blessed are the poor in spirit" (Matt. 5:3; Luke 6:20).
- TRUST IN GOD: "Therefore do not be anxious about tomorrow, for tomorrow will be anxious for itself" (Matthew 6:34).
- NON-VIOLENCE: "If anyone strikes you on the right cheek, turn to him the other also" (Matthew 5:39).
- DETACHMENT: "If anyone would sue you and take your coat, let him have your cloak as well" (Matthew 5:40).
- GENEROSITY AND SERVICE: "If anyone forces you to go one mile, go with him two miles" (Matthew 5:41).
- SAGACIOUS HUMILITY: "When you are invited, go and sit in the last place" (Luke 14:9).
- PROPHETIC COMMITMENT: "Blessed are you when men hate you, and when they exclude you and revile you for my sake" (Luke 6:22).
- CHRISTIAN LOVE: "Love your enemies and pray for those who persecute you" (Matthew 5:44).
- WISDOM AND RENUNCIATION: "Those who try to gain their own life will lose it, and those who lose their life for my sake will find it" (Matthew 10:39).[26]

To reach such sublime ideals, Arrupe believed that profound conversion was necessary:

True experience of God is a liberating experience. It is an experience in which religious persons, enthralled by God's absolute nature, voluntarily make themselves vulnerable and available; they place themselves in God's hands and so discover in this active trusting their own fullness as persons. By centering all their existence in God, they are happily freed from the most painful servitude of all, the interior dissolution that comes from not perceiving life to be a gift, from not experiencing the fullness of life in history as a gift.[27]

---

26   *Hambre de pan y de evangelio.*
27   *La identidad del jesuita.*

This was Arrupe's own experience, which he expressed with one simple phrase, "being in love":

> *Nothing is more practical than finding God,*
> *   that is, than falling in love with God in a quite absolute, final way.*
> *What you are in love with,*
> *   what seizes your imagination, will affect everything.*
> *It will decide what gets you out of bed in the morning,*
> *   what you do with your evenings,*
> *   how you spend your weekends,*
> *   what you read, the people you know,*
> *   what breaks your heart and*
> *   what fills you with joyous amazement and gratitude.*
> *Fall in love, stay in love, and that will decide everything.*[28]

For all these reasons, the figure of Don Pedro has kept growing over time. During the last few years, he has become a symbol of Christian courage and evangelical commitment. I conclude this epilogue with a statement of famous theologian Gustavo Gutiérrez, a Peruvian priest who recently became a Dominican. He summed up well the role played by Arrupe both in the church and in the larger society: "Arrupe was one of the great men of the church of our time. He was someone who, according to the beautiful expression of John XXIII, knew how to look into the distance."[29]

---

28   United States. Date and place of these words are unknown.

29   See José A. García, *Orar con el P. Arrupe* (Bilbao: Mensajero, 2007).

Appendix 1
Genealogical Tree of Father Arrupe (SP 541)

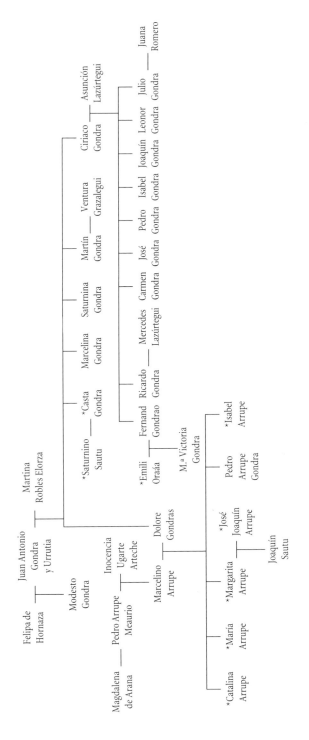

* Closest relatives of Pedro Arrupe

483

Appendix 2
Letter of Father Arrupe, January 3, 1983 (SP 542)

PRÆPOSITI GENERALIS
SOCIETATIS IESU
IMA · Borgo S. Spirito, 5

3 de enero de 1983

Muy querida Mariví y Guillermo

Es la primera carta que escribo en 1983, y por tanto, la comienzo deseándoos un felícimo año, que prácticamente está entero.

Lo que me ha impulsado a escribiros es la agradable sorpresa que me dió hace dos dias una carta de mi hermana Isabel, a la que unía un recorte de periódico, con la inesperada noticia de que María Victoria Gondra Araá "será investida esta tarde en la biblioteca de la Diputación como la primera mujer vizcaina admitida como miembro de número en la REAL SOCIEDAD BASCONGADA DE AMIGOS DEL PAIS.

Dejando aparte que tales Sociedades las fundó nuestro "amigo" Carlos III, puedes imaginarte mi sorpresa y alegría. Isabel me decía muy complacida que eso honra a la familia. Así lo creo yo, y me apresuro a felicitarte muy efusivamente. En adelante no dirán Mariví la sobrina del General de la Compañía, sino dirán Arrupe, el tio de la Primera Dama etc. Lo acepto con gusto. Los jóvenes nos echais a los viejos.

Qué tal habeis pasado las Navidades?. Yo, como podeis suponer, con más deseos que nunca de estar unido con Dios hecho niño, aprendiendo las lecciones de amor y obediencia a los decretos del Eterno Padre, que le envía a amar a los hombres, a sufrir por ellos y a interceder. El Señor me conceda esa gracia de conocerle internamente para más amarle y seguirle, como dice nuestro Padre San Ignacio.

Claro que también he hecho mis escapaditas. Estuve visitando a un grupo de refugiados que atendemos desde la Curia. Y el 31 fui al Gesù al solemne Te Deum tradicional presidido por el Santo Padre. Tuve el consuelo de saludarle, y él estuvo sumamente afectuoso, rogándome con insistencia que pida al Señor por él. Luego, ya en la ceremonia, sin que yo lo esperase, se acercó a darme la comunión, y lo mismo al P. Dezza y a mi fiel enfermero, H. Bandera. Fue un detalle lleno de bondad y afecto.

Por lo demás, sigo tal cual, según creo yo, y haciendo aún algún lento progreso al decir de los que me rodean. He tenido muy abundantes felicitaciones y visitas, y me conforta saber que tante gente pide por mí. Bien lo necesito. Y a todos procuro corresponder con lo mismo.

Repito mi felicitación, y envío un cordialísimo saludo a Guillermo. Y ya seguiremos la lista de tus publicaciones. Saludos también a tio Fernando.
Un abrazo,

Pedro

Appendix 3
Be Good

Therefore, I tell you: Be good!

Evil seems to be taking control of the world; malevolence and malignancy take up more and more space and penetrate ever more deeply.

Be good!

The priest must certainly be a man of holiness, faith, hope, joy, speech, silence, sorrow. But he should above all be good: he should be a man of love.

If a priest entering a parish or any other place where people come together should find indifference, distance, conflict, and coldness, but he himself is and appears *good*, then he will certainly not be able to work miracles and will have to wait, but his waiting will never be useless, and almost certainly it will not be prolonged or burdensome.

Be good!

Good in your expression, which should be relaxed, serene, and smiling; good in your gaze, which should first surprise and then attract.

Divinely good was the gaze of Jesus. Do you remember? When Peter was caught and pierced by that divine and human gaze, he wept bitterly.

Be good in the way you listen!

Thus you will experience, again and again, patience, love, attention, and the reception of eventual callings.

Be good with your hands!

Hands that give, that help, that wipe away tears; hands that hold the hands of the poor and the sick to infuse courage; hands that embrace adversaries and bring them to agreement; hands that write a lovely letter to one who is suffering, above all if we are to blame; hands that know how to ask humbly for oneself and for those in need; hands that know how to serve the infirm; hands that know how to do the humblest tasks.

Be good in speaking and in judging!

Be good, if you are young, with old people; and if you are old, be good with young people.

Be contemplatives in action!

Looking at Jesus, be an "image of him"; be in this world and in the church contemplatives in action; transform your ministerial activity into a means for union with God.

Be always open and attentive to any gesture of God the Father and of all God's children, who are our brothers and sisters.

Be holy!

The holy person finds a thousand ways, even revolutionary ways, to reach without delay the place where the need is urgent; the holy person is bold, ingenious, and modern; the holy person does not wait for innovations and dispositions to arrive from on high; the holy person overcomes obstacles and, if need be, burns up the old structures while superseding them.

But always with the love of God and in absolute fidelity to the church, which we serve humbly because we love it passionately.

—Pedro Arrupe
(Priests' retreat in Cagliari, Italy, March 11, 1976)

Bibliography

Alcalá, Manuel. "La dimisión de Arrupe." In *Pedro Arrupe, general de la Compañía de Jesús: Nuevas aportaciones a su biografía*, edited by Gianni La Bella, 913–56. Bilbao: Ediciones Mensajero, 2007.

———. "Gozo y martirio en España." In *Pedro Arrupe: Así lo vieron*, edited by Manuel Alcalá, Stefan Bamberger, Jean-Yves Calvez, Ignacio Ellacuría, Vincent O'Keefe, Robert T. Rush, and Vitus Seibel, 65–101. Santander: Sal Terrae, 1986.

———. "Pedro Arrupe y la vida religiosa en el posconcilio." In *Pedro Arrupe, general de la Compañía de Jesús: Nuevas aportaciones a su biografía*, edited by Gianni La Bella, 672–709. Bilbao: Ediciones Mensajero, 2007.

Alperovitz, Gar. *Atomic Diplomacy: Hiroshima and Potsdam*. New York: Simon & Schuster, 1965.

Álvarez Bolado, Alfonso. "La Congregación General 32." In *Pedro Arrupe, general de la Compañía de Jesús: Nuevas aportaciones a su biografía*, edited by Gianni La Bella, 251–350. Bilbao: Ediciones Mensajero, 2007.

Anonymous. "El P. Arrupe, misionero y maestro de novicios." *El siglo de las misiones* 148 (October 1950): 395.

Araiza, Manuel Acevez, S.J. *P. Arrupe: Tres ensayos y un anecdotario*. México: Jus, 1989.

Arnold, Paul. *El zen en la tradición japonesa*. Bilbao: Ediciones Mensajero, 1979.

Arranz, Miguel. "Contactos con la Iglesia Ortodoxa rusa." In *Pedro Arrupe, general de la Compañía de Jesús: Nuevas aportaciones a su biografía*, edited by Gianni La Bella, 620–35. Bilbao: Ediciones Mensajero, 2007.

Arrisue, S. *Memoirs*. Tokyo, 1974.

Arrupe, Pedro. *Aquí me tienes, Señor: Apuntes de sus Ejercicios espirituales (1965)*. Bilbao: Mensajero, 2002.

———. "Carta convocando la Congregación general 32." *Acta Romana S.I.* 16 (1973): 126–27.

———. *En él solo la esperanza*. Bilbao: Mensajero, 1983.

———. *Escala en España*. Madrid: Apostolado de la Prensa, 1971.

———. *Este Japón increíble (Memorias del P. Arrupe)*. Bilbao Mensajero, 1959.

———. *Hombres para los demás*. Barcelona: Diáfora, 1983.

———. *Nuestra vida consagrada*. Madrid: Apostolado de la prensa, 1972.

———. *La identidad del jesuita en nuestros tiempos*. Santander: Sal Terrae, 1981.

———. *La iglesia de hoy y del future*. Bilbao: Mensajero, 1982.

———. *La vida religiosa ante un reto histórico*. Santander: Sal Terrae, 1978.

———. *Yo viví la bomba atómica*. México: Patria, 1965.

Ashi, S. *A Bomb*. Hiroshima, 1972.

Baatz, Ursula. *H. Enomiya Lassalle, jesuita y maestro zen*. Barcelona: Herder Editorial, 2005.

———. *H. Enomiya Lassalle: Una vida entre dos mundos; Biografía*. Bilbao: Desclée de Brouwer, 2001.

Ballester, Mariano. "Recuerdo del P. Arrupe y el A.O." *Oración y servicio* 4 (October–December 1991): 297–302.

Bangert, William V. *Historia de la Compañía de Jesús*. Santander: Editorial Sal terrae, 1981.

Cahill, Lisa Sowle. "Catholic Sexual Ethics and the Dignity of the Person: A Double Message." *Theological Studies* 50 (1989): 120–50.

Calvez, Jean-Yves. "Diálogo, cultura, evangelio." In *Pedro Arrupe, general de la Compañía de Jesús: Nuevas aportaciones a su biografía*, edited by Gianni La Bella, 805–28. Bilbao: Ediciones Mensajero, 2007.

———. *El padre Arrupe: Profeta de la iglesia del concilio*. Bilbao: Mensajero, 1998.

———. *Foi et justice: La dimensión sociale de l'évangélisation*. Paris: Desclée de Brouwer, 1985.

———. *Padre Arrupe: La Chiesa dopo il Vaticano II*. Milan: Paoline Editoriale Libri, 1998.

———. *La pensée de Karl Marx*. Paris: Éditions du Seuil, 2006.

———. *Le père Arrupe: L'église après le concile*. Paris: Cerf, 1997.

Campbell, John W. *The Atomic Story*. New York: H. Holt and Co., 1947.

Caporale, Rocco. *Vaticano II: El último de los concilios*. Barcelona: Nova Terra, 1966.

Caprile, Giovanni. *Il Concilio Vaticano II: Cronache del Concilio Vaticano II*. 4 Vols. Rome: Ed. "La civiltà cattolica," 1965–68.

Cartier, Raymond. *La seconde guerre mondiale*. 2 Vols. Paris: Larousse, 1966.

Castella, G. [Gastón]. *Historia de los papas*. Vol. 3. Madrid: Espasa-Calpe, 1970.

Churchill, Winston. *Memorias, La segunda guerra mundial*, vol. 3, *La gran alianza*. Barcelona: José Janés, 1950.

Codina, Victor. "La noche oscura del P. Arrupe: Una carta autógrafa inédita." *Manresa* 62 (April/June 1990): 165–72.

Committee of Japanese Citizens, Hiroshima–Nagasaki. *Days to Remember: An Account of the Bombings of Hiroshima and Nagasaki*. Tokyo: Hiroshima–Nagasaki Publishing Committee, 1981.

Congar, Yves. *Le Concile Vatican II: Son église, peuple de Dieu et corps du Christ*. Paris: Beauchesne, 1984.

———. *El concilio día a día*. Madrid: Estela, 1963.

———. *Diario del concilio*. 3 Vols. Barcelona: Estela, 1967.

———. *Mon journal du concile*. Paris: Cerf, 2002.

Cuyás, Manuel. "En torno a la *Humanae vitae*." In *Selecciones de libros: Actualidad bibliográfica de filosofía y teología; Boletines, libros, notas*, 10–46. Barcelona: Facultades de Filosofía y Teología San Francisco de Borja, 1969.

Daishi, Yoka. *El canto del Inmediato Satori*. Barcelona: Kairós, 2001.

Dietsch, Jean-Claude. *Pedro Arrupe: Itinéraire d'un jesuite*. Paris: Éditions du Centurion, 1982.

Documentos de la Congregación General XXXI. Zaragoza: Hechos y Dichos, 1966.

Documentos del Vaticano II. Madrid: BAC, 1985.

Dumoulin, Heinrich. *Zen: El camino de la iluminación en el Budismo*. Bilbao: Desclée de Brouwer, 2002.

———. *La esencia del Zen: Los textos clásicos de los maestros chinos*. Edited by Thomas Leary. Barcelona: Kairós, 1991.

Dürckheim, Karlfried Graf. *Hara, Centro vital del hombre*. Bilbao: Mensajero, 1987.

————. *Meditar, ¿cómo y por qué?* Bilbao: Mensajero, 1989.

————. *Práctica el camino interior.* Bilbao: Mensajero, 1994.

Duval [Lucien], Aime, S.J. *El niño que jugaba con la luna.* Santander: Sal Terrae, 1984.

Echániz, Ignacio. "Si el grano de trigo […]." In *Pedro Arrupe, general de la Compañía de Jesús: Nuevas aportaciones a su biografía,* edited by Gianni La Bella, 978–52. Bilbao: Ediciones Mensajero, 2007.

Ellacuría, Ignacio. "Pedro Arrupe, renovador de la vida religiosa." In In *Pedro Arrupe: Así lo vieron,* edited by Manuel Alcalá, Stefan Bamberger, Jean-Yves Calvez, Ignacio Ellacuría, Vincent O'Keefe, Robert T. Rush, and Vitus Seibel, 141–72. Santander: Sal Terrae, 1986.

Enomiya-Lassalle, Hugo. *Zen y mística cristiana.* Madrid: Ed. Paulinas, 1991.

————. *Zen, un camino hacia la propia identidad.* Bilbao: Ediciones Mensajero, 1975.

————. *Zen weg zur erleuchtung.* Vienna: Herder, 1974.

Feis, Herbert. *The Atomic Bomb and the End of World War Two.* Princeton: Princeton University Press, 1966.

Floristán, Casiano, and Juan-José Tamayo. *El Vaticano II, veinte años después.* Madrid: Cristiandad, 1985.

García Gutiérrez, Fernando, S.J. *El padre Arrupe en Japón.* 2nd ed. Seville: Ediciones Guadalquivir, 1992.

García, José A., ed. *Orar con el padre Arrupe.* Bilbao: Editorial Mensajero, 2007.

García, Matías. "Arrupe y la justicia." In *Pedro Arrupe, general de la Compañía de Jesús: Nuevas aportaciones a su biografía,* edited by Gianni La Bella, 753–91. Bilbao: Ediciones Mensajero, 2007.

Gondra y Oráa, María Victoria de. *El Bilbao de Julio Lazúrtegui: La acertada visión del futuro industrial y mercantil del País Vasco adelantada por un bilbaino del XIX.* Bilbao: Cámara Oficial de Comercio, Industria y Navegación de Bilbao, 1984.

González, Manuel Revuelta. "La Compañía de Jesús renovada (1965–2003)." In *Los jesuitas en España y en el mundo hispánico,* edited by Teófanes Egido, 399–445. Madrid: Marcial Pons; Fundación Carolina, Centro de Estudios Hispánicos e Iberoamericanos, 2004.

Gutierrez, Alberto. "Arrupe y América Latina." In *Pedro Arrupe, general de la Compañía de Jesús: Nuevas aportaciones a su biografía,* edited by Gianni La Bella, 399–426. Bilbao: Ediciones Mensajero, 2007.

Hachiya, Michihiko. *Hiroshima Diary.* 10th ed. Chapel Hill, NC: University of North Carolina Press, 1985 [1955].

Heredia, Rudolf C. "Arrupe y la India." In *Pedro Arrupe, general de la Compañía de Jesús: Nuevas aportaciones a su biografía,* edited by Gianni La Bella, 563–83. Bilbao: Ediciones Mensajero, 2007.

Hernando, Bernardino M. *Los pasillos de Puebla.* Madrid: PPC, 1979.

Ibuse, Masuji. *Black Rain.* Palo Alto: Kodansha, 1969.

Iglesias, Ignacio. "Una aportación del testimonio y del magisterio de Pedro Arrupe: El discernimiento spiritual." In *Testigos del siglo XX: Maestros del siglo XXI,* edited by María Teresa Alonso Baquer et al., 243–63. XIII Simposio de Historia de la Iglesia en España y América, Academia de Historia Eclesiástica, Sevilla, April 8, 2002. Córdoba: Publicaciones Obra Social y Cultural CajaSur, 2003.

————. "Aportaciones a su biografía interior." In *Pedro Arrupe, general de la Compañía de Jesús: Nuevas aportaciones a su biografía*, edited by Gianni La Bella, 991–92. Bilbao: Ediciones Mensajero, 2007.

Iturrioz, Jesús. "Pedro Arrupe, cincuenta años de sacerdocio." *Mensajero* 1149 (Bilbao, July 1986): 23–27.

Jedin, H. [Hubert], and K. [Konrad] Repgen. *Manual de historia de la iglesia*. Vol. 9. Barcelona: Herder, 1984.

John Paul II. *Cruzando el umbral de la esperanza*. Barcelona: Plaza-Janés, 1994.

Kerkhofs, Jan. "Arrupe y Europa." In *Pedro Arrupe, general de la Compañía de Jesús: Nuevas aportaciones a su biografía*, edited by Gianni La Bella, 403–28. Bilbao: Ediciones Mensajero, 2007.

La Bella, Gianni. "La crisis del cambio." In *Pedro Arrupe, general de la Compañía de Jesús: Nuevas aportaciones a su biografía*, edited by Gianni La Bella, 811–41. Bilbao: Ediciones Mensajero, 2007.

————. *Los jesuitas: Del Vaticano II al papa Francisco*, Mensajero, Bilbao 2019.

Lamet, Pedro Miguel. *El aventurero de Dios: Francisco de Javier*. Madrid: La Esfera de los Libros, 2006.

————. *Un cristiano protesta*. Barcelona: Biblograf, 1980.

————. *Del papa Montini al papa Wojtyla (Los setenta y cinco días que estremecieron a la iglesia)*. Bilbao: Mensajero, 1979.

————. *Díez Alegría, un jesuita sin papeles*. Madrid: Temas de Hoy, 2005.

————. *Juan Pablo II, hombre y papa*. Madrid: Espasa Calpe, 2005.

M'nteba, Simon-Pierre Metena. "Arrupe y África," In *Pedro Arrupe, general de la Compañía de Jesús: Nuevas aportaciones a su biografía*, edited by Gianni La Bella, 356–70. Bilbao: Ediciones Mensajero, 2007.

Madrigal, Santiago. "Su sentido de iglesia siguiendo la estela del Vaticano II." In *Pedro Arrupe, general de la Compañía de Jesús: Nuevas aportaciones a su biografía*, edited by Gianni La Bella, 635–67. Bilbao: Ediciones Mensajero, 2007.

————. *Vaticano II: Remembranza y actualización*. Santander: Editorial Sal Terrae, 2002.

Margenat, José María. "De Bilbao a Japón (1907–1938)." In *Pedro Arrupe, general de la Compañía de Jesús: Nuevas aportaciones a su biografía*, edited by Gianni La Bella, 53–110. Bilbao: Ediciones Mensajero, 2007.

Martialay, Roberto. *Comunidad en sangre*. Bilbao: Mensajero, 1983.

Martín Descalzo, José Luis. *El concilio de Juan y Pablo*. Madrid: La Editorial Católica, 1966.

————. *Un periodista en el concilio*. 4 Vols. Madrid: Propaganda Popular Católica, 1963–66.

McCormick, Richard A. "Moral Theology 1940–1989." *Theological Studies* 50 (1989): 3–24.

Morton, W. Scott. *The Japanese: How They Live and Work*. Tokyo: Tuttle, 1979.

O'Keefe, Vincent. "En las huellas de San Ignacio." *Testimonio* 130 (March/April 1992): 18.

O'Neill, Charles E., and Joaquín María Domínguez, eds. *Diccionario histórico de la Compañía de Jesús: Biográfico–temático II*. Rome: Institutum Historicum S.I., 2005.

Ortí, Vicente Cárcel. *Pablo VI y España: Fidelidad, renovación y crisis (1963–1978)*. Madrid: Biblioteca Autores Cristianos, 1997.

Padberg, John W. *Together as a Companionship: A History of the Thirty-First, Thirty-Second, and Thirty-Third General Congregations of the Society of Jesus.* St. Louis, MO: Institute of Jesuit Sources, 1994.

Paul VI. "Litterae autographae S. Pontificis relatae ad futuram congregationem generalem." *Acta Romana S.I.* 16 (1973): 15–26.

Pfister, Paul, S.J. *Semblanzas espirituales de los santos y beatos de la Compañía de Jesús.* Madrid: Eapsa, 1974.

Pratt, James F. X. "Pedro Arrupe, catalizador de la reforma de los Estados Unidos." In *Pedro Arrupe, general de la Compañía de Jesús: Nuevas aportaciones a su biografía,* edited by Gianni La Bella, 585–620. Bilbao: Ediciones Mensajero, 2007.

Pyle, Leo. *Pope and Pill.* London: Darton, Longman & Todd, 1968.

Royón, Elías. "Su modo de gobernar." In *Pedro Arrupe, general de la Compañía de Jesús: Nuevas aportaciones a su biografía,* edited by Gianni La Bella, 711–51. Bilbao: Ediciones Mensajero, 2007.

Rush, Robert T. "Pedro Arrupe, misionero: Un corazón tan grande como el mundo." In *Pedro Arrupe: Así lo vieron,* edited by Manuel Alcalá, Stefan Bamberger, Jean-Yves Calvez, Ignacio Ellacuría, Vincent O'Keefe, Robert T. Rush, and Vitus Seibel, 43–65. Santander: Sal Terrae, 1986.

Salvat, Ignacio. "Lo que permanece." In *Pedro Arrupe: Memoria siempre viva,* edited by Norberto Alcover, 191–218. Bilbao: Mensajero, 2002.

Suzuki, Daisetz Teitaro. *El ámbito del Zen.* Barcelona Editorial Kairós, 1981.

———. *El ámbito del Zen Vivir el Zen.* Barcelona: Kairós, 1995 [1949].

———. *Budismo zen y psicoanalisis.* Madrid: Fondo de Cultura Económica, 1979.

Thomas, Gordon, and Max Morgan Witts. *Enola Gay.* New York: Stein & Day, 1985 [1977].

Valero, Urbano. "Al frente de la Compañía: La Congregación 31." In *Pedro Arrupe, general de la Compañía de Jesús: Nuevas aportaciones a su biografía,* edited by Gianni La Bella, 139–71. Bilbao: Ediciones Mensajero, 2007.

———. *Pablo VI y los jesuitas: Una relación intensa y complicada, (1963–1978),* Mensajero, Bilbao, 2018.

Vera, José María de. "Misionero en Japón." In *Pedro Arrupe, general de la Compañía de Jesús: Nuevas aportaciones a su biografía,* edited by Gianni La Bella, 111–38. Bilbao: Ediciones Mensajero, 2007.

Villot, Jean-Marie. "Sensus Summi Pontificis relate ad propositum indicendi Congregationem Generalem." *Acta Romana S.I.* 15 (1972): 827–28.

Yuki, Diego R., S.J. [Diego Pacheco, S.J.]. "Nagasaki: La colina de los mártires." *Missionalia hispanica* 17 (1961): 229–45.

Index